D0199245

# Rome

"All you've got to do is decide to go
and the hardest part is over.

## So go!"

TONY WHEELER, COFOUNDER – LONELY PLANET

THIS EDITION WRITTEN AND RESEARCHED BY
Duncan Garwood, Abigail Hole

# Contents

Left: Spanish Steps (p105)

Above: Pantheon (p75)

Right: Basilica di Santa Maria in Trastevere (p171)

Villa Borghese & Northern Rome p205

Vatican City, Borgo & Prati p182

Tridente, Trevi & the Quirinale p103

Centro Storico p73

Monti, Esquilino & San Lorenzo p126

Ancient Rome p56

Trastevere & Gianicolo p169

San Giovanni to Testaccio p147

Southern Rome p158

# Welcome to Rome

*History, human genius and the hot midday sun have conspired to make Rome one of the world's most seductive and thrilling cities.*

## Artistic Grandeur

With an artistic heritage dating back to Etruscan times, Rome is one of the world's great art cities. Throughout history, it has played a starring role in the major upheavals of Western art and the results are there for all to see – amazing classical statues, stunning Renaissance frescoes, breathtaking baroque decor. Walk around the centre and even without trying you'll come across masterpieces by the greats of the artistic pantheon – sculptures by Michelangelo, paintings by Caravaggio, frescoes by Raphael and fountains by Bernini. In Rome, art is not locked away from view, it's quite literally all around you.

## Historical Legacies

For much of its history Rome has been at the centre of world events, first, as *caput mundi* (capital of the world), the glittering hub of the vast Roman Empire, then for centuries as the seat of papal power. It was a city that counted and this is writ large on its historic streets – the Colosseum reminds of glorious imperial days, Castel Sant'Angelo testifies to violent dramas and St Peter's Basilica stands as a monument to artistic genius and papal ambition. Elsewhere, ancient ruins, buried houses and roadside shrines (*maddonelle*) tell of past lives and local beliefs.

## Roman Feasting

A trip to Rome is as much about lapping up the lifestyle as it is gorging on art and historic sights. And there's no better way of getting into the local spirit of things than by eating and drinking well. Food and wine are central to Roman social life and the hundreds of pizzerias, trattorias, restaurants and gelaterie that crowd the city centre do as much business catering to locals as to tourists and out-of-towners. Do as the Romans do, says the proverb, and there's nothing more typically Roman than enjoying a tasty wood-fired pizza in a packed pizzeria or dining al fresco on a glorious city-centre piazza.

## Rome Capital

But there's more to Rome than history, fine art and great food. Rome is Italy's capital and largest city, and while history reverberates all around, modern life is lived to the full. Rome is Italy's political and religious heartbeat and the twin presence of government and Church dominates the city. Many city-centre *palazzi* (mansion) house government offices while over in the Vatican the dome of St Peter's Basilica lords it over the skyline, reminding everyone of the pope's presence. Political intrigue is thick in the air and as tourists tuck into their lunch politicians hunker down to hatch plots over pasta and coffee.

## Why I Love Rome

By Duncan Garwood, Author

Even after more than 10 years living in Rome I am still struck by its beauty. This is a city where the Colosseum and Pantheon, two of the most celebrated buildings in the Western world, are part of the family furniture. And it's this that I love about Rome, the juxtaposition of modern life as lived on such an amazing stage.

On a more earthy level, I also love Italian food and enjoy a good heated discussion over a bottle of local wine – a very Roman experience.

**For more about our authors see p368.**

Above: St Peter's Basilica, as seen from Capitoline Museum

# Rome's
# Top 13

### Colosseum (p58)

**1** Rome's most iconic monument, the Colosseum is a compelling sight. You'll know what it looks like but no photograph can prepare you for the thrill of seeing it for the first time. For 2000 years, this muscular arena has stood as the symbol of Roman power, as the striking embodiment of the terrible awe that Rome once inspired. As you climb its steeply stacked stands, try to image them full of frenzied spectators screaming for blood – a chilling thought.

⊙ *Ancient Rome*

### Palatino (p60)

**2** Rome's seven hills offer some superb vantage points. One of the best is the Palatino (Palatine hill), a gorgeous green expanse of evocative ruins, towering pine trees and sweeping views that rises above the Roman Forum. This is where it all began, where Romulus supposedly killed Remus and founded the city in 753 BC, and where the ancient Roman emperors lived in unimaginable luxury. Nowadays, it's a truly haunting spot, and as you walk the gravel paths you can almost sense the ghosts in the air.

⊙ *Ancient Rome*

2

## Museo e Galleria Borghese (p207)

**3** Everybody's heard of Michelangelo and the Sistine Chapel, but Rome is as much about baroque art as it is the Renaissance, and the lovely Museo e Galleria Borghese is the place to see it. You'll need to book ahead but it's a small price to pay to see Bernini's amazing baroque sculptures, as well as works by Canova, Caravaggio, Raphael and Titian. And when you've finished, the surrounding Villa Borghese park is the perfect place to digest what you've just seen.

**⊙ Villa Borghese & Northern Rome**

## Pantheon (p75)

**4** The best preserved of Rome's ancient monuments, the Pantheon is a truly remarkable building. Its huge columned portico and thick-set walls impress, but it's only when you get inside that you get the full measure of the place. It's vast, and you'll feel very small as you look up at the record-breaking dome soaring above your head. Adding to the effect are the shafts of light that stream in through the central oculus (the circular opening at the dome's apex), illuminating the royal tombs set into the circular marble-clad walls. (INTERIOR OF THE PANTHEON)

**⊙ Centro Storico**

## Vatican Museums (p189)

**5** Rome boasts many artistic highlights, but few are as overpowering as Michelangelo's frescoes in the Sistine Chapel. A kaleidoscopic barrage of colours and images, they come as the grand finale of the Vatican Museums, Rome's largest and most popular art museum. Inside the vast complex, kilometre upon kilometre of corridors are lined with classical sculptures, paintings and tapestries as they lead inexorably towards the Raphael Rooms, a suite of four rooms brilliantly frescoed by Raphael, and, beyond that, the Sistine Chapel. (STAIRCASE, VATICAN MUSEUMS)

**⊙ Vatican City, Borgo & Prati**

## St Peter's Basilica (p184)

**6** You don't have to be a believer to be bowled over by St Peter's Basilica, Rome's largest and most spectacular church. Everything about the place is astonishing, from the sweeping piazza that announces it to the grandiose facade and unbelievably opulent interior. Topping everything is Michelangelo's extraordinary dome, a mould-breaking masterpiece of Renaissance architecture and one of Rome's landmark sights. This is a building that was designed to awe, and even in a city of churches like Rome it stands head and shoulders above everything else.

⊙ *Vatican City, Borgo & Prati*

## Ostia Antica (p220)

**7** Not many people make it out to Ostia Antica, Rome's version of Pompeii. But make the effort and you'll find that its wonderfully preserved ruins are easily on a par with the more famous sites in the city centre. They are certainly easier to follow. Walk along the central strip, the Decumanus Maximus, or potter around the Thermopolium, an ancient cafe, and you'll get a much better idea of what a working Roman town looked like than you ever will by exploring the Roman Forum. (ROMAN THEATRE AT OSTIA ANTICA)

⊙ *Day Trips*

## Dining al Fresco *(p31)*

**8** Eating out is one of the great pleasures of Rome, especially in summer when it's warm enough to dine al fresco and the city's animated streets are packed until the early hours. There's nothing like sitting out on a beautiful cobbled lane to dine on fine Italian food and lusty local wine while all around you the city plays out its daily show. And with everything from refined romantic restaurants to brash, noisy pizzerias and sumptuous gelaterie you'll be sure to find somewhere to suit your style.

✕ *Eating*

## Capitoline Museums (p67)

**9** In ancient times, the Campidoglio (Capitoline hill) was home to Rome's two most important temples. Nowadays, the main reason to make the short, steep climb to the top is to admire the views and visit the Capitoline Museums on Piazza del Campidoglio. The world's oldest public museums, these harbour some fantastic classical statuary, including the celebrated *Lupa Capitolina* (Capitoline Wolf), an icon of early Etruscan art, and some really wonderful paintings. And make sure to bring your camera for the masonry littered around the entrance courtyard. (STATUE OF ROMULUS AND REMUS)

◉ *Ancient Rome*

## Roman Forum (p63)

**10** To walk through the tumbledown ruins of the Roman Forum is to retrace the footsteps of the great figures of Roman history, people like Julius Caesar and Pompey, who both led triumphal marches up Via Sacra, the Forum's central axis. The Forum is today one of Rome's most visited sights but crowds are nothing new here. In ancient times this was the city's busy, chaotic centre, humming with activity as everyone from senators to slaves went about their daily business.

◉ *Ancient Rome*

## Rome's Piazzas (p84)

**11** Hanging out on Rome's showcase piazzas is part and parcel of Roman life. Having an ice cream at a pavement cafe on Piazza Navona, people-watching on Piazza del Popolo, queuing on Piazza San Pietro – these are all quintessential Roman experiences. For millennia, the city's piazzas have been at the centre of city life, hosting markets, ceremonies, games and even executions, and still today they attract cheerful crowds of locals, tourists, hipsters, diners and street artists. (PIAZZA NAVONA)

◉ *Centro Storico*

RUTH EASTHAM & MAX PAOLI / LONELY PLANET IMAGES ©

## Viterbo *(p229)*

**12** For a break from the bluster of Rome, head up to Viterbo. The pace of life here is slower and you'll never have to fight through the crowds as you wander its handsome medieval streets. Viterbo was an important medieval centre and many of its most impressive buildings date to its time as the seat of the papal court in the 13th century. You can visit on a day trip but consider stopping for a couple of days and exploring Lazio's rugged northern reaches. (MEDIEVAL OLD TOWN AND TOWER OF PALAZZO DEI PRIORI)

◉ *Day Trips*

DAVID BORLAND / LONELY PLANET IMAGES ©

TONY BURNS / LONELY PLANET IMAGES ©

## People-Watching on Piazza di Spagna *(p105)*

**13** Rising up from Piazza di Spagna, the Spanish Steps are a favourite perch and a prime people-watching spot. Visitors have been hanging out here since the 18th century and still they come – local lotharios to flirt with the foreigners, red-faced tourists to catch their breath, street touts to sell their plastic tat. Below the Steps, well-heeled shoppers exercise their credit cards at the area's boutiques and flagship designer stores.

◉ *Tridente, Trevi & the Quirinale*

# What's New

## Colosseum

You can now go underground at the Colosseum and visit the hypogeum, the complex of corridors beneath the main arena, and used as a backstage area. Explore the tunnels where wild animals were caged, gladiators psyched themselves up for their bouts and condemned prisoners shivered at the sound of the baying crowds overhead. (p58)

## MAXXI

A stunning work of modern architecture, the Museo Nazionale delle Arti del XXI Secolo (MAXXI) has finally opened its doors to the public more than 10 years after it was commissioned. (p213)

## Museo Nazionale Romano: Palazzo Massimo alle Terme

The superb Roman frescoes on the 3rd floor are looking better than ever thanks to a new layout that better reflects they way they would have originally been placed. (p128)

## Beer

Rome's beer drinkers have never had it so good as a trend for artisanal brews sweeps the city. Have a taste at Open Baladin (p96) or Ma Che Siete Venuti a Fà. (p177)

## Palazzo Valentini

After years of excavation work, a number of ancient Roman houses have gone on show beneath Palazzo Valentini, the seat of Rome's provincial administration. (p109)

## Salotto Locarno

This debonair art deco bar in the gorgeous Locarno Hotel is the perfect place to dress up and drink elegant cocktails. (p120)

## Villa Spalletti Trivelli

Live like a local aristocrat at this refined city-centre country house, a fabulous addition to Rome's luxury accommodation scene. (p243)

## Salotto Gianicolo

A chic summer bar in a romantic setting on the Gianicolo hill. Sit back with something cool and bask in heavenly views. (p120)

## Casa Coppelle

A short hop from the Pantheon, this chilled and romantic restaurant has proved a big hit since opening a couple of years ago. (p89)

## L'Asino d'Oro

This minimalist trattoria brings the earthy tastes of the Umbrian countryside to the bohemian lanes of the Monti district. (p135)

## Argentina Residenza

A discreet, boutique guest house with six quiet rooms on Largo di Torre Argentina, the busy piazza where Julius Caesar was supposedly assassinated. (p241)

## Pastificio San Lorenzo

One of Rome's hot dining venues is this chic restaurant in the industrial-arthouse setting of San Lorenzo's Pastificio Cerere. (p140)

## Museo Missionario di Propaganda Fide

A museum showcasing the art that Catholic missionaries have collected on their travels in the past 350 years. (p109)

For more recommendations and reviews, see **www.lonelyplanet.com/Rome.**

# Need to Know

## Currency
Euro (€)

## Language
Italian

## Visas
Not required by EU citizens. Not required by nationals of Australia, Canada, New Zealand and the USA for stays of up to 90 days.

## Money
ATMs are widespread. Major credit cards are widely accepted but some smaller shops, trattorias and *pensioni* (small, often family-run, hotels or guesthouses) might not take them. Keep cash for immediate expenses.

## Mobile Phones
Local SIM cards can be used in European, Australian and unlocked US phones. Other phones must be set to roaming.

## Time
Western European Time (GMT/UTC plus one hour)

## Tourist Information
Information points (⊙9.30am-7pm) around town for maps, brochures and the Roma Pass. Also a telephone line (☑06 06 08) for events, hotels and transport information.

## Your Daily Budget

### Budget under €70
➡ Dorm beds €15-35

➡ Pizza meal plus beer €15

➡ Save by drinking coffee standing at the bar

➡ Have an *aperitivo* (aperative) and eat for the price of a drink

### Midrange €70-200
➡ Double room €120-250

➡ Three-course restaurant meal €30-50

➡ OK to mix and match courses when eating out

➡ B&Bs are often better value than hotels in the same category

### Top End over €200
➡ Double room €250 plus

➡ City taxi ride €5-15

➡ Auditorium concert tickets €25-90

## Advance Planning

**Two months** Book high season accommodation.

**Three to four weeks** Check for concerts at www.auditorium.it, www.operaroma.it, www.circoloartisti.it.

**One to two weeks** Reserve tables at A-list restaurants. Sort out tickets to the pope's weekly audience at St Peter's.

**Few days** Check www.estate romana.comune.roma.it for free summer events. Phone for tickets for the Museo e Galleria Borghese (compulsory) and book for the Vatican Museums (advisable to avoid queues).

## Useful Websites

➡ **Lonely Planet** (www.lonelyplanet.com/rome) Destination lowdown, hotels and traveller forum.

➡ **060608** (www.060608.it) Rome's official tourist website.

➡ **Pierreci** (www.pierreci.it) Information and ticket booking for Rome's monuments.

➡ **Vatican** (www.vatican.va) Book tickets for the Vatican Museums.

➡ **Auditorium** (www.auditorium.com) Check concert listings.

## WHEN TO GO

In spring (April to June) and early autumn (September and October) there's good weather and many festivals and outdoor events. It's also busy and peak rates apply.

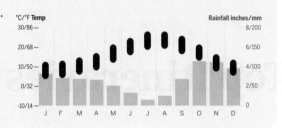

## Arriving in Rome

**Leonardo da Vinci (Fiumicino) Airport** Direct trains to Stazione Termini 6.38am-11.38pm, €14; slower trains to Trastevere, Ostiense and Tiburtina stations, 5.43am-11.38pm, €8; buses to Stazione Termini 8.30am-12.30am and at 1.15am, 2.15am, 3.30am and 5am, €4.50-8; private transfers €25-37 per person; taxis €40.

**Ciampino Airport** Buses to Stazione Termini 7.45am-12.15am, €4-6; private transfers €25-37 per person; taxis €30.

For much more on **arrival**, see p300.

## Getting Around

Rome's public transport system includes buses, trams, metro and a suburban train network. The main hub is Stazione Termini, the only point at which the city's two metro lines cross. The metro is quicker than surface transport but the network is limited and the bus is often a better bet. Children under 10 travel free.

➡ **Metro** Two lines A (orange) and B (blue). Runs 5.30am to 11.30pm (to 1.30am on Friday and Saturday).

➡ **Buses** Most routes pass through Stazione Termini. Buses run 5.30am until midnight, with limited services throughout the night.

For much more on **getting around**, see p301.

## Sleeping

Rome is expensive and with the city busy year-round, you'll want to book as far ahead as you can to secure the best deal and the place you want.

Accommodation options range from palatial five-star hotels to hostels, B&Bs, convents and *pensioni*. Hostels are the cheapest, offering dorm beds and private rooms. Bed and breakfasts range from simple home-style set-ups to chic boutique outfits with prices to match, while religious institutions provide basic, value-for-money accommodation but may insist on a curfew. Hotels are plentiful and there are many budget, family-run *pensioni* in the Termini area.

### Useful Websites

➡ **060608** (www.060608.it) Lists all official accommodation options (with prices).

➡ **Santa Susanna** (www.santasusanna.org/comingToRome/convents.html) Has information on religious accommodation.

➡ **Bed & Breakfast Italia** (www.bbitalia.com) Rome's longest-established B&B network.

For much more on **accommodation**, see p236.

## ORGANISED TOURS

Taking a tour is a good way of seeing a lot in a short time or investigating a sight in depth. There are several outfits running hop-on hop-off bus tours, typically costing about €20 per person. Both the Colosseum and Vatican Museums offer official guided tours but for a more personalised service you'll be better off with a private guide. For more details see p305.

# Top Itineraries

## Day One

### Ancient Rome (p56)

 Start the day at the **Colosseum**, Rome's huge gladiatorial arena – try to get there early to avoid the worst of the queues. Then head down to the **Palatino** to poke around crumbling ruins and admire sweeping views. From the Palatino, follow the path down into the **Roman Forum**, an evocative area of tumbledown temples, sprouting columns and ruined basilicas.

 **Lunch** Hostaria da Nerone (p72) is a traditional, old-school Roman trattoria.

### Ancient Rome (p56)

After lunch climb the **Cordonata** to **Piazza del Campidoglio** and the **Capitoline Museums**. Here you'll find some stunning ancient sculpture and paintings by a selection of big-name artists. To clear your head afterwards, pop next door to **Il Vittoriano** (you can't miss it) and take the lift to the top for Rome's best 360-degree views.

**Dinner** Dine on Roman-Jewish food at Giggetto al Portico d'Ottavia (p94)

### Centro Storico (p73)

Spend the evening in the **Jewish Ghetto**. There are some wonderful eateries here, including **Giggetto al Portico d'Ottavia**, a landmark restaurant that has been feeding the Ghetto since 1929. Round the day off with a late drink at **Bartaruga**.

## Day Two

### Vatican City, Borgo & Prati (p182)

On day two, hit the Vatican. First up, grab a *cornetto* from **Dolce Maniera**, then plunge into the **Vatican Museums**. Once you've blown your mind on the Sistine Chapel and the other highlights, complete your Vatican tour at **St Peter's Basilica**. If the queues are bad, though, or you're suffering art overload, stop first for an early lunch.

 **Lunch** Snack at Mondo Arancina (p201) or Angeli a Borgo (p201).

### Centro Storico (p73)

Dedicate the afternoon to sniffing around the historic centre. Here you'll come across some of Rome's great sights, including **Piazza Navona** and the **Pantheon**. Art lovers can admire paintings by Caravaggio in the **Chiesa di San Luigi dei Francesi** and fashion-conscious shoppers can browse the modish boutiques on **Via del Governo Vecchio**.

 **Dinner** Romantic Casa Coppelle (p89) offers fine French-inspired food.

### Centro Storico (p73)

After dinner stop in the centre for a taste of *dolce vita* bar life. Depending on what you're after, you could spend a relaxed evening at **Etablì** near Piazza Navona, join the student drinkers on **Campo de' Fiori**, or chat over coffee at **Caffè Sant'Eustacchio**.

# Day Three

### Villa Borghese & Northern Rome (p205)

 Day three starts with a trip to the **Museo e Galleria Borghese** to marvel at amazing baroque sculpture. Afterwards, walk off what you've just seen in the shady avenues of **Villa Borghese** and check what's going on at Rome's buzzing cultural centre, the **Auditorium Parco della Musica**.

>  **Lunch** Pop up to Piazzale Ponte Milvio (p215) in the Flamino district.

### Tridente, Trevi & the Quirinale (p103)

 In the afternoon investigate the area around **Piazza di Spagna**. Plan your moves while sitting on the **Spanish Steps** then dive down **Via dei Condotti** to window shop at the flagship designer stores. From Via del Corso, at the bottom, you can make your way up to the **Trevi Fountain**, where tradition dictates you throw in a coin to ensure your return to Rome.

> **Dinner** Trastevere (p174) heaves with restaurants, pizzerias and trattorias.

### Trastevere & Gianicolo (p169)

Over the river, the charmingly photogenic **Trastevere** neighbourhood bursts with life in the evening as locals and tourists flock to its many eateries and bars. Get into the mood with an aperitif at **Freni e Frizioni** before pizza at **Bir & Fud** or a refined dinner at **Glass Hostaria**.

# Day Four

### Southern Rome (p158)

 On day four it's time to venture out to **Via Appia Antica**. The main attraction here are the catacombs and it's a wonderfully creepy sensation to duck down into these sinister pitch-black tunnels. Back above ground, you'll find the remains of an ancient racetrack in the grounds of the nearby **Villa di Massenzio**.

>  **Lunch** Book a table at highly regarded Trattoria Monti (p138)

### Monti, Esquilino & San Lorenzo (p126)

Start the afternoon off by visiting the **Museo Nazionale Romano: Palazzo Massimo alle Terme**, a really superb museum full of classical sculpture and stunning mosaics. Then drop by the monumental **Basilica di Santa Maria Maggiore**, famous for its mosaics, and the **Basilica di San Pietro in Vincoli**, home to Michelangelo's muscular Mosè sculpture. Finish up by exploring the pretty lanes of the **Monti** district.

> **Dinner** Head out to student enclave San Lorenzo (p140) and see what's cooking.

### Monti, Esquilino & San Lorenzo (p126)

Step out with the students in **San Lorenzo**, where there's always something going on in the chic restaurants, cheap student haunts and bars. Further out, you'll find plenty of after-dark action in trendy **Pigneto**.

# If You Like...

## Museums & Galleries

**Vatican Museums** One of the world's great museum's with a vast collection of classical art and sculpture culminating in the Sistine Chapel. (p189)

**Museo e Galleria Borghese** Houses the best baroque sculpture in town and some seriously good Old Masters. (p207)

**Museo Nazionale Romano: Palazzo Massimo alle Terme** Fabulous Roman frescoes and wall mosaics are the highlight of this overlooked gem. (p128)

**Capitoline Museums** The world's oldest public museums are a must for anyone interested in ancient sculpture. (p67)

**Museo Nazionale Etrusco di Villa Giulia** A lovely museum housing a huge collection of Etruscan art and artefacts, most from sites in northern Lazio. (p213)

**Palazzo e Galleria Doria Pamphilj** Hidden behind a grimy exterior this lavish private gallery is full of major works by big-name Italian artists. (p79)

**Galleria Nazionale d'Arte Antica – Palazzo Barberini** A sumptuous baroque palace laden with paintings by such giants as Caravaggio, Raphael and Hans Holbein. (p110)

**Museo Nazionale Romano: Palazzo Altemps** Classical sculpture is set against a backdrop of baroque frescoes at this excellent museum in the historic centre. (p82)

**Museo dell'Ara Pacis** A huge block of sculpted marble, the Ara

WILL SALTER / LONELY PLANET IMAGES ©

Hall of Philosophers in the Capitoline Museums (p67)

Pacis is housed in a controversial modern pavilion (p107)

**MAXXI** This gallery of contemporary art is worth seeing as much for the stunning museum building as the art it displays. (p213)

## Roman Relics

**Colosseum** One of the world's most famous buildings, this breathtaking arena encapsulates all the drama of ancient Rome. (p58)

**Pantheon** With its revolutionary design and amazing dome, this awe-inspiring Roman temple has served as an architectural blueprint for millennia. (p75)

**Palatino (Palatine hill)** Ancient emperors languished in luxury on the Palatino, the oldest and poshest part of imperial Rome. (p60)

**Terme di Caracalla** The hulking remains of this vast baths complex hint at the scale that ancient Rome was built to. (p156)

**Ostia Antica** An ancient port preserved over the millennia, Ostia Antica gives a good impression of a working Roman town. (p220)

**Via Appia Antica** March down Rome's oldest road, built in the 4th century BC, en route to the catacombs. (p160)

**Imperial Forums** The highlight of these sprawled ruins is the Mercati di Traiano, a multi-storey shopping centre dating to the 2nd century. (p69)

**Roman Forum** This was ancient Rome's bustling city centre full of temples, basilicas, shops and streets. (p63)

## Baroque Flair

**St Peter's Basilica** It's impressive from outside but what really takes your breath away is the opulent, marble-clad baroque interior. (p184)

**Piazza Navona** Rome's outdoor salon, this elegant piazza boasts works by Bernini and Borromini, the two giants of the Roman baroque. (p77)

**Chiesa di Santa Maria della Vittoria** This otherwise innocuous church boasts one of the great works of European baroque, Bernini's *Teresa traffitta dall'amore di Dio* (p111)

**Museo e Galleria Borghese** Marvel at Bernini's ability to tease life out of cold, hard marble at this stately museum. (p207)

**Palazzo del Quirinale** The palatial home of the President of the Italian Republic was built by a phalanx of big-name baroque architects. (p110)

**Galleria Nazionale d'Arte Antica – Palazzo Barberini** Students of the baroque shouldn't miss the *Trionfo della Divina Provvidenza,* a spectacular fresco by Pietro da Cortona. (p114)

**Chiesa di San Carlo alle Quattro Fontane** Borromini's tiny church is a study in baroque design, featuring many clever architectural tricks. (p111)

**Chiesa di San Luigi dei Francesi** Gaze on great art for free at this church near Piazza Navona, home to three Caravaggio paintings. (p86)

**Trevi Fountain** Rome's celebrated fountain dates to the rococo 18th century but it exudes all the flamboyance of baroque at its most fanciful. (p108)

**For more top Rome spots see**

➡ Eating (p31)

➡ Drinking & Nightlife (p38)

➡ Entertainment (p43)

➡ Shopping (p49)

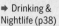

## Frescoes

**Sistine Chapel** Michelangelo's ceiling frescoes and his *Giudizio Universale* are among the greatest works of art on the planet (p196)

**Chiesa del Gesù** Heavenly visions adorn Rome's premier Jesuit church, in the form of a technicolour ceiling fresco by Il Baciccia. (p81)

**Museo Nazionale Romano: Palazzo Massimo alle Terme** The stunning frescoes on show here were used by ancient Roman aristocrats to decorate their lavishly appointed villas. (p128)

**Villa Farnesina** This refined Renaissance villa displays a series of wonderful frescoes by Raphael, Sebastiano del Piombo and Baldassare Peruzzi. (p175)

**Palazzo Farnese** The French Embassy boasts frescoes by Annibale Carracci that some consider the equal of Michelangelo's works in the Sistine Chapel. (p81)

**Galleria Nazionale d'Arte Antica – Palazzo Barberini** Pietro da Cortona's exuberant *Trionfo della Divina Provvidenza* is a masterpiece of 17th-century fresco painting. (p110)

**Chiesa di Sant'Ignazio di Loyola** Home to a famous trompe l'oeil fresco that plays with your sense of perception. (p87)

**Basilica di Santa Cecilia in Trastevere** It's not entirely intact but Pietro Cavallino's 13th-century fresco of the *Giudizio Universale* is still a memorable work. (p198)

**Chiesa di Santo Stefano Rotondo** One of Rome's earliest churches, this is decorated with explicit frescoes depicting the tortures suffered by early Christian martyrs. (p152)

# Going Underground

**Basilica di San Clemente** Descend into the bowels of this multi-layered basilica to discover a pagan temple and a 1st-century house. (p153)

**Vatican Grottoes** Extending beneath St Peter's Basilica, these underground chambers contain the tombs of several popes, including Pope John Paul II. (p188)

**Catacombs** Via Appia Antica is riddled with underground tunnels – the catacombs – where the early Christians buried their dead. (p160)

**Colosseum** Recently opened to guided tours, the hypogeum is the complex of corridors and lifts that lay beneath the arena. (p58)

**Case Romane** Poke around the houses where Saints John and Paul lived before they were executed. (p152)

## Parks & Gardens

**Villa Borghese** Rome's most central park, Villa Borghese is a refined oasis with a small lake, landscaped avenues and some fine museums. (p212)

**Villa Celimontana** A tranquil pocket of greenery on the Celio hill, Villa Celimontana is a great escape from the hustle of the nearby Colosseum area. (p152)

**Villa Ada** With its extensive woods and wild stretches, this sprawling park feels a million miles from Rome. (p214)

**Villa Torlonia** Locals love this small park on Via Nomentana and it is a pretty spot with its swaying palm trees and neoclassical villas. (p215)

**Orto Botanico** Rome's 12-hectare botanical gardens rise up the Gianicolo hill behind Trastevere. (p173)

# Legends

**Palatino (Palatine hill)** The Palatino is where the wolf saved Romulus and Remus and Rome was founded in 753 BC. (p60)

**Largo di Torre Argentina** The spot is not marked but Julius Caesar was assassinated near the Teatro Argentina. (p78)

**Chiesa del Domine Quo Vadis?** Here St Peter supposedly asked a vision of Jesus: *'Domine, quo vadis?'* ('Lord, where are you going?') (p164)

**Carcere Mamertino** St Peter conjured up a miraculous stream of water to baptise his gaolers while holed up here. (p68)

**Chiesa di Santa Maria in Aracoeli** This is where the Tiburtine Sybil foretold the birth of Jesus to the emperor Augustus. (p69)

**Bocca della Verità** Legend holds that if you tell a lie with your hand in the mouth of truth it will be bitten off. (p70)

**Campidoglio** Sacred geese alerted sentries to a night attack during a Gallic siege of Rome in the 4th century BC. (p68)

# Sweeping Views

**Il Vittoriano** Not recommended for vertigo sufferers, the summit of this marble monolith towers over the rest of Rome (p69)

**St Peter's Basilica** Climb the dome and you're rewarded with huge 360-degree views. (p184)

**Gianicolo** Rising above Trastevere, the Gianicolo hill affords sweeping panoramas over Rome's rooftops. (p173)

**Priorato dei Cavalieri di Malta** Look through the keyhole for a perfectly framed picture of St Peter's dome. (p152)

**Orti Farnesiani** A viewing terrace in the Palatino's medieval gardens commands grandstand views over the Roman Forum. (p61)

# Streetlife

**Trastevere** Students, tourists, locals, diners, drinkers, junkies and street-hawkers mingle on Trastevere's vivacious streets (p169)

**Spanish Steps** Find a space, park yourself on a step and settle back to watch the ever-changing spectacle on the square below. (p105)

**Piazza Navona** This beautiful baroque arena provides the stage for a colourful cast of street artists, performers, waiters and tourists. (p77)

**Pigneto** With its noisy market and vibrant bar and restaurant scene, this hip district is always lively. (p142)

**Campo de' Fiori** Market stall holders holler at each other during the day and student drinkers strut their stuff by night. (p80)

# Month by Month

## TOP EVENTS

**Natale di Roma**, April

**Estate Romana**, June to October

**Villa Celimontana Jazz**, July

**Festa di Noantri**, July

**Romaeuropa**, October to November

## January

As New Year celebrations fade, the winter cold digs in. It's a quiet time of year but the winter sales are a welcome diversion.

### 🔒 Shopping Sales

Running from early January to mid-February, the winter sales offer savings of between 20% and 50%. Action is particularly frenzied around Piazza di Spagna and on Via del Corso.

## February

Rome's winter quiet is shattered by high-spirited carnival celebrations, while romance comes to town for St Valentine's Day (14 February). Restaurants do a roaring trade in tables for two, so book ahead.

### 🎭 Carnevale

The week before Lent is a technicolour spectacle as children take to the streets in fancy dress and throw *coriandoli* (coloured confetti) over each other. Costumed processions add to the fun – see www.carnevale.roma.it for details.

## March

The onset of spring brings blooming flowers, rising temperatures and unpredictable rainfall. Unless Easter falls in late March, the city is fairly subdued and low season prices still apply.

### 🏃 Maratona di Roma

Sight-seeing becomes sport at Rome's annual marathon. The 42km route starts and finishes near the Colosseum, taking in many of the city's big sights. Details online at www.maratonadiroma.it.

## April

April is a great month with lovely, sunny weather, fervent Easter celebrations, a week of free museums, azaleas on the Spanish Steps and Rome's birthday

festivities. Expect high-season prices.

### 🎭 Easter

In the capital of the Catholic world, Easter is big business. On Good Friday the pope leads a candle-lit procession around the Colosseum. At noon on Easter Sunday he blesses the crowds in Piazza San Pietro.

### 👁 Settimana della Cultura

During Culture Week admission is free to many state-run monuments, museums, galleries and otherwise closed sites. Dates change annually so check www.beniculturali.it (in Italian).

### 🎭 Natale Di Roma

Rome celebrates its birthday on 21 April with music, historical recreations, fireworks and free entry to many museums. Events are staged throughout the city but the focus is Campidoglio and Circo Massimo.

### 👁 Mostra Delle Azalee

From mid-April to early May, the Spanish Steps are decorated with 600 vases of blooming, brightly coloured azaleas – a perfect photo opportunity.

# May

**May is a busy, high-season month. The weather's perfect – it's generally warm enough to eat outside – and the city is looking gorgeous with blue skies and spring flowers.**

## ☆ Primo Maggio

Hundreds of thousands of fans troop to Piazza di San Giovanni in Laterano for Rome's annual May Day rock concert. It's a mostly Italian affair with big-name local performers but you might catch the occasional foreign guest star.

# June

**The summer has arrived and with it hot weather, the school vacations and a full festivals programme. Stages, stalls and open-air bars are set up across the city creating a laid-back holiday atmosphere.**

## ✯ Estate Romana

Between June and October, Rome's big summer festival involves everything from concerts and dance performances to book fairs, puppet shows and late-night museum openings. Check the website – www.estate romana.comune.roma.it.

## ✯ Roma Incontro Il Mondo

Villa Ada is transformed into a colourful multi-ethnic village for this popular annual event. There's a laid-back party vibe and an excellent programme of concerts – in 2011 Goran Bregovic, Suzanne Vega and Sud Sound System

headlined. Check www. villaada.org.

## ✯ Festa dei Santi Pietro e Paolo

On 29 June, Romans celebrate its two patron saints, Peter and Paul, with a mass at St Peter's Basilica and a street fair on Via Ostiense near the Basilica di San Paolo Fuori-le-Mura.

# July

**Hot summer temperatures make sightseeing a physical endeavour, but come the cool of evening, the city's streets burst into life as locals come out to enjoy summer festivities.**

## ✯ Villa Celimontana Jazz

Rome's best jazz festival is held in the ravishing Villa Celimontana park on the Celio hill. Concerts are held every night throughout the month attracting quality performers and passionate audiences. Get programme details at www.villaceli montanajazz.com.

## ✯ Festa di Noantri

Trastevere celebrates its roots with a raucous street party in the last two weeks of the month. Centred on Piazza Santa Maria in Trastevere, events kick off with a religious procession and continue with much eating, drinking, dancing and praying.

# August

**Rome melts in the heat as locals flee the city for their summer hols. Many businesses shut down**

around 15 August but hoteliers offer discounts and there are loads of summer events to enjoy.

## ◉ Festa della Madonna della Neve

On 5 August, rose petals are showered on celebrants in the Basilica di Santa Maria Maggiore to commemorate a miraculous 4th-century snowfall. This impressive miracle is celebrated at the Basilica di Santa Maria Maggiore on 5 August.

# October

**Autumn is a good time to visit – the warm weather is holding, Romaeuropa ensures plenty of cultural action and, with the schools back, there are far fewer tourists around.**

## ✯ Romaeuropa

Established international performers join emerging stars at Rome's premier dance and drama festival. Events, staged throughout October and November, range from avant-garde dance performances to installations, multimedia shows, recitals and readings. Get details at http://romaeuropa.net/.

## ✯ Festival Internazionale del Film di Roma

Held at the Auditorium Parco della Musica, Rome's film festival rolls out the red carpet for Hollywood hotshots and bigwigs from Italian cinema. Consult the programme at www.roma cinemafest.org.

(Top) Palm Sunday Mass in St Peter's Square, the prelude to a Roman Easter

(Bottom) Fireworks over St Peter's Basilica

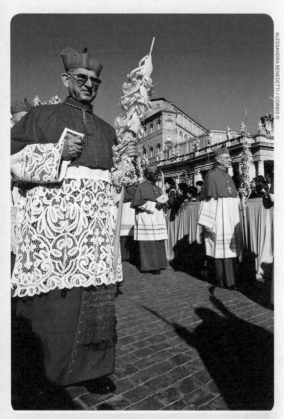

ALESSANDRA BENEDETTI / CORBIS ©

PAOLO COCCO / REUTERS ©

PLAN YOUR TRIP MONTH BY MONTH

# November

**Although the wettest month, November has its compensations – low season prices, excellent jazz concerts and no queues outside the big sights. Autumn is also great for foodies.**

### ✰ Roma Jazz Festival

Jazz masters descend on the Auditorium Parco della Musica for the three-week Roma Jazz Festival (www.romajazzfestival.it). Recent performers have included Macy Gray, Francesco Bearzatti and Nicola Conte.

### ✰ Festival Internazionale di Musica e Arte Sacra

Over four days in mid-November, the Vienna Philharmonic Orchestra and other top ensembles perform a series of classical concerts in Rome's four papal basilicas. Check the programme on www.festivalmusicaeartesacra.net.

# December

**The build-up to Christmas is a jolly time. Crowds brave the cold temperatures to shop for gifts and enjoy the festive lights that adorn much of the city centre.**

### Piazza Navona Christmas Fair

Rome's most beautiful baroque square becomes a big, brash marketplace as brightly lit market stalls set up shop, selling everything from nativity scenes to stuffed toys and teethcracking *torrone* (nougat).

# With Kids

*Despite a reputation as a highbrow cultural destination, Rome has a lot to offer kids. Child-specific sights might be thin on the ground but if you know where to go there's plenty to keep the little 'uns occupied and Mum and Dad happy.*

Investigating the ruins at the Roman Forum (p63)

## Colosseum

Everyone wants to see the Colosseum (p58) and it doesn't disappoint, especially if accompanied by tales of bloodthirsty gladiators and hungry lions. For maximum effect prep your kids beforehand with some Rome-based films – perhaps the *Lizzie McGuire Movie* or the Olsen Twins *When in Rome*; for older teenagers *Gladiator* is a good bet. Your children might well want a photo with one of the costumed Roman legionnaires outside but note that these guys will expect payment for posing with you – €5 is more than enough.

## Museums

Rome's big art museums and galleries are not ideal for rampaging toddlers, but many of the bigger ones now offer educational services and children's workshops, and some host kid-friendly events. There are also some excellent museums for children. Not far from Piazza del Popolo, Explora – Museo del Bambini di Roma (p214) is a museum for kids under 12, with interactive displays and, outside, a free play park open to all.

Out in the distant suburb of EUR, the Museo della Civiltà Romana (p167) is a good bet. With its recreations of ancient bridges, forts and monuments, as well as the room-size model of 4th-century Rome, it provides a great introduction to the city, useful for kids and adults alike.

For something completely different, Rome's cheesy wax museum, the Museo delle Cere (p114), gives the chance to go face to face with popes, rockstars, footie players and opera singers.

## Villa Borghese, Parks & the Zoo

When the time comes to let the kids off the leash, head to Villa Borghese (p212), the most central of Rome's main parks. Here there's plenty of space to run around in – though it's not absolutely car-free – and bikes to hire. The park is also home to Bioparco (p212), Rome's zoo. It isn't cheap, and it's not the best zoo in the world, but after dragging your loved ones to all those churches and museums, it is an option.

PHILIP & KAREN SMITH / LONELY PLANET IMAGES ©

But you don't have to go to the zoo to see animals. There are hundreds of animal sculptures around the city. Kids should look out for an elephant (outside Chiesa di Santa Maria Sopra Minerva), lions (at the foot of the Cordonata staircase up to Piazza del Campidoglio), bees (in Bernini's fountain just off Piazza Barberini), horses, eagles and, of course, Rome's trademark wolf.

Other parks good for a run around include Villa Celimontana (p152), with a popular playground, and Villa Torlonia (p215) on Via Nomentana.

## Creepy Stuff

Rome is full of dark, dank creepy places. Most famously there are the catacombs (p160) on Via Appia Antica. These underground tunnels are fascinating but not suitable for kids under about seven, especially as visits are in guided groups.

Another morbid site is the Capuchin Cemetery under the Chiesa di Santa Maria della Concezione (p114) near Barberini metro station. Again, this isn't one for impressionable toddlers as the spine-chilling crypt is full of skulls and bones, the remains of 4000 Capuchin monks.

## Cinema

A sure-fire kid pleaser, although not for the under 5s, is the Time Elevator (p111) just off Via del Corso. Claiming to be Rome's first ever 5D cinema, it screens the popular film *Time Elevator Rome,* a virtual romp through Roman history that will have you rolling in your seat (quite literally). Less high-tech is the record-breaking Cinema dei Piccoli (p212) in Villa Borghese, which is said to be the world's smallest cinema. It shows kids films most afternoons, although mostly in Italian.

## Ostia Antica

Many of Rome's ancient ruins can be boring for children – they just look like piles of old stones – but Ostia Antica (p220) is different. Here your kids can run along the ancient town's streets, among shops, and up the tiers of its impressive amphitheatre. A trip to Ostia also means a quick ride on a train. However, note that there's little shade on the site so bring water and hats, and take all the usual precautions.

Further afield, and fun to explore with kids, are the Etruscan necropolises at Cerveteri (p225) and Tarquinia (p228).

## Pizza & Ice Cream

Pizza *al taglio* (by the slice) is a godsend for parents of flagging children. It's cheap (about €1 buys two slices of pizza *bianca* – with salt and olive oil), easy to get hold of (there are hundreds of takeaways across town) and works wonders. Ice cream is also manna from heaven, served in *coppette* (tubs) or *coni* (cones) with child-friendly flavours: *fragola* (strawberry), *cioccolato* (chocolate) and *bacio* (with hazelnuts).

# Like a Local

*Gregarious and convivial, the Romans enjoy their city. They love hanging out in its piazzas and speeding around the streets in small cars; they like to dress up and they adore going out. They know theirs is a beautiful city, but they're not jealous and everyone is welcome.*

## Coffee

What tea is for the Brits, coffee is for the Romans, and no day starts without one. As a rule, locals will stop at a bar twice a day for coffee, once in the morning and once after lunch. These are generally drunk fairly quickly during the week but the ritual becomes more leisurely at weekends.

## Going Out

Whether it's teens hanging out on Piazza di Spagna or drinkers spilling out onto Trastevere's piazzas, Romans love to socialise in groups. Friends will go out for a pizza en masse or meet up over an evening *aperitvo,* or simply walk around town together. The early evening *passeggiata* (promenade) is a quintessential Italian experience that is particularly colourful at weekends when families, friends and lovers take to the streets to parade up and down. They won't have a destination in mind as the point isn't actually to go anywhere, but simply to be out there, chatting, flirting, eating ice cream, eyeing each other up. Via del Corso and the streets around Piazza di Spagna are popular *passeggiata* spots.

## Exhibitions, Concerts & Calcio

Romans are great exhibition-goers and while the city's big museums are mainly left to out-of-towners, temporary exhibitions are eagerly supported by locals. Similarly, concerts attract passionate audiences to venues across town, most noticeably the Auditorium Parco della Musica (p212). Football is another local passion, but to avoid gaffes make sure you know the basics – Roma play in red and yellow and their supporters stand in the Curva Sud at the Stadio Olimpico (p213); Lazio play in sky blue and their fans fill the Curva Nord.

# For Free

*Although Rome is an expensive city, you don't have to break the bank to enjoy it. A surprising number of its big sights are free and it costs nothing to stroll the historic streets, piazzas and parks, basking in their extraordinary beauty.*

Strolling past St Peter's Basilica (p184)

## Churches, Museums & Galleries

All of Rome's churches and basilicas are free to enter. Some might have attached museums, cloisters or underground excavations that charge admission but you won't have to pay anything to go into the main church. This means that two of Rome's most famous attractions are completely free: St Peter's Basilica (p184) and the Pantheon (p75), which started life as a pagan temple but is now a church, the Basilica di Santa Maria ad Martyres.

And it's worth noting that many of Rome's churches are laden with priceless art. For example, you'll find sculptures by Michelangelo in St Peter's Basilica (p184), the Basilica di San Pietro in Vincoli (p130), and the Chiesa di Santa Maria Sopra Minerva (p78), and paintings by Caravaggio in the Chiesa di San Luigi dei Francesi (p86), the Chiesa di Sant'Agostino (p80) and the Chiesa di Santa Maria del Popolo (p106).

Many of Rome's museums and galleries are free to EU citizens under 18 and over 65 with discounts available to anyone between 18 and 24. Free to all, however, are the Vatican Museums (p189) on the last Sunday of the month.

## Free (or Nearly Free) Monuments

Some of Rome's best-known monuments are free to enjoy. You don't have to spend a penny to admire the Trevi Fountain (p108), although if you're like most people you'll probably throw a coin or two into the water to ensure you return to the Eternal City.

Another tradition that many enjoy testing is the myth that holds that the Bocca della Verità (p70), will bite your hand off if you tell a lie with your hand in the mouth. Try it, it won't cost you more than a €0.50 donation.

The Spanish Steps (p105) are another free attraction. Rising from Piazza di Spagna, these are a popular site for a sit-down, and as long as you don't eat anything while you're sitting there, you can hang around for as long as you like.

PAOLO CORDELLI / LONELY PLANET IMAGES ©

For a more highbrow experience, sign up for a free guided tour of Palazzo Farnese (p81). This majestic Renaissance palace, now home to the French Embassy, boasts some of Rome's finest frescoes. Note, however, that you'll need to arrange the visit in advance, that tours are in Italian and French only, and that children under 15 are not allowed.

## Piazzas & Parks

Hanging out on Rome's piazzas is a signature Roman experience that doesn't have to cost a *centesimo*. Sure you can pay to eat at a sidewalk cafe on Piazza Navona (p77), but you can equally well sit down on one of the stone benches and enjoy the scenery for nothing. Similarly, on Campo de' Fiori (p80) you can grab a drink at one of the many square-side bars or wander around the daily market for free. Another good people-watching spot is Piazza del Popolo (p107), where you can sit on the steps at the bottom of the central obelisk.

It doesn't cost anything to explore Rome's parks, such as Villa Borghese (p212), Villa Torlonia (p215) or Villa Celimontana (p152). And rising behind Trastevere, the Gianicolo hill (p173) offers some superb views over Rome – yours for nothing more than the effort it takes to walk up there.

## Settimana della Cultura

Usually held in April, this is a week of free admission to Rome's state-run monuments, museums and galleries. This includes big-name sights such as the Colosseum (p58), Palatino (p60) and Roman Forum (p63), as well as top museums like the Museo e Galleria Borghese (p207), Castel Sant'Angelo (p200), the Museo Nazionale Romano: Palazzo Massimo alle Terme (p128) and the Museo Nazionale d'Arte Antica – Palazzo Barberini (p110).

## Eating & Drinking

In Rome you can eat cheaply on takeaway pizza and ice cream but if you want something more varied you'll have to splash out. A good way to eat well for very little is to have an early evening *aperitivo* (aperitif). This allows you to dine on pastas, snacks, rice salads and other nibbles, often in a trendy and good-looking bars, for no more than the price of a drink (generally around €8).

To slate your thirst on free natural spring water, fill up at one of the many drinking fountains across town. It won't save you a fortune but the water is fresh, cool and perfectly safe to drink.

## May Day & Festivals

The main event on Rome's 1 May public holiday is the free rock concert (p24) on Piazza di San Giovanni in Laterano. Organised each year by Italy's biggest trade union, it's massive event attracting hundreds of thousands of fans and some of Italy's top rock gods.

Rome's big public holidays and festivals are a great way of experiencing the city. Summer is an especially good time with many free events staged in atmospheric city-centre locations, but there's action year-round: February means Carnevale (p23) and children in fancy dress, while Rome celebrates its birthday, the so-called Natale di Roma (p23), on 21 April with fireworks and historical processions.

## Public Transport

Children under 10 travel free on Rome's metro and all buses and trams within the city limits. Holders of the Roma Pass (p309) are also entitled to free travel in the city and on selected services in the surrounding Lazio region.

Dining al fresco at Ciampini (p98)

# Eating

*This is a city that lives to eat, rather than eats to live. There is an obsession with the best seasonal ingredients, and some of the city's corners of gastronomic heaven are deceptively simple: home-cooked trattoria food or heaven-sent slices of pizza. However, nowadays there are also many chances to sample cucina creativa (creative cooking), where masterful chefs concoct awe-inspiring takes on Roman cuisine.*

## Roman Cooking

Petronius wrote a satirical account of the banquet of the newly wealthy Trimalchio in the 1st century AD, which fixed in the collective consciousness that ancient Romans ate dormice seasoned with poppies and honey. But the basics of Roman cuisine have remained the same throughout history, resting on the availability of local ingredients: olives, olive oil, pulses, cured pork, lamb, offal, vegetables, wild greens, pecorino cheese, ricotta, wood-baked bread, pasta and fish.

Innards yes, mice no. Like many other Italian cuisines, Roman cooking was born of careful use of the ingredients available – making use of the cheaper cuts of meat, like *guanciale* (pig's cheek), and greens that could be gathered wild from the fields.

### CLASSIC DISHES

Roman favourites are all comfort foods that are seemingly simple (yet notoriously difficult to prepare well) and remarkably tasty. In the classic Roman comedy *I Soliti Ignoti* (Big Deal on Madonna Street; 1958) inept

## NEED TO KNOW

### Prices

The pricing in this chapter refers to the average cost of a meal that includes *primo* (first course), *secondo* (second course) and *dolce* (dessert), plus a glass of wine. Don't be surprised to see *pane e coperto* (bread and cover charge; €1 to €5 per person) added to your bill.

| € | under €25 |
|---|---|
| €€ | €25 to €50 |
| €€€ | over €50 |

### Opening Hours

➡ Most restaurants: noon-3pm & 7.30-11pm, usually closing one day per week (usually Sunday or Monday).

➡ Most eateries close for at least a week in August, but the timings vary from year to year. We have listed here where restaurants close for the whole month. With others it's advisable to ring first in August to check that everyone hasn't gone to the beach.

### Etiquette

➡ Brush up when eating out; Italians dress relatively smartly at most meals.

➡ Bite through hanging spaghetti rather than slurping it up.

➡ Pasta is eaten with a fork (not fork and spoon).

➡ It's OK to eat pizza with your hands.

➡ In an Italian home you may *fare la scarpetta* (make a little shoe) with your bread and wipe plates clean of sauces.

➡ If invited to someone's home, traditional gifts are a tray of *dolci* (sweets) from a *pasticceria* (pastry shop), a bottle of wine or flowers.

### Tipping

Although service is included, leave a tip: anything from 5% in a pizzeria to 10% in a more upmarket place. At least round up the bill.

thieves break through a wall to burgle a safe, but find themselves in a kitchen by mistake, and console themselves by cooking *pasta e ceci* (pasta with chickpeas). Other iconic Roman dishes include *carbonara* (pasta with lardons and egg), *amatriciana* (with tomato and lardons) and *cacio e pepe* (with cheese and pepper), appear on almost every menu in Rome.

The city's conservatism might be measured by its menus, on which belly-warming old favourites are always top of the pots. But nowadays there are ever-increasing Michelin-starred and *cucina creativa* (creative cooking) eateries, where inventive chefs do clever things with Roman staples – adding new ingredients and cooking them in delicate, witty ways.

### ROMAN-JEWISH CUISINE

Most entrenched in culinary tradition is the Jewish Ghetto area, with its hearty Roman-Jewish cuisine, including deep-fried delights and particularly spectacular takes on the artichoke. Deep-frying is a staple of *cucina ebraico-romanesca* (Roman-Jewish cooking), and dates to the period between the 16th and 19th centuries when the Jews were confined to the city's ghetto. To add flavour to their limited ingredients – those spurned by the rich, such as courgette (zucchini) flowers – they began to fry everything from mozzarella to *baccalà* (salted cod).

### THE CULINARY CALENDAR

According to the culinary calendar, which was initiated by the Catholic Church to vary the nutrition of its flock, fish is eaten on Friday, and *baccalà* (salted cod) is often eaten with *ceci* (chickpeas), usually on Wednesday.

Thursday is the day for gnocchi (dumplings). The traditional, heavy Roman recipe uses semolina flour, but you can also find the typical gnocchi with potatoes.

### OFFAL SPECIALITIES

For the heart (and liver and brains) of the *cucina Romana,* head to Testaccio, a traditional working-class district, clustered around the city's former slaughterhouse. This proximity led to the area specialising in offal – a major feature of Roman cooking. In the past, butchers who worked in the city abattoir were often paid in meat as well as money. But they got the cuts that the moneyed classes didn't want, the offal, and so they developed ways to cook them – usually extremely slowly, to develop the flavour and disguise their origins. The Roman staple *coda alla vaccinara* translates as 'oxtail cooked butcher's style'.

A famous Roman dish that's not for the fainthearted is pasta with *pajata*, made

## THE POWER OF PASTA

In *Un Americano a Roma* (An American in Rome; 1954), Roman actor Alberto Sordi wants to be an American. He comes home to a bowl of his mamma's pasta, but rejects it, trying instead to eat bread with milk before spitting it out. The power of pasta is too strong. Exasperated, he says, 'Maccarone, why are you looking at me? You provoke me and I shall destroy you!' A black-and-white photo of Sordi forking the spaghetti into his mouth is probably a more commonly reproduced image than that of the Sistine Chapel.

with the entrails of young veal calves, considered a delicacy since they contain the mother's congealed milk. If you see the word *coratella* in a dish, it means you'll be eating lights (lungs), kidneys and hearts. Often the offal is cooked with *carciofi* (artichokes), which cuts its richness and leaves the palate refreshed. At other times tomato is used, and the expression *in umido,* while normally meaning cooked in a broth, in Lazio tends to mean cooked in a tomato-scented broth.

### SEAFOOD

It's by no means all about cheap cuts of meat. Seafood can be excellent in Rome; it's fished locally in Lazio. There are lots of dedicated seafood restaurants, usually upper-range places with delicate takes on fish such as sea bass, skate and tuna.

### DESSERT

*Dolci* (desserts) tend to be the same at every trattoria: tiramisù, *pannacotta* ('cooked cream', with added sugar and cooled to set) and so on, but for a traditional Roman *dolce* you should look out for ricotta cakes – with chocolate chips or cherries or both – at a local bakery. Many Romans eat at a restaurant and then go elsewhere for a gelato and a coffee to finish off the meal.

### Eat as the Romans Do

For *colazione* (breakfast), most Romans head to a bar for a cappuccino and *cornetto* – a croissant filled with *cioccolata* (chocolate), *marmellata* (marmalade) or *crema* (custard cream).

The main meal of the day is *pranzo* (lunch), eaten at about 1.30pm. Many shops and businesses close for three to four hours every afternoon to accommodate the meal and siesta that follows. On Sundays *pranzo* is sacred.

*Cena* (dinner), eaten any time from about 8.30pm, is usually a simple affair, although this is changing as fewer people make it home for the big lunchtime feast.

A full Italian meal consists of an antipasto (starter), a *primo piatto* (first course), a *secondo piatto* (second course) with an *insalata* (salad) or *contorno* (vegetable side dish), *dolci* (sweet), fruit, coffee and *digestivo* (liqueur). When eating out, however, you can do as most Romans do, and mix and match: order, say, a *primo* followed by an *insalata* or *contorno*.

### Vegetarians & Vegans

Panic not, vegetarians, you can eat well in Rome, with the choice of bountiful antipasti, pasta dishes, *insalati* (salad), *contorni* (side dishes) and pizzas. There are a couple of extremely good vegetarian restaurants, and some of the more creative restaurants have greater choice of vegetarian dishes.

Be mindful of hidden ingredients not mentioned on the menu – for example, steer clear of anything that's been stuffed (like courgette flowers, often spiced up with anchovies) or check that it's *senza carne o pesce* (without meat or fish). Note that to many Italians vegetarian means you don't eat red meat.

Vegans are in for a tougher time. Cheese is used universally, so you must specify that you want something *'senza formaggio'* (without cheese). Also remember that *pasta fresca,* which may also turn up in soups, is made with eggs. The safest bet is to self-cater or try a dedicated vegetarian restaurant, which will always have some vegan options.

### Where to Eat

Eateries are divided into several categories.

#### FAST FOOD

A *tavola calda* (hot table) offers cheap, pre-prepared pasta, meat and vegetable dishes. Quality is usually reasonable while atmosphere takes a back seat. In Ostia Antica (p220) you can see the *tavola calda*'s ancient ancestor, a *thermopile* complete with frescoed menu.

## FEASTING, FASTING

The classic way to celebrate any feast day in Italy is to precede it with a day of eating *magro* (lean) to prepare for the overindulgence to come. On Vigilia (Christmas Eve), for example, tradition dictates that you eat little during the day and have a fish-based dinner as a prelude to the excesses of the 25th. Many special days have dishes associated with them: on Ferragosto (Feast of the Assumption; 15 August) Romans eat *pollo e peperoni* (chicken with peppers).

Most festivals have some kind of food involved, but many of them have no other excuse than food. These are called *sagre* (feasting festivals) and are usually celebrations of local specialities such as hazelnuts, wine and sausages.

A *rosticceria* sells cooked meats but often has a larger selection of takeaway food. There are also takeaway pizza joints serving ready *pizza al taglio* (by the slice). When it's good, it's very good.

### ENOTECHE (WINE BARS)

You can eat well at many *enoteche,* ie wine bars that usually serve snacks (such as cheeses or cold meats, *bruschette* and *crostini*) and some hot dishes. Where these are so good they are worth dining out at, they're listed under 'Eating' in the neighbourhood chapters.

### TRATTORIA, OSTERIA OR RESTAURANT?

Usually for a full meal you'll want a trattoria, an *osteria* (neighbourhood inn), a *ristorante* (restaurant) or a pizzeria.

It was the growing numbers of pilgrims from the 14th century onwards in Rome that saw a proliferation of taverns and *osterie* (neighbourhood inns), which usually specialised in one dish and *vino della casa* (house wine). Grand Tourists (rich pilgrims, in search of Art rather than God) arrived in the 18th century, and *osterie* became more sophisticated.

The difference between the different types of eateries is now fairly blurred. Traditionally, trattorias were family-run places that offered a basic, affordable local menu, and there are still lots of these around. There are also new incarnations of these, which use the faithful formula (ging-

ham tablecloths, old friends on the menu) but offer innovative cuisine and scholarly wine lists – places such as Ditirambo (p93), Tram Tram (p140) and Matricianella (p95). *Ristoranti,* however, offer more choice and smarter service, and are more expensive.

Ethnic restaurants are more prevalent these days, though in Rome Italian food remains king. Even the way people eat is changing. Hip young Romans do brunch and graze on *aperitivo* (early-evening snacks and drinks), creative Italian restaurants turn food into art, farmers' markets trade at weekends, and '0km' (the ultimate in local produce) is in danger of becoming a culinary cliche.

However, the old stalwart trattoria is still where every Roman returns, and some of the city's most memorable culinary experiences are to be had enjoying home-cooked food served by a shuffling matriarch.

### Aperitivo

Aperitivo is a trend from Milan that's been taken up with gusto in Rome – a buffet of snacks to accompany evening drinks in bars and some restaurants, usually from around 6pm till 9pm, and costing around €8-10 for a drink and unlimited platefuls. The younger generation sometimes turn *aperitivo* into a replacement for dinner (but don't tell their parents).

### Pizza

Remarkably, pizza was only introduced to Rome post-WWII, by southern immigrants. But it's like it's been here forever, and every Roman's favourite casual meal remains the gloriously simple pizza, with Rome's signature wafer-thin, bubbling-topped pizzas slapped down on tables by waiters on a mission. A pizzeria will, of course, serve pizza, but many also offer a full menu including antipasti, pasta, meat and vegetable dishes. They're often only open in the evening. Most Romans will precede their pizza with a starter of *bruschetta* or *fritti* (mixed fried things, such as zucchini flowers, potato, olives etc) and wash it all down with beer.

For a snack on the run, Rome's *pizza al taglio* (pizza by the slice) places are hard to beat, with some combinations loaded atop thin, crispy, light-as-air, slow-risen bread that verge on the divine.

## Markets

Rome's fresh-produce markets are a fabulous feature of the city's foodscape. Go to see what's in season and enter the fray with the neighbourhood matriarchs. The markets operate from around 7am to 1.30pm, Monday to Saturday.

Rome's most famous markets:

➡ **Campo de' Fiori** (Map p346; 🚍Corso Vittorio Emanuele II) The most picturesque, but also the most expensive. Prices are graded according to the shopper's accent.

➡ **Nuovo Mercato Esquilino** (Map p340; Via Lamarmora; Ⓜ Vittorio Emanuele) One of Rome's cheapest markets and the best place to find exotic herbs and spices.

➡ **Piazza dell' Unità** (Map p364; 🚍Piazza del Risorgimento) Near the Vatican, perfect for stocking up for a picnic.

➡ **Piazza San Cosimato** (Map p360; 🚍or 🚊Viale di Trastevere) Trastevere's neighbourhood market, still the business with foodstuffs.

➡ **Testaccio** (Map p356; Piazza Testaccio; 🚍or 🚊Via Marmorata) The most Roman of all. Sharpen your elbows and admire the queuing techniques of the elderly. It's noted for its excellent quality and good prices.

## Self-catering

For deli supplies and wine, shop at *alimentari,* which generally open 7am to 1.30pm and 5pm to 8pm daily except Thursday afternoon and Sunday (during the summer months they will often close on Saturday afternoon instead of Thursday). See also the Markets, above.

You can stock up at the small supermarkets dotted around town:

➡ **Conad** (Stazione Termini)

➡ **DeSpar** (Via Giustiniani 18b-21) Near the Pantheon.

➡ **DeSpar** (Via Nazionale 212-213) Near Piazza della Republica.

➡ **Dì per Dì** (Via Vittoria) Near the Spanish Steps.

➡ **Sir** (Piazza dell'Indipendenza 28)

➡ **Todis** (Via Natale del Grande 24) In Trastevere.

## Ice Cream

Eating gelato is as much part of Roman life as the morning coffee – try it and you'll understand why. The city has some of the world's finest ice-cream shops, which use only the finest seasonal ingredients. In these artisanal gelatarie you won't find strawberry icecream in winter, for example, and ingredients are sourced from where they are reputedly the best, so, pistachios from Bronte, almonds from Avola. It's all come a long way since Nero snacked on snow mixed with fruit pulp and honey.

The following are all shining stars of the ice-cream scene, but a rule of thumb for elsewhere is to check the colour of the pistachio: ochre-green = good, bright-green = bad. Most places open from around 8am to 1am, though hours are shorter in winter. Prices range from around €1.50 to €3.50 for a *cona* (cone) or *coppetta* (tub). Here follows a highly controversial top five.

➡ **Alberto Pica** (see p94)

➡ **Fior di Luna** (see p120).

➡ **Il Caruso** (see p120)

➡ **Palazzo del Freddo di Giovanni Fassi** (see p138)

➡ **San Crispino** (see p120)

## Seasonal Calendar

Although nowadays you can, of course, get some produce year round, Rome's kitchens still remain true to what is best for the time of year.

### SPRING

Spring is prime time for lamb, perfect roasted with potatoes – *agnello al forno con patate.* Sometimes it's described as *abbacchio* (Roman dialect for lamb) *scottadito* ('hot enough to burn fingers').

May and June are favourable fishing months, and thus good for cuttlefish and octopus, as well as other seafood.

March to April is the best season for *carciofo alla giudia* (Jewish-style artichoke), when the big round artichokes from Cerveteri appear on the table (smaller varieties are from Sardinia).

Grass-green *fave* (broad beans) are eaten after a meal in the countryside, best accompanied by some salty *pecorino* cheese. A big day for doing this is May 1.

It's also time to tuck into *risotto con asparagi di bosco* (rice with woodland asparagus), as asparagus comes into its prime.

You'll see two types of courgette on Roman market stalls; the familiar dark-green kind, and the lighter green, fluted *zucchine romanesche* (Roman courgette), usually with the flowers still attached – these orange petals, deep-fried, are a delectable feature of Roman cooking.

This the time to visit Nemi in the Castelli Romani, to eat its famous wild strawberries.

## Summer

*Tonno* (tuna) comes fresh from the seas around Sardinia; *linguine ai frutti di mare* and *risotto alla pescatora* are good light summer dishes.

Summertime is *melanzane* (aubergine) time: tuck into them grilled as antipasti or fried and layered with rich tomato sauce in *melanzane alla parmagiana,* or try *melanzane e peperoni stufati (*stuffed aubergine and peppers).

Summer is the season for leafy greens, and Rome even has its own lettuce, the sturdy, flavourful *lattuga romana*. It's usually eaten in a fresh green or mixed salad, dressed simply with olive oil, vinegar and salt.

Tomatoes are at their full-bodied finest – it's the ideal moment for a light *spaghetti al pomodoro* (with fresh tomatoes and basil).

Seductive heaps of *pesche* (peaches) and *albicocche* (apricots) dominate market stalls.

Luscious, succulent, fleshy *fichi* (figs) begin in June, perfect with some salty *proscitto crudo* (cured ham).

### AUTUMN

*Alla cacciatora* (hunter-style) dishes are sourced from Lazio's hills, with meats such as *cinghiale* (boar) and *lepre* (hare).

Fish is also good in autumn; you could try fried fish from Fiumicino, such as *triglia* (red mullet), or mixed small fish, such as *alici* (anchovies).

Autumn also equals mushrooms – the meaty porcini, *galletti* and *ovuli* – and *broccoletti* (also called *broccolini*), a cross between broccoli and asparagus, appears at Roman markets as summer begins to fade; it's often served fried with *aglio* (garlic) and *olio* (olive oil). Other autumnal vegetables include cauliflower and *spinaci* (spinach), while aubergine, peppers and tomatoes continue. *Cicoria selvatica (*wild chicory) has dark-green leaves and a bitter taste, and is at its best sautéed with spicy pepper and garlic. Fruitwise, heaping the markets are *uva* (grapes), *pere* (pears) and *meloni* (melon).

Nuts are now in season, and creamy *nocciola* (hazelnut) and *marron* (chestnut) will be adorning ice-cream cones all over the city.

### WINTER

Winter is the ideal time to eat dishes with *ceci* (chickpeas) and minestrone, as well as herb-roasted *porchetta di Ariccia* (pork from Ariccia).

*Puntarelle* ('little points' – Catalonian chicory), a green found only in Lazio, is a delicious, slightly bitter winter green, often tossed with a dressing of anchovy, garlic and olive oil. *Finnochio* (fennel) is a favourite winter vegetable, eaten in salads or on its own. *Broccolo Romanesco* (Roman broccoli) looks like a cross between broccoli and a cauliflower.

Markets are piled high with *aranci* (oranges) and *mandarini* (mandarins), their brilliant orange set off by dark-green leaves.

In February, look out for *frappé* (strips of fried dough sprinkled with sugar), eaten at carnival time.

## Food & Wine Courses

Check out the **Città di Gusto** (City of Taste; Map p358; [☎]06 551 12 21; Via Enrico Fermi 161), a six-storey shrine to food created by Italian foodie organisation **Gambero Rosso** (www.gamberorosso.it, in Italian). It has cooking courses starring Rome's top chefs, a wine bar, pizza workshop, cookbook shop and the **Teatro del Vino** for demonstrations, tastings and lessons. For taste-sensation culinary events featuring the best in local produce, there's Rome's **Slow Food movement** (www.slowfoodroma.com, in Italian).

Cookery writer Diane Seed (*The Top One Hundred Pasta Sauces*) runs her **Roman Kitchen** (Map p346; [☎]06 678 57 59; http://italiangourmet.com/) several times a year from her kitchen in the Palazzo Doria Pamphilj. There are one-day courses (which include a market visit) costing €200 per day and week-long courses for €1000.

## Lonely Planet's Best

**La Rosetta** (p89) Sublime, classy fish restaurant in view of the Pantheon.

**Forno di Campo de'Fiori** (p93) If angels made pizza by the slice, this is how it'd taste.

**Glass Hostaria** (p176) Italian cuisine as a creative art in Trastevere.

**Open Colonna** (p139) Cooking with verve, wit and flair under a glass roof.

**L'Asino d'Oro** (p135) Fantastic food, stunning value and Umbrian flavours.

## Best Creative

Agata e Romeo (p138)

Glass Hostaria (p176)

Ristorante L'Arcangelo (p202)

Open Colonna (p139)

Ditirambo (p93)

## Best Pizzerias

Pizzeria Ivo (p176)

Panattoni (p175)

Pizzeria al Leoncino (p95)

Bir & Fud (p175)

Pizzeria da Baffetto (p91)

## Best Pizza by the Slice

Pizzarium (p203)

Antico Forno Roscioli (p93)

Forno di Campo de' Fiori (p93)

Da Michele (p119)

Panella l'Arte del Pane (p138)

## Best-Value Eats

L'Asino d'Oro (p135)

Casa Coppelle (p89)

Open Colonna (p139)

Sora Margherita (p94)

Cacio e Pepe (p202)

## Best Settings

Il Palazzetto (p118)

Osteria Ar Galletto (p93)

La Veranda de l'Hotel Columbus (p201)

Open Colonna (p139)

Casa Bleve (p91)

## Best Regional

Palatium (p117)

L'Asino d'Oro (p135)

Colline Emiliane (p120)

Trattoria Monti (p138)

Gelarmony (p201)

## Best See & Be Seen

Pastificio San Lorenzo (p140)

Said (p140)

Dal Bolognese (p115)

Settembrini Café (p202)

Ristorante L'Arcangelo (p202)

An evening drink at La Maison (p96)

# 🍷 Drinking & Nightlife

*There's simply no city with better backdrops for a drink. You can sip a cappuccino overlooking the Roman Forum or crack open the Campari while watching the light bounce off baroque fountains. Often the best way to enjoy nightlife in Rome is to wander from restaurant to bar, getting happily lost down picturesque cobbled streets and being serendipitously awestruck by ancient splendour.*

## Rome After Dark

Rome, like most cities, is a collection of districts, all with their particular character, and different areas attract different crowds when night falls.

The *bella figura* (loosely translated as 'looking good') is important. The majority of locals spend evenings looking beautiful, checking each other out, partaking of the odd ice cream, and not getting drunk – that would be most unseemly. However, this is

changing and certain areas – particularly those popular with a younger crowd – can get rowdy with tipsy teens (for example, around Campo de' Fiori and parts of Trastevere). To try to combat late-night rowdiness, there are strict new regulations in force that mean that drinks may not be taken out onto the street beyond the terrace area of a particular bar.

If you're looking for a chance to go dancing, bear in mind that although the city is no Berlin or London, there's still plenty of after-dark fun to be had. Up-for-it Romans tend to eat late, then drink at bars before heading off to a club at around 1am. It can be difficult to get around, as some of the most interesting places are far-flung – despite drink-and-drive rules, most locals drive, which partly explains the alarming road-accident statistics.

## Enoteche (Wine Bars)

The *enoteca* was where the old boys from the neighbourhood used to drink rough local wine poured straight from the barrel. Times have changed: nowadays they tend to be sophisticated if still atmospheric places, offering Italian and international vintages, delicious cheeses and cold cuts. Some are so good that they are listed in the Eating rather than the Drinking sections of the relevant neighbourhood. However, their main purpose is wine, and you'll find an incredible choice of wines from all over Italy in these places.

## Bars & Pubs

You'll find there are numerous pubs dotted around Rome. They are based on the Irish or British model and look like the real thing, but are generally populated with better-groomed people. In recent years, beer drinking has really taken off in Rome (see p40).

Bars range from regular Italian cafe-bars that have remained the same for centuries, to chic, carefully styled places just made for esoteric cocktails (such as Salotto Locarno p120, close to Piazza del Popolo), to laid-back, perennially popular haunts (such as Freni e Frizioni in Trastevere, that have a longevity rarely seen in other cities.

## Nightclubs

Rome has a range of nightclubs with music policies ranging from lounge and jazz to mainstream house, and from retro burlesque to dancehall and hip hop, so you're bound to find something to suit your taste. Clubs tend to get busy after midnight, or even after 2am. Often admission is free, but drinks are expensive. Cocktails can cost from €10 to €16, but you can drink much more cheaply in the student clubs of San Lorenzo, Pigneto and the *centri sociali* (social centres).

## NEED TO KNOW

**Opening hours**
➡ Most cafes: 7.30am to 8pm
➡ Traditional bars: 7.30am to 1am or 2am.
➡ Most bars, pubs and *enoteche* (wine bars): lunchtime or 6pm to 2am.
➡ Nightclubs: 10pm to 4am.

**Dress Codes**
Romans tend to dress up to go out, and most people will be looking pretty sharp in the smarter clubs and bars in the Centro Storico and Testaccio. However, over in Pigneto and San Lorenzo or at the *centri sociali* (social centres) the look of choice is much more grungy – men without some sort of facial hair may look out of place!

**Online resources**
➡ Rome C'e www.romace.it/home
➡ Roma 2 Night http://roma.2night.it
➡ Zero http://roma.zero.eu/

**Door Policies**
Some of the more popular nightclubs have a seemingly whimsical door policy, and men, whether single or in groups, will often find themselves turned away. At many clubs both men and women will have to dress up to get in or fit in.

## Centri Sociali

Rome's flip side is a surprising alternative underbelly, centred on left-wing *centri sociali* grungy squatter arts centres that often have live music and contemporary arts events, and where dressed down is the look. These centres of anti-establishment counterculture were set up in the 1970s in disused public buildings, such as factories, garages or industrial estates. Then, squatters regularly battled with police, while nowadays most have been around long enough to be part of the establishment. However, they still offer Rome's most unusual and alternative nightlife option, including gigs, club nights and exhibitions, and follow a left-wing political agenda. They're also a bargain, in accordance with their ethic of accessible culture.

Most important are Rialtosantambrogio (p98), Brancaleone (p217) and Villaggio Globale (p156). There's also **Forte**

## FREE WI-FI

More and more Roman bars and cafes have free wi-fi. Some of the nicest locations to check your mail include:

**Barnum Cafe** (p96)

**Etablì** (p96)

**Circus** (p96)

**Chiostro del Bramante Caffè** (p91)

**0,75** (p72)

**TAD** (p122)

**Prenestino** (Map p340; ☑06 218 07 855; www. forteprenestino.net; Via F Delpino Centocelle), housed in a fort east of the city centre, where there are gigs, vintage markets and much more, including a fantastic alternative May Day festival (forget the famous mainstream concert at San Giovanni and head here).

### Rome in Summer

From around mid-June to mid-September, many nightclubs and live-music venues close, some moving to EUR, or the beaches at Fregene or Ostia. The area around the Isola Tiberina throngs with life nightly during the **Lungo er Tevere...Roma**, which sprouts bars, stalls and an open-air cinema.

This chapter supplies venues' regular hours, but be aware that in winter bars often close earlier in the evening, particularly in areas where the norm is to drink outside.

### Listings

For listings check *Trovaroma* (an insert in daily newspaper *La Repubblica*) on Thursday and *Roma C'è* on Wednesday, both of which have a short English section, or the English-language *Wanted in Rome* magazine, published every second Wednesday. Also, in bars and cafes look out for the free nightlife listings in monthly listings guide *Zero*. See also online resources under Need to Know.

### Gay & Lesbian Rome

There's no openly gay part of town and only a smattering of dedicated clubs and bars, though many clubs host regular gay and lesbian nights, listed throughout this chapter. You usually have to ring a bell to gain entry to Rome's gay bars, an indication of the underground feel to the scene. However, Rome's pinker side is by no means invisible: there's a Gay Pride march annually in mid-June, the 10-week **Gay Village** (www.gayvillage.it; ⊙Jul–mid-Sep), a temporary complex of bars, clubs, cinema and even fitness areas, hosting lots of different gigs and club nights, such as the special Bears in Rome (www.bears inrome.it) event. It has run in different locations (usually in EUR) for more than five years.

For local information, pick up a copy of the monthly magazine *AUT,* which has up-to-date listings and is published by **Circolo Mario Mieli** (p308). **AZ Gay** (www.azgay.it) also produces an annual gay guide to Rome, available at tourist kiosks. Lesbians can find out more about the local scene at **Coordinamento Lesbiche Italiano** (p308), which has a recommended women-only restaurant, Luna e L'Altra (men are allowed at lunch time).

Most gay venues (bars, clubs and saunas) require you to have an **Arcigay** (www. arcigayroma.it) membership card. These cost €15/8 per year/three months and are available from any venue that requires one.

### Social Networking

**Friends in Rome** (www.friendsinrome.com) is a social organisation that offers a chance to mingle with an international crowd – a mix of expats, locals and out-of-towners – and find out about the local social scene. The friendly organisers arrange regular social events, including *aperitivi* (aperative) evenings and film showings.

### Beer Revolution

In recent years the microbrewery has taken off in Italy, making this one of the best places in the world to sample artisanal beers. In Rome, the place to head to try out beers such as 'Brewfist Spaceman' or the 'Blind Eye' is Trastevere, especially Ma Che Siete Venuti a Fà (p177), which has a fantastic range of specialist, vintage and rare brews, Bir & Fud (p175), just across the road, which serves fragrant beers up with organic pizzas, or Open Baladin (p96), with its long bar lined with around 40 taps.

## Lazio Wines

Lazio wines may not yet be household names, but it's well worth trying some local wines while you're here. Although whites dominate Lazio's production – 95% of the region's Denominazione di Origine Controllata (DOC; the second of Italy's four quality classifications) wines are white – there are a few notable reds worth dipping into as well. To try any wines from Lazio, Palatium (p117) is the place.

### WHITES

Most of the house white you'll guzzle in Rome will be from the Castelli Romani area to the southeast of Rome, centred on Frascati and Marino. It arrives by truck: robust and honest, usually mixed from Trebbiano and Malvasia grapes.

However, as Italian wine producers have raised their game to face international competition, so Lazio's winemakers have joined the fray. New production techniques have led to a lighter, drier wine that is beginning to be taken seriously. Frascati Superiore is now an excellent tipple, Castel de Paolis' Vigna Adriana wins plaudits, while the emphatically named Est! Est!! Est!!!, produced by the renowned wine house Falesco, which is based in Montefiascone on the volcanic banks of Lago Bolsena, is becoming increasingly drinkable.

---

### ROME'S BEST GAY VENUES AND NIGHTS

→ **Hangar** (p143) A cruisy, long-standing gay bar that hosts various special nights.

→ **Coming Out** (p155) Under the shadow of the Colosseum on what's sometime nicknamed 'gay street', this popular laid-back bar is more out than most – it spills onto the street and there's no doorbell.

→ **Omogenic** (p142) Circolo degli Artisti's weekly gay night.

→ **Venus Rising** (p166) The capital's only lesbian night: last Sunday of the month at Goa.

→ **Max's Bar** (p143) Welcoming Max's is a long-running favourite.

→ **Muccassassina** (p307) Weekly extravaganza at Qube.

---

### REDS

Falesco, based in Lazio, also produces the excellent Montiano, blended from Merlot grapes. Colacicchi's Torre Ercolana from Anagni is another opulent red, which blends local Cesanese di Affile with Cabernet Sauvignon and Merlot. Velvety, complex and fruity, this is a world-class wine.

## Coffee

For Romans, coffee punctuates and marks the process of the day, from the morning and mid-morning cappuccino, to the afternoon espresso pick-me-up, or summertime granita with cream.

To do as the Romans do, you have to be precise about your coffee needs. For an espresso (a shot of strong black coffee), ask for *un caffè;* if you want it with a drop of hot/cold milk, order *un caffè macchiato* ('stained' coffee) *caldo/freddo.* Long black coffee (as in a weaker, watered-down version) is known as *caffè lungo* (an espresso with more water) or *caffè all'american* (a filter coffee). If you fancy a coffee but one more shot will catapult you through the ceiling, you can drink *orzo,* made from roasted barley but served like coffee.

Then, of course, there's the cappuccino (coffee with frothy milk, served warm rather than hot). If you want it without froth, ask for a *cappuccino senza schiuma;* if you want it hot, ask for it *ben caldo.* Italians drink cappuccino only during the morning and never after meals; to order it after 11am would be, well, foreign. In summer *cappuccino freddo* (iced coffee with milk, usually already sugared), a *caffè freddo* (iced espresso) or *granita di caffè* (frozen coffee, usually with cream) top the charts. A *caffè latte* is a milkier version of the cappuccino with less froth and *latte macchiato* is even milkier (warmed milk 'stained' with a spot of coffee). A *caffè corretto* is an espresso 'corrected' with a dash of grappa or something similarly strong.

There are two ways to drink coffee in a Roman bar-cafe: you can either take it standing up at the bar, in which case pay first at the till and then, with your receipt, order at the counter; or you can sit down at a table and enjoy waiter service. In the latter case you'll pay up to double what you'd pay at the bar.

## Drinking & Nightlife by Neighbourhood

**Centro Storico** (p95) Bars and a few clubs, a mix of touristy and sophisticated.

**Trastevere** (p177) Everyone's favourite place for a *passeggiata* (evening stroll), with plenty of bars and cafes.

**Testaccio** (p154) With a cluster of mainstream clubs, there's something for almost every taste.

**Ostiense** (p166) Home to Rome's cooler nightclubs, mostly housed in ex-industrial venues.

**San Lorenzo** (p141) Favoured by students; concentration of bars and alternative clubs; cheaper than the city centre.

**Ponte Milvio** (p216) Top of the pops with Rome's Smart car-driving, designer-clad bank-of-mama-and-papa youth.

## Lonely Planet's Top Choices

**Ai Tre Scalini** (p141) Buzzing *enoteca* that feels as convivial as a pub.

**Ma Che Siete Venuti a Fa'** (p177) Tiny pub that's the heart of Rome's artisanal beer explosion.

**Il Barretto** (p180) Chic, off-the-track, stylishly designed Gianicolo bar.

**Caffè Sant'Eustachio** (p96) Serves Rome's best coffee, with a secret recipe.

**Salotto Locarno** (p120) Beautiful, sympathetically made-over art deco bar that's perfect for cocktails.

## Best Cafes

Caffè Sant'Eustachio (p96)

Caffè Tazza d'Oro (p96)

Bar della Pace (p96)

Caffè Farnese (p97)

## Best for a Lazy Drink

La Bottega del Caffé (p141)

Ombre Rosse (p180)

Necci (p142)

Bar della Pace (p96)

Panella l'Arte del Pane (p138)

## Best for Dancing

Circolo degli Artisti (p142)

Goa (p166)

Rashomon (p167)

La Saponeria (p167)

Rialtosantambrogio (p98)

## Best Enoteche

Ai Tre Scalini (p141)

Cavour 313 (p72)

Casa Bleve (p91)

La Meschita (p180)

Palatium (p117)

## Best Settings

Chiostro del Bramante Caffè (p91)

Caffè Capitolino (p72)

Aroma (p155)

Il Baretto (p180)

Salotto Gianicolo (p120)

## Best Museum Cafes

Caffè Capitolino (p72)

MAXXI (p213)

Auditorium Parco della Musica (p217)

Galleria Nazionale d'Arte Moderna (p212)

Castel Sant'Angelo (p200)

Concert during Rome international film festival (p45)

#  Entertainment

*Watching the world go by in Rome is often entertainment enough, but don't let that make you overlook the local arts and sports scene. Rome is home to the extraordinary Auditorium Parco della Musica, which hosts scores of international artists of all genres. The city also has myriad arts festivals, especially in summer, performances in its venues and churches, and football games that split the city in twain.*

## Music

Music in Rome is thriving, and the city's abundance of beautiful settings makes Rome a superb place to catch a concert, be it classical, jazz or pop. These days myriad international stars play in the Eternal City, and this artistic revolution is all down to one building: the Auditorium Parco della Musica is a state-of-the-art, modernist complex that combines architectural innovation with stunning looks and perfect acoustics, and hosts a remarkable range of gigs and concerts of all genres.

### CLASSICAL

Music in Rome is not just about the Auditorium, however. There are concerts by the Accademia Filarmonica Romana at Teatro Olimpico (p217); academy members have included Verdi and Rossini, and it still attracts star performers. Rome's premier classical music venue before the Auditorium was opened, Auditorium Conciliazione (p204) is also still a force to be reckoned with, and hosts some fine music and dance performances, as does the **Istituzione Universitaria dei Concerti** (☑06 361 00 51; www.concertiiuc.

## NEED TO KNOW

### Listings

**Roma C'è** (www.romace.it, in Italian; €1) is Rome's most comprehensive listings guide, and comes complete with a small English-language section; it's published every Wednesday. Another useful guide is *Trova Roma*, which comes as a free insert with *La Repubblica* every Thursday.

**Wanted in Rome** (www.wantedinrome. com; €1) is an English-language magazine that contains listings in English, and is published every second Wednesday. Free listings booklet **Zero** (www.zero.eu) contains a wide range of entertainment.

### Internet Resources

➡ Comune di Roma (www.comune. roma.it; www.060608.it)

➡ In Rome Now (www.inromenow.com)

➡ Roma Musica (www.romamusica.it)

➡ Tutto Teatro (www.tuttoteatro.com, in Italian)

### Tickets

Tickets for concerts, live music and theatrical performances are widely available across the city. Prices range enormously depending on the venue and artist. Hotels can often reserve tickets for guests, or you can contact the venue or organisation directly – check listings publications for booking details. Otherwise you can try:

➡ **Comune di Roma** (www.060608.it)

➡ **Hellò Ticket** (☑800 90 70 80, 06 480781; www.helloticket.it, in Italian)

➡ **Orbis** (☑06 474 47 76; Piazza dell'Esquilino 37; ☺9.30am-1pm & 4-7.30pm Mon-Fri, closed Aug) Near the Basilica di Santa Maria Maggiore.

it; Piazzale Aldo Moro 5), with a season of concerts featuring lots of guest international artists and orchestras from October to May, held in the Aula Magna of La Sapienza University.

Free classical concerts are often held in many of Rome's churches, especially at Easter and around Christmas and New Year. Seats are available on a first-come, first-served basis, and the programmes usually feature beautiful renditions of classical music – look out for local listings or information at Rome's tourist kiosks.

The Chiesa di Sant'Ignazio di Loyola (p87) is a popular venue for choral masses, as are the Pantheon (p75) and Basilica di San Giovanni in Laterano (p149). The Basilica di San Paolo Fuori le Mura (p133) hosts an important choral mass on 25 January and the hymn *Te Deum* is sung at the Chiesa del Gesù (p81) on 31 December.

### OPERA

Historically, opera in Rome was long opposed by the papacy, and although the first public opera house opened here in the 17th century, it was only after independence that Rome's opera scene began to develop. Mascagnai's *Cavalleria Rusticana,* Puccini's *Tosca* and Rossini's operas *Il Barbiere di Siviglia* and *La Cenerentola* all premiered here.

Rome's opera house, the Teatro dell'Opera di Roma, is a magnificent, grandiose venue, lined in gilt and red, but productions can be a bit hit and miss. For an experience even more spectacular than an opera in these gilded surroundings, catch a performance when the company moves outdoors for the summer season at the ancient Roman Terme di Caracalla (see p156), an unparalleled location.

You can also see opera in various other outdoor locations, which vary from year to year: check current listings or at the tourist information kiosks (p312) for details. During the summer season, the marvellous Concerti del Tempietto (see Arts Festivals, p46) hosts chamber concerts hosted at the Teatro di Marcello.

### JAZZ, ROCK & POP

Major concerts are held indoors or outdoors at the Auditorium della Musica (p212), with recent gigs over a typical month having included performances by Burt Bacharach, Elton John, Primal Scream and Lou Reed.

Large concerts also take place at Rome's sports stadiums, including Stadio Olimpico (☑06 368 57 520; Viale dei Gladiatori).

Jazz is a popular soundtrack for the Eternal City, and there are numerous jazz and blues clubs, including Big Mama in Trastevere, Gregory's in Tridente, Alexanderplatz close to the Vatican, the Charity Café in Monti and the Casa del Jazz in southern Rome. In summer there's the glorious Villa Celimontana Jazz Festival, which takes place under the stars, shaded by umbrella palms, in the central park of

Villa Celimontana, with lots of international stars.

Many nightclubs also host live gigs. Places such as Locanda Atlantide in San Lorenzo, and Fanfulla 101 and Circolo degli Artisti, in and around Pigneto, host alternative rock and pop acts, and also organise outdoor events in some of Rome's most atmospheric locations, such as the amphitheatre at Ostia Antica, the Terme di Caracalla and Villa Ada, with concerts over the last few years having included Peaches, Sonic Youth, Patti Smith, Dinosaur Jr and Joan As Policewoman. In summer, regular concerts have been taking place in the wonderful setting of Centrale Montemartini (see p165), an ex-power station filled with classical sculpture, and at Open Colonna – the glass-roofed restaurant at the Palazzo delle Esposizioni on Via Nazionale. Other clubs, such as Contestaccio in Testaccio, line up acts from extreme electro to U2 tribute bands. Micca Club, in southern Rome, close to San Giovanni, hosts an eclectic mix, including cabaret and burlesque acts galore.

The Centri Sociali (Social Centres), alternative arts centres set up in venues around Rome, are also good places to catch a gig, especially Rialtosantambrogio in the Centro Storico, Brancaleone in northern Rome, and Villagio Globale in Testaccio, with music policies encompassing hip hop, electro, dubstep, reggae and dancehall.

## Dance

Dance is not an art form that receives much patronage in Italy, and the best dancers tend to go abroad to work. But visiting dance companies are often class acts, and they're enthusiastically supported. The Teatro dell'Opera di Roma is home to Rome's official Corps de Ballet, and has a ballet season running in tandem with its opera performances. In summer, as for the opera, performances of classical ballets such as Swan Lake move outside to the fantastic setting of the Terme di Caracalla, with dancers flitting through the artfully lit ruins. The Auditorium Conciliazione (www.auditoriumconciliazione.it/) is another good place to catch contemporary dance companies. Invito alla Danza (p46) is a contemporary dance festival in July that encompasses tango, jazz dance, contemporary and more.

## Film

With such a backdrop, it's no surprise that Rome has a close relationship with the cinema. Rome's cinematic heyday was in the 1960s, with Fellini producing films like La Dolce Vita and Roma, and in the 1970s when Cinecittà (Film City) studios churned out enough spaghetti westerns to keep you entertained for life. But Rome's cinema scene has recently seen something of its former glory, even if it's not home-grown. Major international films recently produced at Cinecittà include Ocean's Twelve, Mission Impossible 3 and the TV series Rome and Dr Who. The studios, built by Mussolini in 1937, suffered a setback in 2007, when around 3000 sq m of the complex were destroyed by fire – it actually started in storage lots for the Rome set, though no-one could confirm if Nero was fiddling as it burned. The studios did arise, phoenix-like, from the ashes but have been even worse afflicted by the cheaper studio alternatives in Eastern Europe. However, recent movies made here include Nanni Moretti's latest Habemus Papam (2011; We have a Pope!).

In 2006, Rome began holding a star-studded international film festival, **Festival Internazionale del Film di Roma** (www.romacinemafest.it), which has since taken place every year in November.

Filmgoing has always remained popular, and there are some 80-odd cinemas dotted around the city. Many of these are small, single-screen affairs, although the number of multiscreen complexes is increasing. Most foreign films are dubbed into Italian;

---

### CINEMA UNDER THE STARS

There are various atmospheric outdoor summer film festivals; check current listings, but these take place annually.

➡ **Isola del Cinema** (www.isoladel cinema.com) Independent films in the romantic setting of the Isola Tiberina (Map p346) in July and August. This runs in conjunction with the Lungo il Tevere festival.

➡ **Notti di Cinema a Piazza Vittorio** (☎06 444 04 31; www.agisanec.lazio.it, in Italian) Italian and international releases at two open-air screens in Piazza Vittorio Emanuele II (Map p340) from June to September. Tickets cost €6.

those shown in the original language are indicated in listings by *versione originale* or VO after the title – there are several cinemas that regularly show English versions, and these are listed in the neighbourhood chapters.

Tickets cost around €8. Afternoon and early-evening screenings are generally cheaper, while all tickets are discounted on Wednesday. Check the listings press or daily papers for schedules and ticket prices.

A fantastic feature of Rome's cinema scene is the summer festival period, when films are shown outdoors at various locations (see p45).

## Theatre

Rome has a thriving local theatre scene, with more than 80 theatres dotted across town, which include both traditional places and an increasing number of smaller experimental venues. It's in the larger city-centre theatres that the programmes tend to be conservative, and performances are usually in Italian.

Particularly wonderful are the summer festivals that make use of Rome's archaeological scenery – no city backdrop could be better suited to classic drama. Performances take place in settings such as Villa Adriana in Tivoli, Ostia Antica's Roman theatre and the Teatro di Marcello. In summer the **Miracle Players** (www.miracleplayers.org) perform classic English drama or historical comedy in English next to the Roman Forum and other open-air locations. Performances are usually free.

## Arts Festivals

Rome hosts a marvellous array of arts and cultural festivals, especially in the long and sultry summer. Here is a sampling of some of the gems. For more on Rome's festivals see p23.

Concerti del Tempietto (www.tempietto.it, in Italian) The ancient Teatro di Marcello (p86) is the dramatic venue for a summer concert series in from June to September, when piano and chamber music bounces off the rugged stone nightly from 8.30pm.

**Festival Internazionale di Villa Adriana** (✆06 802 41 281; www.auditorium.com/villaadriana/) This arts festival occupies the magnificent ruins of Emperor Hadrian's country villa in Tivoli (p221) with concerts, international theatre and dance in archaeological settings (June to July).

**Lungo il Tevere** (www.lungoiltevereroma.it) Summer-long festival, with comedy acts, jazz, film, craft stalls and bars, clustered around the banks of Tiberina island in the middle of the river.

**Invito alla Danza** (✆06 3973 8323; www.invitoalladanza.it) This mammothly popular modern-dance festival, which started in 1980, draws international performers (anything from tango to jazz) and passionate crowds to the beautiful parklands of Villa Doria Pamphilj (Map p360; Via di San Pancrazio 10), south of the Vatican, in July. Tickets cost around €20.

**Roma Incontra il Mondo** (www.villaada.org; Villa Ada) This fabulous world music festival takes place lakeside in June, in the breathtaking setting of Villa Ada, and shows Rome's alternative side, with regular appearances by bands from the Italian deep south, such as Sud Sound System, as well as international greats such as Goran Bregovich playing wild gypsy music.

## Spectator Sports
### FOOTBALL

In this country of great passions, Il Calcio (football) is one of the greatest. After Italy won the World Cup in 2006, half a million people filled Circo Massimo to see the captain, Fabio Cannavaro, parade the trophy. From September to May, Romans flock to their largest temple of worship, the Stadio Olimpico (p213).

In Rome you're either for AS Roma (*giallorossi* – yellow and reds) or Lazio (*biancazzuri* – white and blues). Both Rome's teams play in Serie A (Italy's premier league), at the Stadio Olimpico in the Foro Italico, north of the city centre. Both sides are considered solid, top-level performers, but Lazio has run into problems in recent years, while Roma has seen patchy success. Financial problems have beset both clubs, forcing them to sell top players and rely on one or two star performers.

Lazio's fans traditionally come from the provincial towns outside Rome, while Roma's supporters, known as *romanisti,* are historically working class, from Rome's Jewish community and from Trastevere, Testaccio and Garbatella. Both sets of supporters have an unfortunate controversial minority who have been known to cause trouble at matches.

From September to June there's a game at home for Roma or Lazio almost every weekend and a trip to Rome's football stadium, the **Stadio Olimpico** (Map p366;

## AS ROMA VS LAZIO

The Rome derby is one of the football season's highest-profile games. The rivalry between Roma and Lazio is fierce and little love is lost between the fans. If you go to the Stadio Olimpico, make sure you get it right – Roma fans (in deep red with a natty orange trim) flock to the Curva Sud (southern stand), while Lazio supporters (in light blue) stand in the Curva Nord (northern stand). If you want to sit on the fence, head to the Tribuna Tevere or Tribuna Monte Mario.

For more details on the clubs, check out www.asroma.it and www.sslazio.it (both in Italian).

☑ 06 368 57 520; Viale dei Gladiatori), is an unforgettable experience. Note that ticket purchase regulations are far stricter than they used to be. Tickets have to bear the holder's name and passport or ID number, and you must present a photo ID at the turnstiles when entering the stadium. Two tickets are permitted per purchase for Serie A, Coppa Italia and UEFA Champions League games – if you want to buy more, you can, but they will probably not be together. Tickets cost from €40 to €100. You can buy them from www.ticketone.it, www.listicket.it, from ticket agencies or at one of the AS Roma or Lazio stores around the city (see p102 and p213). To get to the stadium take metro line A to Ottaviano–San Pietro and then bus 32.

### Basketball

Basketball is a popular spectator sport in Rome, though it inspires nothing like the fervour of football. Rome's team, Virtus Roma, plays throughout the winter months at the **Palalottomatica** (☑ 199 12 88 00; Viale dell' Umanesimo; M EUR Palasport) in EUR.

### Rugby Union

Every time a Six Nations game is played in Rome, the city fills with a swell of foreign spectators, easily discernible by their penchant for amusing hats and beer.

Italy's rugby team, the Azzurri (the Blues), entered the Six Nations tournament in 2000, and has been the competition underdog ever since. There is a distinct lack of local media interest in the game. Big matches might get a paragraph or two in national newspapers, while TV coverage is limited to the nation's smallest channel, La7. Public interest is further hampered by the complexity of the rules, which no-one quite understands, as Italian schools don't teach rugby. However, in 2007 Italy won against both Scotland and Wales and finished in 4th place, which sparked an unprecedented wave of pride and coverage, and in 2011 they secured their first Six Nations win over France, which again turned a media spotlight on the sport, and set off a wave of public support.

The team plays home international games at Rome's **Stadio Flaminio** (Map p366; www.federugby.it; ☑ 06 368 57 309; Viale Maresciallo Pilsudski), which is still in use despite the discovery and excavations of an ancient Roman necropolis beneath the stadium.

### Tennis

Italy's premier tennis tournament, the Italian International Tennis Championships, is one of the most important events on the European tennis circuit. Every May the world's top players meet on the clay courts at the monumental, Fascist-era **Foro Italico** (Map p366; ☑ 06 368 58 218; Viale del Foro Italico). Tickets can be bought at the Foro Italico each day of the tournament, except for the final days, which are sold out weeks in advance.

### Equestrian Events

Rome's top equestrian event is the **Piazza di Siena showjumping competition** (☑ 06 638 38 18; www.piazzadisiena.com), an international annual event held in May, gorgeously set in Villa Borghese (Map p366). An important fixture on the high-society calendar, it attracts a moneyed Anglophile crowd.

## Lonely Planet's Top Choices

**Auditorium Parco della Musica** (p217) An incredible venue hosting an eclectic, must-see programme of music, art and more.

**Opera di Roma at Terme di Caracalla** (p156) Opera and ballet set against an unforgettable ancient Roman backdrop.

**Silvano Toti Globe Theatre** (p217) Like the Globe Theatre in London, but with much better weather.

**Estate Romana** (p24) Great umbrella festival that sees arts events all summer long.

## Best Classical Venues

Auditorium Parco della Musica (p217)

Teatro dell'Opera di Roma (p145)

Terme di Caracalla (p156)

Auditorium Conciliazione (p204)

## Best for Live Gigs

Circolo degli Artisti (p142)

Fanfulla 101 (p142)

Villaggio Globale (p156)

Micca Club (p143)

## Best Theatres

Silvano Toti Globe Theatre (p217)

Ostia Antica (p220)

Teatro Argentina (p98)

Teatro Palladium (p168)

Teatro Valle (p98)

## Best Festivals

Estate Romana (p24)

Lungo il Tevere (p45)

Concerti dei Tempietto (p46)

Roma Incontra il Mondo (p46)

Classic style at Davide Cenci (p102)

# Shopping

*Rome's shops, studios and boutiques make retail therapy diverting enough
to distract you from the incredible cityscape. Wander the backstreets and
you'll find yourself glancing into dusty workshops: framers and furniture
restorers. Narrow lanes are dotted by beautiful boutiques and department
stores have an old-style glamour. That's not to say that there are no chain
stores in Rome, but the city is still dominated by the individual shop.*

## What to Buy

Italy's reputation for quality is deserved, and
Rome is a splendid place to shop for designer
clothes, shoes and leather goods. The grid of
streets around Via dei Condotti and Piazza
di Spagna is high-fashion central: even if you
can't afford to buy, it's worth a gape.

There is also a wonderful array of small
designers selling one-off, hand-made outfits,
places to buy bespoke shoes, and work-of-art
jewellery and leather goods. Foodstuffs are,
of course, the tops, and heavenly temples to
food abound – delis, bakeries, *pasticcerie*
and chocolate shops. Designer homewares

are another Italian speciality, and many
shops focus on covetable stainless-steel
kitchenware, glass baubles and super-sleek
interior design.

## High Fashion

Big-name designer boutiques glitter and
gleam in the grid of streets between Piazza di
Spagna and Via del Corso. The great Italian
and international names are represented, as
well as many more off-centre designers, selling clothes, shoes, accessories and dreams.
The immaculately clad high-fashion spine is
Via dei Condotti, but there's also lots of high

## NEED TO KNOW

### Opening Hours

➡ Most city-centre shops: 9am-7.30pm (or 10am-8pm) Mon-Sat; some close Mon morning

➡ Smaller shops: 9am-1pm & 3.30-7.30pm (or 4-8pm) Mon-Sat

### Prices & Sales

While prices here are not as steep as they are in, say, London or Paris, they're still not cheap. To grab a bargain, you should try to time your visit to coincide with the *saldi* (sales). Winter sales run from early January to mid-February and summer sales from July to early September.

### Payment & Receipts

Most shops accept credit cards and many accept travellers cheques. Note that you're required by Italian law to have a *ricevuta* (receipt) for your purchases (see p311).

### Taxes & Refunds

Non-EU residents who spend more than €155 at shops with a 'Tax Free for Tourists' sticker are entitled to a tax rebate. You'll need to fill in a form in the shop and get it stamped by customs as you leave Italy. For more details, see p311.

fashion in Via Borgognona, Via Frattina, Via della Vite and Via del Babuino.

Downsizing a euro or two, Via Nazionale, Via del Corso, Via dei Giubbonari and Via Cola di Rienzo are good for midrange clothing stores, with some enticing small boutiques set amid the chains.

### ONE-OFF BOUTIQUES & VINTAGE

Best for cutting-edge designer boutiques and vintage clothes is bohemian Via del Governo Vecchio, running from a small square just off Piazza Navona towards the river. Other places for one-off boutiques are Via del Pellegrino and around Campo de' Fiori. Via del Boschetto and Via dei Soldati in the Monti area feature unique designers and jewellery makers, antique sellers and artists. Head to San Lorenzo for edgy arts and crafts, with boutiques turning out stunning art works; preview at **Made in San Lorenzo** (www.madeinsanlorenzo.it, in Italian).

### ANTIQUES

For antiques shopping, Via dei Coronari, Via Margutta, Via Giulia and Via dei Banchi Vecchi are the best places to look – quality is high, as are the prices.

### ARTISANS

Rome's shopping scene has a surprising number of artists and artisans who create their goods on the spot in hidden workshops. There are several places in Tridente where you can get a bag, wallet or belt made to your specifications; in other shops you can commission lamps or embroidery. These are part of what makes shopping in Rome special, and they're often found in the Centro Storico and around Tridente.

### FOODSTUFFS

You're in the Italian capital, so of course it's deli heaven. Prepare to enter some of the world's great temples to food, breathe in sweet and savoury scents, and get lost among all the tantalising jars and bottles. Prime among Rome's foodstuff stores are Castroni (p204), Vineri Roscioli Salumeria (p93) and Teichner (p123), and also well worth a visit are Rome's many local food markets (see p35), where you can buy cheese, salami and other delicious stuff.

### ECCLESIASTICAL

South of the Pantheon, a string of ecclesiastical shops has clerics from all over the world trying out ceremonial capes for their swish factor, eyeing up lecterns and stocking up on suitably stern undies. If you want an icon or a pair of (glorious!) cardinal's socks (available in poppy red or ecclesiastical purple), Via dei Cestari is where to head, though bear in mind that idle browsing is not the done thing.

**Ghezzi** (Map p346; ☑06 686 97 44; Via dei Cestari 32-33) The least daunting of the shops.

**Anniable Gamarelli** (Map p346; ☑06 680 13 14; Via di Santa Chiara 34) If nothing but the pope's tailors will do.

**Statuaria – Arte Sacra** (Map p346; ☑06 679 37 53; Via dei Cestari 2) For a life-sized statue of the Virgin Mary or a host of smaller icons.

**Centro Russia Ecumenica il Messaggio dell'Icona** (Map p364; ☑06 689 66 37; Borgo Pio 141) Near St Peter's; sells original painted icons, some glinting with real gold leaf.

## Lonely Planet's Top Choices

**Confetteria Moriondo & Gariglio** (p102) A magical-seeming, stuck-in-time chocolate shop.

**Vertecchi** (p122) Art emporium with beautiful paper and notebooks.

**Lucia Odescalchi** (p122) Exotic, thoroughly modern jewellery – works of art housed in a palace.

**Armando Rioda** (p122) Artisans in an upstairs workroom create luscious handbags at non-designer prices.

**Bottega di Marmoraro** (p124) Have the motto of your choice carved into a marble slab at this delightful shop.

## Rome Souvenirs

Vertecchi (p122)

Bottega di Marmoraro (p124

Bookàbar (p146)

AS Roma Store (p102)

## Artisanal

Claudio Sanò (p146)

Bottega di Marmoraro (p124)

Armando Rioda (p122)

Artigiani Pellettieri – Marco Pelle/Di Clemente (p124)

Aldo Fefè (p100)

La Cravatta su Misura (p181)

## Clothing

Eleonora (p124)

Luna & l'Altra (p99)

daDADA 52 (p101)

Abito (p146)

Scala Quattrodici (p181)

## Shoes

Borini (p101)

AVC by Adriana V Campanile(p124)

Mada (p125)

Fausto Santini (p125)

Danielle (p122)

# Explore Rome

## ROME'S TOP SIGHTS

# Neighbourhoods at a Glance

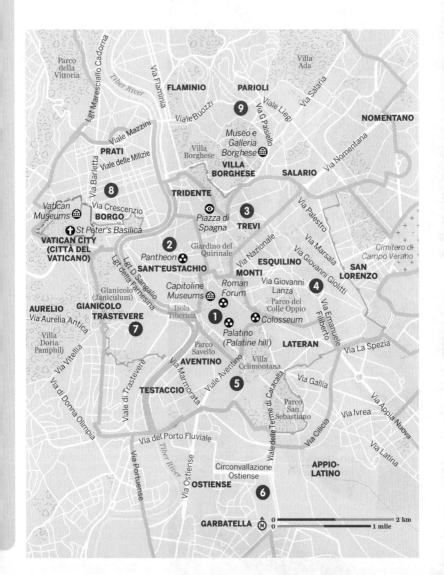

# ❶ Ancient Rome (p56)

In a city of extraordinary beauty, Rome's ancient heart stands out. It's here that you'll find the great icons of Rome's past: the Colosseum, the Palatino (Palatine hill), the forums, and Campidoglio (Capitoline hill). Touristy by day, it's quiet at night with few after-hours attractions.

# ❷ Centro Storico (p73)

The tangled historic centre is the Rome that many come to see – cobbled alleyways, animated piazzas, Renaissance *palazzi* (mansions), cafes and stylish bars. The Pantheon and Piazza Navona are the star turns, but you'll also find a host of monuments, museums and churches, many with works by Michelangelo, Caravaggio and Bernini.

# ❸ Tridente, Trevi & the Quirinale (p103)

Counting the Trevi Fountain and the Spanish Steps among its big sights, this area is glamorous, debonair and touristy. The streets around Piazza di Spagna ooze money with their designer boutiques, fashionable bars and swish hotels, while the Trevi Fountain area swarms with overpriced eateries and brassy souvenir shops.

# ❹ Monti, Esquilino & San Lorenzo (p126)

Centred on Stazione Termini, this is a large and cosmopolitan district. Hidden behind its busy roads you'll find some amazing churches, one of Rome's best museums (Palazzo Massimo alle Terme) – and any number of cool bars and restaurants, mostly located in the Monti, San Lorenzo and Pigneto districts.

# ❺ San Giovanni to Testaccio (p147)

This sweeping, multifaceted area has something for everyone: medieval churches and monumental basilicas (Basilica di San Giovanni in Laterano above all); towering ruins (Terme di Caracalla), and tranquil parkland (Villa Celimontana). Down by the river, Testaccio is an earthy, workaday district known for its traditional trattorias and thumping nightlife.

# ❻ Southern Rome (p158)

Boasting a wealth of diversions, from ancient catacombs to futuristic ministries and cutting-edge clubs, this huge region extends to Rome's southern limits. Interest centres on Via Appia Antica, the ancient Appian Way, which was home to the early Christian catacombs; Via Ostiense, populated with clubs and popular eateries; and EUR, a modernistic purpose-built suburb in the extreme south of the city.

# ❼ Trastevere & Gianicolo (p169)

With its picture-perfect lanes, colourful *palazzi* and boho vibe, this is one of Rome's most vibrant neighbourhoods. Formerly a bastion of working-class independence, it's now a trendy hang-out full of restaurants, cafes, pubs and pizzerias. Behind it, the Gianicolo hill is a lovely, romantic spot commanding superb views.

# ❽ Vatican City, Borgo & Prati (p182)

Over the river from the historic centre, the Vatican is home to two of Rome's top attractions – St Peter's Basilica and the Vatican Museums (where you'll find the Sistine Chapel) – as well as hundreds of overpriced restaurants and souvenir shops. In contrast, nearby Prati offers excellent accommodation, eating and shopping.

# ❾ Villa Borghese & Northern Rome (p205)

This moneyed, cultured part of Rome encompasses the city's most famous park (Villa Borghese) and its most sought-after residential district (Parioli). Concert-goers head to the Auditorium Parco della Musica while art-lovers choose between contemporary exhibitions at MAXXI or baroque marvels at the Museo e Galleria Borghese, one of Rome's best galleries.

# Ancient Rome

COLOSSEUM | FORUMS | CAMPIDOGLIO | PIAZZA VENEZIA | BOCCA DELLA VERITÀ & FORUM BOARIUM

## Five Top Experiences

**1** Getting your first glimpse of the **Colosseum** (p58). Rome's towering gladiatorial amphitheatre is both an architectural masterpiece, the blueprint for much modern stadium design, and a stark, spine-tingling reminder of the brutality of ancient times.

**2** Exploring the haunting ruins of the **Palatino** (p60), ancient Rome's most exclusive neighbourhood.

**3** Coming face to face with centuries of awe-inspiring art at the historic **Capitoline Museums** (p67).

**4** Walking up Via Sacra, the once grand thoroughfare of the **Roman Forum** (p63).

**5** Surveying the city spread out beneath you from atop **Il Vittoriano** (p69)

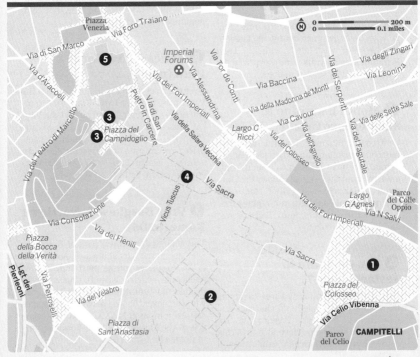

For more detail of this area see Map p344 ➡

# Explore: Ancient Rome

Located to the south of the city centre, this area contains the great ruins of the ancient city, all concentrated within walking distance of each other. They start to get crowded mid-morning and throng with tourists until mid- to-late afternoon, although in peak season they can be busy all day. Apart from the big sights, which you can comfortably cover in a couple of days, there's little in the way of nightlife or after-hours action.

The area has two focal points: the Colosseum to the east, and the Campidoglio (Capitoline hill) to the west. In between lie the forums: the more famous Roman Forum on the left of Via dei Fori Imperiali as you walk up from the Colosseum, and the Imperial Forums on the right. Rising above the Roman Forum, is the Palatino, and behind that the Circo Massimo. Continuing northwest from the Circo Massimo brings you to the Forum Boarium, ancient Rome's cattle market and river port, where you'll find the Bocca della Verità, Rome's mythical lie detector.

To explore the area, the obvious starting point is the Colosseum, which is easily accessible by metro. From here you could go directly up to the Roman Forum but if you go first to the Palatino (your Colosseum ticket covers the Palatino and Roman Forum) you'll get some wonderful views over the forums. From the Palatino enter the Forum and work your way up to Piazza del Campidoglio and the Capitoline Museums. Nearby, the mammoth white Vittoriano is difficult to miss.

## Local Life

➡ **Exhibitions** While tourists climb all over Il Vittoriano (p69), locals head inside it to catch an exhibition at the Complesso del Vittoriano.

➡ **Celebrations** Join Romans to celebrate the city's birthday, the Natale di Roma, on 21 April. Events and historical re-enactments are held in and around Rome's ancient sights.

➡ **Jogging** Don your trainers and run with the Romans on the Circo Massimo, a popular jogging venue (p68).

## Getting There & Away

➡ **Bus** Frequent buses head to Piazza Venezia, including numbers 40, 64, 87, 170, 492, 916 and H.

➡ **Metro** Metro line B has stops at the Colosseum (Colosseo) and Circo Massimo. At Termini follow signs for metro Line B direzione Laurentina.

## Lonely Planet's Top Tip

The big sights in this part of Rome are among the city's most visited. To avoid the worst of the crowds try to visit early morning or in the late afternoon, when it's cooler and the light is much better for taking photos.

Bring bottled water and eats with you as the bars and snack trucks on Via dei Fori Imperiali are a real rip-off.

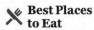

## Best Places to Eat

➡ Hostaria da Nerone (p72)
➡ San Teodoro (p72)
➡ Ara Coeli (p72)

For reviews see p72 ➡

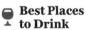

## Best Places to Drink

➡ Caffé Capitolino (p72)
➡ Cavour 313 (p72)
➡ 0,75 (p72)

For reviews see p72 ➡

## Best Lookouts

➡ Il Vittoriano (p69)
➡ Orti Farnesiani (p61)
➡ Tabularium, Capitoline Museums (p67)
➡ Cordonata, Piazza del Campidoglio (p69)

For reviews see p68 ➡

# TOP SIGHTS
## COLOSSEUM

A monument to raw, merciless power, the Colosseum (Colosseo) is the most thrilling of Rome's ancient sights. It's not just the amazing completeness of the place, or its size, but the sense of violent history that resonates: it was here that gladiators met in mortal combat and condemned prisoners fought off wild beasts in front of baying, bloodthirsty crowds. Two thousand years on and it is Italy's top tourist attraction, drawing between 16,000 and 19,000 people on an average day.

Built by Vespasian (r AD 69–79) in the grounds of Nero's vast Domus Aurea complex, the Colosseum was inaugurated in AD 80. To mark the occasion, Vespasian's son and successor Titus (r AD 79–81) staged games that lasted 100 days and nights, during which some 5000 animals were slaughtered. Trajan (r 98–117) later topped this, holding a marathon 117-day killing spree involving 9000 gladiators and 10,000 animals.

The 50,000-seat arena was originally known as the Flavian Amphitheatre, and although it was Rome's most fearful arena, it wasn't the biggest – the Circo Massimo could hold up to 250,000 people. The name Colosseum, when introduced in medieval times, was not a reference to its size but to the *Colosso di Nerone,* a giant statue of Nero that stood nearby.

With the fall of the Roman empire in the 6th century, the Colosseum was abandoned and gradually became overgrown. In the Middle Ages it became a fortress, occupied by two of the city's warrior families, the Frangipani and the Annibaldi. It was later used as a quarry for travertine and marble, and in more recent times pollution and vibrations caused by traffic and the metro have taken a toll. The battle to maintain it is continuous and conservation work is on-going. The immediate priorities are the outer walls, the un-

## DON'T MISS...

- ⇒ The stands
- ⇒ The arena
- ⇒ The hypogeum

## PRACTICALITIES

- ⇒ Map p344
- ⇒ ☑06 399 67 700
- ⇒ www.pierreci.it
- ⇒ Piazza del Colosseo
- ⇒ Adult/reduced incl Roman Forum & Palatino €12/7.50, audioguides €5.50
- ⇒ ⊘8.30am-1hr before sunset
- ⇒ Ⓜ Colosseo

derground sections and the monument's electrical systems, but longer term plans call for the building of a new underground entrance complex.

## The Exterior

The outer walls have three levels of arches, articulated by Ionic, Doric and Corinthian columns. They were originally covered in travertine, and marble statues once filled the niches on the 2nd and 3rd storeys. The upper level had supports for 240 masts that held up a canvas awning over the arena. The entrance arches, known as *vomitoria,* allowed the spectators to enter and be seated in a matter of minutes. And as for modern games, tickets were numbered and spectators were assigned a specified seat in a specified sector.

## The Interior

The interior was divided into the arena, *cavea* and podium. The arena had a wooden floor covered in sand to prevent the combatants from slipping and to soak up the blood. It could also be flooded for mock sea battles. Trapdoors led down to the hypogeum, an underground complex of corridors, cages and lifts beneath the arena floor.

The *cavea,* for spectator seating, was divided into three tiers: magistrates and senior officials sat in the lowest tier, wealthy citizens in the middle and the plebs in the highest tier. Women (except for vestal virgins) were relegated to the cheapest sections at the top. The podium, a broad terrace in front of the tiers of seats, was reserved for emperors, senators and VIPs.

## Hypogeum

The hypogeum, along with the top tier, have recently been opened to the public. Visits, which cost €8 on top of the normal Colosseum ticket and are by guided tour only, require advance booking.

The hypogeum extended under the main arena and served as the stadium's backstage area. Here, scenery for the elaborate performances would be put together and hoisted up by a complex system of lifts and pulleys. Gladiators would enter the hypogeum directly from the nearby gladiator school and wild animals would be brought in from the 'zoo' on the Celio hill and kept in cages built into the walls.

### BEAT THE QUEUES

The Colosseum gets very busy and long queues are the norm. Buy your ticket from the Palatino entrance (about 250m away at Via di San Gregorio 30) or the Roman Forum entrance (Largo della Salara Vecchia). Get the Roma Pass, which is valid for three days and a whole host of sites. Book your ticket online at www.pierreci.it (plus booking fee of €1.50). Join an official English-language tour – €4 on top of the regular Colosseum ticket price.

**Outside the Colosseum, you'll almost certainly be hailed by centurions offering to pose for a photo. They are not doing this for love and will expect payment. There's no set rate but €5 is more than enough – and that's €5 full stop, not €5 per person.**

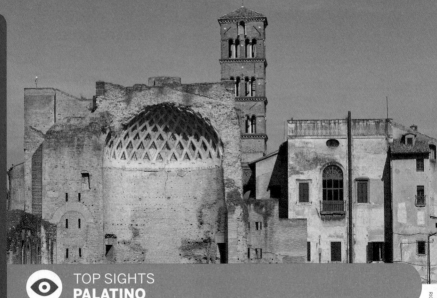

## TOP SIGHTS
## PALATINO

**Sandwiched between the Roman Forum and the Circo Massimo, the Palatino (Palatine hill) is an atmospheric area of towering pine trees, majestic ruins and memorable views. According to legend, this is where Romulus and Remus were saved by a wolf and where Romulus founded Rome in 753 BC. Archaeological evidence cannot prove the legend but it has dated human habitation to the 8th century BC.**

As the most central of Rome's seven hills, and because it was close to the Roman Forum, the Palatino was ancient Rome's poshest neighbourhood. Augustus lived all his life here and successive emperors built increasingly opulent palaces. But after Rome's fall, it fell into disrepair and in the Middle Ages churches and castles were built over the ruins. Later, during the Renaissance, wealthy families established gardens on the hill.

Most of the Palatino as it appears today is covered by the ruins of Emperor Domitian's vast complex, which served as the main imperial palace for 300 years. Divided into the Domus Flavia (imperial palace), Domus Augustana (the emperor's private residence) and a *stadio* (stadium), it was built in the 1st century AD.

### DON'T MISS...

➡ Stadio
➡ Domus Augustana
➡ Casa di Augusto
➡ Orti Farnesiani

### PRACTICALITIES

➡ Map p344
➡ ☎ 06 399 67 700
➡ www.pierreci.it
➡ Via di San Gregorio 30
➡ Adult/reduced incl Colosseum & Roman Forum €12/7.50, audioguides €5;
➡ ⏱ 8.30am-1hr before sunset
➡ Ⓜ Colosseo

### Stadio

On entering the Palatino from Via di San Gregorio, head uphill until you come to the first recognisable construction, the *stadio*. This sunken area, which was part of the main imperial palace, was used by the emperor for private games. Adjoining the stadium to the southeast, but closed to the public, are the impressive remains of a complex built by Septimius Severus, comprising baths (the **Terme di Settimio Severo**) and a palace (the **Domus Severiana**).

## Domus Augustana & Domus Flavia

Next to the *stadio* are the ruins of the **Domus Augustana**, the emperor's private residence. Over two levels, rooms lead off a *peristilio* (garden courtyard) on each floor. You can't get to the lower level, but from above you can see the basin of a fountain and beyond it rooms that were paved with coloured marble.

Over on the other side of the Museo Palatino, is the **Domus Flavia**, the public part of Domitian's palace complex. The Domus was centred on a grand columned peristyle – the grassy area with the base of an octagonal fountain – off which the main halls led. To the north was the emperor's vast throne room (the *aula regia*); to the west, a basilica, which was used by the emperor to meet his advisers; and to the south, a large banqueting hall, the *triclinium*.

## Museo Palatino

The **Museo Palatino** (admission incl in Palatino ticket; ☺8am-4pm) houses a small collection of finds from the Palatino. The downstairs section illustrates the history of the hill from its origins to the Republican age, while upstairs you'll find artefacts from the Imperial age, including a beautiful 1st-century bronze, the *Erma di Canefora*.

## Casa di Livia & Casa di Augusto

Among the best-preserved buildings on the Palatino is the **Casa di Livia**, northwest of the Domus Flavia. Home to Augustus' wife Livia, it was built around an atrium leading onto what were once frescoed reception rooms. In front is the **Casa di Augusto** (☺11am-4.30pm Mon, Wed, Sat & Sun), Augustus' separate residence, which contains superb frescoes in vivid reds, yellows and blues. Enter in groups of five.

## Criptoportico

Reached from near the Orti Farnesiani, the *criptoportico* is a 128m tunnel where Caligula is said to have been murdered and which Nero used to connect his Domus Aurea with the Palatino. Lit by a series of windows, it originally boasted elaborate stucco decorations and is now used to stage temporary exhibitions.

## Orti Farnesiani

In the northwest corner of the Palatino, and covering Domus Tiberiana (once Tiberius' palace), Orti Farnesiani are one of Europe's earliest botanical gardens. Named after Cardinal Alessandro Farnese, who had them laid out in the mid-16th century, they boast lovely perfumed hedges and shady pines. Twin pavilions at the garden's northernmost point command breathtaking views over the Roman Forum.

## ROMULUS & REMUS

The Palatino is closely associated with the legend of Romulus and Remus. Rome's mythical founders were said to have been brought up here by the shepherd Faustulus after a wolf had saved them from death. From near the Casa di Augusto you can look down into the 8th-century BC Capanne Romulee (Romulean Huts) where the twins supposedly lived with their adopted father. In 2007 the discovery of a mosaic-covered cave 15m beneath the Domus Augustana reignited interest in the legend. According to some scholars, this was the Lupercale, the cave believed by ancient Romans to be where Romulus and Remus were suckled by a wolf. Others vigorously contested this, and the mystery remains.

**The best spot for a picnic is the Vigna Barberini (Barberini Vineyard), near the Orti Farnesiani. It is signposted off the path to the Roman Forum.**

Orti Farnesiani●

●Criptoportico

Entrance/Exit
from/to
Roman Forum
●

●Capanne Romulee
●Casa di Livia
●Casa di Augusto

●Domus Flavia

Vigna
Barberini

●Museo Palatino
●Domus Augustana

●Stadio

●Entrance

●Terme di Settimio Severo

●Domus Severiana

TOP SIGHTS
PALATINO

## TOP SIGHTS
## ROMAN FORUM

Once the gleaming heart of the ancient world, a grandiose ensemble of marble-clad temples, proud basilicas and vibrant public spaces, the Roman Forum (Foro Romano) is now a collection of impressive but badly labelled ruins that can leave you drained and confused. But if you can set your imagination going, there's something undeniably compelling about walking in the footsteps of Julius Caesar and the great emperors of Roman history.

Originally an Etruscan burial ground, the Forum was first developed in the 7th century BC and expanded over subsequent centuries to become the centre of the Roman Republic. In the Middle Ages it was reduced to pastureland – the so-called Campo Vaccino (literally 'Cow Field') – and extensively plundered for its marble. The area was systematically excavated in the 18th and 19th centuries and work continues to this day.

### Via Sacra Towards Campidoglio

Entering the Forum from Largo della Salara Vecchia – you can also enter directly from the Palatino – you'll see the **Tempio di Antonino e Faustina** ahead to your left. Erected in AD 141, this was later transformed into a church, so the soaring columns now frame the **Chiesa di San Lorenzo in Miranda**. To your right the **Basilica Fulvia Aemilia**, built in 179 BC, was a 100m-long public hall, with a two-storey porticoed facade.

At the end of the short path, you come to **Via Sacra**, the Forum's main throughfare. Opposite the basilica stands the **Tempio di Giulio Cesare** (Temple of Julius Caesar) built by Augustus in 29 BC. Head right up Via Sacra and you reach the **Curia**, the meeting place of the Roman Senate. This was

### DON'T MISS...

➡ Curia
➡ Arco di Settimio Severo
➡ Tempio di Saturno
➡ Casa delle Vestali
➡ Basilica di Massenzio
➡ Arco di Tito

### PRACTICALITIES

➡ Map p344
➡ ☎06 399 67 700
➡ www.pierreci.it
➡ Largo della Salara Vecchia
➡ Adult/reduced incl Colosseum & Palatino €12/7.50, audioguides €5;
➡ ⊙8.30am-1hr before sunset
➡ ⓂColosseo

In ancient times, a forum was a market place, civic centre and religious complex all rolled into one, and the greatest of all was the Roman Forum (Foro Romano). Situated between the Palatino (Palatine Hill), ancient Rome's most exclusive neighbourhood, and the Campidoglio (Capitoline Hill), it was the city's busy, bustling centre. On any given day it teemed with activity. Senators debated affairs of state in the **Curia 1**, shoppers thronged the squares and traffic-free streets, crowds gathered under the **Colonna di Foca 2** to listen to politicians holding forth from the **Rostrum 2**. Elsewhere, lawyers worked the courts in basilicas including the **Basilica di Massenzio 3**, while the Vestal Virgins quietly went about their business in the **Casa delle Vestali 4**. Special occasions were also celebrated in the Forum: religious holidays were marked with ceremonies at temples such as the **Tempio di Saturno 5** and the **Tempio di Castore e Polluce 6**, and military victories were honoured with dramatic processions up Via Sacra and the building of monumental arches like the **Arco di Settimio Severo 7** and the **Arco di Tito 8**.

The ruins you see today are impressive but they can be confusing without a clear picture of what the Forum once looked like. This spread shows the Forum in its heyday, complete with temples, civic buildings and towering monuments to heroes of the Roman Empire.

## TOP TIPS

➡ Get grandstand views of the Forum from the Palatino and Campidoglio.

➡ Visit first thing in the morning or late afternoon; crowds are worst between 11am and 2pm.

➡ In summer it gets hot in the Forum and there's little shade, so take a hat and plenty of water.

**Colonna di Foca & Rostrum**
The free-standing, 13.5m-high Column of Phocus is the Forum's youngest monument, dating to AD 608. Behind it, the Rostrum provided a suitably grandiose platform for pontificating public speakers.

**Campidoglio (Capitoline Hill)**

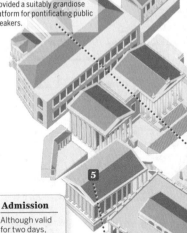

### Admission

Although valid for two days, admission tickets only allow for one entry into the Forum, Colosseum and Palatino.

**Tempio di Saturno**
Ancient Rome's Fort Knox, the Temple of Saturn was the city treasury. In Caesar's day it housed 13 tonnes of gold, 114 tonnes of silver and 30 million *sestertii* worth of silver coins.

JONATHAN SMITH / LONELY PLANET IMAGES ©

GEOFF STRINGER / LONELY PLANET IMAGES ©

**Tempio di Castore e Polluce**
Only three columns of the Temple of Castor and Pollux remain. The temple was dedicated to the Heavenly Twins after they supposedly led the Romans to victory over the Etruscans.

### Arco di Settimio Severo

One of the Forum's signature monuments, this imposing triumphal arch commemorates the military victories of Septimius Severus. Relief panels depict his campaigns against the Parthians.

### Curia

This big barnlike building was the official seat of the Roman Senate. Most of what you see is a reconstruction, but the interior marble floor dates to the 3rd-century reign of Diocletian.

### Basilica di Massenzio

Marvel at the scale of this vast 4th-century basilica. In its original form the central hall was divided into enormous naves; now only part of the northern nave survives.

### Julius Caesar RIP

Julius Caesar was cremated on the site where the Tempio di Giulio Cesare now stands.

**Via Sacra**

**Tempio di Giulio Cesare**

### Casa delle Vestali

White statues line the grassy atrium of what was once the luxurious 50-room home of the Vestal Virgins. The virgins played an important role in Roman religion, serving the goddess Vesta.

### Arco di Tito

Said to be the inspiration for the Arc de Triomphe in Paris, the well-preserved Arch of Titus was built by the emperor Domitian to honour his elder brother Titus.

## THE VESTAL VIRGINS

Despite privilege and public acclaim, life as a vestal virgin was no bed of roses. Every year, six physically perfect patrician girls between the ages of six and 10 were chosen by lottery to serve Vesta, goddess of hearth and household. Once selected, they faced a 30-year period of chaste servitude at the Tempio di Vesta. During this time their main duty was to ensure that the temple's sacred fire never went out. If it did, the priestess responsible would be flogged. The wellbeing of the state was thought to depend on the cult of Vesta, and on the vestals' virginity. If a priestess were to lose her virginity she risked being buried alive and the offending man being flogged to death.

**If you're caught short, there are some loos by the Chiesa di Santa Maria Antiqua.**

rebuilt on various occasions and what you see today is a 1937 reconstruction of Diocletian's Curia.

In front of the Curia, and hidden by scaffolding, is the **Lapis Niger**, a large piece of black marble that covered a sacred area said to be the tomb of Romulus.

At the end of Via Sacra stands the 23m-high **Arco di Settimio Severo** (Arch of Septimius Severus), dedicated to the eponymous emperor and his two sons, Caracalla and Geta. Nearby, at the foot of the Tempio di Saturno, is the **Millarium Aureum**, from where distances to the ancient city were measured.

On your left are the remains of the **Rostrum**, an elaborate podium where Shakespeare had Mark Antony make his famous 'Friends, Romans, countrymen...' speech. In front of this, the **Colonna di Foca** (Column of Phocas) marks the centre of the Piazza del Foro, the forum's main square.

The eight granite columns that rise up behind the Colonna are all that remain of the **Tempio di Saturno** (Temple of Saturn), an important temple that doubled as the state treasury. Behind it, are (from north to south): the ruins of the **Tempio della Concordia** (Temple of Concord), the **Tempio di Vespasiano** (Temple of Vespasian and Titus) and the **Portico degli Dei Consenti**.

## Tempio di Castore e Polluce & Casa delle Vestali

Passing over to the path that runs parallel to Via Sacra, you'll see the stubby ruins of the **Basilica Giulia**, which was begun by Julius Caesar and finished by Augustus. At the end of the basilica, the three columns you see belong to the 5th-century BC **Tempio di Castore e Polluce** (Temple of Castor and Pollux). Near the temple, the **Chiesa di Santa Maria Antiqua** is the oldest Christian church in the Forum, and the **Casa delle Vestali** (House of the Vestal Virgins) was home to the virgins who tended the flame in the adjoining **Tempio di Vesta**.

## Via Sacra Towards the Colosseum

Heading up Via Sacra past the **Tempio di Romolo** (Temple of Romulus), you come to the **Basilica di Massenzio**, the largest building on the forum. Started by the Emperor Maxentius and finished by Constantine (it's also known as the Basilica di Costantino), it covered an area of approximately 100m by 65m.

Continuing, you come to the **Arco di Tito** (Arch of Titus), built in AD 81 to celebrate Vespasian and Titus' victories against Jerusalem.

TOP SIGHTS
ROME FORUM

## TOP SIGHTS
# CAPITOLINE MUSEUMS

The world's oldest national museums are housed in two stately *palazzi* on the Michelangelo-designed Piazza del Campidoglio. Their origins date to 1471, when Pope Sixtus IV donated a number of bronze statues to the city, forming the nucleus of what is now one of Italy's finest collections of classical art. The main entrance is in Palazzo dei Conservatori, where you'll find the original core of the sculptural collection and, on the 2nd floor, an art gallery with a number of important works. Over the piazza, Palazzo Nuovo is crammed to its elegant 17th-century rafters with classical Roman sculpture.

### DON'T MISS...

➡ *Lupa Capitolina*
➡ *Spinario*
➡ *La Buona Ventura*
➡ *Galata Morente*
➡ *Venere Capitolina*

### PRACTICALITIES

➡ Map p344
➡ ☑06 06 08
➡ www.museicapito lini.org
➡ Piazza del Campidoglio 1
➡ Adult/reduced €12/10, audioguides €5
➡ ⊙9am-8pm Tue-Sun, last admission 7pm
➡ 🚌Piazza Venezia

## Palazzo dei Conservatori

Before you head upstairs, take a moment to admire the ancient masonry littered around the ground-floor courtyard, most notably a mammoth head, hand and foot. These all came from a 12m-high statue of Constantine that originally stood in the Basilica di Massenzio in the Roman Forum.

Of the sculpture on the 1st floor, the Etruscan *Lupa Capitolina* (Capitoline Wolf) is the most famous. Located in the Sala Della Lupa, this 5th-century-BC bronze wolf stands over her suckling wards Romulus and Remus, who were added to the composition in 1471. Other crowd-pleasers include the *Spinario,* a delicate 1st-century-BC bronze of a boy removing a thorn from his foot and Gian Lorenzo Bernini's *Medusa*. Also on this floor, in the Exedra of Marcus Aurelius, is the original of the equestrian statue that stands in the piazza outside.

The 2nd floor is given over to the Pinacoteca, the museum's picture gallery, with paintings by such heavyweights as Titian, Tintoretto, Reni, van Dyck and Rubens. Sala di Santa Petronilla has a number of important canvases, including two by Caravaggio: *La Buona Ventura* (The Fortune Teller; 1595), which shows a gypsy pretending to read a young man's hand but actually stealing his ring, and *San Giovanni Battista* (John the Baptist; 1602), a sensual and unusual depiction of the saint.

## Tabularium

A tunnel links Palazzo dei Conservatori to Palazzo Nuovo on the other side of the square via the Tabularium, ancient Rome's central archive, beneath Palazzo Senatorio.

## Palazzo Nuovo

Palazzo Nuovo contains some real show-stoppers. Chief among them is the *Galata Morente* (Dying Gaul) in the Sala del Gladiatore. A Roman copy of a 3rd-century-BC Greek original, it movingly captures the quiet, resigned anguish of a dying Frenchman. Also in this room, the *Satiro in Riposo* (Resting Satyr) is said to have inspired Nathaniel Hawthorne to write his novel *The Marble Faun*. Another superb figurative piece is the sensual yet demure portrayal of the *Venere Capitolina* (Capitoline Venus) in the Gabinetto della Venere.

# ◉ SIGHTS

## ◉ Colosseum & Palatino

### COLOSSEUM
MONUMENT
See p58.

### ARCO DI COSTANTINO
MONUMENT
Map p344 (Via di San Gregorio; MColosseo) The Arco di Costantino (Arch of Constantine) was built in 312 to commemorate Constantine's victory over his rival Maxentius at the Battle of Ponte Milvio. One of the last great Roman monuments, it incorporates stonework dating to Domitian's reign (AD 81–96) and eight large medallions produced in Hadrian's time (117–138).

### PALATINO
ANCIENT RUINS
See p60.

### CIRCO MASSIMO
HISTORICAL SITE
Map p344 (Via del Circo Massimo; MCirco Massimo) Now just a basin of grass, gravel and dust, the Circo Massimo (Circus Maximus) was 1st-century Rome's biggest stadium with a capacity of 250,000. The 600m racetrack circled a wooden dividing island with ornate lap indicators and Egyptian obelisks.

## ◉ The Forums & Around

Before venturing into the forums, take a minute to prepare yourself at the **Centro Espositivo Informativo** (✆06 679 77 02; Via dei Fori Imperiali; ⊙9.30am-6.30pm; MColosseo), an information centre dedicated to the area.

### MAPS & GUIDES

As fascinating as Rome's ruins are, they are not well labelled and it can be hard to know what you're looking at without a map or specialist guide. Lozzi's Archaeo Map (€4) is useful, with clearly illustrated plans of the Roman and Imperial Forums, Colosseum and the Palatino. Electa produces a number of insightful guides, including the *Guide to Ancient Rome* (€9.50) and the *Archaeological Guide to Rome* (€11.90), both available at the Colosseum and Roman Forum bookshops.

### ROMAN FORUM
ANCIENT RUINS
See p63.

### BASILICA DI SS COSMA E DAMIANO
CHURCH
Map p344 (Via dei Fori Imperiali; ⊙9am-1pm & 3-7pm; MColosseo) Backing onto the Roman Forum, this 6th-century basilica incorporates parts of the **Foro di Vespasiano** and **Tempio di Romolo**, visible through the glass wall at the end of the nave. The real reason to visit, though, are the vibrant 6th-century apse mosaics, depicting Christ's Second Coming. Also worth a look is the huge 18th-century Neapolitan **presepio** (nativity scene; admission €1 donation; ⊙10am-1pm & 3-6pm Fri-Sun) in a room off the tranquil 17th-century cloisters.

### MERCATI DI TRAIANO MUSEO DEI FORI IMPERIALI
MUSEUM
Map p344 (✆06 06 08; www.mercatiditraiano.it; Via IV Novembre 94; adult/reduced €11/9; ⊙9am-7pm Tue-Sun, last entry 6pm) Housed in Trajan's 2nd-century market complex, this striking museum provides a fascinating introduction to the Imperial Forums with detailed explanatory panels and a smattering of archaeological artefacts. From the main hallway, a lift whisks you up to the **Torre delle Milizie** (Militia Tower), a 13th-century red-brick tower, and the upper levels of the Mercati di Traiano (Trajan's Markets). These markets, housed in a three-storey semicircular construction, were home to hundreds of traders selling everything from oil and vegetables to flowers, silks and spices.

### CARCERE MAMERTINO
HISTORICAL SITE
Map p344; Clivo Argentario 1; €10; ⊙9.30am-7pm summer, 9.30am-5pm winter, last admission 40min before closing time; ▢Piazza Venezia) At the foot of the Campidoglio, the Mamertine Prison was ancient Rome's maximum-security prison. St Peter did time here and while imprisoned supposedly created a miraculous stream of water to baptise his jailers. On the bare stone walls you can make out early Christian frescoes depicting Jesus and Saints Peter and Paul.

## ◉ Campidoglio

Rising above the Roman Forum, the Campidoglio (Capitoline hill) was one of the seven hills on which Rome was founded. At its summit were Rome's two most im-

## TOP SIGHTS
## IMPERIAL FORUMS

The ruins over the road from the Roman Forum are known collectively as the Imperial Forums (Fori Imperiali). Constructed between 42 BC and AD 112, they were largely buried in 1933 when Mussolini built Via dei Fori Imperiali. Excavations have since unearthed much of them but visits are limited to the Mercati di Traiano (Trajan's Markets), accessible through the Museo dei Fori Imperiali.

Little recognisable remains of the Foro di Traiano (Trajan's Forum), except for some pillars from the Basilica Ulpia and the Colonna di Traiano (Trajan's Column), whose minutely detailed reliefs celebrate Trajan's military victories over the Dacians (from modern-day Romania).

To the southeast, three temple columns rise from Foro di Augusto (Augustus' Forum), now mostly under Via dei Fori Imperiali. The 30m-high wall behind the forum was built to protect it from the frequent fires in the area.

The Foro di Nerva (Nerva's Forum) was also buried by Mussolini's road-building, although part of a temple dedicated to Minerva still stands. Originally, it would have connected the Foro di Augusto to the 1st-century Foro di Vespasiano (Vespasian's Forum). Over the road, three columns are the most visible remains of the Foro di Cesare (Caesar's Forum).

### DON'T MISS...

➡ Mercati di Traiano
➡ Colonna di Traiano
➡ Basilica Ulpia

### PRACTICALITIES

➡ Map p344
➡ Ⓜ Colosseo

---

portant temples: one dedicated to Jupiter Capitolinus (a descendant of Jupiter, the Roman equivalent of Zeus) and the other (which housed Rome's mint) to the goddess Juno Moneta. More than 2000 years on, the hill still wields considerable clout as seat of Rome's municipal government.

**PIAZZA DEL CAMPIDOGLIO**　　　PIAZZA
Map p344 (🚇Piazza Venezia) Designed by Michelangelo in 1538, this elegant piazza is one of Rome's most beautiful squares. You can reach it from the Roman Forum but the most dramatic approach is via the **Cordonata**, the graceful staircase that leads up from Piazza d'Ara Coeli. At the top of the stairs, the piazza is bordered by three *palazzi*: **Palazzo Nuovo** to the left, **Palazzo Senatorio** straight ahead, and **Palazzo dei Conservatori** on the right. Together, Palazzo Nuovo and Palazzo dei Conservatori house the **Capitoline Museums**, while Palazzo Senatorio is home to Rome's city council.

In the centre, the bronze equestrian **statue of Marcus Aurelius** is a copy. The original, which dates from the 2nd century AD, is in the Capitoline Museums.

**CAPITOLINE MUSEUMS**　　　MUSEUM
See p67.

**CHIESA DI SANTA MARIA IN ARACOELI**　　　CHURCH
Map p344 (Piazza Santa Maria in Aracoeli; ☻9am-12.30pm & 3-6.30pm; 🚇Piazza Venezia) Marking the highest point of the Campidoglio, this 6th-century church sits on the site of the Roman temple to Juno Moneta. According to legend it was here that the Tiburtine Sybil told Augustus of the coming birth of Christ, and the church still has a strong association with the nativity. Features to note include the Cosmatesque floor and an important 15th-century fresco by Pinturicchio.

## ⊙ Piazza Venezia

**IL VITTORIANO**　　　MONUMENT
Map p344 (Piazza Venezia; admission free; ☻9.30am-5.30pm summer, 9.30am-4.30pm winter; 🚇Piazza Venezia) Love it or loathe it, as most locals do, you can't ignore Il Vittoriano, the massive mountain of white marble that towers over Piazza Venezia. Known

**LOCAL KNOWLEDGE**

## BARBARA NAZZARO: ARCHITECT

••••••••••••••••••••••••••••••••••••••••••

The Technical Director at the Colosseum, Barbara Nazzaro, explains what went on in the Colosseum's hypogeum.

'Gladiators entered the hypogeum through an underground corridor which led directly in from the nearby Ludus Magnus (gladiator school). In side corridors, which stand over a natural spring, boats were kept. When they wanted these boats up in the arena they would let the spring water in and flood the tunnels. Later these passages were used for winch mechanisms, all of which were controlled by a single pulley system. There were about 80 lifts going up to the arena as well as cages where wild animals were kept. You can still see the spaces where the cages were.'

also as the Altare della Patria (Altar of the Fatherland), it was begun in 1885 to commemorate Italian unification and honour Vittorio Emanuele II, Italy's first king and the subject of its gargantuan equestrian statue. It also hosts the Tomb of the Unknown Soldier.

Whatever you might think of this monument, there's no denying that the 360-degree views from the top are quite stunning. To get to the top, take the glass lift, **Roma dal Cielo** (adult/reduced €7/3.50; ◷9.30am-6.30pm Mon-Thu, to 7.30pm Fri-Sun), from the side of the building.

Inside the body of the structure, the **Museo Centrale del Risorgimento** (Via di San Pietro in Carcere; admission free; ◷9.30am-6pm), often referred to as the Complesso del Vittoriano, hosts temporary art exhibitions and has a collection of military knickknacks documenting the history of Italian unification.

PALAZZO VENEZIA                    MUSEUM

Map p344 (◨Piazza Venezia) On the western side of Piazza Venezia, this was the first of Rome's great Renaissance palaces, built between 1455 and 1464. For centuries it served as the embassy of the Venetian Republic, although its best known resident was Mussolini, who famously made speeches from its balcony.

Nowadays, the *palazzo* houses the **Museo Nazionale del Palazzo Venezia** (◷06 678 01 31; Via del Plebiscito 118; adult/reduced €4/2; ◷8.30am-7.30pm Tue-Sun) with its collection of superb Byzantine and early Renaissance paintings, jewellery, ceramics, arms and armour.

BASILICA DI SAN MARCO               CHURCH

Map p344 (Piazza di San Marco; ◷8.30am-noon & 4-6.30pm Mon-Sat, 9am-1pm & 4-8pm Sun; ◨Piazza Venezia) The early 4th-century Basilica di San Marco stands over the house where St Mark the Evangelist is said to have stayed while in Rome. Its main attraction is the golden 9th-century apse mosaic.

# ◉ Forum Boarium & Around

BOCCA DELLA VERITÀ               MONUMENT

Map p344 (Piazza della Bocca della Verità 18; donation €0.50; ◷9.30am-4.50pm; ◨Via dei Cerchi) A round piece of marble that was once part of an ancient fountain, or possibly an ancient manhole cover, the *Bocca della Verità* (Mouth of Truth) is one of Rome's most photographed curiosities. According to legend, if you put your hand in the carved mouth and tell a lie, it will bite your hand off.

The mouth lives in the portico of the **Chiesa di Santa Maria in Cosmedin**, one of Rome's most beautiful medieval churches. Originally built in the 8th century, the church was given a major revamp in the 12th century, when the bell tower and portico were added and the floor was decorated with Cosmati inlaid marble.

FORUM BOARIUM               HISTORICAL SITE

Map p344 (Piazza della Bocca della Verità; ◨Via dei Cerchi) Car-choked Piazza della Bocca della Verità stands on what was once ancient Rome's cattle market (Forum Boarium). Opposite Chiesa Santa Maria in Cosmedin are two tiny Roman temples dating to the 2nd century BC: the round **Tempio di Ercole Vincitore** and the **Tempio di Portunus**, dedicated to the god of rivers and ports, Portunus. Just off the piazza, the **Arco di Giano** (Arch of Janus) is a four-sided Roman arch that once covered a crossroads. Beyond it is the medieval **Chiesa di San Giorgio in Velabro** (Via del Velabro 19; ◷10am-12.30pm & 4-6.30pm Tue, Fri & Sat), a beautiful church whose original 7th-century portico was destroyed by a Mafia bomb attack in 1993.

START **PALATINO**

END **PIAZZA DEL CAMPIDOGLIO**

DISTANCE **1.2KM**

DURATION **ALL MORNING/ AFTERNOON**

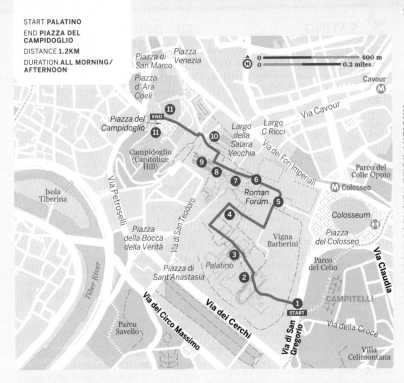

Neighbourhood Walk

# Explore the Ruins

Follow in the footsteps of an ancient Roman on this whistle-stop tour of the city's most famous ruins.

Ancient Rome's most sought-after neighbourhood was the **1 Palatino**, where the emperor lived alongside the cream of imperial society. The ruins here are confusing but their scale gives some sense of the luxury in which the ancient VIPs liked to live. You can still make out parts of the **2 Domus Augustana**, the emperor's private residence, and the **3 Domus Flavia**, where he would hold official audiences. From the Domus find your way up to the **4 Orti Farnesiani**. These gardens weren't part of the ancient city but they're worth a quick look for the views they command over the Roman Forum. Once you've got your photos, head down to the Forum. Coming down from the Palatino you'll enter the Forum near the

**5 Arco di Tito**, one of the Forum's great triumphal arches. Beyond this, bear right and pick up **6 Via Sacra**, the Forum's main drag. Follow this down and after a few hundred metres you'll come to the **7 Casa delle Vestali**, where the legendary Vestal Virgins lived tending to their duties and guarding their virtue. Beyond the three columns of the **8 Tempio di Castore e Polluce**, you'll see a flattened area littered with column bases and brick stumps. This is the **9 Basilica Giulia**, where lawyers and magistrats worked dispensing justice in the crowded law courts. Meanwhile senators debated matters of state at the **10 Curia**, over on the other side of the Forum. From near the Curia, exit the Forum and climb up the Campidoglio (Capitoline hill) to the magnificent **11 Capitoline Museums**.

# EATING

### HOSTARIA DA NERONE
TRATTORIA €€

Map p344 (06 481 79 52; Via delle Terme di Tito; meals €35; ☺Mon-Sat lunch & dinner; MColosseo) This old-school, family-run trattoria is not the place for a romantic dinner or a special-occasion splurge but if you're after a good earthy meal after a day's sightseeing, it does the job admirably. Tourists tuck into classic Roman pastas and salads outside while in the yellowing, woody interior visiting businessmen cut deals over saltimbocca and tiramisu.

### SAN TEODORO
MODERN ITALIAN €€€

Map p344 (☑06 678 09 33; www.st-teodoro.it; Via dei Fienili 49-50; meals €80; ☺Mon-Sat lunch & dinner; ☐Via del Teatro di Marcello) Hidden away on a picturesque corner behind the Palatino, San Teodoro is a refined seafood restaurant. Sit in the cool, minimalist interior or outside on the covered terrace and enjoy sophisticated creations like lasagna with zucchini flowers, scampi and pecorino cheese.

### ARA COELI
GELATERIA €

(Piazza d'Ara Coeli 9; ☺11am-11pm; ☐Piazza Venezia) Close to the base of the Campidoglio, Ara Coeli has more than 40 flavours of excellent organic ice cream, semicold varieties, Sicilian *granita* (flavoured shaved ice) and yoghurt.

# DRINKING & NIGHTLIFE

### CAFFÉ CAPITOLINO
CAFE

Map p344 (Capitoline Museums, Piazzale Caffarelli 4; ☺Tue-Sun; ☐Piazza Venezia) Hidden behind the Capitoline Museums, this stylish rooftop cafe commands memorable views. It's a good place to take a museum timeout and relax with a drink or snack (*panini*, salads and pizza), although you don't need a ticket to drink here – it's accessible via an independent entrance on Piazzale Caffarelli.

### CAVOUR 313
WINE BAR

Map p344 (☑06 678 54 96; www.cavour313. it; Via Cavour 313; ☺10am-3.30pm & 7pm-midnight; MCavour) Close to the Forum, wood-panelled, intimate wine-bar Cavour 313 attracts everyone from actors to politicians to tourists. Sink into its pub-like cosiness and while away hours over sensational wine (over 1200 labels) accompanied by cold cuts and cheese or a light meal.

### 0,75
BAR

Map p344 (www.075roma.com; Via dei Cerchi 65; ☺11am-2am; ☐Via dei Cerchi) A funky bar on the Circo Massimo, good for a lingering drink, weekend brunch (11am-3pm), an *aperitivo*, or a light lunch. It's a friendly place with a laid-back vibe, an attractive exposed-brick look and cool tunes. Free wi-fi.

# Centro Storico

PANTHEON | PIAZZA NAVONA | CAMPO DE' FIORI | JEWISH GHETTO | ISOLA TIBERINA

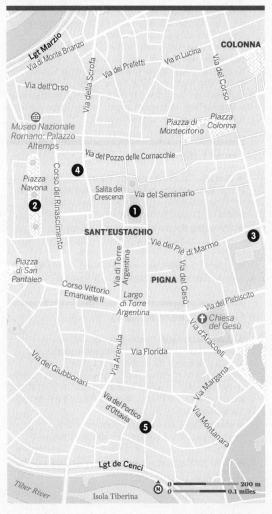

## Neighbourhood Top Five

**1** Stepping into the **Pantheon** (p75) and feeling the same sense of awe that the ancients must have felt 2000 years ago. The sight of the dome soaring up above you is a genuinely jaw-dropping spectacle.

**2** Exploring **Piazza Navona** (p77) and the picturesque streets that surround it.

**3** Browsing the fabulous art collection at the **Palazzo e Galleria Doria Pamphilj** (p77).

**4** Catching three Caravaggio masterpieces at the **Chiesa di San Luigi dei Francesi** (p86).

**5** Escaping the crowds in the shadowy lanes of the **Jewish Ghetto** (p83).

For more detail of this area, see Map p346 ➡ and Map p350 ➡

## Lonely Planet's Top Tip

The *centro storico* is the perfect area to ditch your guidebook and go it alone. You'll probably get lost at some point, but don't worry if you do. Sooner or later you'll emerge on a main road or find a recognisable landmark.

See masterpieces by the likes of Michelangelo, Raphael, Caravaggio and Bernini for absolutely nothing by visiting the area's churches, which are all free to enter.

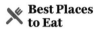

### Best Places to Eat

➡ Casa Coppelle (p89)

➡ Giggetto al Portico d'Ottavia (p94)

➡ Pizzeria da Baffetto (p91)

➡ La Rosetta (p89)

For reviews see p89 ➡

### Best Places to Drink

➡ Caffè Sant'Eustachio (p96)

➡ Open Baladin (p96)

➡ Salotto 42 (p97)

➡ Etablì (p96)

For reviews see p95 ➡

### Best Art Churches

➡ Chiesa di San Luigi dei Francesi (p86)

➡ Chiesa del Gesú (p81)

➡ Chiesa di Sant'Ignazio di Loyola (p88)

➡ Chiesa di Santa Maria Sopra Minerva (p78)

For reviews see p78 ➡

## Explore: Centro Storico

Rome's historic centre is made for leisurely strolling and although you could spend weeks exploring its every corner, you can cover most of the main sights in two or three days. Many people enter the area by bus, getting off at Largo di Torre Argentina, from where it's a short walk up to the Pantheon and beyond that to Rome's political nerve-centre Piazza Colonna. Nearby, on Via del Corso, the Palazzo e Galleria Doria Pamphilj houses one of the capital's finest private art collections. Art is thick on the ground in these parts and many of the centre's churches harbour extraordinary frescoes and sculptures. To the west of the Pantheon, the streets around Piazza Navona, itself one of Rome's great must-see sights, are a magnet for tourists and hip Romans with their bohemian boutiques, cool bars and popular pizzerias.

Over on the other side of Corso Vittorio Emanuele II, the main road that bisects the area, all streets lead to Campo de' Fiori, home to a colourful daily market and hectic late-night drinking scene. From 'il Campo' you can shop your way down to the medieval Jewish Ghetto, a wonderfully atmospheric area of romantic corners, hidden piazzas and authentic eateries.

## Local Life

➡ **Piazzas** The restaurants on Piazza Navona and Piazza Rotonda attract a touristy crowd while Campo de' Fiori pulls in boozing students. Locals head to places in the quieter back streets.

➡ **Shopping Strips** Browse retro fashions and second-hand threads on Via del Governo Vecchio (p79); Via dei Giubbonari is good for frocks and heels.

➡ **Aperitif** Young Romans love to meet over an evening *aperitivo* in the bars around Piazza Navona.

## Getting There & Away

➡ **Bus** The best way to access the *centro storico*. A whole fleet serve the area from Termini, including Nos 40 and 64, which both stop at Largo di Torre Argentina and continue down Corso Vittorio Emanuele II. From Barberini metro station, bus 116 stops at Corso Rinascimento (for Piazza Navona), Piazza Farnese and Via Giulia.

➡ **Metro** There are no metro stations in the neighbourhood but it's within walking distance of Barberini, Spagna and Flaminio stations, all on line A.

➡ **Tram** No 8 connects Largo di Torre Argentina with Trastevere.

## TOP SIGHTS
### PANTHEON

Along with the Colosseum, the Pantheon is one of Rome's iconic sights. A striking 2000-year-old temple, now a church, it is the city's best preserved ancient monument and one of the most influential buildings in the Western world. Over the centuries its innovative design and revolutionary build have served to inspire generations of architects and engineers. And while the greying, pockmarked exterior is looking its age, inside it's a different story, and it remains a unique and exhilarating experience to pass through the towering bronze doors and have your vision directed upwards to the world's largest unreinforced concrete dome.

## History

In its current form the Pantheon dates to around AD 120, when the emperor Hadrian built over an earlier temple. Originally, Marcus Agrippa, son-in-law of the emperor Augustus, had constructed a temple here in 27 BC, but it burnt down in AD 80, and although it was rebuilt by Domitian, it was destroyed for a second time in AD 110 after being struck by lightning. The emperor Hadrian rebuilt it once again, and it's this version that you see today.

Hadrian's temple was dedicated to the classical gods – hence the name Pantheon, a derivation of the Greek words *pan* (all) and *theos* (god) – but in AD 608 it was consecrated as a Christian church in honour of the Madonna and all martyrs after the Byzantine emperor Phocus donated it to Pope Boniface IV. (It's official name is now the Basilica di Santa Maria ad Martyres.) Thanks to this consecration the Pantheon was spared the worst of the medieval plundering that reduced many of Rome's ancient buildings to their bare bones. However, it wasn't totally safe from plundering hands. The gilded-bronze roof tiles were removed and, in the 17th century, the Barberini Pope Urban VIII had the portico's bronze

### DON'T MISS...

➡ The entrance doors
➡ The dome
➡ Raphael's Tomb

### PRACTICALITIES

➡ Map p346
➡ Piazza della Rotonda
➡ Admission free
➡ Audioguide €5
➡ ⊘8.30am-7.30pm Mon-Sat, 9am-6pm Sun
➡ 🚍🚍Largo di Torre Argentina

## THE INSCRIPTION

For centuries the Latin inscription over the Pantheon's entrance led historians to believe that the current temple was Marcus Agrippa's original. Certainly, the wording would suggest so, reading: 'M.AGRIPPA.L.F.COS. TERTIUM.FECIT' or 'Marcus Agrippa, son of Lucius, consul for the third time, built this'. However, excavations in the 19th-century revealed traces of an earlier temple and scholars realised that Hadrian had simply reinstated Agrippa's original inscription over his new temple.

**According to the attendants who work at the Pantheon, the question tourists most often ask is: what happens when it rains? (Rain gets in through the open oculus.) The answer is that the rainwater drains away through 22 almost-invisible holes in the sloping marble floor.**

ceiling melted down to make 80 canons for Castel Sant'Angelo and the baldachino over the main altar of St Peter's Basilica.

During the Renaissance the Pantheon was much studied – Brunelleschi used it as inspiration for his Duomo in Florence – and it became an important burial chamber. Today you'll find the tomb of the artist Raphael here, alongside those of kings Vittorio Emanuele II and Umberto I.

## Exterior

Originally, the Pantheon was on a raised podium, its entrance facing out onto a rectangular porticoed piazza. Nowadays, the dark-grey pitted exterior faces the busy, cafe-lined Piazza della Rotonda. And although it's somewhat the worse for wear, the facade is still an imposing sight. Most impressively, the monumental entrance portico is made up of 16 Corinthian columns, each 13m high and made of Egyptian granite, supporting a triangular pediment. Little remains of the ancient decor, although rivets and holes in the brickwork indicate where the marble-veneer panels were once placed, and the towering 20-tonne bronze doors are 16th-century restorations of the originals.

## Interior

Although impressive from outside, it's only when you get inside the Pantheon that you can really appreciate its full size. With light streaming in through the oculus (the 8.7m-diameter hole in the centre of the dome), the marble-clad interior seems absolutely vast, an effect that was deliberately designed to cut worshippers down to size in the face of the gods.

Opposite the entrance is the church's main altar, over which hangs a 7th-century icon of the Madonna and Child. To the left (as you look in from the entrance) is the tomb of Raphael, marked by Lorenzetto's 1520 sculpture of the *Madonna del Sasso* (Madonna of the Rock), and next door, the tombs of King Umberto I and Margherita of Savoy. Over on the opposite side of the rotunda is the tomb of King Vittorio Emanuele II.

## The Dome

The Pantheon's dome, considered the Romans' most important architectural achievement, was the largest in the world until the 15th century and is still today the largest unreinforced concrete dome ever built. Its harmonious appearance is due to a precisely calibrated symmetry – the diameter is equal to the building's interior height of 43.3m. Light enters through the central oculus, which served as a symbolic connection between the temple and the gods as well as an important structural role – it absorbs and redistributes the huge tensile forces.

TOP SIGHTS
**PANTHEON**

# TOP SIGHTS
## PIAZZA NAVONA

With its ornate fountains, exuberant baroque palazzi and pavement cafes, Piazza Navona is central Rome's showcase square. Long a hub of local life, it hosted Rome's main market for close on 300 years, and today attracts a daily circus of street performers, hawkers, artists, tourists, fortune-tellers and pigeons.

Like many of the city's great landmarks, it sits on the site of an ancient monument, in this case the 1st-century-AD **Stadio di Domiziano** (📞06 0608; Piazza Tor Sanguigna 13; ⊘closed for restoration). This 30,000-seat stadium, remains of which can be seen from Piazza Tor Sanguigna, used to host games – the name Navona is a corruption of the Greek word *agon,* meaning public games. Inevitably, though, it fell into disrepair and it wasn't until the 15th century that the crumbling arena was paved over and Rome's central market transferred here from Campidoglio.

### DON'T MISS...

➡ Fontana dei Quattro Fiumi
➡ Chiesa di Sant'Agnese in Agone
➡ Palazzo Pamphilj

### PRACTICALITIES

➡ Map p346
➡ 🚇Corso del Rinascimento

## Fontana dei Quattro Fiumi

Of the piazza's three fountains, it's Gian Lorenzo Bernini's high-camp **Fontana dei Quattro Fiumi** (Fountain of the Four Rivers) that dominates. Commissioned by Pope Innocent X and completed in 1651, it depicts the Nile, Ganges, Danube and Plate, representing the then-known four continents of the world, and is festooned with a palm tree, lion and horse, and topped by an obelisk. Legend has it that the figure of the Nile is shielding his eyes from the nearby Chiesa di Sant'Agnese in Agone designed by Bernini's hated rival, Francesco Borromini. In truth, it simply indicates that the source of the Nile was unknown at the time the fountain was created.

The **Fontana del Moro** at the southern end of the square was designed by Giacomo della Porta in 1576. Bernini added the Moor holding a dolphin in the mid-17th century, but the surrounding Tritons are 19th-century copies. The 19th-century **Fontana del Nettuno** at the northern end of the piazza depicts Neptune fighting with a sea monster, surrounded by sea nymphs.

## Chiesa di Sant'Agnese in Agone

With its stately, yet vibrantly theatrical facade, the **Chiesa di Sant'Agnese in Agone** (📞06 681 92 134; www.santagneseinagone.org; ⊘9.30am-12.30pm & 3.30-7pm Tue-Sat, 9am-1pm & 4-8pm Sun) is typical of Francesco Borromini's baroque style. The church, which occasionally hosts classical music concerts, is said to stand on the spot where the virgin martyr Agnes performed a miracle before being killed. According to legend, she was stripped naked by her executioners but miraculously grew her hair to cover her body and preserve her modesty.

## Palazzo Pamphilj

The largest building in the square is this elegant baroque *palazzo,* built between 1644 and 1650 by Girolamo Rainaldi and Borromini to celebrate Giovanni Battista Pamphilj's election as Pope Innocent X. Inside there are some impressive frescoes by Pietro da Cortona, but the building, which has been the Brazilian Embassy since 1920, is not open to the general public.

# ◉ SIGHTS

**Bound by the River Tiber and Via del Corso, the** *centro storico* **(historic centre) is made for aimless wandering. Even without trying you'll come across some of Rome's great sights: the Pantheon, Piazza Navona and Campo de' Fiori, as well as a host of monuments, museums and churches. To the south, the Jewish Ghetto has been home to Rome's Jewish community since the 2nd century BC.**

## ◉ Pantheon & Around

### PANTHEON                           CHURCH
See p75.

### ELEFANTINO                         MONUMENT
Map p346 (Piazza della Minerva; ▣Largo di Torre Argentina) A short skip south of the Pantheon stands the Elefantino, a curious and much-loved sculpture of a puzzled elephant carrying a 6th-century-BC Egyptian obelisk. Unveiled in 1667 and designed to glorify Pope Alexander VII, the elephant, symbolising strength and wisdom, was sculpted by Ercole Ferrata to a design by Bernini. The obelisk was taken from the nearby Chiesa di Santa Maria Sopra Minerva.

### CHIESA DI SANTA MARIA SOPRA MINERVA                             CHURCH
Map p346 (Piazza della Minerva; ⊘8am-7pm Mon-Fri, 8am-1pm & 3.30-7pm Sat & Sun; ▣ ▣Largo di Torre Argentina) Built on the site of an ancient temple to Minerva, the Dominican Chiesa di Santa Maria Sopra Minerva is Rome's only Gothic church, although little remains of the original 13th-century design.

Inside, in the Cappella Carafa (also called the Cappella della Annunciazione), you'll find two superb 15th-century frescoes by Filippino Lippi and the majestic tomb of Pope Paul IV. Left of the high altar is one of Michelangelo's lesser-known sculptures, *Cristo Risorto* (Christ Bearing the Cross; 1520). An altarpiece of the Madonna and Child in the second chapel in the northern transept is attributed to Fra Angelico, the Dominican friar and painter, who is also buried in the church.

The body of St Catherine of Siena, minus her head (which is in Siena), lies under the high altar, and the tombs of two Medici popes, Leo X and Clement VII, are in the apse.

### LARGO DI TORRE ARGENTINA          ANCIENT RUINS
Map p346 (▣ ▣Largo di Torre Argentina) A busy transport hub, Largo di Torre Argentina is set around the sunken **Area Sacra** and the remains of four Republican-era temples, all built between the 2nd and 4th centuries BC. These ruins are off-limits to humans but home to a thriving population of 250 stray cats and a **cat sanctuary** (www.roman cats.com; ⊘noon-6pm).

On the piazza's western flank is Rome's premier theatre, the Teatro Argentina.

### MUSEO NAZIONALE ROMANO: CRYPTA BALBI              MUSEUM
Map p346 (✆06 399 67 700; www.pierreci.it; Via delle Botteghe Oscure 31; adult/reduced €7/3.50; ⊘9am-7.45pm Tue-Sun, last admission 7pm; ▣Piazza Venezia) The least known of the Museo Nazionale Romano's four museums, the Crypta Balbi provides a fascinating insight into Rome's multilayered past. More than the exhibits, it's the structure of the building itself that's the main interest. It's built around the ruins of medieval and Renaissance structures, themselves set on top of the Teatro di Balbus (13 BC). You can duck down into the underground excavations before perusing artefacts taken from the Crypta, as well as items found in the forums and on the Oppio and Celio hills. On entry, there's a possible €3 exhibition supplement charge.

## ◉ Piazza Navona & Around

### PIAZZA NAVONA                      PIAZZA
See p77.

### VIA DEI CORONARI                   STREET
Map p346 (▣Corso del Rinascimento) Named after the *coronari* (rosary-bead sellers) who used to work here, this elegant pedestrian street is famous for its antique shops. A lovely, quiet place for a stroll, it follows the course of the ancient Roman road that connected Piazza Colonna with the River Tiber and was once a popular thoroughfare for pilgrims.

### CHIESA DI SANTA MARIA DELLA PACE & CHIOSTRO DEL BRAMANTE      CHURCH
Map p346 (✆06 686 09 035; www.chiostrodel bramante.it; Vicolo dell'Arco della Pace 5; exhibitions adult/reduced €10/8; ⊘church 9am-noon Mon, Wed & Sat, cloisters 10am-11pm daily, exhibitions 10am-8pm Tue- Sun; ▣Corso Vittorio Emanuele II) Tucked away in the backstreets

## TOP SIGHTS
# PALAZZO E GALLERIA DORIA PAMPHILJ

You wouldn't know it from the grimy exterior but this *palazzo* houses one of Rome's richest private art collections, with works by Raphael, Tintoretto, Brueghel, Titian, Caravaggio, Bernini and Velázquez.

Palazzo Doria Pamphilj dates to the mid-15th century, but its current look was largely the work of the current owners, the Doria Pamphilj family, who acquired it in the 18th century. The Pamphilj's golden age, during which the family collection was started, came during the papacy of one of their own, Innocent X (r 1644–55).

The picture gallery has 10 rooms, chronologically ordered and hung with floor-to-ceiling paintings. Masterpieces abound, but look out for Titian's *Salomè con la testa del Battista* (Salome with the Head of John the Baptist) and two early Caravaggios: *Riposo durante la fuga in Egitto* (Rest During the Flight into Egypt) and *Maddalene Penitente* (Penitent Magdalen). The undisputed star is the Velázquez portrait of an implacable Pope Innocent X, who grumbled that it was 'too real'. The *Gabinetto di Velázquez* is Bernini's interpretation of the same subject.

The excellent free audioguide, narrated by Jonathan Pamphilj, brings the place alive with family anecdotes and background information.

### DON'T MISS...

➡ *Salome con la testa del Battista*

➡ *Riposo durante la fuga in Egitto*

➡ *Ritratto di papa Innocenzo X*

### PRACTICALITIES

➡ Map p346

➡ ☑06 679 73 23

➡ adult/reduced €10.50/7.50

➡ ☉10am-5pm, last admission 4.15pm

➡ ☒Via del Corso

near Piazza Navona, this small 15th-century church boasts an elaborate porticoed exterior and a minor Raphael fresco, *Sibille* (Sibyls). Next door, the Chiostro del Bramante (Bramante Cloisters) is a masterpiece of Renaissance styling, its classic lines providing a marked counterpoint to the church's undulating facade. The cloisters, which you can visit freely by popping up to the first floor shop or cafe, are now used to host art exhibitions and cultural events.

### PASQUINO                                    MONUMENT
Map p346 (Piazza Pasquino; ☒Corso Vittorio Emanuele II) Recently scrubbed back to a virginal white, this unassuming sculpture is Rome's most famous 'talking statue'. During the 16th century, when there were no safe outlets for dissent, a Vatican tailor named Pasquino began sticking notes to the statue with satirical verses lampooning the church and aristocracy. Others joined in and soon there were talking statues all over town. Until a few years ago, Romans were still writing messages, known as *pasquinade,* and sticking them to the statue.

### VIA DEL GOVERNO VECCHIO              STREET
Map p346 (☒Corso Vittorio Emanuele II) Striking off west from Piazza Pasquino, Via del Governo Vecchio is a lively, atmospheric street full of boutiques, eateries and vintage clothes shops. The road, once part of the papal thoroughfare from Palazzo Laterano in San Giovanni to St Peter's Basilica, acquired its name in 1755 when the papal government relocated from **Palazzo Nardini** at No 39 to Palazzo Madama on the other side of Piazza Navona. Bramante is thought to have lived at No 123.

### CHIESA NUOVA                                CHURCH
Map p346 (Piazza della Chiesa Nuova; ☉7.30am-noon & 4.30-7.15pm Mon-Sat, 8am-1pm & 4.30-7.15pm Sun; ☒Corso Vittorio Emanuele II) Not exactly new as the name 'New Church' would suggest, this imposing baroque church was built in 1575 as part of a complex to house Filippo Neri's Oratorian order. Originally Neri had wanted a large, plain church, but after his death in 1595 the artists moved in – Rubens painted over the high altar, and Pietro da Cortona decorated the dome, tribune and nave. Neri was canonised in 1622 and is buried in a chapel to the left of the apse.

Next to the church is Borromini's **Oratorio dei Filippini** and behind it is the **Torre dell'Orologio**, a clock tower built to decorate the adjacent convent.

### MUSEO DI ROMA
MUSEUM

Map p346 ([📞]06 820 59 127; www.museodiroma. it; Piazza di San Pantaleo 10; adult/reduced €9/7; ⊙9am-7pm Tue-Sun, last admission 6pm; [🚇]Corso Vittorio Emanuele II) The baroque Palazzo Braschi houses the Museo di Roma's eclectic collection of paintings, photographs, etchings, clothes and furniture, charting the history of Rome from the Middle Ages to the early 20th century. But as striking as the collection are the *palazzo's* beautiful frescoed halls, including the extravagant Sala Cinese and the Egyptian-themed Sala Egiziana. Among the paintings, look out for Raphael's 1511 portrait of Cardinal Alessandro Farnese, the future Pope Paul III.

### CHIESA DI SANT'IVO ALLA SAPIENZA
CHURCH

Map p346 (Corso del Rinascimento 40; ⊙9am-noon Sun; [🚇]Corso del Rinascimento) Hidden in the porticoed courtyard of **Palazzo della Sapienza**, this tiny church is a masterpiece of baroque architecture. Built by Francesco Borromini between 1642 and 1660, and based on an incredibly complex geometric plan, it combines alternating convex and concave walls with a circular interior topped by a twisted spire.

Palazzo della Sapienza, seat of Rome's university until 1935 and now home to the Italian state archive, is often used to stage temporary exhibitions.

---

**LOCAL KNOWLEDGE**

### ARCO DEGLI ACETARI

For one of Rome's most picture-perfect scenes, head to Via del Pellegrino 19, just off Campo de' Fiori. Here you'll come across a dark archway called the **Arco degli Acetari** (Vinegar-Makers' Arch; Map p346). This in itself isn't especially memorable but if you duck under it you'll emerge onto a tiny medieval square enclosed by rusty orange houses and full of colourful cascading plants. Cats and bicycles litter the cobbles, while overhead washing hangs off pretty flower-lined balconies.

---

### [FREE] PALAZZO MADAMA
PALAZZO

Map p346 ([📞]06 670 62 430; www.senato.it; Piazza Madama 11; ⊙guided tours 10am-6pm, 1st Sat of month; [🚇]Corso del Rinascimento) Seat of the Italian Senate since 1871, the regal Palazzo Madama was originally the 16th-century residence of Giovanni de' Medici, the future Pope Leo X. It was enlarged in the 17th century, when the baroque facade was added together with the decorative frieze, and later provided office space for several pontifical departments. The name 'Madama' is a reference to Margaret of Parma, the illegitimate daughter of the Holy Roman Emperor Charles V, who lived here from 1559 to 1567.

### CHIESA DI SANT'AGOSTINO
CHURCH

Map p346 (Piazza di Sant'Agostino; ⊙7.45am-noon & 4-7.30pm; [🚇]Corso del Rinascimento) This early Renaissance church is a favourite of soon-to-be mums, who pop in to pay their respects to Jacopo Sansovino's sculpture of the Virgin Mary, the *Madonna del Parto* (1521). The Madonna also features in Caravaggio's *Madonna dei Pellegrini* (Madonna of the Pilgrims), which caused uproar when it was unveiled in 1604, due to its depiction of Mary as barefoot and her two devoted pilgrims as filthy beggars. Painting almost a century before, Raphael provoked no such scandal with his fresco of *Isaiah,* visible on the third pilaster on the left in the nave.

---

## ◉ Campo De' Fiori & Around

### CAMPO DE' FIORI
PIAZZA

Map p346 ([🚇]Corso Vittorio Emanuele II) Noisy and colourful, 'Il Campo' is a major focus of Roman life: by day it hosts a much-loved market, while at night it turns into a raucous open-air pub. For centuries, it was the site of public executions, and in 1600 the philosophising monk Giordano Bruno, immortalised in Ettore Ferrari's sinister statue, was burned at the stake here for heresy.

Many of the streets surrounding Il Campo are named after the artisans who traditionally occupied them: Via dei Cappellari (hatters), Via dei Baullari (trunk makers) and Via dei Chiavari (key makers). Via dei Giubbonari (jacket makers) is still full of clothing shops.

# TOP SIGHTS
## CHIESA DEL GESÙ

An imposing example of late 16th-century Counter-Reformation architecture, this is Rome's most important Jesuit church. The facade by Giacomo della Porta is impressive, but it's the awesome gold and marble interior that is the real attraction. Of the art on display, the most astounding work is the *Trionfo del Nome di Gesù* (Triumph of the Name of Jesus), the swirling, hypnotic vault fresco by Giovanni Battista Gaulli (aka Il Baciccia), who also painted the cupola frescoes and designed the stucco decoration.

Baroque master Andrea Pozzo designed the **Cappella di Sant'Ignazio** in the northern transept. Here you'll find the tomb of Ignatius Loyola, the Spanish soldier and saint who founded the Jesuits in 1540. The altar-tomb is an opulent marble-and-bronze affair with columns encrusted with lapis lazuli. On top, the terrestrial globe, representing the Trinity, is the largest solid piece of lapis lazuli in the world. On either side are sculptures of *Fede che vince l'Idolatria* (Faith Defeats Idolatry) and *Religione che flagella l'Eresia* (Religion Lashing Heresy).

The Spanish saint lived in the church from 1544 until his death in 1556. His private **rooms** (⊙4-6pm Mon-Sat, 10am-noon Sun), with a masterful trompe l'oeil by Andrea del Pozzo, are right of the main church.

### DON'T MISS...
➡ The *Trionfo del Nome di Gesù* fresco
➡ Cappella di Sant'Ignazio

### PRACTICALITIES
➡ Map p346
➡ www.chiesa delgesu.org
➡ Piazza del Gesù
➡ ⊙7am-noon & 4-7.45pm
➡ 🚌🚊Largo di Torre Argentina

---

**FREE** PALAZZO FARNESE  PALAZZO

Map p346 (☎06 688 92 818; www.ambafrance-it.org in Italian & French; Piazza Farnese; under 15yr not admitted; ⊙tours 3, 4 & 5pm Mon & Thu, by appt only; 🚌Corso Vittorio Emanuele II) Dominating the elegant piazza of the same name, Palazzo Farnese is one of Rome's greatest Renaissance *palazzi*. It was started in 1514 by Antonio da Sangallo the Younger, continued by Michelangelo, who added the cornice and balcony, and finished by Giacomo della Porta. Nowadays, it's the French Embassy and open only to visitors who've booked a place on the biweekly guided tour. The 50-minuite visits (with commentary in Italian or French) take in the garden, courtyard and Galleria dei Carracci, home to a series of superb frescoes by Annibale Carracci, said by some to rival those of the Sistine Chapel. Booking forms can be downloaded from the website and should be sent one to four months before you want to visit. Photo ID is required for entry.

The twin fountains in the square are enormous granite baths taken from the Terme di Caracalla.

PALAZZO SPADA  PALAZZO

Map p346 (☎06 683 24 09; www.galleriaborghese.it; Via Capo di Ferro 13; adult/reduced €5/2; ⊙8.30am-7.30pm Tue-Sun; 🚌Corso Vittorio Emanuele II) The central attraction of this 16th-century *palazzo* is Francesco Borromini's famous perspective. What appears to be a 25m-long corridor lined with columns leading to a hedge and life-sized statue is, in fact, only 10m long. The sculpture, which was a later addition, is actually hip-height and the columns diminish in size not because of distance but because they actually get shorter. And look closer at that perfect-looking hedge – Borromini didn't trust the gardeners to clip a real hedge precisely enough so he made one of stone.

Upstairs, the four-room **Galleria Spada** houses the Spada family art collection, with works by Andrea del Sarto, Guido Reni, Guercino and Titian.

VIA GIULIA  STREET

Map p346 (🚌Via Giulia) Designed by Bramante in 1508, Via Giulia is a charming road lined with colourful Renaissance *palazzi* and potted orange trees. At its southern end, the **Fontana del Mascherone** (Map p350)

# TOP SIGHTS **MUSEO NAZIONALE ROMANO: PALAZZO ALTEMPS**

Just north of Piazza Navona, Palazzo Altemps is a beautiful, late 15th-century *palazzo,* housing the best of the Museo Nazionale Romano's formidable collection of classical sculpture. Many pieces come from the celebrated Ludovisi collection, amassed by Cardinal Ludovico Ludovisi in the 17th century. Prize exhibits include the beautiful 5th-century *Trono Ludovisi* (Ludovisi Throne), a carved marble throne depicting Aphrodite being plucked from the sea as a newborn babe. It shares a room with two colossal heads, one of which is the goddess Juno and dates from around 600 BC. The wall frieze (about half of which remains) depicts the 10 plagues of Egypt and the Exodus.

Equally affecting is the sculptural group *Galata Suicida* (Gaul's Suicide), a melodramatic depiction of a Gaul knifing himself to death over a dead woman.

The building's baroque frescoes provide an exquisite decorative backdrop. The walls of the Sala delle Prospettive Dipinte are decorated with landscapes and hunting scenes seen through trompe l'oeil windows. These frescoes were painted for Cardinal Altemps, Pope Pius IV's nephew, who bought the *palazzo* in the late 16th century.

The museum also houses the Museo Nazional Romano's Egyptian collection.

## DON'T MISS...

➡ Trono Ludovisi
➡ *Galata Suicida*

## PRACTICALITIES

➡ Map p346
➡ 06 683 35 66
➡ www.pierreci.it
➡ Piazza Sant'Apollinare 44
➡ adult/reduced €7/3.50, plus possible €3 exhibition supplement
➡ 9am-7.45pm Tue-Sun, last admission 7pm
➡ Corso del Rinascimento

---

depicts a 17th-century hippy surprised by water spewing from his mouth. Just beyond it, and spanning the road, is the ivy-clad **Arco Farnese**, designed by Michelangelo as part of an ambitious, unfinished project to connect Palazzo Farnese with Villa Farnesina on the opposite side of the Tiber.

Continuing north, on the left, in Via di Sant'Eligio, is the lovely Raphael-designed **Chiesa di Sant'Eligio degli Orefici** (9am-1pm Mon-Fri).

### MUSEO CRIMINOLOGICO                          MUSEUM
Map p346 (06 688 99 442; www.museocriminologico.it; Via del Gonfalone 29; admission €2; 9am-1pm Tue-Sat & 2.30-6.30pm Tue & Thu; Via Giulia) Check out Rome's dark side at this macabre museum of crime. Housed in a 19th-century prison, its gruesome collection runs the gauntlet from torture devices and murder weapons to fake Picassos, confiscated smut and the red cloak of Massimo Titta, Rome's most famous axeman. As the Papal States' official executioner, Titta is said to have carried out a total of 516 executions between 1796 and 1865.

### CHIESA DI SAN GIOVANNI BATTISTA DEI FIORENTINI          CHURCH
Map p346 (Via Acciaioli 2; 7.30am-noon & 5-7pm; Ponte Vittorio Emanuele II) The last resting place of Francesco Borromini and Carlo Maderno, this graceful 16th-century church was commissioned by the Medici Pope Leo X as a showcase for Florentine artistic talent. Jacopo Sansovino won a competition for its design, which was then executed by Antonio Sangallo the Younger and Giacomo della Porta. Carlo Maderno completed the elongated cupola in 1614, while, inside, the altar is by Borromini.

A favourite venue for concerts, the church's 17th-century organ is played at noon Mass every Sunday.

### PALAZZO DELLA CANCELLERIA          PALAZZO
Map p346 (Piazza della Cancelleria; Corso Vittorio Emanuele II) As impressive an example of Renaissance architecture as you'll find in Rome, this huge *palazzo* was built for Cardinal Raffaele Riario between 1483 and 1513. It was later acquired by the Vatican and became the seat of the Papal Chancellory. It is still Vatican property and these days

houses the Tribunal of the Roman Rota, the Holy See's highest ecclesiastical court.

The *palazzo* is sometimes used to stage exhibitions and if you get the chance you should nip through to the courtyard to take a peek at Bramante's glorious double loggia. Next door, and incorporated into the *palazzo*, is the 4th-century **Basilica di San Lorenzo in Damaso** (☉7.30am-noon & 4.30-8pm), one of Rome's oldest churches.

### MUSEO BARRACCO DI
### SCULTURA ANTICA                           MUSEUM

Map p346 (www.museobarracco.it; Corso Vittorio Emanuele II 166; adult/reduced €5.50/4.50; ☉9am-7pm Tue-Sun; ☐Corso Vittorio Emanuele II) This charming museum boasts a fascinating collection of early Mediterranean sculpture. You'll find Greek, Etruscan, Roman, Assyrian, Cypriot and Egyptian works, all donated to the state by Baron Giovanni Barracco in 1902.

The *palazzo* housing the museum, known as the Piccolo Farnesina, was built for a French clergyman, Thomas Le Roy, in 1523.

### CHIESA DI SANT'ANDREA
### DELLA VALLE                                  CHURCH

Map p346 (Corso Vittorio Emanuele II 6; ☉7.30am-noon & 4.30-7.30pm Mon-Sat, 7.30am-12.45pm & 4.30-7.45pm Sun; ☐Corso Vittorio Emanuele II) A must for opera fans, this towering 17th-century church is where Giacomo Puccini set the first act of *Tosca*. Its most obvious feature is Carlo Maderno's soaring dome, the highest in Rome after St Peter's, but its bombastic baroque interior reveals some wonderful frescoes by Mattia Preti, Domenichino and, in the dome, Lanfranco. Competition between the artists was fierce and rumour has it that Domenichino once took a saw to Lanfranco's scaffolding, almost killing him in the process.

# ⊙ Jewish Ghetto

Centred on lively Via Portico d'Ottavia, the Jewish Ghetto is a wonderfully atmospheric area studded with artisans' studios, vintage clothes shops, kosher bakeries and popular trattorias.

Rome's Jewish community dates back to the 2nd century BC, making it one of the oldest in Europe. At one point there were as many as 13 synagogues in the city but

Titus's defeat of Jewish rebels in Jerusalem in AD 70 changed the status of Rome's Jews from citizen to slave. Confinement to the Ghetto came in 1555 when Pope Paul IV ushered in a period of official intolerance that lasted, on and off, until the 20th century. Ironically, though, confinement meant that Jewish cultural and religious identity survived intact.

### MUSEO EBRAICO
### DI ROMA                       SYNAGOGUE, MUSEUM

Map p350 (Jewish Museum of Rome; ☑06 684 00 661; www.museoebraico.roma.it; Via Catalana; adult/reduced €10/4; ☉10am-6.15pm Sun-Thu, 10am-3.15pm Fri summer, 10am-4.15pm Sun-Thu, 9am-1.15pm Fri winter; ☐Lungotevere de' Cenci) The historical, cultural and artistic heritage of Rome's Jewish community is chronicled in this small but engrossing museum. Housed in the city's early 20th-century synagogue, Europe's second largest, it presents harrowing reminders of the hardships experienced by the city's Jewry. Exhibits include copies of Pope Paul IV's papal bull confining the Jews to the ghetto and relics from the Nazi concentration camps.

You can also book one-hour guided walking tours of the Ghetto (adult/reduced €8/5) at the museum.

### PALAZZO CENCI                               PALAZZO

Map p350 (Vicolo dei Cenci; ☐☐Via Arenula) A real-life house of horrors, Palazzo Cenci was the scene of one of the 16th century's most infamous crimes, the murder of Francesco Cenci by his daughter Beatrice and wife Lucrezia (see p97). Shelley based his tragedy *The Cenci* on the family, and a famous portrait of Beatrice by Guido Reni hangs in the Galleria Nazionale d'Arte Antica – Palazzo Barberini. It shows a sweet-faced young girl with soft eyes and fair hair.

### FONTANA DELLE TARTARUGHE      MONUMENT

Map p350 (Piazza Mattei; ☐☐Via Arenula) This playful 16th-century fountain depicts four boys gently hoisting tortoises up into a bowl of water. Apparently, Taddeo Landini created it in a single night in 1585 on behalf of the Duke of Mattei, who had gambled his fortune away and was on the verge of losing his fiancée. On seeing the fountain, Mattei's future father-in-law was so impressed that he relented and let Mattei marry his daughter. The tortoises were added by Bernini in 1658.

# Showtime on Rome's Piazzas

**From the baroque splendour of Piazza Navona to the clamour of Campo de' Fiori and the majesty of St Peter's Square, Rome's showcase piazzas encapsulate much of the city's beauty, history and drama.**

### Piazza Navona

**1** In the heart of the historic centre, Piazza Navona (p77) is the picture-perfect Roman square. Graceful baroque *palazzi* (mansions), flamboyant fountains, packed pavement cafes and cleverly costumed street artists set the scene for the daily invasion of camera-toting tourists.

### Piazza San Pietro

**2** The awe-inspiring approach to St Peter's Basilica, St Peter's Square (p200) is a masterpiece of 17th-century urban design. The work of Gian Lorenzo Bernini, it's centred on a towering Egyptian obelisk and flanked by two grasping colonnaded arms.

### Piazza del Popolo

**3** Neoclassical Piazza del Popolo (p107), once the city's main northern entrance, is a vast, sweeping space. In centuries past, executions were held here; nowadays crowds gather for political rallies, outdoor concerts or just to hang out.

### Piazza del Campidoglio

**4** The centrepiece of the Campidoglio (Capitoline hill; p69)), the Michelangelo-designed Piazza del Campidoglio is thought by many to be the city's most beautiful piazza. Surrounded on three sides by *palazzi* (palaces), it's home to the Capitoline Museums.

### Campo de' Fiori

**5** Campo de' Fiori (p80) is the cousin of the more refined Piazza Navona. While Piazza Navona has street artists and baroque baubles, Campo de' Fiori has market traders and an unpretentious atmosphere.

**Clockwise from top left**
1. Piazza Navona 2. Piazza San Pietro
3. Piazza del Popolo

# TOP SIGHTS
# CHIESA DI SAN LUIGI DEI FRANCESI

Church to Rome's French community since 1589, this opulent baroque church boasts no less than three paintings by Caravaggio. In the Cappella Contarelli, to the left of the main altar, crowds gather to admire the *Vocazione di San Matteo* (The Calling of Saint Matthew), the *Martiro di San Matteo* (The Martyrdom of Saint Matthew) and *San Matteo e l'angelo* (Saint Matthew and the Angel), together known as the St Matthew cycle. These are among Caravaggio's earliest religious works, painted between 1599 and 1602, but they are inescapably his, featuring down-to-earth realism and stunning use of chiaroscuro (the bold contrast of light and dark). Caravaggio's refusal to adhere to artistic conventions and glorify his religious subjects often landed him in hot water and his first version of *San Matteo e l'angelo*, which depicted St Matthew as a bald, bare-legged peasant, was originally rejected by his outraged patron, Cardinal Matteo Contarelli.

Before you leave the church, take a moment to enjoy Domenichino's faded 17th-century frescoes of St Cecilia in the second chapel on the right. St Cecilia is also depicted in the altarpiece by Guido Reni, a copy of a work by Raphael.

## DON'T MISS...

→ *Vocazione di San Matteo*

→ *Martiro di San Matteo*

→ *San Matteo e l'angelo*

## PRACTICALITIES

→ Map p346

→ Piazza di San Luigi dei Francesi

→ ⊘10am-12.30pm & 4-7pm, closed Thu afternoon pm

→ ▣Corso del Rinascimento

---

FREE **AREA ARCHEOLOGICA DEL TEATRO DI MARCELLO E DEL PORTICO D'OTTAVIA** ARCHAEOLOGICAL SITE
Map p350 (Via del Teatro di Marcello 44; ⊘9am-7pm summer, 9am-6pm winter; ▣Via del Teatro di Marcello) To the east of the ghetto, the **Teatro di Marcello** is the star turn of this dusty archaeological area. Although originally planned by Julius Caesar, the 20,000-seat theatre was completed by Augustus in 11 BC and named after a favourite nephew, Marcellus. In the 16th century, a *palazzo* was built onto the original building, which now houses some exclusive apartments lived in by a few lucky Romans.

Beyond the theatre, the **Portico d'Ottavia** is the oldest *quadriporto* (four-sided porch) in Rome. The dilapidated columns and fragmented pediment once formed part of a vast rectangular portico, supported by 300 columns, that measured 132m by 119m. Erected by a builder called Octavius in 146 BC, it was rebuilt in 23 BC by Augustus, who kept the name in honour of his sister Octavia. From the Middle Ages until the late 19th century, the portico housed Rome's fish market.

**CHIESA DI SAN NICOLA IN CARCERE** CHURCH
Map p350 (☑347 381 18 74; www.sotterranei diroma.it; Via del Teatro di Marcello 46; admission church free, excavations €3; ⊘10.30am-7pm; ▣Via del Teatro di Marcello) An innocuous-looking building on busy Via del Teatro Marcello, this 11th-century church harbours some fascinating Roman excavations. Beneath the main church you can poke around the claustrophobic foundations of three Republican-era temples, over which the church was built, and the remnants of an Etruscan vegetable market. Marble columns from the temples were incorporated into the church's structure and are still visible today. Visits are by guided tour only.

---

# ◉ Isola Tiberina

The world's smallest inhabited island, the Isola Tiberina (Tiber Island) has been associated with healing since the 3rd century BC, when the Romans adopted the Greek god of healing Asclepius (aka Aesculapius) as their own and erected a temple to him on the island. Today, the island is home to the Ospedale Fatebenefratelli.

To reach the Isola from the Jewish Ghetto, cross Rome's oldest standing bridge, the 62 BC **Ponte Fabricio**. Visible to the south of the island are the remains of **Ponte Rotto** (Broken Bridge), Ancient Rome's first stone bridge, which was all but swept away in a 1598 flood.

### CHIESA DI SAN BARTOLOMEO    CHURCH
Map p350 (⊙9am-1pm & 3.30-5.30pm Mon-Sat, 9am-1pm & 7-8pm Sun; 🚇Lungotevere dei Pierleoni) Built on the ruins of the Roman temple to Aesculapius, the Greek god of healing, the island's 10th-century church is an interesting hybrid of architectural styles: the facade is baroque, as is the richly frescoed ceiling; the belltower is 12th-century Romanesque, and the 28 columns that divide the interior date to ancient Roman times. Inside, there's a marble wellhead, which is thought to stand over the spring that provided the temple's healing waters.

## ◉ Piazza Colonna & Around

### PIAZZA COLONNA    PIAZZA
Map p346 (🚇Via del Corso) Together with Piazza di Montecitorio, this stylish piazza is Rome's political nerve centre. On its northern flank, the 16th-century **Palazzo Chigi** (www.governo.it, in Italian; Piazza Colonna 370; admission free; ⊙guided visits 9am-2pm Sat Sep-Jun, booking obligatory) has been the official residence of Italy's prime minister since 1961.

Rising 30m above the piazza, the **Colonna di Marco Aurelio** was completed in AD 193 to honour Marcus Aurelius' military victories. The vivid reliefs depict scenes from battles against the Germanic tribes (169–173) and, further up, the Sarmatians (174–176). In 1589 Marcus was replaced on the top of the column with a bronze statue of St Paul.

South of the piazza, in **Piazza di Pietra**, is the **Tempio di Adriano**. Eleven huge Corinthian columns, now embedded in what used to be Rome's stock exchange, are all that remain of Hadrian's 2nd-century temple.

### FREE PALAZZO DI MONTECITORIO    PALAZZO
Map p346 (☑800 01 29 55; www.camera.it; Piazza di Montecitorio; ⊙guided visits 10am-5.30pm, 1st Sun of month; 🚇Via del Corso) Home to Italy's Chamber of Deputies, this baroque *palazzo* was built by Bernini in 1653, expanded by Carlo Fontana in the late 17th century, and given an art nouveau facelift in 1918. Visits take in the palazzo's lavish reception rooms and the main chamber where the 630 deputies debate beneath a beautiful art nouveau skyline.

The **obelisk** outside was brought from Heliopolis in Egypt by Augustus to celebrate victory over Cleopatra and Mark Antony in 30 BC.

### CHIESA DI SANT'IGNAZIO DI LOYOLA    CHURCH
Map p346 (Piazza Sant'Ignazio; ⊙7.30am-7pm Mon-Sat, 9am-7pm Sun; 🚇Via del Corso) Rome's most important Jesuit church after the Chiesa del Gesù, this lordly building flanks Piazza Sant'Ignazio, an exquisite rococo square laid out in 1727 to resemble a stage set. Note the exits into 'the wings' at the northern end and how the undulating surfaces create the illusion of a larger space.

The church, built by the Jesuit architect Orazio Grassi in 1626, boasts a Carlo Maderno facade and a celebrated trompe l'oeil ceiling fresco by Andrea Pozzo (1642–1709) depicting St Ignatius Loyola being welcomed into paradise by Christ and the Madonna. For the best views of the fresco, stand on the small yellow spot on the nave floor and look up. The ceiling, which is, in fact, absolutely flat, appears to curve. But walk a little further into the church and the carefully created perspective stops working and the deception becomes clear.

### ROME'S FAVOURITE FOOT

It doesn't appear on any tourist brochures and you could easily pass by without noticing it. But the **Piè di Marmo** is one of the Romans' favourite monuments. A giant marble foot, now on Via di Santo Stefano del Cacco, it started life attached to statue in a 1st-century temple dedicated to the Egyptian gods Isis and Serapis. Some 1600 years later it cropped up on the street that now bears its name, Via del Piè di Marmo. It was placed in its current position in 1878 to clear the path for King Vittorio Emanuele II's funeral procession to reach the Pantheon.

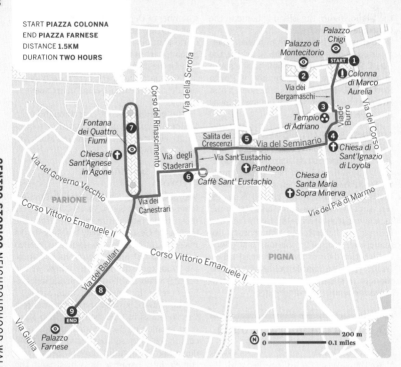

START **PIAZZA COLONNA**
END **PIAZZA FARNESE**
DISTANCE **1.5KM**
DURATION **TWO HOURS**

Neighbourhood Walk
## Centro Storico Piazzas

This walk takes in some of Rome's most celebrated piazzas, as well as several beautiful but lesser-known squares.

Start in ❶ **Piazza Colonna**, a grand square dominated by the 30m-high Colonna di Marco Aurelio and flanked by Palazzo Chigi, the official residence of the Italian prime minister. Next door, and facing onto ❷ **Piazza di Montecitorio**, is the equally impressive seat of the Chamber of Deputies, Palazzo di Montecitorio. From Piazza Colonna follow Via dei Bergamaschi down to ❸ **Piazza di Pietra**, a refined rectangular space overlooked by the 2nd-century Tempio di Adriano. Continue past the columns down Via de' Burro to ❹ **Piazza di Sant'Ignazio Loyola**, a small stagy piazza overlooked by the church of the same name. From here, it's a short walk along Via del Seminario to busy ❺ **Piazza della Rotonda** where the Pantheon needs no introduction.

Leaving the Pantheon, head up Salita dei Crescenzi and then go left along Via Sant'Eustachio to ❻ **Piazza Sant'Eustachio**. On this small, workaday square you'll find the Caffè Sant'Eustachio, a busy and unremarkable -ooking cafe that serves the best espresso in town. With a new spring in your step, follow Via degli Staderari to Corso del Rinascimento, drop a quick left followed by a short right and you're into Rome's showpiece square, ❼ **Piazza Navona**. Here, among the street artists, tourists and pigeons, you can compare the two giants of Roman baroque – Gian Lorenzo Bernini, creator of the Fontana dei Quattro Fiumi, and Francesco Borromini, author of the Chiesa di Sant'Agnese in Agone. Exit the piazza southwards, cross Corso Vittorio Emanuele II, the busy road that bisects the historic centre, and follow Via dei Baullari to the noisy market square, ❽ **Campo de' Fiori**. Just beyond the Campo, ❾ **Piazza Farnese** presents an altogether more sober spectacle, overshadowed by the Renaissance Palazzo Farnese.

### CHIESA DI SAN LORENZO
### IN LUCINA
CHURCH

Map p346 (Piazza San Lorenzo in Lucina 16; ⊙8am-8pm; 🚇Via del Corso) Little remains of the original 5th-century church that was built here atop an ancient well sacred to Juno. But that shouldn't detract from what is a very pretty church, complete with Romanesque bell tower and a long 12th-century columned portico. Inside, the otherwise standard baroque decor is elevated by Guido Reni's *Crocifisso* (Crucifixion) above the main altar, and a fine bust by Bernini in the fourth chapel on the southern side. The French painter Nicholas Poussin, who died in 1655, is buried in the church.

# EATING

Around Piazza Navona, Campo de' Fiori and the Pantheon you'll find an array of eateries, including some of the capital's best restaurants (both contemporary and traditional Roman). Again, beware of overpriced tourist traps. The atmospheric Jewish Ghetto is famous for its unique Roman-Jewish cooking.

## 🍴 Pantheon & Around

### ᴛᴏᴘ CASA COPPELLE
ᴄʜᴏɪᴄᴇ
MEDITERRANEAN €€

Map p346 (🗹06 688 91 707; www.casacoppelle. it; Piazza delle Coppelle 49; meals €35; 🚇Largo di Torre Argentina) Intimate and elegant with wonderful French-inspired food and a warm, attractive buzz, this is a great find. Brick walls, books, flowers and subdued lighting set the romantic stage for simple yet delicious food. Kick off with *millefoglie di bufala e melanzane,* a vibrant mix of pungent buffalo mozzarella and sliced aubergine, before moving onto the main event, superbly cooked steak with delicious, thinly sliced potato crisps. Service is quick and attentive.

### LA ROSETTA
SEAFOOD €€€

Map p346 (🗹06 686 10 02; www.larosetta.com; Via della Rosetta 8; lunch menu €50, tasting menu €140; ⊙closed Sun lunch & 3 weeks Aug; 🚇Largo di Torre Argentina) Run by Roman super-chef Massimo Riccioli, La Rosetta is one of the capital's oldest and best-known seafood restaurants. The menu, which makes no compromises for vegetarians or meat-eaters, features classic fish dishes alongside more elaborate creations such as scallops with cream of artichoke and mint. Bookings are essential, and it's more affordable at lunchtime.

### MACCHERONI
TRATTORIA €€

Map p346 (🗹06 683 07 895; Piazza delle Coppelle 44; meals €40; 🚇Largo di Torre Argentina) With its classic vintage interior – think plain, bottle-lined walls and hanging strands of garlic – attractive setting and traditional menu, Maccheroni is the archetypal *centro storico* trattoria. Locals and tourists flock here to dine on Roman stalwarts like *tonnarelli al cacio e pepe* (pasta with cheese and pepper) and *carciofo alla Romana* (Roman style artichoke).

### ARMANDO AL PANTHEON
TRATTORIA €€

Map p346 (🗹06 688 03 034; www.armando alpantheon.it; Salita dei Crescenzi 31; meals €40; ⊙closed Sat dinner & Aug; 🚇Largo di Torre Argentina) A family-run trattoria, Armando's is a wood-panelled, inviting, authentic institution close to the Pantheon. Always busy, it's fed the likes of philosopher Jean-Paul Sartre and footballer Pelè. It specialises in traditional Roman fare but you can also branch out on dishes like guinea fowl with porcini mushrooms and black beer and spaghetti with truffles. Book ahead.

### OSTERIA SOSTEGNO
TRATTORIA €€

Map p346 (🗹06 679 38 42; www.ilsostegno.it; Via delle Colonnelle 5; meals €35-40; ⊙Tue-Sun; 🚇Largo di Torre Argentina) Follow the green neon arrow to the end of a narrow alley and you'll find this well-kept secret. It's intimate, a favourite of journalists and politicians, with excellent dishes such as *caprese* (tomato and buffalo mozzarella salad) and *ravioli di ricotta e spinaci con limone e zafferano* (ricotta and spinach ravioli with lemon and saffron). Nearby, the **Ristorante Settimio** (Map p346; 🗹06 678 96 51; Via delle Colonnelle 14; meals €35-40) is run by the same family.

### LA CANTINA DI NINCO
### NANCO
TRADITIONAL ITALIAN €€

Map p346 (🗹06 681 35 558; Via del Pozzo delle Cornacchie 36; meals €40; 🚇Largo di Torre Argentina) Go down the steep stairs to this great little restaurant housed in a vaulted underground cellar. Decorated with simple rustic charm, it specialises in cooking from the southern region of Basilicata, so expect

## ROME'S HISTORIC FAMILIES

### The Farnese
At home at **Palazzo Farnese**, the all-powerful Farnese dynasty was one of Renaissance Rome's most celebrated families. Originally landed gentry in northern Lazio, they hit the big time in 1493 when Giulia Farnese became the mistress of Pope Alexander VI. Hardly an official post, it nevertheless gave Alessandro, Giulia's brother, enough influence to secure his election as Pope Paul III (r 1534–49).

### The Borghese
Originally from Siena, the Borghese moved to Rome in the 16th century and quickly established themselves in high society. It was Camillo Borghese's election as Pope Paul V (r 1605–21) that opened the family's path to untold wealth. They became one of Rome's leading landowners and Scipione Borghese, Camillo's nephew, established himself as the city's most influential art patron – his collection is now on show at the **Museo e Galleria Borghese** in his former residence.

### The Chigi
Agostino Chigi (1465–1520), one of the richest men in early 16th-century Rome, was the star of the Chigi banking family. A close confidant of Pope Julius II (the man who commissioned Michelangelo to paint the Sistine Chapel), he was celebrated for his lavish entertaining at **Villa Farnesina**, his palatial residence. Later, the Chigi amassed further fortunes under Pope Alexander VII (r 1655–67), aka Fabio Chigi.

### The Barberini
The only one of Rome's great families to have a metro station named after it, the Barberini arrived in Rome in the early 16th century, escaping their native Tuscany and a dangerous rivalry with the Florentine Medici. They settled well and in 1623 Maffeo Barberini was elected Pope Urban VIII, opening the floodgates to the usual round of family appointments and extravagant building projects, including the lavish **Palazzo Barberini**.

### The Borgias
A byword for intrigue and excess, the Spanish Borgias shocked Renaissance Rome with their murderous ambition and unbridled debauchery. The family patriarch, Rodrigo, served as Pope Alexander VI (r 1492–1503), while his two illegitimate children Cesare (said to have been the model for Machiavelli's *Il Principe*) and Lucrezia (a supposed serial poisoner) earned reputations for deviousness and cruelty.

plenty of delicious salamis, sausages and full-on cheeses. For a taste try the pasta with tomato, *guanciale* (cured pig's cheek) and *cacciaricotta* cheese.

### ENOTECA CORSI                           OSTERIA €
Map p346 (📋06 679 08 21; Via del Gesù 87; meals €20-25; ☉lunch Mon-Sat; 🚇🚌Largo di Torre Argentina) Merrily worse for wear, family-run Corsi is a genuine old-style Roman eatery. The look is rustic – bare wooden tables, paper tablecloths, wine bottles – and the atmosphere one of controlled mayhem. The menu, chalked up on a blackboard, offers no surprises, just honest, homey fare like *melanzane parmigiana* or roast chicken with potatoes.

### IL BACARO                           RISTORANTE €€€
Map p346 (📋06 687 25 54; www.ilbacaro.com; Via degli Spagnoli 27; meals €45-50; ☉lunch Mon-Fri, dinner Mon-Sat; 🚌Corso del Rinascimento) Not an easy one to find, this cosy, romantic restaurant is tucked away in a tiny piazza north of the Pantheon. But it's worth persevering because the food is top notch. Imaginative primi include risottos and soups, while mains feature both fish and meat dishes. Summer seating spills out under a vine-covered pergola. Booking is recommended.

### OBIKÀ                           CHEESE BAR €€
Map p346 (📋06 683 26 30; www.obika.it; Piazza di Firenze; meals €30; ☉10am-midnight; 🚌Via del Corso) This slick, modern set-up – think sushi bar with cheese not fish – serves spec-

tacular mozzarella from Italy's southern Campania region. Try it on its own or with accompaniments such as grilled vegetables or Tuscan salami. There's also a full menu of salads, starters and pasta dishes, and aperitivo is served from 7.30pm. There's a second **branch** (Campo de' Fiori 16; ☻8am-2am).

### GREEN T
ASIAN €€€

Map p346 (☏06 679 86 28; www.green-tea.it; Via del Piè di Marmo 28; lunch menus fish/meat/veg €17/15/13.50, meals €50; ☻Mon-Sat; 🚌🚇Largo di Torre Argentina) It's unusual to find good Asian food in Rome, and this elegant five-room restaurant is something entirely different: a tearoom and boutique, serving street food, meat and fish dishes, as well as a selection of sushi and dim sum. Save money at lunch by opting for one of the daily menus.

### ZAZÀ
PIZZA AL TAGLIO €

Map p346 (☏06 688 01 357; Piazza Sant'Eustachio 49; pizza slice around €3; ☻9am-10pm Mon-Sat; 🚌Corso del Rinascimento) Handily sandwiched between Piazza Navona and the Pantheon, this hole-in-the-wall *pizza al taglio* (pizza by the slice) takeaway hits the spot with its tasty, low-cal organic pizza. It also does home delivery from 4pm to 10pm.

## ✖ Piazza Navona & Around

### PIZZERIA DA BAFFETTO
PIZZERIA €

Map p346 (☏06 686 16 17; Via del Governo Vecchio 114; pizzas €6-9; ☻6.30pm-1am; 🚌Corso Vittorio Emanuele II) For the full-on Roman pizza experience get down to this local institution. Meals here are raucous, chaotic and fast, but the thin-crust pizzas are spot on and the vibe is fun. To partake, join the queue and wait to be squeezed in wherever there's room. Start off with tasty fried courgette flowers and *olive ascolane* (olives stuffed with meat) before moving onto the pizzas, bubbling hot from the wood-fired oven. There's a **Baffetto 2** (Map p346; Piazza del Teatro Valle 18; ☻6.30pm-12.30am Mon-Fri, 12.30-3.30pm & 6.30pm-12.30am Sat & Sun) offering more of the same near Campo de' Fiori.

### CASA BLEVE
WINE BAR, GASTRONOMIC €€€

Map p346 (☏06 686 59 70; www.casableve.it; Via del Teatro Valle 48-49; meals €60; ☻Tue-Sat, closed Aug; 🚌🚇Largo di Torre Argentina) This gorgeous, stately wine bar is a gourmet

delight. Its wine collection is one of the best in town; the dining hall is a picture, set in a column-lined courtyard capped by stained glass; and the food is top class. To accompany your wine there's a formidable selection of cheeses and cold cuts while in the evening choose from the full à la carte menu of creative Italian dishes.

### LILLI
TRATTORIA €€

Map p346 (☏06 686 19 16; Via Tor di Nona 23; meals €25-30; ☻Tue-Sun; 🚌Corso del Rinascimento) Eat like a local at this authentic neighbourhood trattoria on a cobbled cul de sac five minutes' walk from Piazza Navona. Few tourists make it here but it still gets frantically busy at lunchtime, with diners digging into *cacio e pepe* (pasta with *pecorino* cheese and ground black pepper) and other old-school Roman favourites.

### CAMPANA
TRATTORIA €€

Map p346 (☏06 687 52 73; Vicolo della Campana 18; meals €35; ☻Tue-Sun; 🚌🚇Largo di Torre Argentina) Caravaggio, Goethe and Federico Fellini are among the luminaries who have dined at what is said to be Rome's oldest trattoria, dating back to around 1518. Nowadays, local families crowd its two dining rooms to dine on fresh fish and traditional Roman cuisine served by proficient, black-waistcoated waiters.

### CHIOSTRO DEL BRAMANTE CAFFÈ
MODERN ITALIAN €

Map p346 (☏06 688 09 036, ext 26; www.chiostrodelbramante.it; Via della Pace; dishes €10; ☻10am-11pm; 🚌Corso del Rinascimento; 🛜) This swish bistro-cafe is beautifully located, overlooking Bramante's elegant Renaissance cloisters. It's open throughout the day, so you can have a drink, snack, or lunch on salads, quiches and light pastas, all the while making use of the free wifi. Aperitifs are served from 7pm.

### LES AFFICHES
MEDITERANNEAN €

Map p346 (Via Santa Maria dell'Anima 52; meals €10-15; 🚌Corso del Rinascimento) If you're after a light lunch or a tasty pick-me-up, this relaxed bar-cum-bistro hits the spot. There's a good selection of baguettes and imaginative specials, as well as a daily buffet lunch spread. Later in the day, its excellent cocktails, vintage Parisian ambience and late-night closing (2am) ensure a cool crowd of laid-back locals.

### LO ZOZZONE
SANDWICH SHOP €

Map p346 (☑06 688 08 575; Via del Teatro Pace 32; panini from €6; ☺Mon-Sat; 🚇Corso del Rinascimento) With a few inside tables and a mile-long menu of *panini,* the affectionally named 'dirty one' is a top spot for a cheap lunchtime bite. The filling, delicious *panini* are made with *pizza bianca* and combinations of cured meats, cold cuts, cheeses and vegetables.

### CUL DE SAC
WINE BAR, TRATTORIA €€

Map p346 (☑06 688 01 094; www.enotecaculdesac.com; Piazza Pasquino 73; meals €30; ☺noon-4pm & 6pm-12.30am daily; 🚇Corso Vittorio Emanuele II) A popular little wine bar, just off Piazza Navona, with an always busy terrace and narrow, bottle-lined interior. Choose from the encyclopedic wine list and ample menu of Gallic-inspired cold cuts, pates, cheeses and main courses. Book ahead in the evening.

### GELATERIA DEL TEATRO
GELATERIA €

Map p346 (Via di San Simone 70; cones €2; 🚇Corso del Rinascimento) In a cute alleyway just off pedestrian Via dei Coronari, this lovely little gelateria offers up to 40 flavours. The standouts are the Sicilian-inspired flavours like *cannolo siciliano* (based on Sicily's signature ricotta pastry tubes) and *pistachio* (with nuts from the Sicilian town of Bronte).

### DA TONINO
TRATTORIA €

Map p346 (Via del Governo Vecchio 18; meals €20; ☺Mon-Sat; 🚇Corso Vittorio Emanuele II) You'll be hard-pressed to find a cheaper place for a sit-down meal in this neck of central Rome. Unsigned Tonino's might be defiantly low-key with its simple wooden tables and yellowing pictures, but it's almost always packed. There's no menu: the waiter will reel off the choices of rib-sticking Roman staples, such as hearty *pasta alla gricia.*

### ALFREDO E ADA
TRATTORIA €

Map p346 (☑06 687 88 42; Via dei Banchi Nuovi 14; meals €20; ☺Mon-Fri; 🚇Corso Vittorio Emanuele II) For a taste of an authentic Roman cooking, head to this much-loved place with its wood panelling and spindly marble-topped tables. It's distinctly no-frills – the wine list consists of two choices, red or white – but the food, whatever is put in front of you (there's no menu), is filling and warming, just like your Italian *nonna* would have cooked it.

### LA FOCACCIA
PIZZERIA €

Map p346 (☑06 688 03 312; Via del Pace 11; pizzas from €7.50; ☺11pm-12.30am; 🚇Corso del Rinascimento) Hotfoot it to one of the few outside tables at this unsigned pizzeria, facing the beautiful Chiostro del Bramante, or settle for a place in the surprisingly large interior. As well as tasty bruschetta, the wood-fired pizzas are the real thing and the desserts are worth leaving space for.

### GELATERIA GIOLITTI
GELATERIA €

Map p346 (Via degli Uffici del Vicario 40; 🚇Corso del Rinascimento) Rome's most famous gelateria started as a dairy in 1900 and still keeps the hordes happy with succulent sorbets and creamy combinations. Gregory Peck and Audrey Hepburn swung by in *Roman Holiday* and it used to deliver marron glacé to Pope John Paul II. More recently Barrack Obama's daughters swung by during a G8 summit.

### DA FRANCESCO
TRATTORIA, PIZZERIA €€

Map p346 (☑06 686 40 09; Piazza del Fico 29; pizzas €6-9, meals €30; ☺closed Tue; 🚇Corso Vittorio Emanuele II) Gingham, paper tablecloths, frazzled waiters, groaning plateloads of pasta, tasty pizza: this quintessential Roman kitchen has character coming out of its ears, and tables and chairs spilling out onto the pretty piazza. Rock up early or queue. No credit cards.

### PIZZERIA LA MONTECARLO
PIZZERIA €

Map p346 (☑06 686 18 77; www.lamontecarlo.it; Vicolo Savelli 11-13; pizzas from €4.50; ☺noon-3pm & 6.30pm-1am Tue-Sun; 🚇Corso Vittorio Emanuele II) La Montecarlo, another true Roman pizzeria full of raucous charm, is a favourite with sightseers exploring the *centro storico,* although it also attracts its fair share of locals and even the occasional city celeb. Expect thin, wood-charred pizzas, paper tablecloths, milling queues and turbocharged waiters.

### FIOCCO DI NEVE
GELATERIA €

Map p346 (Via del Pantheon 51; cones €2; 🚇Largo di Torre Argentina) Tiny place, grumpy staff, natural colours – this has all the hallmarks of a good Roman gelateria. Romans come to the 'Snowflake', near the Pantheon, when they're in the mood for something creamy. Try the house speciality, *affogato di zabaglione al caffè,* a delicious coffee and zabaglione creation.

# ✗ Campo De' Fiori & Around

## FORNO DI CAMPO
### DE' FIORI
BAKERY, PIZZA AL TAGLIO €

Map p346 (Campo de' Fiori 22; pizza slices about €3; ☺7.30am-2.30pm & 4.45-8pm Mon-Sat; ☐Corso Vittorio Emanuele II) This is one of Rome's best takeaway joints, serving bread, *panini* and delicious straight-from-the-oven pizza *al taglio* (by the slice). Aficionados say to go for the pizza *bianca* (white pizza with olive oil, rosemary and salt) but the *panini* and pizza *rossa* ('red' pizza, with olive oil, tomato and oregano) are just as good.

## DITIRAMBO
MODERN ITALIAN €€

Map p346 (☑06 687 16 26; www.ristorante ditirambo.it; Piazza della Cancelleria 72; meals €35-40; ☺closed Mon lunch; ☐Corso Vittorio Emanuele II; ☑) This hugely popular new-wave trattoria offers a laid-back, unpretentious atmosphere and innovative, organic cooking. The menu changes according to what's good at the market but the focus is on a fresh, creative approach. Vegetarians are well catered for, with dishes like *vellutata di ceci con rughetta e riduzione di aceto balsamico* (cream of chickpeas with rocket and a balsamic vinegar reduction) and *polpette di melanzane* (aubergine meatballs). Book ahead.

## GRAPPOLO D'ORO
MODERN ITALIAN €€

Map p346 (☑06 689 70 80; Piazza della Cancelleria 80; meals €35-40; ☺closed Tue-Fri lunch; ☐Corso Vittorio Emanuele II) More contemporary looking than nearby Ditirambo, this informal, stylish eatery stands out among the sometimes lacklustre options around Campo de' Fiori. The food is creative without being over-designed, and includes old favourites such as *spaghetti alla carbonara* (among the best in Rome, according to local foodie bible *Gambero Rosso*).

## RENATO E LUISA
MODERN ITALIAN €€

Map p346 (☑06 686 96 60; www.renatoeluisa. it; Via dei Barbieri 25; meals €40-45; ☺8.30-12.30pm Tue-Sun; ☐Via Arenula) A favourite among vivacious young Romans, this backstreet trattoria is always packed. Chef Renato takes a creative approach to classic Roman cuisine, resulting in dishes that are modern, seasonal and undeniably local. Typical of this approach is his delectable *spaghetti con alici fresche e pecorino* (with fresh anchovies and pecorino cheese).

## VINERIA ROSCIOLI
### SALUMERIA
GASTRONOMIC, DELICATESSEN €€€

Map p346 (☑06 687 52 87; Via dei Giubbonari 21; meals from €50; ☺Mon-Sat; ☐Via Arenula) This deli-cum-wine bar-cum-restaurant is a foodie paradise. Under the brick arches, you'll find a mouth-watering array of olive oils, conserves, cheeses (around 450 varieties), Italian and Spanish and hams, and much, much more. Out back in the chic restaurant, you can dine on sophisticated Italian food accompanied by some truly outstanding wines – the wine list, which runs to some 1100 labels, contains some truly superlative Italian and French vintages. Reservations recommended.

## ANTICO FORNO
### ROSCIOLI
BAKERY, PIZZA AL TAGLIO €

Map p346 (Via dei Chiavari 34; pizza slice from €2; ☺7.30am-8pm Mon-Fri, 7.30am-2.30pm Sat; ☐Via Arenula) Not the Roscioli's renowned delicatessen and wine bar, but its brother bakery around the corner. Join the lunchtime crowds for a slice of delicious pizza (the *pizza bianca* is legendary) or a freshly baked pastry. There's also a counter serving hot pastas and vegetable side dishes.

## OSTERIA AR GALLETTO
OSTERIA €€

Map p346 (☑06 686 17 14; www.ristoranteargal lettoroma.com; Piazza Farnese 102; meals €35-40; ☺Mon-Sat; ☐Corso Vittorio Emanuele II) You wouldn't expect there to be anywhere reasonably priced on Piazza Farnese, one of Rome's most refined piazzas, but this long-standing *osteria* is the real thing, with good, honest Roman food, a warm local atmosphere and dazzlingly set exterior tables. Roast chicken is the house speciality (*galletto* means little rooster), but there's also a good selection of grilled meats and fish dishes.

## SERGIO ALLE GROTTE
TRADITIONAL ITALIAN €€

Map p346 (☑06 686 42 93; Vicolo delle Grotte 27; meals €30-35; ☺12.30-3.30pm & 6.30pm-1am Mon-Sat; ☐Via Arenula) A flower's throw from the Campo, Sergio's is a textbook Roman trattoria: chequered tablecloths, dodgy wall murals, bustling waiters, and steaming plateloads of pasta. A loyal following enjoys classic hearty Roman pastas – *cacio e pepe, carbonara, amatriciana* – and large steaks grilled over hot coals. In the summer there are tables outside on the cobbled, ivy-hung lane.

### FILETTI DI BACCALÀ
STREET FOOD €

Map p346 (Largo dei Librari 88; meals €20; ⓧ5-10.40pm Mon-Sat; ⓦVia Arenula) On a pretty, scooter-strewn piazza, this tiny stuck-in-time institution is a classic old-fashioned Roman *friggitoria* (shop selling fried food). The house speciality is battered cod but you can also have crispy battered veggies, such as *puntarella* (chicory) and crisp-fried zucchini flowers.

## ✕ Jewish Ghetto

### GIGGETTO AL PORTICO D'OTTAVIA
TRADITIONAL ITALIAN €€

Map p350 (ⓐ06 686 11 05; www.giggettoal portico.it; Via del Portico d'Ottavia 21a; meals €40; ⓧTue-Sun; ⓐⓦPiazza B Cairoli) An atmospheric setting in the Ghetto, rustic interiors, white-jacketed waiters, *fabuloso* Roman-Jewish cooking – this is a quintessential Roman restaurant. Celebrate all things fried by tucking into the marvellous *carciofi alla giudia, fiore di zucca* (zucchini or squash flowers) and *baccalà* (cod) and follow on with a *zuppa di pesce* (fish soup) or *rigatoni alla gricia*.

### GIGGETTO 2
TRADITIONAL ITALIAN €€

Map p350 (ⓐ06 64760369; Via Angelo in Pescheria 13-14; meals €20; ⓐⓦPiazza B Cairoli) For those on a budget, this simple cafe sits behind its older and better known parent, Giggetto al Portico d'Ottavia. It serves no-nonsense pasta and meat dishes, as well as pizza and very drinkable wine at €8 per bottle.

### PIPERNO
TRADITIONAL ITALIAN €€€

Map p350 (ⓐ06 688 06 629; www.ristorante piperno.it; Via Monte de' Cenci 9; meals €55; ⓧclosed Mon & Sun dinner; ⓐⓦVia Arenula) This Roman-Jewish institution is tucked away in a quiet corner of the Ghetto. It's formal without being stuffy, a wood-panelled restaurant of the old school, where white-clad waiters serve wonderful deep-fried *filetti di baccalà* (cod fillets) and *tagliolini alla pescatora* (long ribbon pasta with seafood). To finish, try the delicious *palle del Nonno* ('grandpa's balls' or ricotta and chocolate puffs). Booking is essential for Sunday.

### ALBERTO PICA
GELATERIA €

Map p350 (Via della Seggiola; cones/tubs from €1.50; ⓐⓦVia Arenula) This is a historic Roman gelateria, open since 1960. In summer, it offers flavours such as *fragoline di bosco* (wild strawberry) and *petali di rosa* (rose petal), but rice flavours are specialities year-round (resembling frozen rice pudding – yum).

### SORA MARGHERITA
TRATTORIA €€

Map p350 (ⓐ06 687 42 16; Piazza delle Cinque Scole 30; meals €30; ⓧclosed dinner Mon-Thu, all day Sun; ⓐⓦVia Arenula) No-frills Sora Margherita started as a cheap kitchen for hungry locals, but word has spread and it's now a popular lunchtime haunt of slumming uptowners. Expect dog-eat-dog queues, a rowdy Roman atmosphere, and classic Roman-Jewish dishes such as *carciofi alla giudia* (fried artichoke). Service is prompt and you're expected to be likewise.

### L'ARTE DEL PANE
BAKERY, PIZZA AL TAGLIO €

Map p350 (Piazza Costaguti 31; pizza slices from €2; ⓧclosed Sat afternoon & Sun afternoon; ⓐⓦPiazza B Cairoli) Come mid-morning and you'll find this popular Ghetto bakery packed with locals in for their mid-morning snack. And once you get a whiff of the yeasty smells wafting out from the counters laden with pizza, freshly baked breads, biscuits and focaccias, you'll probably want to follow suit.

### VECCHIA ROMA
TRADITIONAL ITALIAN €€€

Map p350 (ⓐ06 686 46 04; www.ristorantevec chiaroma.com; Piazza Campitelli 18; meals €60; ⓧThu-Tue, closed 3 weeks Aug; ⓦVia del Teatro di Marcello) This old-fashioned restaurant is the very picture of formal elegance with chandeliers and gilt-framed oil paintings, and a candle-lit terrace on a picturebook cobbled corner. Impeccably groomed white-jacketed waiters attend the clientele of sparkling celebrities and scheming politicians, serving fabulous summer salads, warming winter polentas and top-drawer pastas.

### LA TAVERNA DEGLI AMICI
TRADITIONAL ITALIAN €€

Map p350 (ⓐ06 699 20 637; Piazza Margana 37; meals €45; ⓧclosed Sun dinner & Mon; ⓦPiazza Venezia) A smart trattoria in a delightful medieval setting, the Taverna sits on a pretty ivy-draped piazza on the edge of the Jewish Ghetto. It serves consistent classics like *saltimbocca alla romana* ('leap in the mouth' veal with sage), plus delicious fish and homemade desserts. There's also an excellent wine list.

### BOCCIONE
BAKERY €

Map p350 (☑06 687 86 37; Via del Portico d'Ottavia 1; ⊙8am-7.30pm Sun-Thu, 8am-3.30pm Fri; 🚇🚍Piazza B Cairoli) This tiny, unsigned Jewish bakery on the corner with Piazza Costaguti is where the locals come to buy their special occasion *dolci*. The burnished cakes are bursting with fruit and sultanas, and specialities include ricotta cake with chocolate flakes and cherries, marzipan amaretto biscuits, and *mostacciolo romano* (a kind of sweet biscuit) – all served by authentically grumpy elderly ladies.

### LA DOLCEROMA
BAKERY €

Map p350 (☑06 689 21 96; www.ladolceroma.com; Via del Portico d'Ottavia 20; pastries from €2; ⊙8am-8pm Tue-Sat, 10am-1.30pm Sun; 🚇🚍Piazza B Cairoli) Bringing the sweet taste of Vienna to the Roman Ghetto, this well-known bakery specialises in delicious strudel and Sacher torte, as well as carrot cake, pumpkin pie (October and November only), pastries, muffins, cookies and splendid ice cream. Everything's made on the premises.

## ✖ Isola Tiberina

### SORA LELLA
TRADITIONAL ITALIAN €€€

Map p350 (☑06 686 16 01; www.soralella.com; Via Ponte Quattro Capi 16; meals €65; ⊙daily; 🚇🚍Viale di Trastevere) You can't beat the romance of Sora Lella's setting on the river Tiber's tiny island. Ring the doorbell to gain entrance to this timeless institution, named after the much-loved Roman TV star (the owner's mother), and family-run since 1940. The classic Roman menu has some twists, including some wonderful fish dishes – try the standout *paccheri con ragù di pesce* (giant pasta tubes served with a tomato seafood sauce).

## ✖ Piazza Colonna & Around

### MATRICIANELLA
TRADITIONAL ITALIAN €€

Map p346 (☑06 683 21 00; www.matricianella.it; Via del Leone 2/4; meals €40; ⊙Mon-Sat; 🚍Via del Corso) With its gingham tablecloths and chintzy murals, this popular trattoria is loved for its traditional Roman cuisine. You'll find all the usual menu stalwarts as well as some great Roman-Jewish dishes. Romans go crazy for the fried antipasti, the artichoke *alla giudia* (fried, Jewish style) and the meatballs. Booking is essential.

### PIZZERIA AL LEONCINO
PIZZERIA €

Map p346 (☑06 686 77 57; Via del Leoncino 28; pizzas €6-8.50; ⊙closed Wed; 🚍Via del Corso) Some places just never change and fortunately for us, this boisterous neighbourhood pizzeria is one of them. A bastion of budget eating in an otherwise expensive area, it has a wood-fired oven, two small rooms, cheerful decor and gruff but efficient waiters who will serve you an excellent Roman-style pizza and ice-cold beer faster than you can say '*delizioso*'.

### GINO
TRATTORIA €€

Map p346 (☑06 687 34 34; Vicolo Rosini 4; meals €30; ⊙Mon-Sat; 🚍Via del Corso) Hidden away down a narrow lane close to parliament, Gino's is perennially packed with gossiping politicians. Join the right honourables for well-executed staples such as *rigotoni alla gricia* (pasta with cured pig's cheek) and meatballs, served under hanging garlic and gaudily painted vines. No credit cards.

### OSTERIA DELL'INGEGNO
MODERN ITALIAN €€€

Map p346 (☑06 678 06 62; Piazza di Pietra 45; meals €50; ⊙Mon-Sat; 🚍Via del Corso) Not far from the Italian parliament, this casually chic restaurant-cum-bar is much frequented by Italian politicians and their glamorous entourages. Sit down to large salads, creative pastas and meaty mains in the cosy crimson-painted interior or, better still, on the charming piazza overlooking the columns of the Tempio di Adriano.

### SAN CRISPINO
ICECREAM €€

Map p346 (Piazza della Maddalena 3; tubs about €3; ⊙midday-12.30pm Sun-Thu, midday-1.30am Fri & Sat; 🚍Largo di Torre Argentina) A branch of the celebrated Roman gelateria that dishes up what many claim is the best ice cream in town. Flavours such as *pompelmo e rum* (grapefruit and rum) or *limone e pistacchio* (lemon and pistachio) are based on fresh natural ingredients and served in tubs only.

##  DRINKING & NIGHTLIFE

The *centro storico* is home to a couple of nightlife centres: the area around Piazza Navona, with a number of elegant bars and clubs catering to the beautiful, rich and stylish (and sometimes all three); and the rowdier area around Campo de' Fiori, where the crowd is younger and the drinking is heavier. This is where people tend to congregate after football games and foreign students head out on the booze. The *centro storico* also harbours Rome's best cafes.

## ☕ Pantheon & Around

### CAFFÈ SANT'EUSTACHIO                    CAFE
Map p346 (Piazza Sant'Eustachio 82; ☺8.30-1am Sun-Thu, to 1.30am Fri, to 2am Sat; ▣Corso del Rinascimento) This small unassuming cafe, generally three-deep at the bar, serves Rome's best coffee. The famous *gran caffè* is created by beating the first drops of espresso and several teaspoons of sugar into a frothy paste, then adding the rest of the coffee on top. It's superbly smooth and guaranteed to put zing into your sightseeing. Specify if you want it *amaro* (bitter) or *poco zucchero* (with a little sugar).

### CAFFÈ TAZZA D'ORO                    CAFE
Map p346 (Via degli Orfani 84; ☺Mon-Sat; ▣Via del Corso) Head here for caffeine heaven. A busy, stand-up bar with burnished wood and brass fittings, this place serves superb coffee. Its espresso hits the mark perfectly and there's a range of delicious coffee concoctions, such as *granita di caffè,* a crushed-ice coffee with a big dollop of cream, and *parfait di caffè,* a €3 coffee mousse.

## ☕ Piazza Navona & Around

### ETABLÌ                    BAR
Map p346 (✆06 97 616 694; www.etabli.it; Vicolo delle Vacche 9a; ☺6pm-2am Tue-Sun, restaurant 7.30pm-midnight; ▣Corso del Rinascimento) Housed in an airy 17th-century *palazzo,* Etablì is a fab rustic-chic lounge bar-cum-restaurant where Roman lovelies float in to have a drink, read the paper, indulge in *aperitivo* and use the wifi. It's laid-back and good-looking, with an eclectic soundtrack and original French country decor – think lavender tones, wrought-iron fittings, and comfy armchairs. Restaurant meals average about €35.

### CIRCUS                    BAR
Map p346 (Via della Vetrina 15; ☺10am-2am Tue-Sun; ▣Via del Corso) A great little cafe-bar, tucked around the corner from Piazza Navona. It's a funky, informal place to lounge and chat, and there's DJs on Fridays,

art exhibitions and lots of books to browse. Popular with American students from the nearby school. Free wifi.

### BAR DELLA PACE                    BAR
Map p346 (Via della Pace 5; ☺9am-3am Tue-Sun, 4pm-3am Mon; ▣Corso Vittorio Emanuele II) The quintessential *dolce vita* cafe. Inside it's all gilded baroque, polished surfaces and mismatched wooden tables; outside locals and tourists strike poses over their Camparis against a backdrop of ivy. The perfect people-watching spot.

### LA MAISON                    NIGHTCLUB
Map p346 (www.lamaisonroma.it; Vicolo dei Granari 4; ▣Corso Vittorio Emanuele II) Chandeliers and long, low banquettes provide a sexy backdrop for a see-and-be-seen crowd, who flirt and frolic to a soundtrack of poppy tunes and commercial house. It's smooth, mainstream and exclusive, yet more fun than you might expect. Entrance is free, if you can get past the door police, but drinks are about €15 a throw.

## ☕ Campo de' Fiori & Around

### OPEN BALADIN                    BAR
Map p350 (www.openbaladin.com; Via degli Specchi 6; ☺12.30pm-2am; ▣Corso Vittorio Emanuele II) A designer beer bar near Campo de' Fiori, Open Baladin is leading the way in the recent beer trend that is sweeping the city. It's a slick, stylish place with more than 40 beers on tap and up to 100 bottled beers, many produced by Italian artisanal breweries. There's also a decent food menu with *panini,* burgers and daily specials.

### BARNUM CAFE                    CAFE
Map p346 (www.barnumcafe.com; Via del Pellegrino 87; ☺9.30am-midnight; ▣Corso Vittorio Emanuele II) A relaxed spot to check your email over a freshly squeezed orange juice (€3) or spend a pleasant hour or so reading a newspaper on one of the tatty old armchairs in the white bare-brick interior. Light lunches are served and aperitif hour starts at 7.30pm.

### FEMME                    BAR
Map p346 (Via del Pellegrino 14; ☺6pm-2am Tue-Sun ▣Corso Vittorio Emanuele II) Entering this bar, with its funky sounds and silver-seated modernist look, is like wandering

## LEGENDARY CRIMES

On the Ides of March (15 March) 44 BC, Julius Caesar was stabbed to death in the Curia of the Teatro di Pompeo – a vast theatre complex that covered much of what is now the Largo di Torre Argentina. The exact spot is not marked but it's generally reckoned to be under where the Teatro Argentina now stands.

Violent crime is a recurring feature of Rome's long and tortuous history. The city was founded on the back of a murder – Romulus' killing of his twin Remus on the Palatino – and blood stains many of the city's *palazzi*. One of the city's most notorious crimes took place in Palazzo Cenci in the Jewish Ghetto. Here Beatrice Cenci, a young aristocrat, was driven by years of abuse to murder her tyrannical father. After a long and brutal investigation she and her accomplice, her stepmother Lucrezia, were beheaded on 11 September 1599 in front of a vast and largely sympathetic crowd on Ponte Sant'Angelo.

into a Calvin Klein advert. Everywhere you look there are ubercool stunners preening, flirting and working to be seen – it's a great laugh. The cocktails (€6) are the business and the splendid *aperitivo* is almost worth losing one's cool over.

### CAFFÈ FARNESE                                   CAFE
Map p346 (Via dei Baullari 106; ☺7am-2am; ⬛Corso Vittorio Emanuele II) We're with Goethe, who thought Piazza Farnese one of the world's most beautiful squares. Judge for yourself from the vantage of this unassuming cafe. On a street between Campo de' Fiori and Piazza Farnese, it's ideally placed for whiling away the early afternoon hours. Try the *caffè alla casa* (house coffee) – made to a secret recipe.

### IL GOCCETTO                                 WINE BAR
Map p346 (Via dei Banchi Vecchi 14; ☺11.30am-2pm & 6.30pm-midnight Mon-Sat, closed Aug; ⬛Corso Vittorio Emanuele II) Draw up a chair and join the cast of loquacious regulars at this old-style *vino e olio* (wine and oil) shop to imbibe delicious drops by the glass (there are more than 800 labels to choose from), snack on tasty cheese and salami, and get to grips with all the neighbourhood banter.

### L'ANGOLO DIVINO                             WINE BAR
Map p346 (Via dei Balestrari 12; ☺10am-2.30pm & 5pm-2am Mon-Sat; ⬛Corso Vittorio Emanuele II) A hop and a skip from the busy *campo* lies another *vini e olio* shop, somewhat updated, yet on the go since 1946. It's an oasis of genteel calm, with a carefully selected wine list, including French and New World labels, and delectable bites.

### VINERIA REGGIO                              WINE BAR
Map p346 (Campo de' Fiori 15; ☺8.30am-2am; ⬛Corso Vittorio Emanuele II) The pick of the bars and cafes on Campo de' Fiori, this has a small, bottle-lined, cosy interior and outside tables looking out on the human traffic on the piazza. Busy from lunchtime onwards, it attracts tourists and *fighi* (cool) Romans like bees to a honey pot. Wine by the glass from €4.

## 🍷 Jewish Ghetto

### BARTARUGA                                        BAR
Map p350 (www.bartaruga.com; Piazza Mattei 9; ☺6pm-late Tue-Sun; ⬛⬛Via Arenula) A high-camp blast of baroque and art deco, this velvet-lined, chandelier-slung bar is a theatrical choice for a theatrical crowd. Outside, a few humble wooden tables face the Ghetto's much-loved turtle fountain, the Fontana delle Tartarughe. The soundtrack is lounge and jazzy, the mood laid-back and chatty.

## 🍷 Piazza Colonna & Around

### SALOTTO 42                                        BAR
Map p346 (www.salotto42.it; Piazza di Pietra 42; ☺10am-2am Tue-Sat, to midnight Sun & Mon; ⬛Via del Corso) On a picturesque piazza, facing the columns of the Tempio di Adriano, this is a hip, glamorous lounge bar, complete with an ivy-clad facade, vintage armchairs, sleek sofas and a collection of heavy, coffee-table design books. Run by an Italian-Swedish couple, it has an excellent *aperitivo* spread and serves a Sunday brunch (€15).

### CIAMPINI
CAFE

Map p346 (Piazza di San Lorenzo in Lucina; ☺7.30am-8.30pm, to midnight summer; 🚇Via del Corso) The graceful, traffic-free Piazza di San Lorenzo in Lucina is an ideal stop for an al fresco coffee among the well-heeled folk of the neighbourhood. Bring your big sunglasses and little dog. Sitting outside is pricey, so remember it's an investment and settle. There's also a full food menu and tip-top gelato.

### GRAN CAFFÈ LA CAFFETTIERA
CAFE

Map p346 (Piazza di Pietra 65; ☺8am-9pm Mon-Fri, from 9am Sat; 🚇Via del Corso) This stately, art deco cafe is famous for its Neapolitan cakes – try the *sfogliatelle* (a flaky pastry stuffed with ricotta and pieces of candied fruit) for something sweet, or the *rustici* (cheese-and-tomato-filled pastry puffs) for something savoury. Sit in the elegant interior, or outside to watch life on the attractive square.

# ☆ ENTERTAINMENT

### RIALTOSANTAMBROGIO
CULTURAL CENTRE

Map p350 (📞06 68133 640; www.rialto.roma.it; Via di San'Ambrogio 4; 🚇🚇Via Arenula) This ancient courtyard-centred building is Rome's most central *centro sociale* (social centre), with an art-school vibe and an edgy programme of theatre, exhibitions and art-house cinema. It also stages seriously kicking club nights and central Rome's best gigs – check the website for upcoming events.

### TEATRO ARGENTINA
THEATRE

Map p346 (📞06 684 00 01; www.teatrodiroma. net; Largo di Torre Argentina 52; tickets €12-27; 🚇🚇Largo di Torre Argentina) Rome's top theatre is one of the two official homes of the Teatro di Roma; the other is the Teatro India. Founded in 1732, it retains its original frescoed ceiling and a grand gilt-and-velvet auditorium. Rossini's *Barber of Seville* premiered here and today it stages a wide-ranging programme of drama (mostly in Italian) and high-profile dance performances. Book early for the dance productions, which often sell out.

### TEATRO VALLE
THEATRE

Map p346 (📞06 688 03 794; www.teatrovalle.it; Via del Teatro Valle 21; tickets €16-31; 🚇🚇Largo di Torre Argentina) Another of Rome's historic stages, this perfectly proportioned 18th-century theatre is like a pocket opera house, with three levels of red-and-gold private boxes. Its interesting programme spans everything from old classics to ballet, rock opera and recitals. English-language works are sometimes performed in English with Italian subtitles.

### TEATRO DELL'OROLOGIO
THEATRE

Map p346 (📞06 683 92 214; www.teatroorologio. it; Via dei Filippini 17a; 🚇Corso Vittorio Emanuele II) A well-known experimental theatre, the Orologio offers a varied programme of contemporary and classic works, with occasional performances in English.

### ENGLISH THEATRE OF ROME
THEATRE

Map p346 (📞06 444 13 75; www.rometheatre. com; Teatro L'Arciliuto, Piazza Monte Vecchio 5; tickets €12-15; ☺Oct-Jun; 🚇Corso Vittorio Emanuele II) The English Theatre of Rome stages a mix of contemporary and classic plays, comedies and bilingual productions, mainly at the Teatro L'Arciliuto, near Piazza Navona, and occasionally at other venues.

# 🛍 SHOPPING

## 🛍 Pantheon & Around

### SPAZIO SETTE
HOME & GARDEN

Map p346 (www.spaziosette.it, in Italian; Via dei Barbieri 7; 🚇🚇Largo di Torre Argentina) Even if you don't buy any of the designer homeware at Spazio Sette, it's worth popping in to see sharp modern furniture set against 17th-century frescoes. Formerly home to a cardinal, the *palazzo* now houses a three-floor shop full of quality furniture, kitchenware, tableware and gifts.

### SCIÙ SCIÀ
SHOES

Map p346 (Via di Torre Argentina 8; 🚇🚇Largo di Torre Argentina) Walk past and you'd miss it but the local ladies love Sciù Scià for its own range of handmade shoes and multi-coloured suede bags. Styles are sensible but chic, classic with a twist, and the quality is excellent. Bank on at least €90 for flats, €150 plus for a bag.

## STILO FETTI
PENS

Map p346 (www.stilofetti.it, in Italian; Via degli Orfani 82; ☐Via del Corso) Technology might have largely done for fountain pens but they still make excellent gifts, and this old-fashioned family-run pen shop, on the go since 1893, has a wonderful selection. All styles are covered and many top brands are represented, from Parker to Mont Blanc and Graf von Faber-Castell.

## FELTRINELLI
BOOKSTORE

Map p346 (www.lafeltrinelli.it, in Italian; Largo di Torre Argentina 11; ⏱9am-8pm Mon-Fri, 9am-10pm Sat, 10am-9pm Sun; ☐☐Largo di Torre Argentina) Italy's most famous bookseller (and publisher) has shops across the capital. This one has a wide range of books (in Italian) on art, photography, cinema and history, as well as an extensive selection of Italian literature and travel guides in various languages, including English. You'll also find CDs, DVDs and a range of stationery products.

## ALBERTA GLOVES
ACCESSORIES

Map p346 (Corso Vittorio Emanuele II 18; ⏱10am-6.30pm; ☐Corso Vittorio Emanuele II) From elbow-length silk gloves for a grand premiere to crochet for first communions; from tan-coloured driving mitts for touring the Alps to black fingerless numbers for kinky nights out; from fur-lined kid to polkadots, this crammed, tiny shop has gloves for every conceivable occasion. And woolly hats too.

## Piazza Navona & Around

### TEMPI MODERNI
FASHION, JEWELLERY

Map p346 (Via del Governo Vecchio 108; ⏱9.30am-8pm Mon-Sat; ☐Corso Vittorio Emanuele II) Bart Simpson ties and Ferragaomo fashions sit side by side at this kooky little shop on Via del Governo Vecchio. It's packed with quality vintage costume jewellery, wonderful '20s and '30s Bakelite pieces, art nouveau and art deco trinkets, pop art bangles, 19th-century resin brooches, and pieces by couturiers such as Chanel, Dior and Balenciaga. You can also mix and match with the fine array of vintage designer clothing.

### RETRÒ
DESIGN

Map p346 (www.retrodesign.it, in Italian; Piazza del Fico 20; ⏱11am-1pm & 4-8pm Tue-Sat, 4-8pm Mon; ☐Corso del Rinascimento) Design buffs, prepare to swoon over the rainbow rows of sexy 1950s and '60s glassware, Bakelite jewellery, pop art carpets, vintage designer furniture and iconic chairs by the likes of Italian design great Giò Ponti and influential French designer Pierre Paulin.

### OFFICINA PROFUMO FARMACEUTICA DI SANTA MARIA NOVELLA
COSMETICS

Map p346 (Corso del Rinascimento 47; ☐Corso del Rinascimento) Step in for the scent of the place, if nothing else. This bewitching shop – the Roman branch of one of Italy's oldest pharmacies – stocks natural perfumes and cosmetics as well as herbal infusions, teas and pot pourri, all carefully shelved in wooden cabinets under a giant Murano-glass chandelier. It was founded in Florence in 1612 by the Dominican monks of Santa Maria Novella, and many of its cosmetics are based on original 17th-century herbal recipes.

### NARDECCHIA
ANTIQUES

Map p346 (Piazza Navona 25; ☐Corso del Rinascimento) You'll be inviting people to see your etchings after a visit to this historic Piazza Navona shop, famed for its antique prints. Nardecchia sells everything from 18th-century etchings by Giovanni Battista Piranesi to more affordable 19th-century panoramas. Bank on about €120 for a small framed print.

### CUADROS ROMA
DESIGN

Map p346 (www.cuadrosroma.com; Via del Governo Vecchio 11; ⏱11.30am-7.30pm Mon, Wed, Fri & Sat, 3-7.30pm Tue & Thu, 2.30-7.30pm Sun; ☐Corso Vittorio Emanuele II) Interior design made easy. That's the thinking behind this colourful, arty shop and its collection of fashionable modern wallpaper, floor stickers and self-adhesive wall tattoos. The designs are sharp, fresh and original and, with prices starting at €12.90, easy on the pocket.

### LUNA & L'ALTRA
FASHION

Map p346 (Piazza Pasquino 76; ☐Corso Vittorio Emanuele II) A must-stop on any Roman fashion trail, this is one of a number of independent boutiques on and around Via del Governo Vecchio. In its austere, gallery-like interior, clothes and accessories by hip designers Issey Miyake, Dries Van Noten, Rick Owen and Yohji Yamamoto are exhibited in reverential style.

### ALDO FEFÈ ARTISANAL

Map p346 (Via della Stelletta 20b; ☐ Corso del Rinascimento) Started by the owner's father in 1932, this tiny arched workshop produces beautifully handpainted paper. Products include wrapping paper, little chests of drawers, leather-bound notebooks (€26), writing paper, picture frames and beautiful photo albums (€49).

### ZOUZOU FASHION

Map p346 (www.zouzou.it; Vicolo della Cancelleria 9a; ☐ Corso Vittorio Emanuele II) Spice up your Roman romance with a trip to this upmarket lingerie and 'sensual entertainment' shop just off Via del Governo Vecchio. Set up like a Victorian boudoir with crimson walls and corseted mannequins, it has a range of lingerie, toiletries and toys that's sure to bring out the hidden bad girl in every lady.

### VESTITI USATI CINZIA FASHION

Map p346 (Via del Governo Vecchio 45; ☐ Corso Vittorio Emanuele II) Cinzia remains one of the best vintage shops on Via del Governo Vecchio, owned by a former costume designer. There are jackets (in leather, denim, corduroy and linen), slouchy boots, screenprinted T-shirts, retro skirts and suede coats, and you can snap up vintage designer sunglasses.

### OMERO E CECILIA FASHION

Map p346 (Via del Governo Vecchio 110; ☐ Corso Vittorio Emanuele II) In this historic street of vintage shops, this is a wonderful tunnel of a place, stashed full of second-hand leather bags, '70s velvet coats, tweed jackets, '60s Italian dresses, old Burberry trenchcoats and so on. It's a browser's heaven.

### AI MONASTERI COSMETICS

Map p346 (www.monasteri.it; Corso del Rinascimento 72; ☉4.30-7.30pm Mon, Wed & Fri, 10am-1pm Sat; ☐ Corso del Rinascimento) This apothecary-like, wonderfully scented shop sells herbal essences, spirits, soaps, balms, and liqueurs, all created by monks and beautifully packaged. You can stock up on everything from sage toothpaste to rose shampoo, cherry brandy and a mysterious-sounding elixir of love, though quite why monks are expert at this is anyone's guess.

### CASALI ART

Map p346 (Via dei Coronari 115; ☐ Corso del Rinascimento) On Via dei Coronari, a lovely pedestrian street known for its antique furniture shops, Casali deals in antique prints, many delicately hand-coloured. The shop is small but the choice is not, ranging from 16th-century botanical manuscripts to €3 postcard prints of Rome.

### BERTÈ TOYS

Map p346 (Piazza Navona 107-111; ☐ Corso del Rinascimento) On Piazza Navona, this is one of Rome's great toy shops, an emporium specialising in wooden dolls and puppets, but with a great mishmash of other stuff, from tractors to pushchairs, doll houses and tea sets. Perfect for pre-/post-sightseeing bribes.

### COMICS BAZAR ANTIQUES

Map p346 (Via dei Banchi Vecchi 127-128; ☐ Corso Vittorio Emanuele II) Not a comic in sight – this attic-like treasure-trove is crammed to its rafters with antiques. Wade through the lamps that hang everywhere like jungle creepers and you'll find old dolls, framed prints and furniture dating from the 19th century to the 1940s, including pieces by the 19th-century Viennese designer Thonet. You might even find the shopkeeper hidden away among it all.

### CITTÀ DEL SOLE TOYS

Map p346 (www.cittadelsole.it; Via della Scrofa 65; ☉10am-7.30pm, closed Mon morning & Sun; ☐ Corso del Rinascimento) Città del Sole is a parent's dream, a treasure-trove of imaginative toys created to stretch the growing mind rather than numb it. From well-crafted wooden trains to insect investigation kits, here you'll find toys to (with any luck) keep your children occupied for hours.

### LE TELE DI CARLOTTA ARTISANAL

Map p346 (Via dei Coronari 228; ☉10.30am-1pm & 3.30-7pm; ☐ Corso Vittorio Emanuele II) This tiny little sewing box of a shop is a delicate concoction of hand-embroidered napkins, bags and antique pieces of jewellery, ranging from 19th century to 1930s. You can have pieces embroidered on request, if you have enough time in Rome. Heirlooms in the making.

### AL SOGNO TOYS

Map p346 (www.alsogno.com; Piazza Navona 53; ☉10am-10pm; ☐ Corso del Rinascimento) Even from outside you know that Al Sogno, with its elaborate, elegant window displays, is more than your average toy shop. Inside is a wonderland of puppets, trolls, fairies and fake Roman weapons, while upstairs, the mezzanine floor strains under the weight of dolls and stuffed animals. The don't-touch atmosphere is best suited to well-behaved little darlings.

## 🔒 Campo De' Fiori & Around

### IBIZ – ARTIGIANATO IN CUOIO    ACCESSORIES
Map p346 (Via dei Chiavari 39; ☐Corso Vittorio Emanuele II) In this pint-sized workshop, Elisa Nepi and her father craft exquisite, well-priced leather goods, including wallets, bags, belts and sandals, in simple but classy designs and myriad colours. With €40 you should be able to pick up a wallet, purse or pair of sandals.

### RACHELE    FASHION
Map p346 (Vicolo del Bollo 6; ⊘closed Mon; ☐Corso Vittorio Emanuele II) Mums looking to update their kids' (under 12s) wardrobe would do well to look up Rachele in her delightful little shop. With everything from hats and mitts to romper suits and jackets, all brightly coloured and all handmade, this sort of shop is a dying breed. Most items are around the €40 to €50 mark, but the house speciality, a portable, and washable, changing board, costs €75.

### ARSENALE    FASHION
Map p346 (www.patriziapieroni.it; Via del Pellegrino 172; ☐Corso Vittorio Emanuele II) Arsenale is a watchword with fashion-conscious Roman women and the virgin-white shop marries urban minimalism with heavy, rustic fittings to create a clean, contemporary look. Roman designer Patrizia Pieroni started Arsenale over 15 years ago, but it still feels cutting edge with its interestingly structured clothes in rich, luscious fabrics.

### LIBRERIA DEL VIAGGIATORE    BOOKSTORE
Map p346 (Via del Pellegrino 78; ☐Corso Vittorio Emanuele II) If Rome is only a stop on your Grand Tour, this beguiling old-fashioned bookshop is a must. Small but world-encompassing, it's crammed with guides and travel literature in various languages and has a huge range of maps, including hiking maps.

### MONDELLO OTTICA    ACCESSORIES
Map p346 (www.mondelloottico.it; Via del Pellegrino 97-98; ⊘Tue-Sat; ☐Corso Vittorio Emanuele II) If you're in Rome, you need shades. And this is the place to look. Known for its hip window displays, Mondello Ottica is a sparkling white temple of sunglasses with frames by leading designers, including Anne et Valentin, l.a.Eyeworks, Cutler and Gross, and Theo. Prescription glasses can be ready the same day.

### BORINI    SHOES
Map p350 (Via dei Pettinari 86-87; ☐☐Via Arenula) Don't be fooled by the discount, workaday look – those in the know pile into this unglitzy shop, run by the Borinis since 1940, to try on the cool, candy-coloured shoes. Whatever is 'in' this season, Borini will have it, at reasonable prices and in a cover-every-eventuality rainbow palette.

### DADADA 52    FASHION
Map p346 (www.dadada.eu; Via dei Giubbonari 52; ☐Corso Vittorio Emanuele II) Every young Roman fashionista makes a stop at daDADA, for its funky cocktail dresses, bright print summer frocks and eclectic coats. Prices start at around €100 but most items are north of €200. There's also a second branch at Via del Corso 500.

### ETHIC    FASHION
Map p350 (www.3ndlab.com, in Italian; Piazza B Cairoli 11; ⊘10am-7.30pm Tue-Sat, 11.30am-7.30pm Sun & Mon; ☐☐Via Arenula) This hint-of-boho place is an Italian clothing chain, with retro-influenced, bold designs and its own line of girls' clothes. Clothes come in interesting colours, fabrics and designs, and everything is reasonably priced. There are many other branches across town.

### LOCO    SHOES
Map p346 (Via dei Baullari 22; ☐Corso Vittorio Emanuele II) Sneaker fetishists should hotfoot it to Loco for the very latest in big-statement footwear. It's a small shop, but full of attitude, with an interesting collection of original sneakers (for boys and girls), winged boots and suede sandals by international and Italian designers.

### POSTO ITALIANO    SHOES
Map p346 (Via dei Giubbonari 37a; ☐☐Via Arenula) Reasonably priced Posto Italiano has an always-beguiling collection of fashionable, accessible and highly wearable women's shoes. A showcase for emerging Italian designers, it also stocks more established brands.

## 🔒 Jewish Ghetto

**LEONE LIMENTANI**                    HOME & GARDEN

Map p350 (www.limentani.com; Via del Portico d'Ottavia 47; ⊘9am-1pm & 3.30-7pm Mon-Fri, 10am-7.30pm Sat; 🚇🚇Via Arenula) Family-run for seven generations, this well-stocked basement store has a huge, rambling choice of kitchenware and tableware, expensive porcelain and knick-knacks, crockery, cutlery and crystal, all at bargain prices.

## 🔒 Piazza Colonna & Around

**TOP CHOICE** **CONFETTERIA MORIONDO & GARIGLIO**                    CHOCOLATE

Map p346 (Via del Piè di Marmo 21-22; ⊘9am-7.30pm Mon-Sat; 🚇🚇Largo di Torre Argentina) Roman poet Trilussa dedicated several sonnets to this shop, and you can see why. This is no ordinary sweetshop, but a veritable temple to bonbons. Rows of handmade chocolates and sweets (more than 80 varieties) lie in ceremonial splendour in old-fashioned glass cabinets set against dark crimson walls. Moriondo and Gariglio were Torinese cousins who moved to Rome after the unification of Italy, and many of the chocolates are handmade to their original recipes.

**TARTARUGHE**                    FASHION

Map p346 (Via del Piè di Marmo 17; ⊘10am-8pm Tue-Sat, 12.30-8pm Mon; 🚇🚇Largo di Torre Argentina) Tartarughe sells grown-up clothes that are pleasingly frivolous. Designer Susanna Liso's outfits include whispery chiffon tops, multicoloured dresses and knitwear, strikingly cut jackets and coats, and novel accessories in stone, glass and perspex.

**BARTOLUCCI**                    TOYS

Map p346 (www.bartolucci.com; Via dei Pastini 98; 🚇Via del Corso del Rinascimento) You can't miss this woodtastic toy shop, where everything's crafted in pine by the Bartolucci family (often you can see work being done in the shop). It's guarded by a cycling Pinocchio and a full-sized wooden motorbike, and within are ticking clocks, rustic cars, rocking horses, planes and more Pinocchios than you've ever seen in your life.

**DAVIDE CENCI**                    FASHION

Map p346 (www.davidecenci.com; Via di Campo Marzio 1-7; 🚇Via del Corso) For a look that discreetly whispers old money (think blazers, brogues, tweed and flannels) head to Davide Cenci, an old-school clothes shop that has been dressing Rome's finest since 1926. It carries a selection of impeccable Italian and international labels (Ralph Lauren, Tod's, Hogan, Ballantyne, Pucci) as well as its own house brand.

**AS ROMA STORE**                    SPORTSWEAR

Map p346 (Piazza Colonna 360; 🚇Via del Corso) An official club store of AS Roma, one of Rome's two top-flight football teams. The club has been through the mill in recent times, so help boost the team's coffers by buying a replica shirt or keyring, or indeed anything from the selection of branded clothes and trinkets. You can also buy match tickets here.

**DE SANCTIS**                    ARTISANAL

Map p346 (www.desanctis1890.com, in Italian; Piazza di Pietra 24; ⊘10am-1.30pm & 3-7.30pm Mon-Sat, closed Tue morning; 🚇Via del Corso) De Sanctis – in business since 1890 – is full of impressive Italian ceramics from Sicily and Tuscany, with sunbursts of colour decorating candleholders, vases, tiles, urns and plates. De Sanctis ships all over the world.

# Tridente, Trevi & the Quirinale

PIAZZA DI SPAGNA & THE SPANISH STEPS | PIAZZA DEL POPOLO & AROUND | TREVI TO THE QUIRINALE | WEST OF VIA DEL CORSO | PIAZZA BARBERINI & VIA VENETO

## Neighbourhood Top Five

**1** People watching, chattering, photo-snapping and dreaming on the **Spanish Steps** (p105), with a view down the glittering backbone of the Tridente district, designer-store-lined Via Condotti.

**2** Gazing in wonder at the Caravaggio masterpieces in **Chiesa di Santa Maria del Popolo** (p106).

**3** Visiting the **Trevi Fountain** (p108) late in the evening, when the crowds have ebbed away.

**4** Hearing a concert in the Cortona-designed chapel after a Sunday visit to the **Palazzo del Quirinale** (p110).

**5** Seeing **Palazzo Barberini's** (p110) architectural treasures, and feasting your eyes on the gallery's Italian masters.

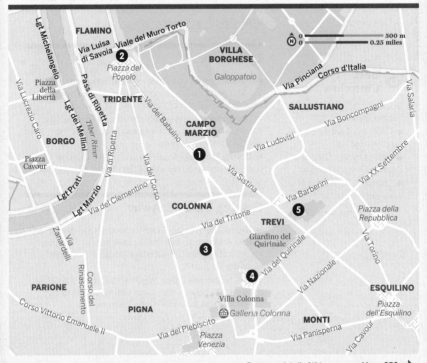

For more detail of this area, see Map p352 ➡

## Lonely Planet's Top Tip

Note that local churches are usually locked up for two to three hours over lunch, so if you want to visit the interiors, time your visit for the morning or late afternoon.

### ✕ Best Places to Eat

➤ Palatium (p117)

➤ Nino (p117/)

➤ Dal Bolognese (p115)

➤ Babette (p115)

➤ Colline Emiliane (p120)

For reviews see p115 ➤

### 🍷 Best Places to Drink

➤ Salotto Locarno (p120)

➤ Stravinkij Bar – Hotel de Russie (p121)

➤ Canova Tadolini (p121)

➤ Ciampini 2 (p121)

For reviews see p120 ➤

### ⊙ Best Churches

➤ Chiesa di Santa Maria del Popolo (p106)

➤ Chiesa di Sant'Andrea al Quirinale (p111)

➤ Chiesa di San Carlo alle Quattro Fontane (p111)

➤ Chiesa di Santa Maria della Vittoria (p111)

For reviews see p107 ➤

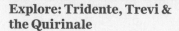

## Explore: Tridente, Trevi & the Quirinale

Tridente is Rome's most glamorous district, full of designer boutiques, fashionable bars and swish hotels. However, it's not just about shopping, dining and drinking. The area also contains the splendid vast neoclassical showpiece, Piazza del Popolo, the Spanish Steps, the Museo dell'Ara Pacis, a controversial modern museum designed by US architect Richard Meier, and several masterpiece-packed churches. To see all the sights here, factoring in some window shopping, would take around a day, and it's all easily walkable – a short walk from the Centro Storico or Piazza Venezia – and easily accessible from Spagna and Flaminio Metro stations.

Alongside Tridente, one of Rome's hills, the Quirinale encompasses the extraordinary Trevi Fountain and the imposing presidential Palazzo del Quirinale, as well as important churches by the twin masters of Roman baroque, Gian Lorenzo Bernini and Francesco Borromini. Other artistic hotspots in the area include the lavish Galleria Colonna and the Galleria Nazionale d'Arte Antica – Palazzo Barberini, a fabulous gallery containing works by a who's who of Renaissance and baroque artists – to see all this at leisure you'll need several days. The Trevi and Quirinale's principal gateway is the Barberini Metro stop. Frenetic during the day, both Tridente and the Quirinale are by no means nightlife zones – they're almost snoozily quiet after dark.

## Local Life

➤ **Socializing** In laid-back, cobbled and ivy-draped Via Margutta (p118), you can experience the upscale neighbourhood feel of this distinctive district.

➤ **Shopping** Commission yourself a handmade bag, a unique lamp or a marble motto from one of the district's artisanal shops.

➤ **Coffee** Do as the locals do and grab a caffeine hit propping up the bar at one of the district's iconic cafes.

## Getting There & Away

➤ **Metro** The Trevi and Quirinale areas are closest to Barberini Metro stop, while Spagna and Flaminio stations are perfectly placed for Tridente. All three stops are on line A.

➤ **Bus** Numerous buses run down to Piazza Barberini or along Via Veneto, and many end up at Piazza San Silvestro, ideal for a foray into Tridente.

## TOP SIGHTS
# PIAZZA DI SPAGNA & THE SPANISH STEPS

**The Piazza di Spagna and the Spanish Steps (Scalinata della Trinità dei Monti) are the focal point of the Tridente district, and most visitors will settle down here to take stock at some point. The area has been a magnet for foreigners since the 1800s. When Dickens visited in the 19th century he reported that 'these steps are the great place of resort for the artists' 'Models,'...The first time I went up there, I could not conceive why the faces seemed familiar to me...I soon found that we had made acquaintance, and improved it, for several years, on the walls of various Exhibition Galleries.'**

### DON'T MISS...

➡ View from the top of the Spanish Steps
➡ Barcaccia

### PRACTICALITIES

➡ Map p352
➡ Admission free
➡ Ⓜ Spagna, Flaminio

## Piazza di Spagna

The Piazza di Spagna was named after the Spanish Embassy to the Holy See, although the staircase, designed by the Italian Francesco de Sanctis and built in 1725 with a legacy from the French, leads to the French Chiesa della Trinità dei Monti. In the late 1700s the area was much loved by English visitors on the Grand Tour and was known to locals as *er ghetto de l'inglesi* (the English ghetto). Keats lived for a short time in an apartment overlooking the Spanish Steps, and died here of TB at the age of 25. The rooms are now a museum (see p108) devoted to the Romantics, especially Keats.

## Barcaccia

At the foot of the steps, the fountain of a sinking boat, the **Barcaccia** (1627), is believed to be by Pietro Bernini, father of the more famous Giani Lorenzo. It's fed from a low-pressure aqueduct, hence the low-key nature of the central fountain. Bees and suns decorate the structure, symbols of the commissioning Barbarini family. Opposite, Via dei Condotti is Rome's most exclusive shopping street, glittering with big-name designers such as Gucci, Bulgari and Prada.

To the southeast of the piazza, adjacent Piazza Mignanelli is dominated by the **Colonna dell'Immacolata**, built in 1857 to celebrate Pope Pius IX's declaration of the Immaculate Conception.

A magnificent repository of art, this is one of Rome's earliest and richest Renaissance churches. Artists including Pinturicchio worked on the building in the 15th century, while Bramante and Bernini added later architectural elements. The lavish chapels, decorated by Caravaggio, Bernini, Raphael and others, were commissioned by local noble families.

**DON'T MISS...**

➡ Caravaggio's paintings, Cerasi Chapel

➡ Chigi Chapel

**PRACTICALITIES**

➡ Map p352

➡ Admission free

➡ ⏲7am-noon & 4-7pm Mon-Sat, 8am-1.30pm & 4.30-7.30pm Sun

➡ Ⓜ Flaminio, Spagna

## The Church

The first chapel was built here in 1099, over the tombs of the Domiti family, to exorcise the ghost of Nero, who was secretly buried on this spot and whose malicious spirit was thought to haunt the area. Some 400 years later, in 1472, it was given a major overhaul by Pope Sixtus IV. Pinturicchio was called in to decorate the pope's family chapel, the Cappella Delle Rovere, and to paint a series of frescoes on the apse, itself designed by Bramante. Also in the apse are Rome's first stained-glass windows, crafted by Frenchman Guillaume de Marcillat in the early 16th century. The altar houses the 13th-century painting Madonna del Popolo, and the altarpiece of the Assumption is by Annibale Carracci.

The former Augustinian convent adjoining the church hosted Martin Luther during his month-long mission here in 1511.

## Chigi Chapel

Raphael designed the Cappella Chigi, dedicated to his patron Agostino Chigi, but never lived to see it completed. Bernini finished the job for him more than 100 years later, contributing statues of Daniel and Habakkuk to the altarpiece, which was built by Sebastiano del Piombo. The most famous feature is the 17th-century mosaic of a kneeling skeleton, placed there to remind the living of the inevitable end.

## Cerasi Chapel

The church's absolute highlight, however, is the Cappella Cerasi with its two Caravaggios: the Conversione di San Paolo (Conversion of St Paul) and the Crocifissione di San Pietro (Crucifixion of St Peter). Both are exquisitely spotlit via the artist's use of light and shade. The latter is frighteningly realistic: the artist has used perspective to emphasise the weight of the cross as it's turned upside down and St Peter's facial expression as he is upturned is heartrendingly human, yet sorrowful rather than afraid.

## Della Rovere Chapel

The frescoes in the lunettes and the Nativity above the altar in this chapel were painted by Pinturicchio in the 15th century.

# ⊙ SIGHTS

The Piazza del Popolo, the Spanish Steps, the Trevi Fountain, Rome's most designer district, Palazzo Barberini and a sprinkling of Caravaggios, all a hop and a skip from Villa Borghese (see p205) when you're in need of a breather: this area is one of Rome's richest, in terms of, cuisine, art and culture, as well as hard cash, and offers an embarrassment of riches for the visitor.

## ⊙ Piazza del Popolo & Around

**CHIESA DI SANTA MARIA DEL POPOLO**     CHURCH
See p106.

**PIAZZA DEL POPOLO**     PIAZZA
Map p352 (⊠Flaminio) For centuries the site of public executions, this elegant neoclassical piazza is a superb people-watching spot. It was originally laid out in 1538 to provide a grandiose entrance to the city – at the time, and for centuries before, it was the main northern gateway into the city. Since then it has been extensively altered, most recently by Giuseppe Valadier in 1823. Guarding its southern entrance are Carlo Rainaldi's twin 17th-century baroque churches, **Chiesa di Santa Maria dei Miracoli** and **Chiesa di Santa Maria in Montesanto**. These had to appear symmetrical, though occupying slightly different footprints, so the architect gave that on the right (dei Miracoli) a circular dome, and that on the left an oval one, while keeping the bases the same. Over on the northern flank of the piazza is the **Porta del Popolo**, created by Bernini in 1655. In the centre, the 36m-high Egyptian **obelisk** was moved here from the Circo Massimo in the mid-16th century. To the east are the Pincio Hill Gardens.

**PINCIO HILL GARDENS**     PARK
Map p352 (⊠Flaminio) Overlooking Piazza del Popolo, the 19th-century Pincio Hill Gardens are named after the Pinci family, who owned this part of Rome in the 4th century. It's quite a climb up from the piazza, but at the top you're rewarded with lovely views over to St Peter's and the Gianicolo hill. From the gardens you can strike out to explore Villa Borghese or head up to the Chiesa della Trinità dei Monti at the top of the Spanish Steps.

## ⊙ West of Via Del Corso

**MUSEO DELL'ARA PACIS**     MUSEUM
Map p352 (☑06 820 59 127; www.arapacis.it; Lungotevere in Augusta; adult/reduced €9/7; ⊙9am-7pm Tue-Sun; ☐Lungotevere in Augusta) The first modern construction in Rome's historic centre since WWII, Richard Meier's minimalist glass-and-marble pavilion echoes the surrounding Fascist architecture. Many Romans detest the first modern construction in Rome's historic centre since WWII. The wall dividing the busy Lungotevere Augusta from Piazza Augusto Imperatore, which has been criticised for obscuring the baroque facade of the church of S. Rocco all'Augusteo, is to be dismantled, according to new plans approved by the architect.

Inside is the less-controversial Ara Pacis Augustae (Altar of Peace), Augustus' great monument to peace. One of the most important works of ancient Roman sculpture, the vast marble altar (it measures 11.6m by 10.6m by 3.6m) was completed in 13 BC and positioned near Piazza San Lorenzo in Lucina, slightly to the southeast of its current site. The location was calculated so that on Augustus' birthday the shadow of a huge sundial on Campus Martius would fall directly on it.

---

### ROME'S OPTICAL ILLUSIONS

Aptly for such a theatrical city, Rome contains some magical visual tricks. Overlooking Piazza del Popolo, there are the seemingly twin churches: constructed to look identical while occupying different-sized sites. Then, there's Borromini's perspective-defying corridor at **Palazzo Spada**; Andrea Pozzo's amazing trompe l'oeil at the **Chiesa di Sant'Ignazio di Loyola** and the secret keyhole view from **Piazza dei Cavalieri di Malta**. Strangest of all is the view of St Peter's Dome from **Via Piccolomini** near **Villa Doria Pamphilj**. Here the dome looms, filling the space at the end of the road, framed by trees. But the really curious thing is that as you move towards the cupola it seems to get smaller rather than larger as the view widens.

Over the centuries the altar fell victim to Rome's avid art collectors, and panels ended up in the Medici collection, the Vatican and the Louvre. However, in 1936 Mussolini unearthed the remaining parts and decided to reassemble them in the present location.

Of the reliefs, the most important depicts Augustus at the head of a procession, followed by priests, the general Marcus Agrippa and the entire imperial family.

**MAUSOLEO DI AUGUSTO**    MONUMENT

Map p352 (Piazza Augusto Imperatore; Piazza Augusto Imperatore) Once one of Ancient Rome's most imposing monuments, this is now an unkempt mound of earth, overgrown with weeds and surrounded by unsightly fences. Plans for a revamp have been on the table for some years, but there's still no sign of activity.

The mausoleum, which was built in 28 BC, is the last resting place of Augustus, who was buried here in AD 14, and his favourite nephew and heir Marcellus. Mussolini had it restored in 1936 with an eye to being buried here himself.

TRIDENTE, TREVI & THE QUIRINALE SIGHTS

## ⊙ Piazza di Spagna & Around

**PIAZZA DI SPAGNA & THE SPANISH STEPS**    PIAZZA, MONUMENT
See p105.

**KEATS-SHELLEY HOUSE**    MUSEUM

Map p352 (☎06 678 42 35; www.keats-shelley -house.org; Piazza di Spagna 26; adult/reduced €4.50/3.50; ☺10am-1pm & 2-6pm Mon-Fri, 11am-2pm & 3-6pm Sat; MSpagna) Next to the Spanish Steps, the Keats-Shelley House is where Romantic poet John Keats died of TB in February 1821. He'd come to Rome a year earlier, on an unsuccessful trip to try to improve his health in the Italian climate, but it didn't, and he died at the age of 25. A year later, fellow poet Percy Bysshe Shelley drowned off the coast of Tuscany. The house is now a small museum crammed with memorabilia relating to the poets and their colleagues Mary Shelley and Lord Byron.

**VIA DEI CONDOTTI**    STREET

Map p (MSpagna) The place to head for high-rolling shoppers, this is Rome's smartest

---

## ⊙ TOP SIGHTS
# TREVI FOUNTAIN

Rome's most famous fountain, Fontana di Trevi, is a baroque extravaganza that almost fills an entire piazza. The foaming masterpiece is famous as the place where Anita Ekberg waded in a gown for Fellini's *La Dolce Vita* (1960).

The flamboyant baroque ensemble was designed by Nicola Salvi in 1732 and depicts Neptune's chariot being led by Tritons with sea horses – one wild, one docile – representing the moods of the sea. The water still comes from the aqua virgo, an underground aqueduct that is over 2000 years old, built by General Agrippa under Augustus and that brings water from the Salone springs around 19 kilometres away. The name Trevi refers to the *tre vie* (three roads) that converge at the fountain.

The famous tradition is to toss a coin into the fountain, thus ensuring your return. According to the same tradition if you throw in a second coin you'll fall in love with an Italian, while a third will have you marrying him or her. Around €3000 is thrown into the Trevi on an average day. It's accepted practice that this money is collected daily and goes to the Catholic charity Caritas, but in 2002, it was discovered that a man had been taking the change for himself. There are now plans to pass legislation to make removal of coins from the fountain an offence.

**DON'T MISS...**

➡ The contrasting seahorses, or moods of the sea.

➡ Throwing a coin or three in the fountain.

**PRACTICALITIES**

➡ Map p352
➡ Admission free
➡ MBarberini

# TOP SIGHTS
# PALAZZO DEL QUIRINALE

Overlooking the high-up Piazza del Quirinale is the imposing presidential palace, formerly the papal summer residence, open to the public on Sundays. There are also exhibitions in the neighbouring Scuderie Papali.

The immense Palazzo del Quirinale served as the papal summer residence for almost three centuries until the keys were begrudgingly handed over to Italy's new king in 1870. Since 1948, it has been home of the Presidente della Repubblica, Italy's head of state.

Pope Gregory XIII (r 1572–85) originally chose the site and over the next 150 years the top architects of the day worked on it, including Bernini, Domenico Fontana and Carlo Maderno.

On the other side of the piazza, the palace's former stables, the **Scuderie Papali al Quirinale** (🖉06 399 67 500; www.scuderiequirinale.it; Via XXIV Maggio 16; ⊘depends on exhibition), is now a magnificent space that hosts excellent art exhibitions.

## DON'T MISS...

➡ Sunday concert in the chapel designed by Carlo Moderno.

➡ Splendid temporary exhibitions in the former stables, the Scuderie Papali.

## PRACTICALITIES

➡ Map p352

➡ 🖉06 4 69 91

➡ www.quirinale.it

➡ Piazza del Quirinale

➡ Adult €5; if you have a bag, ensure you have €1 for a locker.

➡ ⊘8.30am-noon Sun mid-Sep–mid-Jun

➡ Ⓜ Barberini

shopping strip. At the eastern end, near Piazza di Spagna, Caffè Greco (p121) was a favourite meeting point of 18th- and 19th-century writers. Other top shopping streets in the area include **Via Frattina, Via della Croce, Via delle Carrozze** and **Via del Babuino**.

**CHIESA DELLA TRINITÀ DEI MONTI**    CHURCH
Map p352 (🖉06 679 41 79; Piazza Trinità dei Monti; ⊘7am-1pm & 3-7pm Tue-Sun; Ⓜ Spagna) Looming over the Spanish Steps, this landmark church was commissioned by King Louis XII of France and consecrated in 1585. Apart from the great views from outside, it boasts some wonderful frescoes by Daniele da Volterra. His *Deposizione* (Deposition), in the second chapel on the left, is regarded as a masterpiece of mannerist painting. If you don't fancy climbing the steep steps, there's a lift up from Spagna metro station.

**MUSEO MISSIONARIO
DI PROPAGANDA FIDE**    MUSEUM
Map p352 (🖉06 6988 0266; Via di Propaganda 1; admission €8; ⊘2.30-6pm Mon, Wed & Fri; Ⓜ Spagna) Rome's 'propogation of faith' museum is housed in a 17th-century Baroque

architectural masterpiece designed by Bernini (Gianlorenzo) and Francesco Borromini. Not only is this recently opened museum the first chance the public has had to peer inside, but it also has an eclectic, interesting collection of items brought back from overseas missions, including paintings of Japanese life in the 1930s, plus the recently discovered Canova portrait of Ezzelino Romano. But the true highlight is the opportunity to peer into Bernini's wooden library with its ceiling carved with Barberini bees and Borromini's Chapel of the Magi, where the Wise Men's Epiphany acts an allegory for converts to Christianity.

**PALAZZO VALENTINI**    ARCHAEOLOGICAL SITE
Map p352 (🖉06 32810; Via IV Novembre 119/A; adult/reduced €6/4, advance booking fee €1.50; ⊘9.30am-5pm Wed-Mon, tours every 45 min; Ⓜ Spagna) Underneath a grand mansion that's been the seat of the Province of Rome since 1873, the archaeological remains of several lavish ancient Roman houses have been uncovered, and the excavated fragments have been turned into a fascinating multi-media 'experience', which takes you on a virtual tour of the dwellings, complete

TRIDENTE, TREVI & THE QUIRINALE SIGHTS

with sound effects, projected frescoes and glimpses of ancient life as it might have been lived in the area around the buildings.

**CASA DI GOETHE**                        MUSEUM

Map p352 (☑06 326 50 412; www.casadigoethe. it; Via del Corso 18; adult/reduced €4/3; ⊙10am-6pm Tue-Sun; Ⓜ Flaminio) A gathering place for German intellectuals, the Via del Corso apartment where Johann Wolfgang von Goethe enjoyed a happy Italian sojourn from 1786 to 1788, but complained of the noisy neighbours, is now a lovingly maintained museum. Exhibits include documents and some fascinating drawings and etchings. With advance permission, ardent fans can use the library full of first editions.

**VILLA MEDICI**                          PALAZZO

Map p352 (☑06 6 76 11; www.villamedici.it, in French & Italian; Viale Trinità dei Monti 1; ⊙open for events; Ⓜ Spagna) This striking Renaissance palace has been home to the French Academy since the early 19th century. It was built for Cardinal Ricci da Montepulciano in 1540, but Ferdinando dei Medici bought it in 1576 and it remained in Medici hands until Napoleon acquired it in 1801 and gave it to the French Academy. Its most famous resident was Galileo, who was imprisoned here between 1630 and 1633 during his trial for heresy, though Keith Richards and Anita Pallenberg also hung out here, dropping acid in the 1960s.

These days, the only way to get inside is to visit one of the regular art exhibitions or take a guided tour of the finely landscaped **gardens** (adult/reduced €9/7; ⊙guided tours in Italian & English).

## ⊙ Trevi Fountain to the Quirinale

**TREVI FOUNTAIN**                        MONUMENT

See p108.

**PALAZZO DEL QUIRINALE**                 PALAZZO

See p109.

**PIAZZA DEL QUIRINALE**                  PIAZZA

Map p352 (Ⓜ Barbarini)

A wonderful spot to enjoy a glowing Roman sunset, this piazza marks the summit of the Quirinale hill. The central **obelisk** was moved here from the Mausoleo di Augusto

---

⊙ TOP SIGHTS **GALLERIA NAZIONALE D'ARTE ANTICA – PALAZZO BARBERINI**

The sumptuous Palazzo Barberini is an architectural feast before you even consider the National Art Collection that it houses. Among the artworks are paintings by Caravaggio, Raphael, Fra Filippo Lippi and Holbein, to name a few.

The Palazzo Barberini was commissioned by Urban VIII to celebrate the Barberini family's rise to papal power. Many high-profile baroque architects worked on it, including Carlo Moderno and rivals Bernini and Borromini.

The palace houses part of the Galleria Nazionale d'Arte Antica. Besides works by Raphael, Caravaggio, Guido Reni, Bernini, Filippo Lippi, Holbein, Titian and Tintoretto, there is the mesmerising ceiling of the main salon, the *Triumph of Divine Providence* (1632–39) by Pietro da Cortona. Don't miss Hans Holbein's famous portrait of a portly Henry VIII (c 1540) and Filippo Lippi's luminous *Annunciazione e due devoti*. Caravaggio masterpieces include *St Francis in Meditation*, *Narcissus* (c 1571–1610), and the mesmerizingly horrific *Judith Beheading Holophernes* (c 1597–1600). Another must-see is Raphael's lovely *La Fornarina* (The Baker's Girl), a portrait of his mistress Margherita Luti.

**DON'T MISS...**

➡ Pietro da Cortona's painted ceiling

➡ Raphael's *La Fornarina*

➡ Works by Caravaggio

**PRACTICALITIES**

➡ Map p352

➡ ☑06 225 82 493

➡ www.galleria borghese.it

➡ Via delle Quattro Fontane 13

➡ adult/reduced €5/2.50

➡ ⊙9am-7.30pm Tue-Sun, ticket office closes 7pm

➡ Ⓜ Barberini

in 1786 and is flanked by 5.5m statues of **Castor** and **Pollux** reining in a couple of rearing horses.

If you're in the neighbourhood on a Sunday you can catch the weekly changing of the guard (6pm in summer, 4pm the rest of the year).

### GALLERIA COLONNA
GALLERY

See p115.

### CHIESA DI SANTA MARIA DELLA VITTORIA
CHURCH

Map p352 (☑06 482 61 90; Via XX Settembre 17; ⏱8.30am-noon & 3.30-6pm Mon-Sat, 3.30-6pm Sun; ⓂRepubblica) On a busy road junction, this modest church is an unlikely setting for one of the great works of European art – Bernini's extravagant and sexually charged *Santa Teresa traffita dall'amore di Dio* (Ecstasy of St Teresa). In the last chapel on the left, this daring sculpture depicts Teresa, engulfed in the folds of a flowing cloak, floating in ecstasy on a cloud while a teasing angel pierces her repeatedly with a golden arrow. Watching the whole scene from two side balconies are a number of figures, including Cardinal Federico Cornaro, for whom the chapel was built. It's a stunning work, bathed in soft natural light filtering through a concealed window. Go in the afternoon for the best effect.

### CHIESA DI SANT'ANDREA AL QUIRINALE
CHURCH

Map p352 (☑06 474 08 07; Via del Quirinale 29; ⏱8.30am-noon & 3.30-7pm Mon-Sat, 9am-noon & 4-7pm Sun; ⓠVia Nazionale) It's said that in his old age Bernini liked to come and enjoy the peace of this late-17th-century church, regarded by many as one of his greatest. Faced with severe space limitations, he managed to produce a sense of grandeur by designing an elliptical floor plan with a series of chapels opening onto the central area. The opulent interior, decorated with polychrome marble, stucco and gilding, was a favourite of Pope Alexander VII, who used it while in residence at the Palazzo del Quirinale.

### CHIESA DI SAN CARLO ALLE QUATTRO FONTANE
CHURCH

Map p352 (☑06 488 31 09; Via del Quirinale 23; ⏱10am-1pm & 3-6pm Mon-Fri, 10am-1pm Sat, noon-1pm Sun; ⓠVia Nazionale) It might not look it, with its filthy facade and unappealing location, but this tiny church is a

## ROME'S VERSAILLES

If Napoleon had had his way, the Palazzo del Quirinale would have been Rome's Versailles. Journalist and author Corrado Augias explains:

'Napoleon actually chose Rome as his second capital after Paris. He wanted Versailles at Paris and the Palazzo del Quirinale – incidentally, Rome's greatest and most beautiful palace – in Rome. He set artists and architects to prepare it for him and sent down furniture from Paris. In the end he never came and when he was defeated in 1815 the popes took the *palazzo* back for themselves.'

masterpiece of Roman baroque. It was Borromini's first church and bears all the hallmarks of his genius. The elegant curves of the facade, the play of convex and concave surfaces, the dome illuminated by hidden windows, all combine to transform a minuscule space into a light, airy interior.

The church, completed in 1641, stands at the road intersection known as the **Quattro Fontane**, after the late-16th-century fountains on its four corners, representing Fidelity, Strength and the Rivers Arno and Tiber.

### TIME ELEVATOR
CINEMA

Map p352 (☑06 977 46 243; www.time-elevator. it; Via dei Santissimi Apostoli 20; adult/reduced €12/9; ⏱10.30am-7.30pm; ⓠPiazza Venezia) Just off Via del Corso, the Time Elevator cinema is ideal for armchair sightseers. There are three programmes, but the one to see is *Time Elevator Rome*, a 45-minute trip through 3000 years of Roman history. Shows kick off every hour, and children and adults alike will love the panoramic screens, flight-simulator technology and surround-sound system. Note that children under five aren't admitted and anyone who suffers from motion sickness should probably give it a miss.

### BASILICA DEI SANTI APOSTOLI
CHURCH

Map p352 (☑06 69 95 71; Piazza dei Santissimi Apostoli; ⏱7am-noon & 4-7pm; ⓠVia IV Novembre) This much-altered 6th-century church is dedicated to the apostles James and Philip, whose relics are in the crypt. Its most obvious attraction is the portico with its Renaissance arches and the two-tier

**1**

**3**

RICHARD I'ANSON / LONELY PLANET IMAGES ©

# Rome at the Movies

Rome's local film industry took off in the 1950s, but the city has long served as an inspiration to filmmakers, while its films have helped cement the legend of Rome.

Most iconic are *Roman Holiday* and Federico Fellini's *La Dolce Vita* (The Sweet Life; 1960), starring Marcello Mastroianni, which saw Anita Ekberg splash into cinematic history via the Trevi Fountain.

More recently Rome has looked bewitchingly beautiful in Peter Greenaway's *Belly of an Architect* (1987) and Anthony Minghella's *The Talented Mr Ripley* (1999). The touching, atmospheric *Pranzo di Ferragosto* (Midsummer Lunch; 2008) is a portrait of a middle-aged man who is unable to join Rome's mass summer exodus, while Rome in its guise as political powerhouse may be seen in Paolo Sorrentino's brilliant *Il Divo* (The Master; 2008), about controversial politician Giulio Andreotti, starring Toni Servillo.

Characters bounced between locations in Dan Brown's *Angels & Demons* (2009) while the postcard-pretty *Eat, Pray, Love* (2010) stars Julia Roberts and various Italian stereotypes.

For a grittier perspective, there are the neorealist films of the 1940s and '50s, such as *Roma Citta Aperta* (Rome, Open City; 1945; Roberto Rossellini) and Paolo Pasolini's *Accattone* (The Scrounger; 1961).

TONY BURNS / LONELY PLANET IMAGES ©

### TOP 5 ROME MOVIES

- ➡ *Roman Holiday* (1953)
- ➡ *La Dolce Vita* (The Sweet Life; 1960)
- ➡ *Roma, Città Aperta* (Rome, Open City; 1945)
- ➡ *Pranzo di Ferragosto* (Midsummer Lunch; 2008)
- ➡ *Il Divo* (The Master; 2008)

#### Clockwise from top left

**1.** Bocca della Verità (p70) featured in *Roman Holiday* **2.** Via dei Condotti leading up to the Spanish Steps (p105) as seen in *The Talented Mr Ripley* **3.** Trevi Fountain (p108) used in *La Dolce Vita*

## SPAS IN ROME

The admission charge of €45 is a bargain when you consider that **Hotel De Russie Wellness Zone** Map p352 (☑06 328 88 820; www.hotelderussie.it; Via del Babuino 9; ☉7am-10pm; ⓜFlaminio), a glamorous and gorgeous day spa, is in one of Rome's best hotels, and factor in the remote possibility of bumping into Brad Pitt in the Turkish bath, sauna or gym. Treatments are also available, including shiatsu and deep-tissue massage; a 50-minute massage costs around €95.

facade topped by 13 towering figures. Inside, the flashy baroque interior was completed in 1714 by Carlo and Francesco Fontana. Highlights include the ceiling frescoes by Baciccia and Antonio Canova's grandiose tomb of Pope Clement XIV.

Surrounding the basilica are two imposing baroque *palazzi*: at the end of the square, **Palazzo Balestra**, which was given to James Stuart, the Old Pretender, in 1719 by Pope Clement XI, and opposite, **Palazzo Odelscalchi**, with its impressive Bernini façade.

**MUSEO DELLE CERE**                    MUSEUM
Map p352 (☑06 679 64 82; www.museodelle cereroma.com; Piazza dei Santissimi Apostoli 67; adult/reduced €8/6; ☉9.30am-12.30pm & 5-8pm; ☐Via IV Novembre) Rome's waxwork museum is said to have the world's third largest collection, which comprises more than 250 figures, ranging from Barak Obama to Snow White, footballer Francesco Totti and a whole cast of mostly recognisable popes, poets, politicians and murderers. You can also visit the laboratory where the waxworks are created.

# ☉ Piazza Barberini & Via Veneto

**PIAZZA BARBERINI**                    PIAZZA
Map p352 (ⓜBarberini) More a traffic thoroughfare than a place to linger, this noisy square is named after the Barberini family, one of Rome's great dynastic clans (see the boxed text, p90). In the centre, the Bernini-designed **Fontana del Tritone** (Fountain of the Triton) depicts the sea-god Triton blowing a stream of water from a conch while seated

in a large scallop shell supported by four dolphins. Bernini also crafted the **Fontana delle Api** (Fountain of the Bees) in the northeastern corner, again for the Barberini family, whose crest featured three bees in flight.

**GALLERIA NAZIONALE D'ARTE ANTICA – PALAZZO BARBERINI**    GALLERY
See p110.

**CHIESA DI SANTA MARIA DELLA CONCEZIONE**                    CHURCH
Map p352 (☑06 487 11 85; Via Vittorio Veneto 27; admission by donation; ☉9am-noon & 3-6pm Fri-Wed; ⓜBarberini) There's nothing special about this 17th-century church but dip into the **Capuchin cemetery** below and you'll be gobsmacked. Everything from the picture frames to the light fittings is made of human bones. Between 1528 and 1870 the resident Capuchin monks used the bones of 4000 of their departed brothers to create the mesmerising and macabre display. There's an arch crafted from hundreds of skulls, vertebrae used as fleurs-de-lys, and light fixtures made of femurs.

**VIA VITTORIO VENETO**                    STREET
Map p352 (ⓜBarberini) Curving up from Piazza Barberini to Villa Borghese, Via Vittorio Veneto is the spiritual home of *la dolce vita*. The atmosphere of Fellini's Rome has long gone, and the street today, while still impressive, is largely given over to tourism. Luxury hotels occupy many of the towering streetside *palazzi* while waistcoated waiters stand on the tree-lined pavement, tempting passers-by into their overpriced restaurants. The huge building on the right as you walk up is the US embassy.

**GAGOSIAN GALLERY**                    GALLERY
Map p352 (☑06 420 86 498; www.gagosian. com; Via Francesco Crispi 16; admission free; ☉10.30am-7pm Tue-Sat; ⓜBarberini) Since it opened in 2007, the Rome branch of Larry Gagosian's contemporary art empire has hosted the big names of modern art: Cy Twombly, Damien Hirst and Lawrence Weiner, to name a few. The gallery, which was designed by Roman architect Firouz Galdo and Englishman Caruso St John, offers 750 sq m of exhibition space in a stylishly converted 1920s bank, complete with a theatrical neoclassical colonnaded facade.

#  EATING

Rome's designer shopping district may be fashionista heaven, but it retains a neighbourhood feel, albeit a wealthy one. Lots of classy eateries are sandwiched between the boutiques.

You have to take care choosing a restaurant around the Trevi Fountain, as there are a lot of unexciting just-for-tourists restaurants. But some gems sparkle among the stones – follow this guide and you can't go wrong. There are some splendid restaurants around the presidential palace and parliament – Italian politicians are a discerning bunch when it comes to dining out.

## ✕ Piazza del Popolo & Around

**DAL BOLOGNESE**  TRADITIONAL ITALIAN €€€

Map p352 (📞06 361 14 26; Piazza del Popolo 1; meals €70; ⊘Tue-Sun, closed Aug; Ⓜ Flaminio) The moneyed and models mingle at this historically chic restaurant. Dine inside surrounded by wood panelling and exotic flowers, or outside, people-watching with views over Piazza del Popolo. As the name suggests, Emilia-Romagna dishes are the name of the game; everything is good, but try the tortellini in soup, tagliatelle with ragú, or the damn fine fillet steak.

**BABETTE**  ITALIAN €€€

Map p352 (📞06 321 15 59; Via Margutta 1; meals €55; ⊘closed Jan & Aug; Ⓜ Spagna or Flaminio; ✿) You're in for a feast at Babette's, which has a chic yet unpretentious brasserie-style interior of exposed brick walls and vintage painted signs. Food is delicious, with a sophisticated, creative, French twist (think *tortiglioni* with courgette and pistachio pesto), and the wine list is short but super. There's a daily buffet (€10 Tuesday to Friday, €25 weekends).

**EDY**  TRATTORIA €€

Map p352 (📞06 360 01 738; Vicolo del Babuino 4; meals €50; ⊘Mon-Sat; Ⓜ Spagna) This classy neighbourhood restaurant's high-ceilinged, intimate interior is peppered with paintings. Despite the tourist-central location, it caters to mainly Italian clientele, and food, such as *linguine al broccoletti,* is delicious. There are a few outside tables on the cobbled street.

## ◉ TOP SIGHTS
## GALLERIA COLONNA

The only part of Palazzo Colonna open to the public, this incredibly opulent gallery houses the Colonna family's small but stunning private art collection. The polished yellow columns represent the 'Colonna' (which means column) of the family name.

The only part of the palace open to the public is the purpose-built gallery (constructed by Antonio del Grande from 1654 to 1665). Its six rooms are crowned by fantastical ceiling frescoes, all dedicated to Marcantonio Colonna, the family's greatest ancestor, who defeated the Turks at the naval Battle of Lepanto in 1571. Works by Giovanni Coli and Filippo Gherardi in the Great Hall, Sebastiano Ricci in the Landscapes Room and Giuseppe Bartolomeo Chiari in the Throne Room all commemorate his efforts. Note also the cannonball lodged in the gallery's marble stairs, a vivid reminder of the 1849 siege of Rome.

The art on display features a fine array of 16th- to 18th- century paintings, the highlight of which is Annibale *Carracci's vivid Mangiafagioli* (The Bean Eater).

### DON'T MISS...

➡ Fantastic ceiling frescoes

➡ Annibale Carracci's *The Bean Eater*

### PRACTICALITIES

➡ Map p352

➡ 📞06 225 82 493

➡ www.galleria colonna.it

➡ Via della Pilotta 17

➡ adult/reduced €10/8

➡ ⊘9am-1.15pm Sat, daily private tours on request, closed Aug

➡ 🚌Via IV Novembre

START **PINCIO GARDENS**
END **KEATS-SHELLEY HOUSE**
DISTANCE **1KM**
DURATION **TWO HOURS**

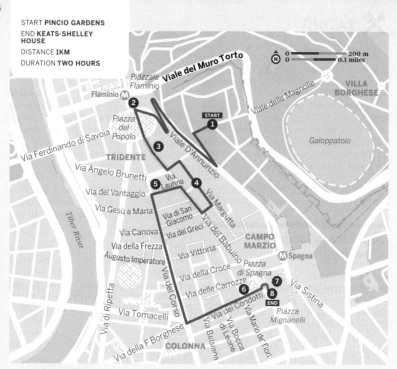

## TRIDENTE, TREVI & THE QUIRINALE NEIGHBOURHOOD WALK

Neighbourhood Walk
## Literary Footsteps

This walk explores the literary haunts, both real and fictional, which speckle the lovely Tridente district.

Begin your walk in ❶ **Pincio Gardens**, where Henry James' Daisy Miller walked with Winterborne, attracting attention for her prettiness. Then make your way downhill to Piazza del Popolo, and visit the church of ❷ **Santa Maria del Popolo**. Dan Brown's *Da Vinci Code* made use of this stunning church as an important keystone in its convoluted plot, making much of the skeleton mosaic on the floor.

From here it's merely a few steps to ❸ **Hotel de Russie**, favoured by the artistic avant garde in the early 20th century. Jean Cocteau stayed here with Picasso, and wrote a letter home in which he described plucking oranges from outside his window.

Running parallel to Via Babuino is ❹ **Via Margutta**. Famous for its artistic and cinematic connections, this picturesque cobbled street was where Truman

Capote came and settled when he visited Rome, writing his short story *Lola* about a raven who lived with him at his apartment.

Next make your way to Via del Corso, to see the ❺ **Casa di Goethe**. Like many literary big guns in the 18th century, Goethe spent time in Rome, having a whale of a time at this apartment from 1786 to 1788. Walk further along the Via del Corso, you can turn left up into Via Condotti, stopping for some refreshment at ❻ **Caffè Greco**, a former haunt of Casanova, Goethe, Keats, Byron and Shelley. Leaving here, you're almost at the ❼ **Spanish Steps**, which Dickens described in his *Pictures from Italy* with some amusement, seeing the characterful artists' models waiting to be hired here. Just south of the steps, overlooking them, is the apartments where Keats died of TB, aged just 25. The ❽ **Keats-Shelley House** is now a fascinating small museum and the ideal place to end your tour.

## TATI' AL 28 INTERNATIONAL €€

Map p352 (☑06 681 342 21; meals €45; ⊙8am-2am; ☐Piazza Augusto Imperatore) Also a 'Gusto (this page) concern, chic Tati is a cafe-bar and restaurant with a chic white-and-black interior and gleaming white-tableclothed tables outside, Tati' al 28 offers a range of cuisines, including Indian dishes and hamburgers. The midday buffet (€10) is a steal, as is the weekend unlimited brunch (€18); there's also aperitivo.

## 'GUSTO OSTERIA WINE BAR €€

Map p352 (☑06 322 62 73; Via della Frezza; meals €45; ☐Piazza Augusto Imperatore) Part of the 'Gusto (below) complex, della Frezza is trendy yet simple, with white-tiled, photo-covered walls. It's part *osteria*, part *enoteca*. As well as selections of meat or cheese, you can order brasserie-style mains such as braised beef and mash, plus lighter meals such as pasta, omelettes and salads.

## BUCCONE WINE BAR €

Map p352 (☑06 36 12 154; Via di Ripetta 19; meals €20; ⊙lunch Mon-Sat, dinner Fri & Sat; Ⓜ Flaminio) Step through the door, under the faded gilt and mirrored sign, and you'll feel as though you've gone back in time. Once a coach house, then a tavern, in the 1960s this building became Buccone, furnished with 19th-century antiques and lined with around a thousand Italian wines as well as a good selection of international tipples. It's perfect for a light meal, with salads, cured meats, cheeses, *torta* (cakes) etc.

## BUCA DI RIPETTA TRADITIONAL ITALIAN €€

Map p352 (☑06 321 93 91; Via di Ripetta 36; meals €50; Ⓜ Flaminio) Popular with actors and directors from the district, who know a good thing when they see it, this value-for-money foodie destination offers robust Roman cuisine. Try the *zuppa rustica con crostini do pane aromatizzati* (country-style soup with rosemary-scented bread) or the *matolino do latte al forno alle erbe con patate* (baked suckling pork with potatoes) and you'll be fuelled either for more sightseeing or for a lie down.

## 'GUSTO PIZZERIA €

Map p352 (☑06 322 62 73; Piazza Augusto Imperatore 9; pizza €6-9.50; ☐Piazza Augusto Imperatore) This mould-breaking warehouse-style gastronomic complex, all exposed brick-work and industrial chic, is still buzzing after all these years. It's a great place to sit on the terrace and eat Neapolitan-style pizzas (rather than the upmarket restaurant fare, which receives mixed reports). There's live music on Tuesday and Thursday evenings.

## MARGUTTA RISTORANTE VEGETARIAN €€

Map p352 (☑06 678 60 33; Via Margutta 118; meals €50; Ⓜ Spagna or Flaminio; ☑) Vegetarian restaurants in Rome are rarer than parking spaces, and this airy art gallery–restaurant is an unusually chic way to eat your greens. Most dishes are excellent, with offerings such as artichoke hearts with potato cubes and smoked provolone cheese. There's an impressive wine list and staff are friendly and bilingual. Best value is the Saturday/Sunday buffet brunch (€15/25). It also offers a four-course vegan menu (€32).

# ✖ West of Via del Corso

## ACHILLI ENOTECA
## AL PARLAMENTO ROMAN €€€

Map p352 (☑06 687 3446; Via dei Prefetti 15; meals €75; ⊙Tue-Sat, closed Aug; Ⓜ Spagna) This new, intimate temple of gastronomy, part of a historic wine bar, specialises in Roman cuisine such as *amatriciana* (pasta with tomato and pancetta sauce), *cacio e pepe* (pasta with Pecorino cheese and black pepper) and carbonara, as well as elegant combinations of seasonal ingredients such as pumpkin and truffles. The wine list is, unsurprisingly, excellent.

# ✖ Piazza di Spagna & Around

## PALATIUM WINE BAR €€

Map p352 (☑06 692 02 132; Via Frattina 94; meals €40; ⊙11am-11pm Mon-Sat, closed Aug; ☐Via del Corso) Conceived as a showcase of Lazio's bounty, this sleek wine barclose to the Spanish Steps serves excellent local specialities, such as *porchetta* (pork roasted with herbs), artisan cheese and delicious salami, as well as an impressive array of Lazio wines (try lesser-known drops such as Aleatico). *Aperitivo* is a good bet too.

## THE ARTISTS' STREET

Via Margutta has long been associated with art and artists, and today it is still lined with antique shops and art galleries.

'The street's reputation goes back to the 16th century, when it was declared a tax-free zone for artists,' explains Valentina Moncada, owner of the eponymous **gallery** at Via Margutta 54.

'If you were an artist and a resident, you paid no taxes, so artists came from all over Europe. Also there was Villa Medici nearby and all the winners of the Prix de Rome (a prestigious French art scholarship) would often come down here.'

By the late 1800s, the studio that Valentina's family had established in the mid-19th century had grown into a popular meeting point for visiting artists, writers and musicians.

'A string of important musicians visited, including all the Italian opera greats – Puccini, Verdi, Mascagni – as well as the composers Wagner, Liszt and Debussy. The Italian futurists also held their first meetings here and in 1917 Picasso worked here; he met his wife, Olga, in the courtyard of number 54.'

Of the street's more recent residents, the most famous is film director Federico Fellini, who lived at No 110 with his wife Giulietta Masina until his death in 1993.

### NINO
TUSCAN €€

Map p352 (⟳06 679 5676; Via Borgognona 11; meals €60; ⊙lunch & dinner Mon-Sat; MSpagna) With a look of wrought-iron chandeliers, polished dark wood and white tablecloths, which is surely pretty unchanged since it opened in 1934, Nino is enduringly popular with the rich and famous. Waiters can be brusque if you're not on the A-list, but the food is good hearty fare, including memorable steaks and Tuscan bean soup.

### IL PALAZZETTO
CREATIVE ITALIAN €€€

Map p352 (⟳06 699 341 000; Via del Bottino 8; meals €75; ⊙Tue-Sun, closed Aug; MSpagna) Despite its sumptuous deep-red interior, this restaurant's spangling jewel is the sun-trap shaded terrace hidden at the top of the Spanish Steps. It's perfect for a glass of *prosecco* (sparkling wine) and a salad or pasta dish on a sunny day or, for more formal dining, there is a wow-factor tasting menu. The *palazzo* also houses the wine academy, and it's also open as a wine bar from 4pm.

### FIASCHETTERIA BELTRAMME
TRATTORIA €€

Map p352 (Via della Croce 39; meals €45; MSpagna) With a tiny dark interior whose walls are covered in paintings and sketches right up to the high ceilings, Fiaschetteria (meaning 'wine-sellers') is a discreet, intimate, stuck-in-time place with a short menu and no telephone. Expect fashionistas with appetites digging into traditional Roman dishes (*pasta e ceci* and so on).

### PASTICCIO
FAST FOOD €

Map p352 (Via della Croce; pasta dish €4; ⊙1-3pm Mon-Sat; MSpagna) A great find in this pricey 'hood. Pasticcio is a pasta shop that serves up around two choices of pasta at lunch time. It's fast food, Italian style – great fresh pasta with tasty sauces.

### OSTERIA MARGUTTA
TRATTORIA €€€

Map p352 (⟳06 323 10 25; Via Margutta 82; meals €65; MSpagna) Theatrical Osteria Margutta is colourful inside and out: inside combines blue glass, rich reds and fringed lampshades, while outside flowers and ivy cover the quaint entrance (snap up a terrace table in summer). Plaques on the chairs testify to the famous thespian bums they have supported. The menu combines classic and regional dishes, with fish served fresh on Tuesday, Friday and Saturday; desserts are homemade, and there's a top wine list.

### OTELLO ALLA CONCORDIA
TRATTORIA €€

Map p352 (⟳06 679 11 78; Via della Croce 81; meals €40; ⊙lunch & dinner Mon-Sat; MSpagna) A perennial favourite with both tourists and locals, Otello is a haven near the Spanish Steps. Outside dining is in the vine-covered courtyard of an 18th-century *palazzo*, where, if you're lucky, you can dine in the shadow of the wisteria-covered pergola.

### ANTICA ENOTECA
WINE BAR €€

Map p352 (⟳06 679 08 96; Via della Croce 76b; meals €35; ⊙11am-1am; MSpagna) Near the Spanish Steps, locals and tourists alike prop up the 19th-century wooden bar, or sit at outside tables or those in the back room, sampling wines by the glass, snacking on antipasti, and ordering well-priced soul food such as pasta or polenta.

### GINA
CAFE €

Map p352 (☑06 678 02 51; Via San Sebastianello 7a; snacks €7-14; ☺11am-8pm; Ⓜ Spagna) Around the corner from the Spanish Steps, this is an ideal place to drop once you've shopped. Comfy white seats are strewn with powder-blue cushions, and it gets packed by a Prada-clad crowd, gossiping and flirting over sophisticated salads and perfect *panini*. You can also order a €40 picnic-for-two to take up to Villa Borghese.

## ✕ Trevi Fountain to the Quirinale

### DA MICHELE
PIZZA AL TAGLIO €

Map p352 (☑349 252 53 47; Via dell'Umiltà 31; pizza slices from €2; ☺8am-5pm Mon-Fri, to 8pm summer; ☐ Via del Corso) A handy address in Spagna district: buy your fresh, light and crispy *pizza al taglio*, and you'll have a delicious fast lunch.

### LE TAMERICI
SEAFOOD €€€

Map p352 (☑06 692 00 700; Vicolo Scavolino 79; meals €70; ☺Mon-Sat, closed Aug; ☐ Via del Tritone) Tucked-away Le Tamerici impresses with its wine list and range of *digestivi*, as well as with its classy food, including light-as-air homemade pasta. The two intimate rooms with bleached-wood beamed ceilings are a great place to settle for an epicurean lunch.

### VINERIA CHIANTI
WINE BAR €€

Map p352 (☑06 678 75 50; Via del Lavatore 81-82; meals €35; ☐ Via del Tritone) This pretty ivy-clad wine bar is bottle-lined inside, with watch-the-world-go-by streetside seating in summer. Cuisine is Tuscan, so the beef is particularly good, but it also serves up imaginative salads, and pizza in the evenings.

### AL PRESIDENTE
SEAFOOD €€€

Map p352 (☑06 679 73 42; Via Arcione 95; meals €75; ☺Tue-Sun, closed Jan & Aug; ☐ Via del Tritone) Al Presidente is a discreet, greenery-shrouded place, under the walls of the presidential palace and which also has outdoor seating in summer. Its sophisticated air is matched by the seafood-centred menu. Innovative dishes include *baccalà* whisked into polenta and grilled, and *trippa di coda di rospo* (tripe of angler-fish tail), but it also does a lipsmacking *pasta all'amatriciana*.

### ANTICO FORNO
FAST FOOD €

Map p352 (☑06 679 28 66; Via delle Muratte 8; panini €3; ☺7am-9pm; ☐ Via del Tritone) A mini-supermarket opposite the Trevi Fountain, this busy place has a well-stocked deli counter where you can choose a filling for your freshly baked *panino* or *pizza bianca*, plus an impressive selection of focaccia and pizza.

---

### MIRACULOUS MADONNAS

Overlooking Vicolo delle Bollette, a tiny lane near the Trevi Fountain, there's a small, simple painting of the Virgin Mary. This is the *Madonna della Pietà,* one of the most famous of Rome's *madonnelle* (small madonnas). There are estimated to be around 730 of these roadside madonnas in Rome's historic centre, most placed on street corners or outside historic *palazzi*. Many were added in the 16th and 17th centuries, but their origins date to pagan times when votive wall shrines were set up at street corners to honour the Lares, household spirits believed to protect passers-by. When Christianity emerged in the 4th century AD, these shrines were simply rededicated to the religion's new icons.

The subject of much popular devotion, they are shrouded in myth. The most famous legend dates to 1796 when news of a French invasion is said to have caused 36 *madonnelle,* including the *Madonna della Pietà,* to move their eyes and some even to cry. A papal commission set up to investigate subsequently declared 26 madonnas to be officially miraculous.

As well as food for the soul, the madonnas also provided a valuable public service. Until street lamps were introduced in the 19th century, the candles and lamps that lit up the images were the city's only source of street lighting.

## ✖ Piazza Barberini & Via Veneto

**COLLINE EMILIANE**  EMILIA-ROMAGNA €€

Map p352 (☑06 481 75 38; Via degli Avignonesi 22; meals €45; ☺Tue-Sat, Sun lunch, closed Aug; Ⓜ Barberini) This welcoming, tucked-away restaurant just off Piazza Barberini flies the flag for Emilia-Romagna, the well-fed Italian province that has given Parmesan, balsamic vinegar, bolognese sauce and Parma ham to the world. On offer here are delicious meats, homemade pasta, rich *ragùs,* and desserts worthy of a moment's silence.

**SAN CRISPINO**  ICECREAM €

Map p352 (☑06 679 39 24; Via della Panetteria 42; ☺midday-12.30pm Sun-Thu, midday-1.30am Fri & Sat) Possibly the best gelato in Rome. What? You want a cone? The delicate, strictly natural and seasonal flavours are served only in tubs (cones would detract from the taste).

**SANTOPADRE**  ROMAN €€

Map p352 (☑06 474 54 05; Via Collina 18; meals €45; ☺dinner Mon-Sat; Ⓜ Termini) Plastered with photos of horses and jockeys, this little neighbourhood restaurant is a local favourite that's been cooking up Roman faves such as *pasta alla gricia* (pasta with pancetta and onion), *involtini* (rolls of finely sliced beef) and *trippa alla Romana* (tripe Roman-style) since 1946. The antipasti is delicious – think delicate marinated vegetables and melt-in-the-mouth meatballs.

**IL CARUSO**  ICECREAM €

Map p352 (Via Collina 15; ☺11am-midnight; Ⓜ Termini) Spot Il Caruso by the gelato-licking hordes outside. This artisanal geletaria only does a few, strictly seasonal, flavours but these it produces to perfection. Try the incredibly creamy pistachio.

#  DRINKING

## 🍷 Piazza del Popolo & Around

**SALOTTO LOCARNO**  BAR

Map p352 (Via della Penna 22; ☺noon-3am; Ⓜ Flaminio) Sister to city-centre venue Salotto 42 and summer-only Salotto Giani-

---

### BERNINI VS BORROMINI

Born within a year of each other, the two giants of Roman baroque hated each other with a vengeance. Gian Lorenzo Bernini (1598-1680), suave, self-confident and politically adept, was the polar opposite of his great rival Francesco Borromini (1599–1677), a solitary and peculiar man who often argued with clients and once had a man beaten half to death.

Their paths first crossed at St Peter's Basilica. Borromini, who had been working as an assistant to Carlo Maderno, a distant relative and the basilica's lead architect, was furious when Bernini was appointed to take over the project on Maderno's death. Nevertheless he stayed on as Bernini's chief assistant and actually contributed to the design of the baldachin – a work for which Bernini took full public credit. To make matters worse, Bernini was later appointed chief architect on Palazzo Barberini, again in the wake of Maderno, and again to Borromini's disgust.

Over the course of the next 45 years, the two geniuses competed for commissions and public acclaim. Bernini flourished under the Barberini pope Urban VIII (r 1623–44) and Borromini under his Pamphilj successor Innocent X (r 1644–1655), but all the while their loathing simmered. Borromini accused Bernini of profiting from his (Borromini's) talents while Bernini claimed that Borromini 'had been sent to destroy architecture'. Certainly, both had very different views on architecture: for Bernini it was all about portraying an experience to elicit an emotional response, while Borromini favoured a more geometrical approach, manipulating classical forms to create dynamic, vibrant spaces.

Of the two, Bernini is generally reckoned to have had the better of the rivalry. His genius was rarely questioned and when he died he was widely regarded as one of Europe's greatest artists. Borromini, on the other hand, struggled to win popular and critical support and after a life of depression committed suicide in 1677.

colo,–this attracts a similar mix of fashionistas and stylish Romans. As part of the art deco Hotel Locarno, it's got a lovely Agatha Christie-era feel, and a greenery-shaded outdoor terrace in summer. Cocktails cost a chi-chi €16, proving that you do have to suffer for beauty.

### STRAVINKIJ BAR – HOTEL DE RUSSIE    BAR
Map p352 (☎06 328 88 70; Via del Babuino 9; ⓂFlaminio) Can't afford to stay at the celeb-magnet Hotel de Russie? Then splash out on a drink at its enchanting bar, set in the courtyard, with sunshaded tables overlooked by terraced gardens. Impossibly romantic in the best *dolce vita* style, it's perfect for a cocktail and some posh snacks.

### ROSATI    CAFE
Map p352 (☎06 322 58 59; Piazza del Popolo 5; Ⓞ7.30am-11.30pm; ⓂFlaminio) Rosati, overlooking the vast disc of Piazza del Popolo, was once the hang-out of the left-wing chattering classes. Authors Italo Calvino and Alberto Moravia used to drink here while their right-wing counterparts went to the **Canova** (Map p352; ☎06 361 22 31; Piazza del Popolo 16; Ⓝ8am-midnight; ✹) over the square. Today tourists are the main clientele, and the views are as good as ever.

## 🍷 Piazza Di Spagna & Around

### CAFFÈ GRECO    CAFE
Map p352 (☎06 679 17 00; Via dei Condotti 86; Ⓝ9am-8pm; ⓂSpagna) Caffè Greco opened in 1760 and retains the look: penguin waiters, red flock and gilt mirrors. Casanova, Goethe, Wagner, Keats, Byron, Shelley and Baudelaire were all regulars. Now there are fewer artists and lovers and more shoppers and tourists. Prices reflect this, unless you do as the locals do and have a drink at the bar.

### CANOVA TADOLINI    CAFE
Map p352 (☎06 321 10 702; Via del Babuino 150a/b; Ⓝ9am-10.30pm Mon-Sat; ⓂSpagna) In 1818 sculptor Canova signed a contract for this studio that agreed it would be forever preserved for sculpture. The place is still stuffed with statues, and it's a unique experience to sit among the great maquettes and sup an upmarket tea or knock back some wine and snacks.

### CIAMPINI 2    CAFE
Map p352 (☎06 681 35 108; Viale Trinità dei Monti; Ⓝ8am-9pm May-Oct; ⓂSpagna) Hidden away a short walk from the top of the Spanish Steps towards the Pincio, this graceful cafe has a garden-party vibe, with green wooden latticework surrounding the outside tables. There are lovely views over the backstreets behind Spagna, and the ice cream is renowned (particularly the truffle).

## 🍷 Piazza Barberini & Via Veneto

### MOMA    CAFE
Map p352 (☎06 420 11 798; Via di San Basilio; Ⓝ7am-11pm Mon-Sat, closed Aug; ⓂBarberini) *Molto* trendy: this cafe-restaurant is a find. It's sleekly sexy and popular with workers from nearby offices. There's a small stand-up cafe downstairs, with a nice little deck outside where you can linger longer over coffee and delicious *dolcetti*. Upstairs is a *cucina creativa* (creative cuisine) restaurant (meals €65).

## ☆ ENTERTAINMENT

### GREGORY'S    LIVE MUSIC
Map p352 (☎06 679 63 86; www.gregorysjazz.com; Via Gregoriana 54d; Ⓝ7pm-2am Tue-Sun Sep-Jun; ⓂBarberini/Spagna) If it were a voice tone, it'd be husky: unwind in the downstairs bar then unwind some more on squashy sofas upstairs to some slinky live jazz, with quality local performers. Gregory's is a popular hang-out for local musicians.

### TEATRO QUIRINO    THEATRE
Map p352 (☎06 679 45 85; www.teatroquirino.it, in Italian; Via delle Vergini 7; ⒹVia del Tritone) Within splashing distance of the Trevi Fountain, this grand 19th-century theatre produces the odd new work and a stream of well-known classics – expect to see works (in Italian) by Arthur Miller, Tennessee Williams, Shakespeare, Seneca and Luigi Pirandello.

### TEATRO SISTINA    THEATRE
Map p352 (☎06 420 07 11; www.ilsistina.com, in Italian; Via Sistina 129; ⓂBarberini) Big-budget theatre spectaculars, musicals and comic star turns are the staples of the Sistina's ever-conservative, ever-popular repertoire.

# 🛍 SHOPPING

## 🛍 Piazza del Popolo & Around

### VERTECCHI
ART

Map p352 (🖉Via della Croce 70; ⊘3.30am-7.30pm Mon, 10am-7.30pm Tue-Sat; Ⓜ Spagna) Ideal for last-minute gift buying, this large paperware and art shop has beautiful printed paper, and an amazing choice of notebooks, art stuff and trinkets.

### LUCIA ODESCALCHI
JEWELLERY

Map p352 (🖉06 699 25506; Palazzo Odescalchi, Piazza Santissimi Apostoli 81; Ⓜ Spagna) If you're looking for a unique piece of statement jewellery that will make an outfit, this is the place to head. Housed in the evocative archives of the family palazzo, the avant-garde pieces often have an almost medieval beauty, and run from incredible polished steel and chain mail to pieces created out of pearls and fossils. Beautiful. Prices start at around €140.

### DANIELLE
SHOES

Map p352 (🖉06 6792467; Via Frattina 85a; Ⓜ Spagna) If you're female and in need of an Italian shoe fix, this is an essential stop on your itinerary, for both classic and fashionable styles – foxy heels, boots and ballet pumps – made in soft leather, in myriad colours and at extremely reasonable prices.

### ARMANDO RIODA
ARTISANAL

Map p352 (🖉06 6992 4406; Via Belsiana 90; Ⓜ Spagna) Looking longingly at the accessory shops of Via Condotti, but can't afford an exquisitely made, big-name handbag? Climb the well-worn stairs to this workshop, choose from a swatch of the softest leathers, and you can shortly be the proud owner of a handmade, designer-style bag, wallet, belt or briefcase. If you have a bag specially made, you're looking at around €200 to €250.

### TAD
DEPARTMENT STORE

Map p352 (🖉06 326 95 131; Via del Babuino 155a; Ⓜ Flaminio/Spagna) TAD is a cutting-edge conceptual department store that sells an entire lifestyle. Here you can buy clothes by Chloë, Balenciaga and more, have a haircut, buy scent and flowers, and furnish your apartment with wooden daybeds and Perspex dining chairs. Don't forget to pick up soundtracks to your perfect life from the CD rack. The serene courtyard cafe is the perfect ladies-who-lunch pitstop, offering appropriately stylish Italian-Asian morsels.

### MYCUPOFTEA
ARTISANAL

Map p352 (🖉06 3265 1061; Via del Babuino 61; Ⓜ Spagna) This is a creative open-plan space,

---

**LOCAL KNOWLEDGE**

### UNIQUE SHOPPING IN ROME

Rome born and bred, Barbara Lessona, an Italian contessa who works as a facilitator and personal shopper in Rome, has a passion for finding the city's unique and special places, and tells us a few of her favourites.

➡ **Mycupoftea** (p122) This is a kind of gallery – a window for unknown designers. The good thing about this shop is that there are always two to three exhibitors at any one time, so you can always find something fun, from dresses, to purses, to jewellery.

➡ **Lucia Odescalchi** (p122) This designer creates amazing jewellery, created out of Perspex, metal, agate, platinum. It's all made in Italy and remarkably unique, and her showroom is housed in the beautiful Palazzo Odelscalchi.

➡ **Vignano** (p125) This is a really cool men's store, with men's coats of extreme quality – such as 'cooked wool' Casentino coats from Tuscany, every imaginable model of hat, fedoras, panamas and so on. It's a wonderful, typical Roman place – he opens when he feels like it! If you want a touch of gentlemen's style, this is where to come.

➡ **Campo Marzio** (p123) This is a very sophisticated perfume store, with beautiful artisanal, specialist perfumes. You can also buy perfumed flowers and candles that make great presents.

➡ **Eleonora** (p124) From the outside, this looks like it could be quite trashy, but in reality it's got a great collection, with Missoni, Fendi, Dolce & Gabbana and hard-to-find Giambattista Valli – it's the trendiest spot in Tridente.

run by women, that showcases the work of two or three designers or artists at a time, selling interesting, individual and afford-able jewellery, art and design.

**BORSALINO** ACCESSORIES

Map p352 (✒06 326 50 838; Piazza del Popolo 20; MFlaminio) Italians really cut a dash in a hat, but don't fret, you can learn. Borsalino is *the* Italian hatmaker, favoured by 1920s criminal Al Capone, Japanese Emperor Hirohito and Humphrey Bogart. Think fedoras, pork-pie-styles, felt cloches and woven straw caps.

**ALINARI** ANTIQUES, BOOKSTORE

Map p352 (✒06 679 29 23; Via Alibert 16; MSpagna) This is the oldest photographic business in the world. The Florentine Ali-nari brothers founded their enterprise in 1852, and produced more than a million plate-glass negatives in their lifetimes. At their Rome shop you can buy beautiful prints of their work depicting the city in the 19th century, as well as some meaty coffee-table books on photography.

**CAMPO MARZIO** PERFUME

Map p352 (✒06 9797739; Via Vittoria 52; MSpagna) A temple-like boutique that's more like a gallery than a perfumerie, this place sells selective, artisanal perfumery, such as Tauer's Pentachords, each of which comprises five notes.

**ANIMALIER E OLTRE** ANTIQUES

Map p352 (✒06 320 82 82; Via Margutta 47; MSpagna) This basement appears to be full of the cast-offs of an eccentric, aristocratic family, with bric-a-brac, curios, antiques and unique furniture. Wrought-iron fur-niture and leather sofas sit alongside a selection of animal-shaped antiques that includes reproductions of 19th-century French *animalier* sculptures.

**IL MARE** BOOKSTORE

Map p352 (✒06 361 20 91; Via di Ripetta 239; MFlaminio) Ahoy there. Specialising in every-thing *mare* (sea) related, this friendly book-shop has maritime books in Italian, English and French, nautical charts, binoculars, pirate flags, model yachts, posters, Lonely Planet guidebooks, videos and CD-ROMs.

**ARTEMIDE** HOMEWARES

Map p352 (✒06 360 01 802; Via Margutta 107; MFlaminio) For lamps that light up the world of interior design, head to Artemide. Wheth-

er moonlike white globes, or lamps that are so minimalist you hardly notice them till you clock the price tag, this is light as art.

**FLOS** HOMEWARES

Map p352 (✒06 320 76 31; Via del Babuino 84-85; MSpagna) Since 1962, light design house Flos has been responsible for a firmament of de-sign classics, including Marc Newson's Hel-ice aluminium floor lamp and many Philippe Starck designs. The look varies from primary-coloured plastic to steely and sleek.

# 🏛 West of Via Del Corso

**TEICHNER** FOOD

Map p352 (✒06 687 14 49; Piazza San Lorenzo in Lucina; 🚊Via del Corso) This is one of Rome's many temples to food, so wander in, inhale the delicious scents and select from cheese, hams, pickles, pestos and so on. There are also a select few ready dishes, such as au-bergine (eggplant) *parmigiana*.

**ENOTECA AL PARLAMENTO** WINE

Map p352 (✒06 687 34 46; Via dei Prefetti 15; 🚊Via del Corso) A delectable mingling of scents – wine, chocolate, fine meats and cheeses – greets you as you enter this state-ly, old-fashioned shop, an empire of taste, walled with wine. Try some caviar tartines, sample the wines, consult the helpful staff, and even dine at the restaurant (see p117).

**LAVORI ARTIGIANI**
**ROMANI (LAR)** HOMEWARES

Map p352 (✒06 687 81 75; Via del Leoncino 29; ☺9am-7pm Mon-Fri, 9am-1pm Sat; 🚊Via del Corso) Lamps have been created here by this artisan family business since 1938, in materials such as wood, brass and parch-ment. Their creations look like vintage finds – from great white cylinders to metal-lic cubist sculptures. If you want to design a lamp, these are the people to talk to.

**MERCATO DELLE STAMPE** MARKET

Map p352 (Largo della Fontanella di Borghese; ☺7am-1pm Mon-Sat; 🚊Piazza Augusto Impera-tore) The Mercato delle Stampe (Print Mar-ket) is well worth a look if you're a fan of vintage books and old prints. Squirrel through the permanent stalls and among the tired posters and dusty back editions, and you might turn up some interesting music scores, architectural engravings or chromolithographs of Rome.

### L'OLFATTORIO
PERFUME

Map p352 (✆06 361 23 25; Via di Ripetta 34; ⊙10.30am-1.30pm & 2.30-7.30pm Tue-Sat; Ⓜ Flaminio) Like a bar, but with perfume instead of drinks, with scents made by names such as Artisan Parfumeur, Diptyque, Les Parfums de Rosine and Coudray. The bartender will guide you through different combinations of scents to work out your ideal fragrance. Exclusive handmade French perfumes are available to buy. Smellings are free but you should book ahead.

### TOD'S
SHOES

Map p352 (✆06 682 10 066; Via della Fontanella di Borghese 56; 🚌 Via del Corso) The trademark of Tod's is its rubber-studded loafers (the idea was to reduce those pesky driving scuffs), perfect weekend footwear for kicking back at your country estate.

## 🏛 Piazza di Spagna & Around

### BOTTEGA DI MARMORARO
ARTISANAL

Map p352 (Via Margutta 53b; Ⓜ Flaminio) A particularly charismatic hole-in-the-wall shop, lined with marble carvings, where you can get marble tablets engraved with any inscription you like (€15). Peer inside at lunchtime and you might see the *marmoraro* cooking a pot of tripe for his lunch on the open log fire.

### ARTIGIANI PELLETTIERI – MARCO PELLE/ DI CLEMENTE
ARTISANAL

Map p352 (✆06 361 34 02; Via Vittoria 15, int 2; Ⓜ Spagna) Ring the bell at this unassuming doorway and hurry up flights of stairs to a family-run leather workshop that feels like it hasn't changed for decades. The elderly artisans create belts (€70 to €100), watch straps (€40 to €90), bags, picture frames, travel cases and other such elegant stuff. You can take along a buckle or watch, to which you want a belt or strap fitted.

### AVC BY ADRIANA V CAMPANILE
SHOES

Map p352 (✆06 699 22 355; Piazza di Spagna 88; Ⓜ Spagna) Designer Campanile started with a small shop in Parioli, and nowadays her heels stalk the city. You can see why: AVC shoes and boots are covetably wearable, stunningly chic and practical – and not insanely priced.

### ELEONORA
CLOTHING

Map p352 (✆06 6919 0554; Via del Babuino 97; ⊙10am-7.30pm Mon-Sat, 11am-7.30pm Sun;

Ⓜ Spagna) The brash exterior disguises a tardis of a shop; venture inside this Tridente hotspot and you'll find that its finger is on the pulse, with a very classy selection of designers, including Dolce & Gabbana, Fendi, Missoni, Marc Jacobs and Sergio Rossi.

### FURLA
ACCESSORIES

Map p352 (✆06 692 00 363; Piazza di Spagna 22; Ⓜ Spagna) Simple, good-quality bags in soft leather and a brilliant array of colours is why the handbagging hordes keep flocking to Furla, where all sorts of accessories, from sunglasses to shoes, are made. There are many other branches dotted all over Rome.

### SERMONETA
ACCESSORIES

Map p352 (✆06 679 19 60; Piazza di Spagna 61; Ⓜ Spagna) Buying leather gloves in Rome is a rite of passage for some, and its most famous glove-seller is the place to do it. Choose from a kaleidoscopic range of quality leather and suede gloves lined with silk and cashmere. An expert assistant will size up your hand in a glance. Just don't expect them to smile.

### ANGLO-AMERICAN BOOKSHOP
BOOKSTORE

Map p352 (✆06 679 52 22; Via della Vite 102; Ⓜ Spagna) Particularly good for university reference books, the Anglo-American is well stocked and well known. It has an excellent range of literature, travel guides, children's books and maps, and if it hasn't got a book you want, you can order it.

### LION BOOKSHOP
BOOKSTORE

Map p352 (✆06 326 54 007; Via dei Greci 33-36; Ⓜ Spagna) This fabulous, long-running English bookshop has English-speaking staff and is well stocked with classics, travel guides, the latest fiction and children's books.

### FENDI
CLOTHING

Map p352 (✆06 69 66 61; Largo Goldoni 420; Ⓜ Spagna) A temple to subtly blinging accessories, this multi-storey art deco building is the Fendi mothership. The look is old-style glamour, with beauty and distinction. Fendi is famous for fur and leather products.

### GALLO
CLOTHING

Map p352 (✆06 360 02 174; Via Vittoria 63; Ⓜ Spagna) Gallo provides the preferred socks of the Italian well-heeled and has a distinctive style: this small store is stripier than a Missoni-wearing tiger. There are horizontally striped knee socks, children's clothes and very soft tights, all adored by chic Romans. Fine knit cotton bikinis are true originals.

### LAURA BIAGIOTTI — CLOTHING
Map p352 (⌨06 679 12 05; Via Mario de' Fiori 26; Ⓜ Spagna) Exquisite creations from cashmere and silk shimmer enticingly in this new boutique – the magical creations of this venerable Roman designer, the 'Queen of Cashmere'.

### TEBRO — DEPARTMENT STORE
Map p352 (⌨06 687 34 41; Via dei Prefetti; Ⓜ Spagna) An old-style department store that has kept wealthy locals in linen, socks, ties, swimwear and underwear for over 140 years. You can even have sheets made to measure for your yacht.

### FOCACCI — FOOD
Map p352 (⌨06 679 12 28; Via della Croce 43; ⊙8am-8pm Mon-Fri, 8am-3pm Sat; Ⓜ Spagna) One of several smashing delis along this pretty street, this is where to buy cheese, cold cuts, smoked fish, caviar, pasta and olive oil as well as wines.

### FRATELLI FABBI — FOOD
Map p352 (⌨06 679 06 12; Via della Croce 27; Ⓜ Spagna) A small but flavour-packed delicatessen, this is a good place to pick up all sorts of Italian delicacies – fine cured meats, buffalo mozzarella from Campania, *parmigiano reggiano,* olive oil, *porchetta* from Ariccia – as well as Iranian caviar.

### MADA — SHOES
Map p352 (⌨06 679 86 60; Via della Croce 57; Ⓜ Spagna) Blink-and-you'll-miss-it Mada is one of those shops that transcends fashion, supplying supremely elegant, beautifully made shoes (€210 to €380) to discerning Italian women of all ages. Pure old-school Italian quality.

### BULGARI — JEWELLERY
Map p352 (⌨06 679 38 76; Via dei Condotti 10; Ⓜ Spagna) If you have to ask the price, you can't afford it. Sumptuous window displays mean you can admire the world's finest jewellery without spending a *centesimo.*

### FAUSTO SANTINI — SHOES
Map p352 (⌨06 678 41 14; Via Frattina 120; Ⓜ Spagna) Rome's best-known shoe designer, Fausto Santini is famous for his beguilingly simple, architectural shoe designs. Colours are beautiful, quality impeccable.

## 🅰 Trevi Fountain to the Quirinale

### VIGNANO — ACCESSORIES
Map p352 (⌨06 679 51 47; Via Marco Minghetti; ⌨Via del Corso) Piled high with head candy, Vignano opened in 1873 and sells top hats, bowlers and deerstalkers, as well as hacking jackets, to a princely clientele, as if nothing much has changed since it first opened its doors. The hours are exhilaratingly Roman – they open when they feel like it.

### LIBRERIA GIUNTI AL PUNTO — BOOKSTORE
Map p352 (⌨06 699 41 045; Piazza dei Santissimi Apostoli 59-65; ⊙10am-8pm Mon-Sat May-Oct, 9.30am-7.30pm Mon-Sat Nov-Apr, 10.30am-1pm & 4-7.30pm Sun year-round; ⌨Piazza Venezia) The 'Straight to the Point' children's bookshop is an ideal place to distract your kids. Large, colourful and well stocked, it has thousands of titles in Italian and a selection of books in French, Spanish, German and English, as well as a good range of toys, from Play Doh to puzzles.

### LA RINASCENTE — DEPARTMENT STORE
Map p352 (⌨06 679 76 91; Largo Chigi 20; ⌨Via del Corso) La Rinascente is a stately, upmarket department store, with a particularly buzzing cosmetics department, all amid art nouveau interiors.

### GALLERIA ALBERTO SORDI — SHOPPING CENTRE
Map p352 (Piazza Colonna; ⊙10am-10pm; ⌨Via del Corso) This elegant stained-glass arcade appeared in Alberto Sordi's 1973 classic, *Polvere di Stelle,* and has since been renamed for Rome's favourite actor, who died in 2003. It's a serene place to browse stores such as Zara, AVC, Feltrinelli, Coccinelle, Gusella and the Bridge, and there's an airy cafe ideal for a quick coffee break.

## 🅰 Piazza Barberini & Via Veneto

### UNDERGROUND — MARKET
Map p352 (⌨06 360 05 345; Ludovisi underground car park, Via Francesco Crispi 96; ⊙3-8pm Sat & 10.30am-7.30pm Sun 2nd weekend of the month Sep-Jun; Ⓜ Barberini) Monthly market held underground, in a subterranean car park near Villa Borghese. There are more than 150 stalls selling everything from antiques and collectables to clothes and toys.

TRIDENTE, TREVI & THE QUIRINALE SHOPPING

# Monti, Esquilino & San Lorenzo

MONTI | ESQUILINO | PIAZZA DELLA REPUBBLICA & AROUND | SAN LORENZO & BEYOND

## Neighbourhood Top Five

**1** Enjoying the splendours of one of Rome's finest yet lesser-known museums, housed in the **Palazzo Massimo Alle Terme** (p128); the highlight being its incredible Ancient Roman frescoes.

**2** Enjoying a drink in a sun-dappled cafe in the bohemian yet chic neighbourhood of **Monti** (p141).

**3** Having a night out in **Pigneto** (p142), the iconic working-class district immortalised by Pasolini.

**4** Wandering around the splendours of **Santa Maria Maggiore** (p129).

**5** Dining in San Lorenzo, the down-at-heel student zone that harbours some of the capital's trendiest restaurants (p140).

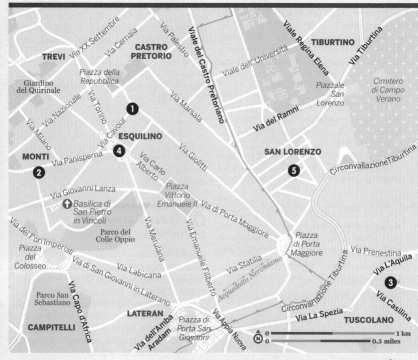

For more detail of this area see Map p340 and Map p339 ➡

# Explore: Monti, Esquilino & San Lorenzo

Although Esquilino covers a large chunk of east-central Rome, the term is used to describe the scruffy area around Stazione Termini and Piazza Vittorio Emanuele II. Near Termini the Museo Nazionale Romano: Palazzo Massimo alle Terme displays stunning classical art, and the area is dotted with some of Rome's finest medieval churches.

Heading downhill, Monti was the ancient city's notorious Suburra slum – a red-light district and the childhood home of Julius Caesar – but is now a charming neighbourhood of inviting eateries, shops and *enoteche* (wine bars). You could say Monti is Rome's Greenwich Village, and, as if to put the seal on its accelerating gentrification, Woody Allen filmed parts of *The Bop Decameron* here in 2011.

San Lorenzo is a lively student quarter east of Termini, home to a beautiful, little-visited patriarchal basilica. It was the area most damaged by Allied bombing during WWII, ironically given the area's vehemently anti-Fascist politics. By day the area feels hungover, a grid of graffitied streets that nonetheless harbour some gemlike boutiques, but after dark it shows its true colours as a student nightlife haunt; it's also home to some excellent restaurants.

A quick tram ride southeast, Pigneto is even more bohemian, the Roman equivalent of London's Shoreditch. House prices are rising and its bars and funky offbeat shops attract a regular crowd of artists and fashion-conscious urbanites.

## Local Life

➡ **Hangouts** While away an hour or more at the Bottega del Caffè (p141) in Monti, watching the world go by.

➡ **Shopping** Find exotic spices and foodstuffs at the Nuovo Mercato Esquilino, Rome's most eclectic food market, next to Piazza Vittorio Emanuele.

➡ **Dining** Make like a tortured artist while noshing on classic Roman dishes, hobnobbing with Rome's arty and media set at Pastificio (p140), San Lorenzo.

## Getting There & Away

➡ **Metro** Cavour Metro stop is most convenient for Monti, while Termini, Castro Pretorio and Vittorio Emanuele stations are useful for Esquilino.

➡ **Bus** Termini is the city's main bus hub, connected to places all over the city; Monti is accessible by buses stopping on Via Nazionale or Via Cavour. San Lorenzo (buses 71, 140 and 492) and Pigneto (buses 81, 810 and 105, and night bus n12) are best reached by bus or tram.

➡ **Tram** This is an easy way to access San Lorenzo (tram 3) or Pigneto (trams 5, 14 or 19).

## Lonely Planet's Top Tip

Don't neglect to visit the oft-overlooked patriarchal Basilica di San Lorenzo Fuori le Mura (p134). It's starkly beautiful.

## ✕️ Best Places to Eat

➡ L'Asino d'Oro (p135)

➡ Trattoria Monti (p138)

➡ Agata e Romeo (p138)

➡ Open Colonna (p139)

➡ Panella l'Arte del Pane (p138)

For reviews see p135 ➡

## ◻ Best Places to Drink

➡ Tre Scalini (p141)

➡ Bottega del Caffè (p141)

➡ Il Tiaso (p142)

➡ Vini e Olii (p142)

For reviews see p141 ➡

## ◉ Best Works of Art

➡ Frescoes at Palazzo Massimo alle Terme (p128)

➡ Michelangelo's colossal Moses (p130)

➡ Fuga's 13th-century facade mosaics (p129)

➡ Richard Meier's modernist Chiesa Dio Padre Misericordioso (p135)

For reviews see p131 ➡

**MONTI, ESQUILINO & SAN LORENZO**

 TOP SIGHTS **MUSEO NAZIONALE ROMANO: PALAZZO MASSIMO ALLE TERME**

One of Rome's finest museums, this light-filled museum that's packed with spectacular classical art remains off the beaten track. However, it's not to be missed.

## Sculpture

The ground and 1st floors are devoted to sculptural masterpieces, including the mesmerising 'Boxer', a crouching Aphrodite from Villa Adriana (p222), the softly contoured, 2nd-century BC 'Sleeping Hermaphrodite', and the ideal vision of the Discus Thrower.

## Frescoes & Mosaics

However, the sensational frescoes on the 2nd floor blow everything else away. The rooms are arranged as they were within the villas. Lighting brings out the colours of the frescoes, which include scenes from nature, mythology, domestic and sensual life in the intimate cubicula (bedrooms), and delicate landscapes from the winter triclinium (dining room).

The showstopping highlight is the room (30 BC to 20 BC) from Villa Livia, one of the homes of Augustus' wife Livia Drusilla. The frescoes depict realistic yet paradisical garden full of roses, pomegranates, iris and camomile, and once decorated a summer triclinium, a living room built half underground as an escape from the heat.

Also on display are the paintings of Columbarium found in Doria Pamphilj, friezes that depict the joys of life and the reality of death. There are also fine mosaics and frescoes from Termini, an area of the city built in the Hadrianic period (2nd century AD).

### DON'T MISS...

➡ The Boxer
➡ Sleeping Hermaphrodite
➡ Frescoes from Villa Livia

### PRACTICALITIES

➡ Map p340
➡ ☎06 399 67 700
➡ www.pierreci.it
➡ Largo di Villa Peretti 1
➡ adult/reduced €7/3.50
➡ audioguide €4
➡ ⊙9am-7.45pm Tue-Sun
➡ ☐ⓂTermini

# TOP SIGHTS
## BASILICA DI SANTA MARIA MAGGIORE

Featuring one of Rome's richest interiors, Santa Maria is one of the capital's great basilicas, dating from the 5th century. One of Rome's four patriarchal basilicas, this monumental church stands on the summit of the Esquilino hill, on the spot where snow is said to have miraculously fallen in the summer of AD 358. To commemorate the event, every year on 5 August thousands of white petals are released from the basilica's coffered ceiling. The basilica's treasures include beautiful 13th-century mosaics on the facade and, within the apse, an exquisite Cosmatesque floor, and a gilded coffered ceiling dating from the 15th century.

### DON'T MISS...

- ➡ Fuga's 13th-century facade mosaics
- ➡ Cosmatesque floor
- ➡ Jacopo Torriti apse mosaics

### PRACTICALITIES

- ➡ Map p340
- ➡ ☑06 698 86 800
- ➡ Piazza Santa Maria Maggiore
- ➡ audioguide €5
- ➡ ⊘7am-7pm
- ➡ Ⓜ Spagna, Flaminio

### Exterior

Santa Maria Maggiore was built on the summit of the Esquilino in the 5th century. Outside, the 18.78m-high column in the Piazza di Santa Maria Maggiore came from the basilica of Massenzio in the Roman Forum, and the church exterior is decorated by glimmering 13th-century mosaics, protected by a baroque porch with five openings, designed by Ferdinando Fuga in 1741. The 75m belfry, the highest in Rome, is 14th-century Romanesque.

### Paving & Mosaics

The great interior retains its original 5th-century structure despite the basilica having been much altered over the centuries. The nave floor is a fine example of 12th-century Cosmati paving. Particularly spectacular are the 5th-century mosaics in the triumphal arch and nave, depicting Old Testament scenes. Binoculars will help discern the detail. The central image in the apse, signed by Jacopo Torriti, dates from the 13th century and represents the coronation of the Virgin Mary.

### The Altar

The baldachin over the high altar seethes with gilt cherubs; the altar itself is a porphyry sarcophagus, which is said to contain the relics of St Matthew and other martyrs. The Madonna col Bambino (Madonna and Child) panel above the altar, surrounded by lapis lazuli and agate, is believed to date from the 12th to 13th centuries. A plaque to the right of the altar marks the spot where Gianlorenzo Bernini and his father Pietro are buried. Steps lead down to the confessio (a crypt in which relics are placed), where a statue of Pope Pius IX kneels before a reliquary containing a fragment of Jesus' manger.

### Chapels

The sumptuously decorated Cappella Sistina was built by Domenico Fontana in the 16th century and contains the tombs of Popes Sixtus V and Pius V. Opposite is the flamboyant Cappella Paolina Borghesiana, erected in the 17th century by Pope Paul V.

### Museum

Through the souvenir shop on the right-hand side of the church is a **museum** (adult/reduced €4/2; ⊘9am-6pm) with a motley collection of religious artefacts. More interesting is the upper **loggia** (☑06 698 86 802; admission €5; ⊘2-5pm), where you'll find some iridescent 13th-century mosaics.

## TOP SIGHTS
# BASILICA DI SAN PIETRO IN VINCOLI

Pilgrims and art lovers flock to this 5th-century church for two reasons: to marvel at Michelangelo's macho sculpture of Moses and to see the chains that bound St Peter when he was imprisoned in the Carcere Mamertino.

### St Peter's Shackles
The church was built in the 5th century specially to house these shackles, which had been sent to Constantinople after the saint's death but were later returned as relics. They arrived in two pieces and legend has it that when they were reunited they miraculously joined together. They are now displayed under the altar.

### Michelangelo's Moses
To the right of the altar, Michelangelo's colossal Moses (1505) forms the centrepiece of Pope Julius II's unfinished tomb. On either side of the prophet are statues of Leah and Rachel, probably completed by Michelangelo's students. Moses, who sports a magnificent waist-length beard and two small horns sticking out of his head, has been studied for centuries, most famously by Sigmund Freud in a 1914 essay, *The Moses of Michelangelo*. The horns were inspired by a mistranslation of a biblical passage: where the original said that rays of light issued from Moses' face, the translator wrote 'horns'. Michelangelo was aware of the mistake, but he gave Moses horns anyway.

Despite the tomb's imposing scale, it was never completed – Michelangelo originally envisaged 40 statues but he got sidetracked by the Sistine Chapel, and Pope Julius was buried in St Peter's Basilica.

### DON'T MISS...
➡ Michelangelo's sculpture of Moses
➡ St Peter's chains

### PRACTICALITIES
➡ Map p340
➡ ☑06 488 28 65
➡ Piazza di San Pietro in Vincoli 4a
➡ ◷ 8am-12.30pm & 3.30-7pm Apr-Sep, 8am-12.30pm & 3-6pm Oct-Mar
➡ Ⓜ Cavour

# ◉ SIGHTS

The sometimes scruffy district of Esquilino is lined by grand 19th-century buildings. It might not be Rome's prettiest district, but it's studded with some stupendous art and museums, including one of Rome's finest patriarchal basilicas in Santa Maria Maggiore and two outposts of the Museo Nazionale Romano, containing a staggering array of treasures.

## ◉ Esquilino

**BASILICA DI SANTA MARIA MAGGIORE** CHURCH

**BASILICA DI SAN PIETRO IN VINCOLI** CHURCH

See p130.

**DOMUS AUREA** SITE

Map p340 (☑06 399 67 700; www.pierreci.itt; Viale della Domus Aurea; adult/reduced €6/3; ⊗closed for restoration; ⓜColosseo) A monumental exercise in vanity, the Domus Aurea (Golden House) was Nero's great gift to himself. Built after the fire of AD 64 and named after the gold that covered its facade, it was a huge complex covering up to a third of the city.

It's estimated only around 20% remains of the original complex. Nero's successors attempted to raze all trace of his megalomania. Vespasian drained Nero's ornamental lake and, in a highly symbolic gesture, built the Colosseum in its place, Domitian built a palace on the Palatino, and Hadrian, having sacked the palace, then entombed it in earth. This process formed Colle Oppio, a hill atop which Hadrian constructed a baths complex. The baths were abandoned by the 6th century, and it is this area that is currently being excavated. It has frequently had to be closed for repairs following flooding and was last open in 2010.

During the Renaissance, artists (including Ghirlandaio, Perugino and Raphael) lowered themselves into the ruins in order to study the frescoed grottoes and to doodle on the walls. All of them later used motifs from the Domus Aurea frescoes in their work.

**MUSEO NAZIONALE D'ARTE ORIENTALE** MUSEUM

Map p340 (☑06 469 74 832; www.museoorientale.it; Via Merulana 248; adult/reduced €6/3; ⊗9am-2pm Tue, Wed & Fri, 9am-7.30pm Thu, Sat & Sun; ⓜVittorio Emanuele) Rome's little-known but impressive National Museum of Oriental Art is housed in the 19th-century Palazzo Brancaccio. It makes for a rewarding visit, with a rich collection of Near and Far Eastern artefacts. The collection starts on a high with some exquisite items from Iran and Central Asia, such as Iranian glassware dating from the 5th to 6th century BC, and goes on to encompass fascinating items from the ancient settlement of Swat in Pakistan, 12th-century homewares from Afghanistan, engraved ritual vessels from China dating 800 to 900 years before Christ, and Ming porcelain figures. There are also Nepalese, Indian and Korean works of art.

**CHIESA DI SANTA CROCE IN GERUSALEMME** CHURCH

Map p339 (☑06 701 47 69; Piazza di Santa Croce in Gerusalemme 12; ⊗7am-1pm & 2-7.30pm; ⓙPiazza di Porta Maggiore) One of Rome's seven pilgrimage churches, the Chiesa di Santa Croce in Gerusalemme was founded in 320 by St Helena, mother of Emperor Constantine, in the grounds of her palace. It takes its name from the Christian relics, including a piece of Christ's cross and St Thomas' doubting finger, that St Helena brought to Rome from Jerusalem. The relics are housed in a chapel at the end of the left-hand aisle.

Of particular note are the lovely 15th-century Renaissance apse frescoes representing the legends of the Cross.

In 2011, the monks who lived in the adjoining monastery were ousted by Pope Benedict XVI following accusations of financial mismanagement and lifestyles that were perceived to be not in keeping with being a monk, including having a former lap dancer perform and running a hotel within the building.

**CHIESA DI SANTA PUDENZIANA** CHURCH

Map p340 (☑06 481 46 22; Via Urbana 160; ⊗8.30am-noon & 3-6pm; ⓜCavour) This, the church of Rome's Filipino community, boasts a sparkling 4th-century apse mosaic, the oldest of its kind in Rome. An enthroned Christ is flanked by two female figures who are crowning St Peter and St

Paul; on either side of them are the apostles dressed as Roman senators. Unfortunately, you can only see 10 of the original 12 apostles, as a barbarous 16th-century facelift lopped off two of them and amputated the legs of the others.

### CHIESA DI SANTA PRASSEDE    CHURCH

Map p340 (☑06 488 24 56; Via Santa Prassede 9a; ☺7.30am-noon & 4-6.30pm; ☐Piazza Santa Maria Maggiore) Famous for its brilliant mosaics, this 9th-century church is dedicated to St Praxedes, an early Christian heroine who hid Christians fleeing persecution and buried those she couldn't save in a well. The position of the well is now marked by a marble disc on the floor of the nave.

The mosaics, produced by artists whom Pope Paschal I had brought in specially from Byzantium, bear all the hallmarks of their eastern creators, with bold gold backgrounds and a marked Christian symbolism. The apse mosaics depict Christ flanked by Saints Peter, Pudentiana and Zeno on the right, and Paul, Praxedes and Pope Paschal on the left. All the figures have golden halos except for Paschal, whose head is shadowed by a blue nimbus to indicate that he was still alive at the time. Further treasures await in the heavily mosaiced **Cappella di San Zenone**, including a piece of the column to which Christ was tied when he was flogged, brought back from Jerusalem – it's in the glass case on the right.

### CHIESA DI SAN MARTINO
### AI MONTI    CHURCH

Map p340 (☑06 487 31 66; Viale del Monte Oppio 28; ☺7.30am-noon & 4-7pm; Ⓜ️Cavour) This was already a place of worship in the 3rd century – Christians would meet here, in what was then the home of a Roman named Equitius. In the 4th century, after Christianity was legalised, a church was constructed, later rebuilt in the 6th and 9th centuries. It was then completely transformed by Filippo Gagliardi in the 1650s. It's of particular interest for Gagliardi's frescoes of the Basilica di San Giovanni in Laterano before it was rebuilt in the mid-17th century and St Peter's Basilica before it assumed its present 16th-century look. Remnants of the more distant past include the ancient Corinthian columns dividing the nave and the aisles.

### CHIESA DI SANTA LUCIA IN SELCI    CHURCH

Map p340 (☑06 482 76 23; Via in Selci 82; ☺9.30-10.30am Sun; Ⓜ️Cavour) A small church best known for its 17th-century Borromini interior, Chiesa di Santa Lucia in Selci dates to some time before the 8th century. It's not open to the public, except for Mass on Sunday morning, but if you ring the bell and ask the resident nuns nicely they'll probably let you in.

### PIAZZA VITTORIO EMANUELE II    PIAZZA

Map p340 (Ⓜ️Vittorio Emanuele) Laid out in the late 19th century as the centrepiece of an upmarket residential district, Rome's biggest square is a grassy expanse with a down-at-heel feel, surrounded by speeding traffic, porticoes and bargain stores. Within the fenced-off central section are the ruins of **Trofei di Mario**, once a fountain at the end of an aqueduct. In the northern corner, the **Chiesa di Sant'Eusebio** (☺7.30-noon & 5-7pm Tue-Sat Oct-Jun, 7.30-8.30am & 6.30-7.30pm Mon, 7.30am-11am & 6-8pm Tue-Sat Jul-Sep) is popular with pet-owners who bring their animals to be blessed on St Anthony's feast day (17 January).

The square itself hosts cultural festivals throughout the year and an outdoor film festival in the summer.

### NATIONAL MUSEUM OF MUSICAL
### INSTRUMENTS    MUSEUM

Map p339 (☑06 32810; Piazza di Santa Croce in Gerusalemme; adult/reduced €4/2; ☐Piazza di Porta Maggiore) This little-known museum behind the church of Santa Croce stands on the site of the former home of St Helena, mother of Constantine. It's undeservedly and refreshingly deserted, with a collection of over 3000 exquisite musical instruments that includes African mandolins made from Armadillo shells, gorgeously painted, handle-operated street pianos from Naples, and one of the world's first pianos, built in 1722.

---

## RADISSON BLU

At this swish, cutting-edge **hotel** (Map p340; ☑06 44 48 41; www.radissonblu.com/eshotel-rome; Via Filippo Turati 171; ☺May-Sep; Ⓜ️Vittorio Emanuele) close to Termini, the sexy rooftop pool has a cocktail bar and restaurant alongside, and is open to nonguests for €45/55, with a 50% discount for children (under 3 years old free).

**PORTA MAGGIORE**                    MONUMENT

Map p339 (Piazza di Porta Maggiore; ⊠ Porta Maggiore) Porta Maggiore was built by Claudius in AD 52. Then, as now, it was a major road junction under which passed the two main southbound roads, Via Prenestina and Via Labicana (modern-day Via Casilina). The arch supported two aqueducts – the Acqua Claudia and the Acqua Aniene Nuova – and was later incorporated into the Aurelian Wall.

**MUSEO STORICO DELLA
LIBERAZIONE**                         MUSEUM

Map p339 (🗐 06 700 38 66; www.viatasso.eu; Via Tasso 145; admission free; ⊘ 9.30am-12.30pm Tue-Sun & 3.30-7.30pm Tue, Thu & Fri; Ⓜ Manzoni) Now a small museum, Via Tasso 145 was the headquarters of the German SS during the Nazi occupation of Rome (1943–44). Members of the Resistance were interrogated, tortured and imprisoned in the cells and you can still see graffiti scrawled on the walls by condemned prisoners. Exhibits, which include photos, documents and improvised weapons, chart the events of the occupation with particular emphasis on the persecution of the Jews, the underground resistance and the Fosse Ardeatine massacre (p161).

---

**⊙ Piazza Della
Repubblica & Around**

**MUSEO NAZIONALE ROMANO: PALAZZO
MASSIMO ALLE TERME**                  MUSEUM

See p128.

**MUSEO NAZIONALE ROMANO: TERME DI
DIOCLEZIANO**                         MUSEUM

Map p340 (🗐 06 399 67 700; www.pierreci.it; Viale Enrico de Nicola 78; adult/reduced €7/3.50, valid for three days for all four Museo Nazionale Romano, audioguide €5; ⊘ 9am-7.45pm Tue-Sun; 🗐 Ⓜ Termini) Over the road from Piazza dei Cinquecento are the remains of the Terme di Diocleziano (Diocletian's Baths), Ancient Rome's largest baths complex, which covered about 13 hectares and could hold up to 3000 people. It was completed in the early 4th century but fell into disrepair after invaders destroyed the feeder aqueduct in about 536.

Through memorial inscriptions and other artefacts the museum supplies a fascinating insight into the structure of Roman society, with exhibits relating to cults and the development of Christianity and Judaism. Upstairs delves into even more ancient history, with tomb objects dating from the 9th to 11th centuries BC, including jewellery and amphorae.

Outside, the vast, elegant cloister was constructed from drawings by Michelangelo. It's lined with classical sarcophagi, headless statues, and huge sculpted animal heads, thought to have come from the Foro di Traiano. To the north, the **Aula Ottagona** (Piazza della Repubblica; admission free; ⊘ 9am-2pm Mon-Sat, 9am-1pm Sun), which is often closed due to staff shortages, houses yet more Roman sculpture.

**CHIESA DI SANTA MARIA
DEGLI ANGELI**                        CHURCH

Map p340 (🗐 06 488 08 12; www.santamaria degliangeliroma.it; Piazza della Repubblica; ⊘ 7am-6.30pm Mon-Sat, 7am-7.30pm Sun; Ⓜ Repubblica) This hulking basilica occupies what was once the central hall of Diocletian's baths complex. It was originally designed by Michelangelo, but only the great vaulted ceiling remains from his plans. Today the chief attraction is the 18th-century double meridian in the transept, one tracing the polar star and the other telling the precise time of the sun's zenith (sunlight enters through a hole to the right of the window above the entrance to the church's right wing). Until 1846, this sundial was used to regulate all Rome's clocks.

**CHIESA DI SAN PAOLO
ENTRO LE MURA**                       CHURCH

Map p340 (🗐 06 488 33 39; www.stpaulsrome. it; cnr Via Nazionale & Via Napoli; ⊘ 9.30am-4.30pm Mon-Fri; 🗐 Via Nazionale) With its stripy neo-Gothic exterior and prominent position, Rome's American Episcopal church is something of a landmark in this city. Inside, the unusual 19th-century mosaics, designed by the Birmingham-born artist and designer Edward Burne-Jones, feature the faces of his famous contemporaries. In his representation of *The Church on Earth,* St Ambrose (on the extreme right of the centre group) has JP Morgan's face, and General Garibaldi and Abraham Lincoln (wearing a green tunic) are among the warriors. In the small garden outside the church there are a number of modern sculptures.

## VILLA ALDOBRANDINI

If you're in need of a breather around Via Nazionale, or are in search of somewhere for a picnic, then take Via Mazzarino off the main road and walk up the steps, past 2nd-century ruins, where you'll find a graceful, sculpture-dotted garden (open dawn until dusk), with gravelled paths and tranquil lawns, raised around 10m above street level. These are the grounds of Villa Aldobrandini, overlooked by the house built here in the 16th century by Cardinal Pietro Aldobrandini to house his extensive art collection. Today the villa is closed to the public and houses the headquarters of an international law institute.

**PALAZZO DELLE ESPOSIZIONI**     GALLERY

Map p340 (✒06 399 67 500; www.palazzo esposizioni.it, in Italian; Via Nazionale 194; ⊙depends on exhibition; 🚇Via Nazionale) This huge neoclassical palace was built in 1882 as an exhibition centre. After a dazzling five-year makeover, it emerged in 2007 as a splendid cultural hub, with cathedral-scale exhibition spaces and sleekly designed art labs, bookshop, cafe and top-notch, glass-roofed restaurant (see p139) that's also an excellent place for a laidback lunch. The building hosts everything from multimedia events and art exhibitions to concert performances, film screenings and conferences. It frequently hosts blockbuster exhibitions such as 'One Hundred Masterpieces from the Städel Museum of Frankfurt', which featured impressionist and expressionist paintings. In various former lives, the *palazzo* served as HQ for the Italian Communist Party, a mess for Allied servicemen, a polling station and even a public loo.

**PIAZZA DELLA REPUBBLICA**     PIAZZA

Map p340 (Ⓜ Repubblica) Flanked by grand 19th-century neoclassical colonnades, this landmark piazza was laid out as part of Rome's post-unification makeover. It follows the lines of the semicircular *exedra* (benched portico) of Diocletian's baths complex (p133) and was originally known as Piazza Esedra. In the centre, the **Fontana delle Naiadi** aroused puritanical ire when it was unveiled by architect Mario Rutelli in 1901. The nudity of the four naiads or water nymphs, who surround the central figure of Glaucus wrestling a fish, was considered too provocative – how Italy has changed. Each reclines on a creature symbolising water in a different form: a water snake (rivers), a swan (lakes), a lizard (streams) and a sea-horse (oceans).

# San Lorenzo & Beyond

**BASILICA DI SAN LORENZO FUORI LE MURA**     CHURCH

Map p339 (✒06 49 15 11; Piazzale San Lorenzo; ⊙8am-noon & 4-6.30pm; 🚇Piazzale del Verano) St Lawrence Outside the Walls is one of Rome's four patriarchal basilicas, and is an atmospheric, tranquil edifice that's starker than many of the city's grand churches, a fact that only adds to its breathtaking beauty. It was the only one of Rome's major churches to have suffered bomb damage in WWII, and is a hotchpotch of rebuilds and restorations, yet still has the serenity of a harmonious whole.

St Lawrence was burned to death in AD 258, and Constantine had the original basilica constructed in the 4th century over his burial place, but it was rebuilt 200 years later. Subsequently a nearby 5th-century church dedicated to the Virgin Mary was incorporated into the building, resulting in the church you see today. The nave, portico and much of the decoration date to the 13th century.

Highlights are the Cosmati floor and the frescoed portico, depicting events from St Lawrence's life. The remains of St Lawrence and St Stephen are in the church crypt beneath the high altar. A pretty barrel-vaulted cloister contains inscriptions and sarcophagi and leads to the **Catacombe di Santa Ciriaca**, where St Lawrence was initially buried.

**CIMITERO DI CAMPO VERANO**     CEMETERY

Map p339 (✒06 492 36 349; Piazzale del Verano; ⊙7.30am-6pm Apr-Sep, 7.30am-5pm Oct-Mar; 🚇Piazzale del Verano) The city's largest cemetery dates to the Napoleonic occupation of Rome between 1804 and 1814, when an edict ordered that the city's dead must be buried outside the city walls. Between the

1830s and the 1980s virtually all Catholics who died in Rome (with the exception of popes, cardinals and royalty) were buried here. If you are in the area, it is worth a look for its grand tombs, but try to avoid 2 November (All Souls' Day), when thousands of Romans flock to the cemetery to leave flowers on the tombs of loved ones.

### PASTIFICIO CERERE
GALLERY

Map p339 ([🕿]06 4470 3912; www.pastificio cerere.com; Via degli Ausoni 7; ⊙3-7pm Mon-Fri; [🚇]Via Tiburtina) This hub of Rome's contemporary art scene started life as a pasta factory in 1905. Abandoned in 1960, it came to prominence as home of the Nuova Scuola Romana (New Roman School), a group of six artists who set the nation's art scene alight in the early 1980s, and who are still the organisation's historic resident artists, but added to their number is a new generation, including Maurizio Savini, famous for his sculptures in pink chewing gum. There are regular shows in the building's gallery and courtyard exhibition spaces, often featuring works created especially for the site.

### CHIESA DIO PADRE MISERICORDIOSO
CHURCH

([🕿]06 231 58 33; www.diopadremisericordioso. it; Via Francesco Tovaglieri 147; ⊙9am-6pm Mon-Fri, 7.30am-12.30pm & 3.30-7.30pm daily; [🚇]Via Francesco Tovaglieri) Rome's first minimalist church, this beautiful white Richard Meier creation has a remarkable and appropriate purity, and for lovers of contemporary architecture, it is well worth the trek out to the suburbs to see it. Built out of white concrete, stucco, gleaming travertine and 976 sq m of glass, it is an exercise in dazzling lightness and white, making use of the play of light both inside and out. The structure is flanked on one side by three graduated concrete, sail-like shells, while on the other side a four-storey atrium connects the church with a community centre.

## ✖ EATING

**Monti, conveniently just north of the Colosseum if you're looking for somewhere nearby, has some wonderful choices. An ancient slum, it's one of Rome's most interesting up-and-coming districts, with intimate bars, wine bars, restaurants and boutiques.**

**In the busy, hotel-packed district around Stazione Termini it's harder to find a good eaterie, but there are some notable classic trattorie, restaurants and *artisanal gelaterie*, and this area contains Rome's best ethnic eats.**

## ✖ Monti

### L'ASINO D'ORO
MODERN ITALIAN €€

Map p340 ([🕿]06 4891 3832; Via del Boschetto 73; meals €40; [Ⓜ]Cavour) This fabulous restaurant has been transplanted from Orvieto and its Umbrian origins resonate in Lucio Sforza's delicious, exceptional cooking. It's unfussy yet innovative, with dishes featuring lots of flavourful contrasts, such as slow-roasted rabbit in a rich berry sauce and desserts that linger in the memory. For such excellent food, this intimate, informal yet classy place is one of Rome's best deals, especially for the set lunch.

### LA CARBONARA
TRATTORIA €€

Map p340 ([🕿]06 482 51 76; Via Panisperna 214; meals €35; ⊙Mon-Sat; [Ⓜ]Cavour) On the go since 1906, this busy restaurant was favoured by the infamous Ragazzi di Panisperna (named after the street), the group of young physicists, including Enrico Fermi, who constructed the first atomic bomb. The waiters are brusque, it crackles with energy and the interior is covered in graffiti – tradition dictates that diners should leave their mark in a message on the wall. The speciality is the eponymous carbonara.

### CIURI CIURI
PASTICCERIA €

Map p340 ([🕿]06 454 44 548; Via Leonina 18; snacks around €2.50; ⊙10am-midnight; [Ⓜ]Cavour) A Sicilian ice-cream and pastry shop where you can pop by (and eat in) for delectable homemade sweets such as *cannoli* (a type of pastry), cassata and *pasticini di mandorla* (almond pastries), all available in moreish bite-sized versions, and created using the freshest of ingredients. There are rib-sticking *arancini* (fried rice balls), and they also have the best ice-cream in the neighbourhood.

### DA VALENTINO
TRATTORIA €€

Map p340 ([🕿]06 4880 643; Via del Boschetto; meals €30; ⊙Mon-Sat; [Ⓜ]Cavour) The vintage 1930s sign outside says 'Birra Peroni', and inside the lovely old-fashioned feel indicates that not much has changed here for years,

JON DAVISON / LONELY PLANET IMAGES ©

**1. Basilica di Santa Maria Maggiore (p129)**
A view of a dome of Santa Maria Maggiore, one of the great papal basilicas of Rome.

**2. Basilica di San Giovanni in Laterano (p149)**
Interior of San Giovanni, the first Christian basilica to be built in Rome.

**3. Chiesa di Santa Maria in Montesanto (p107)**
Chiesa di Santa Maria in Montesanto from Piazza del Popolo.

**4. Basilica di San Paolo Fuori Le Mura (p163)** Basilica di San Paolo Fuori Le Mura with courtyard garden.

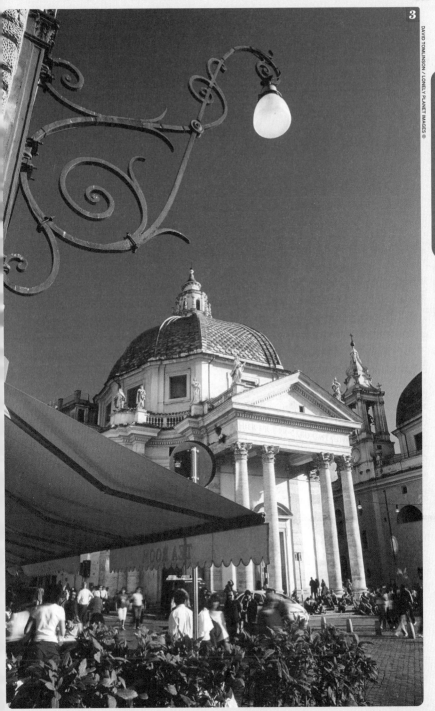

with black-and-white photographs on the walls, white tablecloths and tiled floors. Come here when you're in the mood for grilled *scamorza* (a type of Italian cheese, similar to mozzarella), as this is the main focus of the menu, with myriad variations: served with tomato and rocket, tomato and gorgonzola, cheese and artichokes, grilled meats, hamburgers and so on.

### SWEETY ROME
CAFE €

Map p340 (☑06 4891 3713; Via Milano 48; cupcakes from €3; ⓂCavour) This is an unusual proposition in Rome: delectable cupcakes (including irresistible red velvet options), all topped with a swirl of beautiful creamy icing. Sweety Rome also proffers a great Sunday brunch (€8), plus excellent breakfasts to those who are tiring of the cafe-*cornetto* combination, featuring pancakes, eggs and muffins.

### URBANA 47
MODERN ITALIAN €€

Map p340 (☑06 4788 4006; Via Urbana 47; meals €40; ⓂCavour) Opened by owners of a vintage furniture store, this indeed urbane, informal restaurant is filled with retro furnishings that are all for sale, so if you like the look of the leather armchair in which you settle, it could be yours. On the menu are delicious creations from seasonal, organic and above all local produce by chef Alessandro Miotto, who as far as possible operates the '0km' rule, meaning that most things you eat here will be sourced from nearby. Attracts a chic crowd.

## ✕ Esquilino

### AGATA E ROMEO
MODERN ITALIAN €€€

Map p340 (☑06 446 61 15; Via Carlo Alberto 45; meals €120; ⓁMon-Fri; ⓂVittorio Emanuele) This elegant, restrained place was one of Rome's gastronomic pioneers, and still holds its own as one of the city's most gourmet takes on Roman cuisine. Chef Agata Parisella designs and cooks menus, offering creative uses of Roman traditions; husband Romeo curates the wine cellar; and daughter Maria Antonietta chooses the cheeses. Bookings essential.

### TRATTORIA MONTI
TRATTORIA €€

Map p340 (☑06 446 65 73; Via di San Vito 13a; meals €45; Ⓛlunch & dinner Tue-Sat, lunch Sun; ⓂVittorio Emanuele) The Camerucci family

runs this elegant, intimate, brick-arched place, where the air of contentment is palpable as you enter – a reflection of the top-notch traditional cooking from the Marches region, with an unusual menu that includes lots of daily specials. There are wonderful fried things, delicate pastas and ingredients such as *pecorino di fossa* (sheep's cheese aged in caves), goose, swordfish, sultanas, mushrooms and truffles. Try the speciality egg-yolk *tortelli* pasta. Desserts are delectable, including apple pie with *zabaglione* that's worthy of a postcard home. Word has spread, so book ahead.

### PANELLA L'ARTE DEL PANE
FAST FOOD €

Map p340 (☑06 487 24 35; Via Merulana 54; pizza slices €2.50-5; Ⓛ8am-11pm Mon-Thu, 8am-midnight Fri & Sat, 8.30am-4pm Sun; ⓂVittorio Emanuele) With a sumptuous array of *pizza al taglio*, *supplì* (fried rice balls), focaccia and fried croquettes, this is a sublime express lunch stop, where you can sip a glass of chilled *prosecco* while eyeing up the array gastronomic souvenirs on display in the deli.

### PALAZZO DEL FREDDO
### DI GIOVANNI FASSI
ICE CREAM €

Map p339 (☑06 446 47 40; Via Principe Eugenio 65; from €2; Ⓛnoon-12.30am Sat, 10am-midnight Sun, noon-midnight Tue-Thu; ⓂVittorio Emanuele) A great back-in-time barn of a place, sprinkled with marble tabletops and vintage gelato-making machinery, Fassi offers fantastic classic flavours, such as riso (rice), pistachio and nocciola (hazelnut). The granita, served with dollops of cream, deserves special mention. Curiously, there is only one outlet in Rome but a further 82 in Korea.

### TRIMANI
WINE BAR €€

Map p340 (☑06 446 96 30; Via Cernaia 37b; meals €45; ⓁMon-Sat; 🚈ⓂTermini) Part of the Trimani family's wine empire (their shop just round the corner stocks about 4000 international labels), this is an unpretentious yet highly professional *enoteca*, with knowledgeable, multilingual staff. It's Rome's biggest wine bar and has a vast selection of Italian regional wines as well as an ever-changing food menu – tuck into local salami and cheese or fresh oysters. Book ahead to take one of the regular wine-tasting courses.

# EATING IN ROME

Rome resident Elizabeth Minchilli, a prolific food journalist and blogger at www.eliza bethminchilliinrome.com, shares some top tips.

I always suggest going first to the markets to see what's fresh, because so much has to do with what's seasonal. Besides the regular city markets, there are also weekend farmers' markets, including one at Circus Maximus, **Il Farmer's Market della Capitale** (Via San Teodoro; ⊙9am-6pm Sat & Sun).

You should try piazza bianca (white pizza), which is typical Roman street food, and there is always a discussion about who has the best. Most people cite the Forno de Campo de' Fiori (p93), but I prefer Roscioli (p93) for pizza bianca. If you want pizza with red sauce, go to Antico Forno Urbani (Piazza Costaguti 30) in the Ghetto. You won't find any foreigners there, it's all Italians. The pizza rossa is very thin, covered with just a little bit of tomato sauce, really caramelised and fantastic.

In the last few years Rome has been having this renaissance of pizza-makers. The king of pizza is Gabriele Bonci; people come from all over the world to have his pizza, so it's well worth going to Pizzarium (p203) if you're near the Vatican.

Another thing to try is icecream. You'll pass lots of places with huge fluffy mounds: ignore those and try and look for the artisanal gelato-makers. Again seasonal is always good, so you'll get strawberry in the summer, chestnut in the winter. For example, over near Piazza Navona is Gelateria del Teatro (p92).

Lately one of my favourite restaurants is L'Asino d'Oro (p135), in Monti, which has a really affordable lunch menu. I'd also recommend Settembrini (p202), near the Vatican, La Campana (p91), which is very old fashioned, and I also love Giggetto (p94) in the Ghetto. It has really great *carciofi alla giudia* (deep-fried artichokes). While you're in the Ghetto, stop at the Jewish bakery (Boccione; p95) to get the *pizza ebraica* (Jewish pizza), a sort of dried-fruit cake; it weighs a ton, but it's delicious!

And finally, Rome's beer scene is exploding, and at places like Bir & Fud (p175) you can eat pizza and try lots of different beers on tap.

## ROSCIOLI
FAST FOOD €

Map p340 (Via Buonarroti 48; pizza €2-3; ⊙7am-8.15pm Mon-Sat; MVittorio Emanuele) Off-the-track branch of this splendid deli-bakery-pizzeria, in a road leading off Piazza Vittorio Emanuele, with delish *pizza al taglio*, pasta dishes and so on that make it ideal for a swift lunch or picnic stock-up.

## DA DANILO
TRATTORIA €

Map p340 (☑06 482 5176; Via Petrarca 13; meals €50; ⊙Tue-Sat lunch, Mon-Sat dinner) MVittorio Emanuele) Ideal if you're looking for a fine robust meal a short walk from Termini – in a street leading off Piazza Vittorio Emanuele II – this classic neighbourhood place offers icons of Roman cooking in a rustic, eternal-Roman-trattoria atmosphere. Good for digging into a dish of *cacio e pepe* or carbonara, which are reliable favourites.

## INDIAN FAST FOOD
INDIAN €

Map p340 (☑06 446 07 92; Via Mamiani 11; curries €5.50-7.50; ⊙11am-10.30pm; MVittorio Emanuele) Formica tables, Hindi hits, neon lights, chapatti and naan, lip-smacking samosas and bhajis, and a simple selection of main curry dishes: you could almost imagine yourself in India when you're feasting at this authentic joint.

# ✗ Piazza Della Republica & Around

## OPEN COLONNA
MODERN ITALIAN €€€

Map p340 (☑06 478 22 641; Via Milano 9a; meals €20-80; ⊙noon-midnight Tue-Sat & Sun lunch; ⌕Via Nazionale; ✸) Spectacularly set at the back of Palazzo delle Esposizioni, superchef Antonello Colonna's superb, chic restaurant is tucked onto a mezzanine floor under an extraordinary glass roof. The cuisine is new Roman: innovative takes on traditional dishes, cooked with wit and flair. The best thing? There's a more basic but still delectable fixed two-course lunch or buffet for €15, and Saturday and Sunday brunch at €28, served in the dramatic, glass-ceilinged hall, with a terrace for sunny days.

**DOOZO**  JAPANESE €€

Map p340 (☑06 481 56 55; Via Palermo 51; sushi €6-10, dishes & sets €12-30; ☺dinner Tue-Sun, lunch Tue-Sat; ◻Via Nazionale) Doozo (meaning 'welcome') is a spacious, Zen restaurant-bookshop and gallery that offers tofu, sushi, *soba* (buckwheat noodle) soup and other Japanese delicacies, plus beer and green tea in wonderfully serene surroundings. On the street parallel to noisy Via Nazionale, it's a little oasis, particularly the tree-shade courtyard garden. The perfect escape if you're craving a break from pasta.

**DA RICCI**  PIZZERIA €

Map p340 (☑06 488 11 07; Via Genova 32; pizzas €6-12; ☺7pm-midnight Tue-Sun; ◻Via Nazionale; ✱) In a tranquil, cobbled cul-de-sac a step away from smoggy Via Nazionale, Rome's oldest pizzeria started life as a wine bar in 1905, and its wood-panelled interior feels like it hasn't changed much since. The sign says Est! Est!! Est!!! – Da Ricci's other name (after its white wine from the north of Lazio). Pizzas are thick-based Neapolitan style (though you can get thin-based if you like), and work best with lots of toppings.

# ✖ San Lorenzo & Beyond

In San Lorenzo, the vibrant boho student area east of Termini, you'll find an enticing mix of extraordinarily good, trendy restaurants and dirt-cheap pizzerias.

**TRAM TRAM**  TRATTORIA €€

Map p339 (☑06 49 04 16; Via dei Reti 44; meals €45; ☺Tue-Sun; ◻ ◻Via Tiburtina) This trendy, yet old-style, lace-curtained trattoria takes its name from the trams that rattle past outside. It offers tasty traditional dishes, such as *involtini di pesce spada con patate* (rolls of swordfish with potato). Book ahead.

**POMMIDORO**  TRATTORIA €€

Map p339 (☑06 445 26 92; Piazza dei Sanniti 44; meals €50; ☺Mon-Sat, closed Aug; ◻Via Tiburtina, ◻Via dei Reti) Throughout San Lorenzo's metamorphosis from down-at-heel working-class district to down-at-heel bohemian enclave, Pommidoro has remained the same. A much-loved local institution, it's a century-old trattoria, with high star-vaulted ceilings, a huge fireplace and out-door conservatory seating. It was a favourite of controversial film director Pier Paolo Pasolini, and contemporary celebs stop by – from Nicole Kidman to Fabio Cappello – but it's an unpretentious place with superb-quality traditional food, specialising in magnificent grilled meats.

**SAID**  MODERN ITALIAN €€

Map p339 (☑06 446 92 04; Via Tiburtina 135; meals €50; ◻Via Tiburtina, ◻Via dei Reti) Said is one of San Lorenzo's chicest haunts, housed in a 1920s chocolate factory. It includes a glorious chocolate shop, selling delights like Japanese pink-tea pralines, and a stylish restaurant-bar, all cosy urban chic, with battered sofas, industrial antiques and creative cuisine.

**PASTIFICIO SAN LORENZO**  MODERN ITALIAN €€€

Map p339 (☑06 972 7 3519; Via Tiburtina 135; meals €50; ☺from 7pm; ◻Via Tiburtina, ◻Via dei Reti) The biggest buzz in San Lorenzo is to be found at this brasserie-style restaurant, housed in a corner of the former pasta factory that is now Rome's contemporary art hub as it's also home to a collective of artists' studios. The place is packed, the vibe is 'this is where it's at', and the food.... is fine – nothing to shout about, but perfectly scrumptious old favourites with pappadelle and ragu, served up in a stylish fashion with equivalent prices.

**SUSHIKO**  JAPANESE €€

Map p340 (☑06 443 40 948; Via degli Irpini 8; sushi menus from €40; ☺1-2.30pm Tue-Sat & 8pm-midnight Mon-Sat ◻Via Tiburtina) This nondescript San Lorenzo lane is an unlikely place to find Rome's best sushi, but here it is, with the freshest fish served up as sushi and sashimi, plus rolls, tempura and teppanyaki. It's tiny, with only 24 covers, so book ahead. It makes financial sense to go set menu rather than à la carte.

**FORMULA UNO**  PIZZERIA €

Map p340 (☑06 445 38 66; Via degli Equi 13; pizzas from €6; ☺6.30pm-1.30am Mon-Sat; ◻Via Tiburtina, ◻Via dei Reti) As adrenaline-fuelled as its name: at this basic, historic San Lorenzo pizzeria, under whirring fans, waiters zoom around delivering tomato-loaded bruschetta, fried courgette flowers, *supplì al telefono* and bubbling thin-crust pizza, to eternal crowds of feasting students.

# 🍷 DRINKING & NIGHTLIFE
🍸

The Monti area, north of the Colosseum, is splendid for *aperitivo*, a meal, or after-dark drinks, with lots of charming candlelit wine bars and even a couple of bar-clubs to lengthen your evening.

If you want to keep it real, head down to San Lorenzo, the student district, packed with pubs, bars, clubs and some surprisingly chic restaurants. Less studenty but still with a gritty feel is the happening nightlife district of Pigneto (p142).

## 🍷 Monti

### AI TRE SCALINI                          WINE BAR
Map p340 (Via Panisperna 251; ⊘12.30pm-1am Mon-Fri, 6pm-1am Sat & Sun; 🅼Cavour) The Three Steps is always packed, with crowds spilling out into the street. Apart from a tasty choice of wines, it sells the damn fine Menabrea beer, brewed in northern Italy. You can also tuck into a heart-warming array of cheeses, salami, and dishes such as *porchetta di Ariccia con patate al forno* (roasted Ariccia pork with roast potatoes).

### LA BOTTEGA DEL CAFFÈ                    CAFE
Map p340 (Piazza Madonna dei Monti 5; ⊘8am-2am; 🅼Cavour) Ideal for frittering away any balmy section of the day, this appealing cafe-bar has greenery-screened tables out on the captivatingly pretty Piazza Madonna dei Monti with its fountain. As well as drinks, it serves lipsmacking snacks, from simple pizzas to cheeses and salamis.

### AL VINO AL VINO                         WINE BAR
Map p340 (Via dei Serpenti 19; 🅼Cavour) A studiously rustic, vine-decorated place, mixing ceramic tabletops and contemporary paintings, this is an attractive and good-value spot to linger over a fine collection of wines, particularly *passiti* (sweet wines). The other speciality is *distillati* – grappa, whisky and so on. And of course there are snacks too, including some Sicilian delicacies.

### LA BARRIQUE                             WINE BAR
Map p340 (Via del Boschetto 41b; ⊘1-3pm & 7pm-1.30am Mon-Fri, 7pm-1.30am Sat; 🅼Cavour) A dark and cool, softly lit, bottle-lined wine bar, La Barrique offers excellent French and Italian wines – including many by

the glass – and 120 types of Champagne, divinely accompanied by *bruchettine* (little bruschettas) and *crostone*. *Aperitivi* are served from 7pm.

### BOHEMIEN                                BAR
Map p340 (Via degli Zingari 36; ⊘6pm-2am Wed-Sun; 🅼Cavour) This little bar lives up to its name, and feels like something you might stumble on in Left Bank Paris: small, with mismatched chairs and tables and an eclectic, fittingly boho crowd drinking wine by the glass or cups of tea.

### ICE CLUB                                BAR
Map p340 (www.iceclubroma.it; Via Madonna dei Monti 18; ⊘6pm-2am; 🅼Colosseo) Novelty value is what the Ice Club, most tempting in summer, is all about. Pay €15 (you get a free vodka cocktail served in a glass made of ice), put on a thermal cloak and mittens, and enter the bar, in which everything is made of ice (temperature: -5 degrees C). Most people won't chill here for long – the record is held by a Russian (four hours).

## 🍷 Esquilino

### BAR ZEST AT THE RADISSON BLU            BAR
Map p340 (Via Filippo Turati 171; ⊘10.30am-1am; 🚇Via Cavour) In need of a cocktail in the Termini district? Then pop up to the 7th-floor bar at the slinkily designed Radisson Blu. Waiters are cute, chairs are by Jasper Morrison, views are through plate-glass, and there's a sexy rooftop pool.

### CASTRONI                                CAFE
Map p340 (Via Nazionale 7; ⊘8am-8pm; 🚇Via Cavour) This gourmet foodshop sells foodstuffs from all over the world, and although this branch doesn't have as large a range as that on Via Cola di Rienzo, it still has the fab cafe, which has great coffee, panini and other snacks, and you can stand at the bar or sit at a few booth tables.

### FIDDLER'S ELBOW                         PUB
Map p340 (Via dell'Olmata 43; ⊘5pm-2am; 🚇Via Cavour) Near the Basilica di Santa Maria Maggiore, the granddaddy of Rome's Irish pubs sticks to the formula that has served it so well over the last 25 years or so: Guinness, darts, crisps, and football and rugby showing when there's a big game on, attracting a mix of Romans, expats and tourists.

**WORTH A DETOUR**

## DETOUR: PIGNETO & AROUND

Pigneto is emerging as Rome's nuovo-hip district, a rapid metamorphosis from the working-class quarter it has been for decades. However, it has long been part of the Roman artistic consciousness, immortalised by filmmaker Pasolini, who used to hang out at Necci, and filmed *Accattone* (1961) here. There's a small-town feel, with decaying low-rise houses and graffiti-covered narrow streets. The action is on Via Pigneto: its liveliest half is pedestrianised with a busy market by day; bars spread across the street at night.

➡ **Primo** (Map p339; ☎06 701 3827; Via del Pigneto 46; ⌂Circonvallazione Casilina; ☎) Flagship of the Pigneto scene, Primo is still buzzing after several years, with lots of outdoor tables and a vaguely industrial-brasserie-style interior.

➡ **Osteria Qui se Magna!** (off Map p339; ☎06 274803; Via del Pigneto 307; meals €25; ⌂Circonvallazione Casilina) A small, simple place adorned with gingham paper tablecloths with a couple of outside tables, here you can eat heavenly, hearty, home-cooked food, such as *carciofi con patata* (artichokes with potatoes).

➡ **Pigneto Quarantuno** (Map p339; ☎06 7039 9483; Via del Pigneto 41; meals €50; ☉Tue-Sun; ⌂Circonvallazione Casilina) New kid on the scene, this is a chic addition in the Primo mould, proffering delicious Roman classics such as *cacio e pepe* as well as grilled steak and *baccalà* (cod).

➡ **Il Tiaso** (Map p339; ☎333 28 45 283; Via Perugia 20; ⌂Circonvallazione Casilina; ☎) Think living room, with zebra-print chairs, walls of indie art, Lou Reed biographies shelved between wine bottles, and 30-something owner Gabriele playing his latest New York Dolls album to neo-beatnik chicks, corduroy professors and the odd neighbourhood dog. Well-priced wine, an intimate chilled vibe, and regular live music.

➡ **Vini e Olii** (Map p340; Via del Pigneto 18; ⌂Circonvallazione Casilina) Forget the other bars that line Pigneto's main pedestrianised drag, with their scattered outside tables and styled interiors. *This* is where the locals head. This traditional 'wine and oil' shop has sold cheap beer and wine (bottles from €7.50) for over 70 years, though not so much oil these days. It's outside seating only.

➡ **Necci** (off Map p339; ☎06 976 01 552; Via Fanfulla da Lodi 68; ⌂Circonvallazione Casilina; ☎) To start your exploration of this bar-studded area, try the iconic Necci, opened as an ice-cream parlour in 1924. Today a bar-restaurant, it was also film director Pasolini's old stomping ground in the late '50s and early '60s, and recently Necci appeared in Francesca Archibugi's *Una questione di Cuore*. It caters to an eclectic crowd of all ages, with a lovely, leafy garden-terrace (ideal for families).

➡ **Circolo degli Artisti** (Map p339; ☎06 703 05 684; www.circoloartisti.it; Via Casilina Vecchia 42; ☉various; ⌂Via Casilina) For the sound of the underground, Circolo is one of Rome's best nights out, serving up a fine menu of fun: there's Screamadelica, with Italy's alternative music oracle Fabio Luzzietti; Friday cracks open the electronica and house for gay night Omogenic. Regular gigs see names from Terry Poison to Billy Bragg. The large garden area is ideal for chilling out. Sunday is vintage market day.

➡ **Fanfulla 101** (off Map p339; Via Fanfulla da Lodi 101; ⌂Circonvallazione Casilina) Behind an unmarked door, this is a cultural association, a book-lined old hall that's all vintage chic and left-leaning punters. There are regular live indie, jazz, reggae and rock gigs, plus jam sessions, art-house films, documentaries and poetry readings. June to September, events transfer to **Forte Fanfulla** (Via Fanfulla da Lodi 5; ☉10am-2am).

➡ **Nuovo Cinema Aquila** (Map p339; ☎06 703 99 408; www.cinemaaquila.com; Via L'Aquila 68; ☉Sep-May; ⌂or⌂Via Prenestina) Pigneto's retro cinema is a classic building that had a makeover to go with the rest of the district. It's the neighbourhood's cultural hang-out, with three luxe cinemas, exhibition spaces, bar and bookshop.

➡ **Iosselliani** (Map p339; Via del Pigneto 39; ☉6pm-midnight Tue-Sat, 6-10pm Sun; ⌂Circonvallazione Casilina) Beautiful exotic jewellery that is the work of the artistic partnership of Roberta Paolucci and Paolo Giacomelli.

**FINNEGANS**                                   PUB
Map p340 (Via Leonina 66; ⓂCavour) At first
glance this seems like an Irish pub anywhere in the world, but look closer and it
has some Italian twists – the clientele are
well-groomed expats and fresh-faced Romans, and you can order Bellinis as well as
Guinness. It's Irish-run and shows all the
big football and rugby games, and there's
occasional live music.

**DRUID'S DEN**                                 PUB
Map p340 (Via San Martino ai Monti 28; ◷5pm-
1.30am; ⓂCavour) An Irish nook of a pub,
the Druid's Den attracts a crowd of young
expats and Roman Anglophiles. It meets
all your Irish pub needs: the atmosphere
is convivial, the walls are wood-panelled,
Celtic paraphernalia is everywhere, Guinness is on tap, and it shows all the big
games.

**HANGAR**                                 NIGHTCLUB
Map p340 (Via in Selci 69; ◷10.30pm-2.30am
Wed-Mon, closed 3 weeks Aug; ⓂCavour) A gay
landmark since 1984, Hangar is friendly
and welcoming, with a cruisey vibe, and
attracts locals and out-of-towners, with
porn nights on Monday and strippers on
Thursday. Feeling frisky? Head to the dark
room.

# San Lorenzo & Beyond

**MICCA CLUB**              NIGHTCLUB, LIVE MUSIC
Map p339 (www.miccaclub.com; Via Pietra Micca
7a; ◷10pm-2am Mon, Tue & Thu, 10pm-4am Fri
& Sat, 6pm-1am Sun Sep-Apr, Fri & Sat only May);
ⓂVittorio Emanuele) At eclectic Micca, pop
art and jelly-bright lighting fills ancient
arched cellars. The programme features
everything from burlesque and the Italian
Torture Garden, to glam rock and swing,
with loads of live gigs. There's an admission
fee if a gig's on and at the weekend. Register
online for discounts.

**LOCANDA ATLANTIDE**      NIGHTCLUB, LIVE MUSIC
Map p339 (☎06 447 04 540; www.locandatlan
tide.it; Via dei Lucani 22b; ◷9pm-2am Oct-Jun;
ⓂVia Tiburtina, ⓆScalo San Lorenzo) Come,
tickle Rome's grungy underbelly, and descend into this cavernous place, decked
out in retro junk, packed to the rafters
with attitude-free alternative crowds,

and an always entertaining programme
featuring everything from experimental
theatre to DJ-spun electro music. It's good
to know that punk is not dead.

**SOLEA CLUB**                                  BAR
Map p339 (☎328 925 29 25; Via dei Latini 51;
◷9am-2am; ⓂVia Tiburtina, ⓆScalo San Lorenzo) With vintage sofas, chairs, and cushions on the floor, this slightly grungy place
has the look of a chill-out room in a decadent baroque mansion, and is full of San
Lorenzo hipsters lounging all over the floor,
drinking the mean mojitos. Fun.

**ARCO DEGLI AURUNCI**                     CAFE-BAR
Map p339 (☎06 445 44 25; Via degli Aurunci
42; ◷8am-2am; ⓆVia Tiburtina, ⓆVia dei Reti)
On the corner of San Lorenzo's most happening piazza, this is a relaxed place for a
drink and some snacks (mixed plate of salami and cheeses €14). The interior is airy,
with warm orange walls, brick arches and
blown-up photos, and there's occasional
live music.

**DIMMIDISÍ**                              NIGHTCLUB
Map p339 (☎06 446 18 55; www.dimmidisiroma.
it; Via dei Volsci 126B; ◷6pm-2am Thu-Mon Sep-
May; bVia Tiburtina, ⓆVia dei Reti) This intimate, small-scale white-walled loft of a club
is devoted to new music, including jazz,
soul, dub, electronica and breakbeat. There
are regular DJs and it's a good place to see
live bands.

**ESC ATELIER OCCUPATO**                   NIGHTCLUB
Map p339 (Via dei Volsci 159; ◷11pm-4am; ⓆVia
Tiburtina, ⓆVia dei Reti) The 'occupied studio'
is a squatter-style arts centre, hosting gigs,
club nights, exhibitions, political events
and more. It also organises Dinamo Fest in
July at Città dell'altra Economia, which featured such events as a live set from Richard
Dorfmeister in 2011. Admission and drinks
are cheap.

**MAX'S BAR**                              NIGHTCLUB
Map p339 (☎06 702 01 599; Via Achille Grandi 3a;
admission varies; ◷10.30pm-3.30am Thu-Sun;
ⓆRoma Laziali) Max is a gay Rome institution, and its unthreatening, welcoming
vibe, backed by a hip-wiggling soundtrack
of commercial house, is what has endeared
it to so many men for so long.

START **LA BOTTEGA DEL CIOCCOLATA**
END **BOOKÀBAR**
DISTANCE **1KM**
DURATION **TWO HOURS**

Neighbourhood Walk
# San Lorenzo Walking Tour Monti Shopping

This walk visits the shopping highlights of the Monti district, once an ancient Roman slum, today home to a number of appealing wine bars, restaurants and unique boutiques.

First stop is ❶ **La Bottega del Cioccolata**, filled with enticing rows of handmade chocolates. In the runup to Christmas, Easter or Valentine's Day, the shop is dominated by beautifully presented sweets. After breathing in the chocolate scents and deciding which to sample, turn right into Via dei Serpenti. Crossing the Piazza Madonna dei Monti, the district's picturesque hub, the first shop you'll see is the very chic clothing shop ❷ **B** (Piazza Madonna dei Monti 1). Go in if only to marvel at its strict aesthetic: it stocks black or monochrome clothing, with the odd pop of colour supplied by carefully chosen accessories.

Next, cross to continue your walk along via del Boschetto, where you'll find tiny ❸ **I Vetri di Passagrilli**, where the owner creates works of art out of molten glass. Walking up to the junction with Via Panisperna, there is a cluster of shops. Particularly eye-catching is ❹ **Fabio Piccioni**, filled with vintage, recreated costume jewellery. Suitably adorned, tear yourself away, and settle down for a drink and a snack at ❺ **Ai Tre Scalini**, everyone's favourite Monti wine bar. A few paces away is ❻ **Creje**, where you can find leather bags, wallets and belts and statement silver jewellery, all at reasonable prices. Amble further up the street and you'll find ❼ **Archivia**, a gem of a shop featuring unusual homewares such as silver cutlery with twig-shaped handles. A few steps away is ❽ **Perlei**, with hand-made modernist jewellery made from polished stones, plastic, metal, wood, and burnished gold and silver. For your last stop, cross busy Via Nazionale and dive into the tempting booklined ❾ **Bookàbar**, a great place to browse books on art and Rome as well as curious objects of design; its entrance being to the side of the magnificent Palazzo delle Esposizioni.

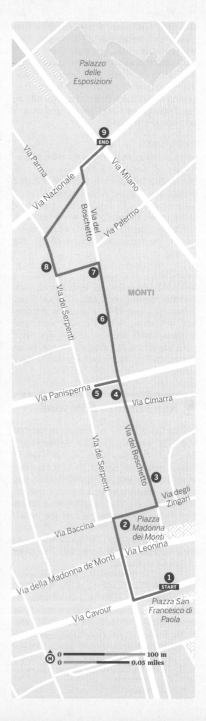

# ⭐ ENTERTAINMENT

**TEATRO DELL'OPERA DI ROMA** OPERA, BALLET
Map p340 (IUC; ☑06 481 601; www.operaroma.
it; Piazza Beniamino Gigli; ⓂRepubblica) It is
functional and Fascist-era outside, but the
interior of Rome's premier opera house – all
plush red and gilt – is a stunning surprise.
This theatre has an impressive history: it
premiered Puccini's *Tosca,* and Maria Cal-
las sang here. Built in 1880, it was given
a Fascist makeover in the 1920s. Contemporary productions don't always match
the splendour of the setting, but you may
get lucky. It's also home to Rome's official
Corps de Ballet; tickets for the ballet cost
anywhere between €13 and €65; for the opera you'll be forking out between €12 and
€80. First-night performances cost more.
From July to mid-August, performances
of both opera and ballet shift outdoors to
the monumental setting of the old Roman
baths, the Terme di Caracalla (p156).

**CHARITY CAFÉ** LIVE MUSIC
Map p340 (☑06 478 25 881; www.charitycafe.it;
Via Panisperna 68; ⓘusually 6pm-2am; ⓂCavour)
Think narrow space, spindly tables, dim
lighting and a laidback vibe: this is a place
to snuggle down and listen to some slinky
live jazz. Supremely civilised, relaxed, un-
touristy and very Monti.

**ISTITUZIONE UNIVERSITARIA DEI
CONCERTI** LIVE MUSIC
Map p339 (IUC; ☑06 361 00 51; www.concertiiuc.
it, in Italian; Piazzale Aldo Moro 5; ⓂCastro Pretorio) The IUC organises a season of concerts
in the Aula Magna of La Sapienza University, including many visiting international
artists and orchestras. Held from October
to June, performances cover a wide range
of musical genres, including baroque, classical, contemporary and jazz – with anything from jazz quartets to Rachmaninov
and Schumann.

**TEATRO AMBRA JOVINELLI** THEATRE
Map p339 (☑06 8308 2620; www.ambrajovi
nelli.org, in Italian; Via G Pepe 43-47; ⓂVittorio
Emanuele) A home away from home for many
famous Italian comics, the Ambra Jovinelli
is a historic venue for alternative comedi-
ans and satirists. Between government-
bashing, the theatre hosts productions of
classics, musicals, opera, new works and
the odd concert.

**WARNER VILLAGE MODERNO** CINEMA
Map p340 (☑892 111; Piazza della Repubblica 45;
ⓂRepubblica) Film premieres are often held
at this multiplex, which screens blockbust-
ers from Hollywood (both in English and
Italian) and major-release Italian films.

# 🛍 SHOPPING

## 🏠 Monti

**LA BOTTEGA DEL CIOCCOLATO** FOOD
Map p340 (☑06 482 14 73; Via Leonina 82;
ⓘ9.30am-7.30pm Oct-Aug; ⓂCavour) Run
by the younger generation of Moriondo &
Gariglio (see p102) is a magical world of
scarlet walls and old-fashioned glass cabinets set into black wood, with irresistible
smells wafting in from the kitchen and
rows of lovingly homemade chocolates on
display.

**I VETRI DI PASSAGRILLI** GLASSWARE
Map p340 (☑06 474 70 22; www.ivetridipassa
grilli.it; Via del Boschetto 94; ⓂCavour) Domenico Passagrilli has had his workshop for
more than 25 years, specialising in fusion
glassware – creating beautiful artworks
through heating glass and moulds in a kiln.
Each of the organic-seeming pieces – plates,
lamps, tiles and window panes – is unique,
and he also restores stained glass.

**FABIO PICCIONI** JEWELLERY
Map p340 (☑06 474 16 97; Via del Boschetto 148;
ⓘ10.30am-1pm Tue-Sat, 2-8pm Mon-Sat; ⓂCa-
vour) A sparkling Aladdin's Cave of decadent one-of-a-kind, costume jewellery;
artisan Fabio Piccioni recycles old trinkets
to create remarkable art deco–inspired
jewellery.

**PERLEI** JEWELLERY
Map p340 (☑06 48 91 38 62; Via del Boschetto
35; ⓂCavour) Beautiful women's jewellery, created by Noritamy, a collaboration
between Tammar Edelman and Elinor
Avni. Their work features bright polished
stones, organic shapes and architectural
structures. The necklaces are particularly
unusual and spectacular, and prices are
reasonable.

### ABITO
CLOTHING

Map p340 (☑06 4881 017; Via Panisperna 61; MCavour) Wilma Silvestre designs elegant clothes with a difference. Choose from the draped, chic, laid-back styles on the rack, and you can have one made up just for you in a day or just a few hours – choose the fabric and the colour. There's usually one guest designer's clothes also being sold at the shop, and it sometimes holds vintage sales downstairs.

### CREJE
CLOTHING

Map p340 (☑06 4890 5227; Via del Boschetto 5A; ☺10am-2.30pm & 3-8pm; MCavour) This Monti boutique sells a mix of clothing sourced from exotic places, including Indian dresses, plus dramatic silver costume jewellery and soft leather bags. Its interesting collection is eclectic and inexpensive.

### FAUSTO SANTINI OUTLET
SHOES

Map p340 (☑06 488 09 34; Via Cavour 106; MCavour) Close to the Basilica di Santa Maria Maggiore, this store is named after Fausto Santini's father, Giacomo. It sells end-of-line and sale Fausto Santini boots, shoes and bags, and is well worth a look for a bargain for his signature architectural designs in butter-soft leather at a fraction of the retail price. Sizes are limited, however.

## 🏠 Esquilino

### BOOKÀBAR
BOOKSTORE

Map p340 (☑06 489 13 361; Via Milano 15-17; ☺10am-8pm Mon-Thu, 10am-10.30pm Fri & Sat, 10am-8pm Sun; ☒Via Nazionale) In Firouz Galdo–designed, cool, gleaming white rooms, Bookàbar – the bookshop attached to Palazzo delle Esposizioni – is just made for browsing. There are books on art, architecture and photography, DVDs, CDs, vinyl, children's books and gifts for the design-lover in your life.

### MAS
DEPARTMENT STORE

Map p340 (☑06 446 80 78; Via dello Statuto 11; ☺9am-12.45 & 3.45-7.45pm daily; MVittorio Emanuele) Glorious MAS (Magazzino allo Statuto) is a multistorey temple of glorious didn't-know-I-needed-it, cheap-as-chips practical goods, thermal vests, bags, watches, pants and the kitchen sink, all piled high and at bargain prices – you can pick up a hat here for a couple of euro, or a pair of silk pyjamas for €5.

## 🏠 Piazza Della Repubblica & Around

### FELTRINELLI INTERNATIONAL
BOOKSTORE

Map p340 (☑06 482 78 78; Via VE Orlando 84; MRepubblica) The international branch of Italy's ubiquitous bookseller has a splendid collection of books in English, plus Spanish, French, German and Portuguese. You'll find everything from recent-release bestsellers to dictionaries, travel guides, DVDs and an excellent assortment of maps.

### MEL BOOKSTORE
BOOKSTORE

Map p340 (☑06 488 54 05; Via Nazionale 254-255; MRepubblica) Mel's, on three floors, has a good range of Italian literature, reference books and travel guides, as well as CDs, half-priced books (general-fiction paperbacks), a cheery children's section and a few books in English and French.

## 🏠 San Lorenzo & Beyond

### LA GRANDE OFFICINA
JEWELLERY

Map p339 (☑06 445 03 48; Via dei Sabelli 165B; ☺11am-7.30pm Tue-Fri, 1-7.30pm Mon; ☒Via Tiburtina) Under dusty workshop lamps, husband-and-wife team Giancarlo Genco and Daniela Ronchetti turn everything from old clock parts and Japanese fans into beautiful work-of-art jewellery. Head here for something truly unique.

### CLAUDIO SANÒ
ARTISANAL

Map p339 (☑06 446 92 84; www.claudiosano.it; Largo degli Osci 67A; ☺10am-1pm & 4.30-8pm Mon-Sat; ☒Via Tiburtina) Claudio Sano creates gleaming moulded works of art in leather that are beautiful, witty and surreal, such as a briefcase with a keyhole through it, another with a bite taken out of it, and a handbag in the shape of a fish. They're not cheap, but masterpieces seldom are.

# San Giovanni to Testaccio

SAN GIOVANNI | CELIO | AVENTINO | TESTACCIO

## Neighbourhood Top Five

**1** Facing up to the overpowering splendour of the monumental **Basilica di San Giovanni in Laterano** (p149). You'll feel very small as you explore the echoing baroque interior of Rome's oldest Christian basilica.

**2** Going underground through layers of history at the **Basilica di San Clemente** (p153).

**3** Being over-awed by the towering ruins of the **Terme di Caracalla** (p156).

**4** Enjoying a quiet moment in the tranquil **Basilica di Santa Sabina** (p155).

**5** Looking through the keyhole of the **Priorato dei Cavalieri di Malta** (p152).

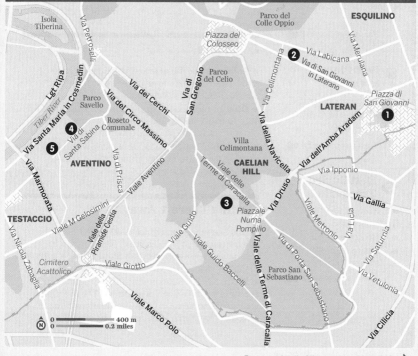

For more detail of this area see Map p356 ➡

## Lonely Planet's Top Tip

If you like opera, check www.operaroma.it for details of summer performances at the Terme di Caracalla. Also, if you visit the Terme di Caracalla, note that the admission ticket includes access to two other sites: the Mausoleo di Cecilia Metella and the Villa dei Quintili. However, these are both some distance from the Terme – the Mausoleo on Via Appia Antica and Villa dei Quintili on Via Appia Nuova – and will require a bus journey to reach.

### ✕ Best Places to Eat

➡ Da Felice (p154)

➡ Il Bocconcino (p154)

➡ Checchino dal 1887 (p154)

For reviews see p154 ➡

### 🍷 Best Places to Drink

➡ Il Pentagrappolo (p154)

➡ L'Oasi della Birra (p155)

➡ Aroma (p155)

For reviews see p154 ➡

### 👁 Best Buried Treasures

➡ Basilica di San Clemente (p153)

➡ Case Romane (p152)

➡ Cimitero Acattolico per Gli Stranieri (p152)

For reviews see p151 ➡

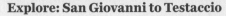

## Explore: San Giovanni to Testaccio

This area extends to the east and south of the Colosseum. It encompasses a lot of ground but can easily be divided into two separate patches: San Giovanni and the Celio; and Aventino and Testaccio. A day in each is sufficient to cover the main sights.

Start off at the landmark Basilica di San Giovanni in Laterano, the focal point of the largely residential Lateran district. It's easily accessible by metro and quite magnificent, both inside and out. Once you've explored the cathedral and surrounding piazza, head down Via di San Giovanni in Laterano towards the Colosseum. Near the bottom, the Basilica di San Clemente is a fascinating church with some thrilling underground ruins. From here, you can walk across to the Celio, the green hill that rises south of the Colosseum. There's not a lot to see around here but the graceful Villa Celimontana park is a great place to escape the crowds. Further south, the Terme di Caracalla is one of the neighbourhood's highlights, easily on a par with anything in the city.

Further west, on the banks of the Tiber, the traditional working-class area of Testaccio is a bastion of old-school Roman cuisine with a number of excellent trattorias, and a popular nightlife district. Rising above it, the Aventino boasts a number of wonderful medieval churches, including the magnificent Basilica di Santa Sabina. Up here you'll also find one of Rome's great curiosities – the famous keyhole view of St Peter's dome.

## Local Life

➡ **Romance** Local Lotharios out to impress their loved ones take them to enjoy the views from the Parco Savello (p152) on the Aventino.

➡ **Offal** Testaccio is the spiritual home of 'blood-and-guts' Roman cooking and its popular trattorias and restaurants are the place to try it (p154).

➡ **Parks** You'll often see locals relaxing with a book or going for a leisurely lunchtime stroll in Villa Celimontana (p152).

## Getting There & Away

➡ **Bus** Useful bus routes include 85 and 87, both of which stop near the Basilica di San Giovanni in Laterano; 714, which serves San Giovanni and the Terme di Caracalla; and 175, which runs to the Aventino.

➡ **Metro** San Giovanni is accessible by metro line A. For Testaccio take line B to Piramide. The Aventino is walkable from Testaccio and Circo Massimo (line B), although from Circo Massimo it's a bit of a hike.

## TOP SIGHTS
# BASILICA DI SAN GIOVANNI IN LATERANO

**For a thousand years this monumental cathedral was the most important church in Christendom. Founded by the Emperor Constantine in the fourth century, it was the first Christian basilica to be built in Rome and, until the 14th century, was the pope's main place of worship. The Vatican still has extraterritorial authority over it, despite it being Rome's official cathedral and the pope's seat as Bishop of Rome.**

The oldest of Rome's four papal basilicas (the others are St Peter's, the Basilica di San Paolo Fuori le Mura and the Basilica di Santa Maria Maggiore), it was constructed during the building boom that followed Constantine's accession to power in 312, and consecrated by Pope Sylvester I in 324. From then until 1309, when the papacy moved to Avignon, it was the principal pontifical church, and the adjacent Palazzo Laterano was the pope's official residence. Both buildings fell into disrepair during the papacy's French interlude, and when Pope Gregory XI returned to Rome in 1377 he preferred to decamp to the fortified Vatican rather than stay in the official papal digs.

Over the course of its long history, the basilica has been vandalised by invading barbarians and twice destroyed by fire. It was rebuilt each time and the basilica you see today is a culmination of several comprehensive makeovers.

### The Facade

Surmounted by fifteen 7m-high statues – Christ with St John the Baptist, John the Evangelist and the 12 Apostles – Alessandro Galilei's monumental white facade is a mid-18th-century work of late-baroque classicism, designed to convey the infinite authority of the Church. Behind the colossal columns, the portico gives onto five sets of doors. The central **bronze doors** were moved here from the Curia in the Roman Forum while, to their right, the wooden **Holy Door** is only opened in Jubilee years.

### DON'T MISS...

➡ Monument to Pope Sylvester II
➡ The baldachin
➡ The cloister

### PRACTICALITIES

➡ Map p356
➡ Piazza di San Giovanni in Laterano 4
➡ audioguide €5
➡ ⊘7am-6.30pm
➡ Ⓜ San Giovanni

## BASILICA LEGENDS

There are various legends associated with the basilica. One holds that if a pregnant woman touches the basilica's main bronze doors she will give birth to a baby boy. Inside, on the first pilaster in the right-hand nave you'll see traces of a fresco by Giotto depicting Pope Boniface VIII declaring the first Jubilee in 1300. While admiring this, cock your ear towards the next pilaster, where a monument to Pope Sylvester II (r 999–1003) is said to sweat and creak when the death of a pope is imminent. Outside on the western side of the cloister, four columns support a slab of marble that medieval Christians believed represented the height of Jesus. A similar story surrounds a piece of porphyry on which it's said Roman soldiers threw lots to win the robes of the crucified Christ.

**As President of the French Republic, Nicolas Sarkozy is the current holder of the title 'Proto-canonico d'onore del capitolo della basilica lateranense' or 'honorary canon of the Basilica of St John in Lateran'.**

## The Interior

The interior has been revamped on numerous occasions, although it owes much of its present look to Francesco Borromini, who was called in by Pope Innocent X to decorate it for the 1650 Jubilee. Divided into a central nave and four minor aisles, it's a breathtaking sight, measuring 130m (length) by 55.6m (width) by 30m (height). Up above, the spectacular gilt **ceiling** was created at different times, but the central section, which is set around Pope Pius IV's carved coat of arms, dates to the 1560s. Beneath your feet, the beautiful inlaid mosaic **floor** was laid down by Pope Martin V in 1425.

The central nave is lined with 18th-century sculptures of the apostles, each 4.6m high and each set in a heroic pose in its own dramatic niche. At the head of the nave, the pointed Gothic **baldachin** that rises over the papal altar is one of the few features that survived Borromini's 17th-century facelift. It's a dramatic work, set atop four columns and decorated with pictures of Jesus, the Virgin Mary and the saints. Up top, behind a grill are the remaining relics of the heads of St Peter and St Paul. In front of the altar, a double staircase leads to the **confessio**, which houses the Renaissance tomb of Pope Martin V.

Behind the altar, the massive apse is decorated with sparkling mosaics, parts of which date to the 4th century, but most of which was added in the 19th century.

## The Cloister

To the left of the altar, the beautiful **cloister** (admission €2; ⊙9am-6pm) was built by the Vassalletto family in the 13th century. It's a lovely, peaceful place with graceful Cosmatesque twisted columns set around a central garden. These columns were once completely covered with inlaid marble mosaics, remnants of which can still be seen. Lining the ambulatories are marble fragments of the original basilica, including the remains of a 5th-century papal throne and inscriptions of a couple of papal bulls.

TOP SIGHTS **BASILICA DI SAN GIOVANNI IN LATERANO**

# ⊙ SIGHTS

## ⊙ San Giovanni

### BASILICA DI SAN GIOVANNI
### IN LATERANO                    CHURCH
See p149.

### PALAZZO LATERANO
### & BATTISTERO          PALAZZO, CHURCH
Map p356 (Piazza San Giovanni in Laterano; admission battistero free; ☺battistero 7.30am-12.30pm & 4-6.30pm; Ⓜ San Giovanni) Flanking Piazza San Giovanni in Laterano, itself dominated by Rome's oldest and tallest **obelisk**, is Domenico Fontana's 16th-century **Palazzo Laterano**. Part of the original 4th-century basilica complex, it was the official papal residence until the popes moved to the Vatican in 1377, and today houses offices of the diocese of Rome.

Just around the corner is the fascinating octagonal **battistero** (baptistry; ☺7.30am-12.30pm & 4-6.30pm). Built by Constantine in the 4th century, it served as the prototype for later Christian churches and bell towers. The chief interest, apart from the architecture, are the decorative mosaics, some of which date back to the 5th century.

### SCALA SANTA & SANCTA
### SANCTORUM                      CHURCH
Map p356 (Piazza di San Giovanni in Laterano 14; Scala/Sancta free/€3.50; ☺Scala 6.15am-noon & 3.30-6.45pm summer, 6.15am-noon & 3-6.15pm winter, Sancta Sanctorum 10.30-11.30am & 3-4pm, closed Wed am & Sun year-round; Ⓜ San Giovanni) The Scala Santa is said to be the staircase that Jesus walked up in Pontius Pilate's palace in Jerusalem. It was brought to Rome by St Helena in the 4th century, and is considered so sacred that you can only climb it on your knees, saying a prayer on each of the 28 steps. At the top of the stairs, and accessible by two side staircases if you don't fancy the knee-climb, is the **Sancta Sanctorum** (Holy of Holies), once the pope's private chapel. A spectacular sight, it's richly decorated with stunning mosaics and frescoes.

Behind the Scala building you'll see what appears to be a cut-off cross-section of a building, adorned with a showy gold mosaic. This is the **Triclinium Leoninum**, an 18th-century reconstruction of the end wall of the banqueting hall in the original Palazzo Laterano.

## ⊙ Celio

### CHIESA DI SS
### QUATTRO CORONATI               CHURCH
Map p356 (Via dei Santissimi Quattro Coronati 20; ☺church 6.15am-8pm Mon-Sat, 6.45am-12.30pm & 3-7.30pm Sun, Cappella di San Silvestro & cloisters 9.30am-noon & 4.30-6pm Mon-Sat, 9-10.40am & 4-5.45pm Sun; ☐Via Labicana) This brooding 4th-century church, rebuilt as a fortified convent after it was destroyed during the 1084 Norman sack of Rome, is dedicated to four Christian sculptors who were killed by Diocletian for refusing to make a statue of a pagan god. As a result, it's still revered by stone-cutters and masons. The most famous feature is the Cappella di San Silvestro and its well-preserved 13th-century frescoes depicting the story of the Donation of Constantine, a famous document by which Constantine ceded control of Rome and the Western Roman Empire to the papacy – see the History Chapter, p259, for more on this.

SAN GIOVANNI TO TESTACCIO SIGHTS

### SUBTERRANEAN CULT
..............................................................................
Mithraism was a cult that was hugely popular with the ancient Roman military. According to its mythology, Mithras, a young, handsome god, was ordered to slay a wild bull by the Sun. As the bull died, it gave life, as its blood flow caused wheat and other plants to grow. In Mithraic iconography, a serpent and dog are usually shown attacking the bull to try to prevent this, while a scorpion attacks its testicles. Mithraic temples are always deep and dark, but the cult's fascination with dank, dark caves doesn't reflect a sinister undercurrent. Rather, its cave-temples represented the cosmos, because it was created from the earth. Here devotees underwent complex processes of initiation, and ate bread and water as a representation of the body and the blood of the bull. Sound familiar? The early Christians thought so too, and were fervently against the cult, feeling its practices were too close to their own.

Also of interest are the beautiful 13th-century cloisters off the northern aisle (ring the bell for admission).

### CHIESA DI SS GIOVANNI E PAOLO & CASE ROMANE
CHURCH, ROMAN RUINS

Map p356 (Piazza di SS Giovanni e Paolo; ⊙8.30am-noon & 3.30-6pm Mon-Thu; ⓂColosseo or Circo Massimo) While there's little of interest in this much-tweaked 4th-century church, the Roman houses that lie beneath it are fascinating. According to tradition, the apostles John and Paul lived in the **Case Romane** (⌖06 704 54 544; www.caseromane.it; adult/reduced €6/4; ⊙10am-1pm & 3-6pm Thu-Mon) before they were beheaded by Constantine's anti-Christian successor, Julian. There's no direct evidence for this, although research has revealed that the houses were used for Christian worship. There are more than 20 rooms, many of them richly decorated. Entry is to the side of the church on Clivo di Scauro.

### CHIESA DI SAN GREGORIO MAGNO
CHURCH

Map p356 (Piazza di San Gregorio 1; ⊙9am-1pm & 3.30-7pm; ⓂColosseo or Circo Massimo) You have to ring the bell for admission to this looming church, which is built on the site where Pope Gregory the Great is said to have dispatched St Augustine to convert the British to Christianity. Originally it was the pope's family home but in 575 he converted it into a monastery. It was rebuilt in the 17th century and the interior was given a baroque facelift a century later.

Inside, the stately 1st-century-BC marble throne in the **Cappella di San Gregorio** is believed to have been St Gregory's personal perch. Outside, the **Cappella di Sant'Andrea** (⊙9.30am-12.30pm Tue, Thu, Sat & Sun) is the most interesting of three small chapels, with frescoes by Domenichino, Guido Reni and Giovanni Lanfranco.

### VILLA CELIMONTANA
PARK

Map p356 (⊙7am-sunset; ⍰Via della Navicella) With its lawns and colourful flower beds, this leafy walled park is a wonderful place to escape the crowds and enjoy a summer picnic. Romantic couples can seek out shady corners while parents can earn goodwill by letting their loved ones loose at the playground. At the centre of the park is a 16th-century villa that was once owned by the Mattei family but now houses the Italian Geographical Society. Each summer the park stages the popular Villa Celimonta Jazz Festival.

### CHIESA DI SANTO STEFANO ROTONDO
CHURCH

Map p356 (www.santo-stefano-rotondo.it; Via di Santo Stefano Rotondo 7; ⊙9.30am-12.30pm Tue-Sun & 2-5pm Tue-Sat winter, 9.30am-12.30pm Tue-Sun & 3-6pm Tue-Sat summer; ⍰Via della Navicella) 'Such a panorama of horror and butchery no man could imagine in his sleep, though he were to eat a whole pig, raw, for supper.' So wrote Charles Dickens after seeing the 16th-century frescoes that circle this otherwise tranquil church. The X-rated images – and they really are pretty graphic – depict the many tortures suffered by the early Christian martyrs.

The church, one of Rome's oldest, dates to the late 5th century, although it was subsequently altered in the 12th and 15th centuries.

## ⊙ Aventino & Around

### PARCO SAVELLO
GARDEN

Map p356 (Via di Santa Sabina; ⊙dawn-dusk; ⍰Lungotevere Aventino) Known to Romans as the *Giardino degli Aranci* (Orange Garden), this pocket-sized park is a romantic haven. Grab a perch at the small panoramic terrace and watch the sun set over the Tiber and St Peter's dome. In summer, theatre performances are sometimes staged among the perfumed orange trees.

### PIAZZA DEI CAVALIERI DI MALTA
PIAZZA

Map p356 (Via di Santa Sabina; ⍰Lungotevere Aventino) At the southern end of Via di Santa Sabina, this ornate cypress-shaded square takes its name from the Cavalieri di Malta (Knights of Malta), who have their Roman headquarters here, in the **Priorato dei Cavalieri di Malta**. Although it's closed to the public, the priory offers one of Rome's most charming views: look through the keyhole and you'll see the dome of St Peter's perfectly aligned at the end of a hedge-lined avenue.

## ⊙ Testaccio

### CIMITERO ACATTOLICO PER GLI STRANIERI
CEMETERY

Map p356 (Via Caio Cestio 5; voluntary donation €2; ⊙9am-5pm Mon-Sat, 9am-1pm Sun; ⓂPiramide) Despite the busy roads that surround it, Rome's 'Non-Catholic Cemetery for For-

# TOP SIGHTS
## BASILICA DI SAN CLEMENTE

This fascinating basilica provides a vivid glimpse into Rome's multilayered past: a 12th-century basilica built over a 4th-century church, which, in turn, stands over a 2nd-century pagan temple and 1st-century Roman house. Beneath everything are foundations dating to the Roman Republic.

The medieval church features a marvellous 12th-century apse mosaic depicting the *Trionfo della Croce* (Triumph of the Cross), with 12 doves symbolising the apostles and a crowd of bystanders including the Madonna, St John, St John the Baptist and other saints. Equally impressive are Masolino's 15th-century Renaissance frescoes in the Chapel of St Catherine, which recount biblical scenes and episodes from the life of St Catherine.

Steps lead down to the 4th-century *basilica inferiore*, mostly destroyed by Norman invaders in 1084, but with some faded 11th-century frescoes illustrating the life of San Clement. Follow down another level and you'll find yourself walking an ancient lane leading to the Roman house and a dark temple of Mithras, which contains an altar depicting the god slaying a bull. Beneath it all, you can hear the eerie sound of a subterranean river, running through a Roman Republic–era drain.

### DON'T MISS...

➡ *Trionfo della Croce*
➡ Chapel of St Catherine
➡ Basilica Inferiore
➡ Temple of Mithras

### PRACTICALITIES

➡ Map p356
➡ www.basilicasan clemente.com
➡ Via di San Giovanni in Laterano
➡ admission church/ excavations free/€5
➡ ⊘9am-12.30pm & 3-6pm Mon-Sat, noon-6pm Sun
➡ Ⓜ Colosseo

---

eigners' (aka the Protestant Cemetery) is a surprisingly restful place. As the traffic thunders past, you can wander the lovingly tended paths contemplating Percy Bysshe Shelley's words: 'It might make one in love with death to think that one should be buried in so sweet a place.' And so he was, along with fellow Romantic poet John Keats and a whole host of luminaries, including Antonio Gramsci, the revered founder of the Italian Communist Party.

**PIRAMIDE DI CAIO CESTIO**  LANDMARK
Map p356 (ⓂPiramide) Sticking out like, well, an Egyptian pyramid, this distinctive landmark stands in the Aurelian Wall at the side of a massive traffic junction. A 36m-high marble-and-brick tomb, it was built for Gaius Cestius, a 1st-century-BC magistrate, and some 200 years later was incorporated into the Aurelian fortification near Porta San Paolo. The surrounding area is today known as Piramide.

**MONTE TESTACCIO**  HISTORICAL SITE
Map p356 (✆06 06 08; Via Galvani 24; adult/reduced €3/2; ⊘visits allowed in groups by appointment only; ⓂPiramide) Right in the centre of the neighbourhood, this artificial hill is made almost entirely of smashed amphorae. Between the 2nd century BC and the 3rd century AD, Testaccio was Rome's river port. Supplies of wine, oil and grain were transported here in huge terracotta amphorae, which, once emptied, were dumped in the river. When the Tiber became almost unnavigable as a consequence, the pots were smashed and the pieces stacked methodically in a pile, which over time grew into a large hill – Monte Testaccio.

**MACRO FUTURE**  ART GALLERY
Map p356 (✆06 574 26 47; www.macro.roma. museum; Piazza Orazio Giustiniani 4; adult/reduced €5/3; ⊘4pm-midnight Tue-Sun; ⓂPiramide) Housed in Rome's ex-slaughterhouse, MACRO's second gallery (the main one is in northern Rome – see p214) serves up contemporary art in two cavernous industrial halls. Note that the gallery opens only when there is an exhibition on – check the website for details.

# EATING

## San Giovanni

### IL BOCCONCINO
TRATTORIA €€

Map p356 (☑06 770 791 75; www.ilbocconcino.com; Via Ostilia 23; meals €30-35; ⊙Thu-Tue, closed Aug) Visited the Colosseum and *need* lunch in a local trattoria? Try 'the little mouthful' in the area heading up towards San Giovanni. Its gingham tablecloths, outdoor seating and cosy interior look like all the others in this touristy neighbourhood but it serves excellent pastas and imaginative meat and fish mains such as *rombo in impanatura di agrumi* (turbot with citrus fruit coating).

### TAVERNA DEI QUARANTA
TRATTORIA €€

Map p356 (☑06 700 05 50; www.tavernadeiquaranta.com; Via Claudia 24; pizzas from €7, meals €25-30; ⊙Mon-Sat; Ⓜ Colosseo) Tasty traditional food, honest prices, near the Colosseum but off the beaten track – there's a lot to like about this laid-back, airy trattoria. There are no great surprises on the menu but daily specials add variety and all the desserts are homemade – always a good sign.

## Testaccio

### DA FELICE
TRADITIONAL ITALIAN €€

Map p356 (☑06 574 68 00; www.feliceatestaccio.com; Via Mastro Giorgio 29; meals €40; ⊙Mon-Sat; 🚇 or 🚊Via Marmorata) Locals and foodies swear by this Testaccio stalwart, famous for its traditional Roman cuisine. The decor might be post-industrial chic – exposed brick walls, chequered marble floor, hanging lamps – but the menu is stolidly traditional, following a classic weekly routine. Highlights include the Tuesday *tonnarelli cacio e pepe* (square-shaped spaghetti with pecorino Romano cheese and black pepper) and the Thursday *coda alla vaccinara* (oxtail).

### TRATTORIA DA BUCATINO
TRATTORIA €€

Map p356 (☑06 574 68 86; Via Luca della Robbia 84; meals €30; ⊙Tue-Sun; 🚇 or 🚊Via Marmorata) This laid-back neighbourhood trattoria is hugely popular. Ask for a table upstairs (with wood panels, Chianti bottles and a mounted boar's head) and dig into huge portions of Roman soul food. The *bucatini all'amatriciana* is a must and meaty *secondi* are also excellent, but do try to save room for a home-cooked dessert.

### CHECCHINO DAL 1887
TRADITIONAL ITALIAN €€€

Map p356 (☑06 574 63 18; Via di Monte Testaccio 30; meals €60; ⊙Tue-Sat, closed Aug; 🚇 or 🚊Via Marmorata) A pig's whisker from the city's former slaughterhouse, Checchino is one of the grander restaurants specialising in the *quinto quarto* (fifth quarter – or insides of the animal). It was here that the Roman recipe for *coda all vaccinara* (oxtail stew) was first developed and it's here that you'll get Rome's best *rigatoni alla gricia* (pasta tubes with pecorino cheese, black pepper and pancetta) according to the local Gambero Rosso food critics.

### PIZZERIA REMO
PIZZERIA €

Map p356 (☑06 574 62 70; Piazza Santa Maria Liberatrice 44; pizzas from €6; ⊙7pm-1am Mon-Sat; 🚇 or 🚊Via Marmorata) Not the place for a romantic dinner, Pizzeria Remo is one of the city's most popular pizzerias, always full of noisy young Romans. The pizzas are thin Roman-style with toppings loaded onto a crisp, charred base. Place your order by ticking your choices on a sheet of paper slapped down by an overstretched waiter. Expect to queue.

### VOLPETTI PIÙ
TRADITIONAL ITALIAN €

Map p356 (Via Volta 8; meals under €15; ⊙10.30am-3.30pm & 5.30-9.30pm Mon-Sat; 🚇 or 🚊Via Marmorata) One of the few places in town where you can sit down and eat well for less than €15, Volpetti Più is a sumptuous *tavola calda,* offering an opulent choice of pizza, pasta, soup, meat, vegetables and fried nibbles. It adjoins Volpetti's to-die-for deli.

# DRINKING & NIGHTLIFE

## San Giovanni

### IL PENTAGRAPPOLO
WINE BAR

Map p356 (Via Celimontana 21b; ⊙noon-3pm & 6pm-1am Tue-Sun; Ⓜ Colosseo) A few blocks from the Colosseum, these smooth star-vaulted rooms offer 250 labels to choose from and about 15 wines by the glass. The bar attracts a mellow, local crowd who sip to the sounds of live jazz or soul on Thursday, Friday and Saturdays nights. There's also a daily *aperitivo* between 6pm and 8.30pm.

### AROMA BAR

Map p356 (Hotel Gladiatori, Via Labicana 125; ⊘4pm-midnight; MColosseo) Romance your partner with a drink or two at the gorgeous, flower-ringed rooftop bar of the five-star Hotel Gladiatori. For maximum effect, head up there at sundown for a twilight cocktail and some magical 'marry-me' views over the Colosseum.

### COMING OUT BAR

Map p356 (www.comingout.it; Via di San Giovanni in Laterano 8; ⊘10.30am-2am; MColosseo) Spot this easygoing gay bar in the shadow of the Colosseum by the rainbow sign and the mixed, convivial crowds spilling out into the street. It's a popular pre-clubbing stop and features regular drag acts and DJ sets.

## Testaccio

### L'OASI DELLA BIRRA BAR

Map p356 (☎06 574 61 22; Piazza Testaccio 41; ⊘5pm-1am Mon-Thu & Sun, to 2am Fri & Sat; MPiramide) Underneath the Palombi wine bar, this rustic watering hole is exactly what it says it is – an Oasis of Beer. With everything from Teutonic heavyweights to boutique brews, as well as an ample selection of wines and a menu of cheeses, cold cuts, stews and the like, it's ideal for an evening of dedicated eating and drinking. It gets very busy, particularly on Saturdays when you'll need to book.

### CONTESTACCIO NIGHTCLUB

Map p356 (www.myspace.com\contestaccio; Via di Monte Testaccio 65b; ⊘8pm-5am Tue-Sun, closed end Jun–mid-Sep; MPiramide) With an under-the-stars terrace, restaurant and cool, arched interior, Contestaccio is one of the most popular venues on the Testaccio clubbing strip, serving up a regular menu of DJs and live gigs. Admission is usually free during the week and cocktails are around €8.

## TOP SIGHTS
## BASILICA DI SANTA SABINA

This magnificent, solemn basilica was founded by Peter of Illyria in around AD 422. It was enlarged in the 9th century and again in 1216, just before it was given to the newly founded Dominican order – look out for the mosaic tombstone of Muñoz de Zamora, one of the order's founding fathers, in the nave floor. A 20th-century restoration returned it to its original look.

One of the few surviving 4th-century elements are the basilica's cypress-wood doors. They feature 18 carved panels depicting biblical events, including one of the oldest Crucifixion scenes in existence. It's quite hard to make out in the top left, but it depicts Jesus and the two thieves although, strangely, not their crosses.

Inside, the three naves are separated by 24 Corinthian columns, which support an arcade decorated with a faded red-and-green frieze. Light streams in from high nave windows that were added in the 9th century, along with the carved choir, pulpit and bishop's throne.

Behind the church is a garden and a meditative 13th-century cloister, where St Dominic is said to have planted Italy's first ever orange tree.

### DON'T MISS...
➡ The main doors
➡ Tombstone of Muñoz de Zamora

### PRACTICALITIES
➡ Map p356
➡ Piazza Pietro d'Illiria 1
➡ ⊘8.15am-12.30pm & 3.30-6pm
➡ Lungotevere Aventino

SAN GIOVANNI TO TESTACCIO DRINKING & NIGHTLIFE

# TOP SIGHTS
## TERME DI CARACALLA

The remnants of the emperor Caracalla's vast baths complex are among Rome's most awe-inspiring ruins. Inaugurated in 216, the original 10-hectare complex comprised baths, gymnasiums, libraries, shops and gardens. Between 6000 and 8000 people were thought to pass through everyday while, underground, hundreds of slaves sweated in 9.5km of tunnels, tending to the plumbing systems. The baths remained in continuous use until 537, when the Visigoths smashed their way into Rome and cut off its water supply. Later excavations in the 16th and 17th centuries unearthed important sculptures, many of which found their way into the Farnese family art collection.

Most of the skeletal ruins are what's left of the central bath house. This was a huge rectangular edifice, measuring 218m by 112m, centred on the *frigidarium* (cold room), where bathers would stop after spells in the warmer *tepidarium* and before that the dome-capped *caldaria* (hot room). Opening onto the *frigidarium* was the *natatio*, a big open-air swimming pool, while two lateral *palestre* (gyms) provided space for a pre-bath workout.

In summer the ruins are used to stage spectacular opera performances – see p145) for further details.

### DON'T MISS...

➡ Frigidarium
➡ Palestre
➡ Caldaria

### PRACTICALITIES

➡ Map p356
➡ ☑06 399 67 700
➡ Viale delle Terme di Caracalla 52
➡ adult/reduced incl Mausoleo di Cecilia Metella & Villa dei Quintili €6/3
➡ audioguide €5
➡ ☉9am-1hr before sunset Tue-Sun, 9am-2pm Mon year-round
➡ ☒Via delle Terme di Caracalla

---

**LINARI** CAFE

Map p356 (Via Nicola Zabaglia 9; ☉7am-11pm Wed-Mon; ☒ or ☒Via Marmorata) Spot this by the crowds of part-of-the-furniture locals. It has the busy clatter of a good bar, with excellent pastries, splendid coffee and barside banter. There are some outside tables, ideal for a cheap lunch (pastas/main courses €5.50/6.50), but you'll have to arm-wrestle the elderly neighbourhood ladies to get one.

**VILLAGGIO GLOBALE** NIGHTCLUB, LIVE MUSIC

Map p356 (www.ecn.org/villaggioglobale/joomla; Lungotevere Testaccio 1; ☒Piramide) For a warehouse-party vibe, head to Rome's best-known *centro sociale,* originally a squat, occupying the city's graffiti-sprayed former slaughterhouse. Thirty years have passed and it's now part of the (anti-) establishment. Entrance is usually around €5, beer is cheap, and the music focuses on dance-hall, reggae, dubstep and drum 'n' bass.

**L'ALIBI** NIGHTCLUB

Map p356 (www.lalibi.it; Via di Monte Testaccio 44; ☉11pm-5am Thu-Sun; ☒Piramide) One of Rome's historic gay clubs, L'Alibi does high-camp with style, putting on kitsch shows and playing sultry, soulful house to a mixed gay and straight crowd. Its spread over three floors and if the sweaty atmosphere in the dance halls gets too much, head up to the huge summer roof terrace. Thursday nights are big with the ever-popular Gloss party.

**AKAB** NIGHTCLUB

Map p356 (www.akabcave.com; Via di Monte Testaccio 68-69; ☉11pm-4am Tue-Sat, closed end Jun–mid-Sep; ☒Piramide) This eclectic former workshop has an underground cellar, an upper floor, a garden and a whimsical door policy. It gets crammed at weekends with local (often cover) bands on Friday, and R&B and house on Saturday. Tuesday is another big night, it's L'Etrika a must for house and electronica fans. Entrance is usually around €15, including a complimentary drink.

**IL SEME E LA FOGLIA** BAR

Map p356 (Via Galvani 18; ☉8am-2am Mon-Sat, 6pm-2am Sun; ☒Piramide) Thanks to its position at the edge of Testaccio's nightlife strip, this innocuous-looking bar is a popular pre-club stop. Groups of dressed-up clubbers gather here to decide their next move and grab a beer in the tiny tangerine bar.

# 🛍 SHOPPING

## VOLPETTI
DELICATESSEN

Map p356 (www.volpetti.com; Via Marmorata 47; 🚇 or 🚋 Via Marmorata) It's not cheap but quality costs and the gourmet delights you'll find here, at what many claim is Rome's best deli, are top of the range. Helpful staff will guide you through the extensive selection that runs the gamut from smelly cheese and homemade pasta to olive oil, vinegar, salami, veggie pies, wine and grappa. You can also order online.

## RGB 46
BOOKSTORE, ART GALLERY

Map p356 (www.grb46.it; Piazza Santa Maria Liberatrice 46; ◎4pm-1am Mon, 10am-1pm & 4pm-1am Tue-Sat; 🚇 or 🚋 Via Marmorata) Specialising in art and design books (mostly in Italian), this laid-back store is as much a gallery as a bookshop with original works of contemporary art on the bare white walls and a small bar serving wine and teas. And to put you in the mood for buying, there's a happy hour each Thursday, Friday and Saturday between 7 and 9pm, free wi-fi and the occasional DJ-set.

## SUZUGANARU
FASHION

Map p356 (Via di San Giovanni in Laterano 206; ◎closed Aug; Ⓜ Colosseo) Photographer–designer Marcella Manfredini sells whimsical, individual women's clothes at this low-key, unpretentious boutique. She makes some of the clothes herself, while also stocking accessories such as bright lacquer bangles, felt bags and belts.

## CALZATURE BOCCANERA
SHOES

Map p356 (Via Luca della Robbia 36; 🚇 or 🚋 Via Marmorata) This well-known Testaccio shoe store stocks big designer names at big designer prices. You'll find everything from Clark's desert boots to Gucci slip-ons, Prada heels and Tod's loafers, as well as bags, belts and leather luxuries. It's particularly worth a look at sale time.

## SOUL FOOD
MUSIC STORE

Map p356 (Via di San Giovanni in Laterano 192; Ⓜ Colosseo) Run by **Hate Records** (www.haterecords.com), Soul Food presents rare vintage vinyl to make every true funkster's heart beat faster: rock, punk, '60s garage, jazz, rockabilly, glam. You name it, they've got it, plus retro-design T-shirts, fanzines and other groupie clobber.

## VIA SANNIO
MARKET

Map p356 (◎8am-1pm Mon-Sat; Ⓜ San Giovanni) This morning market in the shadow of Porta San Giovanni, near the basilica, is awash with wardrobe staples. It has a good assortment of new and vintage clothes, shoes at bargain prices, and a good range of jeans and leather jackets.

**SAN GIOVANNI TO TESTACCIO** SHOPPING

# Southern Rome

VIA APPIA ANTICA | OSTIENSE, SAN PAOLO & GARBATELLA | EUR

## Neighbourhood Top Five

**1** Walking or cycling along the **Via Appia Antica** (p160), tracing the route of a thousand ancient Roman footsteps.

**2** Exploring Rome's Christian burial catacombs, such as the **Catacombe di San Sebastiano** (p1p64).

**3** Wandering around the genius location for the overflow from the Capitoline Museums: **Centrale Montemartini** (p165).

**4** Going clubbing in Ostiense and dancing your arse off somewhere like **La Saponeria** (p167).

**5** Feeling dwarfed by the majesty of **San Paolo Fuori La Mura** (p166).

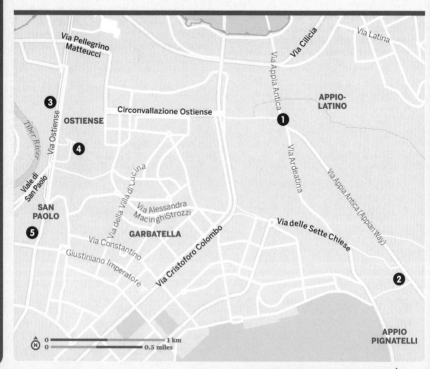

For more detail of this area see Map p358 ➡

# Explore: Southern Rome

Southern Rome is a sprawling neighbourhood that comprises three distinct areas that are of particular interest to the visitor: Via Appia Antica, famous for its catacombs; trendy Via Ostiense; and EUR, Mussolini's futuristic building development. It's all quite spread out, but public transport connections are good.

Heading southeast from Porta San Sebastiano, Via Appia Antica (the Appian Way) is one of the world's oldest roads and a much-prized Roman address. It's a beautiful part of town, with crumbling ruins set amid pea-green fields and towering umbrella. Besides hulking Roman ruins, there are some 300km of underground tunnels here that were used as burial chambers by the early Christians, and three of the networks are open to visitors.

Via Ostiense presents a very different picture. Busy and traffic-clogged, it runs through one of the capital's hippest districts. Disused factories and warehouses harbour restaurants, pubs, clubs and bars, and a couple of gem-like sights: Centrale Montemartini, a great disused power plant housing superb classical statuary, and Basilica di San Paolo fuori le Mura, the world's third-largest church. Over the road, the character-filled Garbatella district merits exploration for its original architecture while, further south, EUR is a world apart. Built by Mussolini as a showcase for his Fascist regime, it's a fascinating, Orwellian quarter of wide boulevards and linear buildings.

## Local Life

→ **Clubbing** Some of Rome's coolest clubs are clustered around Via Ostiense.

→ **Cycling** Escaping from the frenetic city centre along the beautiful Appian Way.

→ **Hangouts** Feeling the laidback, local atmosphere of arty, art deco–style Garbatella.

## Getting There & Away

→ **Metro** Metro line B runs to Piramide, Garbatella, Basilica San Paolo, EUR Palasport and EUR Fermi.

→ **Bus** There are bus connections to Porta San Sebastiano (118, 218 and 714), Via Ostiense (23 and 716) and Via Appia Antica (118, 218 and 660).

→ **Archeobus** If you're spending the day here and want to see several sights, the hop-on hop-off Archeobus (€12) departs from Termini every hour.

## Lonely Planet's Top Tip

On Sunday, Appia Antica is traffic free. On other days bear in mind that the first section, from Porta San Sebastiano for about three miles, isn't pedestrian friendly. The most atmospheric stretch is from the Tempio di Romolo to the Via Appia Nuova junction, and this section is virtually traffic free every day.

If you're not planning to visit lots of sights, take the local bus rather than buying an Archeobus ticket.

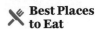 **Best Places to Eat**

→ Trattoria Priscilla (p165)

→ Da Enzo (p165)

→ Hostaria Zampagna (p165)

→ Doppiozeroo (p166)

For reviews see p165 →

 **Best Places to Drink**

→ Doppiozeroo (p166)

→ Il Melograno (p167)

→ Caffè Letterario (p168)

→ Rising Love (p167)

→ Rashomon (p167)

For reviews see p166 →

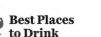 **Best Entertainment**

→ La Casa del Jazz (p168)

→ Teatro India (p168)

→ Teatro Palladium (p168)

→ Piscina delle Rose (p167)

For reviews see p168 →

**SOUTHERN ROME**

## TOP SIGHTS
## VIA APPIA ANTICA

**Heading southeast from Porta San Sebastiano, the Appian Way was known to the Romans as the regina viarum (queen of roads). Named after Appius Claudius Caecus, who laid the first 90km section in 312 BC, it was extended in 190 BC to reach Brindisi, some 540km away on the southern Adriatic coast. Flanked by some of the city's most exclusive private villas, as well as Roman tombs, the long cobbled road is a great place for a walk or cycle.**

### DON'T MISS...

➡ The catacombs
➡ Cycling along the Appia
➡ Villa dei Quintilli

### PRACTICALITIES

➡ Map p358
➡ ☎06 513 53 16
➡ www.parcoappia antica.org
➡ Via Appia Antica
➡ ▣Via Appia Antica

### Burial Chambers & Catacombs

The Appia Antica, peaceful today, resounds with history: it's where Spartacus and 6000 of his slave rebels were crucified in 71 BC, and around it lie 300km of underground tunnels carved out of soft tufa rock, used as burial chambers by the early Christians. Corpses were wrapped in simple white sheets and usually placed in rectangular niches carved into the walls, which were then closed with marble or terracotta slabs. You can't visit all 300km, but three major catacombs (San Callisto, San Sebastiano and Santa Domitilla) are open for guided exploration.

### Cards, Bikes & Tours

If you're planning on really doing the sights, think about buying the Appia Antica Card (see p309). Near the start of the road, the Appia Antica Regional Park Information Point is very informative. You can buy a map of the park here and hire bikes (per hour/day €3/10). The park authorities organise a series of free guided tours, on foot and by bike, on Sunday mornings. You can also download a free audioguide to the Caffarella Valley on the website. In addition, Darwin Cooperative (www.cooperativadarwin.it) leads group walking or biking tours in English, French, Spanish and German.

#  SIGHTS

The awe-inspiring Appian Way stretches south of Rome, dotted by Roman ruins above and riddled with catacombs underground. Elsewhere Southern Rome offers such treasures as the patriarchal basilica San Paolo Fuori le Mura and the Capitoline Museum collection at Centrale Montemartini.

# ⊙ Via Appia Antica

### BASILICA & CATACOMBE DI SAN SEBASTIANO
CHURCH, CATACOMB

See p164.

### VILLA DI MASSENZIO
ANCIENT RUINS

Map p358 (✐06 780 13 24; www.villadimassen zio.it; Via Appia Antica 153; adult/reduced €3/2; ☺9am-1.30pm Tue-Sat; ☐Via Appia Antica) The outstanding feature of Maxentius' enormous 4th-century palace complex is the **Circo di Massenzio**, Rome's best-preserved ancient racetrack – you can still make out the starting stalls used for chariot races. The 10,000-seat arena was built by Maxentius around 309, but he died before ever seeing a race here.

Above the arena are the ruins of Maxentius' imperial residence, most of which are covered by weeds. Near the racetrack, the **Mausoleo di Romolo** (also known as the Tombo di Romolo) was built by Maxentius for his son Romulus. The huge mausoleum was originally crowned with a large dome and surrounded by an imposing colonnade, in part still visible.

### MAUSOLEO DI CECILIA METELLA
ANCIENT RUINS

Map p358 (✐06 399 67 700; Via Appia Antica 161; admission incl Terme di Caracalla & Villa dei Quintili adult/reduced €8/4; ☺9am-1hr before sunset Tue-Sun; ☐Via Appia Antica) Dating to the 1st century BC, this great drum of a mausoleum encloses a burial chamber (built for the daughter of the consul Quintus Metellus Creticus), now roofless. The walls are made of travertine and the sorry-looking interior is decorated with a sculpted frieze featuring Gaelic shields, ox skulls and festoons. In the 14th century it was converted into a fort by the Caetani family, who used to frighten passing traffic into paying a toll.

Beyond the tomb is a picturesque section of the ancient road, excavated in the mid-19th century.

### VILLA DEI QUINTILI
ANCIENT RUINS

off Map p358 (✐06 399 67 700; www.pierreci.it; Via Appia Nuova 1092; adult/reduced incl Terme di Caracalla & Mausoleo di Cecilia Metella €8/4; ☺9am-1hr before sunset Tue-Sun; ☐Via Appia Nuova) Set on lush green fields, this vast 2nd-century villa was the luxurious abode of two brothers who were consuls under Emperor Marcus Aurelius. Alas, the villa's splendour was to be the brothers' downfall – in a fit of jealousy, Emperor Commodus had them both killed, taking over the villa for himself. The highlight is the well-preserved baths complex with a pool, *caldarium* (hot room) and *frigidarium* (cold room).

### CATACOMBE DI SAN CALLISTO
CATACOMB

Map p358 (✐06 513 01 580; www.catacombe. roma.it; Via Appia Antica 110 & 126; adult/reduced €8/4; ☺8.30am-noon & 2.30-5pm Thu-Tue, closed Feb, to 5.30pm Apr-Sep; ☐Via Appia Antica) These are the largest and busiest of Rome's catacombs. Founded at the end of the 2nd century and named after Pope Calixtus I, they became the official cemetery of the newly established Roman Church. In the 20km of tunnels explored to date, archaeologists have found the tombs of 500,000 people and seven popes who were martyred in the 3rd century. The patron saint of music, St Cecilia, was also buried here, though her body was later removed to the Basilica di Santa Cecilia in Trastevere (p171). When her body was exhumed in 1599, more than a thousand years after her death, it was apparently perfectly preserved, as depicted in Stefano Moderno's softly contoured sculpture, a replica of which is here.

### MAUSOLEO DELLE FOSSE ARDEATINE
MONUMENT

Map p358 (✐06 513 67 42; Via Ardeatina 174; admission free; ☺8.15am-3.30pm Mon-Fri, to 4.30pm Sat & Sun; ☐Via Appia Antica) This moving mausoleum is dedicated to the victims of Rome's worst WWII atrocity. Buried here, outside the Ardeatine Caves, are 335 Italians shot by the Nazis on 24 March 1944. Following the massacre, ordered in reprisal for a partisan attack, the Germans used mines to explode sections of the caves and bury the bodies. After the war, the bodies

# Roman Catacombs

According to Roman law, it was forbidden to bury the dead within the city walls. Rome's persecuted Christian community didn't have their own cemeteries and in the 2nd century AD began to build an extensive network of subterranean burial grounds outside the city.

Over time, the burial areas grew larger. The tombs were dug out by specialised gravediggers. Using lamps to light their way, they tunnelled out the galleries.

However, space was limited and became increasingly sought-after. As early as 313, however, the catacombs began to be abandoned, when Constantine issued the Milan decree of religious tolerance.

In about 800, after frequent incursions by invaders, the bodies of the martyrs and first popes were transferred to the basilicas inside the city walls for safe keeping. The catacombs were abandoned and by the Middle Ages many had been forgotten. Those of San Sebastiano were the most frequented as a place of pilgrimage, since they had earlier been the burial place of St Peter and St Paul.

Since the 19th century, more than 30 catacombs have been uncovered in the area. Many contain touching inscriptions.

## TOP 5 CATACOMB READS

➡ *The Roman Catacombs*, by James Spencer Northcote (1859)

➡ *Tombs and Catacombs of the Appian Way: History of Cremation*, by Olinto L. Spadoni (1892)

➡ *Valeria, the Martyr of the Catacombs*, by W H Withrow (1892)

➡ *Christian Rome: Past and Present: Early Christian Rome Catacombs and Basilicas*, by Philippe Pergola (2002)

➡ *The Roman Catacombs*, by Maurus Wolter (2010)

**Clockwise from top left**
1. Detail from 4th century carving in Catacombe di Santa Domitilla (p164) 2. Catacombe di San Callisto (p161)
3. Catacombe di San Sebastiano (p164)

2

were exhumed, identified and reburied in a mass grave, now marked by a huge concrete slab and sculptures.

The site also has a tiny museum dedicated to the Italian Resistance.

### CATACOMBE DI SANTA DOMITILLA
CATACOMB

Map p358 (☑06 511 03 42; Via delle Sette Chiese 283; adult/reduced €8/4; ⊙9am-noon & 2-5pm Wed-Mon, closed Jan; ☐Via Appia Antica) Among Rome's largest and oldest, these catacombs stretch for about 17km. They were established on the private burial ground of Flavia Domitilla, niece of Emperor Domitian and a member of the wealthy Flavian family. They contain Christian wall paintings and the haunting underground **Chiesa di SS Nereus e Achilleus**, a 4th-century church dedicated to two Roman soldiers martyred by Diocletian.

### CHIESA DEL DOMINE QUO VADIS?
CHURCH

Map p358 (Via Appia Antica 51; ⊙8am-6pm; ☐Via Appia Antica) This pint-sized church marks the spot where St Peter, fleeing Rome, met a vision of Jesus going the other way. When Peter asked: *'Domine,*

*quo vadis?'* ('Lord, where are you going?'), Jesus replied, *'Venio Roman iterum crucifigi'* ('I am coming to Rome to be crucified again'). Reluctantly deciding to join him, Peter tramped back into town where he was arrested and executed. In the aisle are copies of Christ's footprints; the originals are in the Basilica di San Sebastiano (p164).

### PORTA SAN SEBASTIANO
MUSEUM

Map p358 (☑06 704 75 284; www.museodellemuraroma.it; Via di Porta San Sebastiano 18; adult/reduced €4/2; ⊙9am-2pm Tue-Sun; ☐Porta San Sebastiano) Marking the start of Via Appia Antica, the 5th-century Porta San Sebastiano is the largest of the gates in the Aurelian Wall. It was originally known as Porta Appia but took on its current name in honour of the thousands of pilgrims who passed under it on their way to the Catacombe di San Sebastiano (p164). During WWII, the Fascist Party secretary Ettore Muti lived here and today it houses the Museo delle Mure, a modest museum illustrating the history of the wall. It's worth a look for the chance to walk along the top of the walls for around 50m.

---

## TOP SIGHTS **BASILICA & CATACOMBE DI SAN SEBASTIANO**

These, the most famous of the catacombs, contain frescoes, stucco work, epigraphs and immaculate mausoleums.

The **Catacombe di San Sebastiano** were the first catacombs to be so called, the name deriving from the Greek *kata* (near) and *kymbas* (cavity), because they were located near a cave. During the persecutory reign of Vespasian, they acted as a safe haven for the remains of St Peter and St Paul and became a popular pilgrimage site. There are three perfectly preserved mausoleums and a plastered wall with hundreds of invocations, engraved by worshippers in the 3rd and 4th centuries.

The 4th-century **basilica** (☑06 780 00 47; Via Appia Antica 136; ⊙8.30am-noon & 2-5pm Mon-Sat, closed Nov, to 5.30pm Apr-Sep), much altered over the years, is dedicated to St Sebastian, who was martyred and buried here in the late 3rd century. In the **Capella delle Reliquie** you'll find one of the arrows used to kill him and the column to which he was tied. On the other side of the church is a marble slab with Jesus' footprints (see p162).

### DON'T MISS...

➡ Graffiti to St Peter & St Paul

➡ Mausoleums

➡ Basilica di San Sebastiano

### PRACTICALITIES

➡ Map p358

➡ ☑06 785 03 50

➡ Via Appia Antica 136

➡ adult/reduced €8/4

➡ ⊙8.30am-noon & 2-5pm Mon-Sat, closed Nov, to 5.30pm Apr-Sept

➡ ☐Via Appia Antica

## ⊙ Ostiense, San Paolo & Garbatella

Heading south from Stazione Roma-Ostia, Via Ostiense encompasses converted warehouses, clubs and hidden sights.

### BASILICA DI SAN PAOLO FUORI LE MURA
CHURCH

See p166.

### CAPITOLINE MUSEUMS AT CENTRALE MONTEMARTINI
MUSEUM

Map p358 (✆06 06 08; www.centralemontemartini.org; Via Ostiense 106; adult/reduced €5.50/4.50, incl Capitoline Museums €14/12, valid 7 days; ☉9am-7pm Tue-Sun; 🚇Via Ostiense) This fabulous outpost of the Capitoline Museums (Musei Capitolini) is a treat. Housed in a former power station, it boldly juxtaposes classical sculpture against diesel engines and giant furnaces. The collection's highlights are in the **Sala Caldaia**, where a giant furnace provides a suitably impressive backdrop. Two of the most beautiful pieces are the *Fanciulla Seduta* and the *Musa Polimnia* gazing dreamily into the distance.

### QUARTIERE GARBATELLA
AREA

Map p358 (Ⓜ Garbatella) A favourite location for TV and filmmakers, Quartiere Garbatella is a wonderfully atmospheric, idiosyncratic district. It was originally conceived as a workers' residential quarter but in the 1920s the Fascists hijacked the project and used the area to house people who'd been displaced by construction work in the city. Many people were moved into *alberghi suburbani* (suburban hotels), big housing blocks designed by Innocenzo Sabbatini, the leading light of the 'Roman School' of architecture. The most famous, **Albergo Rosso** (Piazza Michele da Carbonara) is typical of the style. Other trademark buildings are the **Scuola Cesare Battisti** on Piazza Damiano Sauli and **Teatro Palladium** on Piazza Bartolomeo Romano.

## ✗ EATING

**The increasingly fashionable southern neighbourhoods of Ostiense and Garbatella feature some excellent restaurants, and you can also eat well in a rural setting close to Via Appia Antica.**

## ✗ Via Appia Antica & the Catacombs

### RISTORANTE CECILIA METELLA
TRADITIONAL ITALIAN €€

Map p358 (✆06 511 02 13; Via Appia Antica 125; meals €35; ☉Tue-Sun; 🚇Via Appia Antica) Near the catacombs of San Callisto, the outside seating at Cecilia Metella is great, set on a low hill under a vine canopy and with glimpses of the jewel-green countryside. Inside, the restaurant resembles a wedding-reception room, but it's attractive enough, and the food is reasonable, too – the grilled meats are recommended.

### TRATTORIA PRISCILLA
TRATTORIA €€

Map p358 (✆06 513 63 79; Via Appia Antica 68; meals €30; ☉Mon-Sat, lunch Sun; 🚇Via Appia Antica) Set in a 16th-century former stable, this intimate family-run trattoria has been feeding hungry travellers along the Appian Way for more than a hundred years, serving up traditional *cucina Romana,* so think *carbonara, amatriciana* and *cacio e pepe.*

## ✗ Ostiense, San Paolo & Garbatella

### DA ENZO
TRATTORIA €€

Map p358 (✆06 574 13 64; Via Ostiense 36; meals €30; ☉lunch Tue-Sat, dinner Mon-Sat; Ⓜ Piramide) With just a few tables, this is a classic Roman family-run trattoria that's been here for around 50 years. The chef used to cook at the parliament, and now feeds the workers from the nearby market. The fresh pasta is good, the sausage super and the tiramisu feathery light.

### HOSTARIA ZAMPAGNA
TRATTORIA €€

Map p358 (✆06 574 23 06; Via Ostiense 179; meals €30; ☉Mon-Sat; 🚇Via Ostiense) The trendification of Via Ostiense – with ever-growing numbers of bars and clubs in its side streets – has thankfully bypassed this humble trattoria. As for the past 80 years, you sit down to good hearty, home-cooked food prepared according to the city's weekly calendar. It's all splendid: try *spaghetti alla carbonara, alla gricia* or *all'amatriciana,* then tuck into tripe, beef or *involtini.*

# TOP SIGHTS BASILICA DI SAN PAOLO FUORI LE MURA

The biggest church in Rome after St Peter's (and the world's third-largest), the magnificent, little-visited church of St Paul's stands on the site where St Paul was buried after being decapitated in AD 67. Built by Constantine in the 4th century, it was largely destroyed by fire in 1823 and much of what you see today is a 19th-century reconstruction.

Not all the ancient church was destroyed in the 19th-century fire; many treasures survived, including the 5th-century triumphal arch, with its heavily restored mosaics, and the gothic marble tabernacle over the high altar. This was designed in about 1285 by Arnolfo di Cambio together with another artist, possibly Pietro Cavallini.

Doom-mongers should check out the papal portraits beneath the nave windows. Every pope since St Peter is represented and legend has it that when there is no room for the next portrait, the world will fall.

The stunning 13th-century Cosmati mosaic work in the **cloisters** (admission free; ⊙9am-1pm & 3-6pm) of the adjacent Benedictine abbey also survived the 1823 fire.

### DON'T MISS...

➡ 5th-century triumphal arch and mosaics
➡ Papal portraits
➡ Cloister

### PRACTICALITIES

➡ Map p358
➡ ☑06 80 800
➡ Via Ostiense 190
➡ ⊙ 6.45am-6.30pm
➡ Ⓜ San Paolo

---

# DRINKING & NIGHTLIFE

The ex-industrial area of Ostiense is fertile clubbing land, with its many warehouses, workshops and factories just crying out for a new lease of life as pockets of nightlife nirvana. This is where Rome's serious clubbers lose countless hours worshipping at the shrines of electro, nu-house, nu-funk and all sorts of other eclectica. Nearby, the appealing suburb of Garbatella has long been undergoing trendification, and is a cool, boho district popular with left-leaning hipsters.

### DOPPIOZEROO                    BAR
Map p358 (☑06 573 01 961; Via Ostiense 68; ⊙7am-2am Mon-Sat; ⓂPiramide) This easygoing bar was once a bakery, hence the name ('double zero' is a type of flour). But today the sleek, modern interior attracts hungry, trendy Romans like bees to honey, especially for the famously lavish, dinner-tastic *aperitivo* between 6.30pm and 9pm.

### ALPHEUS                    NIGHTCLUB
Map p358 (☑06 574 78 26; www.alpheus.it in Italian; Via del Commercio 36; ⊙various Tue-Sun Oct-May; ⓂPiramide) Alpheus hosts an eclectic array of sounds in its four rooms, including Argentine tango (plus lessons), hard rock and house – with plenty of live gigs. Saturday is the popular 'Gorgeous, I am' gay night, with lots of go-go dancers and guest DJs.

### DISTILLERIE CLANDESTINE        NIGHTCLUB
Map p358 (☑06 573 05 102; www.distillerie clandestine.com; Via Libetta 13; ⊙11.30pm-4am Thu-Sun Sep-May; ⓂPiramide) A club-bar-restaurant that has a 1930s-meets-Blade Runner decor and keeps the punters dancing with a mix of house, dance and hip hop. As well as a restaurant, there's a ship-shaped American bar lit by a tangle of neon tubes suspended above it.

### GOA                    NIGHTCLUB
Map p358 (☑06 574 82 77; Via Libetta 13; ⊙11pm-4.30am Tue-Sun Oct-May; ⓂGarbatella) Rome's serious super-club, with international names (recent guests include Satoshi Tomiie and M.A.N.D.Y.), a fashion-forward

crowd, podium dancers and heavies on the door. The night to head here, though, is Thursday, when top Italian DJ Claudio Coccoluto showcases the best of Europe's electronic music DJs. Lesbian night, Venus Rising (www.venusrising.it), hits Goa the last Sunday of the month.

### LA SAPONERIA
NIGHTCLUB

Map p358 (☑393 966 1321; Via degli Argonauti 20; ☺11pm-4.30am Tue-Sun Oct-May; Ⓜ Garbatella) Formerly a soap factory, nowadays La Saponeria lathers up the punters with guest DJs spinning everything from nu-house to nu-funk, minimal techno, dance, hip-hop and R&B. Recent guests include Grandmaster Flash.

### RASHOMON
NIGHTCLUB

Map p358 (www.rashomonclub.com; Via degli Argonauti 16; ☺11pm-4.30am Tue-Sun Oct-May; Ⓜ Garbatella) Rashomon is sweaty, not posey, and where to head when you want to dance

your arse off. Shake it to a music-lovers' feast of electro-rock, electronica, indie, reggae, hip hop and dancehall, plus live acts and occasional dancehall lessons.

### RISING LOVE
NIGHTCLUB

Map p358 (☑06 8952 0643; www.risinglove.it; Via delle Conce 14; ☺11pm-4am Tue-Sun Oct-May; Ⓜ Piramide) For those who like their electro, techno, funky groove and an underground vibe, this white, industrial, arty cultural association will tick all the boxes. Guest DJs as well as local talent get the crowd rocking, and there are regular special nights.

### IL MELOGRANO
WINE BAR

Map p358 (☑06 511 56 09; Via Guglielmo Massaia 9; ☺10.30am-3.30pm & 7pm-midnight Mon-Fri, 7pm-midnight Sat; Ⓜ Garbatella) A small, snug wine bar, this is run by two knowledgeable brothers who will suggest the best wines from their 300-strong list without making you feel like an ignoramus. There's a cheap

---

**WORTH A DETOUR**

## EUR

One of the few planned developments in Rome's history, EUR was built for an international exhibition in 1942, and although war intervened and the exhibition never took place, the name stuck – Esposizione Universale di Roma (Roman Universal Exhibition) or EUR. There are a few museums but the area's interest lies in its spectacular rationalist architecture. It's quite unique, if not on a particularly human scale, and the style is beautifully expressed in a number of distinctive *palazzi*, including the iconic **Palazzo della Civiltà del Lavoro** (Quadrato della Concordia; Ⓜ EUR Magliana), dubbed the Square Colosseum. The Palace of the Workers is EUR's architectural icon, a rationalist masterpiece clad in gleaming white travertine. Designed by Giovanni Guerrini, Ernesto Bruno La Padula and Mario Romano, and built between 1938 and 1943, it consists of six rows of nine arches, rising to a height of 50m.

Elsewhere, other monumentalist architecture includes the **Chiesa Santi Pietro e Paolo** (Piazzale Santi Pietro e Paolo), the **Palazzetto dello Sport** (Piazzale dello Sport) and the wonderful **Palazzo dei Congressi** (Piazza JF Kennedy). The area is still a focus for development, with Massimiliano Fuksas' cutting-edge Nuvola ('cloud') congress centre being built here. A steel and Teflon cloud is suspended by steel cables in a glass box – it was inspired by a cloud-gazing daydream.

The **Museo della Civiltà Romana e Planetario** (☑06 06 08; Piazza G Agnelli 10; adult/reduced €.50/5.50, incl Museo Astronomico & Planetario €9.50/7.50; ☺9am-2pm Tue-Sat, 9am-1.30pm Sun; Ⓜ EUR Fermi) is a sure-fire kid-pleaser, founded by Mussolini in 1937 to glorify imperial Rome. A hulking place, it contains intriguing displays, including a giant-scale re-creation of 4th-century Rome, while the **Museo Astronomico & Planetario** (☑06 06 08; www.planetarioroma.it; adult/child €7.50/5.50; ☺9am-2pm Tue-Fri, 9am-7pm Sat & Sun, 8.30-11.30pm Tue-Fri & 4.30-11.30pm Sat & Sun Jul & Aug) will appeal to older children.

Also in EUR is Rome's largest public swimming pool, **Piscina delle Rose** (☑06 542 20 333; www.piscinadellerose.it; Viale America 20; admission from €8; ☺10am-10pm Mon-Fri, 9am-7pm Sat & Sun mid-May–Sep; Ⓜ EUR Palasport). It gets crowded, so arrive early to grab a deck chair.

set-dinner menu or you can choose dishes such as *bruschettine, crostini* and *carpacci* a la carte. Desserts are homemade, best accompanied by fragrant dessert wines.

# ⭐ ENTERTAINMENT

### LA CASA DEL JAZZ                    LIVE MUSIC
Map p358 (☑06 70 47 31; www.casajazz.it; Viale di Porta Ardeatina 55; admission €10-25; ⊗7pm-midnight; Ⓜ Piramide) In the middle of a 2500-sq-m park in the southern suburbs, the Casa del Jazz (House of Jazz) is housed in a three-storey 1920s villa that belonged to a Mafia boss. When he was caught, the Comune di Roma (Rome Council) converted it into a jazz-tastic complex, including a 150-seat auditorium, rehearsal rooms, cafe and restaurant, and it hosts regular shows by international stars, such as Joan as Policewoman. From mid-June to mid-September it hosts the Casa del Jazz Festival.

### CAFFÈ LETTERARIO                    ARTS CENTRE
Map p358 (☑06 5730 2842; www.caffeletterario roma.it; Via Ostiense 83; ⊗various, depending on events; ⬚Via Ostiense) Caffè Letterario is an intellectual hangout housed in the funky converted space of the sometime slaughterhouse of Rome's former Mercati Generali. It combines designer looks, bookshop, gallery, performance space and lounge bar. There are regular live gigs from Italian gypsy music to Indian dance. Check the website for upcoming events.

### TEATRO PALLADIUM                    THEATRE
Map p358 (☑06 4555 3050; www.teatro-palla dium.it, in Italian; Piazza Bartolomeo Romano; tickets €5-25; Ⓜ Garbatella) Once at risk of being turned into a bingo hall, the wonderful Teatro Palladium was rescued for the residents of Garbatella and has been beautifully renovated. The 1920s interior houses an eclectic, fascinating programme of classical music (including the Roma Tre Orchestra), contemporary theatre, children's films and plays, and it's one of the venues for the **Autumn RomaEuropa festival** (http:// romaeuropa.net).

### TEATRO INDIA                    THEATRE
Map p358 (☑06 442 39 286; www.teatrodiroma. net; Lungotevere dei Papareschi; tickets €12-27; ⬚Via Enrico Fermi) Inaugurated in 1999 in the post-industrial landscape of Rome's southern suburbs, the India is the younger sister of the Teatro Argentina. It's a stark modern space in a converted industrial building, a fitting setting for its cutting-edge programme, with a calendar of international and Italian works.

# Trastevere & Gianicolo

EAST OF VIALE DI TRASTEVERE | WEST OF VIALE DI TRASTEVERE | GIANICOLO

## Neighbourhood Top Five

**1** Discovering the Piazza di Santa Maria in Trastevere and visiting its beautiful **church** (p171), with its exquisite interior and exterior mosaics.

**2** Setting down at a bar, such as **Ombre Rosse** (p180), and watching the world go by.

**3** Visiting the nuns' choir of Santa Cecilia in Trastevere to see the **Cavallini fresco** (p171).

**4** Seeing the bird's eye views over Rome from **Gianicolo hill** (p173).

**5** Spending a wonderfully tranquil afternoon amid tall palms and exotic flora in the **Orto Botanico** (p173).

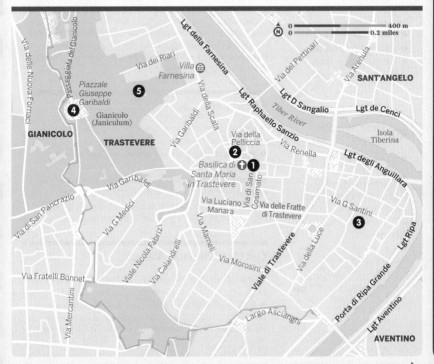

For more detail of this area see Map p360 ➡

## Lonely Planet's Top Tip

Time your visit to Santa Cecilia (p171) so that you can gain entrance to the hushed convent next door to see the Cavallini fresco in the nuns' choir. It feels a tremendous privilege to visit this hidden secret.

 **Best Places to Eat**

➡ Glass Hostaria (p176)

➡ Le Mani in Pasta (p177)

➡ Artigiano Innocenti (p174)

➡ Da Lucia (p176)

➡ Sisini (p175)

For reviews see p174

 **Best Places to Drink**

➡ Ma Che Siete Venuti a Fa' (p177)

➡ Il Barretto (p180)

➡ Ombre Rosse (p180)

➡ Freni e Frizioni (p180)

➡ Bar San Calisto (p177)

For reviews see p177 ➡

**Best Works of Art**

➡ Santa Maria in Trastevere (p171)

➡ Stefano Moderno's sculpture in Santa Cecilia in Trastevere (p171)

➡ Frescoes in Villa Farnesina (p175)

➡ Caravaggio in Galleria Nazionale d'Arte Antica di Palazzo Corsini (p172)

For reviews see p172 ➡

# Explore: Trastevere & Gianicolo

Trastevere is Rome's most vivacious neighbourhood, an outdoor circus of ochre and butterscotch palazzi, ivy-clad facades and photogenic cobbled lanes, peopled with a bohemian and eclectic cast of tourists, travellers, students and street sellers. The bohos and original Romans might be increasingly rubbing shoulders with wealthy expats, as rental prices in this most beguiling district go through the roof, but Trastevere still retains its distinct and very Roman character. The very name means 'across the Tiber' *(tras tevere)*, emphasising the sense of difference.

The area is ideal for aimless, contented wandering, lazy coffees outside piazza cafes, home-cooked meals in local trattorias, and an evening drink to watch the world go by. There are also some beautiful sights here: glittering Basilica di Santa Maria is one of Rome's most charming churches, Villa Farnesina contains superb frescoes by Raphael and others, and exquisitely frescoed Palazzo Corsini is home to an impressive art collection. Close by are the tranquil botanical gardens; hike up Gianicolo (Janiculum hill) to be rewarded by some of Rome's most awe-inspiring views and a chance to see Bramante's perfect little Tempietto. To the east, Basilica di Santa Cecilia is the resting place of Santa Cecilia, patron saint of music, with a wonderful, hidden Cavallini fresco and fascinating excavations.

Despite all this, it's after dark that Trastevere really comes into its own. Narrow alleyways heave late into the night as Romans and tourists flock to the pizzerias, trattorias, bars and cafes that pepper the atmospheric lanes, and on a summer's evening, you can barely move for people in the main streets, as bars overflow and hordes of people enjoy a *passeggiata* (evening stroll).

## Local Life

➡ **Drinking** A coffee or a *sambuca alla mosque* ('with flies' - coffee beans) at Bar San Calisto

➡ **Passegiata** An evening stroll to see and be seen, with a stop for an ice cream.

➡ **Football** Trastevere is a Roma supporters' stronghold: come a big game, the air of excitement is palpable.

➡ **Biscuits** Buying *brutti ma buoni* 'ugly but good' biscuits, from bakery of Artigiano Innocenti (p174).

## Getting There & Away

➡ **Tram** No 8 from Largo di Torre Argentina runs to the main drag of Viale Trastevere.

➡ **Bus** From Termini, bus H runs to Viale di Trastevere. For Gianicolo, if you don't fancy the steep steps from Via G Mameli, take bus 870 from Piazza delle Rovere.

## TOP SIGHTS
## BASILICA DI SANTA MARIA IN TRASTEVERE

**This exquisitely glittering church is said to be the oldest church in Rome dedicated to the Virgin Mary. Its facade is decorated with a beautiful medieval mosaic that depicts Mary feeding Jesus surrounded by 10 women bearing lamps. Two are veiled and hold lamps that have gone out, symbolising widowhood, while the lit lamps of the others represent their virginity.**

### A Fountain of Oil

The church was first constructed in the early 3rd century over the spot where, according to legend, a fountain of oil miraculously sprang from the ground. Its current Romanesque form is the result of a 12th-century revamp. The portico came later, added by Carlo Fontana in 1702, with its balustrade decorated by four popes.

### Mosaics

Inside it's the golden 12th-century mosaics that stand out. In the apse, look out for the dazzling depiction of Christ and his mother flanked by various saints and, on the far left, Pope Innocent II holding a model of the church. Beneath this is a series of six mosaics by Pietro Cavallini (c 1291) illustrating the life of the Virgin.

### Columns, Ceiling & Cosmati

Other features to note include the 21 Roman columns, some plundered from the Terme di Caracalla, the wooden ceiling designed in 1617 by Domenichino; and, on the right of the altar, a spiralling Cosmati candlestick, placed on the exact spot where the oil fountain is said to have sprung. The last chapel on the left-hand side, the Cappella Avila, is also worth a look for its stunning 17th-century dome. The spiralling Cosmatesque floor was relaid in the 1870s, a recreation of the 13th-century original.

### DON'T MISS...

➡ Facade mosaics
➡ 13th-century Cavallini mosaics in the apse
➡ Ancient Roman granite columns

### PRACTICALITIES

➡ Map p360
➡ ☏06 581 48 02
➡ Piazza Santa Maria in Trastevere
➡ ⊘ 7.30am-9pm
➡ ▢or ▢Viale di Trastevere

# ◎ SIGHTS

Trastevere is dotted with exquisite churches, but some of its most wonderful sights are picturesque glimpses down narrow, ochre-and-orange-shaded lanes that will make you catch your breath. For Rome's most spectacular views, stride up the steep slopes of Gianicolo, stopping at the jewel-perfect Tempietto di Bramante on the way.

## ◎ East of Viale di Trastevere

**BASILICA DI SANTA CECILIA IN TRASTEVERE**                         CHURCH
See p171.

**CHIESA DI SAN FRANCESCO D'ASSISI A RIPA**                         CHURCH
Map p360 (⌀06 581 90 20; Piazza San Francesco d'Assisi 88; ⊙7am-noon & 4-7pm Mon-Sat, 7am-1pm & 4-7.30pm Sun; ☐ or ◨Viale di Trastevere) The 17th-century church of St Francis contains the impressive 18th-century Rospigliosi and Pallavici sculptural monuments, but the overriding reason to visit is to gasp at one of Bernini's most daring works, in the Paluzzi-Albertoni chapel. The *Beata Ludovica Albertoni* (Blessed Ludovica Albertoni; 1674) is a work of highly charged sexual ambiguity showing Ludovica, a Franciscan nun, in a state of rapture as she reclines, eyes shut, mouth open, one hand touching her breast.

St Francis of Assisi is said to have stayed on this spot for a period in the 13th century and you can still see the rock that he used as a pillow and his crucifix, in his cell – the church was later entirely rebuilt several times, its current incarnation dating from the 1680s.

## ◎ West of Viale di Trastevere

**BASILICA DI SANTA MARIA IN TRASTEVERE**                         CHURCH
See p171.

**VILLA FARNESINA**                         PALAZZO
See p175.

**GALLERIA NAZIONALE D'ARTE ANTICA DI PALAZZO CORSINI**                         GALLERY
Map p360 (⌀06 688 02 323; www.galleriaborgh ese.it; Via della Lungara 10; adult/child €4/2; ⊙8.30am-7.30pm Tue-Sun; ◨Lungotevere della Farnesina, Piazza Trilussa) Housing part of Italy's national art collection (the rest is in Palazzo Barberini, p110), 16th-century Palazzo Corsini has a distinguished history. Michelangelo, Erasmus and Bramante stayed here but the *palazzo* is most associated with Queen Christina of Sweden, who took up residency in 1662, turning it into a centre of artistic life in Rome, and entertaining a steady stream of lovers in her richly frescoed bedroom. She lived here until her death in 1689. Architect Ferdinando Fuga (who worked on the masterful facades for Trastevere's Santa Maria Maggiore and Santa Cecilia) remodelled the palace in 1746 for the new owner, Cardinal Neri Corsini, rebuilding the facade.

Gallery highlights include Van Dyck's superb, intimate *Madonna della Paglia* (Madonna of the Straw) in room 3, Rubens' haunting *San Sebastiano Liberato dagli Angeli* (St Sebastian liberated by the angels), Poussin's Triumph of David in room 2, and a fantastic Caravaggio, *San Giovanni Battista* (St John the Baptist), full of glowering menace, in Room 7. Look out also for the burnished gold 15th-century *Last Judgement,* by Fra Angelico,

**PIAZZA SANTA MARIA IN TRASTEVERE**                         PIAZZA
Map p360 (☐ or ◨Viale di Trastevere) Trastevere's focal square is a prime people-watching spot. By day it's full of mums with strollers, chatting locals and guidebook-toting tourists; by night it's the domain of foreign students, young Romans and out-of-towners, all out for a good time.

The octagonal fountain in the centre of the square is of Roman origin and was restored by Carlo Fontana in 1692.

**MUSEO DI ROMA IN TRASTEVERE**                         MUSEUM
Map p360 (⌀06 820 59 127; www.museodiromain trastevere.it; Piazza Sant'Egidio 1b; adult/reduced €6.50/5.50; ⊙10am-8pm Tue-Sun; ☐ or ◨Viale di Trastevere) Housed in a former Carmelite convent, adjoining the neighbouring 17th-century church of Sant'Egidio, this small museum hosts interesting photography and art exhibitions, usually depicting past life in Italy. Upstairs the permanent collection contains a small selection of 19th-century watercolours depicting Rome, and also has temporary Rome-related exhibitions, and *Stanza di Trilussa,* an installation that fills an entire small room with manuscripts and domestic items relating to the famous Roman poet, who wrote in the local dialect.

# ◉ TOP SIGHTS **BASILICA DI SANTA CECILIA IN TRASTEVERE**

This church, with its serene courtyard, remarkable frescoes by Pietro Cavallini, and ancient Roman excavations beneath the building, is the last resting place of St Cecilia, the patron saint of music, who was martyred on this site in AD 230.

This basilica stands on the site of an earlier 5th-century church, itself built over the ancient Roman house where it's believed Cecilia was martyred in AD 230. You can visit the network of excavated houses that lie beneath the church. Below the altar, Stefano Moderno's delicate sculpture shows exactly how her miraculously preserved body was found when it was unearthed in the Catacombe di San Callisto (p161) in 1599.

In the apse, look out for the dazzling depiction of Christ and his mother flanked by various saints and, on the far left, Pope Innocent II holding a model of the church. Beneath this is a series of six mosaics by Pietro Cavallini (c 1291) illustrating the life of the Virgin. In the right-hand nave the Cappella del Caldarium, complete with two works by Guido Reni, marks the spot where the saint was allegedly tortured.

But the basilica's pride and joy is the spectacular 13th-century fresco in the nun's choir.

**DON'T MISS...**

➡ Cavallini's *Last Judgement* fresco
➡ Moderno's sculpture
➡ Excavated buildings

**PRACTICALITIES**

➡ Map p360
➡ ☑06 589 92 89
➡ Piazza di Santa Cecilia 22
➡ basilica/fresco/crypt free/€2.50/2.50
➡ ⊘basilica & crypt 9.30am-12.30pm, 4-6.30pm, fresco 10am-12.30pm Mon-Sat
➡ 🚊 or 🚍Viale di Trastevere

---

**PORTA SETTIMIANA**  MONUMENT

Map p360 (🚊Lungotevere della Farnesina, Piazza Trilussa) Resembling a crenellated keep, Porta Settimiana marks the start of Via della Lungara, the 16th-century road that connects Trastevere with the Borgo. It was built in 1498 by Pope Alexander VI over a small passageway in the Aurelian Wall and later altered by Pope Pius VI in 1798.

From Porta Settimiana, Via Santa Dorotea leads to Piazza Trilussa, a popular evening hang-out, and Ponte Sisto, which connects with the *centro storico*.

---

# ◉ Gianicolo

Today a tranquil and leafy area that combines embassies, monuments, piazzas, Rome's botanical gardens and some beautiful architecture, it's difficult to imagine today that in 1849 the Gianicolo was the scene of fierce and bloody fighting. A makeshift army under Giuseppe Garibaldi defended Rome against French troops sent to restore papal rule. The hill today is dotted by monuments to the Italian hero and his army – Garibaldi is commemorated with a massive monument in Piazzale Giuseppe Garibaldi, while his Brazilian-born wife, Anita, has her own equestrian monument about 200m away in Piazzale Anita Garibaldi.

The Gianicolo is a superb viewpoint with sweeping panoramas over Rome's rooftops, and has several summer-only bars that are blessed with thrilling views. There are also regular children's puppet shows on the hill, a long-standing tradition.

**ORTO BOTANICO**  BOTANICAL GARDEN

Map p360 (☑06 499 17 107; Largo Cristina di Svezia 24; adult/reduced €4/2; ⊘9am-6.30pm Mon-Sat Apr–mid-Oct, 9.30am-5.30pm Mon-Sat mid-Oct–Mar; 🚊Lungotevere della Farnesina, Piazza Trilussa) Formerly the private grounds of Palazzo Corsini (p172), Rome's 12-hectare botanical gardens are a little-known gem and the perfect place to unwind in a lush green, tree-shaded expanse covering the steep slopes of the Giancolo. Plants have been cultivated here since the 13th century, but in their present form, the gardens were established in 1883, when the grounds of Palazzo Corsini were given to the University of Rome. They now contain up to 8000 species, including some of Europe's rarest plants. You will find an avenue of dizzying palms, fountains, nature-worn sculptures and Mediterranean, rose and Japanese gardens. There are also some beautiful old glasshouses and an impressive bamboo plantation, as well as a garden with 300 types of medicinal plants (Giardino dei Semplici), a collection of cacti, and an aroma garden (Giardino degli Aromi).

### TEMPIETTO DI BRAMANTE & CHIESA DI SAN PIETRO IN MONTORIO CHURCH

Map p360 (☑06 581 39 40; www.sanpietroinmontorio.it; Piazza San Pietro in Montorio 2; ◷church 8.30am-noon & 3-4pm Mon-Fri, tempietto 9.30am-12.30pm & 4-6pm Tue-Sun Apr-Sep, 9.30am-12.30pm & 2-4pm Tue-Sun Oct-Mar; ◻Via Garibaldi) Considered the first great building of the High Renaissance, Bramante's sublime Tempietto (Little Temple; 1508) stands in the courtyard of the Chiesa di San Pietro in Montorio, on the spot where St Peter is said to have been crucified. It's a small building but its classically inspired design (a circular interior surrounded by 16 columns and topped by a classical frieze, elegant balustrade and proportionally perfect dome) beautifully captured the Renaissance *zeitgeist*. More than a century later, in 1628, Bernini added a staircase. Bernini also contributed a chapel to the adjacent church, the last resting place of Beatrice Cenci.

It's quite a climb uphill, but you're rewarded by the views. To cheat, take bus 870 from Via Paola just off Corso Vittorio Emanuele II near the Tiber.

### FONTANA DELL'ACQUA PAOLA FOUNTAIN

Map p360 (Via Garibaldi; ◻Via Garibaldi) Just up from the Chiesa di San Pietro in Montorio, this monumental white fountain was built in 1612 to celebrate the restoration of

### SUMMER BAR ON THE GIANICOLO

From June to September, the **Gianicolo 150** (Piazzale Giuseppe Garibaldi; ◷7pm-2am) opens an outdoor 'street art cafe', run by the cool cats who are responsible for the uber-chic Salotto Locarno (p120) and Salotto 42 (p97). It's an outdoor living room set on Gianicolo hill, with sofas draped with pretty people, plus even prettier views over Rome.

a 2nd-century aqueduct that supplied (and still supplies) water from Lago di Bracciano, 35km to the north of Rome. Four of the fountain's six pink-stone columns came from the facade of the old St Peter's Basilica, while much of the marble was pillaged from the Roman Forum. Originally the fountain had five small basins, but these were replaced by a large granite basin, added by Carlo Fontana, in 1690.

### VILLA DORIA PAMPHILJ PARK

Map p360 (◷dawn-dusk; ◻Via di San Pancrazio) Rome's largest park is a great place to escape the relentless city noise. Once a vast private estate, it was laid out around 1650 for Prince Camillo Pamphilj, nephew of Pope Innocent X. At its centre is the prince's summer residence, the **Casino del Belrespiro**, and its manicured gardens and citrus trees. It's now used for official government functions.

## ✖ EATING

**Traditionally working-class and poor, now chic and pricey, picturesque Trastevere has a huge number of restaurants, trattorias, cafes and pizzerias. The better places dot the maze of side streets, and it pays to be selective, as many of the restaurants are bog-standard tourist traps. But it's not just tourists here – Romans like to eat in Trastevere too. Find the right spot and you'll have a meal to remember.**

## ✖ East of Viale di Trastevere

### LA GENSOLA SICILIAN €€

Map p360 (☑06 581 63 12; Piazza della Gensola 15; meals €50; ◷closed Sun mid-Jun–mid-Sep; ◻ or ◻Viale di Trastevere;) Tucked away in Trastevere, this tranquil, classy yet unpretentious trattoria thrills foodies with delicious food that has a Sicilian slant and emphasis on seafood, including an excellent tuna tartare, linguine with fresh anchovies and divine *zuccherini* (tiny fish) with fresh mint. The set menu costs €41.

### ARTIGIANO INNOCENTI BAKERY €

Map p360 (☑06 580 39 26; Via delle Luce 21; ◷8am-8pm Mon-Sat, 9.30am-2pm Sun; ◻ or ◻Viale di Trastevere) It's at reassuring spots

# TOP SIGHTS
## VILLA FARNESINA

Villa Farnesina was built in the early 16th century for Agostino Chigi, the immensely wealthy papal banker. The house was bought by Cardinal Alessandro Farnese in 1577, hence its name. This was not the first lavish villa on this site – Julius Caesar's country house was located here, and its great frescoes may be seen in Palazzo Massimo alle Terme (see p128).

This 16th-century villa is a classic Renaissance design, a symmetrical construction with two wings that features some awe-inspiring frescoes by Sebastiano del Piombo, Raphael and the villa's original architect, Baldassare Peruzzi, who had formerly worked as Bramante's assistant.

The most famous frescoes are in the Loggia of Cupid and Psyche on the ground floor, which are attributed to Raphael, who also painted the Trionfo di Galatea (Triumph of Galatea), depicting a beautiful sea nymph, in the room of the same name. The vaulted ceiling of the room is covered with astrological scenes that depict the constellations of the stars at the time of Agostino Chigi's birth.

On the 1st floor, Peruzzi's dazzling frescoes in the Salone delle Prospettive are a superb illusionary perspective of a marble colonnade and panorama of 16th-century Rome.

### DON'T MISS...

➡ Frescoes by Sebastiano del Piombo
➡ Raphael-attributed Loggia decoration
➡ Peruzzi's panorama in the Salone delle Prospettive

### PRACTICALITIES

➡ Map p360
➡ ☑06 680 27 397
➡ Via della Lungara 230
➡ adult/reduced €5/4
➡ ⊙9am-1pm Mon-Sat, tours by reservation only
➡ ⬚or ⬚Viale di Trastevere

TRASTEVERE & GIANICOLO EATING

---

like this that you can feel that the world never changes, in some places. This is a stuck-in-time bakery where the staff chat to the regulars, and you can buy light-as-air *crostate*, and stock up on biscuits such as *brutti ma buoni* (ugly but good).

### DA ENZO
TRATTORIA €

Map p360 (☑06 581 83 55; Via dei Vascellari 29; meals €25; ⊙Mon-Sat; ⬚Piazza Sonnino) This snug dining room with rough yellow walls and lots of character serves up great, seasonally based Roman meals, such as spaghetti with clams and mussels or grilled lamb cutlets. There's a tiny terrace on the quintessential Trastevere cobbled street.

### PANATTONI
PIZZERIA €

Map p360 (☑06 580 09 19; Viale di Trastevere 53; pizzas €6.50-9; ⊙6.30pm-1am Thu-Tue; ⬚ or ⬚Viale di Trastevere) Panattoni is nicknamed *l'obitorio* (the morgue) because of its marble-slab tabletops. Thankfully the similarity stops there. This is one of Trastevere's liveliest pizzerias, with paper-thin pizzas, a clattering buzz, testy waiters, streetside seating and fried starters (specialities are *supplì* and *baccalà*).

### FIOR DI LUNA
ICE CREAM €

Map p360 (☑06 645 61314; Via della Lungaretta 96; from €2; ⊙noon-2am Tue-Sun; ⬚ or ⬚Viale di Trastevere) Perfectly placed for picking up an artisanal icecream to accompany you on your Trastevere meanderings, this busy little hub serves up handmade icecream and sorbet – it's made in small batches and only uses natural, seasonal ingredients, such as hazelnuts from Tonda and pistachios from Bronte.

### SISINI
PIZZERIA €

Map p360 (Via di San Francesco a Ripa 137; pizza & pasta from €2; ⊙9am-10.30pm Mon-Sat, closed Aug; ⬚ or ⬚Viale di Trastevere) Locals love this fast-food joint (the sign outside says 'Supplì'), serving up fresh *pizza al taglio* and different pasta and risotto dishes served in plastic boxes – there's one small table where you can eat standing up, or you can take away. It's also worth sampling the *supplì* and roast chicken.

### BIR & FUD
PIZZERIA €

Map p360 (Via Benedetta 23; meals €25; ⊙6.30pm-1am, closed Aug; ⬚ or ⬚Viale di Trastevere) This orange-and-terracotta, vaulted pizzeria wins plaudits for its organic take

**LOCAL KNOWLEDGE**

## GRATTACHECCA

It's summertime, the living is easy, and Romans like nothing better in the sultry evening heat than to amble down to the river and partake of some *grattachecca* (crushed ice covered in fruit and syrup) down by the banks of the Tiber. It's the ideal way to cool down, and there are kiosks along the riverbank satisfying this very Roman need; try **Sora Mirella Caffè** (grattachecca €3-6; ⊙11am-3am May-Sep), next to Ponte Cestio.

on pizzas, *crostini* and delicious fried things (potato, pumpkin etc) and has a microbrewery on site. Chef Gabriele Bonci of the wonderful Pizzarium (p203) is consultant here. Save room for dessert. Book ahead.

## ✖ West of Viale di Trastevere

### GLASS HOSTARIA CREATIVE ITALIAN €€€

Map p360 (②06 583 35 903; Vicolo del Cinque 58; meals €70; ⊙dinner Tue-Sun; ⊋Piazza Trilussa) Trastevere's foremost foodie address, the Glass Hostaria is a breath of fresh air in the neighbourhood, a modernist-styled, sophisticated setting with cooking to match. Chef Cristina creates inventive, delicate dishes that combine with fresh ingredients and traditional elements to delight and surprise the palate.

### PARIS ROMAN-JEWISH €€

Map p360 (②06 581 53 78; Piazza San Calisto 7; meals €45; ⊙Tue-Sat, lunch Sun, closed 3 weeks Aug; ⊋ or ⊋Viale di Trastevere) Nothing to do with Paris (it's the name of the founder), this is an elegant, old-school Roman restaurant set in a 17th-century building, and it's the best place outside the Ghetto to sample Roman-Jewish cuisine, such as delicate *fritto misto con baccalà* (deep-fried vegetables with salt cod) and *carciofi alla giudia* (Jewish-style artichokes), as well as Roman dishes such as just-right *rigatoni alla carbonara* (pasta with egg and bacon sauce). There's a sunshaded terrace.

### DA LUCIA TRATTORIA €

Map p360 (②06 580 36 01; Vicolo del Mattonato 2; meals €30; ⊙Tue-Sun; ⊋Piazza Trilussa)

Eat beneath the fluttering knickers of the neighbourhood at this terrific trattoria, frequented by hungry locals and tourists, and packed with locals for Sunday lunch. On a cobbled backstreet that is classic Trastevere, it serves up a cavalcade of Roman specialities including *trippa all romana* (tripe with tomato sauce) and *pollo con peperoni* (chicken with peppers), as well as bountiful antipasti and possibly Rome's best tiramisu. Cash only.

### DA AUGUSTO TRATTORIA €

Map p360 (②06 580 37 98; Piazza de' Renzi 15; meals €25; ⊙lunch & dinner Fri-Wed; ⊋Piazza Trilussa) For a true Trastevere feast, plonk yourself at one of Augusto's rickety tables and prepare to enjoy some mammastyle cooking. The hard-working waiters dish out hearty platefuls of *rigatoni all'amatriciana and stracciatella* (clear broth with egg and Parmesan) among a host of Roman classics.

### PIZZERIA IVO PIZZERIA €

Map p360 (②06 581 70 82; Via di San Francesco a Ripa 158; pizzas €6.5-8.80; ⊙dinner Wed-Mon; ⊋ or ⊋Viale di Trastevere) One of Trastevere's most famous pizzerias, Ivo's has been slinging pizzas for some 40 years, and still the hungry come. With the TV on in the corner and the tables full, with a lively strip out on the street when the weather's good enough, Ivo's a noisy and vibrant place where the crispy, though not huge, pizzas are some of Rome's most delicious and traditional, and the waiters fit the gruff-and-fast stereotype.

### DA OLINDO TRATTORIA €

Map p360 (②06 581 88 35; Vicolo della Scala 8; meals €25; ⊙dinner Mon-Sat; ⊋ or ⊋Viale di Trastevere) One of Trastevere's old-style basic kitchens, this is your classic family affair, where the menu is short and the atmosphere is lively. Cuisine is robust, portions are huge. Expect *baccalà con patate* on Fridays and gnocchi on Thursdays, but other dishes – such as *coniglio all cacciatore* (rabbit, hunter-style) or *polpette al sugo* (meatballs in sauce) – whichever day you like.

### LA BOTTICELLA TRATTORIA €€

Map p360 (②06 581 47 38; Vicolo del Leopardo 39a; meals €55; ⊙Wed-Tue; ⊋Piazza Trilussa) On a quiet Trastevere backstreet, La Botticella offers pure Roman cooking, outside under the lines of flapping washing, or inside in the picture-lined salon. Menu stalwarts include tripe and *rigatoni alla paiata* (pasta with calf's intestines), but there are less demanding dishes, such as an excellent *spaghetti all'amatriciana* and *fritto alla botticella (*deep-fried vegetables).

### VALZANI
PASTRIES & CAKES €

Map p360 (☏06 580 37 92; Via del Moro 37; cakes €3; ☺10am-8pm Wed-Sun, 3-8pm Mon & Tue, closed Jul & Aug; 🚊 or 🚊Piazza Sonnino) The speciality of this glorious, stuck-in-time cake shop, opened in 1925 and not redecorated since, is the legendary *torta sacher,* the favourite cake of Roman film director Nanni Moretti. But there are also chocolate-covered *mostaccioli* (biscuits), Roman *pangiallo* (honey, nuts and dried fruit – typical for Christmas) and Roman *torrone* (nougat). If you're here around Easter pop in to see the staggering array of chocolate animals and eggs, all remarkable value.

### FORNO LA RENELLA
PIZZERIA €

Map p360 (☏06 581 72 65; Via del Moro 15-16; pizza slices from €2; ☺9am-1am; 🚊Piazza Trilussa) The wood-fired ovens at this historic Trastevere bakery have been firing for decades, producing a delicious daily batch of pizza, bread and biscuits. Piled-high toppings (and fillings) vary seasonally. Popular with everyone from skinheads with big dogs to elderly ladies with little dogs.

### DAR POETA
PIZZERIA €

Map p360 (☏06 588 05 16; Vicolo del Bologna 46; pizzas €7.50-12; ☺lunch & dinner; 🚊Piazza Trilussa) Dar Poeta, a breezy, cheery pizzeria hidden away in an atmospheric side street, proffers hearty pizzas in a buzzing atmosphere. The base is somewhere between wafer-thin Roman and Neapolitan comfort food, and the slow-risen dough apparently makes it easier to digest. There are also bruschettas and salads, and it's famous for its unique ricotta and Nutella calzone.

### LE MANI IN PASTA
PASTA €

Map p360 (☏06 581 60 17; Via dei Genovesi 37; meals €40; lunch daily, dinner Tue-Sun; 🚊 or 🚊 Viale di Trastevere; ✻👶) Lively and popular, this narrow and secret-feeling place has an open kitchen that serves up delicious fresh pasta topped with whatever's in season, which could be, if you're lucky, *calamari e carciofi* (squid and artichokes).

# 🍷 DRINKING & NIGHTLIFE

**Enchantingly pretty, Trastevere is one of the city's most popular areas to wander, drink and decide what to do afterwards. Foreign visitors love it, as do those who love foreign visitors, but it's also a local haunt. The streets in summer are packed, with the stalls, bars spilling into the street, and a carnival atmosphere – it's even a bit overcrowded and won't be to everyone's taste. To escape the throng, head to the bars on the outskirts of the area, where the vibe is gentler and the body count lower.**

### BAR LE CINQUE
BAR

Map p360 (Vicolo del Cinque 5; ☺6.30am-2am Mon-Sat; 🚊 or 🚊Piazza Sonnino) There's no sign outside, and it looks like a run-down ordinary bar, but this is a long-standing Trastevere favourite, and always has a small crowd clustered around outside; they're here for the pivotal location, easygoing vibe and cheap drinks (€3/5 for a small/large beer).

### MA CHE SIETE VENUTI A FÀ
BAR

Map p360 (Via Benedetta 25; ☺3pm-2am; 🚊 or 🚊Piazza Sonnino) Also known as the Football Pub, the name means 'What did you come here for?' (it's a football chant), but the answer, rather than anything to do with the beautiful game, could be atmosphere and beer. It's pint-sized place, but packs a huge number of artisanal beers into its interior, with delicious caramel-like tipples such as Italiano Bibock (by Birrificio Italiano), Old Man or London Honey. A small/large beer costs €4/6.

### BAR SAN CALISTO
BAR

Map p360 (Piazza San Calisto; ☺5.30am-2am Mon-Sat; 🚊 or 🚊Piazza Sonnino) Those in the know head to the down-at-heel 'Sanca' for its basic, stuck-in-time atmosphere and dirt-cheap prices (a beer costs from €1.50). It attracts everyone from intellectuals to pseudo-intellectuals to keeping-it-real Romans, alcoholics and American students. It's famous for its chocolate – drunk hot with cream in winter, eaten as ice cream in summer. Apparently, unless you have drunk a post-dinner coffee here, or a *Sambuca con la Mosca* ('with flies', with two or three raw coffee beans dropped in the drink), you will not truly know Trastevere.

MARTIN MOOS / LONELY PLANET IMAGES ©

**1. Behind the Bar**
Student bar in Centro Storico.

**2. Drinking in Rome**
Drinks at Rosati (p121).

**3. Rome at Dusk**
Evocative street scene in
Trastevere.

GLENN BEANLAND / LONELY PLANET IMAGES ©

**LOCAL KNOWLEDGE**

### TRASTEVERE STYLE

For a cool haircut in the backstreets of Trastevere, look no further than **Ellefe**, a buzzing salon tucked behind Bar San Calisto. The hairdressers here are experts in laid-back chic, and you can also have a massage in the converted ancient cellar, with the choice of either a massage waterbed or a softly blue-lit cavern.

### BIG STAR                                          BAR

Map p360 (Via G Mameli 25; ⊙6.30pm-2am, closed Aug; 🚇 or 🚊Piazza Sonnino) If the scene in central Trastevere is feeling a bit too mainstream, head to the outskirts to find this unpretentious, grungy bar. It's a red-painted, rock-and-roll, pub-like place, with a cool studenty clientele, masses of beers on tap, from La Trappe to Sierra Nevada, and regular live music.

### FRENI E FRIZIONI                                   BAR

Map p360 (☑06 583 34 210; Via del Politeama 4; ⊙6.30pm-2am; 🚊Piazza Trilussa) Everyone's favourite hip Trastevere hang-out: in a former life, this bar and cafe was a garage, hence its name ('brakes and clutches'). The arty crowd flocks here to slurp well-priced drinks (especially mojitos) and pack the piazza in front. Feast on the good-value *aperitivo*.

### OMBRE ROSSE                                       BAR

Map p360 (☑06 588 41 55; Piazza Sant'Egidio 12; ⊙8am-2am Mon-Sat, 11am-2am Sun; 🚊Piazza Trilussa) Another seminal Trastevere hang-out; grab a table on the terrace and watch the world go by. The cosmopolitan clientele ranges from elderly Italian wide boys to chic city slickers. Tunes are slinky and there's live music (jazz, blues, world) on Thursday and Sunday evenings from September to April.

### LIBRERIA DEL CINEMA                               CAFE

Map p360 (☑06 581 77 24; Via dei Fienaroli 31d; ⊙4-10pm Mon-Fri, 4-11pm Sat, 3-9pm Sun; 🚇 or 🚊Piazza Sonnino) It's difficult to know in which category to put this place, as it's a bookshop and cafe, but we're putting it here as a perfect coffee-and-snack pitstop. There's *aperitivo* from 6pm. And, of course, you can browse the impressive cinema book collection too.

### LA MESCHITA                                  WINE BAR

Map p360 (☑06 583 33 920; Piazza Trilussa 41; 🚊Piazza Trilussa) This tiny bar inside the entrance to upmarket restaurant Enoteca Ferrara serves fantastic *aperitivo* and has a wide range of wines by the glass, from €7. Fancy an intimate tête-à-tête, with fine wines and yummy snacks? This is your place.

## 📍 Gianicolo

### IL BARRETTO                                       BAR

Map p360 (☑06 583 65 422; Via Garibaldi 27; ⊙6am-2am Mon-Sat, 5pm-2am Sun; 🚇 or 🚊Piazza Sonnino) Venture a little way up the Gianicolo, up a steep flight of steps from Trastevere. Go on, it's so worth it: you'll discover this cocktail bar, an architectural triumph. The bar is mostly huge plate-glass windows overlooking the district, and there's a garden terrace. The basslines are meaty, the bar staff hip girls with glossy curtains of hair, the interior mixes vintage with pop art, and it's genuinely cool. A G&T costs €8.

## ☆ ENTERTAINMENT

### BIG MAMA                                   LIVE MUSIC

Map p360 (☑06 581 25 51; www.bigmama.it, in Italian; Vicolo di San Francesco a Ripa 18; annual membership €14; ⊙9pm-1.30am, show 10.30pm Thu-Sat, closed Jun-Sep; 🚇 or 🚊Viale di Trastevere) To wallow in the Eternal City blues, there's only one place to go – this cramped Trastevere basement, hosting jazz, funk, soul and R&B. Weekly residencies from well-known Italian musicians and songwriters, and frequent concerts by international artists.

### LETTERE CAFFÈ GALLERY                      LIVE MUSIC

Map p360 (☑06 972 70 991; Vicolo San Francesco a Ripa 100/101; ⊙ 7pm-2am daily, closed mid-Aug–mid-Sep; 🚊Piazza Trilussa) Like books? Poetry? Blues and jazz? Then you'll love this place – a clutter of barstools and books, where there are regular live gigs, poetry slams, comedy and gay nights, followed by DJ sets playing indie and new wave.

### ANFITEATRO DEL TASSO                          THEATRE

Map p360 (☑06 575 08 27; www.anfiteatroquer ciadeltasso.com; Passaggiata del Gianicolo; ⊙Jul & Aug; 🚊Piazza Garibaldi) The setting is extraordinary: an amphitheatre overlooking Rome's rooftops that was built over 300 years ago. The productions are extraordinary too, for different reasons, featuring hammy turns in Greek and Roman comedy and the odd 18th-century drama, but they're always great fun.

### TEATRO VASCELLO                    THEATRE
Map p360 (📞06 588 10 21; www.teatrovascello.it; Via Giacinto Carini 72, Monteverde; 🚇Via Giacinto Carini) Left-field in vibe and location, this is independent, fringe theatre stages interesting, cutting-edge new work, including avant-garde dance, multimedia events and works by emerging playwrights.

### ALCAZAR                             CINEMA
Map p360 (📞06 588 00 99; Via Merry del Val 14; 🚇 or 🚊Viale di Trastevere) An old-style cinema with plush red seats. On certain days you can see films in their original language (*Lingua originale*) with Italian subtitles.

### NUOVO SACHER                       CINEMA
Map p360 (📞06 581 81 16; www.sacherfilm.eu; Largo Ascianghi 1; 🚇 or 🚊Viale di Trastevere) Owned by cult Roman film director Nanni Moretti, this is the place to catch the latest European art-house flick. Originally designed to support home-grown film talent, it occasionally also screens films in their original language. Summer screenings take place in the courtyard next to the cinema.

# 🛍 SHOPPING

## 🛍 Trastevere

### LA CRAVATTA SU MISURA          ACCESSORIES
Map p360 (📞06 581 66 76; Via Santa Cecilia 12; ⏰10am-2pm & 3.30-7pm Mon-Fri, 10am-2pm Sat; 🚇 or 🚊Viale di Trastevere) With ties draped over the wooden furniture, this inviting shop resembles the study of an absent-minded professor. But don't be fooled: these guys know their ties. Only the finest Italian silks and English wools are used in neckwear made to customers' specifications. At a push, a tie can be ready in a few hours.

### OFFICINA DELLA CARTA             GIFTS
Map p360 (📞06 589 55 57; Via Benedetta 26b; 🚊Piazza Trilussa) A perfect present pitstop, this tiny workshop produces attractive hand-painted paper-bound boxes, photo albums, recipe books, notepads, photo frames, diaries and charming marionette theatres.

### SCALA QUATTORODICI              CLOTHING
Map p360 (📞Via della Scala 13-14; 🚇Piazza Trilussa) Make yourself over à la Audrey Hepburn with these classically tailored clothes in beautiful fabrics – either made-to-measure or off-the-peg. Pricey (a frock will set you back €600 or so) but oh so worth it.

### PORTA PORTESE                     MARKET
Map p360 (⏰7am-1pm Sun; Via Portuense; 🚇 or 🚊Viale di Trastevere) To see another side of Rome head to this mammoth flea market. With thousands of stalls selling everything from rare books to spare bike parts, from Peruvian shawls to iPods, it's crazily busy and a lot of fun. Keep your valuables safe and wear your haggling hat.

### ROMA-STORE                        PERFUME
Map p360 (📞06 581 87 89; Via della Lungaretta 63; ⏰10am-8pm; 🚇 or 🚊Viale di Trastevere) With no sign, Roma-Store is an enchanting perfume shop crammed full of deliciously enticing bottles of scent, including lots of unusual brands as well as English Floris, Italian Aqua di Parma and French Etat Libre d'Orange.

### ALMOST CORNER BOOKSHOP        BOOKSTORE
Map p360 (📞06 583 69 42; Via del Moro 45; ⏰10am-1.30pm & 3.30-8pm Mon-Sat, 11am-1.30pm & 3.30-8pm Sun; 🚇Piazza Trilussa) This is how a bookshop should look: a crammed haven full of rip-roaring reads, with every inch of wall space containing English-language books and travel guides. There's an excellent selection of contemporary novels and bestsellers as well as more obscure titles. If you can't find what you want, the English-speaking staff will order it.

### BIBLI                             BOOKSTORE
Map p360 (📞06 588 40 97; Via dei Fienaroli 28; ⏰5.30pm-midnight Mon, 11am-midnight Tue-Sun; 🚇 or 🚊Viale di Trastevere) On an artsy Trastevere street, Bibli is a buzzing warren that manages to be a bookshop, cultural centre and cafe, with a little courtyard and delectable cakes. A great place to pass a pleasant hour or two browsing, it regularly hosts poetry readings and book presentations. There's a limited selection of books in English. There's *aperitivo* (€15, 6.30pm to 8pm), lunchtime buffet (€10, 12.30pm to 3.30pm) and brunch (€20, from 12.30pm Saturday and Sunday) for peckish intelligentsia.

# Vatican City, Borgo & Prati

VATICAN CITY | BORGO | PRATI | AURELIO

## Neighbourhood Top Five

**1** Gazing heavenwards at Michelangelo's cinematic ceiling frescoes in the **Sistine Chapel** (p193). See God pointing his finger at Adam and pinch yourself that you're looking at the original painting, not a dime-a-dozen poster copy.

**2** Being blown away by the super-sized opulence of **St Peter's Basilica** (p184).

**3** Trying to line up the columns on **Piazza San Pietro** (p200) – it is possible.

**4** Revelling in the wonderful rooftop views from **Castel Sant'Angelo** (p200).

**5** Marvelling at the vibrant colours of the fabulously frescoed **Stanze di Raffaello** (p192).

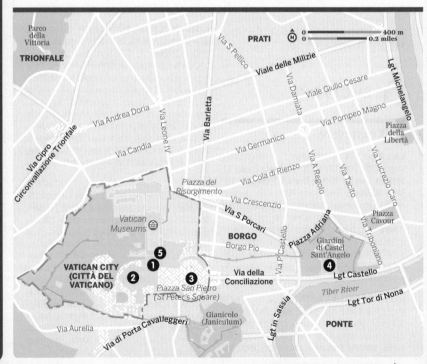

For more detail of this area see Map p364 ➡

# Explore: Vatican City, Borgo & Prati

The Vatican, the world's smallest sovereign state (a mere 0.44 sq km), sits atop the low-lying Vatican hill just a few hundred metres west of the river Tiber. Centred on the domed bulk of St Peter's Basilica and Piazza San Pietro, it boasts some of Italy's most celebrated masterpieces, many housed in the vast Vatican Museums.

You'll need at least a morning to do justice to the Vatican Museums. The highlight is the Michelangelo-decorated Sistine Chapel, but there's enough art on display to keep you busy for years. If you're with a tour guide, or if you can sneakily join a tour group, you can pass directly from the Sistine Chapel through to St Peter's Basilica; otherwise you'll have to walk around and approach from Piazza San Pietro, itself one of the Vatican's most dramatic sights. Once finished in the basilica, you'll probably be ready for a break. There are few good eating options in the Vatican itself, but the graceful residential district of Prati is full of excellent trattorias and restaurants.

Between the Vatican and the river lies the cobbled, medieval district of the Borgo – before Mussolini bulldozed through Via dei Conciliazione, all the streets around St Peter's were like this. The big sight here is Castel Sant'Angelo, the big drum-shaped castle overlooking the river.

The Vatican, Borgo and Prati districts are all easy to reach by public transport. Most people arrive by metro, getting off at Ottaviano–San Pietro metro station, or by bus from Stazione Termini or the *centro storico*.

## Local Life

➡ **Fast Food** Rather than having a full-length sit-down lunch, many local office workers grab a snack at the Sicilian snack bar Mondo Arancina (p201). Next door, Gelarmony (p201) is the place for pudd.

➡ **Shopping Strips** Spearing off Piazza del Risorgimento, Via Cola di Rienzo is lined with busy department stores.

➡ **Live Music** Join the locals for sweet melodies at Alexanderplatz (p203), Rome's top jazz joint. Another favourite venue is the basement pub Fonclea (p203).

## Getting There & Away

➡ **Bus** From Termini, No 40 is the quickest bus to the Vatican – it'll drop you off near Castel Sant'Angelo. You can also take No 64, which runs a similar route but stops more often. No 492 runs to Piazza del Risorgimento from Stazione Tiburtina, passing through Piazza Barberini and the *centro storico*.

➡ **Metro** Take metro line A to Ottaviano–San Pietro. From the station signs direct you to St Peter's.

## Lonely Planet's Top Tip

Be wary of the touts around Ottaviano metro station selling queue-jumping tours of the Vatican Museums. Many of these are not authorised and the tours they offer cost more than those sold by the museums' online ticket office or by the Vatican-sponsored Roma Cristiana (www.operaromanapellegrinaggi.org).

Note that if you want to attend Easter or Christmas mass at St Peter's you have to book tickets through the Prefettura della Casa Pontificia (www.vatican.va).

### ✖ Best Places to Eat

➡ Angeli a Borgo (p201)
➡ Gelarmony (p201)
➡ Pizzarium (p203)
➡ Cacio e Pepe (p202)
➡ Osteria dell'Angelo (p202)

For reviews see p201 ➡

### 🍺 Best Places to Drink

➡ Alexanderplatz (p203)
➡ Passaguai (p203)
➡ Art Studio Café (p203)
➡ Fonclea (p203)

For reviews see p203 ➡

### ⊙ Best Overground & Underground

➡ Dome of St Peter's Basilica (p188)
➡ Terrace of Castel Sant'Angelo (p200)
➡ St Peter's Tomb (p188)
➡ Vatican Grottoes (p188)

For reviews see p200 ➡

**VATICAN CITY, BORGO & PRATI**

## TOP SIGHTS
# ST PETER'S BASILICA

In a city of outstanding churches, none can hold a candle to St Peter's Basilica (Basilica di San Pietro), Italy's biggest, richest and most spectacular church. A monument to centuries of artistic genius, it contains some spectacular works of art, including three of Italy's most celebrated masterpieces: Michelangelo's Pietá, his breathtaking dome, and Bernini's baldachin (canopy) over the papal altar. The basilica is a huge place but it can still get very crowded and on busy days it attracts more than 20,000 visitors. If you want to be one of them, remember to dress appropriately – that means no shorts, miniskirts or bare shoulders.

### DON'T MISS...
➡ *Pietà*
➡ Statue of St Peter
➡ The dome
➡ The baldachin
➡ *Cathedra di San Pietro*
➡ Monument to the Stuarts

### PRACTICALITIES
➡ Map p364
➡ Piazza San Pietro
➡ Admission free
➡ Audioguide €5
➡ ⊙7am-7pm Apr-Sep, 7am-6pm Oct-Mar
➡ Ⓜ Ottaviano-San Pietro

## History

The first basilica was built by Constantine in the 4th century. Standing on the site of Nero's stadium, the Ager Vaticanus, where St Peter is said to have been buried, it was consecrated in AD 326. But like many early churches, it eventually fell into disrepair and it wasn't until the mid-15th century that efforts were made to restore it, first by Pope Nicholas V and then, rather more successfully, by Julius II. In 1506 Bramante came up with a design for a basilica based on a Greek-cross plan, with four equal arms and a huge central dome. It was an audacious plan and when building eventually began, Bramante attracted fierce criticism for destroying the old basilica and many of its Byzantine mosaics and frescoes.

On Bramante's death in 1514, construction work ground to a halt as architects, including Raphael and Antonio da Sangallo, tried to modify his original plans. But little progress was made and it wasn't until Michelangelo took over in 1547 at the age of 72 that the situation changed. Michelangelo simplified Bramante's plans and drew up designs for what was to become his greatest architectural achievement, the dome. He never lived to see it built, though, and it was left to Giacomo della Porta and Domenico Fontana to finish it in 1590.

With the dome in place, Carlo Maderno inherited the project in 1605. He designed the monumental facade and lengthened the nave towards the piazza.

## The Facade

Built between 1608 and 1612, Carlo Maderno's immense facade is 48m high and 118.6m wide. Eight 27m-high columns support the upper attic on which 13 statues stand representing Christ the Redeemer, St John the Baptist and the 11 apostles. The central balcony is known as the Loggia della Benedizione, and it's from here that the pope delivers his *Urbi et Orbi* blessing at Christmas and Easter. Behind the facade is the grand atrium, through which you pass to enter the basilica. Note the first door on the right, the **Porta Santa** (Holy Door), which is opened only in Jubilee Years.

## Interior – Right Nave

At the beginning of the right aisle, Michelangelo's hauntingly beautiful **Pietà** sits in its own chapel behind a panel of bullet-proof glass. Sculpted when he was a little-known 25 year-old (in 1499), it's the only work he ever signed – his signature is etched into the sash across the Madonna's breast.

Nearby, the **red porphyry disk** on the floor inside the main door marks the spot where Charlemagne and later Holy Roman emperors were crowned by the pope.

Paying tribute to a woman whose reputation was far from holy, Carlo Fontana's gilt and bronze **monument to Queen Christina of Sweden** is dedicated to the Swedish monarch who converted to Catholicism in 1655. You'll see it on a pillar just beyond the Pietà.

Moving down the aisle you come to the **Cappella del Santissimo Sacramento**, a small chapel decorated in sumptuous baroque style. The iron grille was designed by Borromini; the gilt bronze ciborium above the altar is by Bernini; and the altarpiece, *The Trinity,* is by Pietro da Cortona.

Just beyond the chapel, the grandiose **Monument to Gregory XIII** sits near the **Cappella Gregoriana**, built by Gregory XIII from designs by Michelangelo. The outstanding work here is the 12th-century fresco of the *Madonna del Soccorso* (Madonna of Succour), which was moved from the original basilica in 1578.

Much of the right-hand transept is roped off but from outside you can still see the **monument of Clement XIII**, one of Antonio Canova's most famous works.

**Free English-language tours of the basilica are run from the Centro Servizi Pellegrini e Turisti, at 9.45am on Tuesday and Thursday and at 2.15pm every afternoon between Monday and Friday.**

## Interior – Central Nave

Dominating the centre of the basilica is Bernini's 29m-high **baldachin**. Supported by four spiral columns and made with bronze taken from the Pantheon, it stands over the papal altar, also known as the Altar of the Confession, which itself sits on the site of St Peter's grave. The pope is the only priest permitted to serve at the high altar. In front, the elaborate **Confessione**, built by Carlo Maderno, is where St Peter was originally buried.

Above the baldachin, Michelangelo's **dome** rises to a height of 119m. Based on Brunelleschi's cupola in Florence, this towering masterpiece is supported by four stone **piers** that rise around the papal altar. They are named after the saints whose statues adorn their Bernini-designed niches – Longinus, Helena, Veronica and Andrew – and decorated with reliefs depicting the *Reliquie Maggiori* (Major Relics): the lance of St Longinus, which he used to pierce Christ's side; the cloth of St Veronica, which bears a miraculous image of Christ; and a piece of the True Cross, collected by St Helena.

At the base of the **Pier of St Longinus**, to the right as you face the papal altar, is a much-loved bronze **statue of St Peter**, believed to be a 13th-century work by Arnolfo di Cambio, whose right foot has been worn down by centuries of caresses. On the Feast Day of St Peter and St Paul (29 June), the statue is dressed in papal robes.

Behind the altar in the tribune at the end of the basilica, the **throne of St Peter** (1665) is the centrepiece of Bernini's extraordinary **Cattedra di San Pietro**. In the middle of the elaborate gilded-bronze throne, supported by statues of Saints Augustine, Ambrose, Athanasius and John Chrysostom, is a wooden seat, which was once thought to have been St Peter's but in fact dates to the 9th century. Above, rays of yellow light shine through a gaudy window, framed by a gilded mass of

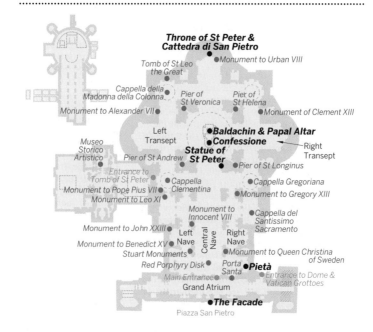

*St Peter's baldachin*

## FACE IN THE BALDACHIN

The frieze on Bernini's baldachin contains a hidden narrative that begins at the pillar to the left (looking with your back to the entrance). As you walk clockwise around the baldachin note the woman's face carved into the frieze of each pillar, at about eye level. On the first three pillars her face seems to express the increasing agony of childbirth; on the last one, it's replaced by that of a smiling baby. The woman was a niece of Pope Urban VIII who gave birth as Bernini worked on the baldachin.

golden angels and in whose central pane flies a dove (representing the Holy Spirit).

To the right of the throne, Bernini's **monument to Urban VIII** depicts the pope flanked by the figures of Charity and Justice.

### Interior – Left Nave

In the roped-off left transept behind the **Pier of St Veronica**, the **Cappella della Madonna della Colonna** takes its name from the image of the Madonna that once adorned the old basilica but now stares out from Giacomo della Porta's marble altar. To its right, above the **tomb of St Leo the Great**, is a particularly fine relief by the baroque sculptor Alessandro Algardi. Opposite it, under the next arch, is Bernini's last work in the basilica, the **monument to Alexander VII**.

About halfway down the left aisle, the cupola of the **Cappella Clementina** is named after Clement VIII (d 1605), who had Giacomo della Porta decorate it for the Jubilee of 1600. Beneath the altar is the **tomb of St Gregory the Great** and, above it, a mosaic representing the *Miracolo di San Giorgio* (Miracle of St George), inspired by a work of Andrea Sacchi. To the left is a classical **monument to Pope Pius VII** by Thorvaldsen.

In the next arch, Alessandro Algardi's 16th-century **monument to Leo XI** depicts the bearded Medici pope seemingly weighed down by the weight of the job. Beyond it, the richly decorated **Cappella del Coro** was created by Giovanni Battista Ricci to

**Contrary to popular opinion, St Peter's Basilica is not the world's largest church – the Basilica of Our Lady of Peace in Yamoussoukro on the Ivory Coast is bigger. Bronze floor plates in the central aisle indicate the respective sizes of the 14 next-largest churches.**

designs by Giacomo della Porta; Bernini designed the elegant choir stalls. The **monument to Innocent VIII** by Antonio Pollaiuolo (in the next aisle arch) is a re-creation of a monument from the old basilica.

Continuing back towards the front of the basilica, the **Cappella della Presentazione** contains two of St Peter's most modern works: a black relief **monument to John XXIII** by Emilio Greco, and a **monument to Benedict XV** by Pietro Canonica. Under the next arch are the so-called **Stuart monuments**. On the right is the monument to Clementina Sobieska, wife of James Stuart, by Filippo Barigioni, and on the left is Canova's vaguely erotic monument to the last three members of the Stuart clan, the pretenders to the English throne who died in exile in Rome.

## Dome

To climb the **dome** (with/without lift €7/5; ◷8am-5.45pm Apr-Sep, 8am-4.45pm Oct-Mar) look for the entrance to the right of the basilica. A small lift takes you halfway up but it's still a long climb to the top (320 steps to be exact). Press on, though, and you'll be rewarded with stunning views. It's well worth the effort, but bear in mind it's steep, long and narrow: not recommended for those who suffer from claustrophobia or vertigo.

## Museo Storico Artistico

Accessed from halfway down the left nave, the **Museo Storico Artistico** (Treasury of St Peter's; adult/reduced €6/4; ◷9am-6.15pm Apr-Sep, 9am-5.15pm Oct-Mar) sparkles with sacred relics and priceless artefacts. Highlights include a tabernacle by Donatello; the Colonna Santa, a 4th-century Byzantine column from the earlier church; the 6th-century *Crux Vaticana* (Vatican Cross), a gift from the emperor Justinian II; and the massive 15th-century bronze tomb of Sixtus IV by Pollaiuolo.

## Tomb of St Peter

Excavations beneath the basilica have uncovered part of the original church and what archaeologists believe is the **Tomb of St Peter** (admission €10, over 15s only). In 1942, the bones of an elderly, strongly built man were found in a box hidden behind a wall covered by pilgrims' graffiti. After more than 30 years of forensic examination, in 1976, Pope Paul VI declared the bones to be those of St Peter.

The excavations can be visited only on a 90-minute guided tour. To book a spot email the **Ufficio Scavi** (Excavations Office; ☏06 698 85 318; scavi@fsp.va), as far in advance as possible.

## Vatican Grottoes

Extending beneath the basilica, the **Vatican Grottoes** (admission free; ◷9am-6pm Apr-Sep, 9am-5pm Oct-Mar) contain the tombs of numerous popes, including John Paul II, whose simple sepulchre contrasts with many of the flamboyant monuments in the basilica above. You can also see several huge columns from the original 4th-century basilica.

# TOP SIGHTS
# VATICAN MUSEUMS

Visiting the Vatican Museums is a thrilling and unforgettable experience. With some 7km of exhibitions and more masterpieces than many small countries, this vast museum complex, housed in the 5.5-hectare Palazzo Apostolico Vaticano, contains one of the world's greatest art collections. You'll never manage to cover the whole collection in one go – it's said that if you spent one minute on every exhibit it would take you 12 years to see everything – but for a whistle-stop tour get to the Pinacoteca, the Museo Pio-Clementino, Galleria delle Carte Geografiche, Stanze di Raffaello (Raphael Rooms) and the Sistine Chapel.

## Pinacoteca

The papal picture gallery boasts some 460 paintings with works by Giotto, Fra Angelico, Filippo Lippi, Guido Reni, Guercino, Nicholas Poussin, Van Dyck and Pietro da Cortona. Look out for Raphael's *Madonna di Foligno* (Madonna of Folignano) and his last painting, *La Trasfigurazione* (Transfiguration), which was completed by his students after he died in 1520. Other highlights include Giotto's *Polittico Stefaneschi* (Stefaneschi Triptych); Giovanni Bellini's *Pietà* and Leonardo da Vinci's unfinished *San Gerolamo* (St Jerome); and Caravaggio's *Deposizione* (Deposition from the Cross).

## Museo Gregoriano Egizio

Founded by Pope Gregory XVI in 1839, this museum contains pieces taken from Egypt in Roman times. The collection is small but there are fascinating exhibits includ-

### DON'T MISS...

➡ Sistine Chapel
➡ *Stanze di Raffaello*
➡ *Apollo Belvedere & Laocoön,* Museo Pio-Clementino
➡ *La Trasfigurazione,* Pinacoteca

### PRACTICALITIES

➡ Map p364
➡ ☎06 698 84 676
➡ http://mv.vatican.va
➡ Viale Vaticano
➡ adult/reduced €15/8, last Sun of the month free
➡ audioguide €7
➡ ⏰9am-6pm Mon-Sat, last admission 4pm, 9am-2pm last Sun of month, last admission 12.30pm
➡ Ⓜ Ottaviano–San Pietro

## JUMP THE QUEUE

Here's how to jump the ticket queue. Book tickets at the museums' online ticket office (http://biglietteriamu sei.vatican.va/musei/ tickets). On payment, you'll receive email confirmation, which you should print and present, along with valid ID, at the museum entrance. Note that tickets bought online incur a €4 booking fee. You can also book guided tours (adult/ reduced €31/24) online. Alternatively, you could book a tour with a reputable guide. On the whole, exhibits are not well labelled, so consider hiring an audioguide or buying the excellent *Guide to the Vatican Museums and City* (€12). Time your visit: Wednesday mornings are good as everyone is at the pope's weekly audience; afternoon is better than the morning; avoid Mondays when many other museums are shut.

**The museums are well equipped for visitors with disabilities and wheelchairs are available free of charge from the Special Permits desk in the entrance hall. They can also be reserved in advance by emailing accoglienza. musei@scv.va. Strollers can be taken into the museums.**

ing the *Trono di Rameses II,* part of a statue of the seated king, vividly painted sarcophagi dating from around 1000 BC, and some macabre mummies.

## Museo Chiaramonti

This museum is effectively the long corridor that runs down the lower east side of the Belvedere Palace. Its walls are lined with thousands of statues representing everything from immortal gods to playful cherubs and ugly Roman patricians. Near the end of the hall, off to the right, is the **Braccio Nuovo** (New Wing), which contains a famous sculpture of Augustus and a statue depicting the Nile as a reclining god covered by 16 babies.

## Museo Pio-Clementino

This spectacular museum contains some of the Vatican Museums' finest classical statuary, including the peerless *Apollo Belvedere* and the 1st-century *Laocoön,* both in the **Cortile Ottagono** (Octagonal Courtyard).

Before you go into the courtyard, take a moment to admire the 1st-century *Apoxyomenos,* one of the earliest known sculptures to depict a figure with a raised arm.

To the left as you enter the courtyard, the *Apollo Belvedere* is a Roman 2nd-century copy of a 4th-century-BC Greek bronze. A beautifully proportioned representation of the sun god Apollo, it's considered one of the great masterpieces of classical sculpture. Nearby, the *Laocoön* depicts a muscular Trojan priest and his two sons in mortal struggle with two sea serpents.

Back inside the museum, the **Sala degli Animali** is filled with sculptures of all sorts of creatures and some magnificent 4th-century mosaics. Continuing through the sala, you come to the **Galleria delle Statue**, which has several important classical pieces; the **Sala delle Buste**, which contains hundreds of Roman busts; and the **Gabinetto delle Maschere**, named after the floor mosaics of theatrical masks. To the east, the **Sala delle Muse** (Room of the Muses) is centred on the *Torso Belvedere,* another of the museum's must-sees. A fragment of a muscular Greek sculpture from the 1st century BC, it was found in Campo de' Fiori and used by Michelangelo as a model for his *ignudi* in the Sistine Chapel.

The next room, the **Sala Rotonda** (Round Room), contains a number of colossal statues, including the gilded-bronze figure of an odd-looking *Ercole* (Hercules) and an exquisite floor mosaic. The enormous basin in the centre of the room was found at Nero's Domus Aurea and is made out of a single piece of red porphyry stone.

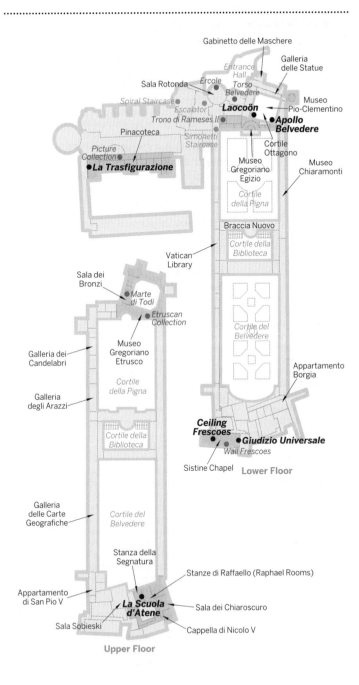

Gabinetto delle Maschere

Galleria delle Statue

Entrance Hall

Sala Rotonda

Ercole

Torso Belvedere

Museo Pio-Clementino

*Laocoön*

Spiral Staircase

Escalator

Trono di Rameses II

*Apollo Belvedere*

Cortile Ottagono

Simonetti Staircase

Pinacoteca

Museo Chiaramonti

Picture Collection

*La Trasfigurazione*

Museo Gregoriano Egizio

Cortile della Pigna

Braccia Nuovo

Cortile della Biblioteca

Vatican Library

Sala dei Bronzi

*Marte di Todi*

Cortile del Belvedere

*Etruscan Collection*

Museo Gregoriano Etrusco

Appartamento Borgia

Galleria dei Candelabri

Cortile della Pigna

Galleria degli Arazzi

Cortile della Biblioteca

*Ceiling Frescoes*

*Giudizio Universale*

*Wall Frescoes*

Sistine Chapel   Lower Floor

Galleria delle Carte Geografiche

Cortile del Belvedere

Stanza della Segnatura

Stanze di Raffaello (Raphael Rooms)

Appartamento di San Pio V

*La Scuola d'Atene*

Sala dei Chiaroscuro

Sala Sobieski

Cappella di Nicolo V

Upper Floor

VATICAN CITY, BORGO & PRATI VATICAN MUSEUMS

## SPIRAL STAIRCASE

One of the most photographed works in the Vatican Museums' – and yes, you can use cameras in the museum, but no flashes and no photos in the Sistine Chapel – is the spiral staircase that you take to leave the museums. The work of the Italian architect Giuseppe Moma, it was made in 1932 and served as the museums' main entrance until 2000. In fact, it is actually two staircases incorporated into a single double-helix structure, just like the human DNA strand.

Images from Raphael's masterwork *La Scuola d'Atene* (The School of Athens) turn up in the most unusual of places. The Guns N' Roses albums *Use Your Illusion I* and *II* both feature a detail from the painting – a boy crouching over to write in a notebook balanced on his raised leg.

## Museo Gregoriano Etrusco

On the upper level of the Belvedere (off the 18th-century Simonetti staircase), Museo Gregoriano Etrusco contains artefacts unearthed in the Etruscan tombs of northern Lazio, and a collection of Greek vases and Roman antiquities. Of particular interest is the *Marte di Todi* (Mars of Todi), a full-length bronze statue of a warrior dating from the 4th century BC, in the **Sala dei Bronzi**.

## Galleria dei Candelabri & Galleria degli Arazzi

Originally an open loggia, the **Galleria dei Candelabri** is packed with classical sculpture and several elegantly carved marble candelabras that give the gallery its name. The corridor continues through to the **Galleria degli Arazzi** (Tapestry Gallery) and its 10 huge tapestries. The best tapestries, those on the left, were woven in Brussels in the 16th century.

## Galleria delle Carte Geografiche & Sala Sobieski

One of the unsung heroes of the Vatican Museums, the 120m-long Map Gallery is hung with 40 huge topographical maps. They were all created between 1580 and 1583 for Pope Gregory XIII, and based on drafts by Ignazio Danti, a leading cartographers of his day.

Beyond the gallery is the **Appartamento di San Pio V**, containing some interesting Flemish tapestries, and the **Sala Sobieski**, named after the enormous 19th-century canvas on its northern wall (depicting the victory of the Polish King John III Sobieski over the Turks in 1683).

## Stanze di Raffaello

Even in the shadow of the Sistine Chapel, the *Stanze di Raffaello* (Raphael Rooms) stand out. They were part of Pope Julius II's private apartment; in 1508 he commissioned the 25-year-old, relatively unknown Raphael to decorate them. The frescoes cemented Raphael's reputation, establishing him as a rising star.

But while they carry his name, not all were completed by Raphael: he painted the **Stanza della Segnatura** (Study) and **Stanza d'Eliodoro** (Waiting Room), while the **Stanza dell'Incendio di Borgo** (Dining Room) and **Sala di Costantino** (Reception Room) were decorated by students following his designs.

The first, **Sala di Costantino**, was finished by Giulio Romano in 1525, five years after Raphael's death. It is dominated by the huge *Battaglia di Costantino contro Maxentius* (Battle of the Milvian Bridge), celebrating the victory of Constantine, Rome's first Christian emperor, over Maxentius.

## SUGGESTED ITINERARY

Follow this three-hour itinerary for the museums' greatest hits.

Once you've passed through the entrance complex, head up the escalator. At the top, signs indicate left for the Sistine Chapel and Stanze di Raffaello (Raphael Rooms). Before following these, nip out to the terrace for views over St Peter's dome and the Vatican Gardens. Re-enter and follow onto the Cortile della Pigna, home to a huge Augustan-era bronze pine cone. Cross the courtyard and enter a long corridor – the Museo Chiaramonti. Don't stop here, but continue left, up the stairs, to the Museo Pio-Clementino. Follow the flow of people through the Cortile Ottagonale and onto the Sala Croce Greca (Greek Cross Room), from where stairs lead up to the Galleria dei Candelabri (Gallery of the Candelabra). It gets very crowded along here as you are funnelled through the Galleria degli Arazzi (Tapestry Gallery) and onto the Galleria delle Carte Geografiche (Map Gallery). At the end of the corridor, carry on through the Sala Sobieski, to the Sala di Costantino, the first of the four Stanze di Raffaello (Raphael Rooms). From the last of these, the one-way system routes you past the modern art and onto the Sistine Chapel.

Leading off this are the **Sala dei Chiaroscuri**, featuring a Raphael-designed ceiling, and the **Cappella di Niccolo V**, Pope Nicholas V's private chapel. Often closed to the public, this tiny chapel features a superb cycle of frescoes by Fra Angelico.

The **Stanza d'Eliodoro**, which was used for private audiences, was painted between 1512 and 1514. It takes its name from the *Cacciata d'Eliodoro* (Expulsion of Heliodorus from the Temple). To the right of this is the *Messa di Bolsena* (Mass of Bolsena), showing Julius II paying homage to the relic of a 13th-century miracle at the lake town of Bolsena. Next is *Incontro di Leone Magno con Attila* (Encounter of Leo the Great with Attila) by Raphael and his school, and on the fourth wall the *Liberazione di San Pietro* (Liberation of St Peter), one of Raphael's most brilliant works.

The **Stanza della Segnatura**, Pope Julius' study and library, was the first room that Raphael painted, and it's here that you'll find his great masterpiece, *La Scuola d'Atene* (The School of Athens) featuring philosophers and scholars gathered around Plato and Aristotle. The seated figure in front of the steps is believed to be Michelangelo, while the figure of Plato is said to be a portrait of Leonardo da Vinci, and Euclide (the bald man bending over) is Bramante. Raphael also included a self-portrait in the lower right corner (he's the second figure from the right in the black hat). Opposite is *La Disputa del Sacramento* (Disputation on the Sacrament), also by Raphael.

The most famous work of the **Stanza dell'Incendio di Borgo** is *Incendio di Borgo* (Fire in the Borgo), which depicts Leo IV extinguishing a fire by making the sign of the cross. The ceiling was painted by Raphael's master, Perugino. From Raphael's rooms, stairs lead to the **Appartamento Borgia** and the Vatican's collection of modern religious art.

## Sistine Chapel

See p196.

## Vatican Library

Founded by Nicholas V in 1450, the Biblioteca Apostolica Vaticana contains more than 1.5 million volumes, including illuminated manuscripts, early printed books, prints and drawings.

TOP SIGHTS
**VATICAN MUSEUMS**

# Sistine Chapel

**The jewel in the Vatican crown, the Sistine Chapel (Cappella Sistina) is home to two of the world's most famous works of art – Michelangelo's ceiling frescoes and his *Giudizio Universale* (Last Judgment).**

But the chapel is more than just an art gallery. It also serves an important religious function as the pope's private chapel, the place where the papal conclave meets to elect a new pope. As a consequence, it's the only place in the Vatican Museums with air-conditioning.

The chapel was originally built for Pope Sixtus IV, after whom it is named, and consecrated on 15 August 1483. It's a big, barn-like structure, measuring 40.2m long, 13.4m wide and 20.7m high – the same size as the Temple of Solomon – and even pre-Michelangelo would have been impressive. Its walls had frescoes by the top artists of the day, the vaulted ceiling had been painted to resemble a blue sky with golden stars, and the floor, which is as you see it today, had been laid out in inlaid polychrome marble.

But although named after Sixtus, the chapel owes its modern fame to Michelangelo and his two unrivalled masterpieces. The first, the ceiling, was commissioned by Pope Julius II and painted between 1508 and 1512; the second, the spectacular *Giudizio Universale* (Last Judgment), was completed almost 30 years later in 1541. Taken together, they cover approximately 1000 sq m and represent one of the greatest feats of painting ever accomplished by a single man.

Both were controversial works – male nudes weren't, and generally aren't, considered appropriate subjects for church decor – and both were influenced by the political ambitions of the popes who commissioned them. The ceiling came as part of Julius II's drive to transform Rome into the Church's showcase capital, while Pope Paul III intended the *Giudizio Universale* (Last Judgment) to serve as a warning to Catholics to toe the line during the Reformation, which was then sweeping through Europe.

In recent years debate has centred on the chapel's multi-million dollar restoration, which finished in 1999 after nearly 20 years. In removing almost 450 years' worth of dust and candle soot, restorers finally revealed the frescoes in their original technicolour glory. But some critics claimed that they also removed a layer of varnish that Michelangelo had added to darken them and enhance their shadows. Whatever the truth, the Sistine Chapel remains a truly spectacular sight.

**Right**
1. Ceiling of the Sistine Chapel

# The Ceiling

**The Sistine Chapel provided the greatest challenge of Michelangelo's career and painting the 800-sq-m vaulted ceiling at a height of more than 20m pushed him to the limits of his genius.**

When Pope Julius II first approached him – some say on the advice of his chief architect, Bramante, who was keen for Michelangelo to fail – he was reluctant to accept. He regarded himself as a sculptor and up until then had had virtually no experience of painting frescoes. However, Julius was determined and in 1508 he persuaded Michelangelo to accept the commission for a fee of 3,000 ducats (more or less €1.5 to 2 million in today's money).

To get the best views of the ceiling stand near the chapel's main entrance – across from the visitors' entrance in the far wall.

## The Central Panels

Pope Julius' original plan had been for Michelangelo to paint the twelve apostles and a series of decorative architectural elements. But the artist rejected this and came up with a much more complex design to cover the entire ceiling. Based on stories from the book of Genesis, this is what you see today.

At the heart of the work are nine central panels depicting the Creation, the story of Adam and Eve, the Fall, and the plight of Noah. Starting at the altar end, these show: *God Separating Light from Darkness; Creation of the Sun, Moon and Planets; Separation of Land from Sea; Creation of Adam; Creation of Eve; Temptation and Expulsion of Adam and Eve from the Garden of Eden; Noah's Sacrifice; The Flood;* and the *Drunkenness of Noah.*

The most famous scene is the *Creation of Adam*, which shows a bearded God pointing his figure at Adam, thus bringing him to life. Another celebrated image is the *Temptation and Expulsion of Adam and*

**Clockwise from top left**
1. Central panels from the ceiling of the Sistine Chapel
2. Detail of *Creation of Adam* fresco

*Eve from the Garden of Eden,* which shows Adam and Eve being sent packing after accepting the forbidden fruit from Satan, represented by a snake with the body of a woman coiled around a tree.

## The Ignudi, Prophets & Sibyls

Set around the central panels are 20 athletic male nudes, known as the *ignudi.* These muscle-bound models caused a scandal when they were first revealed and still today art historians are divided over their meaning – some claim they are angels, others that they represent Michelangelo's neo-Platonic vision of ideal man.

On the lower curved part of the vault and separated by the triangular spandrels and lunettes, are figures of Hebrew prophets and pagan sibyls. These powerful representations – especially the Delphic and Libyan sibyls – are among the most striking and dramatic images on the ceiling. The spandrels contain figures representing the ancestors of Christ.

### MYTHS DEBUNKED

It is often said that Michelangelo worked alone. He didn't. Throughout the job, he employed a steady stream of assistants to help with the plaster work (producing frescoes involves painting directly onto wet plaster).

Another popular myth is that Michelangelo painted lying down, as portrayed by Charlton Heston in the film *The Agony and the Ecstasy*. In fact, Michelangelo designed a curved scaffolding system that allowed him to work standing up, albeit in an awkward backward-leaning position. What the film did get right, though, was the prickly relationship between Michelangelo and Pope Julius.

# Giudizio Universale (Last Judgment)

**Michelangelo's second stint in the Sistine Chapel, from 1535 to 1541, resulted in the *Giudizio Universale* (Last Judgment), the 200-sq-m fresco that covers the wall above the altar.**

The project, which was commissioned by Pope Clement VII and encouraged by his successor Paul III, was controversial from the start. Critics were outraged when Michelangelo destroyed two Perugino frescoes when preparing the wall – it had to be replastered so that it tilted inwards to protect it from dust – and when it was unveiled in 1541, its dramatic, swirling mass of 391 predominantly naked bodies provoked outrage. So fierce were feelings that the Church's top brass, meeting at the 1564 Council of Trent, ordered the nudity to be covered up. The task fell to Daniele da Volterra, one of Michelangelo's students, who added fig leaves and loincloths to 41 nudes, earning himself the nickname *il braghettone* (the breeches maker). But the fresco also had its supporters and many considered it Michelangelo's best work, surpassing all the other paintings in the chapel, including his own ceiling frescoes.

## The Composition

The central focus of the painting is the figure of Christ, near the top. Around him, in a kind of vortex, the souls of the dead are torn from their graves to face his judgment. The saved get to stay up in heaven (the throng of bodies in the upper right quadrant), while the damned are sent down to face the demons in hell (in the bottom right).

An interesting point to note is the striking amount of ultramarine blue in this painting. At the time, this colour was made from the hugely expensive stone lapis lazuli. But as it was the pope who was

**Clockwise from top left**
1. Last Judgment fresco 2. Detail of St Bartholomew from Last Judgment fresco

paying for all the paint Michelangelo had no qualms about applying it in generous measure. In contrast, he didn't use any in his ceiling frescoes because he had to pay for all his own materials on that job.

## In Detail

Look in the bottom right-hand corner and you'll see a nude figure with a snake around him. This is Minos, judge of the underworld, with the face of Biagio de Cesena, the papal master of ceremonies and one of Michelangelo's loudest critics.

Look closer and you'll see that he also has donkey ears and that the snake wrapped around him is actually biting him on his crown jewels.

Further up the painting, just beneath Christ, is the bald, beefy figure of St Bartholomew holding his own flayed skin. The face painted in the skin is said to be a self-portrait of Michelangelo, its anguished look reflecting the artist's tormented faith.

---

### WALL FRESCOES

If you can tear your eyes from the Michelangelos, the Sistine Chapel also boasts some superb wall frescoes. These formed part of the original chapel decoration and were painted between 1481 and 1482 by a crack team of Renaissance artists, including Botticelli, Ghirlandaio, Pinturicchio, Perugino and Luca Signorelli. They represent events in the lives of Moses (to the left, looking at the *Giudizio Universale*) and Christ (to the right).

Highlights include Botticelli's *Temptations of Christ* (the second fresco on the right) and Perugino's superbly composed *Christ Giving the Keys to St Peter* (the fifth fresco on the right).

# ⊙ SIGHTS

Boasting priceless treasures at every turn, the Vatican is home to some of Rome's most popular sights. The Vatican Museums and St Peter's Basilica are the star attractions but Castel Sant'Angelo, one of the city's most recognisable landmarks, is also well worth a visit.

## ⊙ Vatican City

**ST PETER'S BASILICA**                   CHURCH
See p184.

**PIAZZA SAN PIETRO**                      PIAZZA
Map p364 (MOttaviano-San Pietro) One of the world's great public spaces, the piazza was laid out by Gian Lorenzo Bernini between 1656 and 1667 for Pope Alexander VII. Seen from above, it resembles a giant keyhole with two semicircular colonnades, each consisting of four rows of Doric columns, encircling a giant ellipse that straightens out to funnel believers into the basilica. The effect was deliberate – Bernini described the colonnades as representing 'the motherly arms of the church'. The 25m obelisk in the centre was brought to Rome by Caligula from Heliopolis in Egypt and later used by Nero as a turning post for the chariot races in his circus.

The scale of the piazza is dazzling: at its largest it measures 340m by 240m; there are 284 columns and, on top of the colonnades, 140 saints. In the midst of all this the pope seems very small as he delivers his weekly address at noon on Sunday.

**VATICAN MUSEUMS**                        MUSEUM
See p189.

**VATICAN GARDENS**                        GARDEN
Map p364 (http://biglietteriamusei.vatican.va; adult/reduced incl Vatican Museums €31/24) Up to half the Vatican is covered by the perfectly manicured Vatican Gardens, which contain fortifications, grottoes, monuments and fountains dating from the 9th century to the present day. Visits are by two-hour guided tour only, for which you'll need to book at least a week in advance.

## ⊙ Borgo

Overshadowed by Castel Sant'Angelo, this quarter retains a low-key medieval charm despite batteries of restaurants, hotels and pizzerias.

**CASTEL SANT'ANGELO**                     MUSEUM
Map p364 (🖉06 681 91 11; Lungotevere Castello 50; adult/reduced €5/2.50; ⊙9am-7.30pm, last admission 6.30pm Tue-Sun; 🚇Piazza Pia) With its chunky round keep, this castle is an instantly recognisable landmark. Originally a mausoleum for the emperor Hadrian, it was converted into a papal fortress in the 6th century and named after an angelic vision that Pope Gregory had in 590. Thanks to a secret 13th-century passageway to the Vatican palaces, it provided sanctuary to many popes in times of danger, including Clemente VII who holed up here during the 1527 Sack of Rome.

Its upper floors boast lavishly decorated Renaissance interiors, including, on the 4th floor, the beautifully frescoed Sala Paolina. Two stories further up, the terrace, immortalised by Puccini in his opera *Tosca,* offers great views over Rome.

**PONTE SANT'ANGELO**                      BRIDGE
Map p364 (🚇Piazza Pia) Hadrian built the Ponte Sant'Angelo across the River Tiber in 136 to provide an approach to his mausoleum, but it was Bernini who brought it to life with his angel sculptures in the 17th century. The three central arches of the bridge are part of the original structure; the end arches were restored and enlarged in 1892–94 during the construction of the Lungotevere embankments.

### PAPAL AUDIENCES

At 11am on Wednesday, the pope addresses his flock at the Vatican (in July and August in Castel Gandolfo near Rome). For free tickets, download the request form from the Vatican website (www.vatican.va) and fax it to the **Prefettura della Casa Pontificia** (fax 06 698 85 863). Pick up tickets at the office through the bronze doors under the colonnade to the right of St Peter's.

When he is in Rome, the Pope blesses the crowd in St Peter's Square on Sunday at noon. No tickets are required.

## COMPLESSO MONUMENTALE SANTO SPIRITO IN SAXIA
HISTORICAL BUILDING

Map p364 (☏06 683 52 433; www.giubilarte. it; Borgo Santo Spirito 1; group visits only adult/reduced €7.50/6; ☺guided tours 10am & 3.30pm Mon; ▣Piazza Pia) Originally an 8th-century lodging for Saxon pilgrims, this ancient hospital complex was established by Pope Innocent III in the late 12th century. Three hundred years later Sixtus IV added an octagonal courtyard and two vast frescoed halls, known collectively as the Corsia Sistina (Sistine Ward).

## MUSEO STORICO NAZIONALE DELL'ARTE SANITARIA
MUSEUM

Map p364 (☏06 689 30 51; Lungotevere in Sassia 3; group visits only admission €7; ☺by reservation; ▣Piazza Pia) Next to the Pronto Soccorso department of the Ospedale Santo Spirito, this medical museum has a ghoulish collection of surgical instruments, macabre curiosities and anatomical models.

# ✖ EATING

Beware, hungry tourists: there are unholy numbers of overpriced, mediocre eateries around the Vatican and St Peter's, aimed at the thousands who pass through each day and need somewhere to flop and refuel. It's worth making the extra effort to find somewhere listed in this guide, as there are fabulous places amid the follies.

North of the Vatican is Prati, an upmarket, largely residential district and location of the RAI TV headquarters. It has some excellent, interesting restaurants catering to wining and dining media lovelies.

# ✖ Vatican City

### OLD BRIDGE
GELATERIA €

Map p364 (Via dei Bastioni di Michelangelo 5; cones/tubs from €1.50; ▣Piazza del Risorgimento) Ideal for a pre- or post-Vatican pick-me-up, this tiny parlour has been cheerfully dishing up huge portions of delicious ice cream for over 20 years. Try the chocolate or pistachio, and, go on, have a dollop of cream.

## GUIDED TOURS

For details of companies offering guided tours of the Vatican Museums and St Peter's Basilica, see the Tours section of the Transport chapter, p305.

# ✖ Borgo

### ANGELI A BORGO
TRADITIONAL ITALIAN €€

Map p364 (☏06 686 96 74; www.angeliaborgo.com; Borgo Angelico 28; pizzas from €5.50, meals €25-30) It is possible to escape the crowds and eat well near St Peter's. Just a few blocks back from the basilica, this is a laid-back restaurant–pizzeria with a high brick ceiling, yellow walls and an ample menu. There are woodfired pizzas and focaccia, abundant pastas and interesting main courses, including chicken curry. If all else fails, the tiramisu is exceptional.

### LA VERANDA DE L'HOTEL COLUMBUS
MODERN ITALIAN €€€

Map p364 (☏06 687 29 73; www.laveranda.net; Borgo Santo Spirito; meals €70; ▣Piazza del Risorgimento) Dine in romantic splendour under Pinturicchio frescoes in the loggia of the 15th-century Palazzo della Rovere. In line with the setting, dishes are based on superb Italian ingredients, such as Tuscan *chianina* beef, and accompanied by top-quality Italian and international wines. Prices are lower at lunch.

# ✖ Prati

### ⬛TOP CHOICE GELARMONY
GELATERIA €

Map p364 (Via Marcantonio Colonna 34; ice cream from €1.50; ☺10am-late daily) This superb gelateria is the ideal place for a lunchtime dessert, a mid-afternoon treat, an evening fancy – in fact, anything at any time. Alongside delicious ice cream, there's a devilish selection of creamy Sicilian sweets, including the best *cannoli* (pastry tubes filled with sweetened ricotta and candied fruit or chocolate pieces) this side of Palermo.

### MONDO ARANCINA
SICILIAN €

Map p364 (Via Marcantonio Colonna 38; arancine from €2) All sunny yellow ceramics, cheerful crowds and tantalising deep-fried snacks, this bustling takeaway brings a little corner of Sicily to Rome. Star of the show are the classic fist-sized *arancine,* fried rice balls stuffed with ragù and peas. Pay first at the till and then take your receipt to the food counter.

### CACIO E PEPE
TRATTORIA €

Map p364 (☑06 321 72 68; Via Avezzana 11; meals €25; ☺closed Sat dinner & Sun) No-nonsense home-style cooking is why Romans flock to this humble trattoria. If you can find a seat at one of the gingham-clad tables spread across the pavement, keep it simple with *cacio e pepe* – fresh *bucatini* slicked with buttery cheese and pepper – followed by *pollo alla cacciatora* ('hunter's chicken').

### OSTERIA DELL'ANGELO
TRATTORIA €€

Map p364 (☑06 372 94 70; Via Bettolo 24; set menus €25 & €30; ☺closed lunch Mon & Sat, Sun) Former rugby player Angelo presides over this hugely popular neighbourhood trattoria (reservations are a must). The set menu features a mixed antipasti, a robust Roman-style pasta and a choice of hearty mains with a side dish. To finish off, you're offered lightly spiced biscuits to dunk in sweet dessert wine.

### HOSTARIA DINO E TONY
TRATTORIA €€

Map p364 (☑06 397 33 284; Via Leone IV; meals €30-35; ☺Mon-Sat) Something of a rarity, Dino e Tony is an authentic trattoria in the Vatican area. Kick off with the monumental antipasto, a minor meal in its own right, before plunging into its signature dish, *rigatoni all' amatriciana.* Finish up with a *granita di caffè,* a crushed ice coffee served with a full inch of whipped cream. No credit cards.

### SETTEMBRINI CAFÉ
MODERN ITALIAN €

Map p364 (Via Settembrini 25; meals €15) A favourite lunchtime haunt of media execs from the nearby RAI TV offices, this trendy cafe does a roaring trade in tasty bar snacks and fresh pastas. Next door, the main **restaurant** (☑06 323 26 17; Via Settembrini 25; meals €60; ☺closed Sat lunch & Sun) is highly regarded by Roman foodies for its modern cuisine and exemplary wine list.

### DAL TOSCANO
TRADITIONAL ITALIAN €€

Map p364 (☑06 397 25 717; www.ristorantedal toscano.it; Via Germanico 58-60; meals €40; ☺Tue-Sun) Carnivores will adore Dal Toscano, an old-fashioned *ristorante* that serves top-notch Tuscan food, with an emphasis

on superb meats. Start with the hand-cut Tuscan *prosciutto,* before attempting the colossal char-grilled *bistecche alla Fiorentina* (Florentine-style steak). You'll need to book.

### RISTORANTE L'ARCANGELO
MODERN ITALIAN €€€

Map p364 (☑06 321 09 92; Via Belli 59-61; meals €60; ☺closed lunch Sat & Sun) Frequented by politicians and local celebs, this smart restaurant serves traditional Roman staples and innovative modern fare – think tripe with mint and pecorino or spicy pigeon with apples and mustard.

### DOLCE MANIERA
BAKERY €

Map p364 (Via Barletta 27; ☺24hr) This 24-hour basement bakery supplies much of the neighbourhood with breakfast. Head here for cheap-as-chips *cornetti,* slabs of pizza, *panini* and an indulgent array of cakes.

### DEL FRATE
WINE BAR €€

Map p364 (☑06 323 64 37; www.enotecadelf rate.it; Via degli Scipioni 122; meals €40; ☺Mon-Sat; ⓂOttaviano–San Pietro) Locals love this upmarket wine bar with its simple wooden tables and high-ceilinged brick-arched rooms. There's a formidable wine list and a small, but refined, selection of beef and tuna tartares, appetising salads, cheeses and fresh pastas.

### HOSTARIA-PIZZERIA GIACOMELLI
PIZZERIA €

Map p364 (☑06 372 59 10; Via Emilio Faà di Bruno 25; pizzas from €6; ☺Tue-Sat; ⓂOttaviano–San Pietro) This neighbourhood restaurant has them queuing around the block for thin and crispy Roman pizzas. The decor is nothing fancy, but the reliably good food, from the *crostini* to the spicy *diavola* pizza, has locals voting with their feet. No credit cards.

### SHANTI
INDIAN, PAKISTANI €

Map p364 (☑06 324 49 22; www.ristoranteshan ti.it; Via Fabio Massimo 68; curries from €9; ⓂOttaviano–San Pietro) When you need a change from pizza and pasta, this deservedly popular Indian and Pakistani restaurant dishes up delicately spiced dishes (tandooris, dhals and the like) in an appealing setting. Lunch menus (vegetarian/meat €8/10) are a bargain.

## PIZZERIA AMALFI
PIZZERIA €

Map p364 (🖉06 397 33 165; Via dei Gracchi 12; pizzas from €6; ⓂOttavian–San Pietro) While Roman pizzas are thin and crispy, Neapolitan pizzas are thicker and more doughy. And that's what you get at this bustling Naples-themed pizzeria just off the main road from Ottaviano metro stop to St Peter's.

## FRANCHI
DELICATESSEN €

Map p364 (🖉06 687 46 51; Via Cola di Rienzo 198; snacks €2.50-4; ⊙9am-8.30pm; ⓂOttaviano–San Pietro) One of Rome's historic delicatessen, Franchi is great for a swift bite, or to stock up on stuff to take home. White-jacketed assistants work with practised dexterity slicing hams, cutting cheese, weighing olives and preparing *panini,* to take away or eat at stand-up tables.

# ✖ Aurelio

## PIZZARIUM
PIZZA AL TAGLIO €

Map p364 (Via della Meloria 43; pizza slice €2-3) It's worth searching out this unassuming takeaway near the Cipro–Musei Vaticani metro station for superb fried snacks and *pizza a taglio.* Pizza toppings are original and intensely flavoursome and the pizza base manages to be both fluffy and crisp. Eat standing up, and wash it down with a chilled beer.

# 🍷 DRINKING & 🍸 NIGHTLIFE

**The quiet area around the Vatican harbours a few charming wine bars and cafes. For nightlife there are a couple of live-music venues, including Italy's best jazz club.**

# 🍸 Prati

## ALEXANDERPLATZ
LIVE MUSIC

Map p364 (🖉06 397 42 171; www.alexander platz.it; Via Ostia 9; admission €15; ⊙8pm-2am; ⓂOttaviano–San Pietro) Rome's top jazz joint attracts top international performers and a passionate, knowledgeable crowd. You'll need to book a table if you want dinner, and the music starts around 10pm. In July and August the club ups sticks and trans-

fers to the grounds of Villa Celimontana for an enchanting, under-the-stars jazz festival.

## PASSAGUAI
WINE BAR

Map p364 (www.passaguai.it; Via Leto 1; ⊙10am-2am Mon-Sat; 🚇Piazza del Risorgimento) A small, cavelike basement wine bar, Passaguai has a few outdoor tables on a quiet street, and feels pleasingly off-the-radar. It boasts a good wine list and a range of artisanal beers, and the food – think cheese and cold cuts – is tasty too. Free wifi.

## ART STUDIO CAFÉ
CAFE

Map p364 (www.artstudiocafe.it; Via dei Gracchi 187a) A cafe, exhibition space and craft school all in one, this bright and breezy spot serves one of Prati's most popular aperitifs. It's also good for a light lunch – something like chicken couscous or fresh salad – or a restorative mid-afternoon tea.

## FONCLEA
LIVE MUSIC

Map p364 (🖉06 689 63 02; www.fonclea.it; Via Crescenzio 82a; ⊙7pm-2am Sep-May; 🚇Piazza del Risorgimento) Fonclea is a great little pub venue for live music, with bands playing anything from jazz to soul, funk to rockabilly and African sounds (gigs start at around 9.30pm). Get in the mood with a drink during happy hour, every day between 7pm and 8pm. From June to August Fonclea moves to a summer riverside site on the Tiber – check the website for details about the location.

## MAKASAR
TEA ROOM

Map p364 (www.makasar.it; Via Plauto 33; ⊙noon-9.30pm; 🚇Piazza del Risorgimento) Recharge your batteries with a quiet tea at this oasis of oriental tranquility. Pick your tipple from the nine-page tea menu (there's wine if you prefer) and sit back in the charming, ochre-walled interior while poring over a lavish art book.

## CASTRONI
CAFE

Map p364 (Via Cola di Rienzo 196; ⊙8am-8pm; ⓂOttaviano–San Pietro) This landmark food shop has an in-store cafe that does a roaring trade in morning cappuccinos and *cornettos* (Italian croissants). There's a second branch at Via Ottaviano 55 near the Ottaviano metro station.

## ENTERTAINMENT

 ## SHOPPING

### AUDITORIUM CONCILIAZIONE THEATRE

Map p364 (☎899 904 560; www.auditorium conciliazione.it, in Italian; Via della Conciliazione 4; 🚇Piazza Pia) On the main approach road to Piazza San Pietro, this auditorium plays host to performances of the Orchestra Sinfonica Roma (www.orchestrasinfonicadi roma.it) as well as other classical and contemporary concerts, dance spectacles, film screenings, and exhibitions.

### TEATRO GHIONE THEATRE

Map p364 (☎06 637 22 94; www.teatroghione. it, in Italian; Via delle Fornaci 37; 🚇Piazza del Risorgimento 🚇Ottaviano–San Pietro) A former cinema, the Teatro Ghione is a small, beautifully restored theatre near St Peter's that offers a varied programme featuring major international performers. You can catch anything from Pirandello to opera arias, from Chopin to Sarah Kane.

### CASTRONI FOOD

Map p364 (www.castroniocoladirienzo.com, in Italian; Via Cola di Rienzo 196; ⊘8am-8pm; 🚇Ottaviano–San Pietro) An Aladdin's cave full of gourmet treats. Towering shelves groan under the weight of vinegars, truffles, olive oils, pastas, dried mushrooms and chocolates, as well as Vegemite and baked beans. It also has a good in-store cafe.

### ANGELO DI NEPI FASHION

Map p364 (www.angelodinepi.it; Via Cola di Rienzo 267; 🚇Piazza del Risorgimento) Roman designer Nepi adores rich colours, and combines Italian cuts and styles with rich fabrics to make you as pretty as a peacock.

# Villa Borghese & Northern Rome

VILLA BORGHESE | FLAMINIO | PARIOLI | NOMENTANO | SALARIO

## Neighbourhood Top Five

**1** Getting to grips with genius at the lavish **Museo e Galleria Borghese** (p207). Gian Lorenzo Bernini's sculptures are the star of the show but look out for Antonio Canova's racy depiction of the voluptuous Paolina Bonaparte.

**2** Strolling the leafy lanes of Rome's most famous park, **Villa Borghese** (p212).

**3** Catching a world-class concert at the **Auditorium Parco della Musica** (p212).

**4** Applauding the sophistication of Etruscan art at the **Museo Nazionale Etrusco di Villa Giulia** (p213).

**5** Spying some of Christendom's oldest frescoes at the **Mausoleo di Santa Costanza** (p215).

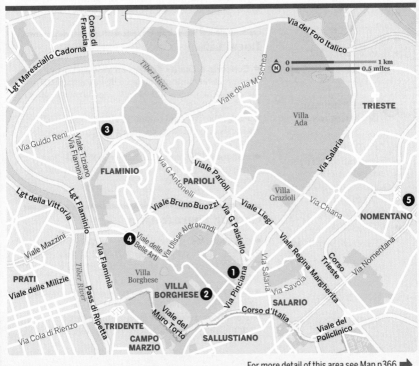

For more detail of this area see Map p366 ➡

## Lonely Planet's Top Tip

Be sure to book your visit to the Museo e Galleria Borghese. It only takes a quick phone call and you won't get in without a reservation, which would be a real shame.

Many of the museums and galleries listed in this chapter have lovely cafes, ideal for a recuperative coffee or small snack.

## ✖ Best Places to Eat

➡ Palotta (p216)

➡ Bar Pompi (p215)

➡ Ensô (p216)

For reviews see p215 ➡

## 🍷 Best Places to Drink

➡ Chioscetto di Ponte Milvio (p216)

➡ Casina del Lago (p216)

➡ Brancaleone (p217)

For reviews see p216 ➡

## 👁 Best Museums & Galleries

➡ Museo e Galleria Borghese (p207)

➡ Museo Nazionale Etrusco di Villa Giulia (p213)

➡ Galleria Nazionale d'Arte Moderna (p212)

➡ MAXXI (p213)

➡ MACRO (p214)

For reviews see p212 ➡

# Explore: Villa Borghese & Northern Rome

Although less packed with traditional sights than elsewhere, this large swathe of northern Rome is well worth investigating. The obvious starting point is Villa Borghese, an attractive park counting the city's zoo, its largest modern art gallery and a stunning Etruscan museum among its myriad attractions. But its *pièce de résistance* is the Museo e Galleria Borghese, one of Rome's top art galleries. The park is easily explored on foot but to get to most of the other sights in this neighbourhood, take public transport.

From Piazzale Flaminio, a tram heads up Via Flaminia to two of Rome's most important modern buildings: Renzo Piano's extraordinary Auditorium Parco della Musica and Zaha Hadid's contemporary art gallery, MAXXI. Continue up the road and you come to Ponte Milvio, a bridge popular with starstruck lovers and scene of an ancient Roman battle. Over the river, and to the west, the Stadio Olimpico is Rome's impressive football stadium.

Over on the eastern side of Villa Borghese, Via Salaria, the old Roman *sale* (salt) road, is now the heart of a smart residential and business district. To the north, the vast Villa Ada park expands northwards while, to the south, Via Nomentana traverses acres of housing as it heads out of town. On Via Nomentana, Villa Torlonia is a captivating park, and the Basilica di Sant'Agnese fuori le Mura claims Rome's oldest Christian mosaic.

# Local Life

➡ **Concerts & Events** Romans are avid supporters of concerts at the Auditorium Parco della Musica (p217). Check also for events at the MAXXI (p213) and MACRO (p214) art galleries.

➡ **Parks** Tourists tend to stop at Villa Borghese (p212) but locals often head to Villa Torlonia (p215) and Villa Ada (p214).

➡ **Hangouts** The bars and eateries on Piazzale Ponte Milvio (p216) are a favourite of lunching locals and a young drinking crowd.

# Getting There & Away

➡ **Bus** Buses 116, 52 and 53 head up to Villa Borghese from Via Vittorio Veneto near Barberini metro station. There are regular buses along Via Nomentana and Via Salaria.

➡ **Metro** To get to Villa Borghese by metro, follow the signs up from Spagna station (line A).

➡ **Tram** Tram 2 trundles up Via Flaminia from Piazzale Flaminio above Flaminio metro station (line A).

## TOP SIGHTS
# MUSEO E GALLERIA BORGHESE

If you have time, or inclination, for only one art gallery in Rome, make it this one. Housing the 'queen of all private art collections', it provides the perfect introduction to Renaissance and baroque art without ever being overwhelming. To limit numbers, visitors are admitted at two-hourly intervals, so you'll need to call to prebook, and then enter at an allotted entry time, but trust us, it's worth it.

The collection, which includes works by Caravaggio, Bernini, Botticelli and Raphael, was formed by Cardinal Scipione Borghese (1579–1633) after whom the museum is named.

## The Villa

Known as the Casino Borghese, the villa was originally built by Cardinal Scipione to house his immense art collection. However, it owes its current neoclassical look to a comprehensive 18th-century facelift carried out by Prince Marcantonio Borghese, a direct descendant of the cardinal. But while the villa remained intact, the collection did not. Much of the antique statuary was carted off to the Louvre in the early 19th century, and other pieces were gradually sold off. In 1902 the Italian State bought the Casino but it wasn't until 1997 that the collection was finally put on public display.

The villa is divided into two parts: the ground-floor museum, with its superb sculptures, intricate Roman floor mosaics and hypnotic trompe l'oeil frescoes; and the upstairs picture gallery.

### DON'T MISS
......................................
➡ Ratto di Proserpina
➡ Venere Vincitrice
➡ Ragazzo col Canestro di Frutta
➡ La Deposizione di Cristo
➡ Amor Sacro e Amor Profano

### PRACTICALITIES
......................................
➡ Map p366
➡ ☎06 3 28 10
➡ Piazzale del Museo Borghese 5
➡ adult/reduced €8.50/5.25
➡ audioguide €5
➡ ☺9am-7pm Tue-Sun, prebooking required
➡ 🚃Via Pinciana

## CARDINAL SCIPIONE BORGHESE

Cardinal Scipione Caffarelli Borghese (1576–1633) was one of the most influential figures in Rome's baroque art world. Blessed with wealth, power and position – he was made a cardinal at age 26 by his uncle Pope Paul V – he sponsored the greatest artists of the day, including contemporaries Caravaggio, Bernini, Domenichino, Guido Reni and Pieter Paul Rubens. Yet while he promoted them he didn't always see eye to eye with them and he was quite prepared to play dirty to get his hands on their works: he had the fashionable painter Cavaliere d'Arpino flung into jail in order to confiscate his canvases, and he had Domenichino arrested to force him to surrender La Caccia di Diana (The Hunt of Diana).

---

The gallery has a bar on the lower ground floor but for a coffee head to the Casina del Lago, near Villa Borghese's pocket-sized lake.

## Ground Floor

The entrance hall features 4th-century floor mosaics of fighting gladiators and a 2nd-century *Satiro Combattente* (Fighting Satyr). High on the wall is a gravity-defying bas-relief of a horse and rider falling into the void, by Pietro Bernini (Gian Lorenzo's father).

Sala I is centred on Antonio Canova's daring depiction of Napoleon's sister, Paolina Bonaparte Borghese, reclining topless as *Venere Vincitrice* (Venus Victrix; 1805–08). Apparently, Paolina had quite a reputation and tales abounded of her shocking behaviour. When asked how she could have posed almost naked, she's said to have replied that it wasn't cold.

But it's Gian Lorenzo Bernini's spectacular sculptures – flamboyant depictions of pagan myths – that really steal the show. Just look at Daphne's hands morphing into leaves in the swirling *Apollo e Dafne* (1622–25) in Sala III, or Pluto's hand pressing into the seemingly soft flesh of Persephone's thigh in the *Ratto di Proserpina* (Rape of Proserpina; 1621-22) in Sala IV.

Caravaggio, one of Cardinal Scipione's favourite artists, dominates Sala VIII. You'll see a dissipated *Bacchus* (1592–95), the strangely beautiful *La Madonna dei Palafrenieri* (Madonna of the Palafrenieri; 1605–06), and *San Giovanni Battista* (St John the Baptist; 1609–10), probably his last work. There's also the much-loved *Ragazzo col Canestro di Frutta* (Boy with a Basket of Fruit; 1593–95) and dramatic *Davide con la Testa di Golia* (David with the Head of Goliath; 1609–10): Goliath's head is said to be a self-portrait.

## Picture Gallery

With works representing the best of the Tuscan, Venetian, Umbrian and northern European schools, the upstairs picture gallery offers a wonderful snapshot of European Renaissance art.

In Sala IX don't miss Raphael's extraordinary *La Deposizione di Cristo* (The Deposition; 1507), and his charming *Dama con Liocorno* (Lady with a Unicorn; 1506). In the same room is the superb *Adorazione del Bambino* (Adoration of the Christ Child; 1499) by Fra Bartolomeo and Perugino's *Madonna col Bambino* (Madonna and Child; early 16th century).

Next door, Correggio's erotic *Danae* (1530–31) shares wall space with a willowy Venus, as portrayed by Cranach in his *Venere e Amore che Reca Il Favo do Miele* (Venus and Cupid with Honeycomb; 1531).

Moving on, Sala XIV boasts two self-portraits of Bernini and Sala XVIII contains two significant works by Rubens: *Deposizione nel sepolcro* (The Deposition; 1602) and *Susanna e I Vecchioni* (Susanna and the Elders; 1605–07). The highlight is Titian's early masterpiece, *Amor Sacro e Amor Profano* (Sacred and Profane Love; 1514) in Sala XX.

**Ground Floor**

**First Floor**

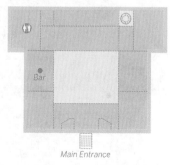

Main Entrance

**Services and Amenities Level**

TOP SIGHTS
**MUSEO E GALLERIA BORGHESE**

AFP / GETTY IMAGES ©

# Treasures of the Museo e Galleria Borghese

**Housed in an ornate 17th-century palace, Museo e Galleria Borghese (p207) has some of the city's finest art treasures, including Gian Lorenzo Bernini's sculptures and Renaissance and baroque paintings.**

### Ratto di Proserpina

**1** One of Bernini's greatest sculptures, *Rape of Proserpina* portrays Pluto, god of the underworld, abducting Proserpina. A work of supreme virtuosity, it shows the artist's ability to craft emotion out of cold, hard marble.

### Venere Vincitrice

**2** Antonio Canova's depiction of a curvaceous Paolina Bonaparte as the goddess *Venere Vincitrice* (Venus Victrix) is typical of his elegant, mildly erotic, neoclassical style.

### Ragazzo col Canestro di Frutta

**3** One of Caravaggio's early works, *Boy with a Basket of Fruit* reveals stylistic techniques that became his trademarks – realism and the use of chiaroscuro to focus attention on the central figures.

### Amor Sacro e Amor Profano

**4** Titian's *Sacred and Profane Love* is one of the museum's most important works, a celebration of heavenly love (represented by the nude figure) and earthly love (the clothed figure).

### La Deposizione di Cristo

**5** A Renaissance masterpiece, Raphael's *Deposition* was originally an altarpiece. Its composition, inspired by ancient Roman tomb reliefs, shows his unsurpassed mastery of perspective in portraying groups of figures.

3

THE ART ARCHIVE / ALAMY ©

**Clockwise from top left**
**1.** *Rape of Proserpina* by Bernini **2.** Paolina Bonaparte Borghese as *Venere Vincitrice* (Venus Victrix) by Canova **3.** *Boy with a Basket of Fruit* by Caravaggio **4.** *Sacred and Profane Love* by Titian

# ◉ SIGHTS

This large and attractive area boasts several fascinating sights including one of the city's best art galleries, a cutting edge cultural centre and a couple of contemporary museums. In the midst of everything, Villa Borghese park provides a welcome escape from the bustle of the city centre.

## ◉ Villa Borghese & Around

### MUSEO E GALLERIA BORGHESE
MUSEUM & ART GALLERY

See p207.

### VILLA BORGHESE
PARK

Map p366 (entrances at Piazzale San Paolo del Brasile, Piazzale Flaminio, Via Pinciana, Via Raimondi; ⊙dawn-dusk; ☐Porta Pinciana) Locals, lovers, tourists, joggers – no one can help heeding the call of this ravishing park just north of the historic centre. Originally the grounds of Cardinal Scipione Borghese's 17th-century residence, the park has various museums and galleries, as well as other attractions such as the 18th-century **Giardino del Lago** and **Piazza di Siena**, an amphitheatre used for Rome's top equestrian event in May. Near the Piazzale San Paolo del Brasile entrance, the **Cinema dei Piccoli** (☑06 855 34 85; www.cinemadeipiccoli.it; Viale delle Pineta 15; tickets €5-5.50) is the world's smallest cinema.

Bike hire is available at various points, including Via delle Belle Arti, for about €5/15 per hour/day.

### BIOPARCO
ZOO

Map p366 (☑06 360 82 11; www.bioparco.it; Viale del Giardino Zoologico 1; adult/child over 1m & under 12yr/child under 1m €12.50/10.50/free; ⊙9.30am-6pm Apr-Oct, 9.30am-5pm Nov-Mar; ☐Bioparco) A tried and tested kid-pleaser, Rome's zoo hosts a predictable collection of animals on a far-from-inspiring 18-hectare site. Quite frankly there are better ways to spend your money, but if your kids are driving you bonkers, it's a thought.

### MUSEO CARLO BILOTTI
ART GALLERY

Map p366 (☑06 06 08; www.museocarlobilotti.it; Viale Fiorello La Guardia; adult/reduced €7/6; ⊙9am-7pm Tue-Sun; ☐Porta Pinciana) The art collection of billionaire cosmetics magnate Carlo Bilotti is stylishly housed in the Orangery of Villa Borghese. It's a small collection (only 22 pieces), but it's interesting and well presented with explanatory panels in English and Italian. Paintings range from a Warhol portrait of Bilotti's wife and daughter to 18 works by Giorgio de Chirico (1888–1978), one of Italy's most important 20th-century artists.

### GALLERIA NAZIONALE D'ARTE MODERNA
ART GALLERY

Map p366 (☑06 322 98 221; www.gnam.arti.beniculturali.it; Viale delle Belle Arti 131; adult/reduced €8/4; ⊙8.30am-7.30pm, last admission 6.45pm Tue-Sun; ☐Piazza Thorvaldsen) This oft-overlooked gallery of modern and contemporary art is definitely worth a visit. Set in a vast belle époque palace are works by some of the most important exponents of modern Italian art. There are canvases by the *macchiaioli* (the Italian Impressionists) and futurists Boccioni and Balla, as well as several impressive sculptures by Canova and major works by Modigliani and De Chirico. International artists are also represented, with works by Degas, Cezanne, Kandinsky, Klimt, Mondrian, Pollock and Henry Moore.

The gallery's charming terrace cafe is the perfect place for a languorous breather. Entrance to the gallery for visitors with disabilities is at Via Antonio Gramsci 73.

## ◉ Flaminio

### AUDITORIUM PARCO DELLA MUSICA
CULTURAL CENTRE

Map p366 (☑06 802 41 281; www.auditorium.com; Viale Pietro de Coubertin 10; guided tours adult/reduced €9/7; ⊙11am-8pm Mon-Fri, 10am-6pm Sat & Sun; ☐☐Viale Tiziano, or shuttle bus from Stazione Termini) Rome's premier concert complex is not what you'd expect. Designed by superstar architect Renzo Piano and inaugurated in 2002, it consists of three grey pod-like concert halls set round a 3000-seat amphitheatre and the remains of a 300 BC Roman villa, discovered shortly after construction work began. It's a truly audacious work of architecture and is now one of Europe's most popular arts centres – in 2010 more than a million people attended more than a thousand cultural events. Guided tours cover the concert halls, amphitheatre (known as the *cavea*) and enormous foyer area, which is itself home to a small archaeology museum and stages temporary exhibitions. Tours depart hourly 11.30am to 4.30pm Saturday and Sunday, by arrangement Monday to Friday.

## MUSEO NAZIONALE DELLE ARTI
## DEL XXI SECOLO (MAXXI) ART GALLERY

Map p366 (☑06 321 01 81; www.fondazione maxxi.it; Via Guido Reni 2f; adult/reduced €11/7; ⊙11am-7pm Tue, Wed, Fri & Sun, 11am-10pm Thu & Sat; 🚌🚊Viale Tiziano) Rome's flagship contemporary art gallery opened in May 2010 to grand fanfare and headlines across the world. The star of the show was, and still is, Zaha Hadid's stunning €150 million, 27,000 sq m gallery, universally hailed as a triumph of modern architecture. Housed in a former barracks, the building is impressive inside and out. The multi-layered geometric facade gives on to a cavernous light-filled interior full of snaking walkways, suspended staircases, glass, cement and steel. There's no set route between the exhibition spaces but it's fascinating to follow the sweeping ramps as they curve around the walls. The gallery has a small permanent collection but more interesting are the temporary exhibitions and installations – check the website for details.

## PONTE MILVIO BRIDGE

Map p366 (🚊Ponte Milvio) A pretty pedestrian footbridge, Ponte Milvio is best known as the site of the ancient Battle of the Milvian Bridge. These days, it's a favourite with love-struck teenagers who come to leave padlocks chained to the railings as a sign of their undying *amore*.

The bridge was first built in 109 BC to carry Via Flaminia over the Tiber and survived intact until 1849, when Garibaldi's troops blew it up to stop advancing French soldiers. Pope Pius IX had it rebuilt a year later. On the northern end, the tower **Torretta Valadier** is sometimes used to stage art exhibitions.

## FORO ITALICO SPORTS CENTRE

Map p366 (Viale del Foro Italico; Ⓜ️Ottaviano-San Pietro & 🚌32) At the foot of Monte Mario, the Foro Italico is a grandiose Fascist-era sports complex, centred on the **Stadio Olimpico**, Rome's 70,000-seater football stadium. Most people pass through en route to the football, but if you're interested in Fascist architecture, it's worth a look. Designed by the architect Enrico Del Debbio, it remains much as it was originally conceived. A

VILLA BORGHESE & NORTHERN ROME SIGHTS

---

## TOP SIGHTS **MUSEO NAZIONALE ETRUSCO DI VILLA GIULIA**

If you're planning to visit Lazio's Etruscan sites, or even if you're not, this wonderful museum is the ideal place to bone up on Etruscan history. Italy's finest collection of Etruscan treasures is considerately presented in Villa Giulia, Pope Julius III's elegant Renaissance palace.

There are thousands of exhibits, many of which came from burial tombs in the surrounding Lazio region, ranging from domestic utensils and terracotta vases to extraordinary bronze figurines, black *bucchero* tableware and dazzling jewellery.

Must-sees include a polychrome terracotta statue of an armless *Apollo*, from the Etruscan town of Veio, just north of Rome. Another headline act is the *Euphronios Krater*, a celebrated Greek vase that was returned to Italy in 2008 after a 30-year tug of war between the Italian government and New York's Metropolitan Museum of Art. But perhaps the museum's most famous piece is the 6th-century BC *Sarcofago degli Sposi* (Sarcophagus of the Betrothed). This astonishing work, originally unearthed in 400 broken pieces in a tomb in Cerveteri, depicts a husband and wife reclining on a stone banqueting couch. Although called a sarcophagus, it was actually designed as an elaborate urn to hold the couple's ashes.

### DON'T MISS

➡ Sarcofago degli Sposi

➡ Apollo di Veio

➡ Euphronios Krater

### PRACTICALITIES

➡ Map p366

➡ ☑06 322 65 71

➡ Piazzale di Villa Giulia

➡ adult/reduced €4/2

➡ ⊙8.30am-7.30pm, last admission 6.30pm Tue-Sun

➡ 🚊Viale delle Belle Arti

## THE BATTLE OF THE MILVIAN BRIDGE

Constantine's defeat of Maxentius at the Battle of the Milvian Bridge on 28 October 312 is one of the most celebrated victories in Roman history.

The battle came as the culmination of a complex seven-year power struggle for control of the Western Roman Empire. Constantine and his vastly outnumbered army approached Rome from the north along Via Flaminia, meeting Maxentius' forces on the northern bank of the Tiber. Fighting was short and bloody, leaving Maxentius dead, his army in tatters and the path to Rome and empire unopposed.

But while this is historically significant, the real reason for the battle's mythical status is the Christian legend that surrounds it. According to the Roman historian Lactantius, Constantine dreamt a message telling him to paint a Christian symbol on his troops' shields. A second historian, Eusebius, provides a more dramatic account, recounting how on the eve of the battle Constantine saw a cross in the sky, accompanied by the words 'In this sign, conquer.' Whatever the case, the reality is that Constantine won a resounding victory and in so doing set the seeds for the spread of Christianity in the Roman world.

17m-high marble **obelisk**, inscribed with the words 'Mussolini Dux', stands at the beginning of a broad avenue leading down to the **Stadio dei Marmi**, a running track surrounded by 60 marble nudes, and the Stadio Olimpico.

### EXPLORA – MUSEO DEI BAMBINI
### DI ROMA
MUSEUM

Map p366 (☑06 361 37 76; www.mdbr.it; Via Flaminia 82; adult/child over 3yr/child 1-3yr/child under 1yr €7/7/3/free; ☺9.30am-7.30pm Tue-Sun Sep-Jul, 11.30am-7pm Tue-Sun Aug; ⓜFlaminio) Rome's only dedicated kids' museum, Explora is aimed at the under-12s. It's set up as a miniature town where children can play at being grown-ups and with everything from a doctor's surgery to a TV studio, it's a hands-on, feet-on, full-on experience that your nippers will love. Outside there's also a free play park open to all.

Booking is advisable on weekdays, essential at weekends.

## ⊙ Salario & Beyond

### MUSEO D'ARTE CONTEMPORANEA
### DI ROMA (MACRO)
ART GALLERY

Map p366 (☑06 06 08; www.macro.roma.mu seum; Via Nizza 138, cnr Via Cagliari; adult/reduced €11/9; ☺11am-10pm Tue-Sun; ⬛Via Nizza) Along with MAXXI, this is Rome's most important contemporary art gallery. Exhibits, which include works by all of Italy's important post-WWII artists, are displayed in what was once a brewery. The sexy black-and-red interior retains much of the building's

original structure but sports a sophisticated steel-and-glass finish thanks to a revamp by French architect Odile Decq.

### CATACOMBE DI PRISCILLA
CATACOMBS

Map p366 (☑06 862 06 272; www.catacombe priscilla.com; Via Salaria 430; guided visit adult/ reduced €8/5; ☺8.30am-noon & 2.30-5pm Tue-Sun; ⬛Via Salaria) In the early Christian period, these creepy catacombs were something of a high-society burial ground, known as the Queen of Catacombs. Seven popes and various martyrs were buried in their 13km of tunnels between 309 and 555. They retain a lot of their original decoration, including the oldest ever image of the Madonna, a scratchy fresco dating to the beginning of the third century.

### VILLA ADA
PARK

Map p366 (entrances at Via Salaria & Via Ponte Salario; ⬛Via Salaria) If you're in this neck of the woods and you need a breather, Villa Ada is the place. A big rambling park with wooded paths, lakes and lawns, it was once the private property of King Vittorio Emanuele III. Outdoor concerts are held here in summer as part of the Roma Incontro il Mondo festival.

## ⊙ Nomentano

### PORTA PIA
LANDMARK

Map p366 (Piazzale Porta Pia; ⬛Via XX Settembre) This imposing crenellated structure, built near the ruins of the Porta Nomentana, one of the original gates in the ancient Aurelian walls, was Michelangelo's last architectural work. It's best known as the scene of bitter street-fighting in 1870 as Italian troops breached the adjacent walls to wrest the city from the pope and claim it for the nascent kingdom of Italy.

### VILLA TORLONIA  PARK

Map p366 (Via Nomentana 70; ⊘dawn-dusk; ⊒Via Nomentana) Full of towering pine trees, atmospheric palms and scattered villas, this splendid 19th-century park once belonged to Prince Giovanni Torlonia (1756–1829), a powerful banker and landowner. His large neoclassical villa, the **Casino dei Principi**, later became the Mussolini family home (1925–43) and, towards the end of WWII, Allied headquarters (1944–47). These days it's used to stage temporary exhibitions.

### MUSEI DI VILLA TORLONIA  MUSEUMS

Map p366 (✆06 06 08; www.museivillatorlonia. it; adult/reduced incl Casino Nobile, Casina delle Civitte & Casino dei Principi €10/8; ⊘9am-7pm Tue-Sun; ⊒Via Nomentana) With its oversized neoclassical facade – designed by Giuseppe Valadier – **Casino Nobile** (adult/reduced incl Casino dei Principi €8/7) makes quite an impression. Inside, in the luxuriously decorated interior, you can admire the Torlonia family's fine collection of sculpture, period furniture and paintings.

To the northeast, the much smaller **Casina delle Civette** (adult/reduced €4/3) is a bizarre mix of Swiss cottage, Gothic castle and twee farmhouse decorated in art nouveau style. Built between 1840 and 1930, it is now a museum dedicated to stained glass with designs and sketches, decorative tiles, parquetry floors and woodwork.

The main ticket office is just inside the Via Nomentana entrance to the park.

### BASILICA DI SANT'AGNESE FUORI LE MURA & MAUSOLEO DI SANTA COSTANZA  CHURCH & CATACOMBS

Off Map p366 (www.santagnese.org, in Italian; Via Nomentana 349; ⊘9am-noon & 4-8pm; ⊒Via Nomentana) Although a bit of a hike, it's well worth searching out this intriguing medieval religious complex. In the 7th-century **Basilica di Sant'Agnese fuori le Mura** look out for the golden apse mosaic depicting St Agnes with the signs of her martyrhood – a flame and sword, standing on the flames that failed to kill her. According to tradition, the 13-year-old Agnes was sentenced to be burnt at the stake but when the flames

failed to kill her she was beheaded on Piazza Navona and buried in the **catacombs** (guided visit adult/reduced €8/5; ⊘closed Sun morning & Nov) beneath this church.

Across the convent courtyard is the 4th-century **Mausoleo di Santa Costanza**. The squat circular building has a dome supported by 12 pairs of granite columns and a vaulted ambulatory decorated with beautiful 4th-century mosaics, said by some to be Christendom's oldest.

## ✗ EATING

**Rome's wealthy northern suburbs are speckled with fine restaurants, and there's a cluster around the happening nightlife district of Ponte Milvio.**

### ✗ Flaminio

TOP CHOICE **BAR POMPI**  GELATERIA, PASTRIES & CAKES €
Map p366 (Via Cassia 8; tiramisu €3; ⊘Tue-Sun; ⊒Ponte Milvio) Just behind happening Piazzale Ponte Milvio on the northern side of the Tiber, this small bar is famous for its tiramisu. And rightly so; it's fabulous. It comes in four forms: classic, strawberry,

---

### QUARTIERE COPPEDÈ

Hidden among the elegant *palazzi* that flank Viale Regina Margherita is the **Quartiere Coppedè** (Map p366; ⊒Viale Regina Margherita), a tiny pocket of fairy-tale buildings and monuments. Tuscan turrets, Liberty sculptures, Moorish arches, Gothic gargoyles, frescoed facades and palm-fringed gardens are all squeezed in to create a truly mesmerising pastiche of architectural styles and influences. The mind behind the madness belonged to a little-known Florentine architect, Gino Coppedè, who designed and built the quarter between 1913 and 1926.

It's best entered from the corner of Via Tagliamento and Via Dora. Highlights include the Fontana delle Rane (Fountain of the Frogs) in Piazza Mincio, a modern take on the better known Fontana delle Tartarughe in the Jewish Ghetto.

pistachio, and banana and nutella. And after much painstaking research, the prize goes to the pistachio.

### PALLOTTA
PIZZERIA €

Map p366 (☑06 333 42 45; Piazzale Ponte Milvio 23; pizzas from €5; ☺Thu-Tue; 🚇Ponte Milvio) Run by the Pallotta family for generations, this is an archetypal old-school pizzeria. It serves great pizzas, plus the usual fried starters and barbecued meats in an atmospheric leafy garden. It's an icon of unpretentious quality in this yuppie area.

### ENSÔ
JAPANESE €€

Map p366 (☑06 332 21 175; www.ensoristorante giapponese.com; Piazzale Ponte Milvio 33; lunch menus €8-15, sushi/sashimi from €5/8; 🚇Ponte Milvio) This friendly Japanese restaurant is a good option if the daily diet of pasta and pizza is beginning to wear thin. There's a full menu of sushi and sashimi, as well as a selection of Asian curries, all served promptly and with a smile. Particularly good value are the lunchtime menus.

### IL GIANFORNAIO
BAKERY €

Map p366 (Piazzale Ponte Milvio 35; snacks/pastas/main dishes from €1/7/8; ☺7.10am-2.30pm & 4.40-7.30pm Mon-Sat; 🚇Ponte Milvio) A busy bakery that does a fantastic range of sweet and savoury snacks – think strudels, *cornettos* (Italian croissants) and thin and crispy pizza slices – as well as pasta and meat dishes to eat at one of the few indoor tables.

### RED
MODERN ITALIAN €€€

Map p366 (☑06 806 91 630; www.redrestau rant.roma.it; Viale Pietro de Coubertin 30; meals €50; ☺noon-late; 🚗 or 🚇Viale Tiziano, or shuttle bus M from Stazione Termini) Mingle with the stars at the fashionable restaurant-bar of the Auditorium Parco della Musica. It's a glamorous, loungey place staffed by black-clad waiters and styled in designer red and apple greens. The food is duly creative with a good selection of pastas and some dishy seafood mains. Also popular is the daily *aperitivo*, served between 6.30pm and 9pm, and the Sunday brunch.

## ✗ Over the River

### AL SETTIMO GELO
GELATERIA €

Map p366 (Via Vodice 21a; ☺Tue-Sun; 🚇Piazza Giuseppe Mazzini) The name's a play on 'seventh heaven' and it's not a far-fetched title

for one of Rome's finest gelaterie with a devotion to the best possible natural ingredients. Try the Greek ice cream or cardamom made to an Afghan recipe.

#  DRINKING & NIGHTLIFE

**Many of the big galleries have excellent on-site cafes. Otherwise the drinking scene is centred on Piazzale Ponte Milvio, which is particularly popular with sashaying under-20s, dressed to the nines and driving tiny cars.**

## ♀ Villa Borghese & Around

### CASINA DEL LAGO
CAFE

Map p366 (Viale dell'Aranciera 2; 🚇Porta Pinciana) This elegant little cafe, housed in a neoclassical pavilion in Villa Borghese, is a lovely place for a coffee or cocktail, particularly in summer when the outdoor deck seating really comes into its own.

## ♀ Flaminio

### CHIOSCHETTO DI PONTE MILVIO
BAR

Map p366 (Ponte Milvio 44; ☺6pm-2am Apr-Oct; 🚇Ponte Milvio) A local landmark, this tiny green kiosk next to the Ponte Milvio bridge has been open since the 1920s and is perennially popular, with lots of pavement tables. It might look like a shack, but the mojitos are the business and not too expensive either.

## ♀ Salario & Beyond

### PIPER CLUB
NIGHTCLUB

Map p366 (www.piperclub.it; Via Tagliamento 9; 🚇Via Salaria) Keeping Rome in the groove since 1965, Piper has worked through its midlife crisis and is starting to rediscover its mojo as the life and soul of Rome's clubbing scene. As well as hosting funky party nights, it also stages some great gigs – previous performers have included White Lies, Nitin Sawney, Babyshambles and Pete Yorn.

#  Nomentano

## BRANCALEONE
NIGHTCLUB

Off Map p366 (www.brancaleone.eu; Via Levanna 11; admission around €10; ⊙Oct-Jun; ᵬVia Nomentana) This former *centro sociale* is now one of Rome's top clubs. Blockbuster DJs ratch up the tempo, pumping up the young, alternative crowd with house, hip-hop, drum'n'bass, reggae and electronica. Everyone from serious musos to skate kids will be in their element. The club is some distance from the city centre, just off Via Nomentana in the outlying Montesacro district.

# ⭐ ENTERTAINMENT

## AUDITORIUM PARCO DELLA MUSICA
CULTURAL CENTRE

Map p366 (☎06 802 41 281; www.auditorium. com; Viale Pietro de Coubertin 30; ᵬ or ᵬViale Tiziano, or shuttle bus M from Stazione Termini) Rome's state-of-the-art concert complex combines architectural innovation with perfect acoustics: architect Renzo Piano apparently studied the interiors of lutes and violins as part of his design process. Its programme is eclectic, featuring everything from classical music concerts to tango exhibitions, book readings, art exhibitions and film screenings.

The Auditorium is also home to Rome's premier classical-music organisation, the Accademia di Santa Cecilia, and its world-class orchestra, the **Orchestra dell' Accademia Nazionale di Santa Cecilia** (www. santacecilia.it), directed by Antonio Pappano. The academy's programme includes a top-class symphonic season – featuring superstar guest conductors – and short festivals dedicated to single composers.

## TEATRO OLIMPICO
THEATRE

Map p366 (☎06 326 59 91; www.teatroolimpico. it, in Italian; Piazza Gentile da Fabriano 17; ᵬ ᵬPiazza Mancini) This is home to the **Accademia Filarmonica Romana** (www.filarmonicaroma na.org, in Italian), one of Rome's major classical music organisations. Past members have included Rossini, Donizetti and Verdi, and it still attracts star performers. Its varied programme concentrates on classical and chamber music but also features opera, ballet and contemporary multimedia events.

## CASA DEL CINEMA
CINEMA

Map p366 (☎06 06 08; www.casadelcinema.it; Largo Marcello Mastroianni 1; ᵬVia Boncompagni) In Villa Borghese, the Casa del Cinema comprises an exhibition space, two projection halls and a popular cafe. It screens everything from documentaries to shorts, indie flicks and arthouse classics, sometimes in their original language, and hosts a regular programme of film-related events and book presentations.

## SILVANO TOTI GLOBE THEATRE
THEATRE

Map p366 (☎06 06 08; www.globetheatreroma. com; Largo Aqua Felix, Villa Borghese; ᵬPiazzale Brasile) Like London's Globe Theatre, but with better weather, this is an open-air Elizabethan theatre in the middle of Villa Borghese. The season – mainly Shakespeare – includes occasional productions in English. Tickets start at €10 for a place in the stalls, rising to €22.

#  SHOPPING

## LIBRERIA L'ARGONAUTA
BOOKSTORE

Map p366 (www.librerialargonauta.com; Via Reggio Emilia 89; ᵬVia Nizza) Off the main tourist trail, this travel bookshop is a lovely place to browse. The serene atmosphere and shelves of travel literature can easily spark daydreams of far-off places. Staff are friendly and happy to let you drift around the world in peace.

## MAXXI
BOOKSTORE

Map p366 (www.fondazionemaxxi.it; Via Guido Reni 2f; ⊙11am-7pm Tue, Wed, Fri & Sun, 11am-10pm Thu & Sat; ᵬ or ᵬViale Tiziano) The bookshop of the MAXXI art museum is in a cool, white space over the courtyard from the main gallery. Its collection is small but specialised with an excellent selection of books on modern art, architecture and design. You can also pick up exhibition catalogues.

## NOTEBOOK
BOOKSTORE, MUSIC

Map p366 (www.notebookauditorium.it, in Italian; Viale Pietro de Coubertin 30; ⊙10am-8pm, closed Aug; ᵬ or ᵬViale Tiziano) Part of the Auditorium Parco della Musica complex, this attractive modern shop offers a sizeable collection of art, film, music, design and travel books (mostly in Italian), as well as CDs, DVDs and Auditorium merchandise. Not surprisingly it's particularly good for classical music.

## SPORTS & ACTIVITIES

**Stadio Olimpico** Map p366 (Viale del Foro Italico; MOttaviano-SanPietro & 🚍32) Watching a football game at Rome's Olympic Stadium is an unforgettable experience, although you'll have to keep your wits about you as crowd trouble is not unheard of. Throughout the season (September to May), there's a game most Sundays involving one of the city's two teams: AS Roma, known as the *giallorossi* (yellow and reds; www.asroma.it), or Lazio, the *biancazzuri* (white and blues; www.sslazio.it, in Italian). Ticket prices start at €10 and can be bought at Lottomatica (lottery centres), the stadium, ticket agencies, www.listicket.it or one of the many Roma or Lazio stores around the city – try the **AS Roma Store** (Piazza Colonna 360) or **Lazio Point** (Via Farini 34).

### BORGO PARIOLI MARKET                                    MARKET

Map p366 (Via Tirso 14 & Via Metauro 21; ⊘10am-8pm Sat & Sun 1st three weekends of the month; 🚍Viale Regina Margherita) Parioli is Rome's most expensive residential area, and its weekend market is a hot date on the capital's monthly shopping calendar. Among the often-expensive bric-a-brac, you'll find original jewellery and accessories from the 1950s onwards, silverware, paintings, antique lamps and old gramophones.

### PONTE MILVIO                                           MARKET

Map p366 (Piazzale Ponte Milvio; ⊘9am-sunset 1st & 2nd Sun of the month, closed Aug; 🚍Ponte Milvio) The 2nd-century-BC Ponte Milvio is the scene of a great monthly antique market along the riverbank. On the first Sunday of every month stalls spring up between Ponte Milvio and Ponte Duca d'Aosta laden with antiques and collectable clobber.

### LORENZA AMBROSETTI                                  ARTISANAL

Map p366 (Via Reggio Emilia 11; ⊘10am-12.30pm & 4-7pm Mon-Fri; 🚍Via Nomentana) Out of this unprepossessing little shop, Signora Ambrosetti sells beautiful, handmade tiles, many of which are created from ancient and historic designs. The polished flooring at the Galleria Doria Pamphilj came from here. Bank on around €70 per sq m.

### GOODY MUSIC                                        MUSIC STORE

Map p366 (Via Cesare Beccaria 2; MFlaminio) This is where DJs go to stock up on tunes, with a trainspotting collection of hip-hop, nu-jazz, deep and funky house, hardstyle and rare grooves, on vinyl and CD. Staff are knowledgeable, and you can also buy equipment and T-shirts.

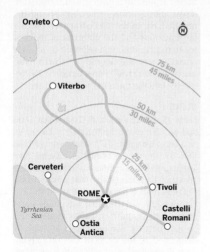

# Day Trips from Rome

### Ostia Antica p220

With preservation in places matching that of Pompeii, at the ancient Roman port of Ostia Antica you can wander through complete streets, gape at Roman toilets, and see an ancient Roman menu.

### Tivoli p221

This hilltop town is home to two Unesco World Heritage sites: Villa Adriana, the mammoth country estate of Emperor Hadrian, and 16th-century Villa d'Este, with its fantastical gardens featuring musical fountains.

### Castelli Romani p223

Studding the hills to the south of Rome are 13 hilltop towns that have long been a greener escape from the city for the Romans, including the Pope, who has his summer residence at Castel Gandolfo.

### Cerveteri p225

Cerveteri (and the further-flung site of Tarquinia) were important Etruscan centres their exquisite tombs and fantastic museums provide a window onto the Etruscan world.

### Viterbo p229

A medieval gem, graceful Viterbo evokes its 13th-century golden age, and is also famous for its health-imbuing hot springs.

### Orvieto p232

The gorgeous hilltop hilltown of Umbria is an easy and rewarding day trip, allowing you to experience one of the highlights of another region.

# Ostia Antica

## Explore

Half a day or more would be ideal to explore the impressive remains of Ostia Antica. This ancient Roman city was a busy working port until 42 AD, and the ruins are substantial and well preserved. The main thoroughfare, the **Decumanus Maximus**, runs over 1km from the city's entrance (the Porta Romana) to the Porta Marina, which originally led to the sea, and it's still the main drag. The site gets busy at weekends, but is usually exhilaratingly empty during the week.

## The best...

➡ **Sight** Thermopolium (p221)
➡ **Place to Eat** Ristorante Cipriani (p221)

## Top tip

Bring a picnic or time your visit so that you can eat at one of the restaurants in the town, as the site cafe feels rather like a canteen and can get busy.

To get the most out of your visit, buy a handy site map from the ticket office (€2).

## Getting There & Away

**Car** Take Via del Mare, parallel to Via Ostiense, and follow the signs for the *scavi* (ruins).

**Train** From Rome, take metro line B to Piramide, then the Ostia Lido train (half-hourly) from Stazione Porta San Paolo, getting off at Ostia Antica. The trip is covered by the standard BIT tickets (see boxed text p302).

## Need to Know

➡ **Area Code** 00119
➡ **Location** 25km southwest of Rome
➡ **Information** Ostia Antica (www.ostiaantica.net)

## ◉ SIGHTS

Founded in the 4th century BC, Ostia (named for the mouth or *ostium* of the Tiber) became a great port and later a strategic centre for defence and trade, with a population of around 50,000, of whom 17,000 were slaves, mostly from Turkey, Egypt and the middle East. In the 5th century AD barbarian invasions and the outbreak of malaria led to its abandonment followed by its slow burial – up to 2nd-floor level – in river silt, hence its survival. Pope Gregory IV re-established the town in the 9th century.

**RUINS**

Ostia (Scavi Archeologici di Ostia Antica; ☎06 563 52 830; www.ostiantica.info, in Italian; Viale dei Romagnoli 717; adult/reduced/child €6.5/3.75/free, car park €2.50; ☺8.30am-7.15pm Tue-Sun Apr-Oct, to 6pm Mar, to 5pm Nov-Feb, last admission 1hr before closing) was a busy working port until it began to decline in the 3rd century AD, and the town was made up of restaurants, laundries, shops, houses and public meeting places. These are clearly delineated in the ruins of the site, giving a good impression of what life must have been like when it was at its busiest.

Either side of the main thoroughfare, **Decumanus Maximus**, there are networks of narrow streets lined by buildings.

At one stage, Ostia had 20 baths complexes, including the **Terme di Foro** – these were equipped with a roomful of stone toilets (the *forica*) that remain largely intact. Pivot-holes show that the entrances had revolving doors, and there are 20 marble seats that remain intact. Water flowed along channels in front of the seats, into which the user would dip a sponge on a stick to clean themselves.

The most impressive mosaics on site are at the huge **Terme di Nettuno**, which occupied a whole block and date from Hadrian's renovation of the port. Make sure you climb the elevated platform and look at the three enormous mosaics here, including Neptune driving his seahorse chariot, surrounded by sea monsters, mermaids and mermen. In an adjacent room is a mosaic with Neptune's wife, Amphitrite, on a hippocampus, accompanied by Hymenaeus – the god of weddings – and tritons. In the centre of the baths complex are the remains of a large arcaded courtyard called the Palaestra, in which athletes used to train. There's an impressive mosaic depicting boxing and wrestling.

Next to the Nettuno baths is a good-sized **amphitheatre**, built by Agrippa and later enlarged to hold 4000 people. Stucco is still discernable in the entrance hall. In late antiquity, the orchestra could be flooded to present watery tableaus. By climbing to the top of the amphitheatre and looking over the site, you'll get a good idea of the original layout of the port and how it would have functioned.

Behind the amphitheatre is the **Piazzale delle Corporazioni** (Forum of the Corporations), the offices of Ostia's merchant guilds, which sport well-preserved mosaics depicting the different interests of each business. These include guilds, shippers, and traders. The pictures represent dolphins, ships, the lighthouse at Portus (the older nearby settlement) and the grain trade. The symbols here indicate just how international the nature of business in Ostia was. Both Latin and Greek graffiti has been discovered on the walls of the city.

The **Forum**, the main square of Ostia, is dominated by the huge Capitolium, which was built by Hadrian, a temple dedicated to the main Roman deities, the Capitoline triad (Jupiter, Juno and Minerva).

Nearby is another of the highlights of the site: the **Thermopolium**, an ancient cafe. Check out the bar counter, surmounted by a frescoed menu, the kitchen and the small courtyard, where customers would have sat next to the fountain and relaxed with a drink.

The site has a complex comprising a cafeteria and bar (but a picnic is always a good idea) and museum, which houses statues and sarcophagi excavated on site.

**CASTELLO DI GIULIO II**   CASTLE
(☑06 563 58 013; Piazza della Rocca; ☺free 20-min guided tours 10am & noon Tue-Sun, plus 3pm Tue & Thu, max 30 people) Near the entrance to the excavations is this castle, an impressive example of 15th-century military architecture, which lost its purpose when a freak flood changed the course of the river, making the location less accessible.

 **EATING**

**RISTORANTE CIPRIANI**   RESTAURANT €€
(☑06 5635; 2956; meals €30; ☺lunch & dinner Thu-Sat, Mon & Tue, lunch Sun) If it's sunny enough to eat outside, this location can't be beat; dine on *cucina Romana*, with dishes such as *pasta alla' Gricia* (with lardons and onion) and *cacio e pepe* (cheese and pepper), while seated in a cobbled street in the old Borgo by the castle.

**RISTORANTE MONUMENTO**   RESTAURANT €€
(☑06 565 00 21; Piazza Umberto I 8; meals €30; ☺lunch & dinner Tue-Sun) This tucked-away restaurant near the ruins specialises in homemade pasta and fish and has a traditional interior decorated by blown-up old black-and-white photos.

# Tivoli

### Explore
For millennia, the hilltop town of Tivoli has been a summer escape for rich Romans, as amply demonstrated by its two Unesco World Heritage sites, both breathtaking hedonistic playgrounds. Villa Adriana was the mammoth country estate of Emperor Hadrian, and the 16th-century Villa d'Este is a wonder of the High Renaissance. You can visit both in a day, though you'll have to start early.

### Best...
➡ **Sight** Villa Adriana's Maritime Theatre (p222)
➡ **Place to Eat** Sibella (p223)

### Top Tip
Take a picnic, or organise your day to eat in Tivoli town before heading over to Villa Adriana (which is a short bus ride out of town).

### Getting There & Away
**Bus** Tivoli is 30km east of Rome and is accessible by Cotral bus from outside the Ponte Mammolo station on metro line B (€1.60, every 15 minutes, 50 minutes). However, it's best to buy a Zone 3 BIRG ticket (€6), which will cover you for the whole day.

The easiest way to visit both sites is to visit the Villa D'Este first, as it is close to Tivoli town centre. Then take the Cotral bus back towards Ponte Mammolo (€1) from Largo Garibaldi, asking the driver to stop close to Villa Adriana. After visiting the villa, you can then take the same bus (€2, 50 minutes) back to Ponte Mammolo.

**Car** Take either Via Tiburtina (SS5) or the faster Rome–L'Aquila autostrada (A24).

**Train** From Stazione Tiburtina (€2.30, 50 minutes to 1 hour 20 minutes, at least hourly).

## Need to Know

➡ **Area Code** 00019

➡ **Location** 30km east of Rome

➡ **Tourist Office** Tourist information point (☏07 743 13 536; ⊙9am–5.30pm) On Piazza Garibaldi, where the bus arrives.

##  SIGHTS

**VILLA ADRIANA**  HISTORICAL SITE

(☏06 399 67 900; adult/reduced €8/4, car park €2; ⊙ 9am-7pm, last admission 5.30pm) Many powerful Romans had villas around Tivoli in ancient times, and this site is Emperor Hadrian's summer residence **Villa Adriana**, 5km outside Tivoli. It set new standards of luxury when it was built between AD 118 and 134, even given the excess of the Roman Empire – it covered around 300 acres, so it was more like a town than a summer house. A model near the entrance gives you an idea of the scale of the original complex, which you'll need several hours to explore. Consider hiring an audioguide (€5), which gives a helpful overview. There's a small cafeteria next to the ticket office, but a nicer option is to bring a picnic lunch or eat in Tivoli.

A great traveller and enthusiastic architect, Hadrian personally designed much of the complex, taking inspiration from buildings he'd seen around the world, in Greece and Egypt. The **pecile**, a large porticoed pool area where the emperor used to stroll after lunch, was a reproduction of a building in Athens. Similarly, the **canopo** is a copy of the sanctuary of Serapis near Alexandria, with a long canal of water, originally surrounded by Egyptian statues, representing the Nile.

To the east of the pecile is one of the highlights, Hadrian's private retreat, the **Teatro Marittimo**. Built on an island in an artificial pool, it was originally a minivilla accessible only by swing bridges, which the emperor would have raised when he felt like retreating into utter solitude. Nearby, the fish pond is encircled by an underground gallery where Hadrian liked to wander. There are also nymphaeums, temples and barracks, and a museum with the latest discoveries from ongoing excavations (often closed).

---

**WORTH A DETOUR**

### SUBIACO & ST BENEDICT

St Benedict is generally regarded as the father of Western monasticism. Fleeing the vice that had so disgusted him as a student in Rome, he sought the gloom of the grotto to meditate and pray. During this time he attracted a large local following that eventually provoked the ire of his fellow friars and forced him onto the road.

Remote-feeling and dramatic, and carved into the rock above the saint's former humble cave, Subiaco is well worth the trip to see its wonderful monasteries and impressive abbey, with breathtaking views across the biblical-seeming countryside. Apart from its stunning setting, described by Petrarch as 'the edge of Paradise', the **Monastery of St Benedict** (☏07 748 50 39; ⊙9am-12.15pm & 3.30-6.15pm) is adorned with rich 13th- to 15th-century frescoes. Halfway down the hill from St Benedict is the **Monastery of St Scholastica** (☏07 748 55 69; ⊙9am-12.30pm & 3-6.30pm, 3.30-7pm Jun-Aug), the only one of the 13 monasteries built by St Benedict still standing in the Valley of the Amiene. It has a restaurant offering set menus for €18 and €26.

To reach Subiaco, you can take a bus direct from Viale Mazzini in Tivoli (one hour, hourly). To get here from Rome, take a Cotral bus to Subiaco's Piazza Falcone (€6.30, 1¼ hours, every 15 to 30 minutes Monday to Friday, less frequently at weekends) from Ponte Mammolo on metro line B. The bus stops a little way from the Monastery of St Scholastica – it's a 3km scenic, if demanding, uphill walk.

## VILLA D'ESTE                                    PALAZZO

(☑199 766 166, 0445 230310; www.villadeste tivoli.info; Piazza Trento; adult/reduced €8/4; ☺8.30am-1hr before sunset Tue-Sun) In Tivoli's hill-top centre, the steeply terraced gardens of Villa d'Este are a superlative example of the High Renaissance garden, dotted by fantastical fountains that are all powered by gravity alone, without pumps. The villa was once a Benedictine convent, converted by Lucrezia Borgia's son, Cardinal Ippolito d'Este, into a pleasure palace in 1550. It was extended by his various successors, but fell into romantic dilapidation in the 18th century.

However, renovations began under the tenure of Cardinal Alessandro d'Este, who also hosted Franz Liszt. The pianist, inspired by the gardens, wrote his compositions 'To the Cypresses of the Villa d'Este', and 'The Fountains of the Villa d'Este' during his stay.

The rich Mannerist frescoes of the villa interior merit a glance, but it's the garden that you're here for: the steep terraces harbour water-spouting gargoyles and elaborate avenues lined by deep-green, knotty cypresses. One fountain (designed by Gianlorenzo Bernini) used its water pressure to play an organ concealed in the top part of its structure, and this plays regularly throughout the day. Another highlight is the 130m-long 'Viale delle Cento Fontaine' – this Path of 100 Fountains is lined by uniquely carved, gargoyle-like images, featuring grotesque faces, ships and eagles, among others, and joins the Fountain of Tivoli to the 'Rometta' (little Rome) fountain. The latter has a model of Tiberina island, with reproductions of the landmarks of Rome, the she-wolf and other symbols.

The villa is a two-minute walk north from Largo Garibaldi. Picnics are not permitted, but there's a stylish cafe.

## VILLA GREGORIANA                              PARK

(☑06 399 67 701; Piazza Tempio di Vesta; adult/ child €5/2.50; ☺10am-6.30pm Tue-Sun Apr–mid-Oct, 10am-2.30pm Mon-Sat, 10am-4pm Sun Mar & mid-Oct–Nov, by appointment Dec-Feb) In 1826, there was a terrible flood when the waters of the Aniene river overflowed its banks, carrying away houses with the force of the water. As a result, Pope Gregory XVI ordered the river waters be diverted through a tunnel, creating a magnificent waterfall over a steep gorge, crashing down 120m to the bottom of the canyon, and known as the Cascata Grande (Great Waterfall). The architects of this used the old riverbed and the gorge, and the thickly wooded setting, full of caves, ravines and archaeological fragments, to create the park of Villa Gregoriana.

 **EATING**

## SIBILLA                                RESTAURANT €€

(☑0774 335281; Via della Sibilla 50; meals €50; ☺May-Sep) Chef Adriano Baldassare, who studied under Antonello Colonna, serves up exciting creative cuisine that combines Roman traditions with innovation at this impressive restaurant, which has a glorious setting overlooked by two ruined temples and overlooking the slopes of Villa Gregoriana. The food lives up to the view, there's an extensive wine list, and it's less expensive than you would expect.

## TRATTORIA DEL FALCONE          TRATTORIA €€

(☑0774 312358; Via del Trevio 34; meals €30; ☺Wed-Mon) In Tivoli town, this is a lively trattoria with exposed stone walls that's been serving up classic pasta dishes since 1918 and is popular with both tourists and locals.

# Castelli Romani

............................................................

## Explore

About 20km south of Rome, the Colli Albani (Alban hills) and their 13 towns are collectively known as the Castelli Romani. For millennia they've provided Romans with a green refuge hot summer weekends, and people still escape here, mainly to wander, eat and drink the fresh white wine for which the area is famous. The most famous towns are Castel Gandolfo, where the pope has his summer residence; Frascati, renowned for its wine; lakeside Nemi, with its Roman boats museum; and Grottaferrata, which has a fine abbey. The other towns are Monte Porzio Catone, Montecompatri, Rocca Priora, Colonna, Rocca di Papa, Marino, Albano Laziale, Ariccia and Genzano.

## Best

➡ **Sight** Lago Albano (p225)
➡ **Place to Eat** Cacciani (p225)
➡ **Place to Drink** Frascati (p225)

## Top Tip

In Frascati, wander around until you find a place serving fresh local wine and porchetta, and settle down for a simple feast (preferably at trestle tables, out on a cobbled street).

If you want to visit several towns, but don't have your own transport, the easiest two to see in a day are Frascati and Castel Gandolfo, as there is a bus linking the two.

## Getting There & Away

**Bus** To get from Frascati to Grottaferrata (€1, 10 minutes, every 30 to 40 minutes), catch a Cotral bus from Piazza Marconi. Buses also leave from here to Genzano di Roma (€1, 45 minutes, about hourly); from where you can catch another bus to Nemi (€1, 10 minutes, about hourly). There are buses from Frascati's Piazza Marconi to Castel Gandolfo (€1, 30 minutes).

**Car** For Frascati and Grottaferrata take Via Tuscolana (SS215); for Castel Gandolfo and Albano Laziale take Via Appia Nuova (SS7) south, following signs for Ciampino Airport.

**Train** There are buses to Frascati, but the best way to reach the city is by train from Stazione Termini (€1.90, 30 minutes, about hourly Monday to Saturday, every two hours Sunday). There are buses from Rome to Castel Gandolfo, but it's far easier to reach by train from Rome's Stazione Termini (€1.90, 40 minutes). It's not possible to catch a train between Frascati and Castel Gandolfo.

## Need to Know

➡ **Area Code** 00444
➡ **Location** 20km southeast of Rome
➡ **Tourist Office** Frascati Point (☑06 940 15 378; ☺8am-8pm)

 **SIGHTS**

### FRASCATI · TOWN

A villa perches over the town above ornamental gardens, its flat-fronted façade like an expensive stage set. It's the 16th-century **Villa Aldobrandini**, designed by Giacomo della Porta and built by Carlo Maderno; it's closed to the public, but you can visit the impressive **gardens** (☺8am-2pm & 3-6pm Mon-Fri). These are a fine example of an early Italian Baroque garden, with the palace as the focal point, set dramatically into the wooded hill. Water features in the garden were designed by Orazio Olivieri, though many of the fountains no longer function.

Also worth a visit in Frascati, sharing the stable building with the tourist office, is the new **Museo Tuscolano** (☑06 941 7195; ☺10am-6pm Tue-Fri, 10am-7pm Sat), with artfully lit republican and imperial artefacts and interesting models of Tuscolo villas.

However, villas and views are all very well, but most people come to Frascati for the food and fresh white wine. You can pick up a *porchetta panini* (sandwich made of pork roasted with herbs) from one of the stands that do a brisk weekend trade around Piazza del Mercato, or head to the cantinas that dot the town, which usually sell *porchetta,* olives, salami and cheeses plus jugs of wine.

### TUSCULUM · RUIN

If you have a car, head up to the ruins of ancient **Tusculum**. All that remains of this once-imposing 4th-century-BC town is a small amphitheatre, a crumbling villa and a small stretch of road leading up to the city, but it's a lovely spot for a walk, and the views are stupendous.

### GROTTAFERRATA ABBEY · CHURCH

(abbazia; ☑06 945 93 09; Viale San Nilo; ☺7am-12.30pm & 3.30pm-1hr before sunset) Another trip that requires you to have your own transport is **Grottaferrata**, where there's a 15th-century **abbey**, founded in 1004. The church interior resembles an incense-perfumed jewellery box, and Mass is particularly atmospheric. The congregation of Greek monks wear distinctive flat-topped black caps.

### CASTEL GANDOLFO · TOWN

Continuing southwest brings you to **Castel Gandolfo**, an impressive, dome-capped hilltop *borgo* (small village) overlooking

Lago di Albano. This is the pope's summer residence, which, although closed to the public, still attracts hordes of tourists to the impressive town square. The small town is a very pretty place for a wander, with views opening out across the lake below.

### LAGO ALBANO                           LAKE
This great azure expanse is simply glorious for a summer swim, and cafes and boating-hire places dot its banks. Filling two volcanic craters, the lake is about 3.5km by 2.3km.

### NEMI                                   TOWN
The town of Nemi is perched high above Lago di Nemi, the smaller of the two volcanic lakes in the Castelli Romani. This area was the centre of a cult to the goddess Diana in ancient times, and favourite holiday spot of the emperor Caligula. Today it's a popular getaway from Rome, and famous for its wild strawberries, best eaten in the early summer. There's a great museum here, the small **Museo delle Navi Romani** (☑06 939 80 40; Via Diana 15; admission €3; ⊘9am-7pm Mon-Sat, 9am-1pm Sun) on the shore of the lake. This was built by Mussolini to house two incredibly preserved wooden Roman boats, dating from Caligula's reign, that had been discovered and salvaged from the lake in 1932. These were tragically destroyed by fire in 1944 – what you see now are scale models.

## ✖ EATING & DRINKING

The Frascati area is famous for its white wine and there are plenty of places where you can try it and other local varieties. Most fun are the town's famous rough-and-ready *cantinas,* which usually sell *porchetta,* olives, salami and cheeses, to go with jugs of the fresh young white wine. You can also pick up a *porchetta panini* from one of the stands that do a brisk weekend trade around Piazza del Mercato.

### LA QUINTESSA                RESTAURANT €€
(☑06 938 020029; Via Spiaggia del Lago 20, Castel Gandolfo; meals €40; ⊘lunch Wed-Tue, dinner Wed-Sun) With fantastic views over the lake, this place has a studied design that wouldn't seem out of place in central Rome, with low-slung ceiling lamps, antique till, suitcases, tailors' dummies and other chic oddities. It also offers food that lives up

to the setting, with tasty Roman cooking, good pizza and more.

### TRATTORIA LA SIRENA DEL LAGO          TRATTORIA €€
(☑06 936 80 20; Via del Plebiscito 26, Nemi; meals €30) At this clifftop favourite, the local game and trout are excellent and the local wine refreshing. Nemi is also famous for its wild strawberries – sprinkled over almost everything (especially ice cream) in season.

### CACCIANI                      RESTAURANT €€
(☑06 942 03 78; Via Al Diaz; meals €55; ⊘Tue-Sat) The town's best restaurant, with fine food and a graceful terrace.

### HOSTERIA SAN ROCCO              OSTERIA €€
(☑06 942 82 786; Via Cadorna, 1; ⊘lunch & dinner) To try a typical *fraschette* (osteria that traditionally served only porchetta and wine) head to 'Da Trinco', as it's nicknamed by locals; it serves up traditional pasta dishes such as spaghetti alla gricia or saltimbocca, and a fine array of antipasti.

# Cerveteri

## Explore
Outside Rome lies an extraordinary, Unesco-listed Etruscan burial complex, a haunting necropolis that is a town of the dead, set around a grid of streets. Spend the morning wandering around the *Lord of the Rings*–style townscape, expecting to see hobbits pop out, then lunch in the town before completing your day with a visit to the Etruscan museum.

**1. Al Fresco Dining in Orvieto (p232)**
Eating outside in Orvieto.

**2. Ostica Antica (p220)**
The ruins of Thermopolium, an ancient bar at Ostica Antica.

**3. Villa Adriana (p222)**
Teatro Marittimo at the Villa Adriana, Tivoli.

## Best...

⇒ **Sight** Necropoli di Banditaccia (p229)
⇒ **Place to Eat** Antica Locanda
le Ginestre (p229)

## Top Tip

Don't miss Cerveteri's fascinating Etruscan museum, which supplies context to the tombs and brings the ancient era alive.

## Getting There & Away

**Bus** Cotral bus (€3.50, 55 minutes, hourly) from outside the Cornelia metro stop on metro line A. Buses leave Cerveteri for Rome from the main square.

**Car** Take either Via Aurelia (SS1) or the Civitavecchia autostrada (A12) and exit at Cerveteri–Ladispoli.

## Need to Know

⇒ **Area Code** 00052
⇒ **Location** 35km northwest of Rome

⇒ **Tourist Office** Tourist information point (☑06 995 52 637; Piazza Aldo Moro; ⊘9.30am-1.30pm)

# ◉ SIGHTS

Cerveteri, or Kysry to the Etruscans and Caere to Latin-speakers, was one of the most important commercial centres in the Mediterranean from the 7th to the 5th centuries BC. However, most of the city was built of wood, and hence there is nothing left. Only the necropolis, carved underground, gives an indication of the splendour that must have been.

As Roman power grew, so Cerveteri's fortunes faded, and in 358 BC the city was annexed by Rome. After the fall of the Roman Empire, the spread of malaria and repeated Saracen invasions caused further decline. In the 13th century there was a mass exodus from the city to the nearby town of Ceri, and Caere became Caere Vetus (Old Caere), from which its current name derives. The

---

**WORTH A DETOUR**

## WORTH THE DETOUR: TARQUINIA

If you've been bitten by the Etruscan bug, Tarquinia is as fascinating as, yet entirely different from, Cerveteri, with beautiful painted tombs that are vivid with detail and colour. The town of Tarquinia alone, with its narrow cobbled streets, perfectly preserved walled city and graceful buildings, merits a visit, especially as it has a fantastic Etruscan museum housed in a medieval palazzo.

On the edge of Tarquinia's *centro storico* lies the **Museo Nazionale Tarquiniese** (☑06 3996 7150; Piazza Cavour; adult/child €6/3, incl necropolis €8/4; ⊘8.30am-7.30pm Tue-Sun), housed in the exquisite 15th-century Palazzo Vitelleschi, a fabulous palace centred around a courtyard. Highlights of its collection are a breathtaking terracotta frieze of winged horses (the Cavalli Alati) and, on the upper floors, several entire frescoed tombs that have been transported here in their entirety, full of incredibly vibrant paintings.

To see the famous painted tombs in situ, head for the **necropolis** (☑06 3996 7150; adult/child €6/3, incl museum adult/child €8/4; ⊘8.30am-1hr before sunset Tue-Sun), 2km from town. It's unlike Cerveteri in that the parts of the tombs above ground have been destroyed, and the treasures beneath are now protected by functional little corrugated huts. But it's what lies beneath the ground that is important.

There are around 6000 tombs in this area, of which around 200 are painted, and around 20 or so are accessible to the public. There are some beautiful hunting and fishing scenes in the Tomba della Caccia e della Pesca; scenes featuring dancers, she-lions and dolphins in the Tomba delle Leonesse; and an insight into Etruscan erotica in the Tomba della Fustigazione (Tomb of the Flogging), where a near-naked woman bends between two naked men, one of whom is raising a whip.

To reach Tarquinia from Cerveteri, take one of the regular Cotral buses from Piazza A. Moro to Ladispoli railway station (6 minutes) to take a train to Tarquinia (€3.20, 35 minutes, every two hours). Returning to Rome from Tarquinia, there are trains direct to Termini (€6.20, 1 hour 20 minutes, half-hourly).

early 19th century saw the first tentative archaeological explorations in the area, and in 1911 systematic excavations began in earnest.

### NECROPOLI DI BANDITACCIA   HISTORICAL SITE

(☑06 399 67 150; Via del Necropoli; admission/reduced €6/3, incl museum €8/4; ⊙8.30am-1hr before sunset) You can get an hourly shuttle bus from the tourist information point to the **necropolis**, the tomb complex 2km out of town. The bus leaves seven to nine times per day starting at 8.30am and finishing at 5pm (earlier in winter; €0.70). The trip takes five minutes and costs €1. Alternatively, follow the well-signposted road – it's a pleasant 15-minute walk.

The 10-hectare necropolis is a townscape of the afterlife, organized with streets, small squares and neighbourhoods. The site contains different types of tombs: some are trenches cut in rock and some, also carved into the rock, are shaped like huts or houses. Most common of all the types of construction is the tumulus, a circular structure cut into the earth and topped by a cumulus – a topping of turf. These various styles of tombs provide the only surviving examples of Etruscan residential architecture. Not much has changed here since DH Lawrence visited and described the tombs in his *Etruscan Places* (1932), writing: 'They are surprisingly big and handsome, these homes of the dead. Cut out of the living rock, they are just like houses. The roof has a beam cut to imitate the roof-beam of the house. It is a house, a home.'

Signs indicate the path to follow and some of the major tombs, such as the 6th-century-BC Tomba dei Rilievi (Tomb of the Bas-Reliefs), are decorated with wonderfully carved reliefs, still bright with paint. This highly decorative tomb features figures from the underworld and, in glorious domestic detail, cooking implements, axes, knives, amphorae and other household items.

### MUSEO NAZIONALE DI CERVETERI   MUSEUM

(Piazza Santa Maria; admission €6/3, incl necropolis €8/4; ⊙8.30am-7.30pm Tue-Sun), Take the bus back into town and you can visit this small but splendid museum housed in the castle that dominates the medieval centre of the town. There are two rooms filled with Etruscan funerary objects, such as amphorae, statuary and ceramics, and the treasures taken from the tombs help to bring the dead to life. The earliest objects found date back to a millennia before Christ.

 **EATING**

### ANTICA LOCANDA LE GINESTRE   RESTAURANT €€

(☑06 994 06 72; Piazza Santa Maria 5; meals €35; ⊙Tue-Sun) This top-notch family-run restaurant offers delicious food, prepared with organically grown local produce and served in the elegant dining room or flower-filled courtyard garden. Book ahead.

# Viterbo

......................................................

## Explore

Viterbo makes a good base for exploring Lazio's rugged north, or it can be visited on a day trip – there are plenty of sights within the town, whose pretty *centro storico* is compact and walkable. It's well worth making the trip out here and spending the whole day, perhaps visiting some of the city's surrounding sights, such as the local hot springs or beautiful Lago Bolsena on the following day or in the afternoon.

......................................................

## Best...

➡ **Sight** Palazzo dei Priori (p231)

➡ **Place to Eat** Ristorante Enoteca la Torre (p232)

➡ **Place to Drink** Gran Caffè Schenardi (p232)

......................................................

## Top Tip

The most hassle-free way to reach Viterbo is by train, as journeys by bus can get snarled in traffic.

......................................................

## Getting There & Away

**Bus** From Rome, Cotral buses (€4.80, every 30 minutes) depart from the Saxa Rubra station on the Ferrovia Roma-Nord train line. Catch the train (standard BIT)

# Viterbo

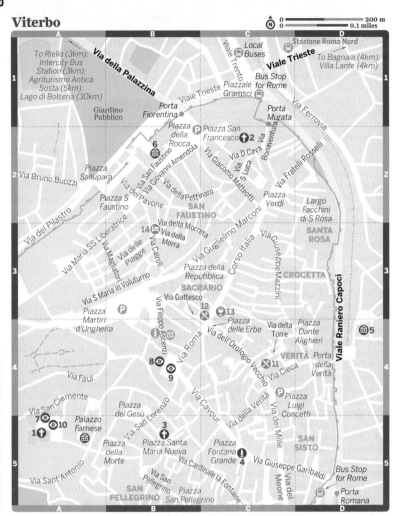

# Viterbo

| ⊙ **Sights** | **(p231)** |
|---|---|
| 1 Cattedrale di San Lorenzo | A5 |
| 2 Chiesa di San Francesco | C2 |
| 3 Chiesa di Santa Maria Nuova | B5 |
| 4 Fontana Grande | C5 |
| 5 Museo Civico | D4 |
|   Museo del Colle del Duomo | (see 1) |
| 6 Museo Nazionale Etrusco | B2 |
| 7 Palazzo dei Papi | A5 |
| 8 Palazzo dei Priori | B4 |
| 9 Piazza del Plebiscito | B4 |

| 10 Piazza San Lorenzo | A5 |
|---|---|
| ⊗ **Eating** | **(p232)** |
| 11 Ristorante Enoteca La Torre | C4 |
| 12 Ristorante Tre Re | C3 |
| ⊙ **Drinking** | **(p232)** |
| 13 Gran Caffè Schenardi | C3 |
| ⊜ **Sleeping** | **(p232)** |
| 14 Tuscia Hotel | B3 |

to Saxa Rubra from Piazzale Flaminio (just north of Piazza del Popolo). Viterbo is covered by a Zone 5 BIRG ticket (€9). In Viterbo, ensure you get off at Porta Romana, not the intercity bus station at Riello, which is a few kilometres north-west of the town. Returning to Rome, take the bus from the Porta Romana or Piazzale Gramsci stops.

**Car** Take Via Cassia (SS2). Once in Viterbo, the best bet for parking is either Piazza Martiri d'Ungheria or Piazza della Rocca.

**Train** Trains depart hourly from Monday to Saturday and every two hours on Sundays from Rome's Ostiense station (get off at Viterbo Porta Romana). The journey takes nearly two hours and costs €4.50 one way.

................................................

### Need to Know

➡ **Area Code** 01100

➡ **Location** 105km northwest of Rome

➡ **Tourist Office** Tourist information office (☑07 6132 5992; www.provincia.vt.it, in Italian; Via Filippo Ascenzi; ☻10am-1pm & 3-6pm Tue-Sun)

## ⊙ SIGHTS

Founded by the Etruscans and eventually taken over by Rome, Viterbo developed into an important medieval centre, and in the 13th century it became the residence of the popes. Papal elections were held in the Gothic Palazzo dei Papi, where in 1271 the entire college of cardinals was briefly imprisoned. The story goes that after three years of deliberation the cardinals still hadn't elected a new pope. Mad with frustration, the Viterbesi locked the dithering priests in a turreted hall and starved them into electing Pope Gregory X.

Apart from its historical appeal, Viterbo is famous for its therapeutic hot springs. The best known is the sulphurous Bulicame pool, mentioned by Dante in the *Divine Comedy*.

### PALAZZO DEI PRIORI                    PALAZZO
(Piazza del Plebiscito; admission free; ☻ 9am-1pm & 3-7pm) Viterbo's walled *centro storico* is small and best covered on foot. The focal

square, the Renaissance **Piazza del Plebiscito**, is dominated by the imposing **Palazzo dei Priori**. Now home to the town council, it's worth venturing inside for the 16th-century frescoes that colourfully depict Viterbo's ancient origins – the finest are in the Sala Regia on the 1st floor. Outside, the elegant courtyard and fountain were added two centuries after the *palazzo* (mansion) was built in 1460.

### PIAZZA SAN LORENZO                    PIAZZA
For an idea of how rich Viterbo once was, head southwest to **Piazza San Lorenzo**, the medieval city's religious heart. It was here that the cardinals came to vote for their popes and pray in the 12th-century **Cattedrale di San Lorenzo**. Built originally to a simple Romanesque design, it owes its current Gothic look to a 14th-century makeover; damage by Allied bombs in WWII meant the roof and nave had to be rebuilt.

### MUSEO DEL COLLE DEL DUOMO            MUSEUM
(adult/reduced incl guided visit to Palazzo dei Papi, Sala del Conclave, Loggia €7/5; ☻10am-1pm & 3-8pm Tue-Sun, to 6pm winter) Next door, the **'museum of the cathedral hill'** displays a small collection of religious artefacts, including a reliquary said to contain the chin (!) of John the Baptist.

### CHIESA DI SANTA MARIA NUOVA         CHURCH
(Piazza Santa Maria Nuova; ☻10am-1pm & 3-5pm) The oldest church in Viterbo, this lovely 11th-century Romanesque building was restored to its original form after WWII bomb damage. The cloisters, believed to date from an earlier period, are particularly lovely.

### PIAZZA SAN PELLEGRINO                PIAZZA
South of here lies the remarkably well-preserved medieval quarter. Wander down Via San Pellegrino with its low-slung arches and claustrophobic grey houses to this pint-sized and picturesque square.

### MUSEO NAZIONALE ETRUSCO             MUSEUM
(☑0761 32 59 29; Piazza della Rocca; admission €6; ☻8.30am-7.30pm Tue-Sun) For a shot of Etruscan culture, head to the **National Etruscan Museum**, housed in an attractive *palazzo* by the northern entrance to the town, with an interesting collection of local Etruscan artefacts.

## SLEEPING IN VITERBO

➧ **Tuscia Hotel** (☑0761 34 44 00; www.tusciahotel.com; Via Cairoli 41; s €44-50, d €68-76; P⊖❋) The best of the city's midrange options, Tuscia Hotel is a central, spick-and-span place that's leagues ahead of the competition in terms of cleanliness and comfort. The rooms here are large, light and kitted out with satellite TV; nine rooms have air-con. There's a sunny roof terrace.

➧ **Agriturismo Antica Sosta** (☑0761 251 369; www.agriturismo anticasosta.it; meals €35, s/d €40/70; P⊖❋) This mansion, set in pea-green countryside, is five kilometres from Viterbo, on SS Cassia Nord, with spacious, simple rooms and a delicious restaurant, serving scrumptious dishes such as *strozzapreti con salsiccia, porcini e pancetta* ('priest-strangler' pasta with sausage, porcini mushrooms and cured ham).

**CHIESA DI SAN FRANCESCO**  CHURCH
(☑0761 34 16 96; Piazza San Francesco; ⊕8am-6.30pm) A short walk away is this Gothic church containing the tombs of two popes: Clement IV (d 1268) and Adrian V (d 1276). Both are attractively decorated, notably that of Adrian, which features Cosmati work (multicoloured marble and glass mosaics set into stone and white marble).

**MUSEO CIVICO**  MUSEUM
(☑0761 34 82 75; Piazza Crispi; admission €3.10; ⊕9am-7pm Tue-Sun summer, to 6pm winter) On the other side of town, the **Civic Museum** features more Etruscan goodies, as well as curious fake antiquities created in the 15th century by Annius of Viterbo, a monk and forger trying to boost Viterbo's reputation. There's also a small art gallery, the highlight of which is Sebastiano del Piombo's *Pietà*.

**FONTANA GRANDE**  FOUNTAIN
In its eponymous piazza, the **'Big Fountain'** lives up to its name, and is also the oldest of Viterbo's Gothic fountains.

**VILLA LANTE**  PALAZZO
For a High Renaissance spectacle, head to the wonderful **Villa Lante**, 4km northeast of Viterbo at Bagnaia. This mannerist drama of terraces, water cascades and gaily waving statues forms part of the bucolic **park** (☑07 612 88 008; admission €2; ⊕8.30am-1hr before sunset Tue-Sun) that surrounds the 16th-century villa. To get to Bagnaia from Viterbo, take the bus from Viale Trieste (€1).

 ## EATING & DRINKING

**RISTORANTE ENOTECA
LA TORRE**  RESTAURANT €€€
(☑0761 22 64 67; Via della Torre 5; meals €65; ⊕lunch Thu-Tue, dinner Thu-Wed) Viterbo's best restaurant is a dream date for foodies: the Japanese chef combines precision and delicacy of presentation with innovative uses of fresh seasonal produce.

**RISTORANTE TRE RE**  RESTAURANT €€
(☑0761 30 46 19; Via Gattesco 3; meals €35; ⊕Fri-Wed) This historic trattoria dishes up steaming plates of tasty local specialities and seasonally driven dishes. None is more typical than the *pollo alla Viterbese,* excellent roast chicken stuffed with spiced potato and green olives.

**GRAN CAFFÈ SCHENARDI**  CAFE €
(☑07 613 45 860; Corso Italia 11-13) The Schenardi has been operating since 1818, and the wonderfully ornate interior looks like it hasn't changed much since.

# Orvieto

### Explore
Crowning a steep hill, beautiful medieval Orvieto is dominated by its awe-inspiring humbug-striped *duomo* (cathedral). Unsurprisingly, it's a tourist honeypot and gets crowded, particularly in summer. But don't let that deter you. This is a wonderful place to wander and makes a perfect day trip from Rome.

### Best...

→ **Sight** Duomo (p234)
→ **Place to Eat** Ristorante la Pergola (p235)
→ **Place to Drink** Caffè Clandestino (p235)

### Top Tip

Stay overnight to experience the atmosphere of the town once all the day trippers have ebbed away.

### Getting There & Away

**Bus Bargagli** (☑057 778 62 23; www.bargagli autolinee.it) runs daily buses to Rome (€8, 1½ hours, 8.10am Monday to Saturday, 7.10pm Sunday). From Rome, buses depart from Stazione Tiburtina (3.15pm, Monday to Saturday, 9pm Sunday).

**Car** The city is on the A1 north–south autostrada. There's plenty of parking space in Piazza Cahen and in several designated areas outside the old city walls.

**Train** Trains depart from Rome's Stazione Termini (€7.10 to €20, 60 to 80 minutes, every two hours). Take the funicular up to Piazza Cahen at the eastern end of the old town, then a shuttle bus (which fills up very quickly) to the Piazza del Duomo. If you can, opt for the very pleasant 20-minute walk uphill.

### Need to Know

→ **Area Code 05010**
→ **Location** 120km northwest of Rome
→ **Tourist Office** (☑07 6334 1772; info@ iat.orvieto.tr.it; Piazza Duomo 24; ⊗8.15am–1.50pm & 4–7pm Mon–Fri, 10am–1pm & 3–6pm Sat, Sun & holidays)

 **SIGHTS**

Perched precariously on a cliff made of the area's tufa stone, besides its magnificent cathedral, Orvieto also houses an important collection of Etruscan artefacts, and the cliff beneath is riddled with a fascinating series of ancient underground caves.

If you're planning extensive sightseeing in the town, a good investment is the **Carta Unica** (adult/concession €18/15), which includes five hours' free parking, a return trip on the cable car, free bus transport, and admission (only once) to the Cappella di San Brizio in the cathedral, Museo Claudio Faina e Civico, Orvieto Underground, Torre del Moro, Museo dell'Opera del Duomo and the Crocifisso del Tufo necropolis (the last is at the foot of the rock massif on which Orvieto stands). It's available at participating sites and next door to the tourist office.

**DAY TRIPS FROM ROME** ORVIETO

> **WORTH A DETOUR**
>
> ### LAGO DI BOLSENA
>
> Surrounded by lush rolling countryside a few kilometres short of the regional border with Umbria, Lago di Bolsena is the largest and northernmost of Lazio's lakes. The lake's main town is Bolsena, a charming, low-key place that, despite a heavy hotel presence, retains its medieval character.
>
> Like many Italian towns, Bolsena has its own miracle story. In 1263 a priest who had been tormented by doubts about the veracity of transubstantiation (the transformation of wine and bread into the blood and body of Christ) was saying Mass when he noticed blood dripping from the bread he was blessing. The bloodstained cloth in which he wrapped the bread may be seen in Orvieto's cathedral (p234), which was built to commemorate the miracle.
>
> In the medieval centre is the 11th-century **Basilica di Santa Cristina** (☑07 6179 9067; www.basilicasantacristina.it; Piazza Santa Cristina; ⊗7.15am-12.45pm & 3-7.30pm Easter-Sep, 7.15am-12.30pm & 3-5.30pm Oct-Easter) where you'll find four stones stained with miraculous blood. The church is named for the martyr, who was daughter of the local prefect and yet was tortured and finally killed for her faith – her story is re-enacted annually on 23 and 24 July. Beneath the basilica are a series of **catacombs**, where the young saint (aged only 12) was buried, and also noteworthy for the number of tombs that are still sealed.

There's a pleasant, tranquil walk around Orvieto's walls (5km) – pick up a map at the tourist office, where you can also enquire about wine tours in the Umbrian countryside. To find out more information on local wine trails, contact **Associazione Strada dei Vini Etrusco Romana in provincial di Terni** (☏0763 306508; www.stradadeivini etruscoromana.it).

### DUOMO
CATHEDRAL

(☏0763 34 11 67; www.opsm.it, in Italian; Piazza Duomo; ☉7.30am-7.30pm Apr-Sep, 7.30am-6.30pm Mar & Oct, 7.30am-1pm & 2.30-5.30pm Nov-Feb) Confoundingly beautiful, Orvieto's **Duomo** is otherworldly in its striped magnificence. Started in 1290, it was originally planned in the Romanesque style but, as work proceeded and architects changed, it became more Gothic. The black-and-white marble banding of the main body of the church is surpassed and complemented by the dancing polychrome colours of the façade.

Pope Urban IV commissioned the cathedral to celebrate the Miracle of Bolsena (see p233) in 1263, but it took 30 years to plan and three centuries to complete. It was probably started by Fra Bevignate and later additions were made by Lorenzo Maitani, Andrea Pisano and his son Nino Pisano, Andrea Orcagna and Michele Sanicheli. The great bronze doors, the work of Emilio Greco, were added in the 1960s.

### CAPPELLA DI SAN BRIZIO
CHAPEL

(admission €3, incl museum €5; ☉9.30am-1pm & 2.30-5pm Mon-Sat, 2.30-5.30 Sun Nov-Feb, 9.30am-6pm Mon-Sat, 1-5.30pm Sun Mar & Oct, 9.30am-7pm Mon-Sat, 1-5.30pm Sun Apr-Sep) Inside, Luca Signorelli's fresco cycle, *Il Giudizio Universale* (The Last Judgment), shimmers with life in this chapel to the right of the altar. Signorelli began work on the series in 1499. Michelangelo is said to have taken inspiration from it for the Sistine Chapel. Indeed, to some, Michelangelo's version runs a close second to Signorelli's work.

### CAPPELLA DEL CORPORALE
CHAPEL

The **'Chapel of the Body'** houses the blood-stained altar linen from Bolsena, and features frescoes by Ugolino di Prete Ilario that depict the miracle.

## SLEEPING IN ORVIETO

➡ **Hotel Maitani** (☏07 6334 2011; www.hotelmaitani.com; Via Lorenzo Maitani 5; s/d €79/130; P) Polished parquet floors, sober antique furnishings and cathedral views (in some rooms) are a winning combination at this thoughtful hotel. Prices quoted are without breakfast.

➡ **B&B Valentina** (☏07 6334 1607; www.bandbvalentina.com; Via Vivaria 7; s €45-60, d €65-90, tr €65-129, apt €130-180) On a cobbled alley, Valentina offers casually elegant, spacious rooms, a couple with kitchen facilities, and also has an apartment sleeping four.

### MUSEO DELL'OPERA DEL DUOMO
MUSEUM

(☏0763 34 35 92; www.opsm.it; Palazzo Soliano & Palazzi Papali, Piazza Duomo; adult €4, incl Cappella di San Brizio €5; ☉10am-1pm & 2-5pm Wed-Mon Nov-Feb, 10am-7pm Wed-Mon Oct & Mar, 9.30am-7pm daily Apr-Sep) Next to the cathedral is the **Museum of the Cathedral**, housed in the former papal palaces, with a clutter of religious relics, as well as Etruscan antiquities and paintings by artists such as Simone Martini, Arnolfo di Cambio and the three Pisanos: Andrea, Nino and Giovanni.

### PALAZZO PAPALE
MUSEUM

Around the corner in the **Papal Palace**, you can see one of Italy's most important collections of Etruscan archaeological artefacts in the **Museo Archeologico Nazionale** (☏/fax 07 6334 1039; Piazza Duomo; adult/reduced €3/1.50; ☉8.30am-7.30pm) and the more interesting **Museo Claudio Faina e Civico** (☏0763 34 15 11; www.museofaina.it; Piazza Duomo 29; adult/concession €4.50/3; ☉9.30am-6pm daily Apr-Sep, 10am-5pm Tue-Sun Oct-Mar), where you'll find some significant Greek ceramic works, mostly found near Piazza Cahen in tombs dating to the 6th century BC.

### TORRE DEL MORO
TOWER

(☏07 6334 4567; Corso Cavour 87; adult/reduced €2.80/2; ☉10am-8pm May-Aug, 10am-7pm Mar, Apr, Sep & Oct, 10.30am-4.30pm Nov-Feb) Head northwest along Via del Duomo to Corso Cavour and the **Moor's Tower**. Climb all 250 steps and you're rewarded with sweeping city views.

### ORVIETO UNDERGROUND  HISTORICAL SITE

(☎07 6334 4891; Parco delle Grotte; adult/reduced €6/5; ☻tours 11am, 12.15pm, 4pm & 5.15pm daily Mar-Jan, more frequent in busy periods, Sat & Sun only Feb) The coolest place in Orvieto, in degrees and atmosphere, is **Orvieto Underground**. Underneath the city, the rock is riddled with 440 caves, which have been used for millennia for various purposes. Tours (with English-speaking guides) take you through caverns variously used as WWII bomb shelters, refrigerators, wells and, during many a siege, dovecotes to trap pigeons for dinner (still seen on local restaurant menus as *palombo*).

### CHIESA DI SANT'ANDREA  CHURCH

(☻8.30am-12.30pm & 3.30-7.30pm) At Orvieto's heart lies Piazza della Repubblica, once the site of Orvieto's Roman Forum and later the centre of the medieval city, where you'll find this 12th-century **church** with its curious decagonal bell tower.

### CHIESA DI SAN GIOVENALE  CHURCH

(Piazza Giovenale; ☻8am-12.30pm & 3.30-6pm) Constructed in the year 1000, this church's interior is brightened by 13th- and 14th-century frescoes, which are fine examples of Romanesque–Gothic art and the later Orvieto school and form a beautiful contrast.

### LA ROCCA  FORT

Standing watch at the town's easternmost tip is the 14th-century rock fortress, **the Rock**, part of which is now a public garden.

### POZZO DI SAN PATRIZIO  NOTABLE BUILDING

(☎07 6334 3768; Viale Sangallo; adult/reduced €5/3.50; ☻9am-7.45pm May-Aug, 9am-6.45pm Mar, Apr, Sep & Oct, 10am-4.45pm Nov-Feb) To the north of the fortress, **St Patrick's Well** is a 60m-deep well, lined by two spiral staircases for water-bearing mules.

 **EATING**

### CANTINA FORESI  WINE BAR €

(☎07 6334 1611; Piazza del Duomo 2; snacks from €5; ☻9am-8pm) Under the shadow of the *duomo,* yet surprisingly reasonable, this family-run *enoteca* (wine bar) serves simple *panini* (bread rolls) and sausages, washed down with local wine.

### RISTORANTE LA PERGOLA  RESTAURANT €€

(☎07 6334 3065; Via dei Magoni 9b; meals €40; ☻Thu-Tue) Intimate and elegant, with a conservatory at the back, this serves great Umbrian cuisine, with plenty of truffles and 'hunter-style' chicken, lamb and boar dishes, all in a warm, welcoming atmosphere.

### RISTORANTE ZEPPELIN  RESTAURANT €€

(☎07 6334 1447; Via Garibaldi 28; meals €35) With high, arched ceilings and an old-fashioned feel, this jazz-cool restaurant produces creative Umbrian food. Expect delicate ravioli combined with ingredients such as sage and almonds, and a dazzling array of rich, meaty *secondi* (second courses).

## 🍷 DRINKING

### CAFFÈ CLANDESTINO  CAFE €

(☎07 6334 0868; Corso Cavour 40; snacks from €3) This cafe-bar has a lively buzz, high ceilings, good coffee, nice snacks and brasserie-style meals, a few outside tables where you can sit with the sun on your face, and regular live music tucked into a relatively small space. What more could you want?

DAY TRIPS FROM ROME ORVIETO

# Sleeping

*From opulent five-star palaces to chic boutique hotels, family-run pensioni, bed and breakfasts, and tranquil convents, Rome has accommodation to please everyone, from the fussiest prince to the most impecunious nun. But while there's plenty of choice, rates are universally high and you'll need to book early to get the best deal.*

## Rates & Payment

Although Rome doesn't have a low season as such, the majority of hotels offer discounts from November to March (excluding the Christmas and New Year period) and from mid-July through August. Expect to pay top whack in spring (April to June) and autumn (September and October) and over the main holiday periods (Christmas, New Year and Easter). Nowadays, the rates that many hotels apply change on a daily basis and can often vary enormously depending on demand, season and booking method (online, through an agency etc). Throughout this chapter we've given prices for the low-season minimum and high-season maximum, unless there's a single year-round price. Most mid- and top-range hotels accept credit cards. Budget places might, but it's always best to check in advance. Many smaller places offer discounts of up to 10% for payment in cash.

## Getting There

All the areas covered in this chapter are a bus ride or metro journey from Stazione Termini. If you come by car, be warned that there is a terrible lack of on-site parking facilities in the city centre, although your hotel should be able to direct you to a private garage. Street parking is not recommended.

## Hotel Tax

As of January 2011, everyone overnighting in Rome has to pay a room occupancy tax on top of their regular accommodation bill. This amounts to:

➡ €1 per person per night for a maximum of five days in campsites

➡ €2 per person per night for a maximum of 10 days in *agriturismi* (farm stay accommodation), B&Bs, guesthouses, and 1-, 2- and 3-star hotels

➡ €3 per person per night for a maximum of 10 days in 4- and 5-star hotels.

The tax is applicable to anyone who is not a resident in Rome.

Prices quoted in this chapter do not include the tax.

## Pensioni & Hotels

The bulk of accommodation in Rome is made up of *pensioni* and *alberghi* (hotels).

A *pensione* is a small, family-run hotel or guesthouse. In Rome, they are generally housed in converted one- or two-floor apartments. Rooms tend to be simple, and although most come with a private bathroom, those that don't will usually have a basin and bidet.

Hotels are bigger and more expensive than *pensioni*, although at the cheaper end of the market, there's often little difference between the two. All hotels are rated from one to five stars, although this rating relates to facilities only and gives no indication of value, comfort, atmosphere or friendliness. Most hotels in Rome's city centre tend to be three-star and up. As a rule a room in a three-star hotel will come with a hairdryer, minibar (or fridge), safe and air-conditioning. Many will also have satellite TV and internet connections.

A common complaint in Rome is that hotel rooms are small. This is especially true in the *centro storico* and Trastevere, where many hotels are housed in converted *palazzi* (mansions). Similarly, a spacious lift is a rare find, particularly in older *palazzi,* and you'll seldom find one that can accommodate more than one average-sized person with luggage.

Breakfast in cheaper hotels is rarely worth setting the alarm for, so, if you have the option, save a few bob and pop into a bar for a coffee and *cornetto* (croissant).

## B&Bs & Guesthouses

Alongside the hundreds of traditional B&Bs (private homes offering a room or two to paying guests), Rome has a large number of boutique-style guesthouses that offer chic, upmarket accommodation at mid- to top-end prices. Note also that breakfast in a Roman B&B is usually a continental combination of bread rolls, croissants, ham and cheese.

## Hostels

Hostels have smartened up in recent years and now cater to everyone from backpackers to budget-minded families. Many of these newer hostels offer traditional dorms as well as smart hotel-style rooms (singles, doubles, even family rooms) with private bathrooms. Curfews are generally a thing of the past and some even offer 24-hour receptions. However, many hostels don't accept prior reservations for dorm beds, so arrive after 10am and it's first come, first served.

For information on Rome, and Italy's official HI hostels, contact the **Italian Youth Hostel Association** (Associazione Italiana Alberghi per la Gioventù; Map p340; ☑ 06 4890 7740; www.aighostels.com; Piazza San Bernardo 107).

## Religious Institutions

Unsurprisingly, Rome is well furnished with religious institutions, many of which offer cheap(-ish) rooms for the night. Bear in mind, though, that many have strict curfews and that the accommodation, while spotlessly clean, tends to be short on frills. Also, while there are a number of centrally located options, many convents are situated out of the centre, typically in the districts north and west of the Vatican. Book well in advance.

## Rental Accommodation

For longer stays, renting an apartment might well work out cheaper than an extended hotel sojourn. Bank on spending about €900 per month for a studio apartment or a small one-bedroom place. For longer-term stays, you will probably have to pay bills on top plus a condominium charge for building maintenance. A room in a shared apartment will cost from €600 per month, plus bills. You'll usually be asked to pay a deposit equal to one or two months' rent and the first month in advance.

For a mini-apartment in a hotel block, go online at www.060608.it and check out the Sleeping section. Several hotels also offer apartment rental, such as the Beehive (p244) and Hotel Campo de' Fiori (p240).

## Accommodation Websites

The **Comune di Roma** (www.060608.it) publishes an extensive list of B&Bs, rentals and hotels (with prices).

### HOTELS

You can consult a list of author-reviewed accommodation options on Lonely Planet (hotels.lonelyplanet.com) and book directly online.

### B&BS

These agencies offer online booking:

**Bed & Breakfast Association of Rome** (www.b-b.rm.it) Lists B&Bs and short-term apartment rentals.

**Bed & Breakfast Italia** (www.bbitalia.com) Rome's longest-established B&B network.

**Cross Pollinate** (www.cross-pollinate.com) Has B&Bs, private apartments and guesthouses.

**Sleeping Rome** (www.sleepingrome.com) Offers B&B and has good short-term flat rentals.

### RELIGIOUS INSTITUTES

Check out www.santasusanna.org/coming ToRome/convents.html for a useful list of religious institutes offering accommodation.

### RENTAL ACCOMMODATION

Useful rental resources:

**Accommodations Rome** (www.accomoda tionsrome.com)

**Flat in Rome** (www.flatinrome.it)

**Flats in Italy** (www.flatsinitaly.com)

**Italy Accom** (www.italy-accom.com)

**Leisure in Rome** (www.leisureinrome.com)

**Rental in Rome** (www.rentalinrome.com)

**Sleep in Italy** (www.sleepinitaly.com)

## NEED TO KNOW

### Price Ranges
In this chapter prices quoted are the minimum-maximum for rooms with a private bathroom, and unless otherwise stated include breakfast. The following price indicators apply (for a high-season double room):

| | |
|---|---|
| € | under €120 |
| €€ | €120 to €250 |
| €€€ | €250 and up |

### Reservations
➡ Always try to book ahead, especially if coming in high season or for a major religious festival.

➡ Ask for a *camera matrimoniale* for a room with a double bed. A *camera doppia* (double room) is a room with twin beds.

➡ There's a **hotel reservation service** (☑06 699 10 00; booking fee €3; ⏰7am-10pm) next to the tourist office at Stazione Termini.

### Checking In & Out
➡ Check out is usually between 10am and noon. In hostels, it's around 9am.

➡ Some guesthouses require you to arrange a time to check in.

➡ If you're going to arrive late, mention this when you book your room.

## Lonely Planet's Favourites

**Villa Laetitia** (p247) A romantic riverside villa with fabulous Fendi decor.

**Donna Camilla Savelli** (p246) Tasteful conversion of a convent designed by baroque maestro Borromini.

**Arco del Lauro** (p246) Minimalist comfort in the heart of medieval Trastevere.

**Villa Spalletti Trivelli** (p243) Bask in country style at this stately city centre mansion.

**Pensione Panda** (p242) Flying the budget flag in Rome's designer shopping district.

**Beehive** (p244) Putting the boutique into hostel accommodation.

## Best by Budget

### €
Pensione Panda (p242)
Okapi Rooms (p242)
Beehive (p244)
La Piccola Maison (p243)
Hotel San Pietrino (p247)

### €€
Arco del Lauro (p246)
Casa Montani (p248)
Hotel Barocco (p243)
Daphne Inn (p243)
Teatropace 33 (p240)
Suites Trastevere (p247)

### €€€
Donna Camilla Savelli (p246)
Portrait Suites (p242)
Villa Laetitia (p247)
Villa Spalletti Trivelli (p243)
Babuino 181 (p241)
Hotel Sant'Anselmo (p246)

## Best for Location
Albergo Abruzzi (p240)
Hotel Navona (p241)
Hotel Scalinata di Spagna (p243)
Hotel Campo de' Fiori (p240)
Casa di Santa Brigida (p241)
Hotel Bramante (p247)

## Best for Romance
Villa Laetitia (p247)
Donna Camilla Savelli (p246)
Hotel Sant'Anselmo (p246)
Hotel Locarno (p242)
Residenza Cellini (p244)

## Best for Traditional Style
Donna Camilla Savelli (p246)
Villa Spalletti Trivelli (p243)
Hotel Due Torri (p240)
Hotel Forum (p240)
Residenza Arco de' Tolomei (p246)

## Best for Views
Hotel Forum (p240)
Hotel Scalinata di Spagna (p243)
Albergo Abruzzi (p240)
Portrait Suites (p242)

## Best for Backpackers
Beehive (p244)
Alessandro Palace Hostel (p245)
Papa Germano (p245)
Yellow (p246)

## Best for Families
Hotel Campo de' Fiori (p240)
Welrome Hotel (p245)
Alessandro Palace Hostel (p245)
Casa Banzo (p241)

# Where to Stay

SLEEPING

| Neighbourhood | For | Against |
| --- | --- | --- |
| Ancient Rome | Close to major sights like Colosseum, Roman Forum and Capitoline Museums; quiet at night. | Not cheap and few budget options; restaurants tend to be touristy. |
| Centro Storico | Most atmospheric part of Rome with everything on your doorstep – Pantheon, Piazza Navona, restaurants, bars and shops. | Most expensive part of town; few budget options; can be noisy. |
| Tridente, Trevi & the Quirinale | Good for Spanish Steps, Trevi Fountain and designer shopping; excellent mid- to top end options; good transport links. | Decidedly upmarket area with prices to match; subdued after dark. |
| Monti, Esquilino & San Lorenzo | Lots of budget accommodation around Stazione Termini; some top eating options in Monti & good nightlife in San Lorenzo; good transport links. | Some dodgy streets in Termini area, which is not Rome's most characterful. |
| San Giovanni to Testaccio | More authentic than many central areas, with good eating and drinking options; Aventino a quiet, romantic area; Testaccio a top nightlife district. | Few options available and away from San Giovanni not many big sights. |
| Trastevere & Gianicolo | Gorgeous, atmospheric area; party atmosphere with hundreds of bars, cafes, restaurants and trattorias; some interesting sights. | Very noisy, particularly on summer nights; expensive; hotel rooms often small. |
| Vatican City, Borgo & Prati | Near St Peter's Basilica and the Vatican Museums; decent range of accommodation; some excellent shops and restaurants; on the metro. | Expensive near St Peter's; not much nightlife; sells out quickly for religious holidays. |
| Villa Borghese & Northern Rome | Largely residential area good for the Auditorium and some top museums; generally quiet after dark. | Out of the centre; few budget choices. |

## Ancient Rome

**HOTEL FORUM** HOTEL €€€

Map p344 (☎06 679 24 46; www.hotelforumrome.com; Via Tor de' Conti 25; s €160-220, d €240-360; Ⓜ Cavour; P ❄ 🛜) The stately Forum offers some of the best views in town. From the rooftop restaurant, you can look down on all of Ancient Rome, from the Campidoglio down to the Colosseum. Inside, the look is olde worlde, with antiques and leather armchairs, wood-panelling and dangling chandeliers.

**FORTY SEVEN** BOUTIQUE HOTEL €€€

Map p344 (☎06 678 78 16; www.fortysevenhotel.com; Via Petroselli 47; s €190-285, d €190-300; 🚌Via Petroselli; ❄ @ 🛜) This lovely retreat sits at the back of the Roman Forum near the Bocca della Verità. The plain grey facade opens onto a bright modern interior, full of sunshine and sharply designed guest rooms. Up top, there's a wonderful rooftop lounge bar, while in the basement you can work off your troubles in the gym and sauna, both included in the rates.

**CAESAR HOUSE** HOTEL €€

Map p344 (☎06 679 26 74; www.caesarhouse.com; Via Cavour 310; s €150-230, d €170-270; Ⓜ Cavour; ❄ 🛜) Quiet, friendly, yet in the thick of it on busy Via Cavour, this is a refined apartment hotel. Its smart public areas are polished and modern while rooms reveal a warm, peachy decor, four-poster beds and small bathrooms. The suite has a view over the forum.

**HOTEL NERVA** HOTEL €€

Map p344 (☎06 678 18 35; www.hotelnerva.com; Via Tor de' Conti 3; s €50-149, d €69-229; Ⓜ Cavour; ❄ 🛜) Cheerful and family run, the Nerva is tucked away on a narrow road behind the Imperial Forums. A small place, it manages to squeeze 22 small-ish peach-coloured rooms onto its three floors as well as plenty of Roman paraphernalia.

## Centro Storico

TOP CHOICE **HOTEL CAMPO DE' FIORI** BOUTIQUE HOTEL €€€

Map p346 (☎06 687 48 86; www.hotelcampodefiori.com; Via del Biscione 6; r & apt €99-599; 🚌Corso Vittorio Emanuele II; ❄ @ 🛜) This rakish four-star has got the lot – sexy decor, an enviable location, attentive staff and a panoramic roof terrace. They even serve scrambled eggs and bacon for breakfast. The 23 rooms are individually decorated but they all feel delightfully decadent with boldly coloured flock walls, gilt mirrors and restored bric-a-brac. The hotel also offers 11 apartments in the vicinity, ideal for families.

**TEATROPACE 33** HOTEL €€

Map p346 (☎06 687 90 75; www.hotelteatropace.com; Via del Teatro Pace 33; s €69-150, d €110-240; 🚌Corso Vittorio Emanuele II; ❄) Near Piazza Navona, this friendly three-star is a class choice with 23 beautifully appointed rooms decorated with parquet flooring, damask curtains and exposed wood beams. There's no lift, just a monumental 17th-century stone staircase and a porter to carry your bags.

**HOTEL DUE TORRI** HOTEL €€

Map p346 (☎06 6880 6956; www.hotelduetorriroma.com; Vicolo del Leonetto 23; s €125-150, d €170-230; 🚌Via di Monte Brianzo; ❄ 🛜) The Hotel Due Torri has always offered discretion – first as a residence for cardinals, then as a brothel, and now as a lovely, refined hotel. The look is classic, with huge gilt-framed mirrors, antiques, parquet floors and plump pot plants, and while rooms aren't huge, they're bright and comfortable.

**ALBERGO ABRUZZI** HOTEL €€

Map p346 (☎06 679 20 21; www.hotelabruzzi.it; Piazza della Rotonda 69; s €110-180, d €120-250; 🚌Largo di Torre Argentina; ❄) This popular three-star, bang opposite the Pantheon, is all about location. But the small rooms are also attractive, with parquet, cherry wood furnishings and soft colour schemes. The one problem is noise – double glazing will keep some of it out but a silent night is unlikely. Breakfast is served in a nearby cafe.

**RELAIS PALAZZO TAVERNA** BOUTIQUE HOTEL €€

Map p346 (☎06 2039 8064; www.relaispalazzotaverna.com; Via dei Gabrielli 92; s €70-140, d €100-210; 🚌Ponte Vittorio Emanuele II; ❄ @) Housed in a 15th-century *palazzo* deep in the heart of the historic centre, this contemporary boutique hotel sets its bold, modern aesthetic against a lovely historic background. Amenities such as plasma-screen satellite TVs, and tea- and coffee-making facilities ice the cake.

### HOTEL TEATRO DI POMPEO                HOTEL €€

Map p346 (☑06 687 28 12; www.hotelteatrodi
pompeo.it; Largo del Pallaro 8; s €140-160, d
€180-210; ☐Corso Vittorio Emanuele II; ✲@☎)
Built on top of a theatre that Pompey constructed in 55 BC (now the breakfast room),
this charming hotel is tucked away behind
Campo de' Fiori. Rooms boast a classic old-
fashioned feel with polished wood–bed-
steads and terracotta floor tiles. The best,
on the 3rd floor, also have sloping wood-
beamed ceilings.

### HOTEL NAVONA                          HOTEL €€

Map p346 (☑06 6821 1392; www.hotelnavona.
com; Via dei Sediari 8; s €120-140, d €160-200;
☐Corso del Rinascimento; ✲☎) This family-
run hotel occupies several floors of a 15th-
century *palazzo* near Piazza Navona.
Rooms vary: on the reception floor they are
small with traditional gilt-framed decor
and antique furniture, while upstairs they
come with medieval ceilings and contemporary silver-grey colours. The same people
also run the **Residenza Zanardelli** (Map
p346; ☑06 6821 1392; www.residenzazanardelli.
com; Via Zanardelli 7; r €100-200; ☐Corso del Rinascimento; ✲) north of Piazza Navona.

### ARGENTINA RESIDENZA        BOUTIQUE HOTEL €€

Map p346 (☑06 6819 3267; www.argentinaresi
denza.com; Via di Torre Argentina 47; r €120-200;
☐Largo di Torre Argentina; ✲☎) This quiet
boutique hotel is hidden on the 3rd floor of
a *palazzo* overlooking busy Largo di Torre
Argentina. But all the bustle of the piazza
will seem a long way away as you slip into
a Jacuzzi bath and relax in one of the six
tastefully modern rooms.

### HOTEL MIMOSA                          PENSIONE €

Map p346 (☑06 688 01 753; www.hotelmimosa.
net; Via di Santa Chiara 61, 2nd fl; s €55-85, d €70-
118, tr €90-160, without bathroom s €45-70, d
€50-98; ☐Largo di Torre Argentina; ✲@) This
long-standing *pensione* is one of the few
budget options in the historic centre. It's all
fairly basic but rooms have recently been
made over and they now come with lami-
nated parquet floors and cooling cream and
brown colours. Payment in cash only.

### CASA BANZO                            B&B €€

Map p350 (☑06 683 39 09; www.casabanzo.
it; Piazza del Monte di Pietà 30; r €100-200, apt
€140-200; ☐Via Arenula; ✲) Not an easy place
to find (there's no sign), Casa Banzo is stunningly close to Campo de' Fiori, and has
seven individually styled rooms, some bigger
and better decorated than others but none
as grand as the 2nd-floor frescoed reception
hall and monumental stone staircase (there's
no lift). On the ground floor, there's a small
apartment suitable for families of up to five.

### CASA DI SANTA
### BRIGIDA                               CONVENT €€

Map p346 (☑06 6889 2596; www.brigidine.org;
Piazza Farnese 96, entrance Via di Monserrato
54; s/d €120/200; ☐Corso Vittorio Emanuele II;
✲@) Housed in a picturesque 14th-century
*palazzo*, this convent is where the Swedish St Brigid lived and died in 1373. It isn't
the cheapest religious accommodation in
Rome, but it's among the best with pleasant, no-frills rooms and a superb location
on Piazza Farnese. Meals are available for
€25.

### ALBERGO DEL SOLE                      PENSIONE €€

Map p346 (☑06 687 94 46; www.solealbiscione.
it; Via del Biscione 76; s €100, d €125-160; ☐Corso
Vittorio Emanuele II; P✲☎) Dating to 1462,
this is said to be the oldest hotel in Rome.
There's nothing special about the functional rooms but there's a pleasant 2nd-
floor roof terrace, wi-fi is available (€1.50),
and the location near Campo de' Fiori is
excellent. Air-con is available only in some
rooms. No credit cards and no breakfast.

# 🛏 Tridente, Trevi & the Quirinale

Rome's glossiest district is chock full of designer boutiques catering to high-rolling
shoppers, and encompasses the Spanish
Steps, Piazza di Spagna and Piazza del Popolo. There are lots of restaurants around
here, but this is a district that's in its element during the day – after dark it's somewhat subdued.

### BABUINO 181                    BOUTIQUE HOTEL €€€

Map p352 (☑06 3229 5295; www.romeluxury
suites.com/babuino; Via del Babuino 181; r €180-
250; ❂✲☎) A beautifully renovated old
palazzo in the heart of the shopping district, Babuino offers discreet luxury, with
modern chic rooms and touches such as a
Nespresso machine and fluffy bath robes.
Breakfast is great, too.

### GREGORIANA
HOTEL €€€

Map p352 (☑06 679 42 69; www.hotelgrego
riana.it; Via Gregoriana 18; s €148-198, d €228-
288; MSpagna; ☺✳) This low-key, polished
art deco hotel is fantastically set behind
the Spanish Steps. Rooms are decorated
by beautiful circular maple-wood headboards, snow-white linen and lots of
gleaming rosewood. Staff are friendly and
unpretentious.

### HOTEL LOCARNO
HOTEL €€€

Map p352 (☑06 361 08 41; www.hotellocarno.
com; Via della Penna 22; s €150-180, d €150-250;
MFlaminio; ☺✳@⊛) With its ivy-clad exterior, stained-glass doors and rattling cage-
lift, the Locarno is an art deco classic – the
kind of place Hercule Poirot might stay if he
were in town. Many rooms have silk wallpaper and period furniture, occasionally a bit
tired but full of period charm, while others
have cream walls and wrought-iron beds.
There's a lovely roof garden, a restaurant
and uber-cool bar.

### PORTRAIT SUITES
BOUTIQUE HOTEL €€€

Map p352 (☑06 6938 0742; www.portraitsuites.
com; Via Bocca di Leone 23; r €410-670; MFlaminio; P☺✳⊛) Owned by the Ferragamo family, this is a discreet, exclusive residence,
with14 exquisitely styled suites and studios
across six floors in an elegant townhouse,
plus a dreamy 360-degree roof terrace and
made-in-heaven staff. There's no restaurant, but you can have meals delivered.
Breakfast is served in your room or on the
terrace.

### CENCI
B&B €€

Map p352 (☑340 355 6788; www.cencibedand
breakfast.it; Vicolo Scavolino 61; d €100-120;
MBarberini; ✳@⊛) There are three rooms,
so only early birds will snag this cool place
with contemporary decor in warm hues
that complement the high ceilings and
sunny rooms and is virtually atop the Trevi
Fountain.

### PENSIONE PANDA
HOTEL €

Map p352 (☑06 678 01 79; www.hotelpanda.
it; Via della Croce 35; s with/without bathroom
€80/68, d with/without bathroom €108/78;
MSpagna; ✳⊛) Only 50m from the Spanish Steps, in an area where a bargain is
a Bulgari watch bought in the sales, the
friendly, efficient Panda is an anomaly, a
budget pension, and a splendid one. The
clean rooms are smallish but nicely furnished, and there are several triples with
a bed on a cosy mezzanine. Air-con costs
€6 per night.

### OKAPI ROOMS
HOTEL €€

Map p352 (☑06 3260 9815; www.okapirooms.it;
Via della Penna 57; s €65-80, d €85-120; MFlaminio; ✳⊛) Run by the owners of Pensione
Panda (p242), 20-room Okapi is housed
in a town house in a great location close
to Piazza del Popolo. Rooms are simple,
small, airy affairs with cream walls, terracotta floors and double glazing. Some are
decorated with ancient-style carvings and
several have small terraces. Bathrooms are
tiny but sparkling clean.

### HOTEL DE RUSSIE
HOTEL €€€

Map p352 (☑06 32 88 81; www.hotelderussie.
it; Via del Babuino 9; d €450-690; MFlaminio;
P✳@) A favourite of Hollywood celebs,
the historic de Russie is almost on Piazza
del Popolo, and has exquisite terraced gardens. The decor is softly luxurious in many
shades of grey, and the rooms offer state-
of-the-art entertainment systems, massive
mosaic-tiled bathrooms and the softest
linen sheets.

### CROSSING CONDOTTI
GUESTHOUSE €€

Map p352 (☑06 6992 0633; www.crossingcon
dotti.com; Via Mario de' Fiori 28; r €180-300;
MSpagna; ☺✳⊛) A five-room place, this
is one of Rome's new breed of upmarket
guest houses, where all the fittings, linen
and comforts are top of the range, and the
pretty, though not large rooms have lots
of character and antique furnishings. No
breakfast, but there's a well-stocked kitch-
en with drinks and a Nespresso machine.

### HASSLER VILLA MEDICI
HOTEL €€€

Map p352 (☑06 69 93 40; www.hotelhassler.
com; Piazza della Trinità dei Monti 6; d €450-500;
MSpagna; ✳@⊛) Sumptuously surmount-
ing the Spanish Steps, the Hassler is a byword for old-school luxury. A long line of
VIPs have stayed here, enjoying the ravishing views and sumptuous hospitality. The
Michelin-starred restaurant Imàgo serves
fine food overlooking amazing panoramas.
Under the same management is nearby
boutique **Il Palazzetto** (☑06 699 341 000;
www.ilpalazzettoroma.com; Vicolo del Bottino 8),
with views over the Spanish Steps, for those
who want a more intimate experience.

### HOTEL MOZART
HOTEL €€

Map p352 (☑06 3600 1915; www.hotelmozart. com; Via dei Greci 23b; s €110-165, d €40-245; Ⓜ Spagna; Ⓟ❄@🛜) A credit-card's flourish from Via del Corso, the Mozart has classic, immaculate rooms, decorated in dove greys, eggshell blues and rosy pinks, with comfortable beds, gleaming linen and polished wooden furniture; deluxe rooms have Jacuzzi baths and small terraces. The lowest prices quoted are without breakfast.

### HOTEL SCALINATA DI SPAGNA
HOTEL €€€

Map p352 (☑06 6994 0896; www.hotelscalinata. com; Piazza della Trinità dei Monti 17; d €150-190; Ⓜ Spagna; ❄@🛜) Given its location – perched alongside the Spanish Steps – the Scalinata is surprisingly modestly priced. An informal and friendly place, it's something of a warren, with a great roof terrace, and low corridors leading off to smallish, old-fashioned, yet romantic rooms. Book early for a room with a view.

### HOTEL MODIGLIANI
HOTEL €€

Map p352 (☑06 4281 5226; www.hotelmod igliani.com; Via della Purificazione 42; s €100-168, d €115-202; Ⓜ Barberini; ❄🛜) Run by an artistic couple, the Modigliani is all about attention to detail and customer service. The 23 dove-grey rooms are spacious and light, and the best have views and balconies, either outside or over the quiet internal courtyard garden.

### DAPHNE INN
HOTEL €€

Map p352 (☑06 8745 0086; www.daphne-rome. com; Via di San Basilio 55; d with/without bathroom €140-235/€100-150; Ⓜ Barberini; ❄@🛜) Boutique B&B Daphne is a gem, with chic, sleek, comfortable rooms, helpful English-speaking staff, and loan of a mobile phone for your stay. There are rooms in two locations – the one off Via Veneto is the pick, but there's a second at Via degli Avvignonesi 20. Book months ahead.

### HOTEL BAROCCO
HOTEL €€

Map p352 (☑06 487 20 01; www.hotelbarocco. com; Piazza Barberini 9; d €160-330; Ⓜ Barberini; ➡❄@🛜) In a superbly convenient location, this well-run, welcoming 41-room hotel overlooking Piazza Barberini (the pricier rooms have views) has a classic feel, with rooms featuring oil paintings, gleaming linen, gentle colour schemes and fabric-covered walls; breakfast is ample and served in a wood-panelled room.

### HOTEL ERCOLI
PENSIONE €

Map p352 (☑06 474 54 54; www.hotelercoli.com; Via Collina 48; s €60-90, d €70-110; ▣Via Piave; ➡❄) Old-fashioned and friendly, the 3rd-floor (there's an elderly cage lift) Ercoli is a straight-up *pensione,* renovated a couple of years back. It's popular with foreign students. The 14 rooms are functional rather than memorable, but they're all sparkling clean with tiled floors, breakfast is included and the air-con works.

### LA PICCOLA MAISON
B&B €

Map p352 (☑06 4201 6331; www.lapiccolamai son.com; Via dei Cappuccini 30; s €50-140, d €70-200; Ⓜ Vittorio Emanuele; ➡❄🛜) The excellent Piccola Maison is housed in a 19th-century building in a great location close to Piazza Barberini, and has pleasingly plain, neutrally decorated rooms and thoughtful staff. It's a great deal.

## 🛏 Monti, Esquilino & San Lorenzo

The bulk of Rome's budget accommodation is concentrated in the Termini area, around the central station. It has its shady sides, but has been cleaned up in recent years and there are now some good places to stay.

Monti, a wealthy yet bohemian district, sandwiched between Via Nazionale and Via Cavour, is a very attractive area that's becoming increasingly popular; San Lorenzo does have a couple of hotels, but isn't recommended as an area to stay, as it tends to be noisy at night.

### VILLA SPALLETTI TRIVELLI
HOTEL €€€

Map p340 (☑06 4890 7934; www.villaspal letti.it; Via Piacenza 4; r €330-345; Ⓜ Spagna; ➡Ⓟ❄@🛜) With 12 rooms in a glorious mansion in central Rome, Villa Spalletti Trivelli has upped the ante for luxurious stays in the capital. Rooms are soberly and elegantly decorated, overlooking the gardens of the Quirinale or the estate's Italian garden. The overall feel is that of staying in the stately home of some aristocratic friends.

### HOTEL DUCA D'ALBA
HOTEL €

Map p340 (☑06 48 44 71; www.hotelducadalba. com; Via Leonina 14; s €90-190, d €100-240; Ⓜ Vittorio Emanuele; ➡❄@🛜) An appealing four-star hotel in the Monti district, this has small but charming rooms: most have fabric-covered or handpainted walls, wood-beamed ceilings, big flat-screeen TVs and sleek button-studded headboards.

### HOTEL ARTORIUS
HOTEL €€

Map p340 (✆06 482 11 96; www.antica-locanda. com; Via del Boschetto 13; d €160-185; ⓂCavour; ✳@🛜) The art deco–flavoured lobby looks promising, and the rest delivers too in this small Monti hotel, with simple, plain rooms – not large, but perfectly comfortable, one (room 109) of which has a terrace – and a family-run feel.

### TARGET INN
INN €€

Map p340 (✆06 474 53 99; www.targetinn.com; Via Modena 5, 3rd fl; s €100-120, d €120-160; ⓂRepubblica; ✳@🛜) Sleek, minimalist Target has only seven rooms, featuring high ceilings, red leather furniture, gleaming white walls, abstract art, black wardrobes and traditional parquet floors. Families should go for the suite, which sleeps four.

### BEEHIVE
HOSTEL €

Map p340 (✆06 4470 4553; www.the-beehive. com; Via Marghera 8; dm €20-25, d without bathroom €70-80; ⓂTermini; ➾@🛜) More boutique chic than backpacker crash-pad, the Beehive is one of Rome's best hostels. Run by a Californian couple, it's an oasis of style with original artworks, funky modular furniture and a vegetarian cafe (prices don't include breakfast). Beds are in a spotless, eight-person mixed dorm or six private double rooms, all with fans. Book ahead.

### NICOLAS INN
B&B €€

Map p340 (✆06 9761 8483; www.nicolasinn. com; Via Cavour 295, 1st fl; s €90-150, d €100-180; ⓂCavour; ➾✳🛜) This sunny B&B is at the bottom of noisy Via Cavour, a stone's throw from the Imperial Forums. Run by a welcoming young couple, it has four big guest rooms, with wrought-iron beds, tiled floors, and colourful pictures. It's remarkably quiet, and has a long line of satisfied customers (none of whom are under-fives, as they're not permitted).

### RESIDENZA CELLINI
GUESTHOUSE €€

Map p340 (✆06 4782 5204; www.residenzacel lini.it; Via Modena 5; d €145-240; ⓂRepubblica; ➾✳@🛜) With grown-up furnishings featuring potted palms, polished wood, pale yellow walls, oil paintings and a hint of chintz, this charming, family-run hotel on

a quiet road parallel to Via Nazionale offers spacious, elegant rooms, all with satellite TV and Jacuzzi or hydro-massage showers. There's a sunny flower-surrounded terrace for summer breakfasts.

### HOTEL OCEANIA
HOTEL €€

Map p340 (✆06 482 46 96; www.hoteloceania. it; Via Firenze 38; s €70-140, d €85-210; ⓂRepubblica; @🛜) The homely, quaint Oceania is a welcome break from the bustle of the streets five floors below. It's an intimate, old-fashioned hotel, with 34 rooms that have fabric-covered walls and heavy curtains, wooden furnishings and brightly tiled bathrooms. Book early.

### 66 IMPERIAL INN
B&B €€

Map p340 (✆06 482 56 48; www.66imperialinn. com; Via del Viminale 66; s €80-180, d €80-210; 🚇Via Nazionale; ✳🛜) This smart B&B underwent renovation in 2010 and has emerged with chic and funky rooms, which combine designer wallpapers and Chinoiserie-styled headboards with hot-pink silks and gleaming white linen. Rooms have high ceilings, and are airy, comfortable and quiet. The bathrooms are spotless and the Jacuzzi showers are a treat.

### HOTEL COLUMBIA
HOTEL €€

Map p340 (✆06 488 35 09; www.hotelcolumbia. com; Via del Viminale 15; d €160-188; ⓂTermini or Repubblica; ✳@🛜) In a workaday area that's an aria from the Opera House, the friendly Columbia sports a polished look with beamed or exposed stone ceilings and dark-wood cabinets. The white-walled rooms are bright and surprisingly full of character – some have beautiful Murano crystal chandeliers. The breakfast is good, and in summer is served on the pretty roof terrace.

### RADISSON BLU
HOTEL €€

Map p340 (✆06 44 48 41; www.radissonblu.com/ eshotel-rome; Via Filippo Turati 171; d €190-225; ⓂVittorio Emanuele; ➾✳@⌾) The Radisson Blu's location is not the best, but it's a popular choice with business travellers and design-conscious customers who appreciate the advance deals, sci-fi decor and hi-tech gadgetry – though the standard rooms verge on the silly, with their central bathroom cubes. The poolside rooftop bar serves swell cocktails and the pool is open to nonguests for €45/55 per day/weekend.

### HOTEL DOLOMITI
HOTEL €€

Map p340 (☑06 495 72 56; www.hotel-dolomiti. it; Via San Martino della Battaglia 11; s €45-130, d €60-170; M Castro Pretorio; ⊖ ✷ @ ☎) Welcoming, family-run Dolomiti has rooms on the 4th floor of an apartment block. The rooms are colour-coordinated with cream walls, cherry-wood furniture, rich-red fabrics and prints of chubby-cheeked cherubs. The same family also manages the Hotel Lachea two floors below. The combined reception is on the 1st floor.

### HOTEL & HOSTEL DES ARTISTES
HOSTEL €, HOTEL €€

Map p340 (☑06 445 43 65; www.hoteldesartistes.com; Via Villafranca 20; dm €14-52; r without bathroom €69-95; M Castro Pretorio; ⊖ ✷ @) The wide range of rooms here are decked out in wood and gold with faux-antique furniture and rich reds, gilt lamps and terracotta or tiled floors, and have decent bathrooms. Offers discounts for longer stays and/or cash payment. The hotel runs the nearby clean and functional hostel **Carlito's Way** (☑06 444 03 84; www.rome-hotel-carlitosway.com; Via Villafranca 10), which also has some smart hotel-style doubles.

### HOTEL GIULIANA
HOTEL €

Map p340 (☑06 488 07 95; www.hotelgiuliana.com; Via Agostino de Pretis 70; s €60-100, d €80-170; M Termini; ⊖ ✷) A cosy little hotel run by a jolly Londoner and her daughter, the Giuliana ticks all the right boxes. Rooms, divided into standard and superior, are dapper; the location, near Via Nazionale, is convenient; and the service is cheery and efficient.

### ALBERGO GIUSTI
RELIGIOUS INSTITUTION €

Map p340 (☑06 7045 3462; http://hotelgiusti. com/en/enhome.html; Via Giusti 5; s €40-50, d €75-90; M Vittorio Emanuele; ✷ @) Run by the sisters of Sant'Anna, this spartan, spotless bed-and-breakfast is a great deal, in a convent in the side streets near the Basilica di Santa Maria Maggiore. Rooms are salmon-pink or minty-green and a few have small balconies. The nuns are hospitable, if rather stern, and it feels very safe – a tranquil haven close to Termini.

### HOSTEL & HOTEL DES ARTISTES
HOTEL €

(Map p340; ☑06 445 43 65; www.hoteldesartistes.com; Via Villafranca 20; dm €14-52; r without bathroom €69-95, r with bathroom €105-119; ⊖ ✷ @) The wide range of rooms here are decked out in wood and gold with faux-antique furniture and rich reds, gilt lamps and terracotta or tiled floors, and have decent bathrooms. Offers discounts for longer stays and/or cash payment.

### WELROME HOTEL
HOTEL €

Map p340 (☑06 4782 4343; www.welrome.it; Via Calatafimi 15-19; s €80-100, d €90-110; M Termini; ⊖ ✷ ☎) The owners of the Welrome have a personal mission to look after guests: not only do they take huge pride in their small, spotless hotel but they also enthusiastically point out the cheapest places to eat, where not to waste your time and what's good to do. Families should go for the huge room named after Piazza di Spagna; a cot will be provided at no extra charge.

### HOTEL CERVIA
PENSIONE €

Map p340 (☑06 49 10 57; www.hotelcerviaroma. com; Via Palestro 55; s €40-70, d €60-90, with shared bathroom s €30-40, d €45-65; M Castro Pretorio; ☎) Considerately run by two friendly multilingual women, the Cervia has been recently restructured and now has a new breakfast room and smartly decorated rooms. Children are welcome, with free cots available on request. On the 2nd floor (no lift) they also run the similar **Hotel Restivo** (☑06 446 21 72; www.hotelrestivo. com). Wi-fi is downstairs only.

### PAPA GERMANO
HOTEL €

Map p340 (☑06 48 69 19; www.hotelpapagermano.it; Via Calatafimi 14a; dm €17-30, d €60-100, with shared bathroom d €50-80; M Termini; ✷ @ ☎) Easygoing and popular, Papa Germano is a budget stalwart. There are various sleeping options, ranging from four-person dorms to private rooms with or without private bathrooms. It feels a bit institutional, but still has a family-run feel, the decor is plain and fairly smart, and all are scrupulously clean. Breakfast is included (though only on request at the lowest prices), and air-con costs €5 per night.

### ALESSANDRO PALACE HOSTEL
HOSTEL €

Map p340 (☑06 446 19 58; www.hostelsalessandro.com; Via Vicenza 42; dm €18-35, d €70-110; M Termini or Castro Pretorio; ✷ @) A long-standing favourite appealing to both budgeting families and backpackers, offering spick-and-span, terracotta-floored doubles, triples and quads, plus dorms sleeping from four to eight, all with cheery bedspreads. Every room has its own bathroom and hairdryer. In some, windows open only a fraction.

### YELLOW
HOSTEL €

Map p340 (☏06 4938 2682; www.the-yellow.com; Via Palestro 44; dm €24-50, d €70; ⓜCastro Pretorio; ✳@⏜) Popular Yellow caters to a youthful, party-loving crowd (there's even an age limit – 18 to 40). Decor is bright, clean and funky, featuring Starsky-and-Hutch stencils on the walls, and mixed dorms sleep between four and 12 people in basic bunks, with barracks-style showers and toilets (bigger dorms have bathrooms down the hall). The bar downstairs (where you can buy breakfast), open till 2am, has outdoor tables. Reception is 24 hours.

### ABERDEEN HOTEL
HOTEL €€

Map p340 (☏06 482 39 20; www.travel.it/roma/aberdeen; Via Firenze 48; s €85-120, d €109-170; ⓜRepubblica; ✳@) This sparkling three-star is a decent, easygoing hotel in a well-connected central location. The spacious rooms feature chequered chessboard floors, comfy beds (orthopaedic mattresses are standard) and spotless mint-green bathrooms. Buffet breakfast is served under a charming coffered wood ceiling and everywhere you go the staff are cheerful, cordial and helpful.

## 🛏 San Giovanni to Testaccio

### TOP CHOICE HOTEL SANT'ANSELMO
HOTEL €€€

Map p356 (☏06 57 00 57; www.aventinohotels.com; Piazza Sant'Anselmo 2; s €130-265, d €150-290; ⏹Via Marmorata; ✳@) Set amid the terracotta villas and umbrella pines of the peaceful Aventino district, this is a delightful romantic hideaway. Its rooms are not the biggest but they are stylish, marrying carved beds, heavy brocades and dripping chandeliers with modern touches and contemporary colours. A few also have terraces offering shimmering views over southern Rome.

### B&B BASILICA SQUARE
B&B €

Map p356 (☏06 7759 0548; www.basilicasquare.com; Piazza San Giovanni in Laterano 26; s €60-90, d €75-120; ⓜSan Giovanni; ✳⏜) Budget accommodation is thin on the ground in this neck of the woods, but this simple B&B does the job nicely enough with four simply decorated rooms in a good location, opposite the Basilica di San Giovanni in Laterano. The Colosseum is within walking distance and there's a metro station nearby.

## 🛏 Trastevere & Gianicolo

Trastevere is beautiful: cobbled narrow streets, ivy-coated terracotta buildings, graceful piazzas – this is the Roman holiday of your dreams. It's also thick with restaurants, pubs and cafes, and gets mind-bogglingly busy, especially on hot summer nights, when in some streets you can hardly move for crowds. So, not a good choice for light sleepers. Its tightly packed streets are dotted by hotels in historic *palazzi*, although note that space is tight and rooms tend to be small.

### DONNA CAMILLA SAVELLI
HOTEL €€€

Map p360 (☏06 58 88 61; www.hotelsavelli.com; Via Garibaldi 27; d €200-260; ⏹ or ⏹Viale di Trastevere; ⏚P✳@⏜) If you have the cash, stay here, in this converted convent that was designed by baroque genius Borromini. It's been beautifully updated; muted colours complement the serene concave and convex curves of the architecture, and service is excellent. The pricier of the 78 rooms overlook the lovely cloister garden or views of Rome and are decorated with antiques, but the cheaper ones are still very lovely.

### RESIDENZA ARCO DE' TOLOMEI
HOTEL €€

Map p360 (☏06 5832 0819; www.bbarcodeitolomei.com; Via Arco de' Tolomei 27; d €145-220; ⏹ or ⏹Viale di Trastevere; ⏚✳⏜) Next to Arco del Lauro, this gorgeous place is decorated with polished antiques and rich contrasting chintzes that make the interiors feel like a country cottage. It's also a lovely place to stay, and the owners are friendly and helpful.

### ARCO DEL LAURO
B&B €€

Map p360 (☏06 9784 0350; www.arcodellauro.it; Via Arco de' Tolomei 27; s €75-125, d €95-145; ⏹Viale di Trastevere; ⏚✳⏜) With only six rooms, this fab B&B in an ancient *palazzo*, through a large stone arch and on a narrow cobbled street,is a find with gleaming white rooms that combine rustic charm with minimalist simplicity. The largest room has a high wood-beamed ceiling. Beds are comfortable, showers are powerful, and the owners are eager to please. Book well ahead.

### BUONANOTTE GARIBALDI
GUESTHOUSE €€

Map p360 (☏06 5833 0733; www.buonanotte garibaldi.com; Via Garibaldi 83; r €150-280; ⏹ or ⏹Piazza Sonnino; ⏚✳@⏜) With only three rooms, this is a haven, an upmarket B&B in a divinely pretty inner-city villa, set around a courtyard. The rooms, themed Green, Orange and Blue, are beautifully decorated and there are works of art and sculpture all over the place – this is an artist's house. The elegant Luisa Longo has her studio in one corner of the courtyard. Pick of the rooms is Blue, upstairs, which opens onto a greenery-shaded terrace.

### HOTEL SANTA MARIA                    HOTEL €€

Map p360 (✆06 589 46 26; www.hotelsanta maria.info; Vicolo del Piede 2; s €90-190, d €130-260; ▣ or ▣Piazza Sonnino; ▣⊝❋@☎]) Walk along the ivy-lined approach and you'll enter a tranquil haven. Surrounding a spacious modern cloister (a former convent site), shaded by orange trees, rooms are cool and comfortable, with slightly fussy decor and terracotta floors. There are some much larger family rooms. Staff are helpful and professional, and it's wheelchair-friendly. Its smaller sister is **Residenza Santa Maria** (✆06 5833 51 03; www.residenzasantamaria. com; Via Dell'Arco Di San Calisto 20), a few streets away.

### VILLA DELLA FONTE                    HOTEL €€

Map p360 (✆580 37 97; www.villafonte.com; Via della Fonte dell'Olio 8; s €110-145, d €135-170; ▣ or ▣Piazza Sonnino; ⊝❋☎) A lovely terracotta-hued gem, Villa della Fonte occupies a 17th-century building, and only has five rooms, all of which are simply decorated but have pretty outlooks, good bathrooms and comfortable beds covered with lovely linen. The sunny garden terrace (for breakfast in warm weather) is a plus.

### SUITES TRASTEVERE                    B&B €€

Map p360 (✆347 074 40 86; www.trastevere. bbsuites.com; Viale Trastevere 248; s €70-105, d €80-160; ▣ or ▣Viale di Trastevere; ⊝❋☎) On the 4th floor of a honey-hued palazzo on the wide main drag and tramway running from Trastevere, this friendly, popular B&B has dramatically frescoed rooms, each themed after local sights, such as the Colosseum and the Pantheon.

### LA FORESTERIA ORSA MAGGIORE    HOSTEL €

Map p360 (✆06 689 37 53; www.casainter nazionaledelledonne.org, in Italian; 2nd fl, Via San Francesco di Sales 1a; dm €26, s/d without bathroom €52/72, s/d with bathroom €75/110; ▣Piazza Trilussa; ⊝@) This lesbian-friendly, women-only guest house (boys aged 12 or younger are welcome) is housed in a restored 16th-century convent. It is run by the Casa Internazionale delle Donne (International Women's House) and offers safe and well-priced accommodation in a quiet corner of Trastevere. The 13 simple rooms sleep two, four, five or eight, and some have views onto the attractive internal garden. There's a 3am curfew. Wheelchair accessible.

## 🛏 Vatican, Borgo & Prati

**TOP CHOICE**⟩ **VILLA LAETITIA**    BOUTIQUE HOTEL €€€

Map p364 (✆06 322 67 76; www.villalaetitia.com; Lungotevere delle Armi 22; d €190-350; ▣Lepanto; ❋☎) It doesn't get any more fab than this, darling. A stunning boutique hotel in a graceful riverside villa owned and styled by members of the famous Fendi fashion family. The 14 gorgeous rooms are all individually decorated – particularly impressive is the Crystal Room with its perspex furniture and the Garden Room with its original Picasso – and each comes with its own kitchen facilities. Breakfast is not included.

### HOTEL SAN PIETRINO                    HOTEL €

Map p364 (✆06 370 01 32; www.sanpietrino. it; Via Bettolo 43; s €45-75, d €65-112, s without bathroom €35-55, d without bathroom €55-85; ▣Ottaviano-San-Pietro; ❋@☎) Not far from Ottaviano metro station, San Pietrino is a lovely little hotel. Its rooms are characterful and prettily decorated, with terracotta floors and the occasional statue. Added bonuses include comfortable beds, wi-fi, and helpful staff.

### HOTEL BRAMANTE                    HOTEL €€

Map p364 (✆06 6880 6426; www.hotelbra mante.com; Vicolo delle Palline 24-25; s €100-160, d €150-220; ▣Ottaviano–San Pietro; ❋☎) In the atmospheric Borgo, Hotel Bramante exudes country-house charm, with 16 quietly elegant rooms – think oriental rugs, wood-beamed ceilings and antiques. It's housed in the 16th-century building where architect Domenico Fontana lived before Pope Sixtus V banished him from Rome.

### BIBI E ROMEO'S HOME                    B&B €

Map p364 (✆346 965 69 37; www.bbromeo. com; Via Andrea Doria 36; s €50-80, d €60-130, tr €90-130, q €100-150; ▣Ottaviano–San Pietro; ❋☎) Up from a broad cafe-lined avenue, this peaceful, personable B&B has rooms that are a cut above the average. They're decorated in stylish mixes of white, brown and grey, with quotes written on the walls by the authors they're themed after: Pablo Neruda, Pessoa, Tersani and Santagostino.

### COLORS HOTEL HOTEL €€

Map p364 (📞06 687 40 30; www.colorshotel.com; Via Boezio 31; s from €30, d from €40; 🚇Piazza del Risorgimento; ❄️@) Popular with young travellers, this is a friendly, laid-back hotel with 23 brightly painted rooms spread over three floors (no lift, though). There are also cheaper rooms with shared bathrooms and, in July and August, six-bed dorms (€18-30 per person).

### HOTEL LADY PENSIONE €

Map p364 (📞06 324 21 12; www.hoteladyroma. it; 4th fl, Via Germanico 198; d €70-100, s without bathroom €45-75, d without bathroom €55-85; 🚇Lepanto; 🛜) A homey old-school *pensione*, the Hotel Lady is a quiet and inviting place. The eight rooms are snug, comfortable, spotless, and rooms 4 and 6 have wood-beamed ceilings. Breakfast, which is optional but costs €5 to €10 extra, is served in the attractive salon.

### HOTEL FLORIDA HOTEL €€

Map p364 (📞06 324 18 72; www.hotelfloridaroma.it; Via Cola di Rienzo 243; s €40-150, d €50-170, tr €65-200, q €80-200; 🚇Piazza del Risorgimento; ❄️🛜) Looking good after a recent makeover, this friendly hotel has decent-sized minimalist rooms and small, en suite designer bathrooms. Breakfast, if you want it, costs €5 per person, but wi-fi is free in the spacious reception area.

### HOTEL GIUGGIOLI HOTEL €€

Map p364 (📞06 3600 5389; www.hotelgiuggiolirome.com; Via Germanico 198; s €60-140, d €70-180; 🚇Lepanto; ❄️🛜) One of several hotels in the same building, the 1st-floor Giuggioli offers nine dapper, pearl-grey rooms with a minimum of furniture and large, comfortable beds. Three floors up, the Giuggioli's sister hotel, the Hotel dei Quiriti, has more old-fashioned rooms for the same price. Wi-fi cost €1 per hour.

### CASA DI ACCOGLIENZA PAOLO VI RELIGIOUS ACCOMMODATION €

Map p364 (📞06 390 91 41; www.ospitiamoconcuore.it; Viale Vaticano 92; s/d/tr/q €35/65/83/95; 🚇Ottaviano-San-Pietro; ❄️) A lovely, palm-shaded convent, right opposite the entrance to the Vatican Museums, where the welcoming sisters offer small, sunny rooms, which are so clean they gleam. Book way ahead. There's no breakfast.

### DOMUS NASCIMBENI RELIGIOUS ACCOMMODATION €

(📞06 662 75 01; www.nascimbeni.it; Via di Torre Rosso 68; s €40-50, d €70-75, tr €90-105; 🚇Via di Torre Rosso; ❄️) This is a good option for large families or groups in need of quiet, cheap digs. It's a big, spotlessly clean place with white, institutional-type rooms and plenty of space in an anonymous suburb northwest of the Vatican – there's a bus stop just outside. Meals are also available for €15.

## 🛏 Villa Borghese & Northern Rome

### CASA MONTANI BOUTIQUE GUESTHOUSE €€

Map p366 (📞06 3260 0421; www.casamontani.com; Piazzale Flaminio 9; d €140-240; 🚇Flaminio; ❄️@🛜) A lovely, upmarket guesthouse with just five rooms. All are slightly different but the overall look is up-to-the-minute cool with grey colour schemes, modern parquet, custom-made furniture and contemporary art. Prices are low, considering the level of comfort, and it's a specially good deal in low season.

# Understand Rome

# Rome Today

In the past decade or so, Rome has done much to pull itself into the 21st century. A major clean-up for the year 2000 Jubilee was followed by an outbreak of artistic and architectural activity in the mid-noughties that put the city back on Europe's cultural map. Since then the pace of renovation has slowed and Rome today is a city of ups and downs, on the one hand striving to deal with economic uncertainty and political upheaval, on the other celebrating papal beatification and gay pride with festive abandon.

## Best on Film

**The Talented Mr Ripley** (1999) Murderous intrigue on Piazza di Spagna and in other Italian locations.

**Roma Città Aperta** (Rome Open City; 1945) A neorealist study of desperation in Nazi-occupied Rome.

**Dear Diary** (1994) Cult director Nanni Moretti scoots around a semi-deserted Rome.

**Rome** (2005 & 2007) TV sword-and-sandal epic covering Rome's transition from Republic to Empire.

**Roman Holiday** (1953) Gregory Peck, Audrey Hepburn, a Vespa and *dolce vita* romance.

## Best in Print

**The Secrets of Rome: Love & Death in the Eternal City** (Corrado Augias; 2007) Journalist Augias muses on little-known historical episodes.

**Imperium** (Robert Harris; 2006) Fictional biography of Cicero by bestselling Brit author.

**Michelangelo & the Pope's Ceiling** (Ross King; 2003) Fascinating account of the painting of the Sistine Chapel.

**The Borgia Bride** (Jeanne Kalogradis; 2006) Dangerous passions let loose in Renaissance Rome.

**Roman Tales** (Alberto Moravia; 1954) Short stories set in Rome's poorest neighbourhoods.

## Rome Celebrates

Despite a reputation as a chaotic and traffic-clogged city – both merited – Rome can put on a superb show when it wants to. On 1 May 2011, Piazza San Pietro provided the lordly setting for the beatification of Pope John Paul II, a ceremony that drew hundreds of thousands of pilgrims from all over the world. Then, a month later, more than 40 heads of state flew into town to join Rome's political leaders celebrate Italy's 150th anniversary. No less heartfelt were the festivities that accompanied the huge Gay Pride rally just a few days later. Up to a million people paraded through the city's streets while out on the Circo Massimo (Circus Maximus) Lady Gaga camped it up in high style.

## Scandal & Political Protest

Politics have always been central to Roman life and the recent scandals surrounding Italian Prime Minister Silvio Berlusconi have been the talk of Rome (and most of Italy) for some time. The most titillating of these, the so-called Rubygate affair, erupted in early 2011 when it emerged that Berlusconi had been hosting 'bunga bunga' sex parties at his villa near Milan. More seriously, it was alleged that he had had sex with an underage prostitute, an exotic dancer called Ruby Rubacuore. Following a criminal investigation, he was officially charged and trial proceedings began in April 2011. This took the number of trials he is currently facing to four – the other three are for business-related corruption and fraud offences.

Predictably, news of Rubygate provoked jokes across the world but few people were laughing in Rome. In fact, tensions had been running high in the capital since December 2010, when violent street rioting had broken out after Berlusconi survived a parliamentary confidence vote. For many Romans, political protests and the disruption they cause – streets cordoned off, traffic in tilt, police everywhere – are part and parcel of everyday life, but few were prepared for the ferocious street battles that erupted on 15 December on Via del Corso and other historic streets. Newspaper reports spoke of the worst rioting for 30 years while Roberto Maroni, Italy's Interior Minister, blamed what he called 'professionals of violence'. Fortunately, the atmosphere in the city has since calmed and while political tensions are still riding high, there's little menace in the Roman air.

## Cultural Ups & Downs

On the cultural front, the last couple of years have been fairly turbulent. There have been successes – a recent Caravaggio exhibition attracted up to 5000 visitors per day and more than a million people attended events at the Auditorium in 2010 – but recent talk has been of spending cuts and the effect they will have on the city's high-maintenance monuments. In an effort to counter these budgetary shortfalls, Rome's right-wing mayor Gianni Alemanno has been actively pursuing private investment, and in spring 2011 he announced that Diego Della Valle, owner of Tod's, had offered to finance restoration work at the Colosseum to the tune of €25 million. The news was hailed as a breakthrough in some quarters but attacked by critics who condemned the idea of a private company having a stake in a national treasure. Under the terms of the deal Della Valle gets exclusive rights to the Colosseum's image for 15 years.

## Tourism on the Up

Surprisingly, though, all this political turmoil has not adversely affected tourism, a mainstay of the Roman economy, and after several bad years, it looks like the downward trend has finally been arrested. According to figures released by the Comune di Roma, 2010 was something of a bumper year with 10.4 million arrivals registered, a record for recent times.

Against this background, Rome's good-humoured citizens continue to enjoy their city, flocking to the many festivals, concerts and events that enliven its hot summer nights, struggling on the desperately overcrowded metro and hanging out in its beautiful, pot-holed streets.

**ROME TODAY**

## population per sq km

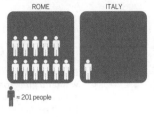

ROME     ITALY

≈ 201 people

## ethnicity
(% of population)

90

10

Italian     Other

## if Rome were 100 people

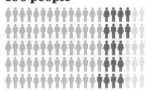

69 drive a car
18 ride a scooter
13 rely exclusive on public transport

# History

Rome's history spans three millennia, from the classical myths of vengeful gods to the follies of Roman emperors, from Renaissance excess to swaggering 20th-century Fascism. Emperors, popes and dictators have come and gone, playing out their ambitions and conspiring for their place in history. Everywhere you go in this remarkable city, you're surrounded by the past. Martial ruins, Renaissance palazzi and flamboyant baroque basilicas all have tales to tell – of family feuding, historic upheavals, artistic rivalries, intrigues and dark passions.

**Historical Reads**

Handbook to Life in Ancient Rome (Lesley Adkins, Roy A. Adkins)

The Colosseum (Keith Hopkins, Mary Beard)

The Oxford History of the Roman World (ed John Boardman, Jasper Griffin, Oswyn Murray)

Rome: The Biography of a City (Christopher Hibbert)

The Families Who Made Rome: a History and a Guide (Anthony Majanlahti)

## ANCIENT ROME, THE MYTH

As much a mythical construct as a historical reality, Ancient Rome's image has been carefully nurtured throughout history. Intellectuals, artists and architects have sought inspiration from this skilfully constructed legend, while political and religious rulers have invoked it to legitimise their authority and serve their political ends.

### Imperial Spin Doctors

Rome's original mythmakers were the first emperors. Eager to reinforce the city's status as *Caput Mundi* (capital of the world), they turned to writers such as Virgil, Ovid and Livy to create an official Roman history. These authors, while adept at weaving epic narratives, were less interested in the rigours of historical research and frequently presented myth as reality. In the *Aeneid,* Virgil brazenly draws on Greek legends and stories to tell the tale of Aeneas, a Trojan prince who arrives in Italy and establishes Rome's founding dynasty. Similarly, Livy, a writer celebrated for his monumental history of the Roman Republic, makes liberal use of mythology to fill the gaps in his historical narrative. Accuracy wasn't considered necessary and Roman officialdom enthusiastically adopted their works as the basis for Rome's history.

Ancient Rome's rulers were sophisticated masters of spin; under their tutelage, art, architecture and elaborate public ceremony were employed to perpetuate the image of Rome as an invincible and divinely sanctioned power. Monuments such as the Ara Pacis, the Colonna di Traiano and the Arco di Costantino celebrated imperial glories, while gladiatorial games

**TIMELINE**

| 753 BC | 509 BC | 146 BC |
| --- | --- | --- |
| According to legend, this is the year Romulus kills his twin brother Remus, and founds Rome. Archaeological evidence exists of an 8th-century settlement on the Palatino. | On the death of the king Tarquinius Superbus, the Roman Republic is founded, giving birth to the acronym SPQR (Senatus Populusque Romanus; the Senate and People of Rome). | Carthage is razed to the ground at the end of the Third Punic War and mainland Greece is conquered by rampant legionaries. Rome becomes undisputed master of the Mediterranean. |

# The Roman Empire

## LEGACY OF AN EMPIRE

Rising out of the bloodstained remnants of the Roman Republic, the Roman Empire was the Western world's first great superpower. At its zenith under Emperor Trajan (r AD 98–117), it extended from Britannia in the north to North Africa in the south, from Hispania (Spain) in the west to Palestina (Palestine) and Syria in the east. Rome itself had more than 1.5 million inhabitants and the city sparkled with the trappings of imperial splendour: marble temples, public baths, theatres, circuses and libraries. Decline eventually set in during the 3rd century and by the latter half of the 5th century Rome was in barbarian hands.

### Europe Divided

The empire's most immediate legacy was the division of Europe into east and west. In AD 285 the emperor Diocletian, prompted by wide-spread disquiet across the empire, split the Roman Empire into eastern and western halves – the west centred on Rome, and the east on

| 73–71 BC | 49 BC | 15 March, 44 BC | AD 14 |
|---|---|---|---|
| Spartacus leads a slave revolt against dictator Cornelius Sulla. Defeat is inevitable; punishment is brutal. Spartacus and 6000 followers are crucified along Via Appia Antica. | *Alea iacta est* ('The die is cast'). Julius Caesar leads his army across the River Rubicon and marches on Rome. In the ensuing civil war, Ceasar defeats rival Pompey. | On the Ides of March, soon after Julius Caesar is proclaimed dictator for life, he is stabbed to death in the Teatro di Pompeo (on modern-day Largo di Torre Argentina). | Augustus dies after 41 years as Rome's first emperor. His reign is successful unlike those of his mad successors Tiberius and Caligula, who go down in history for their cruelty. |

## ROMULUS & REMUS, ROME'S LEGENDARY TWINS

The most famous of Rome's many legends is the story of Romulus and Remus, the mythical twins who are said to have founded Rome on 21 April 753 BC.

Romulus and Remus were born to the Vestal Virgin Rhea Silva after she'd been seduced by Mars. At their birth they were immediately sentenced to death by their great-uncle Amulius, who had stolen the throne of Alba Longa from his brother, Rhea Silva's father, Numitor. But the sentence was never carried out, and the twins were abandoned in a basket on the banks of the Tiber. Following a flood, the basket ended up on the Palatino, where the babies were saved by a she-wolf and later brought up by a shepherd, Faustulus.

Years later, and after numerous heroic adventures, the twins decided to found a city on the site where they'd originally been saved. They didn't know where this was, so they consulted the omens. Remus, on the Aventino, saw six vultures; his brother over on the Palatino saw 12. The meaning was clear and Romulus began building, much to the outrage of his brother. The two subsequently argued and Romulus killed Remus.

Romulus continued building and soon had a city. To populate it he created a refuge on the Campidoglio, Aventino, Celio and Quirinale hills, to which a ragtag population of criminals, ex-slaves and outlaws soon decamped. However, the city still needed women. Romulus therefore invited everyone in the surrounding country to celebrate the Festival of Consus (21 August). As the spectators watched the festival games, Romulus and his men pounced and abducted all the women, an act that went down in history as the Rape of the Sabine Women.

Byzantium (later called Constantinople) – in a move that was to have far-reaching consequences. In the west, the fall of the Western Roman Empire in AD 476 paved the way for the emergence of the Holy Roman Empire and the Papal States, while in the east, Roman (later Byzantine) rule continued until 1453 when the empire was finally conquered by rampaging Ottoman armies.

### Democracy & the Rule of Law

In broader cultural terms, Roman innovations in language, law, government, art, architecture, engineering and public administration remain relevant to this day.

One of the Romans' most striking contributions to modern society was democratic government. Democracy had first appeared in 5th-century BC Athens, but it was the Romans, with their genius for organisation, who took it to another level. Under the Roman Republic (509–47 BC), the Roman population was divided into two categories: the Senate and the Roman people. Both held clearly defined responsibilities.

**Ancient Rome on Screen**

*Spartacus (Stanley Kubrick)*

*Quo Vadis (Mervyn LeRoy)*

*Gladiator (Ridley Scott)*

*I, Claudius (BBC)*

*Rome (HBO)*

| 64 | 67 | 80 | 285 |
|---|---|---|---|
| Rome is ravaged by a huge fire that burns for five and a half days. Some blame Nero, although he was in Anzio when the conflagration broke out. | St Peter and St Paul become martyrs as Nero massacres Rome's Christians. The persecution is a thinly disguised ploy to win back popularity after the great fire of 64 AD. | The 50,000-seat Flavian Amphitheatre, better known as the Colosseum, is inaugurated by Emperor Titus. Five thousand animals are slaughtered in the 100-day opening games. | To control anarchy within the Roman Empire, Diocletian splits it into two. The eastern half is later incorporated into the Byzantine Empire; the western half falls to the barbarians. |

The people, through three assembly bodies – the Centuriate Assembly, the Tribal Assembly and the Council of the People – voted on all new laws and elected two annual tribunes who had the power of veto in the Senate. The Senate, for its part, elected and advised two annual consuls who acted as political and military leaders. It also controlled the Republic's purse strings and, in times of grave peril, could nominate a dictator for a six-month period.

This system worked pretty well for the duration of the Republic, and remained more or less intact during the empire – at least on paper. In practice, the Senate assumed the assemblies' legislative powers and the emperor claimed power of veto over the Senate, a move that pretty much gave him complete command, although in such a way as to preserve the facade of republican government.

The observance of law was an important element in Roman society. As far back as the 5th century BC, the Republic had a bill of rights, known as the Twelve Tables. This remained the foundation stone of Rome's legal system until Emperor Justinian (r 527–565) produced his mammoth *Corpus Iurus Civilis* (Body of Civil Law) in 529. This not only codified all existing laws but also included a systematic treatise on legal philosophy. In particular, it introduced a distinction between *ius civilis* (civil law – laws particular to a state), *ius gentium* (law of nations – laws established and shared by states) and *ius naturale* (natural law – laws concerning male-female relationships and matrimony).

## Latin

But more than the laws themselves, Rome's greatest legacy to the legal profession was the Latin language. Latin was the lingua franca of the Roman Empire and was later adopted by the Catholic Church, a major reason for its survival. It is still today one of the Vatican's official languages and until the 2nd Vatican Council (1962–65) was the only language in which Catholic Mass could be said. As the basis for modern Romance languages such as Italian, French and Spanish, it provides the linguistic roots of many modern words.

## Roman Roads

And just as many words lead to Latin, so all roads lead to Rome. The ancient Romans were the master engineers of their day, and their ability to travel quickly was an important factor in their power to rule. The queen of all ancient roads was Via Appia Antica, which connected Rome with the southern Adriatic port of Brindisi. Via Appia survives to this day, as do many of the other ancient roads: Via Aurelia, Via Cassia, Via Flaminia and Via Salaria are among the most important.

**HISTORY** LEGACY OF AN EMPIRE

VIRGIL

*Virgil (70 BC–19 BC), real name Publius Vergilius Maro, was born near the northern Italian town of Mantua to a wealthy family. He studied in Cremona, Milan, Rome and Naples, before becoming Rome's best-known classical poet. His most famous works are the Eclogues, Georgics and the Aeneid.*

**313**

A year after his victory at the Battle of Milvian Bridge, the Emperor Constantine issues the Edict of Milan, officially establishing religious tolerance and legally ending anti-Christianity persecution.

**476**

The fall of Romulus Augustulus marks the end of the Western Empire. This had been on the cards for years: in 410 the Goths sacked Rome; in 455 the Vandals followed suit.

JONATHAN SMITH / LONELY PLANET IMAGES ©

*Arco di Constantino*

# CHRISTIANITY & PAPAL POWER

For much of its history Rome has been ruled by the pope, and today the Vatican still wields immense influence over the city.

The ancient Romans were remarkably tolerant of foreign religions. They themselves worshipped a cosmopolitan pantheon of gods, ranging from household spirits and former emperors to deities appropriated from Greek mythology (Jupiter, Juno, Neptune, Minerva etc). Religious cults were also popular – the Egyptian gods Isis and Serapis enjoyed a mass

## EMPERORS' WHO'S WHO

Of the 250 or so emperors of the Roman Empire, only a few were truly heroic. Here we highlight 10 of the best, worst and completely mad.

➡ **Augustus (27 BC–AD 14)** Rome's first emperor. Ushers in a period of peace and security; the arts flourish and many monuments are built, including the Ara Pacis and Pantheon.

➡ **Caligula (37–41)** Emperor number 3 after Augustus and Tiberius. Remains popular until illness leads to the depraved behaviour for which he is famous. Is murdered by his bodyguards on the Palatino.

➡ **Claudius (41–54)** Expands the Roman Empire and conquers Britain. Is eventually poisoned, probably at the instigation of Agrippina, his wife and Nero's mother.

➡ **Nero (54–68)** Initially rules well but later slips into insanity – he has his mother murdered, persecutes the Christians and attempts to turn half the city into a palace. He is eventually forced into suicide.

➡ **Vespasian (69–79)** First of the Flavian dynasty, he imposes peace and cleans up the imperial finances. His greatest legacy is the Colosseum.

➡ **Trajan (98–117)** Conquers the east and rules over the empire at its zenith. Back home he revamps Rome's city centre, adding a forum, market place and column, all of which still stand.

➡ **Hadrian (117–38)** Puts an end to imperial expansion and constructs walls to mark the empire's borders. He rebuilds the Pantheon and has one of the ancient world's greatest villas built at Tivoli.

➡ **Aurelian (270–75)** Does much to control the rebellion that sweeps the empire at the end of the 3rd century. Starts construction of the city walls that bear his name.

➡ **Diocletian (284–305)** Splits the empire into eastern and western halves in 285. Launches a savage persecution of the Christians as he struggles to control the empire's eastern reaches.

➡ **Constantine I (306–37)** Although based in Byzantium (later renamed Constantinople in his honour), he legalises Christianity and embarks on a church-building spree in Rome.

| 754 | 800 | 1084 | 1300 |
|---|---|---|---|
| Pope Stephen II and Pepin, king of the Franks, cut a deal resulting in the creation of the Papal States. The papacy is to rule Rome until Italian unification. | Pope Leo III crowns Pepin's son, Charlemagne, Holy Roman Emperor during Christmas mass at St Peter's Basilica. A red disk in the basilica marks the spot where it happened. | Rome is sacked by a Norman army after Pope Gregory VII invites them in to help him against the besieging forces of the Holy Roman Emperor Henry IV. | Pope Boniface VIII proclaims Rome's first ever Jubilee, offering a full pardon to anyone who makes the pilgrimage to the city. Up to 200,000 people are said to have come. |

following, as did Mithras, a heroic saviour-god of vaguely Persian origin, who was worshipped by male-only devotees in underground temples.

## Emergence of Christianity

Christianity entered this religious cocktail in the 1st century AD, sweeping in from Judaea, a Roman province in what is now Israel and the West Bank. Its early days were marred by persecution, most notably under Nero (r 54–68), but it slowly caught on, thanks to its popular message of heavenly reward and the evangelising efforts of Sts Peter and Paul. However, it was the conversion of the Emperor Constantine (r 306–37) that really set Christianity on the path to European domination. In 313 Constantine issued the Edict of Milan, officially legalising Christianity, and later, in 378, Theodosius (r 379–95) made Christianity Rome's state religion. By this time, the Church had developed a sophisticated organisational structure based on five major sees: Rome, Constantinople, Alexandria, Antioch and Jerusalem. At the outset, each bishopric carried equal weight but in subsequent years Rome emerged as the senior party. The reasons for this were partly political – Rome was the wealthy capital of the Roman Empire – and partly religious – early Christian doctrine held that St Peter, founder of the Roman Church, had been sanctioned by Christ to lead the universal Church.

## Papal Control

But while Rome had control of Christianity, the Church had yet to conquer Rome. This it did in the dark days that followed the fall of the Roman Empire by skilfully stepping into the power vacuum created by the demise of imperial power. And although no one person can take credit for this, Pope Gregory the Great (r 590–604) did more than most to lay the groundwork. A leader of considerable foresight, he won many friends by supplying free bread to Rome's starving citizens and restoring the city's water supply. He also stood up to the menacing Lombards, who presented a very real threat to the city.

It was this threat that pushed the papacy into an alliance with the Frankish kings, an alliance that resulted in the creation of the two great powers of medieval Europe: the Papal States and the Holy Roman Empire. In Rome, the battle between these two superpowers translated into endless feuding between the city's baronial families and frequent attempts by the French to claim the papacy for their own. This political and military fighting eventually culminated in the papacy transferring to the French city of Avignon between 1309 and 1377, and the Great Schism (1378–1417), a period in which the Catholic world was headed by two popes, one in Rome and one in Avignon.

**Emperors' Hall of Shame**

Caligula(37–41)

Elagabalus (218–224)

Caracalla (211–217)

Commodus (180–192)

Nero (54–68)

| 1309 | 1347 | 1378–1417 | 1506 |
|---|---|---|---|
| Fighting between French-backed pretenders to the papacy and Roman nobility ends in Pope Clement V transferring to Avignon. Only in 1377 does Pope Gregory XI return to Rome. | Cola di Rienzo, a local notary, declares himself dictator of Rome. Surprisingly, he's welcomed by the people; less surprisingly he's later driven out of town by the hostile aristocracy. | Squabbling between factions in the Catholic Church leads to the Great Schism. The pope rules in Rome while the alternative antipope sits in Avignon. | Pope Julius II employs 150 Swiss mercenaries to protect him. The 100-strong Swiss Guard, all practising Catholics from Switzerland, are still responsible for the pope's personal safety. |

As both religious and temporal leaders, Rome's popes wielded influence well beyond their military capacity. For much of the medieval period, the Church held a virtual monopoly on Europe's reading material (mostly religious scripts written in Latin) and was the authority on virtually every aspect of human knowledge. All innovations in science, philosophy and literature had to be cleared by the Church's hawkish scholars, who were constantly on the lookout for heresy.

## Modern Influence

Almost a thousand years on and the Church is still a major influence on modern Italian life. In recent years, Vatican intervention in political and social debate has provoked fierce divisions within Italy. A case in point was a right-to-die case involving a woman who'd been in a vegetative coma since 1992. In November 2008, the Italian High Court ruled that doctors could cease Eluana Englaro's treatment, something that her father had long maintained was what she wanted. The Church, fearing that this was the first step on the road to euthanasia, opposed the decision and fought to have it overruled. Public opinion was divided on the subject but Berlusconi's right-wing government sided with the Vatican and at the last minute tried to halt proceedings with an emergency decree. This provoked outrage from 'right-to-die' activists and criticism from Italy's Head of State, Giorgio Napolitano, who refused to sign the decree. In the end, the High Court's ruling was carried out and Eluana's treatment was interrupted in February 2009. She died a few days later.

This relationship between the Church and Italy's modern political establishment is a fact of life that dates to the establishment of the Italian Republic in 1946. For much of the First Republic (1946–94), the Vatican was closely associated with the Christian Democrat party (DC, *Democrazia Cristiana*), Italy's most powerful party and an ardent opponent of communism. At the same time, the Church, keen to weed communism out of the political landscape, played its part by threatening to excommunicate anyone who voted for Italy's Communist Party (PCI, *Partito Comunista Italiano*). Today, no one political party has a monopoly on Church favour, and politicians across the spectrum tread warily around Catholic sensibilities. But this reverence isn't limited to the purely political sphere; it also informs much press reporting and even law enforcement. In September 2008, Rome's public prosecutor threatened to prosecute a comedian for comments made against the pope, invoking the 1929 Lateran Treaty under which it is a criminal offence to 'offend the honour' of the pope and Italian president. The charge, which ignited a heated debate on censorship and the right to free speech, was eventually dropped by the Italian justice minister.

Via Appia Antica is named after Appius Claudius Caecus, the Roman censor who initiated its construction in 312 BC. He also built Rome's first aqueduct, the Aqua Appia, which brought in water from the Sabine Hills.

| 1508 | 1527 |
| --- | --- |
| Michelangelo starts painting the Sistine Chapel while down the hall Raphael begins to decorate Pope Julius II's private apartments, better known as the Stanze di Raffaello (Raphael Rooms). | Pope Clement VII takes refuge in Castel Sant'Angelo as Rome is overrun by troops loyal to Charles V, king of Spain and Holy Roman Emperor. |

*Ponte Sant'Angelo with Castel Sant'Angelo in the background*

## DONATION OF CONSTANTINE

The most famous forgery in medieval history, the Donation of Constantine is a document in which the Roman Emperor Constantine purportedly grants Pope Sylvester I (r 314–35) and his successors control of Rome and the Western Roman Empire, as well as primacy over the holy sees of Antioch, Alexandria, Constantinople, Jerusalem and all the world's churches. The alleged reason for such generosity was the gratitude Constantine felt towards Sylvester for having cured him of leprosy.

No one is exactly sure when the document was written but the consensus is that it dates to the mid- or late 8th century. Certainly this fits with the widespread theory that the author was a Roman cleric, possibly working with the knowledge of Pope Stephen II (r 752–57).

For centuries the donation was accepted as genuine and used by popes to justify their territorial claims against the Holy Roman emperors and other rival leaders. But in 1440 the Italian humanist and philosopher Lorenzo Valla proved that it was a forgery. By analysing the Latin used in the document he was able to show that it was inconsistent with the Latin used in the 4th century.

## RENAISSANCE, A NEW BEGINNING

Bridging the gap between the Middle Ages and the modern age, the Renaissance (*Rinascimento* in Italian) was a far-reaching intellectual, artistic and cultural movement. It emerged in 14th-century Florence but quickly spread to Rome, where it gave rise to one of the greatest makeovers the city had ever seen.

### Humanism & Rebuilding

The movement's intellectual cornerstone was humanism, a philosophy that focused on the central role of humanity within the universe, a major break from the medieval world view, which had placed God at the centre of everything. It was not anti-religious, though. Many humanist scholars were priests and most of Rome's great works of Renaissance art were commissioned by the Church. In fact, it was one of the most celebrated humanist scholars of the 15th century, Pope Nicholas V (r 1447–84), who is generally considered the harbinger of the Roman Renaissance.

When Nicholas became pope in 1447 Rome was not in a good state. Centuries of medieval feuding had reduced the city to a semi-deserted battleground, and the city's bedraggled population lived in constant fear of plague, famine and flooding (the Tiber regularly broke its banks). In political terms, the papacy was recovering from the trauma of the Great Schism and attempting to face down Muslim encroachment in the east.

You'll see the letters SPQR everywhere in Rome. They were adopted during the Roman Republic and stand for Senatus Populusque Romanus (the Senate and People of Rome).

| 1540 | 1555 | 1626 | 1632 |
|---|---|---|---|
| Pope Paul III officially recognises the Society of Jesus, aka the Jesuits. The order is founded by Ignatius de Loyola, who spends his last days in the Chiesa del Gesù. | As fear pervades Counter-Reformation Rome, Pope Paul IV confines the city's Jews to the area known as the Jewish Ghetto. Official intolerance continues on and off until the 20th century. | After more than 150 years of construction, St Peter's Basilica is consecrated. The hulking basilica remains the largest church in the world until well into the 20th century. | Galileo Galilei is summoned to appear before the Inquisition. He is forced to renounce his belief that the earth revolves around the sun and is exiled to Florence. |

It was against this background that Nicholas decided to rebuild Rome as a showcase of Church power. To finance his plans, he declared 1450 a Jubilee year, a tried and tested way of raising funds by attracting hundreds of thousands of pilgrims to the city (in a Jubilee year anyone who comes to Rome and confesses receives a full papal pardon).

Over the course of the next 80 years or so, Rome underwent a complete overhaul. Pope Sixtus IV (r 1471–84) had the Sistine Chapel built and, in 1471, gave the people of Rome a selection of bronzes that became the first exhibits of the Capitoline Museums. Julius II (r 1503–13) laid Via del Corso and Via Giulia, and ordered Bramante to rebuild St Peter's Basilica. Michelangelo frescoed the Sistine Chapel and designed the dome of St Peter's, while Raphael inspired a whole generation of painters with his masterful grasp of perspective.

**Longest-Serving Popes**

St Peter (30–67)

Pius XI (1846–78)

John Paul II (1978–2005)

Leo XIII (1878–1903)

Pius Vi (1775–99)

## The Sack of Rome & Protestant Protest

But outside Rome an ill wind was blowing. The main source of trouble was the longstanding conflict between the Holy Roman Empire, led by the Spanish Charles V, and the Italian city states. This simmering tension came to a head in 1527 when Rome was invaded by Charles' marauding army and ransacked as Pope Clement VII (r 1523–34) hid in Castel Sant'Angelo. The sack of Rome, regarded by most historians as the nail in the coffin of the Roman Renaissance, was a hugely traumatic event. It left the papacy reeling and gave rise to the view that the Church had been greatly weakened by its own moral shortcomings. That the Church was corrupt was well known, and it was with considerable public support that Martin Luther pinned his famous 95 Theses to a church door in Wittenberg in 1517, thus sparking off the Protestant Reformation.

The patron saints of Rome, Peter and Paul, were both executed during Nero's persecution of the Christians between 64 and 68. Paul, who as a Roman citizen was entitled to a quick death, was beheaded, while Peter was crucified upside down on the Vatican hill.

## The Counter-Reformation

The Catholic reaction to the Reformation was all-out. The Counter-Reformation was marked by a second wave of artistic and architectural activity, as the Church once again turned to bricks and mortar to restore its authority. But in contrast to the Renaissance, the Counter-Reformation was a period of persecution and official intolerance. With the full blessing of Pope Paul III, Ignatius Loyola founded the Jesuits in 1540, and two years later the Holy Office was set up as the Church's final appeals court for trials prosecuted by the Inquisition. In 1559 the Church published the *Index Librorum Prohibitorum* (Index of Prohibited Books) and began to persecute intellectuals and freethinkers. Galileo Galilei (1564–1642) was forced to renounce his assertion of the Copernican astronomical system, which held that the earth moved around the sun. He was summoned by the Inquisition to Rome in 1632 and exiled to Florence for the rest of his

| 1656–67 | 1798 | 1870 | 1883 |
|---|---|---|---|
| Gian Lorenzo Bernini lays out Piazza San Pietro for Pope Alexander VII. Bernini, along with his great rival Francesco Borromini, are the leading exponents of Roman baroque. | Napoleon marches into Rome, forcing Pope Pius VI to flee. A republic is announced, but it doesn't last long and in 1801 Pius VI's successor Pius VII returns to Rome. | Nine years after Italian unification, Rome's city walls are breached at Porta Pia and Pope Pius IX is forced to cede the city to Italy. Rome becomes the Italian capital. | In the small town of Forlì in Emilia-Romagna, Italy's future dictator Benito Mussolini is born. An ardent socialist, Mussolini rises through the ranks of the Italian Socialist Party. |

life. Giordano Bruno (1548–1600), a freethinking Dominican monk, fared worse. Arrested in Venice in 1592, he was burned at the stake eight years later in Campo de' Fiori. The spot is today marked by a sinister statue.

Despite, or perhaps because of, the Church's policy of zero tolerance, the Counter-Reformation was largely successful in re-establishing papal prestige. And in this sense it can be seen as the natural finale to the Renaissance that Nicholas V had kicked off in 1450. From being a rural backwater with a population of around 20,000 in the mid-15th century, Rome had grown to become one of Europe's great 17th-century cities, home to Christendom's most spectacular churches and a population of some 100,000 people.

## POWER & CORRUPTION

The exercise of power has long gone hand in hand with corruption. As the British historian Lord Acton famously put it in 1887, 'Power tends to corrupt; absolute power corrupts absolutely.' And no one enjoyed greater power than Rome's ancient emperors.

### Caligula

Of all Rome's cruel and insane leaders, few are as notorious as Caligula. A byword for depravity, Caligula was hailed as a saviour when he inherited the empire from his great-uncle Tiberius in AD 37. Tiberius, a virtual recluse by the end of his reign, had been widely hated, and it was with a great sense of relief that Rome's cheering population welcomed the 25-year-old Caligula to the capital.

Their optimism was to prove ill-founded. After a bout of serious illness, Caligula began showing disturbing signs of mental instability and by AD 40 had taken to appearing in public dressed as a god. He made his senators worship him as a deity and infamously tried to make his horse, Incitatus, a senator. He was accused of all sorts of perversions and progressively alienated himself from all those around him. By AD 41 his Praetorian Guard had had enough and on 24 January its leader, Cassius Chaerea, stabbed him to death.

### Papal Foibles

Debauchery on such a scale was rare in the Renaissance papacy, but corruption was no stranger to the corridors of ecclesiastical power. It was not uncommon for popes to father illegitimate children, and nepotism was rife. The Borgia pope Alexander VI (r 1492–1503) fathered two illegitimate children with the first of his two high-profile

POPE STEPHEN II

The pope's personal kingdom, the Papal States were established in the 8th century after the Frankish King Pepin drove the Lombards out of northern Italy and donated large tracts of territory to Pope Stephen II. At the height of their power, the States encompassed Rome and much of central Italy.

| 1885 | 1922 | 1929 | 1946 |
|---|---|---|---|
| To celebrate Italian unification and honour Italy's first king, Vittorio Emanuele II, construction work begins on Il Vittoriano, the mountainous monument dominating Piazza Venezia. | Some 40,000 Fascists march on Rome. King Vittorio Emanuele III, worried about the possibility of civil war, invites the 39-year-old Mussolini to form a government. | Keen to appease the Church, Mussolini signs the Lateran Treaty, creating the state of the Vatican City. To celebrate, Via della Conciliazione is bulldozed through the medieval Borgo. | The republic is born after Italians vote to abolish the monarchy. Two years later, on 1 January 1948, the Italian constitution becomes law. |

mistresses. The second, Giulia Farnese, was the sister of the cardinal who was later to become Pope Paul III (r 1534–59), himself no stranger to earthly pleasures. When not persecuting heretics during the Counter-Reformation, the Farnese pontiff managed to sire four children.

## Tangentopoli

Corruption has also featured in modern Italian politics, most famously during the 1990s *Tangentopoli* (Kickback City) scandal. Against a backdrop of steady economic growth, the controversy broke in Milan in 1992 when a routine corruption case – accepting bribes in exchange for public works contracts – blew up into a nationwide crusade against corruption.

Led by the 'reluctant hero', magistrate Antonio di Pietro, the *Mani Pulite* (Clean Hands) investigations exposed a political and business system riddled with corruption. Politicians, public officials and businesspeople were investigated and for once no one was spared, not even the powerful Bettino Craxi (prime minister between 1983 and 1989), who, rather than face a trial in Italy, fled to Tunisia in 1993. He was subsequently convicted in absentia on corruption charges and died in self-imposed exile in January 2000.

*Tangentopoli* left Italy's entire establishment in shock, and as the economy faltered – high unemployment and inflation combined with a huge national debt and an extremely unstable lira – the stage was set for the next act in Italy's turbulent political history.

### BERLUSCONI, ITALY'S MEDIA KING

Since 1994 Silvio Berlsconi has dominated Italian political and public life like a modern-day colossus. A colourful, charismatic and highly divisive character, he is Italy's longest-serving post-war PM and one of the country's richest men, with a fortune that the US business magazine *Forbes* puts at US$7.8 billion. His business empire spans the media, advertising, insurance, food, construction and sport – he owns Italy's most successful football team, AC Milan.

For much of his controversial political career, he has been criticised for his hold over Italy's media and, in particular, for his control of the nation's TV output. Italian TV is dominated by two networks – RAI, the Rome-based state broadcaster, and Mediaset, Italy's largest private media company – and Berlusconi has major interests in both camps. He's the controlling shareholder of Mediaset and as PM wields enormous influence over RAI. This 'conflict of interest' has long aroused debate, both inside and outside Italy, and is one of the reasons Freedom House, the US-based press watchdog, only gives Italy a 'partly free' freedom of press rating.

For more on Berlusconi's trials and tribulations, see the Rome Today essay, p250.

| 1957 | 1960 |
|---|---|
| Leaders of Italy, France, West Germany, Belgium, Holland and Luxembourg sign the Treaty of Rome establishing the European Economic Community. | Rome stages the Olympic Games while Federico Fellini makes *La Dolce Vita* in Cinecittà film studios. Meanwhile Stanley Kubrick is using Cinecittà to film his Roman epic, *Spartacus*. |

*Cinecittà Film Studios*

Chief among the actors were Francesco Rutelli, a suave media-savvy operator who oversaw a successful citywide cleanup as mayor of Rome (1993–2001), and the larger-than-life media magnate Silvio Berlusconi, whose three terms as prime minister (1994, 200–06 and 2008–) have been dogged by controversy and scandal.

## THE FIRST TOURISTS

As a religious centre Rome has long attracted millions of pilgrims. In 1300 Pope Boniface VIII proclaimed the first Jubilee Year, with the promise of a full pardon for anyone who made the pilgrimage to St Peter's Basilica and the Basilica di San Giovanni in Laterano. Hundreds of thousands came and the Church basked in popular glory. In 2000 some 24 million visitors poured into the city for Pope John Paul II's Jubilee. However, it was in the late 18th and early 19th centuries that Rome's reputation as a tourist destination was born.

### Gentlemen Visitors & Romantic Poets

The Grand Tour, the 18th-century version of the gap year, was considered an educational rite of passage for wealthy young men from northern Europe, and Britain in particular. In the 19th century it became fashionable for young ladies to travel, chaperoned by spinster aunts, but in the late 1700s the tour was largely a male preserve.

The overland journey through France and into Italy followed the medieval pilgrim route, entering Italy via the St Bernard Pass and descending the west coast before cutting in to Florence and then down to Rome. After a sojourn in the capital, tourists would venture down to Naples, where the newly discovered ruins of Pompeii and Herculaneum were causing much excitement, before heading up to Venice.

Rome, enjoying a rare period of peace, was perfectly set up for this English invasion. The city was basking in the aftermath of the 17th-century baroque building boom, and a craze for all things classical was sweeping Europe. Rome's papal authorities were also crying out for money after their excesses had left the city coffers bare, reducing much of the population to abject poverty.

Thousands came, including Goethe, who stopped off to write his 1817 travelogue *Italian Journey,* and Byron, Shelley and Keats, who all fuelled their romantic sensibilities in the city's vibrant streets. So many English people stayed around Piazza di Spagna that locals christened the area *er ghetto de l'inglesi* (the English ghetto). Trade in antiquities flourished and local artists did a roaring business producing etchings for souvenir-hungry visitors.

The Borgias, led by family patriarch Rodrigo, aka Pope Alexander VI (r 1492–1503), were one of Renaissance Rome's most notorious families. Machiavelli is said to have modelled *Il Principe* (*The Prince*) on Rodrigo's son, Cesare, while his daughter, Lucrezia, earned a reputation as a femme fatal with a penchant for poisoning her enemies.

| 1968 | 1978 | 1991 | 1992–93 |
|---|---|---|---|
| Widespread student unrest results in mass protests across Italy. In Rome, students clash with police at La Sapienza's architecture faculty, an event remembered as the Battle of Valle Giulia. | Former PM Aldo Moro is kidnapped and shot by a cell of the extreme left-wing *Brigate Rosse* (Red Brigades) during Italy's *anni di piombo* (years of lead). | On 1 January Italy and 10 other European countries adopt the euro as their official currency. Critics later blame this for the country's economic woes. | A nationwide anti-corruption crusade, *Mani Pulitei* (Clean Hands), shakes the political and business establishment. Many high-profile figures are arrested. |

Artistically, rococo was the rage of the moment. The Spanish Steps, built between 1723 and 1726, proved a major hit with tourists, as did the exuberant Trevi Fountain.

## THE GHOSTS OF FASCISM

Rome's Fascist history is a deeply sensitive and highly charged subject. In recent years historians on both sides of the political spectrum have accused each other of recasting the past to suit their views: left-wing historians have accused their right-wing counterparts of glossing over the more unpleasant aspects of Mussolini's regime, while right-wingers have attacked their left-wing colleagues for whitewashing the facts to perpetuate an over-simplified myth of antifascism.

### Mussolini

Benito Mussolini was born in 1883 in Forlì, a small town in Emilia-Romagna. As a young man he was an active member of the Italian Socialist Party, rising through the ranks to become editor of the party's official newspaper, *Avanti!* However, service in WWI and Italy's subsequent descent into chaos led to a change of heart and in 1919 he founded the Italian Fascist Party. Calling for rights for war veterans, law and order, and a strong nation, the party won support from disillusioned soldiers, many of whom joined the squads of Blackshirts that Mussolini used to intimidate his political enemies.

In 1921 Mussolini was elected to the Chamber of Deputies. His parliamentary support was limited but on 28 October 1922 he marched on Rome with 40,000 black-shirted followers. The march was largely symbolic but it had the desired effect. Fearful of civil war between the Fascists and Socialists, King Vittorio Emanuele III invited Mussolini to form a government. His first government was a coalition of Fascists, nationalists and liberals, but victory in the 1924 elections left him much better placed to consolidate his personal power, and by the end of 1925 he had seized complete control of Italy. In order to silence the Church he signed the Lateran Treaty in 1929, which made Catholicism the state religion and recognised the sovereignty of the Vatican State.

On the home front, Mussolini embarked on a huge building program: Via dei Fori Imperiali and Via della Conciliazione were laid out; parks were opened on the Oppio hill and at Villa Celimontana; the Imperial Forums and the temples at Largo di Torre Argentina were excavated; and the monumental Foro Italico sports complex and EUR were built. Abroad, Mussolini invaded Abyssinia (now Ethiopia) in 1935 and sided with Hitler in 1936. In 1940, from the balcony of Palazzo Venezia, he an-

The Roman Inquisition was set up in the 16th century to counter the threat of Protestantism. It was responsible for prosecuting people accused of heresy, blasphemy, immorality and witchcraft, and although it could, and did, send people for execution, it often imposed lighter punishments such as fines and the recital of prayers.

| 1999 | 2000 | 2001 | 2005 |
|---|---|---|---|
| After 20 years, the Sistine Chapel restoration is finally completed. The Michelangelo frescoes have never looked so vibrant, leading some critics to question the restorers' methods. | Pilgrims pour into Rome from all over the world to celebrate the Catholic Church's Jubilee year. A highpoint is a mass attended by two million people at Tor Vergata university. | Charismatic media tycoon Silvio Berlusconi becomes prime minister for the second time. His first term in 1994 was a short-lived affair; his second lasts the full five-year course. | Pope John Paul II dies after 27 years on the papal throne. He is replaced by his long-standing ally Josef Ratzinger, who takes the name Benedict XVI. |

nounced Italy's entry into WWII to a vast, cheering crowd. The good humour didn't last, as Rome suffered, first at the hands of its own Fascist regime, then, after Mussolini was ousted in 1943, at the hands of the Nazis. Rome was liberated from German occupation on 4 June 1944.

## The Post-War Period

But defeat in WWII didn't kill off Italian Fascism, and in 1946 hardline Mussolini supporters founded the *Movimento Sociale Italiano* (MSI; Italian Social Movement). For close on 50 years this overtly fascist party participated in mainstream Italian politics, while on the other side of the spectrum the *Partito Comunista Italiano* (PCI; Italian Communist Party) grew into Western Europe's largest communist party. The MSI was finally dissolved in 1994, when Gianfranco Fini rebranded it as the post-Fascist *Alleanza Nazionale* (AN; National Alliance). AN remained an important political player until it was incorporated into Silvio Berlusconi's *Popolo delle Libertà* coalition in 2009.

Outside the political mainstream, Fascism (along with communism) was a driving force of the domestic terrorism that rocked Italy during the *anni di piombo* (years of lead), between the late 1960s and early 1980s. In these years, terrorist groups emerged on both sides of the ideological spectrum, giving rise to a spate of politically inspired violence. Most famously, the communist *Brigate Rosse* (Red Brigades) kidnapped and killed former PM Aldo Moro in 1978, and the neo-fascist Armed Revolutionary Nuclei bombed Bologna train station in 1980, killing 85 people and leaving up to 200 injured.

In more recent years, extreme right-wing groups have been connected with organised football hooliganism. According to figures released by Italy's Home Ministry in 2009, up to 234 fan groups have been identified as having political ties, of which 61 are said to be closely associated with extreme right-wing movements.

Fascism once again hit the headlines in April 2008 when Gianni Alemanno, an ex-MSI activist and member of AN, was elected mayor of Rome. In his first year in office, Alemanno had to walk an ideological tightrope as he tried to sell himself as a mayor for everyone. Inevitably, though, his Fascist past aroused discomfort. The sight of supporters hailing his election victory with the Fascist salute – something he was quick to distance himself from – did not go down well in many quarters and in September 2008 he infuriated Rome's Jewish community by refusing to condemn Fascism as 'absolute evil'. Ironically, two months later he won praise from the community's leader for leading a group of 250 schoolchildren to Auschwitz and urging them never to forget the tragedy of the Holocaust.

---

**HISTORY THE GHOSTS OF FASCISM**

In his 1818 work *Childe Harold's Pilgrimage*, the English poet Lord Byron quotes the words of the 8th-century monk Bede: 'While stands the Coliseum, Rome shall stand; When falls the Coliseum, Rome shall fall! And when Rome falls – the World.'

BYRON

---

| 2008–09 | 2008 | 2010 | 2011 |
|---|---|---|---|
| Berlusconi bounces back for a third term as PM after a two-year spell in opposition. In 2009 he hosts the G8 summit in the earthquake-shattered city of L'Aquila. | Gianni Alemanno, a former member of the neo-fascist party MSI (*Movimento Sociale Italiano*), sweeps to victory in Rome's mayoral elections. The news makes headlines across the world. | Berlusconi's right-wing government survives a parliamentary confidence vote leading to rioting in the city centre. Protesters fight police on Piazza del Popolo and other historic streets. | On 1 May, Pope John Paul II is beatified in front of hundreds of thousands of faithful at Piazza San Pietro. Pope Benedict XVI leads the ceremony, the last step before sainthood. |

# The Arts

**Rome's turbulent history and magical cityscape have long provided inspiration for painters, sculptors, filmmakers, writers and musicians. The great classical works of Roman antiquity fuelled the imagination of Renaissance artists; Counter-Reformation persecution led to baroque art and popular street satire; the trauma of Mussolini and WWII found expression in neorealist cinema. More recently, economic difficulties have led to spending cuts and a dip in morale but the setbacks are borne and Rome's arts scene remains defiantly vibrant.**

## PAINTING & SCULPTURE

Home to some of the Western world's most recognisable art, Rome is a visual feast. Its churches alone contain more masterpieces than many midsize countries and the city's galleries are laden with works by the world's most famous artists.

### Etruscan Groundwork

Laying the groundwork for much later Roman art, the Etruscans placed great importance on their funerary rites and they developed sepulchral decoration into a highly sophisticated artform. Elaborate stone sarcophagi were often embellished with a reclining figure or a couple, typically depicted with a haunting, enigmatic smile. A stunning example is the *Sarcofago degli Sposi* (Sarcophagus of the Betrothed) in the Museo Nazionale Etrusco di Villa Giulia. Underground funerary vaults, such as those unearthed at Tarquinia, were further enlivened with bright, exuberant frescoes. These frequently represented festivals or scenes from everyday life, with stylised figures shown dancing or playing musical instruments, often with little birds or animals in the background.

The Etruscans were also noted for their bronze work and filigree jewellery. Bronze ore was abundant and was used to craft everything from chariots to candelabras, bowls and polished mirrors. One of Rome's most iconic sculptures, the 5th-century-BC *Lupa Capitolina* (Capitoline Wolf), now in the Capitoline Museums, is, in fact, an Etruscan bronze. Etruscan jewellery was unrivalled throughout the Mediterranean and goldsmiths produced elaborate pieces using sophisticated filigree and granulation techniques that were only rediscovered in the 20th century.

For Italy's best collection of Etruscan art, head to the Museo Nazionale Etrusco di Villa Giulia; to see Etruscan treasures in situ head out of town to Cerveteri and Tarquinia.

### Roman Developments

In art, as in architecture, the ancient Romans borrowed heavily from the Etruscans and Greeks. In terms of decorative art, the Roman use of floor mosaics and wall paintings was derived from Etruscan funerary decoration. By the 1st century BC, floor mosaics were a popular form of home decor. Typical themes included landscapes, still lifes, geometric patterns and depictions of gods. Wall mosaics, however, were rare, being unaffordable to all but the wealthiest citizens. In the Museo Nazionale Romano: Palazzo Massimo alle Terme, you'll find some spectacular wall mosaics from Nero's villa in Anzio, as well as a series of superb 1st-century-BC frescoes from Villa Livia, one of the homes of Livia Drusilla, Augustus' wife.

---

**Top Galleries & Museums**

Vatican Museums

Museo e Galleria Borghese

Capitoline Museums

Museo Nazionale Romano: Palazzo Massimo alle Terme

---

The best surviving examples of Etruscan frescoes are found in Tarquinia where up to 6000 tombs have been discovered. Particularly graphic are the erotic paintings in the Tomba della Fustigazione (Tomb of the Flogging).

## Sculpture

Sculpture was an important element of Roman art, and was largely influenced by Greek styles. In fact, early Roman sculptures were often made by Greek artists or were, at best, copies of imported Greek works. They were largely concerned with the male physique and generally depicted visions of male beauty in mythical settings – the *Apollo Belvedere* and the *Laocoön* in the Vatican Museums' Museo Pio-Clementino are classic examples.

However, over time differences began to emerge between Greek and Roman styles. Roman sculpture lost its obsession with form and began to focus on accurate representation, mainly in the form of sculptural portraits. Browse the collections of the Museo Palatino or the Museo Nazionale Romano: Palazzo Massimo alle Terme and you'll be struck by how lifelike – and often ugly – so many of the marble busts are.

In terms of function, Greek art was all about beauty, harmony and dramatic expression, while Roman art was highly propagandistic. From the time of Augustus (r 27 BC–AD 14), art was increasingly used to serve the state, and artists came to be regarded as little more than state functionaries. This new narrative art often took the form of relief decoration recounting the story of great military victories. The Colonna di Traiano and Ara Pacis are two stunning examples of the genre.

### Early Christian Art

The earliest Christian art in Rome are the traces of biblical frescoes in the Catacombe di Priscilla on Via Salaria and the Catacombe di San Sebastiano on Via Appia Antica. These, and other early works, are full of stock images: Lazarus being raised from the dead, Jesus as the good shepherd, the first Christian saints. Symbols also abound: the dove representing peace and happiness, the anchor or trident symbolising the cross, and the fish in reference to an acrostic from the Greek word for fish (Ichthys) which spells out Jesus Christ, Son of God, Saviour.

### Mosaics

With the legalisation of Christianity in the 4th century, these images began to move into the public arena, appearing in mosaics across the city. Mosaic work was the principal artistic endeavour of early Christian Rome and mosaics adorn many of the churches built in this period. Stunning examples include the 4th-century apse mosaic in the Chiesa di Santa Pudenziana, the wonderful mosaics in the vaulted ambulatory of the Mausoleo di Santa Costanza and the 5th-century works in the Basilica di Santa Maria Maggiore.

Eastern influences became much more pronounced between the 7th and 9th centuries, when Byzantine styles swept in from the east, leading to a brighter, golden look. Byzantine art tended to de-emphasise the naturalistic aspects of the classical tradition and exalt the spirit over the body, so glorifying God rather than the man or the state. The best examples in Rome are in the Basilica di Santa Maria in Trastevere and the Chiesa di Santa Prassede, a small 9th-century church built in honour of an early Christian heroine.

### The Renaissance

Originating in late 14th-century Florence, the Renaissance had already made its mark in Tuscany and Venice when it arrived in Rome in the latter half of the 15th century.

But over the next few decades it was to have a profound impact on the city as the top artists of the day were summoned to decorate the many new buildings going up around town.

THE ARTS PAINTING & SCULPTURE

Dramatically ensconced in a Richard Meier–designed pavilion, the Ara Pacis is a key work of ancient Roman sculpture. The vast marble altar is covered with detailed reliefs, including one showing Augustus with his family.

## Saints Glossary

As befits the world's Catholic capital, Rome is overrun by saints. Roads are named after them, churches commemorate them and paintings portray them in all their righteous glory. Here we list some of the big-name *santi* (saints) you'll come across in Rome.

**Sant'Agnese** (d 305, b Rome) Patron saint of virgins and Girl Scouts, St Agnes died a martyr at the age of 13. According to tradition, she was beheaded on Piazza Navona, although not before a last-minute miracle. Just before she was executed her tormentors stripped her naked, only to recoil in amazement as her hair instantly grew to cover her body.

**Santa Caterina di Siena** (1347–80, b Siena, Tuscany) An avid letter writer – her 300-plus surviving letters are considered masterpieces of early Tuscan literature – St Catherine worked tirelessly to bring the papacy back from Avignon to Rome. She's now mostly buried in the Chiesa di Santa Maria Sopra Minerva, although her head and right thumb are in Siena and her foot is in Venice.

**Santa Cecilia** (2nd century, b Rome) A popular Roman saint, St Cecilia is the patron of music and musicians. She earned this accolade after singing for three days after her executors botched her beheading. She was buried in the Catacombe di San Callisto and was later moved to the Basilica di Santa Cecilia in Trastevere.

**San Clemente** (d 97, b Rome) St Clement was ordained by St Peter and became the fourth pope in 88 AD. He was later banished to the Crimean mines by Trajan and thrown into the Black Sea by guards fed up with his continual preaching. The sea water receded some time later, revealing a tomb miraculously containing his body.

**Sant'Elena** (c 248–328, b Turkey) St Helena is best known as the mother of Constantine, Rome's first Christian emperor. She traipsed off to the Holy Land in search of the Holy Cross and sent pieces to Rome and Constantinople.

**San Giovanni** (d c 101) Author of the gospel of St John and the Book of Revelation, St John was a travelling companion of Jesus and friend of St Peter. He was tortured by the emperor Domitian but apparently emerged unscathed from a cauldron of boiling oil. The Basilica di San Giovanni in Laterano is dedicated to him and St John the Baptist.

**San Gregorio** (540–604, b Rome) Born into a family of saints, St Gregory made his name as Pope Gregory the Great. He sent St Augustine to convert the Brits, built monasteries and lent his name to a style of liturgical singing – the Gregorian chant. He is the patron saint of choirboys.

**Sant'Ignazio di Loyola** (1491–1556, b Guipuzcoa, Spain) Although Spanish by birth, St Ignatius Loyola earned his Roman colours by founding the Jesuits in Rome in 1540. He spent his last days in a suite of rooms at the Chiesa del Gesù.

**San Lorenzo** (c 225–258, b Huesca, Spain) A canny financial manager, St Lawrence safeguarded the assets of the 3rd-century Roman Church when not helping the sick, poor and crippled. His patronage of chefs and cooks results from his indescribably awful death – he was grilled to death on a griddle iron.

**San Marco** (1st century AD, b Libya) Although a native of Libya and the patron saint of Venice, St Mark is said to have written the second gospel while in Rome. The Basilica di San Marco stands over the house where he used to stay when in town.

**San Matteo** (1st century AD, b Ethiopia) As patron saint of bankers, stockbrokers and accountants, St Matthew will have been in much demand recently. A Roman tax collector turned apostle, he is portrayed by Caravaggio in the Chiesa di Luigi dei Francesi.

**San Paolo** (c 3–65, b Turkey) Saul the Christian hater became St Paul the travelling evangelist after conversion on the road to Damascus. He was eventually decapitated in Rome during Nero's persecution of the Christians. Along with St Peter, he's the capital's patron saint. Their joint feast day, a holiday in Rome, is 29 June.

**San Pietro** (d 64, b Galilee) One of Rome's two patron saints, St Peter is said to have founded the Roman Catholic Church after Jesus gave him the keys to the

One of the greatest artists of the Middle Ages was Pietro Cavallini (c 1240–1330), a Roman-born painter and mosaic designer. Little is known about his life but his most famous work is the *Giudizio Universale* (Last Judgement) fresco in the Chiesa di Santa Cecilia in Trastevere.

Kingdom of Heaven. He was crucified upside down and buried on the spot where St Peter's Basilica now stands. Relics of his head are kept in the Basilica di San Giovanni in Laterano.

**Santa Prassede** (d 164) Daughter of a Roman senator and sister of fellow saint, St Pudenziana, St Praxedes made her name harbouring Christians in a time of persecution and burying their dead in a well on her family estate.

**Santa Pudenziana** (d 160) Little is known of the virgin martyr St Pudenziana, except that she was St Praxedes' sister, and that she appears in the apse mosaic in Chiesa di Santa Pudenziana, one of Rome's oldest churches.

**San Sebastiano** (d c 288, b France) St Sebastian distinguished himself as an officer in Diocletian's imperial army before converting to Christianity. Diocletian wasn't amused and had him tied to a tree and turned into an archery target. He survived only to be beaten to death. He's the patron saint of archers and police officers.

**Santa Teresa** (1515–1582, b Avila, Spain) The Spanish St Theresa is the subject of Bernini's famous sculpture *Santa Teresa traffita dall'amore di Dio*. When not founding Carmelite convents or writing mystical literature, she often experienced bouts of religious ecstasy.

## Michelangelo & the Sistine Chapel

Rome's most celebrated works of Renaissance art are Michelangelo's paintings in the Sistine Chapel – the Genesis ceiling frescoes, painted between 1508 and 1512, and the *Giudizio Universale* (Last Judgment), which he worked on between 1536 and 1541. Regarded as the high point of Western artistic achievement, these two works completely outshine the chapel's wall paintings, themselves masterpieces of 15th-century fresco art painted by Pietro Vannucci (Perugino; 1446–1523), Sandro Botticelli (1445–1510), Domenico Ghirlandaio (1449–94), Cosimo Rosselli (1439–1507), Luca Signorelli (c 1445–1523) and Bernadino di Betto (Pinturicchio; 1454–1513).

Michelangelo Buanarroti (1475–1564), born near Arrezzo in Tuscany, was the embodiment of the Renaissance spirit. A painter, sculptor, architect and occasional poet, he, more than any other artist of the era, left an indelible mark on the Eternal City. The Sistine chapel, his *Pietà* in St Peter's Basilica, his sculptures in the city's churches – his masterpieces are legion and they remain city highlights to this day.

## The Human Form

The human form was central to much Renaissance art, and Michelangelo and Leonardo da Vinci famously studied human anatomy to perfect their representations. Underlying this trend was the humanist philosophy, the intellectual foundation stone of the Renaissance, which held man to be central to the God-created universe and beauty to represent a deep inner virtue.

This focus on the human body led artists to develop a far greater appreciation of perspective. Early Renaissance painters had made great strides in formulating rules of perspective but they found that the rigid formulae they were experimenting with often made harmonious arrangements of figures difficult. This was precisely the challenge that Raffaello Sanzio (Raphael; 1483–1520) tackled in *La Scuola d'Atene* (The School of Athens; 1510–11) in the Stanze di Raffaello in the Vatican Museums and the *Trionfo di Galatea* in Villa Farnesina.

Originally from Urbino, Raphael arrived in Rome in 1508 and went on to become the most influential painter of his generation. A paid-up advocate of the Renaissance exaltation of beauty, he painted many versions of the Madonna and Child, all of which epitomise the Western model of 'ideal beauty' that perseveres to this day.

**THE ARTS** PAINTING & SCULPTURE

Michelangelo and Raphael didn't get on. Despite this, Raphael felt compelled to honour his elder after sneaking into the Sistine Chapel to look at Michelangelo's half-finished ceiling frescoes. He was so impressed with what he saw that he painted Michelangelo into his masterpiece *La Scuola d'Atene*.

**Key Renaissance Works**

*Sistine Chapel frescoes (Vatican Museums)*

*Pietà (St Peter's Basilica)*

*La Scuola d'Atene (Vatican Museums)*

*Deposizione di Cristo (Galleria e Museo Borghese)*

*Christ Giving the Keys to St Peter (Sistine Chapel)*

## Counter-Reformation & The Baroque

The baroque burst onto Rome's art scene in the early 17th century in a swirl of emotional energy. Combining a dramatic sense of dynamism with highly charged emotion, it was enthusiastically appropriated by the Catholic Church. At the time the Church was viciously persecuting Counter-Reformation heresy and the powerful popes of the day saw baroque art as an ideal propaganda tool. They eagerly championed the likes of Caravaggio, Gian Lorenzo Bernini, Domenichino, Pietro da Cortona and Alessandro Algardi.

Not surprisingly, much baroque art has a religious theme and you'll often find depictions of martyrdoms, ecstasies and miracles. The use of coloured marble, gold leaf and ornamental church settings are further trademarks.

An artist, architect and art historian, Giorgio Vasari (1511–1574) was the first person to use the term 'Middle Ages'. He wrote it in his classic work of art history, *The Lives of the Artists* (1550), to describe the period between classical antiquity and the 16th century Renaissance.

### Caravaggio

One of the key painters of the period was Caravaggio (1573–1610), the Milan-born *enfant terrible* of Rome's art world. A controversial and often violent character, he arrived in Rome around 1590 and immediately set about re-writing the artistic rule books. While his peers and Catholic patrons sought to glorify and overwhelm, he painted nature as he saw it. He had no time for 'ideal beauty' and caused uproar with his lifelike portrayal of hitherto sacrosanct subjects – his barefoot depiction of the Virgin Mary in the *Madonna dei Pellegrini* in the Chiesa di Sant'Agostino is typical of his audacious approach. However, not even his harshest critics could question his technical virtuosity, and his skilful use of chiaroscuro as a dramatic device.

### Gian Lorenzo Bernini

But while Caravaggio shocked his patrons, Gian Lorenzo Bernini (1598–1680) delighted them with his stunning sculptures. More than anyone else before or since, Bernini was able to capture a moment, freezing emotions and conveying a sense of dramatic action. His depiction of *Santa Teresa traffita dall'amore di Dio* (Ecstasy of St Teresa) in the Chiesa di Santa Maria della Vittoria does just that, blending realism, eroticism and theatrical spirituality in a work that is widely considered one of the greatest of the baroque period. Further evidence of his genius is on show at the Museo e Galleria Borghese, where you can marvel at his ability to make stone-cold marble seem soft as flesh in the *Ratto di Proserpina* (Rape of Persephone), or his magnificent depiction of Daphne transforming into a laurel tree in *Apollo e Dafne* (Apollo and Daphne).

**Big-Name Baroque Artists**

Annibale Carracci (1560–1609)

Michelangelo Merisi da Caravaggio (1573–1610)

Domenichino (1581–1641)

Pietro da Cortona (1596–1669)

Gia Lorenzo Bernini (1598–1680)

### Frescoes

Fresco painting continued to provide work for artists well into the 17th century. Important exponents include Domenichino (1581–1641), whose decorative works adorn the Chiesa di San Luigi dei Francesi and the Chiesa di Sant'Andrea della Valle; Pietro da Cortona (1596–1669), author of the *Trionfo della Divina Provvidenza* (Triumph of Divine Providence) in Palazzo Barberini; and Annibale Carracci (1560–1609), the genius behind the frescoes in Palazzo Farnese, said by some to equal those of the Sistine Chapel.

### The 20th-century

In artistic terms, the early 20th century was marked by the development of two very different movements: futurism and metaphysical painting (*pittura metafisica*), an early form of surrealism.

## Futurism

Often associated with fascism, Italian futurism was an ambitious movement, embracing not only the visual arts but also architecture, music, fashion and theatre. It started with the publication of Filippo Tommaso Marinetti's *Manifesto del futurismo* (Manifesto of Futurism) in 1909, which was backed up a year later by the futurist painting manifesto written by Umberto Boccioni (1882–1916), Giacomo Balla (1871–1958), Luigi Russolo (1885–1947) and Gino Severini (1883–1966). A rallying cry for modernism and a vitriolic rejection of artistic traditions, these manifestos highlighted dynamism, speed, machinery and technology as their central tenets. They were also nationalistic and highly militaristic.

One of the movement's founding fathers, Giacomo Balla (1871–1958) encapsulated the futurist ideals in works such as *Espansione dinamica Velocità*, one of a series of paintings exploring the dynamic nature of motion, and *Forme Grido Viva l'Italia*, an abstract work inspired by the futurists' desire for Italy to enter WWI. Both are on show at the Galleria Nazionale d'Arte Moderna.

## Metaphysical Painting

In contrast to the brash vitality of futurism, metaphysical paintings were peopled by mysterious images conjured up from the subconscious world. Its most famous exponent was Giorgio de Chirico (1888–1978), whose visionary works were a major influence on the French surrealist movement. With their stillness and sense of foreboding they often show classical subjects presented as enigmatic mannequin-like figures. Good examples include *Ettore e Andromeda* in the Galleria Nazionale d'Arte Moderna, and *Orfeo Solitario* in the Museo Carlo Bilotti.

---

### ROME'S TOP ART CHURCHES

You don't need to visit Rome's galleries or museums to enjoy great art. The city's churches, which are all fee to enter, contain works by many celebrated artists. Here we list 10 of the best.

➡ St Peter's Basilica (p184) Michelangelo's divine *Pietà* is just one of the many masterpieces on display at the Vatican's showcase basilica.

➡ Basilica di San Pietro in Vincoli (p130) Moses stands as the muscular centrepiece of Michelangelo's unfinished tomb of Pope Julius II.

➡ Chiesa di San Luigi dei Francesi (p86) Frescoes by Domenichino are outshone by three Caravaggio canvases depicting the life and death of St Matthew.

➡ Chiesa di Santa Maria del Popolo (p106) A veritable gallery with frescoes by Pinturicchio, a Raphael-designed chapel, and two paintings by Caravaggio.

➡ Chiesa di Santa Maria della Vittoria (p111) The church's innocuous exterior gives no clues that this is home to Bernini's extraordinary *Santa Teresa traffita dall'amore di Dio*.

➡ Chiesa di Santa Prassede (p132) The Cappella di San Zenone features some of Rome's most brilliant Byzantine mosaics.

➡ Chiesa del Gesù (p81) Feast your eyes on the magnificent fresco *Trionfo del Nome di Gesù* (Triumph of the Name of Jesus) at Rome's top Jesuit church.

➡ Basilica di Santa Maria Maggiore (p129) Admire beautiful Cosmati flooring and, high up in the triumphal arch, wonderful 5th-century mosaics.

➡ Chiesa di Santa Maria Sopra Minerva (p78) Rome's only Gothic church boasts its own minor Michelangelo, a sculpture of *Cristo Risorto* (Christ Bearing the Cross).

➡ Chiesa di Sant'Agostino (p80) Houses the *Madonna dei Pellegrini*, one of Caravaggio's most controversial paintings, and a fresco by Raphael.

## Contemporary Scene

Rome's contemporary arts scene was given a major boost by the opening of two flagship arts centres in 2010 and 2011: the Museo Nazionale delle Arti del XXI Secolo, better known as MAXXI, and the Museo d'Arte Contemporanea di Roma, also known by its acronym, MACRO. Both have attracted widespread attention, although the jury is still out as to whether the art they exhibit is equal to the sleek, architecturally innovative buildings that stage it.

Rome's premier modern art event is the annual Road to Contemporary Art fair. The fourth edition, held in May 2011 at MACRO Future, a post-industrial exhibition space in Rome's former slaughterhouse, proved a considerable success, hosting more than 100 international and Italian exhibitors and attracting over 43,000 visitors.

In terms of home-grown talent, Rome's artistic hub is the Pastificio Cerere in San Lorenzo. A pasta factory turned art studio, it is home to a number of working artists, including Maurizio Savini, best known for his sculptures made from pink chewing gum. Other Rome-based artists to look out for include the video-artist Elisabetta Benassi, and Tiziano Lucci, who has exhibited in Britain, Germany, the US and Argentina.

Street art also thrives in Rome, particularly in the suburbs of San Lorenzo, Pigneto and Ostiense, where walls are covered in stencil art, poster work and graffiti.

# LITERATURE

A history of authoritarian rule has given rise to a rich literary tradition, encompassing everything from ancient satires to dialect poetry and anti-fascist prose. As a backdrop, Rome has inspired scribes as diverse as Goethe and Dan Brown.

Artemisia Gentileschi (1593–1653) was one of the few women artists of the Renaissance. Stylistically, she was heavily influenced by Caravaggio and many of her paintings depict strong, aggressive women, a fact often attributed to the rape she suffered as a student.

## Cicero, Virgil et al – the Classics

Famous for his blistering oratory, Marcus Tullius Cicero (106–43 BC) was the Roman Republic's pre-eminent author. A brilliant barrister, he became consul in 63 BC and subsequently published many philosophical works and speeches. Fancying himself as the senior statesman, Cicero took the young Octavian under his wing and attacked Mark Antony in a series of 14 speeches, the *Philippics*. These proved fatal, though, for when Octavian changed sides and joined Mark Antony, he demanded and got – Cicero's head.

### Poetry & Satire

A contemporary of Cicero, Catullus (c 84–54 BC) cut a very different figure. A passionate and influential poet, he is best known for his epigrams and erotic verse.

On becoming emperor, Augustus (aka Octavian) encouraged the arts, and Virgil (70–19 BC), Ovid, Horace and Tibullus all enjoyed freedom to write. Of the works produced in this period, it's Virgil's rollicking *Aeneid* that stands out. A glorified mix of legend, history and moral instruction, it tells how Aeneas escapes from Troy and after years of mythical mishaps ends up landing in Italy where his descendants Romulus and Remus eventually found Rome.

Little is known of Decimus Iunius Iuvenalis, better known as Juvenal, but his 16 satires have survived as classics of the genre. Writing in the 1st century AD, he combined an acute mind with a cutting pen, famously scorning the masses as being interested in nothing but 'bread and circuses'.

## Ancient Histories

The two major historians of the period were Livy (59 BC–AD 17) and Tacitus (c 56–116). Although both wrote in the early days of empire they displayed very different styles. Livy, whose history of the Roman Republic was probably used as a school textbook, cheerfully mixed myth with fact to produce an entertaining and popular tome. Tacitus, on the other hand, took a decidedly colder approach. His *Annals* and *Histories,* which cover the early years of the Roman Empire, are cutting and often witty, although imbued with an underlying pessimism.

## Street Writing & Popular Poetry

Rome's tradition of street writing, which today survives in the form of colourful graffiti art, goes back to the dark days of the 17th century. With the Church systematically suppressing every whiff of criticism, Counter-Reformation Rome was not a great place for budding authors. As a way round censorship, disgruntled Romans began posting *pasquinades* (anonymous messages; named after the first person who wrote one) on the city's so-called speaking statues. These messages, often archly critical of the authorities, were sensibly posted in the dead of night and then gleefully circulated around town the following day. The most famous speaking statue stands in Piazza Pasquino near Piazza Navona.

### Dialect Verse

Poking savage fun at the rich and powerful was one of the favourite themes of Gioacchino Belli (1791–1863), one of a trio of poets who made their names writing poetry in Roman dialect. Born poor, Belli started his career with conventional and undistinguished verse, but found the crude and colourful dialect of the Roman streets better suited to his outspoken attacks on the chattering classes.

Carlo Alberto Salustri (1871–1950), aka Trilussa, is the best known of the trio. He, too, wrote social and political satire, although not exclusively so, and many of his poems are melancholy reflections on life, love and solitude. One of his most famous works, the anti-fascist poem *All'Ombra* (In the Shadow), is etched onto a plaque in Piazza Trilussa, the Trastevere square named in his honour.

The poems of Cesare Pescarella (1858–1940) present a vivid portrait of turn-of-the-century Rome. Gritty and realistic, they pull no punches in describing everyday life as lived by Rome's forgotten poor.

## Rome as Inspiration

With its magical cityscape and historic atmosphere, Rome has provided inspiration for legions of foreign authors.

### Romantic Visions

In the 18th century the city was a hotbed of literary activity as historians and Grand Tourists poured in from northern Europe. The German author Johann Wolfgang von Goethe captures the elation of discovering ancient Rome and the colours of the modern city in his celebrated travelogue *Italian Journey* (1817).

Rome was also a magnet for the English Romantic poets. John Keats, Lord Byron, Percy Bysshe Shelley, Mary Shelley and other writers all spent time in the city. Byron, in a typically over-the-top outburst, described Rome as the city of his soul even though he visited only fleetingly. Keats came to Rome in 1821 in the hope that it would cure his ill health, but it didn't and he died of tuberculosis in his lodgings at the foot of the Spanish Steps.

**Roman Reads**

Roman Tales (Alberto Moravia)

That Awful Mess on Via Merulana (Carlo Emilio Gadda)

The Secrets of Rome, Love & Death in the Eternal City (Corrado Augias)

Later, in the 19th century, American author Nathaniel Hawthorne penned his classic *The Marble Faun* (1860) after two years in Italy. Taking inspiration from a sculpture in the Capitoline Museums, he uses a murder story as an excuse to explore his thoughts on art and culture.

## Modern Takes

In the first decade of the 2000s it became fashionable for novelists to use Rome as a backdrop. Dan Brown's thriller *Angels and Demons* (2001) is set in Rome, as is Kathleen A Quinn's warm-hearted love story *Leaving Winter* (2003). Jeanne Kalogridis transports readers back to the 15th century in her sumptuous historical novel *The Borgia Bride* (2006), a sensual account of Vatican scheming and dangerous passions.

Robert Harris's accomplished fictional biography of Cicero, *Imperium* (2006), is one of a number of books set in 1st-century Rome. Steven Saylor's *The Triumph of Caesar* (2009) skilfully evokes the passion, fear and violence that hung in the air during Julius Caesar's last days. Similarly stirring is *Antony and Cleopatra* (2008), the last in Colleen McCollough's Masters of Rome series, which centres on the doomed love triangle between Octavian, Mark Antony and Cleopatra.

Into this historical genre you can add a further sub-genre – the ancient murder-mystery. A good example is Martha Marks' *Rubies of the Viper* (2010), a feminist-tinged mystery praised for its vivid descriptions and page-turning prose.

## Literature & Fascism

A controversial figure, Gabriele D'Annunzio (1863-1938) was the most flamboyant Italian writer of the early 20th century. A WWI fighter pilot and ardent nationalist, he was born in Pescara and settled in Rome in 1881. Forever associated with fascism, he wrote prolifically, both poetry and novels. Of his books, perhaps the most revealing is *Il Fuoco* (The Flame of Life; 1900), a passionate romance in which he portrays himself as a Nietzschean superman born to command.

### The Anti-Fascists

On the opposite side of the political spectrum, Roman-born Alberto Moravia (1907–90) was banned from writing by Mussolini and, together with his wife, Elsa Morante (1912–85), was forced into hiding for a year. The alienated individual and the emptiness of fascist and bourgeois society are common themes in his writing. In *La Romana* (The Woman of Rome; 1947) he explores the broken dreams of a country girl, Adriana, as she slips into prostitution and theft.

The novels of Elsa Morante are characterised by a subtle psychological appraisal of her characters and can be seen as a personal cry of pity for the sufferings of individuals and society. Her 1974 masterpiece, *La Storia* (History), is a tough tale of a half-Jewish woman's desperate struggle for dignity in the poverty of occupied Rome.

Taking a similarly anti-fascist line, Carlo Emilio Gadda (1893–1973) combines murder and black humour in his classic whodunnit, *Quer Pasticciaccio Brutto de Via Merulana* (That Awful Mess on Via Merulana; 1957). Although the mystery is never solved, the book's a brilliant portrayal of the pomposity and corruption that thrived in Mussolini's Rome.

## The Current Crop

Born in Rome in 1966, Niccolò Ammaniti is the king of Rome's literary young guns. In 2007 he won the Premio Strega, Italy's top literary prize for his novel, *Come Dio comanda* (As God Commands), but he's probably best known for *Io Non Ho Paura* (I'm Not Scared; 2001), a soulful study

In 1559 Pope Paul IV published the *Index Librorum Prohibitorum* (Index of Prohibited Books), a list of books forbidden by the Catholic Church. Over the next 400 years, it was revised 20 times, the last edition appearing in 1948. It was officially abolished in 1966.

Rome's most influential contribution to literature was the Vulgate Bible. This dates to the 4th century when Pope Damasus (r 366–384) had his secretary Eusebius Hieronymous, aka St Jerome, translate the bible into accessible Latin. His version is the basis for the bible currently used by the Catholic Church.

of a young boy's awakening to the fact that his father is involved in a child kidnapping. Striking an altogether different chord, Federico Moccia's brand of romance-lite was raised to cult status after the success of the 2004 film *Tre metri sopra il cielo* (Three Metres Above the Sky), the adaptation of his 1992 book.

Other Roman writers making a mark include Licia Troisa, author of the best-selling trio of fantasy novels *Cronache del Mondo Emerso,* and Letizia Muratori, a journalist and novelist whose latest book *Sole senza nessuno* is a modern period-piece set in the fashion world of 1960s Rome.

# CINEMA & TELEVISION

## Cinema

Rome's October film festival is usually a celebratory affair. Billboards go up across the city and Hollywood hotshots glam it up at the Auditorium Parco della Musica in front of banks of flashing photographers. But things didn't exactly go to plan in 2010 when up to a 1000 screenwriters and directors took to the red carpet to protest against government spending cuts. The Italian government is one of the major financiers of Italian cinema and over the past few years it has been systematically slashing investment. This is felt acutely in Rome, where the film industry is an important employer, and the crowds demonstrating on the red carpets were not protesting on artistic grounds, they were seriously worried about their jobs.

### Cannes & Cinecittà

But despite these setbacks the Italian film industry continues to produce movies. Most are aimed at the Italian market but some do make international waves, like Nanni Moretti's eagerly awaited *Habemus Papam* which debuted to critical praise at the 2011 Cannes Film Festival.

Italian filmmakers have long had a good relationship with Cannes and 2008 was a recent highpoint. Matteo Garrone, a young Roman director, took the Grand Prix for *Gomorra* (Gomorrah), a hard-hitting exposé of the Neapolitan mafia, and Paolo Sorrentino scooped the Special Jury Prize for *Il Divo*, an ice-cold portrayal of Giulio Andreotti, Italy's most famous postwar politician.

Recent years have also witnessed a renewal of interest in Rome's filmmaking facilities. Private investment in Cinecittà has lured a number of big-name directors to Rome's legendary studios, including Ron Howard for his 2009 thriller *Angels and Demons,* Mel Gibson for *The Passion of the Christ* (2004), and Martin Scorsese, who had 19th-century New York recreated for his 2002 epic *Gangs of New York.* But competition from cheaper Eastern Europe countries, and a strong euro, is making it increasingly hard for Rome to attract US producers, a problem that Cinecittà hopes to tackle with a €675 million investment plan.

### Roman Directors

Leading the new wave of Roman filmmakers is Matteo Garrone (b 1968), whose *Gomorra* (Gomorrah; 2008) helped seal a reputation already on the up after his 2002 film *L'Imbalsamatore* (The Embalmer). In 2008, he also produced the award-winning comedy *Si Puo Fare,* directed by fellow Roman Giulio Manfredonia (b 1967).

Other directors who enjoyed critical acclaim in the noughties included Emanuele Crialese (b 1965) who won plaudits for the 2006 film *Nuovomondo* (Golden Door) and Saverio Costanzo (b 1975) who hit the bullseye with his 2010 film adaptation of Paolo Giordano's bestselling book *La solitudine dei numeri primi*. Gabriele Muccino (b 1967), director

DARIO ARGENTO

Throughout the 1960s and '70s Italy was one of the world's most prolific producers of horror films. Rome's master of terror was, and still is, Dario Argento (b 1940), director of the 1975 cult classic *Profondo Rosso* (Deep Red) and more than 20 other movies.

of the 2001 smash *L'Ultimo Bacio* (The Last Kiss) returned to his earlier success in 2010 with *Baciami ancora,* a sequel to *L'UIltimo Baccio.*

Before Muccino, Rome was generally represented by Carlo Verdone (b 1950) and Nanni Moretti (b 1953). A comedian in the Roman tradition, Verdone has made a name for himself satirising his fellow citizens in a number of bittersweet comedies which, at best, are very funny, but which are sometimes repetitive and predictable. His 1995 film *Viaggi di Nozze* (Honeymoons) is one of his best.

Moretti, on the other hand, falls into no mainstream tradition. A politically active writer, actor and director, his films are often whimsical and self-indulgent. Arguably his best work, *Caro Diario* (Dear Diary; 1994) earned him the best director prize at Cannes in 1994 – an award that he topped in 2001 when he won the Palme d'Or for *La Stanza del Figlio* (The Son's Room).

**THE ARTS** CINEMA & TELEVISION

After his savage satire on Berlusconi in the film *Il Caimano,* Nanni Moretti turned his hawkish eye on the Church in *Habemus Papam.* A comedy centred on a pope who resigns after treatment for stress, it provoked a surprisingly muted reaction from the Vatican when it opened in summer 2011.

### The Golden Age

For the real golden age of Roman film-making you have to turn the clocks back to the 1940s, when Roberto Rossellini (1906–77) produced a trio of neorealist masterpieces. The first and most famous was *Roma Città Aperta* (Rome Open City; 1945), filmed with brutal honesty in the Prenestina district east of the city centre. Vittorio de Sica (1901–74) kept the neorealist ball rolling in 1948 with *Ladri di Biciclette* (Bicycle Thieves), again filmed in Rome's sprawling suburbs.

Federico Fellini (1920–94) took the creative baton from the neorealists and carried it into the following decades. His disquieting style demands more of audiences, abandoning realistic shots for pointed images at once laden with humour, pathos and double meaning. Fellini's greatest international hit was *La Dolce Vita* (1960), starring Marcello Mastroianni and Anita Ekberg.

## SERGIO LEONE, MR SPAGHETTI WESTERN

Best known for virtually single-handedly creating the spaghetti western, Sergio Leone (1929–89) is a hero to many. Martin Scorsese, Quentin Tarantino and Robert Rodriguez are among the directors who count him as a major influence, while Clint Eastwood owes him his cinematic breakthrough. Astonishingly, he only ever directed seven films.

The son of a silent-movie director, Leone cut his teeth as a screenwriter on a series of sword-and-sandal epics, before working as assistant director on *Quo Vadis?* (1951) and *Ben-Hur* (1959). He made his directorial debut three years later on *Il Colosso di Rodi* (The Colossus of Rhodes; 1961).

However, it was with his famous dollar trilogy – *Per un pugno di dollari* (A Fistful of Dollars; 1964), *Per qualche dollari in piu* (For a Few Dollars More; 1965) and *Il buono, il brutto, il cattivo* (The Good, the Bad and the Ugly; 1966) – that he really hit the big time. The first, filmed in Spain and based on the 1961 samurai flick *Yojimbo,* set the style for the genre. No longer were clean-cut, morally upright heroes pitted against cartoon-style villains, but characters were more complex, often morally ambiguous and driven by self-interest.

Stylistically, Leone introduced a series of innovations that were later to become trademarks. Chief among these was his use of musical themes to identify his characters. And in this he was brilliantly supported by his old schoolmate, Ennio Morricone. One of Hollywood's most prolific composers, Morricone (b 1928) has worked on more than 500 films, but his masterpiece remains his haunting score for *Il buono, il brutto, il cattivo* (The Good, the Bad and the Ugly). A unique orchestration of trumpets, whistles, gunshots, church bells, harmonicas and electric guitars, it was inducted into the Grammy Hall of Fame in 2009.

The films of Pier Paolo Pasolini (1922–75) are similarly demanding. A communist Catholic homosexual, he made films that not only reflect his ideological and sexual tendencies but also offer a unique portrayal of Rome's urban wasteland.

A contemporary of both Pasolini and Fellini, Sergio Leone (1929–89) struck out in a very different direction – see the boxed text, p276.

## Television

The real interest in Italian TV is not so much what's on the screen as the political shenanigans that go on behind it. Unfortunately, none of this real life drama translates to on-screen programming, which remains ratings-driven and advert-drenched. Soap operas, quizzes and reality shows are staples and homemade drama rarely goes beyond the tried and tested, with an incessant stream of films on popes, saints, priests and martyrs. Scantily-clad women, known as *veline,* appear in droves, particularly on the interminable variety shows that run on Saturday evenings and Sunday afternoons.

Italian broadcasters are, on the whole, fairly liberal when it comes to sex and violence, but censorship remains an issue, particularly in current-affairs and news programming. Critics have long accused Silvio Berlusconi of using his position as PM and majority shareholder in Italy's largest private TV company to influence the TV news agenda. And while he simply denies the accusation, the debate is set to rage for as long as he remains a political force.

# MUSIC

Despite cutbacks in public funding, Rome's music scene is in good health. International orchestras perform to sell-out audiences, jazz greats jam in steamy clubs and rappers rage in underground venues. It wasn't always like this, though, and until the mid-2000s Rome was considered something of a musical backwater. What changed things was the 2002 opening of the Auditorium Parco della Musica and an administration which invested heavily in culture.

Adapted from a book by Giancarlo De Cataldo, the critically-acclaimed TV series *Romanzo Criminale* tells the story of a Rome-based criminal gang. The storyline and characters are based on the real-life Banda della Magliana which dominated Rome's criminal underworld in the late 1970s and early 1980s.

## Castration & Choral Music

In a city of churches, it's little wonder that choral music has deep roots. In the 16th and 17th centuries, Rome's great Renaissance popes summoned the top musicians of the day to tutor the papal choir. Two of the most famous were Giovanni Pierluigi da Palestrina (c 1525–94), one of Italy's foremost Renaissance composers, and the Naples-born Domenico Scarlatti (1685–1757). Girolamo Frescobaldi (1583–1643), admired by the young JS Bach, was twice an organist at St Peter's Basilica.

The papal choirs, originally composed of priests, were closed to women and the high parts were taken by *castrati,* boys who had been surgically castrated before puberty to preserve their high voices. Although castration was punishable by excommunication, the Sistine Chapel and other papal choirs contained *castrati* as early as 1588 and as late as the early 20th century. The last known *castrato,* Alessandro Moreschi (1858–1922), known as *l'angelo di Roma* (the angel of Rome), was castrated in 1865, just five years before the practice was officially outlawed. He entered the Sistine Chapel choir in 1883 and 15 years later became conductor. He retired in 1913, 10 years after Pius X had banned *castrati* from the papal choirs. Boy sopranos were introduced in the 1950s.

In 1585 Sixtus V formally established the Accademia di Santa Cecilia as a support organisation for papal musicians. Originally it was involved in the publication of sacred music, although it later developed

## PIER PAOLO PASOLINI, MASTER OF CONTROVERSY

Poet, novelist and filmmaker, Pier Paolo Pasolini (1922–75) was one of Italy's most important and controversial 20th century intellectuals. His works, which are complex, unsentimental and provocative, provide a scathing portrait of Italy's post-war social transformation.

Although he spent much of his adult life in Rome, he had a peripatetic childhood. He was born in Bologna but moved around frequently and rarely spent more than a few years in any one place. He did, however, form a lasting emotional attachment to Friuli, the mountainous region in northeastern Italy where his mother was from and where he spent the latter half of WWII. Much of his early poetry, collected and published in 1954 as *La meglio gioventù,* was written in Friulano dialect.

Politically, he was a communist, but he never played a part in Italy's left-wing establishment. In 1949 he was expelled from the *Partito Comunista Italiano* (PCI; Italian Communist Party) after a gay sex scandal and for the rest of his career he remained a sharp critic of the party. His most famous outburst came in the poem *Il PCI ai giovani,* in which he dismisses left-wing students as bourgeois and sympathises with the police, whom he describes as '*figli di poveri*' (sons of the poor). In the context of 1968 Italy, a year marked by widespread student agitation, this was a highly incendiary position to take.

Pasolini was no stranger to controversy. His first novel *Ragazzi di Vita* (The Ragazzi), set in the squalor of Rome's forgotten suburbs, earned him success and a court case for obscenity. Similarly, his early films – *Accattone* (1961) and *Mamma Roma* (1962) – provoked righteous outrage with their relentlessly bleak depiction of life in the Roman underbelly.

True to the scandalous nature of his art, Pasolini was murdered in 1975. It was originally thought that his death was linked to events in the gay underworld but revelations in 2005 hinted that it might, in fact, have been a politically motivated killing. The case is still open.

a teaching function, and in 1839 it completely reinvented itself as an academy with wider cultural and academic goals. Today it is one of the world's most highly respected conservatories, with its own orchestra and chorus.

### Opera

Rome is often snobbed by serious opera buffs who prefer their Puccini in Milan, Venice or Naples. However, in recent years the city's main opera company, the Teatro dell'Opera di Roma, has upped its standards and performances are passionately followed. The Romans have long been keen opera-goers – it's said that the Barberini family, one of Rome's most powerful aristocratic dynasties, used to stage spectacular performances in Palazzo Barberini in the 17th century – and in the 19th century a number of important operas were premiered in Rome, including Rossini's *Il Barbiere di Siviglia* (The Barber of Seville; 1816), Verdi's *Il Trovatore* (The Troubadour; 1853) and Giacomo Puccini's *Tosca* (1900).

*Tosca* not only premiered in Rome but is also set in the city. The first act takes place in the Chiesa di Sant'Andrea della Valle, the second in Palazzo Farnese, and the final act in Castel Sant'Angelo, the castle from which Tosca jumps to her death.

### Jazz, Hip hop & the Contemporary Scene

Jazz has long been a mainstay of Rome's music scene. Introduced by US troops during WWII, it grew in popularity during the postwar period and took off in the 1960s with the opening of the mythical Folk-studio club. Since then, it has gone from strength to strength and the city now offers some of Italy's finest jazz clubs. Big names to look out for include Enrico Pieranunzi, a Roman-born pianist and composer, and Doctor 3 whose idiosyncratic sound has earned them considerable acclaim.

Rome also has a vibrant hip hop scene. Hip hop, which arrived in the city in the late 1980s and spread via the *centro sociale* (organised squat) network, was originally highly politicised and many early exponents associated themselves with Rome's alternative left-wing scene. But in recent years exposure and ever-increasing commercialisation has diluted this political element and the scene has largely gone mainstream. A key contributor to this evolution was rapper Piotta whose 1999 hit *Supercafone,* introduced the world to the Roman *coatto* (a working-class tough guy with attitude and bling). For a taste of genuine Roman rap tune into bands like Colle der Fomento, Cor Veleno, or the ragamuffin outfit Villa Ada Posse.

## THEATRE & DANCE

Surprisingly for a city in which art has always been appreciated, Rome has no great theatrical tradition. It has never had a Broadway or West End, and while highbrow imports are greeted enthusiastically, fringe theatre remains something of a novelty. That said, experimental theatre is increasingly finding space in the city's cultural calendar and the Teatro Cometa Off in Testaccio is making a name for itself as host of the Liberi Esperimenti Teatrali, an annual programme of workshops, laboratories and experimental performances.

Although not strictly speaking a Roman, Dacia Maraini (b 1936) has produced her best work while living in Rome. Considered one of Italy's most important feminist writers, she continues to work as a journalist while her all-women theatre company Teatro della Maddalena stages her 30-plus plays. Some of these, including the 1978 *Dialogo di una Prostituta con un suo Cliente* (Dialogue of a Prostitute with Client), have also played abroad.

Gigi Proietti (b 1940), on the other hand, is pure Roman. A hugely popular writer, performer and director, he combines TV acting with dubbing (he's dubbed Robert De Niro, Richard Burton, Marlon Brando and Dustin Hoffman) and theatre work. He's artistic director of the Teatro Brancaccio and regularly plays to full houses.

New York's favourite neurotic, Woody Allen, continues his European tour. After films in London, Barcelona and Paris, his next picture is to be set in Rome.

Dance is a major highlight of Rome's big autumn festival, Romaeuropa. But while popular, performances rarely showcase homegrown talent, which remains thin on the ground. In fact, Rome's reputation in the world of dance rests more on its breakdancers than its corps de ballet. The city's most celebrated crew is Urban Force which often represents the capital in national and international competitions and regularly performs live.

Major ballet performances are staged at the Teatro dell'Opera, home to Rome's principal ballet company, the Balletto del Teatro dell'Opera. The company has long had a shaky reputation but under its internationally renowned director, Carla Fracci (b 1936), production standards improved. But with Fracci's departure in 2010, after clashing with Rome's mayor Gianni Alemanno over proposed spending cuts, a big question mark hangs over the future.

'But in 2010 Fracci departed the company after clashing with Rome's mayor Gianni Alemanno over proposed spending cuts and was replaced by the Belgian choreographer and director, Micha van Hoecke.'

# Architecture

**From ancient ruins and Renaissance basilicas, to baroque churches and hulking fascist *palazzi*, Rome's architectural legacy is unparalleled. Michelangelo, Bramante, Borromini and Bernini are among the architects who have stamped their genius on Rome's remarkable cityscape, which features some of the Western world's most celebrated buildings. But it's not all about history. In recent years a number of high-profile building projects have drawn the world's top architects to Rome, their futuristic designs provoking discussion, debate and soul-searching among the city's loquacious and passionate critics.**

## THE ANCIENTS

Architecture was central to the success of the ancient Romans. In building their great capital, they were the first people to use architecture to tackle problems of infrastructure, urban management and communication. For the first time architects and engineers were asked to design houses, roads, aqueducts and shopping centres alongside temples, tombs and imperial palaces. To do this the Romans advanced methods devised by the Etruscans and Greeks, developing construction techniques and building materials that allowed them to build on a massive and hitherto unseen scale.

### Etruscan Roots

By the 7th century BC the Etruscans were the dominant force on the Italian peninsula, with important centres at Tarquinia, Caere (Cerveteri) and Veii (Veio). These city-states were fortified with defensive walls and although little actually remains – the Etruscans generally built with wood and brick, which hasn't aged well – archaeologists have found evidence of aqueducts, bridges and sewers, as well as sophisticated temples. In Rome, you can still see foundations of an Etruscan temple on the Campidoglio (Capitoline hill).

But much of what we now know about the Etruscans derives from findings unearthed in their elaborate tombs. Like many ancient peoples, the Etruscans placed great emphasis on their dead and they built impressive cemeteries. These were constructed outside the city walls and harboured richly decorated stone vaults covered by mounds of earth. The best examples of Etruscan tombs are to be found in Cerveteri and Tarquinia, north of Rome.

**Architecture Reads**

*Rome (Amanda Claridge)*

*The Genius in the Design: Bernini, Borromini and the Rivalry that Transformed Rome (Jake Morrissey)*

*Rome and Environs: An Archaeological Guide (Filippo Coarelli)*

### Roman Developments

When Rome was founded in 753 BC (if legend is to be believed), the Etruscans were at the height of their power and Greeks colonists were establishing control over southern Italy. In subsequent centuries a three-way battle for domination ensued, with the Romans emerging victorious. Against this background, Roman architects borrowed heavily from Greek and Etruscan traditions, at least until they found their feet and developed their own styles and techniques.

Ancient Roman architecture was monumental in form and often propagandistic in nature. Huge amphitheatres, aqueducts and temples joined muscular and awe-inspiring basilicas, arches and thermal baths in trumpeting the skill and vision of the city's early rulers and the nameless architects who worked for them.

## Temples

Early Republican-era temples were originally based on Etruscan designs but over time the Romans turned to the Greeks for their inspiration. But whereas Greek temples had steps and colonnades on all sides, the classic Roman temple had a high podium with steps leading up to a deep porch. Good examples of this include the Tempio di Portunus near Piazza della Bocca della Verità and, though they're not so well preserved, the temples in the Area Sacra di Largo di Torre Argentina. These temples also illustrate another important feature of Roman architectural thinking. While Greek temples were designed to stand apart and be viewed from all sides – in fact, it's often difficult to know which is the front of a Greek temple – Roman temples were built into the city's urban fabric, set in busy central locations such as the forums, and designed to be approached from the front.

The Roman use of columns was also Greek in origin, even if the Romans favoured the more slender Ionic and Corinthian columns over the plain Doric pillars – to see how the columnar orders differ study the exterior of the Colosseum, which incorporates all three styles.

## Aqueducts & Sewers

One of the Romans crowning architectural achievements was the development of a water supply infrastructure, based on a network of aqueducts and underground sewers. In the early days, Rome got its water from the Tiber and natural underground springs, but as its population grew so demand outgrew supply. To meet this demand, the Romans constructed a complex system of aqueducts to bring water in from the hills of central Italy and distribute it around the city.

The first aqueduct to serve Rome was the 16.5km Aqua Appia, which became fully operational in 312 BC. Over the next 700 years or so, up to 800km of aqueducts were laid out in the city, a network capable of supplying up to one million cubic metres of water a day.

This was no mean feat for a system that depending entirely on gravity. All aqueducts, whether underground pipes, as most were, or vast overland viaducts, were built at a slight gradient to allow the water to flow. There were no pumps to force the water along so this gradient was key to maintaining a continuous and efficient flow.

At the other end of the water cycle, waste water was drained away via an underground sewerage system known as the Cloaca Maxima (Greatest Sewer) and emptied downstream into the river Tiber. The Cloaca, commissioned by Rome's seventh and last king, Tarquin the Proud (r 535–509 BC), as part of a project to drain the valley where the Roman Forum now stands, was originally an open ditch but from the from the beginning of the 2nd century BC it was gradually built over.

## MAIN ARCHITECTURAL PERIODS

### c 8th–3rd centuries BC

The Etruscans in central Italy and the Greeks in the southern Italian colony, Magna Graecia, lay the groundwork for later Roman developments. Particularly influential are Greek temple designs.

### c 4th century BC– 5th century AD

The ancient Romans make huge advances in engineering techniques, constructing monumental public buildings, bridges, aqueducts, houses and an underground sewerage system.

### 4th–12th century

Church building is the focus of architectural activity in the Medieval period as Rome's early Christian leaders seek to stamp their authority on the city.

### 15th–16th century

Based on humanism and a reappraisal of classical precepts, the Renaissance hits an all-time high in the first two decades of the 16th century, a period known as the High Renaissance.

### 17th century

Developing out of the Counter-Reformation, the baroque flourishes in Rome, fuelled by Church money and the genius of Gian Lorenzo Bernini and Francesco Borromini.

ARCHITECTURE THE ANCIENTS

### Residential Housing

While Rome's emperors and aristocrats lived in luxury in vast palaces up on the Palatino (Palatine hill), the city's poor huddled together in large residential blocks called *insulae*. These were huge, poorly built structures, sometimes up to six or seven storeys high, that accommodated hundreds of people in dark, unhealthy conditions. Little remains of these early *palazzi* but near the foot of the Aracoeli staircase – the steps that lead up to the Chiesa di Santa Maria in Aracoeli – you can still see a section of what was once a typical city-centre *insula*.

### Concrete & Monumental Architecture

Most of the ruins that litter modern Rome are the remains of the ancient city's big, show-stopping monuments – the Colosseum, the Pantheon, the Terme di Caracalla, the Forums. These grandiose constructions, still standing some 2000 years after they were built, are not only reminders of the sophistication and intimidatory scale of ancient Rome – just as they were originally designed to be – they are also monuments to the vision and bravura of the city's ancient architects.

Rome's ancient ruins are revealing in many ways, but the one thing they lack is colour. Ancient Rome would have been a vivid, brightly coloured place with buildings clad in coloured marble, gaudily painted temples and multicoloured statues and sculptures.

The Colosseum is not only an icon of Roman might, it is also a masterpiece of 1st-century engineering. Similarly, the Pantheon, with its world-beating dome, is a wonderful example of an imperial-age temple while also being a building of quite staggering structural complexity.

One of the key breakthroughs the Romans made, and one that allowed them to build on an ever-increasing scale, was the invention of concrete in the 1st century BC. Made by mixing volcanic ash with lime and an aggregate, often tufa rock or brick rubble, concrete was quick to make, easy to use and cheap. Furthermore, it freed architects from their dependence on skilled masonry labour (up to that point construction techniques required stone blocks to be specially cut to fit into each other). Concrete allowed the Romans to develop vaulted roofing, which they used to span the Pantheon's ceiling and the huge vaults at the Terme di Caracalla among other places.

Concrete wasn't particularly attractive, though, and while it was used for heavy-duty structural work it was usually lined with travertine and coloured marble, imported from Greece and North Africa. Brick was also an important material, used both as a veneer and for construction.

### ALL ROADS LEAD TO ROME

The Romans were the great road-builders of the ancient world. Approximately 80,000km of surfaced highways spanned the Roman Empire, providing vital military and communication links. Many of modern Rome's roads retain the names of their ancient forebears and follow almost identical routes.

The main roads of ancient times ran from Rome to all corners of the peninsula:

**Via Appia** The 'queen of roads' ran down to Brindisi on the southern Adriatic coast.

**Via Aurelia** Connected Rome with France by way of Pisa and Genoa.

**Via Cassia** Led north to Viterbo, Siena and Tuscany.

**Via Flaminia** Traversed the Apennines to Rimini on the east coast.

**Via Salaria** The old salt road linked with the Adriatic port of Castrum Truentinum, south of modern-day Ancona.

# EARLY CHRISTIAN

The history of early Christianity is one of persecution and martyrdom. Introduced in the 1st century AD, it was legalised by the emperor Constantine in 313 AD and became Rome's state religion in 378. The most startling reminders of early Christian activity are the catacombs, a series of underground burial grounds built under Rome's ancient roads. Christian belief in the resurrection meant that the Christians could not cremate their dead, as was the custom in Roman times, and with burial forbidden inside the city walls they were forced to go outside the city.

## Church Building

The Christians began to abandon the catacombs in the 4th century and increasingly opted to be buried in the churches the emperor Constantine was building in the city. Although Constantine was actually based in Byzantium, which he renamed Constantinople in his own honour, he nevertheless financed an ambitious building programme in Rome. The most notable of the many churches that he commissioned is the Basilica di San Giovanni in Laterano. Built between 315 and 324 and reformed into its present shape in the 5th century, it was the model on which many subsequent basilicas were based. Other showstoppers of the period include the Basilica di Santa Maria in Trastevere and the Basilica di Santa Maria Maggiore.

A second wave of church-building hit Rome in the period between the 8th and 12th centuries. As the early papacy battled for survival against the threatening Lombards, its leaders took to construction to leave some sort of historical imprint, resulting in the Basilica di Santa Sabina, the Chiesa di Santa Prassede and the 8th-century Chiesa di Santa Maria in Cosmedin, better known as home to the Bocca della Verità (Mouth of Truth).

The 13th and 14th centuries were dark days for Rome as internecine fighting raged between the city's noble families. While much of northern Europe and even parts of Italy were revelling in Gothic arches and towering vaults, little of lasting value was being built in Rome. The one great exception is the city's only Gothic church, the Chiesa di Santa Maria Sopra Minerva.

### Basilica Style

In design terms, these early Christian churches were modelled on, and built over, Rome's great basilicas. In ancient times, a basilica was a large rectangular hall used for public functions, but as Christianity took hold they were increasingly appropriated by the city's church-builders. The main reason for this was that they lent themselves perfectly to the new style of religious ceremonies that the Christians were introducing, rites that required space for worshippers and a central focus for the altar. Rome's pagan temples, in contrast, had been designed as symbolic cult centres and were not set up to house the faithful – in fact, most pagan ceremonies were held outside, in front of the temple, not inside as Christian services required.

Over time, basilica design became increasingly standardised. A principal entrance would open onto an atrium, a courtyard surrounded by

**18th century**
A short-lived but theatrical style born out of the baroque, the florid rococo has given Rome some of its most popular sights.

**early 20th century**
Muscular and modern, Italian rationalism plays to Mussolini's vision of a fearless, futuristic Rome, a 20th-century *caput mundi* (world capital).

**1990s–**
Rome provides the historic stage upon which some of the world's top contemporary architects experiment. Controversy, criticism and praise are meted out in almost equal measure.

ARCHITECTURE EARLY CHRISTIAN

Rome's first aqueduct, the Aqua Appia is named after the censor Appius Claudius Caecus, the same man who built Via Appia Antica.

*continued on page 288*

# Rome in Architecture

## Ancient Monuments & Medieval Churches

**Rome's architects and master builders created the greatest city the Western world had ever seen. As Christianity took root, the early popes led a bout of church building.**

### Colosseum

More than any other building, this great amphitheatre (p58) symbolises the power and glory of ancient Rome. Built by the emperor Vespasian and inaugurated in 80 AD by his son and successor, Titus, it dramatically illustrates the Roman use of the arch. Its first three tiers consist of 80 arches framed by columns of different orders: Doric at ground level, Ionic in the middle and Corinthian on the third tier.

### MUST-SEE BUILDINGS

- ➡ Colosseum
- ➡ Pantheon
- ➡ Basilica di Santa Maria Maggiore
- ➡ Tempietto di Bramante
- ➡ St Peter's Basilica
- ➡ Piazza San Pietro
- ➡ Chiesa del Gesù
- ➡ Chiesa di San Carlo alle Quattro Fontane
- ➡ Palazzo della Civiltà del Lavoro
- ➡ Auditorium Parco della Musica

### Pantheon

The Pantheon (p75) is one of the most influential buildings ever constructed. A squat rotunda, preceded by a columned portico and crowned by the largest unreinforced concrete dome ever built, it was revolutionary in both conception and execution. The main technical challenge was how to keep the dome's weight down. To do this, they circled the cupola with five bands of decorative coffers (the rectangular recesses you see on the inside of the dome) and calibrated the concrete to ensure that it was lighter at the top than at the base. In the centre, the 8.7m-diameter oculus acts as a compression ring, absorbing and redistributing the structural forces centred on the dome's apex.

### Basilica di Santa Maria Maggiore

Although much altered over the centuries, this hulking cathedral (p129) is the only one of Rome's four patriarchal basilicas to retain its original 5th-century layout. Key features include the vast central nave, delineated by two rows of 20 columns, and its extensive mosaic decor. Mosaic decor was typical of early Christian design.

**Clockwise from top left**
1. Interior of Basilica di Santa Maria Maggiore 2. The Pantheon

# From Renaissance Basilicas to Contemporary Icons

**Italy's architects remodelled Rome in baroque and Renaissance styles. Mussolini tried to restyle Rome as his Fascist capital. Today Rome applauds the works of some of the world's top architects.**

### Tempietto di Bramante

In architectural terms, Bramante's 1502 Tempietto (p174) is one of Rome's most influential buildings, a masterpiece of harmonious design that encapsulates High Renaissance ideals. A small circular temple capped by a dome and ringed by a columned peristyle, it's symmetrical and perfectly proportioned, its design clearly inspired by Rome's classical temples.

### St Peter's Basilica

The greatest church in the Catholic world, St Peter's (p184) is an amalgamation of designs, styles and plans. Standing at the head of Piazza San Pietro, Gian Lorenzo Bernini's baroque piazza, it was worked on by a small army of Renaissance and baroque architects, including Bramante, Bernini, Raphael and Michelangelo. In architectural terms, the two key features are Michelangelo's extraordinary dome – which at the time was the world's tallest structure – and Carlo Maderno's columned facade. Inside, the look is baroque with acres of polished marble and imposing sculptures set in niches.

### Chiesa di San Carlo alle Quattro Fontane

This petite baroque church (p111), built by Francesco Borromini, incorporates many of his trademark touches – a facade of convex and concave surfaces, the use of hidden

**Clockwise from top left**

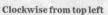
1. Auditorium Parço della Musica 2. Palazzo della Civiltà del Lavora 3. Tempietto di Bramante

windows to stream light onto decorative features, and a complex elliptical plan to exploit the limited space.

## Palazzo della Civiltà del Lavoro

Out in EUR, this iconic building (p167) is a work of 1930s Italian rationalism. With its clean, bold lines and plain, unadorned surfaces, it exudes a sense of macho monumentality – a posture appreciated by Fascist dictator Benito Mussolini.

## Auditorium Parco della Musica

Inaugurated in December 2002, Renzo Piano's startlingly original Auditorium (p212) is the most influential modern building in Rome, not so much in terms of its unique design – an eye-catching ensemble of iron-grey pods centred on an outdoor amphitheatre – as for the boost it has given Rome's cultural scene.

---

### RECYCLING MARBLE

The building booms of the Renaissance and baroque periods transformed Rome in more ways than one for, just as spectacular new churches and *palazzi* (mansions) went up, so the city's ancient buildings were stripped. The ancient Romans imported much of their marble from North Africa and Greece, but the papal paymasters preferred the city's abandoned marble-clad monuments. A particularly rich source was the Colosseum, which was systematically plundered for centuries, and provided marble for St Peter's Basilica and other big projects. Its current form is largely the result of this relentless demolition.

Elsewhere, bronze was taken from the Pantheon for use on Castel Sant'Angelo and for the baldachino at St Peter's, while the great doors of the Basilica di San Giovanni in Laterano were transferred there from the Curia in the Roman Forum.

*continued from page 283*

colonnaded porticoes, which, in turn, would lead to the narthex, or porch. Through the church doors, the interior would be rectangular and divided lengthways by rows of columns into a central nave and smaller, side aisles. At the far end, the main altar and bishop's throne (cathedra) would sit in the semi-circular apse. In some churches a transept would bisect the central nave in front of the apse to form a Latin cross.

## THE RENAISSANCE

Florence, rather than Rome, is generally regarded as Italy's great Renaissance city. But while many of the movement's early architects hailed from Tuscany, the city they turned to for inspiration was Rome. The Eternal City might have been in pretty poor nick in the late 15th century but as the centre of classical antiquity it was much revered by budding architects and a trip to study the Colosseum and the Pantheon was considered a fundamental part of any architect's training.

One of the key aspects they were studying, and which informs much Renaissance architecture, is the idea of harmony. This is achieved, or sought, by the application of symmetry, order and proportion. To this end many Renaissance buildings incorporate structural features copied from the ancients – columns, pilasters, arches and, most dramatically, domes. The Pantheon's dome, in particular, proved immensely influential, serving as a blueprint for many later works.

### Early Years

It's impossible to pinpoint the exact year the Renaissance arrived in Rome, but many claim it was the election of Pope Nicholas V in 1447 that sparked off the artistic and architectural furore that swept the city in the next century or so. Nicholas believed that as head of the Christian world Rome had a duty to impress, a theory that was eagerly taken up by his successors, and it was at the behest of the great papal dynasties – the Barberini, Farnese and Pamphilj – that the leading artists of the day were summoned to Rome.

The Venetian Pope Paul II (r 1464–71) commissioned many works, including Palazzo Venezia, Rome's first great Renaissance *palazzo* (mansion). Built in 1455, when Paul was still a cardinal, it was enlarged in

Even experts are puzzled as to why the Pantheon's dome is still standing. Had it been made from modern concrete it would have collapsed under its own weight long ago.

### BRAMANTE, THE ARCHITECT'S ARCHITECT

One of the most influential architects of his day, Donato Bramante (1444–1514) was the godfather of Renaissance architecture. His peers Michelangelo, Raphael and Leonardo da Vinci considered him the only architect of their era equal to the ancients.

Born near Urbino, he originally trained as a painter before taking up architecture in his mid-30s in Milan. Here he met Leonardo da Vinci, who was to remain a lifelong friend and influence, and worked on a number of prestigious church projects.

However, it was in Rome that he enjoyed his greatest success. Working for Pope Julius II, he developed a monumental style that while classical in origin was pure Renaissance in its expression of harmony and perspective. The most perfect representation of this is his Tempietto, a small but much-copied temple. His original designs for St Peter's Basilica also revealed a classically inspired symmetry with a Pantheon-like dome envisaged atop a Greek-cross structure.

A rich and influential architect, Bramante was also an adept political operator, a ruthless and unscrupulous manipulator who was not above badmouthing his competitors. It's said that he talked Pope Julius II into giving Michelangelo the Sistine Chapel contract in the hope that it would prove the undoing of the young Tuscan artist.

## FIVE FLAMBOYANT FOUNTAINS

**Trevi Fountain** Wild horses rise out of the rocks at this fantastical rococo extravaganza, Rome's largest and most celebrated fountain.

**Fontana dei Quattro Fiumi** Topped by a tapering obelisk, Bernini's opulent baroque display sits in splendour on Piazza Navona.

**Fontana delle Naiadi** The naked nymphs languishing around Piazza della Repubblica's scene-stealing fountain caused scandal when revealed in 1901.

**Fontana dell'Acqua Paola** Known to Romans as *il fontanone del Gianicolo*, this grandiose baroque fountain sits atop the Gianicolo hill.

**Barcaccia** The Spanish Steps lead down to this sunken-ship fountain, supposedly modelled on a boat dumped on the piazza by a flood in 1598.

1464 when he became pope. Sixtus IV (r 1471–84) had the Sistine Chapel built, and enlarged the Chiesa di Santa Maria del Popolo.

## High Renaissance

But it was under Julius II (1503–13) that the Roman Renaissance reached its peak, thanks largely to a classically minded architect from Milan, Donato Bramante (1444–1514).

Considered the high priest of Renaissance architecture, Bramante arrived in Rome in 1499. Here, inspired by the ancient ruins, he developed a refined classical style that was to prove hugely influential. His 1502 Tempietto is a masterpiece of elegance. Similarly harmonious is his beautifully proportioned 1504 cloister at the Chiesa di Santa Maria della Pace near Piazza Navona.

In 1506 Julius commissioned him to start work on the job that would finally finish him off – the rebuilding of St Peter's Basilica (Basilica di San Pietro). The fall of Constantinople's Aya Sofya (Church of the Hagia Sofia) to Islam in the mid-14th century had pricked Nicholas V into ordering an earlier revamp, but the work had never been completed and it wasn't until Julius took the bull by the horns that progress was made. However, Bramante never got to see how his original Greek-cross design was developed, as he died in 1514.

St Peter's Basilica occupied most of the other notable architects of the High Renaissance, including Giuliano da Sangallo (1445–1516), Baldassarre Peruzzi (1481–1536) and Antonio da Sangallo the Younger (1484–1546). Michelangelo (1475–1564) eventually took over the task in 1547, modifying the layout and creating the basilica's crowning dome. Modelled on Brunelleschi's design for the Duomo in Florence, this is considered Michelangelo's finest architectural achievement and one of the most important works of the Roman Renaissance.

## Mannerism

As Rome's architects strove to build a new Jerusalem, the city's leaders struggled to deal with the political tensions arising outside the city walls. These came to a head in 1527 when the city was invaded and savagely routed by troops of the Holy Roman Emperor, Charles V. This traumatic event forced many of the artists working in Rome to flee the city and ushered in a new style of artistic and architectural expression. Mannerism was a relatively short-lived form but in its emphasis on complexity and decoration, in contrast to the sharp, clean lines of traditional Renaissance styles, it hinted at the more ebullient designs that would later arrive with the onset of the 17th-century baroque.

**Early Basilicas**

Basilica di San Giovanni in Laterano

Basilica di Santa Sabina

Basilica di Santa Maria Maggiore

Basilica di Santa Maria in Trastevere

One of mannerism's leading exponents was Baldassarre Peruzzi, whose Villa Farnesina, built in traditional Renaissance style, contrasts with his later Palazzo Massimo alle Colonne on Corso Vittorio Emanuele II, which reveals a number of mannerist elements – a more pronounced facade, decorative window mouldings and the employment of showy imitation stonework.

## THE BAROQUE

**Key Borromini Works**

*Chiesa di San Carlo alle Quattro Fontane*

*Chiesa di Sant'Agnese in Agone*

*Chiesa di Sant'Ivo alla Sapienza*

*Prospettiva (Perspective Corridor), Palazzo Spada*

As the principal motor of the Roman Renaissance, the Catholic Church became increasingly powerful in the 16th century. But with power came corruption and calls for reform. These culminated in Martin Luther's 95 Theses and the far-reaching Protestant Reformation. This hit the Church hard and prompted the Counter-Reformation (1560–1648), a vicious and sustained campaign to get people back into the Catholic fold. In the midst of this great offensive, baroque art and architecture emerged as a highly effective form of propaganda. Stylistically, baroque architecture aims for a dramatic sense of dynamism, an effect that it often achieves by combining spatial complexity with clever lighting and a flamboyant use of decorative painting and sculpture.

One of the first great Counter-Reformation churches was the Jesuit Chiesa del Gesù, designed by the leading architect of the day, Giacomo della Porta (1533–1602). In a move away from the style of earlier Renaissance churches, the facade has pronounced architectural elements that create a contrast between surfaces and a play of light and shade.

The end of the 16th century and the papacy of Sixtus V (1585–90) marked the beginning of major urban-planning schemes. Domenico Fontana (1543–1607) and other architects created a network of major thoroughfares to connect previously disparate parts of the sprawling medieval city, and decorative obelisks were erected at vantage points throughout Rome. Fontana also designed the main facade of Palazzo del Quirinale, the immense palace that served as the pope's summer residence for almost three centuries. His nephew, Carlo Maderno (1556–1629), also worked on the *palazzo* when not amending Bramante's designs for St Peter's Basilica.

### Bernini vs Borromini

No two people did more to fashion the face of Rome than the two great figures of the Roman baroque – Gian Lorenzo Bernini (1598–1680) and Francesco Borromini (1599–1667). Two starkly different characters – Naples-born Bernini was suave, self-confident and politically adept,

---

### ROCOCO FRILLS

In the early days of the 18th century, as baroque fashions began to fade and neoclassicism waited to make its 19th-century entrance, the rococo burst into theatrical life. Drawing on the excesses of the baroque, it was a short-lived fad but one that left a memorable mark.

The **Spanish Steps**, built between 1723 and 1726 by Francesco de Sanctis, provided a focal point for the many Grand Tourists who were busy discovering Rome's classical past. A short walk to the southwest, Piazza Sant'Ignazio was designed by Filippo Raguzzini (1680–1771) in 1728 to provide a suitably melodramatic setting for the **Chiesa di Sant'Ignazio di Loyola**, Rome's second Jesuit church.

Most spectacular of all, however, was the **Trevi Fountain**, one of the city's most exuberant and enduringly popular monuments. It was designed in 1732 by Nicola Salvi (1697–1751) and completed three decades later.

while Borromini, from Lombardy, was a solitary and peculiar man – they led the transition from Counter-Reformation rigour to baroque exuberance.

Bernini is perhaps best known for his work in the Vatican. He designed St Peter's Square (Piazza San Pietro), famously styling the colonnade as 'the motherly arms of the Church', and was chief architect at St Peter's Basilica from 1629. While working on the basilica, he created the baldachin (altar canopy) above the main altar, using bronze stripped from the Pantheon.

Under the patronage of the Barberini pope Urban VIII, Bernini was given free rein to transform the city, and his churches, *palazzi,* piazzas and fountains remain landmarks to this day. However, his fortunes nose-dived when the pope died in 1644. Urban's successor, Innocent X, wanted as little contact as possible with the favourites of his hated predecessor and instead turned to Borromini, Alessandro Algardi (1595–1654) and Girolamo and Carlo Rainaldi (1570–1655 and 1611–91, respectively). Bernini, however, later came back into favour with his magnificent design for the 1651 Fontana dei Quattro Fiumi in the centre of Piazza Navona, opposite Borromini's Chiesa di Sant'Agnese in Agone.

Borromini, the son of an architect and well versed in stonemasonry and construction techniques, created buildings involving complex shapes and exotic geometry. A recurring feature of his designs is the skilful manipulation of light, often obtained by the clever placement of small oval-shaped windows. His most memorable works are the Chiesa di San Carlo alle Quattro Fontane, which has an oval-shaped interior, and the Chiesa di Sant'Ivo alla Sapienza, which combines a complex arrangement of convex and concave surfaces with an innovative spiral tower.

Throughout their careers, the two geniuses were often at each other's throats. Borromini was deeply envious of Bernini's early success and Bernini, in turn, was scathing of Borromini's complex geometrical style. For more on the Bernini–Borromini rivalry see the boxed text, 'Bernini vs Borromini' on p120.

**Key Bernini Works**

---

St Peter's Square
(Piazza San
Pietro)

---

Chiesa di
Sant'Andrea al
Quirinale

---

Fontana dei
Quattro Fiumi

---

Palazzo di
Montecitorio

# FASCISM, FUTURISM & THE 20TH CENTURY

Rome entered the 20th century in good shape. During the last 30 years of the 19th century it had been treated to one of its periodic makeovers – this time after being made capital of the Kingdom of Italy in 1870. Piazzas were built – Piazza Vittorio Emanuele II, at the centre of a new upmarket residential district, and neoclassical Piazza della Repubblica, over Diocletian's bath complex – and roads were laid. Via Nazionale and Via Cavour were constructed to link the city centre with the new railway station, Stazione Termini, and Corso Vittorio Emanuele II to connect Piazza Venezia with the Vatican. To celebrate unification and pander to the ego of the ruling Savoy family, the Vittoriano monument was built between 1885 and 1911.

## Rationalism & Rebuilding

Influenced by the German Bauhaus movement, architectural rationalism was all the rage in 1920s Europe. In its international form it advocated an emphasis on sharply defined linear forms, but in Italy it took on a slightly different look, thanks to the influence of the Gruppo Sette, its main Italian promoters, and Benito Mussolini, Italy's Fascist dictator. Basically, the Gruppo Sette acknowledged the debt Italian architecture owed to its classical past and incorporated elements of that

Via dei Fori Imperiali, the road that divides the Roman Forums from the Imperial Forums, was one of Mussolini's most controversial projects. Inaugurated in 1932, it was conceived to link the Colosseum (representing ancient power) with Piazza Venezia (representing Fascist power) but in the process tarmacked over much of the ancient forums.

tradition into their modernistic designs. Aesthetically and politically, this tied in perfectly with Mussolini's vision of Fascism as the modern bearer of ancient Rome's imperialist ambitions.

A shrewd manipulator of imagery, Mussolini embarked on a series of grandiose building projects, including the 1928–31 Foro Italico sports centre, Via dei Foro Imperiali and the residential quarter of Garbatella. Garbatella, now a colourful neighbourhood in southern Rome, was originally planned as an English-style garden city to house the city's workers, but in the 1920s the project was hijacked by the Fascist regime, which had its own designs. Central to these were innovative housing blocks, known as *alberghi suburbani* (suburban hotels), which were used to accommodate people displaced from the city centre. The most famous of these hotels, the *Albergo Rosso,* was designed by Innocenzo Sabbatini (1891–1983), the leading light of the Roman School of architecture. This local movement looked to ally modern functionalism with a respect for tradition and a utopian vision of urban development.

## EUR

Mussolini's most famous architectural legacy is the EUR district in the extreme south of the city. Built for the Esposizione Universale di Roma in 1942, this strange quarter of wide boulevards and huge linear buildings owes much of its look to the vision of the *razionalisti* (rationalists). In practice, though, only one of their number, Adalberto Libera, actually worked on the project, as by this stage most of the Gruppo Sette had fallen out with the ruling junta. Libera's Palazzo dei Congressi is a masterpiece of rationalist architecture, but EUR's most iconic building is the 'Square Colosseum', the Palazzo della Civiltà del Lavoro, designed by Giovanni Guerrini, Ernesto Bruno La Padula and Mario Romano.

**Modern Icons**

Palazzo della Civiltà del Lavoro

Auditorium Parco della Musica

Museo dell'Ara Pacis

Museo Nazionale delle Arti del XXI Secolo (MAXXI)

## Postwar Developments

For much of the postwar period architects in Rome were limited to planning cheap housing for the city's ever-growing population. Swathes of hideous apartment blocks were built along the city's main arteries, and grim suburbs sprang up on land claimed from local farmers.

The 1960 Olympics heralded a spate of sporting construction, and both Stadio Flaminio and Stadio Olimpico date to this period. Pier Luigi Nervi, Italy's master of concrete and a hugely influential innovator, added his contribution in the form of the Palazzetto dello Sport.

# MODERN ROME

Rome's recent past has witnessed a flurry of architectural activity. A clutch of superstar architects have worked on projects in the city. These include Renzo Piano, Italy's foremost architect; renowned American Richard Meier; Anglo-Iraqi Zaha Hadid; Odile Decq, a major French architect; and Dutch legend Rem Koolhaas. Out in EUR, work continues on Massimiliano Fuksas' cutting-edge Centro Congressi Italia.

## Controversy & Acclaim

The foundations of this building boom date to the early 1990s when the then-mayor Francesco Rutelli launched a major clean-up of the historic centre. As part of the process he commissioned Richard Meier to build a new pavilion for the 1st-century AD Ara Pacis. Predictably, Meier's glass-and-steel Museo dell'Ara Pacis caused controversy when it was unveiled in 2006. Vittorio Sgarbi, an outspoken art critic and politician, claimed that the American's design was the first step to globalising Rome's unique classical heritage. The Roman public appreciated the idea of introducing modern architecture to the city centre, but few were entirely convinced by Meier's design and in 2010 Rome's mayor, Gianni Alemanno, met the architect to discuss modifications. The most important change they agreed on was to knock down the wall that separates the Ara Pacis from the Tiber-front road, as part of a planned renovation of the entire Piazza Augusto Imperatore area.

Meier won far more acclaim for a second project, his striking Chiesa Dio Padre Misericordioso in Tor Tre Teste, a dreary suburb east of the city centre. Another religious project that won widespread applause was Paolo Portoghesi's postmodern mosque, opened in 1995 in the upmarket Parioli district.

Back nearer the centre, Renzo Piano's Auditorium Parco della Musica has had a huge impact on Rome's music and cultural scene. Piano, the man behind the Centre Pompidou in Paris and the *New York Times* building, is one of two Italian architects who can genuinely claim international celebrity status. The other is Massimiliano Fuksas.

## Fuksas & the Cloud

Born in Rome in 1944, Fuksas is known for his futuristic vision and while he has no signature building as such, his design for the Centro Congressi Italia comes as close as any to embodying his style. A rectangular 30m-high glass shell containing a 3500-sq-metre steel-and-Teflon cloud supported by steel ribs and suspended over a vast conference hall, its look is fearlessly modern. Yet it's not without its references to the past: in both scale and form it owes its inspiration to the 1930s rationalist architecture that surrounds it.

## Architecture Glossary

| | |
|---|---|
| **ambulatory** | a place to walk in a cloister; also an aisle, often semicircular, running behind the high altar in a church |
| **apse** | a semicircular or polygonal recess with a domed roof over a church's altar |
| **architrave** | the main beam set atop columns |
| **baldachino** (baldachin) | a stone canopy built over an altar or tomb; often supported by columns and freestanding |
| **baroque** | style of European art, architecture and music of the 17th and 18th centuries |
| **basilica** | an oblong hall with an apse at the end of the nave; used in ancient Rome for public assemblies and later adopted as a blueprint for medieval churches |
| **capital** | the head of a pillar or column |
| **cloister** | enclosed court attached to a church or monastery; consists of a roofed ambulatory surrounding an open area |
| **colonnade** | a row of columns supporting a roof or other structure |
| **cornice** | a horizontal moulded projection that crowns a building; the upper part of an entablature |
| **crypt** | an underground room beneath a church used for services and burials |
| **cupola** | a rounded dome forming part of a ceiling or roof |
| **entablature** | the part of a classical facade that sits on top of the columns; it consists of an architrave, on top of which is a decorative frieze and the cornice |

| | |
|---|---|
| **forum** | in Ancient Rome, a public space used for judicial business and commerce |
| **frieze** | a horizontal band, often with painted or sculptural decoration, that sits between the architrave and cornice |
| **futurism** | Italian early 20th-century artistic movement that embraced modern technology |
| **loggia** | a gallery or room with one side open, often facing a garden |
| **nave** | the central aisle in a church, often separated from parallel aisles by pillars |
| **neoclassi-cism** | dominant style of art and architecture in the late 18th and early 19th centuries; a return to Ancient Roman styles |
| **oculus** | circular opening at the top of a dome |
| **pilaster** | a rectangular column attached to a wall from which it projects |
| **portico** | a porch with a roof supported by columns |
| **rationalism** | international architectural style of the 1920s; its Italian form, often associated with Fascism, incorporates linear styles and classical references |
| **relief** | the projection of a design from a plane surface |
| **Renaissance** | European revival of art and architecture based on classical precedents between the 14th and 16th centuries |
| **rococo** | ornate 18th-century style of architecture |
| **Romanesque** | architectural style used between the 10th and 12th centuries; characterised by vaulting and round arches |
| **stucco** | wall plaster used for decorative purposes |
| **trompe l'oeil** | a visual illusion tricking the viewer into seeing a painted object as a three-dimensional image |
| **transept** | in a cross-shaped church, the two parts that bisect the nave at right angles, forming the short arms of the cross |

# The Roman Way of Life

**As a visitor, it's often difficult to see beyond Rome's spectacular veneer to the large, modern city that lies beneath, a living, breathing capital, home to nearly three million people. So how do the Romans live their city? Where do they work? Who do they live with? How do they let their hair down?**

## A DAY IN THE LIFE

Rome's Mr Average, Signor Rossi, lives with his wife in a small, two-bedroom apartment in the suburbs and works in a government ministry in the city centre. His working day is typical of the many who crowd *i mezzi* (the means, ie public transport) in the morning rush hour.

His morning routine is the same as city dwellers the world over: a quick breakfast – usually nothing more than a sweet, black espresso – followed by a short bus ride to the nearest metro station. On the way he'll stop at an *edicola* (kiosk) to pick up his daily newspaper (*Il Messaggero*) and share a joke with the kiosk owner, a manic Roma supporter. A quick scan of the headlines reveals few surprises – the opposition up in arms about Berlusconi's proposals to reform the justice bill; the Pope reminding everyone of their duty to live according to Christian values; a full page match report on the previous evening's Roma – Lazio derby.

Rome's metro is not a particularly pleasant place to be in *l'ora di punta* (the rush hour), especially in summer when it can get unbearably hot, but the regulars are resigned to the discomfort and bear it cheerfully. On arriving at work Signor Rossi has time for another coffee and a cornetto at the bar underneath his office.

His work, like many in the swollen state bureaucracy, is not the most interesting in the world, nor the best paid, but it's secure and with a *contratto a tempo indeterminato* (permanent contract) he doesn't have to worry about losing it. In contrast, many of his younger colleagues work in constant fear that their temporary contracts will not be renewed when they expire.

Lunch, which is typically taken around 1.30pm, is usually a slice of *pizza al taglio* (pizza by the slice) from a nearby takeaway. It's eaten standing up and followed by a leisurely wander around the surrounding neighbourhood. Before heading back to the office for the afternoon session, another espresso is customary.

Clocking off time in most ministries is typically from 5pm onwards and by about 7pm the evening rush hour is in full swing. Once home, our Signor Rossi changes out of his suit and at about 8.30pm sits down to a pasta supper and a discussion of plans for the weekend. On Saturday he's been invited to a friend's wedding, which means he'll have to find time to shop for a present. On Sunday his partner wants to go to the Caravaggio exhibition at the Quirinale, but that'll be packed, and he'd rather drive out to the Castelli Romani for lunch at Lago di Albano.

## WORK

Employment in the capital is largely based on Italy's bloated state bureaucracy. Every morning armies of suited civil servants pour into town and disappear into vast ministerial buildings to keep the machinery of

The nepotistic system of *raccomandazione* (recommendations) gave birth to a long-running TV show I Raccomandati, a glitzy talent show in which the performing contestants are all presented by so-called VIPs.

Paolo Virzì's 2008 film Tutta la vita davanti won critical praise for its bittersweet portrayal of a philosophy graduate who dreams of a job in research but ends up working the phones in a Roman call centre.

government ticking over. Other important employers include the tourist sector, banking, finance and culture – Italy's historic film industry is largely based in Rome and there are hundreds of museums and galleries across town.

But times are tough and Rome's work environment is looking quite bleak at the moment. Unemployment is on the up – in early 2011 it stood at 9.1% against a national average of 8.4% – and job openings are becoming increasingly rare. To land it lucky you really have to know someone. Official figures are hard to come by, but it's a universally accepted truth that personal connections are the best way of finding work. This system of *raccomandazioni* (recommendations) is widespread and covers all walks of life. In autumn 2010 news emerged that hundreds of wives, sons, in-laws, and friends of powerful local politicians had been given jobs in the city's public transport company, ATAC. The newspapers screamed scandal, but, in truth, no one was all that surprised.

Like everywhere in Italy, Rome's workplace is largely a male preserve, and Italian women continue to work less and earn less than their male counterparts. They also have to face problems that their male colleagues don't. According to figures released by Istat, Italy's official statistics body, up to 800,000 women were forced to leave work in 2008-2009 after giving birth. Italian law legislates against this, but sexual discrimination clearly remains an issue in many work places.

Rome's under 40s are another workplace minority with many young Romans forced to accept short-term contracts for jobs for which they are hugely overqualified such as working in a telephone call centre. These jobs typically offer no job security, no pension benefits and no prospects.

> In 2010, residential property was selling for an average of €4262 per sq m in Rome. For a mid-sized 80 sq m apartment that means an asking price of €340,960. In comparison, Italy's average net income is just under €1300 per month.

## HOME LIFE & THE FAMILY

Romans, like most Italians, live in apartments. These are often small – 75 to 100sq m is typical – and expensive. House prices in central Rome are among the highest in the country and many first time buyers are forced to move out of town or to distant suburbs outside of the GRA (the *grande raccordo anulare*), the busy ring road that marks the city's outer limit.

### RELIGION IN ROMAN LIFE

Rome is a city of churches. From the great headline basilicas in the historic centre to the hundreds of parish churches dotted around the suburbs, the city is packed with places to worship. And with the Vatican in the centre of town, the Church, with a capital C, is a constant presence in Roman life.

Yet the role of religion in modern Italian society is an ambiguous one. On the one hand approximately 90% of Italians consider themselves Catholic; on the other, only about a third attend church regularly. But while Romans don't go to church very often, they are, on the whole, a conformist bunch, and for many the Church remains a point of reference. The Church's line on ethical and social issues might not always meet with widespread support but it's always given an airing in the largely sympathetic national press. Similarly, about 65% of people who get married do so in church and first communions remain an important social occasion entailing gift-giving and lavish receptions.

Catholicism's hold on the Roman psyche is strong, but recent increases in the city's immigrant population have led to a noticeable Muslim presence. This has largely been a pain-free process but friction has flared on occasion and in 2007 Rome's right-wing administration blocked plans to open a mosque in the multi-ethnic Piazza Vittorio Emanuele II area.

Almost all apartments are in self-managed *condominios* (blocks of individually owned flats), a fact which gives rise to no end of neighbourly squabbling. Regular *condominio* meetings are often fiery affairs as neighbours argue over everything from communal repairs and plumbing quotes to noisy dogs and broken lights.

Rates of home ownership are relatively high in Rome and properties are commonly kept in the family, handed down from generation to generation. People do rent but the rental market is largely targeted at Rome's huge student population.

## Staying at Home

Italy's single most successful institution, and the only one in which the innately cynical Romans continue to trust, is the family. Friends might let you down, the state will almost certainly let you down, but when the chips are down you can depend on family. A generalisation, obviously, but the fact remains that while divorce is on the increase and fewer people are getting married, the Roman family survives.

It's still the rule rather the exception for young Romans to stay at home until they marry, which they typically do at around 30. Official figures report that 83.2% of 18 to 29 year old men live with *mamma* and *papa* – the so called *mammoni* (Mummy's boys). For girls of the same age – the *figlie di papa* (Daddy's girls) – the percentage is slightly lower, 71.4%, but still high.

To foreign observers this is all pretty weird but local house prices are high and young Romans are generally reluctant to downgrade and move away from their home patch to a cheaper neighbourhood. In any case, Romans brought up in this tradition know that the *quid pro quo* comes later when they are expected to support their elderly parents. Seen from another perspective, though, it might simply mean that Roman families like living together.

But while faith in the family remains, the family is shrinking. Italy's birth rate is one of the lowest in Europe and almost half of all Italian children (46.5%) have no brothers or sisters. Rome's army of *nonni* (grandparents) berate their children for this as does the Vatican for whom procreation is a fundamental duty of marriage. For their part, Italy's politicians worry that such a perilously low birth rate threatens the future tax returns necessary for funding the country's pension payments.

## PLAY

Despite all the trials and tribulations of living in Rome – dodgy public transport, iffy services and sky-high prices – few Romans would swap their city for anywhere else. They know theirs is one of the world's most beautiful cities and they enjoy it with gusto. You only have to look at the city's pizzerias, trattorias and restaurants – not those in the touristy centre, but those out in the dreary suburbs where most people live – to see that eating out is a much-loved local pastime. Groups of friends and relatives will typically get together in a favourite eatery to catch up over plateloads of pasta and pizza. It's a cliché of Roman life but food really is central to social pleasure.

Drinking, on the other hand, is not a traditional Roman activity, at least not in the sense of piling into a pub for pints of beer. Romans have long enjoyed hanging out looking cool – just look at all those photos of *dolce vita* cafe society – and still today an evening out in a Roman bar is as much about flirting and looking gorgeous as it is about consuming alcohol.

Satirist Beppe Severgnini explains the Italian system of queuing, often a shock to first-time visitors, in *An Italian in Italy:* 'Here we favour more artistic configurations, such as waves, parabolas, herringbone patterns, hordes, groups, and clusters. Our choreography complicates waiting, but brightens our lives.'

## BELLA FIGURA

The concept of cutting a dash (*fare la bella figura*) is important to Romans. For a style-conscious hipster that might mean wearing the latest designer fashions, having your hair cut just so or carrying a top-of-the-range smartphone. A cool car, perhaps a Smart or a SUV, will also help. For a middle-aged banker it will involve being impeccably groomed and dressed appropriately for every occasion. This slavish adherence to style isn't, of course, limited to clothes or accessories. It extends into all walks of life and hip Romans will frequent the same bars and restaurants, drink the same aperitivi and hang out on the same piazzas.

Clothes shopping is another popular Roman pastime alongside cinema-going and football. Interest in Rome's two Serie A teams, Roma and Lazio, has waned a little of late due to disappointing on-field results and turbulent off-pitch politics but a trip to the Stadio Olimpico to watch the Sunday game is still considered an afternoon well-spent by many Romans. Depending on the result, of course.

Romans are inveterate car-lovers and on hot summer weekends they will often drive out to the coast or surrounding countryside. Beach bums make for nearby Ostia or more upmarket Fregene, while those in search of a little greenery make for the Castelli Romani hills, which have the advantage of being easy to get to and well stocked with eateries serving the much-loved local delicacy, *porchetta* (herbed spit-roasted pork).

# Survival Guide

# Transport

## GETTING TO ROME

Most people arrive in Rome by plane, landing at one of its two airports: Leonardo da Vinci, better known as Fiumicino, or Ciampino, the hub for European low-cost airlines. For details of budget airlines flying to Rome check out www.fly cheapo.com. Domestic flights connect Rome with airports across Italy.

As an alternative to short-haul flights, trains serve Rome's main station, Stazione Termini, from a number of European destinations as well as cities across Italy.

Long-distance domestic and international buses arrive at the Autostazione Tiburtina.

You can also get to Rome by boat. Ferries serve Civi-tavecchia, some 80km north of the city, from a number of Mediterranean ports.

Flights, tours and rail tickets can be booked online at lonelyplanet.com/bookings.

## Air

### Leonardo da Vinci Airport

Rome's main international airport, **Leonardo da Vinci** (FCO; ☑06 6 59 51; www.adr.it), aka Fiumicino, is situated on the coast 30km west of the city. It is divided into four terminals: Terminal 1 for domestic flights; Terminal 2 for charter flights; Terminal 3 for international flights; Terminal 5 for flights to the USA and Israel. Terminals

1, 2 and 3 are within easy walking distance of each other in the main airport building; Terminal 5 is accessible by shuttle bus from Terminal 3.

TO/FROM THE AIRPORT
The easiest way to get to/from the airport is by train but there are also bus services and private shuttle services.

**Leonardo Express train** (adult/child €14/free) Runs to/from platforms 27 and 28 at Stazione Termini. Departures from Termini every 30 minutes between 5.52am and 10.52pm, from the airport between 6.36am and 11.36pm. Journey time is 30 minutes.

**FR1 train** (one way €8) Connects the airport to Trastevere, Ostiense and Tiburtina stations, but not Termini. Departures from the airport every 15 minutes (hourly on Sunday and public holidays) between 5.57am and 11.27pm, from Tiburtina between 5.05am and 10.33pm.

**Cotral bus** (www.cotralspa.it; one way €4.50 or €7 if bought on bus) Runs to/from Stazione Tiburtina via Stazione Termini. Eight daily departures including night services from Tiburtina at 12.30am, 1.15am, 2.30am and 3.45am and from the airport at 1.15am, 2.15am, 3.30am and 5am. Journey time is one hour.

**SIT bus** (☑06 591 68 26; www.sitbusshuttle.it; one way €8) Regular departures from Via Marsala outside Stazione Ter-

mini between 5am and 8.30pm, from the airport between 8.30am and 12.30am. Tickets available on the bus. Journey time is one hour.

**Airport Connection Services** (☑06 338 32 21; www. airportconnection.it) Transfers to/from the city centre start at €37 per person.

**Airport Shuttle** (☑06 420 13 469; www.airportshuttle.it) Transfers to/from your hotel for €25 for one person, then €6 for each additional passenger up to a maximum of eight.

**Taxi** The set fare to/from the city centre is €40, which is valid for up to four passengers including luggage. Note that taxis registered in Fiumicino charge a set fare of €60, so make sure you catch a Comune di Roma taxi.

**Car** Follow signs for Roma out of the airport complex and onto the autostrada. Exit at EUR, following signs for the *centro*, to link up with Via Cristoforo Colombo, which will take you directly into the centre. All major car-hire companies are present at Fiumicino.

### Ciampino Airport

**Ciampino** (CIA; ☑06 6 59 51; www.adr.it), 15km southeast of the city centre, is used by European low-cost airlines and charter operators. It's not a big airport but there's a steady flow of traffic and

## CLIMATE CHANGE & TRAVEL

Every form of transport that relies on carbon-based fuel generates $CO_2$, the main cause of human-induced climate change. Modern travel is dependent on aeroplanes, which might use less fuel per kilometre per person than most cars but travel much greater distances. The altitude at which aircraft emit gases (including $CO_2$) and particles also contributes to their climate change impact. Many websites offer 'carbon calculators' that allow people to estimate the carbon emissions generated by their journey and, for those who wish to do so, to offset the impact of the greenhouse gases emitted with contributions to portfolios of climate-friendly initiatives throughout the world. Lonely Planet offsets the carbon footprint of all staff and author travel.

at peak times it can get extremely busy.

TO/FROM THE AIRPORT
The best option is to take one of the regular bus services into the city centre. You can also take a bus to Ciampino station and then pick up a train to Stazione Termini.

**Terravision bus** (www.terravision.eu; one way/return €4/8) Twice hourly departures to/from Via Marsala outside Stazione Termini. From the airport services are between 8.15am and 12.15am, from Via Marsala between 4.30am and 9.20pm. Buy tickets at Terracafé in front of the Via Marsala bus stop. Journey time is 40 minutes.

**SIT bus** (www.sitbusshuttle.com; one way/return €6/8) Regular departures from Via Marsala outside Stazione Termini between 4.30am and 9.30pm, from the airport between 7.45am and 11.15pm. Tickets available on the bus. Journey time is 45 minutes.

**Cotral bus** (www.cotralspa.it; one way/return €3.90/6.90) Runs 15 daily services to/from Via Giolitti near Stazione Termini. **Terravision bus** (www.terravision.eu; one way/return €4/8) Twice hourly departures to/from Via Marsala outside Stazione Termini. Also buses to/from Anagnina metro station (€1.20) and Ciampino train station (€1.20) where you can

connect with trains to Stazione Termini (€1.30).

**Airport Connection Services** (☑06 338 32 21; www.airportconnection.it) Transfers to/from the city centre start at €37 per person.

**Airport Shuttle** (☑06 420 13 469; www.airportshuttle.it) Transfers to/from your hotel for €25 for one person, then €5 for each additional passenger up to a maximum of eight.

**Taxi** The set rate to/from the airport is €30.

**Car** If you want to hire a car, you'll find all the major rental companies in the arrivals hall. Exit the station and follow Via Appia Nuova straight into the city centre.

## Train

Almost all trains arrive at and depart from **Stazione Termini** (Map p340), Rome's main train station and principal transport hub. There are regular connections to other European countries, all major Italian cities, and many smaller towns. Train information is available from the **train information office** (☑6am–midnight) next to platform 1, online at www.ferroviedellostato.it, or, if you speak Italian, by calling ☑89 20 21.

From Termini, you can connect with both metro lines (line A, which is colour-coded orange; and line B, which is marked with blue

signs) or take a bus from the bus station on Piazza dei Cinquecento out front. Taxis are outside the main exit.

## Bus

Long-distance national and international buses use the **Autostazione Tiburtina** (Piazzale Tiburtina). From the bus station cross under the overpass for the Tiburtina train station where you can pick up the metro (line B) and connect with Termini for onward buses, trains or metro line A.

## Boat

Rome's port is at Civitavecchia, about 80km north of Rome. Ferries sail here from destinations across the Mediterranean including Barcelona, Malta and Tunis, as well as Sicily and Sardinia. Check out www.traghettiweb.it for route details, prices and bookings.

From Civitavecchia there are half-hourly trains to Stazione Termini (€4.50 to €12.50, one hour). Civitavecchia's station is about 700m from the entrance to the port.

## GETTING AROUND ROME

Rome is a sprawling city, but the historic centre is relatively compact and it's quite possible to explore much of it on foot. The city's public transport system includes buses, trams, metro and a suburban train system. Tickets, which come in various forms, are valid for all forms of transport.

## Metro

➡ Rome has two metro lines, A (orange) and B (blue), which cross at Termini, the only point at which you can change from one line to the other.

➡ Trains run approximately every five to 10 minutes between 5.30am and 11.30pm (to 1.30am on Friday and Saturday). However, until April 2012 line A is closing at 9pm every day except Saturday for construction work. To replace it there are two temporary bus lines: MA1 from Battistini to Arco di Travertino and MA2 from Piazzale Flaminio to Anagnina.

➡ All the metro stations on line B have wheelchair access except for Circo Massimo, Colosseo and Cavour (direction Laurentina), while on line A Cipro–Musei Vaticani station is one of the few stations equipped with lifts.

➡ Take line A for the Trevi Fountain (Barberini), Spanish Steps (Spagna) and St Peter's (Ottaviano–San Pietro).

➡ Take line B for the Colosseum (Colosseo).
For ticket details, see the boxed text p302.

## Bus & Tram

➡ Rome's buses and trams are run by **ATAC** (☑06 5 70 03; www.atac.roma.it).

➡ The main bus station (Map p340) is in front of Stazione Termini on Piazza dei Cinquecento, where there's an **information booth** (☺7.30am-8pm). Other important bus stops are at Largo di Torre Argentina, Piazza Venezia and Piazza San Silvestro.

➡ Buses generally run from about 5.30am until midnight, with limited services throughout the night.

Rome's night bus service comprises more than 25 lines, many of which pass Termini and/or Piazza Venezia. Buses are marked with an n before the number and bus stops have a blue owl symbol. Departures are usually every 15 to 30 minutes between about 1am and 5am, but can be much slower.

The most useful routes:

**n1** Follows the route of metro line A.

**n2** Follows the route of metro line B.

**n7** Piazzale Clodio, Via Zanardelli, Corso Rinascimento, Corso Vittorio Emanuele II, Largo di Torre Argentina, Piazza Venezia, Via Nazionale and Stazione Termini.

---

### TICKETS, PLEASE

Public-transport tickets are valid on all Rome's bus, tram and metro lines, except for routes to Fiumicino airport. They come in various forms:

**BIT** (biglietto integrato a tempo, a single ticket valid for 75 minutes and one metro ride) €1

**BIG** (biglietto integrato giornaliero, a daily ticket) €4

**BTI** (biglietto turistico integrato, a three-day ticket) €11

**CIS** (carta integrata settimanale, a weekly ticket) €16

**Abbonamento mensile** (a monthly pass) €30
Children under 10 travel free.

You can buy tickets at tabacchi (tobacconist's shop) and newsstands and from vending machines at metro, bus and train stations. They must be purchased before you get on the bus or train, then validated in the yellow machine once on board, or at the entrance gates for the metro. You risk a €50 fine if you're caught without a validated ticket.

The **Roma Pass** (www.romapass.it) comes with a three-day travel pass valid within the city boundaries. The **Vatican and Rome card** (1/3 days €20/25) provides unlimited travel on all public transport within the city and on the Open buses operated by Roma Christiana (see p306).

#### Travelling out of town

For destinations in the surrounding Lazio region, **Cotral** (☑800 174 471; www.cotralspa.it) buses depart from numerous points throughout the city. The company is linked with Rome's public transport system, which means that you can buy tickets that cover city buses, trams, metro and train lines, as well as regional buses and trains. There are a range of tickets but your best bet is a daily BIRG (biglietto integrato regionale giornaliero) ticket, which allows unlimited travel on all city and regional transport. It's priced according to zones: the most expensive, zone 7, costs €10.50; the cheapest, zone 1, is €2.50.

Get tickets from tabacchi and authorised ATAC sellers.

## USEFUL BUS ROUTES

| BUS NO | ROUTE | OPERATING HOURS | FREQUENCY |
| --- | --- | --- | --- |
| H | Stazione Termini, Via Nazionale, Piazza Venezia, Largo di Torre Argentina, Ponte Garibaldi, Viale Trastevere | 6am–midnight | up to 6 hourly |
| 3 | Stazione Trastevere, Testaccio, Circo Massimo, Colosseo, San Giovanni, Porta Maggiore, Policlinico, Villa Borghese | 5.30am–10pm | up to 12 hourly |
| 8 Tram | Largo di Torre Argentina, Trastevere, Stazione Trastevere and Monteverde Nuovo | 5.10am–3am | up to 15 hourly |
| 23 | Piazzale Clodio, Piazza Risorgimento, Ponte Vittorio Emanuele II, Lungotevere, Ponte Garibaldi, Via Marmorata (Testaccio), Piazzale Ostiense and Basilica di San Paolo | 5.15am–midnight | up to 7 hourly |
| 40 | Express Stazione Termini, Via Nazionale, Piazza Venezia, Largo di Torre Argentina, Chiesa Nuova, Piazza Pia (for Castel Sant'Angelo) and St Peter's | 6.30am–12.24am | up to 15 hourly |
| 64 | Stazione Termini to St Peter's Square. It takes the same route as the 40 Express but is more crowded and has more stops | 5.30am–12.30am | up to 13 hourly |
| 170 | Stazione Termini, Via Nazionale, Piazza Venezia, Via del Teatro Marcello and Piazza Bocca della Verità, then south to Testaccio and EUR | 5.30am–midnight | up to 9 hourly |
| 175 | Stazione Termini, Piazza della Repubblica, Piazza Barberini, Colosseum, Via del Circo Massimo, Aventino hill and Piazzale dei Partigiani | 5.30am–midnight | up to 5 hourly |
| 492 | Stazione Tiburtina, San Lorenzo, Stazione Termini, Piazza Barberini, Piazza Venezia, Corso Rinascimento, Piazza Cavour, Piazza Risorgimento and Cipro–Vatican Museums (metro line A) | 5.30am–midnight | up to 5 hourly |
| 590 | Follows the route of metro line A and has special facilities for disabled passengers | 7.30am–10.30pm | 1 hourly |
| 660 | Largo Colli Albani, Via Appia Nuova and Via Appia Antica (near Mausoleo di Cecilia Metella) | 7am–8.45pm | 2 hourly |
| 714 | Stazione Termini, Piazza Santa Maria Maggiore, Piazza San Giovanni in Laterano and Viale delle Terme di Caracalla (then south to EUR) | 5.25am–midnight | up to 8 hourly |
| 910 | Stazione Termini, Piazza della Repubblica, Villa Borghese, Auditorium Parco della Musica, Piazza Mancini | 5.30am–midnight | up to 5 hourly |

## Car & Motorcycle

Driving around Rome is not the quickest or most relaxing way of getting around town. Riding a scooter or motorbike is faster and makes parking a lot easier, but Rome is no place for learners, so if you're not an experienced rider it's probably best to give it a miss. Hiring a car for a day trip out of town is definitely worth considering.

Most of Rome's historic centre is closed to normal traffic from 6.30am to 6pm Monday to Friday, from 2pm to 6pm Saturday, and from 11pm to 3am Friday to Sunday. Restrictions also apply in Trastevere (6.30am-10am Mon-Sat, 11pm-3am Fri-Sun), San Lorenzo (9pm-3am Fri-Sun), Monti (11pm-3am Fri-Sun) and Testaccio (11pm-3am Fri-Sun).

All streets accessing the 'Limited Traffic Zone' (ZTL) have been equipped with electronic-access detection devices. If you're staying in this zone, contact your hotel, which will fax the authorities with your number plate, thus saving you a fine. For further information, check www.agenziamobilita.roma.it or call ☑06 57 003.

Driving out of town can be costly. Tolls apply on autostradas and petrol and diesel are expensive. A good source of general motoring

## BUSES FROM TERMINI

From Piazza dei Cinquecento outside Stazione Termini buses run to all corners of the city.

| DESTINATION | BUS NO |
| --- | --- |
| St Peter's Square | 40 |
| Piazza Venezia | 40/64 |
| Piazza Navona | 40/64 |
| Campo de' Fiori | 40/64 |
| Pantheon | 40/64 |
| Colosseum | 75 |
| Terme di Caracalla | 714 |
| Villa Borghese | 910 |
| Trastevere | H |

information is the **Automobile Club d'Italia** (ACI; www.aci.it, in Italian), Italy's national motoring organisation.

### Driving Licence & Road Rules

All EU driving licences are recognised in Italy. Holders of non-EU licences must get an International Driving Permit (IDP) to accompany their national licence. Apply to your national motoring association.

To ride a scooter up to 125cc, the minimum age is 18 and a licence (a car licence will do) is required. For anything over 125cc you need a motorcycle licence.

Other rules:

➡ Drive on the right, overtake on the left and give way to cars coming from the right.

➡ It's obligatory to wear seat belts, to drive with your headlights on outside built-up areas, and to carry a warning triangle and fluorescent waistcoat in case of breakdown.

➡ Wearing a helmet is compulsory on all two-wheeled vehicles.

➡ The blood alcohol limit is 0.05%.

Unless otherwise indicated, speed limits are as follows:

➡ 130km/h (in rain 110km/h) on autostradas

➡ 110km/h (in rain 90km/h) on all main, non-urban roads

➡ 90km/h on secondary, non-urban roads

➡ 50km/h in built-up areas

### Hire

Car hire is available available at both Rome's airports and Stazione Termini. Reckon on paying from about €50 per day for a small car such as a Fiat Panda or Fiat 500. Note also that most Italian hire cars have manual gear transmission.

**Avis** (www.avisautonoleggio.it, in Italian) Ciampino airport (☑06 793 40 195); Fiumicino airport (☑06 650 11 531); Stazione Termini (☑06 481 43 73)

**Europcar** (www.europcar.com) Ciampino airport (☑06 793 40 387); Fiumicino airport (☑06 657 61 211); Stazione Termini (☑06 488 28 54)

**Hertz** (www.hertz.it, in Italian) Ciampino airport (☑06 793 40 616); Fiumicino airport (☑06 650 11 553); Stazione Termini (☑06 474 03 89)

**Maggiore National** (central bookings ☑199 151 120; www.maggiore.it, in Italian; per day €50-167) Ciampino airport (☑06 793 40 368); Fiumicino airport (☑06 650 10 678); Stazione Termini (☑06 488 00 49)

To hire a scooter, prices range from about €20 for a 50cc scooter to €1265 for a 600cc motorbike. Reliable operators:

**Bici e Baci** (☑06 482 84 43; www.bicibaci.com; Via del Viminale 5)

**Eco Move Rent** (☑06 447 04 518; www.ecomoverent.com; Via Varese 48-50)

**Treno e Scooter** (☑06 489 05 823; www.trenoescooter.com; Piazza dei Cinquecento)

**On Road** (☑06 481 56 69; www.scooterhire.it; Via Cavour 80)

### Parking

Blue lines denote pay-and-display parking spaces with tickets available from meters (coins only) and *tabacchi*. Expect to pay up to €1.20 per hour between 8am and 8pm (11pm in some places). After 8pm (or 11pm) parking is free until 8am the next morning. Traffic wardens are vigilant and fines are not uncommon. If your car gets towed away, check with the **traffic police** (☑06 6 76 91).

Car parks:

**Piazzale dei Partigiani** (Map p358; per hr/day €0.77/5; ⊗24hr)

**Stazione Termini** (Map p340; Piazza dei Cinquecento; per hr/day €2/18; ⊗6am-1am)

**Stazione Tiburtina** (Map p339; Via Pietro l'Eremita; weekday/Sun per hr €2/free; ⊗6am-10pm)

**Villa Borghese** (Map p366; Viale del Galoppatoio 33; per hr/day €2/20; ⊗24hr) There's a comprehensive list of carparks on www.060608.it – click on the transport tab & car parks.

## Bicycle

The centre of Rome doesn't lend itself to cycling: there are steep hills and treacherous cobbled roads, and the traffic is terrible. However, if you want to pedal around town, pick up *Andiamo in Bici a Roma* (€7), a useful map published by L'Ortensia Rossa, which details Rome's main cycle paths.

➡ On Saturdays, Sundays and weekdays after 8pm, you can take your bike on the metro and the Lido di Ostia train. You have to use the front carriage and buy a separate ticket for the bike.

➡ On Sundays and holidays you can carry bikes on bus 791.

➡ On regional trains marked with a bike icon on the timetable, you can carry a bike on payment of a €3.50 supplement.

➡ Rome has a bike-sharing scheme. You can sign up at the ATAC ticket offices at Termini, Spagna and Lepanto metro stations. There's a €5 signing on fee and a €5 minimum charge. On signing up you're provided with a rechargeable smartcard that allows you to pick up a bike from one of the 27 stations across the city, and use it for up to 24 hours within a single day. On the road, you pay €0.50 for every 30 minutes. For further information see www.bikesharing.roma.it or call ☑06 5 70 03.

### Hire

**Appia Antica Regional Park Information Point**
(☑06 513 53 16; www.parcoap piaantica.org; Via Appia Antica 58-60; per hr/day €3/10)

**Bici e Baci** (☑06 482 84 43; www.bicibaci.com; Via del Viminale 5; per hr/day €4/11)

**Eco Move Rent** (☑06 447 04 518; www.ecomoverent. com; Via Varese 48-50; per hr/ day €4/10)

**Treno e Scooter** (☑06 489 05 823; www.trenoescooter. com; Piazza dei Cinquecento; per hr/day €4/10)

**Villa Borghese** (Via delle Belle Arti; per hr/day €4/15)

## Taxi

➡ Official licensed taxis are white with the symbol of Rome and an identifying number on the doors. Always go with the metered fare, never an arranged price (the set fares to and from the airports are exceptions).

➡ In town (within the ring road) flag fall is €2.80 between 7am and 10pm on weekdays, €4 on Sundays and holidays, and €5.80 between 10pm and 7am. Then it's €0.92 per km. Official rates are posted in taxis and on www.viviromaintaxi.eu.

➡ You can hail a taxi, but it's often easier to wait at a rank or phone for one. There are major taxi ranks at the airports, Stazione Termini, Largo di Torre Argentina, Piazza San Silvestro, Piazza della Repubblica, Piazza del Colosseo, Piazza Belli in Trastevere and in the Vatican at Piazza del Pio XII and Piazza Risorgimento.

➡ You can book a taxi by phoning the Comune di Roma's automated **taxi line** (☑060609) or calling a taxi company direct.

**La Capitale** (☑06 49 94)
**Pronto Taxi** (☑06 66 45)
**Radio Taxi** (☑06 35 70)
**Samarcanda** (☑06 55 51)
**Tevere** (☑06 41 57)
The website www.060608. has a list of taxi companies – click on the transport tab, then getting around & by taxi.

Note that when you call for a cab, the meter is switched on straight away and you pay for the cost of the journey from wherever the driver receives the call.

## Train

Apart from connections to Fiumicino airport, you'll probably only need the overground rail network if you head out of town to the Castelli Romani (p223), Os-

tia Antica (p220) or Orvieto (p223).

➡ You can get trains to all these destinations from **Stazione Termini** (Map p340; Piazza dei Cinquecento).

➡ Train information is available at the station's **train information office** (🕑6am-midnight) next to platform 1. Alternatively you can go online at www.ferroviedellostato.it or call ☑89 20 21.

➡ Buy tickets at the windows on the main station concourse, from the automated ticket machines or from an authorised travel agency – look for an FS or *biglietti treni* sign in the window.

➡ Rome's second train station is **Stazione Tiburtina**, four stops from Termini on metro line B. Of the capital's eight other train stations, the most important are **Stazione Roma-Ostiense** (Map p358) and **Stazione Trastevere** (Map p360).

## TOURS

## Walking

**A Friend in Rome** (☑06 661 40 987; www.afriend-inrome.it) Silvia Prosperi organises private tailor-made tours (on foot, by bike or scooter) to suit your interests. She covers the Vatican and main historic centre as well as neighbourhoods such as the Aventino, Trastevere, Celio and the Monti. Rates are €50 per hour, with a minimum of three hours for most tours. Silvia can also arrange mosaic lessons, cooking classes and coastal cruises.

**Dark Rome** (☑06 833 60 561; www.darkrome.com) Runs a range of themed tours, costing from €22 to €91. Popular choices include the Crypts and Catacombs tour, which takes in Rome's buried treasures, and the Semi-Private Vatican Museums Tour, which takes you into the museums before they're opened to the public.

**Enjoy Rome** (Map p340; ☑06 445 18 43; www.enjoy rome.com; Via Marghera 8a) Offers three-hour walking tours of the Vatican (under/over 26 yr €25/30) and Ancient & Old Rome (under/over 26 yr €25/30) as well as various other tours – see the website for further details. Note that tour prices do not cover admission charges to the Vatican Museums and Colosseum.

**Through Eternity Cultural Association** (☑06 700 93 36; www.through eternity.com) Another reliable operator offering a range of private and group tours led by English-speaking experts. Walks include a group twilight tour of Rome's piazzas and fountains (€29, 2½ hours), the Vatican Museums and St Peter's Basilica (€41, five hours), and an Angels and Demons tour (€31, 3½ hours) based on Dan Brown's bestselling book.

**Roma Cristiana** (☑06 698 96 380; www.operaromana pellegrinaggi.org) Runs various walking tours, including visits to the Vatican Museums (adult/reduced €26/17) and St Peter's Basilica (€12). Tickets are available online or at the meeting point just off Piazza San Pietro.

**ArCult** (☑339 650 31 72; www.arcult.it) Run by architects, Arcult offers excellent customisable tours focusing on Rome's contemporary architecture, looking at buildings like the Auditorium Parco della Musica, MACRO, MAXXI and

the Centro Congressi Italia. A half-day tour costs between €200 and €300 for two to 10 people, so it makes sense to get a like-minded group together.

## Bus

**Trambus 110open** (☑800 281 281; www.trambusopen. com; family/adult/reduced €50/20/18; ◷every 15min 8.30am-8.30pm) This open-top, double-decker bus departs from Piazza dei Cinquecento in front of Termini station, and stops at the Colosseum, Bocca della Verità, Piazza Venezia, St Peter's, Ara Pacis and Trevi Fountain. The entire tour lasts two hours, but the tickets, which are available on board, from the info boxes on Piazza dei Cinquecento and at the Colosseum, or from authorised Trambus Open dealers, are valid for 48 hours and allow you to hop off and on as you please.

**Trambus Archeobus** (☑800 281 281; www. trambusopen.com; family/ adult €40/12; ◷every half-hr 9am-4.30pm) A stop-and-go bus that takes sightseers down Via Appia Antica, stopping at points of archaeological interest along the way. It departs from Piazza dei Cinquecento and tickets, valid for 48 hours, can be bought online, on board, at the Piazza dei Cinquecento or Colosseum info boxes and at Trambus Open authorised dealers.

**Open Bus Cristiana** (☑06 698 96 380; www.operaro-manapellegrinaggi.org; 24hr/

one circuit €18/13; ◷every 20 min 8.40am-7pm) The Vatican-sponsored Opera Romana Pellegrinaggi runs a hop-on, hop-off bus departing from Via della Conciliazione and Termini. Tickets are available on board the bus, online or at the meeting point just off Piazza San Pietro.

## Bike & Scooter

**Bici & Baci** (☑06 482 84 43; www.bicibaci.com; Via del Viminale 5; €35; ◷10am, 3pm & 7pm Mar-Oct, on request Nov-Feb) Bici & Baci runs daily bike tours of central Rome, taking in the historic centre, Campidoglio and the Colosseum, as well as tours on vintage Vespas and in classic Fiat 500 cars. For the Vespa and Fiat 500 tours you'll need to book 24 hours ahead. Routes and prices vary according to your requests.

## Boat

**Battelli di Roma** (☑06 977 45 498; www.battellidiroma. it; adult/reduced €16/12) Runs hour-long hop-on hop-off cruises along the Tiber between Ponte Sant'Angelo and Ponte Nenni. Trips depart at 10am from Ponte Sant'Angelo, 10.10pm from Isola Tiberina, and then hourly until 6.30pm. There are also dinner cruises (€58, 2¼ hours), wine-bar cruises (€39, 2¼ hours) and a bus–boat combination tour (adult/reduced €32/19). Tickets are available online or at the embarkation points on Molo Sant'Angelo and Isola Tiberina.

# Directory
# A–Z

## Business Hours

| BUSINESS | HOURS |
|----------|-------|
| Banks | 8.30am-1.30pm & 2.45pm-4.30pm Mon-Fri |
| Bars & cafes | 7.30am-8pm, sometimes until 1am or 2am |
| Shops | 9am-7.30pm or 10am-8pm Mon-Sat, some 11am-7pm Sun; smaller shops 9am-1pm & 3.30-7.30pm (or 4-8pm) Mon-Sat. |
| Clubs | 10pm-4am |
| Restaurants | noon-3pm & 7.30pm-11pm (later in summer) |

## Customs Regulations

Within the European Union you are entitled to Tax Free prices on fragrances, cosmetics and skincare; photographic and electrical goods; fashion and accessories; gifts, jewellery and souvenirs where they are available, and there there are no longer any allowance restrictions on these Tax Free items.

If you're arriving from a non-EU country you can import, duty free, 200 cigarettes, 1L of spirits (or 2L fortified wine), 4L wine, 60ml perfume, 16L beer and goods, including electronic devices, up to a value of €300; anything over this value must be declared on arrival and the duty paid. On leaving the EU, non-EU residents can reclaim value-added tax (VAT) on expensive purchases (see p311).

## Emergency

**Ambulance** (☎118)
**Fire** (☎115)
**Police** (☎113)

## Gay & Lesbian Travellers

Hardly San Fran on the Med, Rome nevertheless has a thriving, if low-key gay scene. The big annual events – Gay Pride in June, Gay Village in the summer – are colourful crowdpleasers, and in 2011 Rome hosted Europride, with

---

### PRACTICALITIES

➡ Vatican Radio (www.radiovaticana.org; 93.3 FM & 105 FM in Rome, in Italian, English and other languages.

➡ RAI-1, RAI-2 and RAI-3 (www.rai.it) National broadcaster.

➡ Radio Città Futura (www.radiocittafutura.it) Good for contemporary music.

➡ State-run TV channels: RAI-1, RAI-2 and RAI-3 (www.rai.it)

➡ Main commercial stations (mostly run by Silvio Berlusconi's Mediaset company): Canale 5 (www.canale5.mediaset.it), Italia 1 (www.italia1.mediaset.it), Rete 4 (www.rete4.mediaset.it) and La 7 (www.la7.it).

➡ Weights & measures use the metric system.

➡ Smoking is banned in public spaces such as bars, cafes and restaurants.

➡ Italy's currency is the euro. The seven euro notes come in denominations of €500, €200, €100, €50, €20, €10 and €5. The eight euro coins are in denominations of €2 and €1, and 50, 20, 10, five, two and one cents.

a huge parade through central Rome. There are numerous gay and mixed nights in clubland, where gay is decidedly 'in' as well as out and proud.

In terms of gay rights, Italy is a late developer. Homosexuality is legal (over the age of 16) and even widely accepted, but it is publicly frowned on by the government, the views of which largely coincide with the Vatican's. And with the Catholic hierarchy decidedly against same-sex marriages and rights for common-law couples, both straight and gay, changes to the statute books are unlikely any time soon.

The main gay cultural and political organisation is the **Circolo Mario Mieli di Cultura Omosessuale** (☑06 541 39 85; www.mariomieli.it, in Italian; Via Efeso 2a), which organises debates, cultural events and social functions, including **Muccassassina** (www.muccassassina.com) clubnights and the city's annual Gay Pride march. It also runs free AIDS/HIV testing and a care centre. Its website has info and listings of forthcoming events.

The national organisation for lesbians is the **Coordinamento Lesbiche Italiano** (CLI; ☑06 686 42 01; www.clrbp. it, in Italian; Via San Francesco di Sales 1b), who hold regular conferences and literary evenings. There is also a women-only hostel, La Foresteria Orsa Maggiore (p247).

Other useful listings guides include the international gay guide *Spartacus*, available at gay and lesbian organisations and in bookshops. You can also go online at www.gayrome.com and www.gayfriendlyitaly.com, which carries listings for Rome.

The following might also be of help:

**Arcigay Roma** (☑06 6450 1102; www.arcigayroma.it; Via Nicola Zabaglia 14) The Roman branch of the national Arcigay organisation. Offers counsel

ling, phone lines and general information.

**Arcilesbica** (☑06 645 01102; www.arcilesbica.roma. it; Viale Stefanini 15) Organises social outings.

**Zipper Travel Association** (☑06 4436 2244; www. zippertravel.it; Via dei Gracchi 17) A specialist gay and lesbian travel agency.

# Electricity

230v/50hz

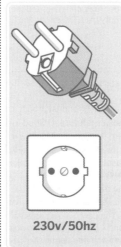

230v/50hz

# Internet Access

There are plenty of internet cafes to choose from, and most hotels have wifi these days, though with signals of varying quality, and there'll usually be at least a fixed computer for guests' use – those that do are indicated with the @ internet and/or 🛜 wi-fi icons. For information on wifi hotspots around the city and how to access them, see the boxed text 'Wi-fi Access', p312. Here is a list of some usefully located and reliable internet cafes, though there are many more:

**Internet Point** (☑06 5833 3316; Piazza Sonnino 27; per hr €4; ☺8.30am-10pm) In Trastevere.

**Internet Point** (☑06 4544 7204; Via dei Serpenti 89; per hr €4; ☺8am-10pm) Close to Via Nazionale.

**Pantheon Internet Point** (Via di Santa Caterina da Siena, 40; per hr €4; ☺10am-8pm Mon-Sat) Near the Pantheon.

# Legal Matters

The most likely reason for a brush with the law is to report a theft. If you do have something stolen and you want to claim it on insurance, you must make a statement to the police as insurance companies won't pay up without official proof of a crime.

The Italian police is divided into three main bodies: the *polizia*, who wear navy-blue jackets; the *carabinieri*, in a black uniform with a red stripe; and the grey-clad *guardia di finanza* (fiscal police), responsible for fighting tax evasion and drug smuggling. If you run into trouble, you're most likely to end up dealing with the *polizia* or *carabinieri*.

If you are detained for any alleged offence, you should be given verbal and written

## DISCOUNT CARDS

| DISCOUNT CARD | PRICE ADULT/ REDUCED | VALIDITY | ADMISSION TO |
|---|---|---|---|
| Appia Antica Card | €6/3 | 7 days | Terme di Caracalla, Mausoleo di Cecilia Metella and Villa dei Quintili. |
| Archaeologia Card | €23/12 | 7 days | Entrance to the Colosseum, Palatino, Terme di Caracalla, Museo Nazionale Romano (Palazzo Altemps, Palazzo Massimo alle Terme, Terme di Diocleziano, Crypta Balbi), Mausoleo di Cecilia Metella and Villa dei Quintili. |
| Roma Pass (www. romapass.it) | €27 | 3 days | Includes free admission to two museums or sites (you choose from a list of 38) as well as reduced entry to extra sites, unlimited public transport within Rome, access to the bike-sharing scheme, and reduced-price entry to other exhibitions and events. Roma & Più pass includes some of the surrounding province. |

Note that EU citizens aged between 18 and 25 generally qualify for a discount at most galleries and museums, while those under 18 and over 65 often get in free. In both cases you'll need proof of your age, ideally a passport or ID card.

notice of the charges laid against you within 24 hours. You have no right to a phone call upon arrest but you can choose not to respond to questions without the presence of a lawyer. For serious crimes it is possible to be held without trial for up to two years.

Rome's **Questura** (police headquarters; ☑06 4 68 61; Via San Vitale 15; ◷9am-midday Mon, Wed & Fri) is just off Via Nazionale.

### Drink & Drugs

Rome is not a good place to be caught with illegal drugs. Under Italian law there's no distinction between hard and soft drugs, so cannabis is effectively on the same legal footing as cocaine, heroin and ecstasy. If you're caught with what the police deem to be a dealable quantity, you risk heavy fines or prison sentences of between six and 20 years. In practice, these draconian punishments are rarely enforced, and if you can prove you're a Rastafarian, you should get off scot-free – in July 2008 the Italian Supreme Court ruled that it

was OK for Rastas to smoke cannabis, as it's part of their religion.

The legal limit for a driver's blood-alcohol reading is 0.05%.

## Medical Services

Italy has a public health system that is legally bound to provide emergency care to everyone. EU nationals are entitled to reduced-cost, sometimes free, medical care with a European Health Insurance Card (EHIC), available from your home health authority; non-EU citizens should take out medical insurance.

For emergency treatment, you can go to the *pronto soccorso* (casualty) section of an *ospedale* (public hospital), where it's also possible to receive emergency dental treatment, but be prepared for a long wait. For less serious ailments call the **Guardia Medica** (☑06 57 06 00).

A more convenient course, if you have insurance and can afford to pay up front, would be to call a private doctor to come to

your hotel or apartment. The callout/treatment fee will probably be around €130. Try **Roma Medica** (☑338 622 48 32; ◷24hr). Pharmacists will serve prescriptions and can provide basic medical advice.

If you need an ambulance, call ☑118.

### Emergency Rooms

**Ospedale Bambino Gesù** (☑06 6 85 91; Piazza di Sant'Onofrio 4) Rome's premier children's hospital, but be warned, the emergency section is very busy and you'll have a long wait if your case isn't urgent.

**Ospedale di Odontoiatria G Eastman** (☑06 84 48 31; Viale Regina Elena 287b) Specialist dental care.

**Ospedale Fatebenefratelli** (☑06 6 83 71; Piazza Fatebenefratelli, Isola Tiberina)

**Ospedale San Camillo Forlanini** (☑06 5 87 01; Circonvallazione Gianicolense 87)

**Ospedale San Giacomo** (☑06 3 62 61; Via A Canova 29)

## NO SMOKE

Smoking is banned in enclosed public spaces, which includes restaurants, bars, shops and public transport. If you want to smoke, ask if there's a smoking room, or go outside.

**Ospedale San Giovanni** (⌀06 7 70 51; Via Amba Aradam 9)

**Ospedale Santo Spirito** (⌀06 6 83 51; Lungotevere in Sassia 1)

**Policlinico Umberto I** (⌀06 4 99 71, first aid 06 499 79 501; Viale del Policlinico 155)

## Pharmacies

Marked by a green cross, *farmacie* (pharmacies) open from 8.30am to 1pm and 4pm to 7.30pm Monday to Friday and on Saturday mornings. Outside these hours they open on a rotational basis, and all are legally required to post a list of places open in the vicinity. Night pharmacies are listed in daily newspapers and in pharmacy windows.

If you think you'll need a prescription while in Rome, make sure you know the drug's generic name rather than the brand name. Regular medications available over the counter – such as antihistamine or paracetamol – tend to be fairly expensive in Italy, so you might want to bring supplies of these with you if you think you're likely to need them.

There's a 24-hour **pharmacy** (⌀06 488 00 19; Piazza dei Cinquecento 51) on the western flank of Piazza dei Cinquecento near Stazione Termini. In the station, you'll find a **pharmacy** (⏱7.30am-10pm) next to platform 1.

In the Vatican, the **Farmacia Vaticana** (⌀06 698 905 651; Palazzo Belvedere; ⏱8.30am-6pm Mon-Fri Sep-Jun, 8.30am-3pm Mon-Fri Jul & Aug, plus 8.30am-1pm Sat year-round) sells certain drugs that are not available in Italian pharmacies, and will fill foreign prescriptions (something local pharmacies can't do).

# Money

Exchange rates are given inside the front cover of this book. For the latest rates, check out www.xe.com. For a guide to costs, see p16.

## ATMs

ATMs (known in Italy as *bancomat*) are widely available in Rome and most will accept cards tied into the Visa, MasterCard, Cirrus and Maestro systems. The daily limit for cash withdrawal is €250. It's a good idea to let your bank know when you are going abroad, in case they block your card when payments from unusual locations appear – if you are registered for online banking, you can usually do this online.

Remember that every time you withdraw cash, you'll be charged a transaction fee (usually around 3% with a minimum of €3 or more) as well as a 1% to 3% conversion charge. Check with your bank to see how much this is.

## Changing Money

You can change your money in banks, at post offices or at a *cambio* (exchange office). There are exchange booths at Stazione Termini (p301) and at Fiumicino and Ciampino airports. In the centre, there are numerous bureaux de change, including **American Express** (⌀06 6 76 41; Piazza di Spagna 38; ⏱9am-5.30pm Mon-Fri, 9am-12.30pm Sat). Post offices and banks tend to offer the best rates. A few banks also provide automatic exchange machines that accept notes from most major currencies.

Always make sure you have your passport, or some form of photo ID, at hand when exchanging money.

## Credit Cards

Credit cards are widely accepted but it's still a good idea to carry a cash back-up. Virtually all midrange and top-end hotels accept credit cards, as do most restaurants and large shops. You can also use them to obtain cash advances at some banks. Some of the cheaper *pensioni* (guesthouses), trattorias and pizzerias accept nothing but cash.

Major cards such as Visa, MasterCard, Eurocard, Cirrus and Eurocheques are widely accepted. Amex is also recognised, although it's less common than Visa or MasterCard.

Note that using your credit card in ATMs can be costly. On every transaction there's a fee, which with some credit-card issuers can reach US$10, as well as interest per withdrawal. Check with your issuer before leaving home.

If your card is lost, stolen or swallowed by an ATM, telephone to have an immediate stop put on its use.

**Amex** (⌀06 7290 0347)

**Diners Club** (⌀800 39 39 39)

**MasterCard** (⌀800 87 08 66)

**Visa** (⌀800 81 90 14)

The Amex office (American Express (⌀06 6 76 41; Piazza di Spagna 38; ⏱9am-5.30pm Mon-Fri, 9am-12.30pm Sat) can issue customers with new cards, usually within 24 hours and sometimes immediately, if they have been lost or stolen.

As for your debit card, let your credit-card company know of your travel plans. Otherwise the bank might block the card when it sees any unusual spending.

## Post

Italy's postal system, **Poste Italiane** (☎803 160; www. poste.it) is not the world's best, but nor is it as bad as it's often made out to be; however, parcels do occasionally go missing. The Vatican postal system, on the other hand, has long enjoyed a reputation for efficiency.

Stamps (francobolli) are available at post offices and authorised tobacconists (look for the official tabacchi sign: a big 'T', usually white on black).

There are local post offices in every district. Opening hours vary but are typically 8.30am to 6pm Monday to Friday and 8.30am to 1pm on Saturday. All post offices close two hours earlier than normal on the last business day of each month.

**Main post office** (Map p352; ☎06 697 37 213; Piazza di San Silvestro 19; ⏰8am-7pm Mon-Sat)

**Vatican post office** (☎06 698 83 406; Piazza San Pietro; ⏰8.30am-6.30pm Mon-Sat) Letters can be posted in blue Vatican post boxes only if they carry Vatican stamps.

### Rates

Letters up to 20g cost €0.65 to Zone 1 (Europe and the Mediterranean Basin), €0.85 to Zone 2 (other countries in Africa, Asia and America) and €1 to Zone 3 (Australia and New Zealand). For more important items, use registered mail (raccomandata), which costs €4.80 to Zone 1, €5.60 to Zone 2 and €6 to Zone 3.

## Public Holidays

Most Romans take their annual holiday in August. This means that many businesses and shops close for at least part of the month, particularly around Ferragosto (Feast of the Assumption) on 15 August. August is not considered high season by Rome's hoteliers (as Italians tend to vacate the city rather than descend on it), many of whom offer discounts to avoid empty rooms.

Italian schools close for three months in summer (from mid-June to mid-September), for three weeks over Christmas (generally the last two weeks of December and the first week of January) and for a week at Easter.

Public holidays:

**Capodanno** (New Year's Day) 1 January

**Epifania** (Epiphany) 6 January

**Pasquetta** (Easter Monday) March/April

**Giorno della Liberazione** (Liberation Day) 25 April

**Festa del Lavoro** (Labour Day) 1 May

**Festa della Repubblica** (Republic Day) 2 June

**Festa dei Santi Pietro e Paolo** (Feast of St Peter & St Paul) 29 June

**Ferragosto** (Feast of the Assumption) 15 August

**Festa di Ognisanti** (All Saints' Day) 1 November

**Festa dell'Immacolata Concezione** (Feast of the Immaculate Conception) 8 December

**Natale** (Christmas Day) 25 December

**Festa di Santo Stefano** (Boxing Day) 26 December

For further details of Rome's holiday calendar, see p23.

## Safe Travel

Rome is not a dangerous city, but petty crime is a notable problem (see the boxed text, p314).

Road safety is also an issue. The highway code is obeyed with discretion, so don't take it for granted that cars and scooters will stop at pedestrian crossings, or even at red lights. The only way to cross the road is to wait for a suitable gap in the traffic and then walk confidently and calmly across, ideally with a group of local nuns.

For issues facing lone women travellers, see p315.

## Taxes & Refunds

A value-added tax of 20%, known as IVA (Imposta di Valore Aggiunto), is slapped on just about everything in Italy. If you are a non-EU resident and you spend more than €180 on a purchase, you can claim a refund when you leave the EU. The refund only applies to purchases from affiliated retail outlets that display a 'Tax Free' sign. When you make your purchase ask for a tax-refund voucher, to be filled in with the date of your purchase and its value. When you leave the EU, get this voucher stamped at customs and take it to the nearest tax-refund counter where you'll get an immediate refund, either in cash or charged your credit card. If there's no refund counter at the airport or you're travelling by sea or overland, you'll need to get the voucher stamped at the port or border crossing and mail it back for refund.

Note that under Italian tax law you are legally required to get a receipt for any purchase you make. Although it's highly unlikely, you could be asked by an officer of the guardia di finanza (fiscal police) to produce one immediately after you leave a shop. Without one, you risk a fine.

## Telephone

### Domestic Calls

Rome's area code is 06. Area codes are an integral part of all Italian phone numbers

## WI-FI ACCESS

Free wi-fi access is available in much of central Rome. Look online at www.wimove.it to see the locations of the hotspots. It's free (for an hour a day) but you will need to register the first time you use it, and to do that you'll need an Italian mobile-phone number. If you've got one, you can sign on by filling in the registration form that appears when you open your browser in a hotspot and validating the account with a quick phone call (from the mobile whose number you've provided). Once registered, you'll only need to log in on subsequent occasions.

Many hotels, bars and cafes also offer wi-fi access, and increasingly it's free; see p40 for a list of cafes where you may find it free of charge.

**Telecom Italia** (www.187.it, in Italian) sells prepaid wi-fi cards for €3 (one hour), €5 (five hours), €15 (24 hours) and €40 (seven days).

and must be dialled even when calling locally. Mobile-phone numbers are nine or 10 digits long and begin with a three-digit prefix starting with a 3. Toll-free numbers are known as *numeri verdi* and usually start with ☑800. Some six-digit national-rate numbers are also in use (such as those for Alitalia and Trenitalia).

For directory inquiries, dial ☑1240.

### International Calls

To call abroad from Italy dial ☑00, then the relevant country and area codes, followed by the telephone number.

Try to avoid making international calls from a hotel, as you'll be stung by high rates. It's cheaper to call from a private call centre or from a public payphone with an international calling card. These are available at newsstands and tobacconists, and are often good value. Another alternative is to use a direct-dialling service such as AT&T's USA Direct (access number ☑800 172 444) or Telstra's Australia Direct (access number ☑800 172 610), which allows you to make a reverse-charge call at home-country rates. Sky-

pe is also available at many internet cafes.

To make a reverse-charge (collect) international call from a public telephone, dial ☑170. All phone operators speak English.

### Mobile Phones

Italian mobile phones operate on the GSM 900/1800 network, which is compatible with the rest of Europe and Australia but not with the North American GSM 1900 or Japanese systems (although some GSM 1900/900 phones do work here).

If you have a GSM dual- or tri-band phone that you can unlock (check with your service provider), it can cost as little as €10 to activate a prepaid *(prepagato)* SIM card in Italy. **TIM** (Telecom Italia Mobile; www.tim.it, in Italian), **Wind** (www.wind.it, in Italian) and **Vodafone** (www.vodafone.it, in Italian) all offer SIM cards and have retail outlets across town. Note that by Italian law all SIM cards must be registered in Italy, so make sure you have a passport or ID card with you when you buy one. Also, if you're buying a SIM card abroad, check that the provider offers a registration service.

### Public Phones

Despite the fact that Italy is one of the most mobile-saturated countries in the world, you can still find public payphones around Rome. Most work and most take telephone cards (*schede telefoniche*), although you'll still find some that accept coins or credit cards. You can buy phonecards (€5, €10 or €20) at post offices, tobacconists and newsstands. Before you use them you need to break off the top left-hand corner of the card.

## Time

Italy is in a single time zone, one hour ahead of GMT. Daylight-saving time, when clocks move forward one hour, starts on the last Sunday in March. Clocks are put back an hour on the last Sunday in October.

Italy operates on a 24-hour clock, so 6pm is written as 18:00.

## Toilets

Public toilets are not widespread and those that do exist are often closed; some make a small charge. The best thing to do is to nip into a cafe or bar, all of which are required by law to have a loo. The law doesn't extend to loo paper, though, so try to have some tissues to hand.

## Tourist Information

### Telephone & Internet Resources

**Comune Call Centre** (☑06 06 06; ⏰24hr) Very useful for practical questions such as: where's the nearest hospital? Where can I park? When are the underground trains running? The centre is staffed 24 hours and there are staff who speak English, French, Arabic, German, Spanish, Italian and Chinese available from 4pm to 7pm.

**Tourist Information Line** (☑06 06 08; www.060608.com; ⊙9am-9pm) A free multilingual tourist information line and website providing information on culture, shows, hotels, transport, etc; you can also book theatre, concert, exhibition and museum tickets on this number. The website is similarly comprehensive and easy to use.

**Turismo Roma** (www.turismoroma.it) The official website of Rome Tourist Board with accommodation and restaurant lists, as well as details of upcoming events, museums and much more.

## Tourist Offices

**Centro Servizi Pellegrini e Turisti** (Map p364; ☑06 6988 1662; Piazza San Pietro; ⊙8.30am-6.15pm Mon-Sat) The Vatican's official tourist office.

**Enjoy Rome** (Map p340; ☑06 445 18 43; www.enjoyrome.com; Via Marghera 8a; ⊙9am-5.30 Mon-Fri, 8.30am-2pm Sat) This is a private tourist office that arranges guided tours and books accommodation.

**Meridiana Information Point** (Map p366; ☑06 8530 4242; www.villaborghese.it; Viale dell'Uccelliera 35; ⊙9am-5pm daily year-round, to 7pm Fri-Sun Apr-Sep) For information on Villa Borghese; closed for renovation at the time of research.

**Rome Tourist Board** (APT; ☑06 06 08; www.turismoroma.it; Terminal B, International Arrivals; ⊙9am-6pm) At Fiumicino airport.
The Comune di Roma also runs tourist information points throughout the city:

**Castel Sant'Angelo** (Map p364; Piazza Pia; ⊙9.30am-7pm)

**Ciampino airport** (International Arrivals, baggage reclaim area; ⊙9am-6.30pm)

**Fiumicino airport** (Terminal C, International Arrivals; ⊙9am-6.30pm)

**Piazza Navona** (Map p346; ⊙9.30am-7pm) Near Piazza delle Cinque Lune.

**Piazza Santa Maria Maggiore** (Map p340; Via dell'Olmata; ⊙9.30am-7pm)

**Piazza Sonnino** (Map p360; ⊙9.30am-7pm)

**Stazione Termini** (Map p340; ⊙8am-8.30pm) Next to platform 24.

**Trevi Fountain** (Map p352; Via Marco Minghetti; ⊙9.30am-7pm) Nearer to Via del Corso than the fountain.

**Via Nazionale** (Map p340; ⊙9.30am-7pm)

At these kiosks pick up the monthly what's-on pamphlet *L'Evento* as well as **Un Ospite a Roma** (A Guest in Rome; www.aguestinrome.com).

# Travellers with Disabilities

Rome isn't an easy city for travellers with disabilities. Cobbled streets, blocked pavements and tiny lifts are difficult for the wheelchair-bound, while the relentless traffic can be disorienting for partially sighted travellers or those with hearing difficulties.

Getting around on public transport is difficult, although efforts are being made to improve accessibility. On metro Line B all stations have wheelchair access except for Termini, Circo Massimo, Colosseo, Cavour and EUR Magliana, while on Line A few of the central stations have facilities except for Cipro–Musei Vaticani. Note that bus 590 covers the same route as metro Line A and is wheelchair accessible. Rome's newer buses and trams can generally accommodate wheelchairs.

If travelling by train, ring the national helpline ☑199 30 30 60 to arrange assistance. At Stazione Termini, the **Sala Blu Assistenza Disabili** (☑06 488 17 26; ⊙7am-9pm) next to platform 1 can provide information on wheelchair-accessible trains and help with transport in the station. Contact the office 24 hours ahead if you know you're going to need assistance. There's a similar office at Stazione Tiburtina.

Airline companies should be able to arrange assistance at airports if you notify them of your needs in advance. Alternatively, contact **ADR Assistance** (www.adrassistance.it) for assistance at Fiumicino or Ciampino airports.

Some taxis are equipped to carry passengers in wheelchairs; ask for a taxi for a *sedia a rotelle* (wheelchair). For contact numbers, see p305.

## Organisations

The best point of reference is **CO.IN** (www.coinsociale.it, in Italian; Via Enrico Giglioli 54/A), an umbrella group for associations and cooperatives across the country, which can provide useful information and local contacts.
Other useful resources:

**Handy Turismo** (☑06 3507 5707; www.handyturismo.it) A comprehensive and easy-to-use website with information on travel, accommodation and access at the main tourist attractions.

**Roma per Tutti** (☑06 5717 7094; www.romapertutti.it, in Italian) A council-backed venture to provide assistance and free guided museum visits.

## Visas

EU citizens do not need a visa to enter Italy. Nationals of some other countries, including Australia, Canada, Israel, Japan, New Zealand, Switzerland and the USA do not need a visa for stays of up to 90 days.

Italy is one of the 15 signatories of the Schengen Convention, an agreement whereby participating countries abolished customs checks at common borders. The standard tourist visa for a Schengen country is valid for 90 days. You must apply for it in your country of residence and you cannot apply for more than two in any 12-month period. They are not renewable inside Italy.

Technically, all foreign visitors to Italy are supposed to register with the local police within eight days of arrival. However, if you're staying in a hotel you don't need to bother as the hotel does this for you.

Up-to-date visa information is available on www.lonelyplanet.com – follow links through to the Italy destination guide.

### Permesso di Soggiorno

A *permesso di soggiorno* (permit to stay, also referred to as a residence permit) is required by all non-EU nationals who stay in Italy longer than three months. In theory, you should apply for one within eight days of arriving in Italy. EU citizens do not require a *permesso di soggiorno* but are required to register with the local registry office (*ufficio anagrafe*) if they stay for more than three months.

To get one, you'll need an application form; a valid passport, containing a stamp with your date of entry into Italy (ask for this, as it's not automatic); a photocopy of your passport with visa, if required; four passport-style photographs; proof of your ability to support yourself financially (ideally a letter from an employer or school/university); and a €14.62 official stamp.

Although correct at the time of writing, the documentary requirements change periodically, so always check before you join the inevitable queue.

Details are available on www.poliziadistato.it – click on the English tab and then follow the links.

The quickest way to apply is to go with the relevant documents to the **Ufficio Immigrazione** (Via Teofilo Patini; ⊗8.30-11.30am Mon-Fri & 3-5pm Tue & Thu) in the city's eastern suburbs.

## Study Visas

Non-EU citizens who want to study at a university or language school in Italy must have a study visa. These can be obtained at your nearest Italian embassy or consulate. You will normally require confirmation of your enrolment, proof of payment of fees and proof that you can support yourself financially. The visa only covers the period of the enrolment. This type of visa is renewable within Italy but, again, only with confirmation of ongoing enrolment and that you are still financially self-supporting.

## Work Visas

To work in Italy all non-EU citizens require a work visa. Apply to your nearest Italian embassy or consulate. You'll need a valid passport, proof of health insurance and a work permit. The work permit is obtained in Italy by your employer and then forwarded to you prior to your visa application.

# Women Travellers

Rome is not a dangerous city for women, but women should take the usual precautions, and, as in most places, avoid wandering around alone late at night, especially in the area around Termini. It's practically unheard of for women to go out in the evening on their own, and if you do, be prepared for some unwanted attention or to feel quite conspicuous.

The most common source of discomfort is harassment. If you find yourself being pestered by local men and ignoring them isn't working, tell them that you are waiting for your husband (*marito*) or boyfriend (*fidanzato*), and if necessary, walk away. Avoid becoming aggressive, as this may result in an unpleasant confrontation.

Gropers, particularly on crowded public transport, can also be a problem. If you do feel someone start to touch you inappropriately, make a fuss – a loud '*che schifo!*' (how disgusting!) should do the job. If a more serious incident occurs, report it to the police, who are then required to press charges.

# Language

When in Rome, you'll find that locals appreciate you trying their language, no matter how muddled you may think you sound.

Italian is not difficult to pronounce as the sounds used in spoken Italian can all be found in English.

Note that ai is pronounced as in 'aisle', ay as in 'say', ow as in 'how', dz as the 'ds' in 'lids', and that r is a strong and rolled sound.

Keep in mind too that Italian consonants can have a stronger, emphatic pronunciation – if the consonant is written as a double letter, it should be pronounced a little stronger. This difference in the pronunciation of single and double consonants can mean a difference in meaning, eg sonno son·no (sleep) versus sono so·no (I am).

If you read our coloured pronunciation guides as if they were English, you'll be understood. The stressed syllables are indicated with italics.

## BASICS

Italian has two words for 'you' – use the polite form Lei lay if you're talking to strangers, officials or people older than you. With people familiar to you or younger than you, you can use the informal form tu too.

In Italian, all nouns and adjectives are either masculine or feminine, and so are the articles il/la eel/la (the) and un/una oon/oo·na (a) that go with the nouns.

In this chapter the polite/informal and masculine/feminine options are included where necessary, separated with a slash and indicated with 'pol/inf' and 'm/f'.

### WANT MORE?

For in-depth language information and handy phrases, check out Lonely Planet's *Italian phrasebook*. You'll find it at **shop.lonelyplanet.com**, or you can buy Lonely Planet's iPhone phrasebooks at the Apple App Store.

| | | |
|---|---|---|
| **Hello.** | *Buongiorno.* | bwon·*jor*·no |
| **Goodbye.** | *Arrivederci.* | a·ree·ve·*der*·chee |
| **Yes.** | *Sì.* | see |
| **No.** | *No.* | no |
| **Excuse me.** | *Mi scusi.* (pol) | mee *skoo*·zee |
| | *Scusami.* (inf) | *skoo*·za·mee |
| **Sorry.** | *Mi dispiace.* | mee dees·*pya*·che |
| **Please.** | *Per favore.* | per fa·*vo*·re |
| **Thank you.** | *Grazie.* | *gra*·tsye |
| **You're welcome.** | *Prego.* | *pre*·go |

**How are you?**
*Come sta/stai?* (pol/inf)   *ko*·me sta/stai

**Fine. And you?**
*Bene. E Lei/tu?* (pol/inf)   *be*·ne e lay/too

**What's your name?**
*Come si chiama?* pol   *ko*·me see *kya*·ma
*Come ti chiami?* inf   *ko*·me tee *kya*·mee

**My name is ...**
*Mi chiamo ...*   mee *kya*·mo ...

**Do you speak English?**
*Parla/Parli*   *par*·la/*par*·lee
*inglese?* (pol/inf)   een·*gle*·ze

**I don't understand.**
*Non capisco.*   non ka·*pee*·sko

## ACCOMMODATION

| | | |
|---|---|---|
| **Do you have a ... room?** | *Avete una camera ...?* | a·*ve*·te *oo*·na *ka*·me·ra ... |
| double | *doppia con letto matrimoniale* | *do*·pya kon *le*·to ma·tree·mo·*nya*·le |
| single | *singola* | *seen*·go·la |
| **How much is it per ...?** | *Quanto costa per ...?* | *kwan*·to *kos*·ta per ... |
| night | *una notte* | *oo*·na *no*·te |
| person | *persona* | per·*so*·na |

**Is breakfast included?**
*La colazione è*    la ko·la·*tsyo*·ne e
*compresa?*    kom·*pre*·sa

| | | |
|---|---|---|
| **air-con** | *aria condizionata* | a·rya kon·dee·tsyo·*na*·ta |
| **bathroom** | *bagno* | ba·nyo |
| **campsite** | *campeggio* | kam·*pe*·jo |
| **guesthouse** | *pensione* | pen·*syo*·ne |
| **hotel** | *albergo* | al·*ber*·go |
| **youth hostel** | *ostello della gioventù* | os·*te*·lo de·la jo·ven·*too* |
| **window** | *finestra* | fee·*nes*·tra |

## DIRECTIONS

**Where's ...?**
*Dov'è ...?*    do·ve ...

**What's the address?**
*Qual'è l'indirizzo?*    kwa·le leen·dee·*ree*·tso

**Could you please write it down?**
*Può scriverlo,*    pwo *skree*·ver·lo
*per favore?*    per fa·*vo*·re

**Can you show me (on the map)?**
*Può mostrarmi*    pwo mos·*trar*·mee
*(sulla pianta)?*    (soo·la *pyan*·ta)

| | | |
|---|---|---|
| **at the corner** | *all'angolo* | a·*lan*·go·lo |
| **at the traffic lights** | *al semaforo* | al se·*ma*·fo·ro |
| **behind** | *dietro* | *dye*·tro |
| **far** | *lontano* | lon·*ta*·no |
| **in front of** | *davanti a* | da·*van*·tee a |
| **left** | *a sinistra* | a see·*nee*·stra |
| **near** | *vicino* | vee·*chee*·no |
| **next to** | *accanto a* | a·*kan*·to a |
| **opposite** | *di fronte a* | dee *fron*·te a |
| **right** | *a destra* | a *de*·stra |
| **straight ahead** | *sempre diritto* | *sem*·pre dee·*ree*·to |

## EATING & DRINKING

**What would you recommend?**
*Cosa mi consiglia?*    *ko*·za mee kon·*see*·lya

**What's in that dish?**
*Quali ingredienti*    *kwa*·li een·gre·*dyen*·tee
*ci sono in*    chee *so*·no een
*questo piatto?*    *kwe*·sto *pya*·to

**What's the local speciality?**
*Qual'è la specialità*    kwa·le la spe·cha·lee·*ta*
*di questa regione?*    dee *kwe*·sta re·*jo*·ne

**That was delicious!**
*Era squisito!*    e·ra skwee·*zee*·to

**Cheers!**
*Salute!*    sa·*loo*·te

### KEY PATTERNS

To get by in Italian, mix and match these simple patterns with words of your choice:

**When's (the next flight)?**
*A che ora è*    a ke o·ra e
*(il prossimo volo)?*    (eel *pro*·see·mo *vo*·lo)

**Where's (the station)?**
*Dov'è (la stazione)?*    *do*·ve (la sta·*tsyo*·ne)

**I'm looking for (a hotel).**
*Sto cercando*    sto cher·*kan*·do
*(un albergo).*    (oon al·*ber*·go)

**Do you have (a map)?**
*Ha (una pianta)?*    a (*oo*·na *pyan*·ta)

**Is there (a toilet)?**
*C'è (un gabinetto)?*    che (oon ga·bee·*ne*·to)

**I'd like (a coffee).**
*Vorrei (un caffè).*    vo·*ray* (oon ka·*fe*)

**I'd like to (hire a car).**
*Vorrei (noleggiare*    vo·*ray* (no·le·*ja*·re
*una macchina).*    *oo*·na ma·*kee*·na)

**Can I (enter)?**
*Posso (entrare)?*    *po*·so (en·*tra*·re)

**Could you please (help me)?**
*Può (aiutarmi),*    pwo (a·yoo·*tar*·mee)
*per favore?*    per fa·*vo*·re

**Do I have to (book a seat)?**
*Devo (prenotare*    *de*·vo (pre·no·*ta*·re
*un posto)?*    oon *po*·sto)

**Please bring the bill.**
*Mi porta il conto,*    mee *por*·ta eel *kon*·to
*per favore?*    per fa·*vo*·re

| | | |
|---|---|---|
| **I'd like to reserve a table for ...** | *Vorrei prenotare un tavolo per ...* | vo·*ray* pre·no·*ta*·re oon *ta*·vo·lo per ... |
| **(two) people** | *(due) persone* | (*doo*·e) per·*so*·ne |
| **(eight) o'clock** | *le (otto)* | le (*o*·to) |

| | | |
|---|---|---|
| **I don't eat ...** | *Non mangio ...* | non *man*·jo ... |
| **eggs** | *uova* | *wo*·va |
| **fish** | *pesce* | *pe*·she |
| **nuts** | *noci* | *no*·chee |
| **(red) meat** | *carne (rossa)* | *kar*·ne (*ro*·sa) |

## Key Words

| | | |
|---|---|---|
| **bar** | *locale* | lo·*ka*·le |
| **bottle** | *bottiglia* | bo·*tee*·lya |
| **breakfast** | *prima colazione* | *pree*·ma ko·la·*tsyo*·ne |

| | | |
|---|---|---|
| cafe | *bar* | *bar* |
| cold | *freddo* | *fre·do* |
| dinner | *cena* | *che·na* |
| drink list | *lista delle bevande* | *lee·sta de·le be·van·de* |
| fork | *forchetta* | *for·ke·ta* |
| glass | *bicchiere* | *bee·kye·re* |
| grocery store | *alimentari* | *a·lee·men·ta·ree* |
| hot | *caldo* | *kal·do* |
| knife | *coltello* | *kol·te·lo* |
| lunch | *pranzo* | *pran·dzo* |
| market | *mercato* | *mer·ka·to* |
| menu | *menù* | *me·noo* |
| plate | *piatto* | *pya·to* |
| restaurant | *ristorante* | *ree·sto·ran·te* |
| spicy | *piccante* | *pee·kan·te* |
| spoon | *cucchiaio* | *koo·kya·yo* |
| vegetarian (food) | *vegetariano* | *ve·je·ta·rya·no* |
| with | *con* | *kon* |
| without | *senza* | *sen·tsa* |

## Meat & Fish

| | | |
|---|---|---|
| beef | *manzo* | *man·dzo* |
| chicken | *pollo* | *po·lo* |
| duck | *anatra* | *a·na·tra* |
| fish | *pesce* | *pe·she* |
| herring | *aringa* | *a·reen·ga* |
| lamb | *agnello* | *a·nye·lo* |
| lobster | *aragosta* | *a·ra·gos·ta* |
| meat | *carne* | *kar·ne* |
| mussels | *cozze* | *ko·tse* |
| oysters | *ostriche* | *o·stree·ke* |
| pork | *maiale* | *ma·ya·le* |
| prawn | *gambero* | *gam·be·ro* |
| salmon | *salmone* | *sal·mo·ne* |

| Signs | |
|---|---|
| **Entrata/Ingresso** | Entrance |
| **Uscita** | Exit |
| **Aperto** | Open |
| **Chiuso** | Closed |
| **Informazioni** | Information |
| **Proibito/Vietato** | Prohibited |
| **Gabinetti/Servizi** | Toilets |
| **Uomini** | Men |
| **Donne** | Women |

| | | |
|---|---|---|
| scallops | *capasante* | *ka·pa·san·te* |
| seafood | *frutti di mare* | *froo·tee dee ma·re* |
| shrimp | *gambero* | *gam·be·ro* |
| squid | *calamari* | *ka·la·ma·ree* |
| trout | *trota* | *tro·ta* |
| tuna | *tonno* | *to·no* |
| turkey | *tacchino* | *ta·kee·no* |
| veal | *vitello* | *vee·te·lo* |

## Fruit & Vegetables

| | | |
|---|---|---|
| apple | *mela* | *me·la* |
| beans | *fagioli* | *fa·jo·lee* |
| cabbage | *cavolo* | *ka·vo·lo* |
| capsicum | *peperone* | *pe·pe·ro·ne* |
| carrot | *carota* | *ka·ro·ta* |
| cauliflower | *cavolfiore* | *ka·vol·fyo·re* |
| cucumber | *cetriolo* | *che·tree·o·lo* |
| fruit | *frutta* | *froo·ta* |
| grapes | *uva* | *oo·va* |
| lemon | *limone* | *lee·mo·ne* |
| lentils | *lenticchie* | *len·tee·kye* |
| mushroom | *funghi* | *foon·gee* |
| nuts | *noci* | *no·chee* |
| onions | *cipolle* | *chee·po·le* |
| orange | *arancia* | *a·ran·cha* |
| peach | *pesca* | *pe·ska* |
| peas | *piselli* | *pee·ze·lee* |
| pineapple | *ananas* | *a·na·nas* |
| plum | *prugna* | *proo·nya* |
| potatoes | *patate* | *pa·ta·te* |
| spinach | *spinaci* | *spee·na·chee* |
| tomatoes | *pomodori* | *po·mo·do·ree* |
| vegetables | *verdura* | *ver·doo·ra* |

## Other

| | | |
|---|---|---|
| bread | *pane* | *pa·ne* |
| butter | *burro* | *boo·ro* |
| cheese | *formaggio* | *for·ma·jo* |
| eggs | *uova* | *wo·va* |
| honey | *miele* | *mye·le* |
| ice | *ghiaccio* | *gya·cho* |
| jam | *marmellata* | *mar·me·la·ta* |
| noodles | *pasta* | *pas·ta* |
| oil | *olio* | *o·lyo* |
| pepper | *pepe* | *pe·pe* |

| rice | riso | ree·zo |
|---|---|---|
| salt | sale | sa·le |
| soup | minestra | mee·nes·tra |
| soy sauce | salsa di soia | sal·sa dee so·ya |
| sugar | zucchero | tsoo·ke·ro |
| vinegar | aceto | a·che·to |

## Drinks

| beer | birra | bee·ra |
|---|---|---|
| coffee | caffè | ka·fe |
| (orange) juice | succo (d'arancia) | soo·ko (da·ran·cha) |
| milk | latte | la·te |
| red wine | vino rosso | vee·no ro·so |
| soft drink | bibita | bee·bee·ta |
| tea | tè | te |
| (mineral) water | acqua (minerale) | a·kwa (mee·ne·ra·le) |
| white wine | vino bianco | vee·no byan·ko |

## EMERGENCIES

**Help!**
Aiuto! — a·yoo·to

**Leave me alone!**
Lasciami in pace! — la·sha·mee een pa·che

**I'm lost.**
Mi sono perso/a. (m/f) — mee so·no per·so/a

**There's been an accident.**
C'è stato un incidente. — che sta·to oon een·chee·den·te

**Call the police!**
Chiami la polizia! — kya·mee la po·lee·tsee·a

**Call a doctor!**
Chiami un medico! — kya·mee oon me·dee·ko

**Where are the toilets?**
Dove sono i gabinetti? — do·ve so·no ee ga·bee·ne·tee

**I'm sick.**
Mi sento male. — mee sen·to ma·le

**It hurts here.**
Mi fa male qui. — mee fa ma·le kwee

**I'm allergic to ...**
Sono allergico/a a ... (m/f) — so·no a·ler·jee·ko/a a ...

| Question Words | | |
|---|---|---|
| How? | Come? | ko·me |
| What? | Che cosa? | ke ko·za |
| When? | Quando? | kwan·do |
| Where? | Dove? | do·ve |
| Who? | Chi? | kee |
| Why? | Perché? | per·ke |

## SHOPPING & SERVICES

**I'd like to buy ...**
Vorrei comprare ... — vo·ray kom·pra·re ...

**I'm just looking.**
Sto solo guardando. — sto so·lo gwar·dan·do

**Can I look at it?**
Posso dare un'occhiata? — po·so da·re oo·no·kya·ta

**How much is this?**
Quanto costa questo? — kwan·to kos·ta kwe·sto

**It's too expensive.**
È troppo caro/a. (m/f) — e tro·po ka·ro/a

**Can you lower the price?**
Può farmi lo sconto? — pwo far·mee lo skon·to

**There's a mistake in the bill.**
C'è un errore nel conto. — che oo·ne·ro·re nel kon·to

| ATM | Bancomat | ban·ko·mat |
|---|---|---|
| post office | ufficio postale | oo·fee·cho pos·ta·le |
| tourist office | ufficio del turismo | oo·fee·cho del too·reez·mo |

## TIME & DATES

| What time is it? | Che ora è? | ke o·ra e |
|---|---|---|
| It's one o'clock. | È l'una. | e loo·na |
| It's (two) o'clock. | Sono le (due). | so·no le (doo·e) |
| Half past (one). | (L'una) e mezza. | (loo·na) e me·dza |

| in the morning | di mattina | dee ma·tee·na |
|---|---|---|
| in the afternoon | di pomeriggio | dee po·me·ree·jo |
| in the evening | di sera | dee se·ra |

| yesterday | ieri | ye·ree |
|---|---|---|
| today | oggi | o·jee |
| tomorrow | domani | do·ma·nee |

| Monday | lunedì | loo·ne·dee |
|---|---|---|
| Tuesday | martedì | mar·te·dee |
| Wednesday | mercoledì | mer·ko·le·dee |
| Thursday | giovedì | jo·ve·dee |
| Friday | venerdì | ve·ner·dee |
| Saturday | sabato | sa·ba·to |
| Sunday | domenica | do·me·nee·ka |

| January | gennaio | je·na·yo |
|---|---|---|
| February | febbraio | fe·bra·yo |
| March | marzo | mar·tso |
| April | aprile | a·pree·le |
| May | maggio | ma·jo |

| | | |
|---|---|---|
| June | *giugno* | *joo·nyo* |
| July | *luglio* | *loo·lyo* |
| August | *agosto* | *a·gos·to* |
| September | *settembre* | *se·tem·bre* |
| October | *ottobre* | *o·to·bre* |
| November | *novembre* | *no·vem·bre* |
| December | *dicembre* | *dee·chem·bre* |

## NUMBERS

| | | |
|---|---|---|
| 1 | *uno* | *oo·no* |
| 2 | *due* | *doo·e* |
| 3 | *tre* | *tre* |
| 4 | *quattro* | *kwa·tro* |
| 5 | *cinque* | *cheen·kwe* |
| 6 | *sei* | *say* |
| 7 | *sette* | *se·te* |
| 8 | *otto* | *o·to* |
| 9 | *nove* | *no·ve* |
| 10 | *dieci* | *dye·chee* |
| 20 | *venti* | *ven·tee* |
| 30 | *trenta* | *tren·ta* |
| 40 | *quaranta* | *kwa·ran·ta* |
| 50 | *cinquanta* | *cheen·kwan·ta* |
| 60 | *sessanta* | *se·san·ta* |
| 70 | *settanta* | *se·tan·ta* |
| 80 | *ottanta* | *o·tan·ta* |
| 90 | *novanta* | *no·van·ta* |
| 100 | *cento* | *chen·to* |
| 1000 | *mille* | *mee·lel* |

## TRANSPORT

**At what time does the ... leave/arrive?**
*A che ora*    a ke o·ra
*parte/arriva ...?*    par·te/a·ree·va ...

| | | |
|---|---|---|
| boat | *la nave* | la na·ve |
| bus | *l'autobus* | low·to·boos |
| ferry | *il traghetto* | eel tra·ge·to |
| metro | *la metro-politana* | la me·tro·po·lee·ta·na |
| plane | *l'aereo* | la·e·re·o |
| train | *il treno* | eel tre·no |
| ... ticket | *un biglietto ...* | oon bee·lye·to |
| one-way | *di sola andata* | dee so·la an·da·ta |
| return | *di andata e ritorno* | dee an·da·ta e ree·tor·no |
| bus stop | *fermata dell'autobus* | fer·ma·ta del ow·to·boos |
| platform | *binario* | bee·na·ryo |
| ticket office | *biglietteria* | bee·lye·te·ree·a |
| timetable | *orario* | o·ra·ryo |
| train station | *stazione ferroviaria* | sta·tsyo·ne fe·ro·vyar·ya |

**Does it stop at ...?**
*Si ferma a ...?*    see fer·ma a ...

**Please tell me when we get to ...**
*Mi dica per favore*    mee dee·ka per fa·vo·re
*quando arriviamo a ...*    kwan·do a·ree·vya·mo a ...

**I want to get off here.**
*Voglio scendere qui.*    vo·lyo shen·de·re kwee

**I'd like to hire a bicycle.**
*Vorrei noleggiare*    vo·ray no·le·ja·re
*una bicicletta.*    oo·na bee·chee·kle·ta

**I have a flat tyre.**
*Ho una gomma bucata.*    o oo·na go·ma boo·ka·ta

**I'd like to have my bicycle repaired.**
*Vorrei fare riparare la*    vo·ray fa·re ree·pa·ra·re la
*mia bicicletta.*    mee·a bee·chee·kle·ta

# MENU DECODER

**abbacchio al forno** – lamb roasted with rosemary and garlic; usually accompanied by rosemary-roasted potatoes

**agnello alla cacciatora** – lamb 'hunter-style' with onion and fresh tomatoes

**baccalà** – salt cod, often served deep fried in the Roman-Jewish tradition

**Bresaola** – wind-dried beef, a feature of Roman-Jewish cuisine; served as a replacement for *prosciutto* (ham)

**bruschette** – *from the Roman dialect bruscare, meaning 'roast over coals', grilled bread rubbed with garlic, splashed with olive oil and sprinkled by salt, most commonly then topped by tomatoes.*

**bucatini all'amatriciana** – thick spaghetti with tomato sauce, onions, pancetta, cheese and chilli; originated in Amatrice, a town east of Rome, as an adaptation of *spaghetti alla gricia*

**cacio e pepe** – pasta mixed with freshly grated *pecorino romano* (a sharp, salty, sheep's milk cheese), ground black pepper and a dash of olive oil

**carciofi alla giudia** – deep-fried 'Jewish-style' artichokes; the heart is soft and succulent, the leaves taste like delicious crisps

**carciofi alla romana** – artichokes boiled with oil, garlic and mint

**coda alla vaccinara** – beef tail stewed with garlic, parsley, onion, carrots, celery and spices; a dish developed when abattoir workers received the cheapest cuts of meat

**fiori di zucca** – courgette flowers, usually stuffed with mozzarella and anchovies and fried

**frutti di mare** – seafood; usually served as a sauce with pasta, comprising tomatoes, clams, mussels, and perhaps prawns and calamari

**gnocchi alla romana** – semolina-based mini-dumplings baked with ragù or tomato sugo; traditionally served on Thursdays

**involtini** – thin slices of veal or beef, rolled up with sage or sometimes vegetables and mozzarella.

**minestra di arzilla con pasta e broccoli** – skate soup with pasta and broccoli; Roman-Jewish dish served only at the most traditional restaurants

**pasta con lenticchie** – popular local dish of pasta with lentils

**pasta e ceci** – pasta with chickpeas; warms the cockles in winter

**pizza bianca** – 'white pizza' unique to Rome; a plain pizza brushed with salt, olive oil and often rosemary; can split and fill to make a sandwich

**pollo alla romana** – chicken cooked in butter, marjoram, garlic, white wine and tomatoes or peppers

**polpette al sugo** – meatballs served with traditional tomato sauce

**porchetta** – a hog roasted on a spit with herbs and an abundance of *finocchio selvatico* (wild fennel); the best comes from Ariccia, in the hills south of Rome

**ragù**– classic Italian meat sauce traditionally made by

slowing stewing cuts of meat, or mince, in a rich tomato sugo

**rigatoni alla pajata** – thick ridged pasta tubes with the small intestine of a milk-fed calf or lamb; a Testaccio speciality

**saltimbocca alla romana** – the deliciously named 'leap in the mouth'; a veal cutlet jazzed up with sparing amounts of *prosciutto* (ham) and sage

**spaghetti alla carbonara** – gorgeous, barely-there sauce of egg, cheese and *guanciale* (cured pig's cheek); the egg is added raw, and stirred into the hot pasta to cook it.

**spaghetti alla gricia** – pasta with *pecorino* cheese, black pepper and pancetta; comes from the town of Griciano (northern Lazio)

**spaghetti con le vongole** – spaghetti with clams and a dash of red chilli to pep things up; sometimes served with tomatoes, sometimes without

**stracciatella** – humble chicken broth given a lift by the addition of Parmesan and whisked egg

**sugo** – all-purpose tomato sauce served in many dishes; it's traditionally combined with *basilico* (basil)

**supplì** – rice balls, like large croquettes; if they contain mozzarella, they're called *supplì a telefono* because when you break one open, the cheese forms a string like a telephone wire between the two halves

**trippa alla romana** – tripe cooked with potatoes, tomato and mint and sprinkled with *pecorino* cheese; a typical Saturday-in-Rome dish

# Behind the Scenes

## SEND US YOUR FEEDBACK

We love to hear from travellers – your comments keep us on our toes and help make our books better. Our well-travelled team reads every word on what you loved or loathed about this book. Although we cannot reply individually to postal submissions, we always guarantee that your feedback goes straight to the appropriate authors, in time for the next edition. Each person who sends us information is thanked in the next edition – and the most useful submissions are rewarded with a free book.

Visit **lonelyplanet.com/contact** to submit your updates and suggestions or to ask for help. Our award-winning website also features inspirational travel stories, news and discussions.

Note: We may edit, reproduce and incorporate your comments in Lonely Planet products such as guidebooks, websites and digital products, so let us know if you don't want your comments reproduced or your name acknowledged. For a copy of our privacy policy visit lonelyplanet.com/privacy.

## OUR READERS

**Many thanks to the travellers who used the last edition and wrote to us with helpful hints, useful advice and interesting anecdotes:**

LW Braber, Badong Abesamis, Joan Brown, Jeroen De Man, Damien Dumas, Jennie Duprey, Jim Eigen, Martin Gascoigne, Emily Harris, Jonathan Holden, Ansh Jain, Laura Koppenberg, Gregory Morrison, Rachel Perella, Tim Powell, Steven Reid, Roberto Terajitis, Hilary Van Der Starre-Phillips, Maaike Wattel, Elyse Williams, Jane Wood

## AUTHOR THANKS

### Duncan Garwood

*Grazie* to everybody who helped me out on this job. A big thank you to Silvia Prosperi for her expert guidance and generous tip-sharing and to Barbara Nazzaro and Piero Meogrossi for their fascinating insights into the Colosseum. Thanks also to Al Rumjen for his company in Testaccio. I'd also like to thank fellow author Abi Hole for her great work and support. Finally, and as always, a huge hug to Lidia, Ben and Nick.

### Abigail Hole

Huge thanks to Duncan Garwood, the excellent coordinating author on this book, and to Joe Bindloss for commissioning me to work on my favourite city. *Molto grazie* to Luca, Gabriel and Jack, to Anna and Marcello, to Carlotta and Alessandro, and to Mum and Dad. A huge thank you to the unparalleled Barbara Lessona for all her kind assistance, to Elizabeth Minchilli for her interview, and to Paola Zagnarelli, Stéphanie Santini, Alessandro Sauda and Francesca Mazzà for their help with research.

## ACKNOWLEDGMENTS

Illustrations p62, pp64-5, p186, p191, p209 by Javier Martinez Zarracina.

Cover photograph: Fiat 500, Trastevere district, Rome. Stephane Frances/Photolibrary.

Many of the images in this guide are available for licensing from Lonely Planet Images: www.lonelyplanetimages.com.

## THIS BOOK

This 7th edition of Lonely Planet's *Rome* guidebook was researched and written by Duncan Garwood and Abigail Hole. The previous two editions were also written by Duncan and Abigail. This guidebook was commissioned in Lonely Planet's London office, and produced by the following:

**Commissioning Editor**
Joe Bindloss
**Coordinating Editor**
Jeanette Wall
**Coordinating Cartographer** Brendan Streager

**Coordinating Layout Designer** Paul Iacono
**Managing Editors** Brigitte Ellemor, Anna Metcalfe
**Managing Cartographers** Alison Lyall, Amanda Sierp
**Managing Layout Designer** Jane Hart
**Assisting Editors** Elisa Arduca, Cathryn Game, Alan Murphy
**Assisting Cartographers** Sonya Brooke, Alex Leung, Peter Shields
**Cover Research** Naomi Parker
**Internal Image Research** Aude Vauconsant
**Indexer** Barbara Delissen

**Language Content**
Laura Crawford, Annelies Mertens
**Thanks to** Helen Christinis, Melanie Dankel, Brendan Dempsey, Janine Eberle, Ryan Evans, Chris Girdler, Victoria Harrison, Liz Heynes, Laura Jane, David Kemp, Alana Mahony, Wayne Murphy, Trent Paton, Piers Pickard, Averil Robertson, Jessica Rose, Lachlan Ross, Michael Ruff, Julie Sheridan, Laura Stansfeld, Rebecca Skinner, Sophie Splatt, John Taufa, Gerard Walker, Clifton Wilkinson

See also separate subindexes for:

✕ **EATING P332**

🍷 **DRINKING & NIGHTLIFE P333**

☆ **ENTERTAINMENT P334**

🔒 **SHOPPING P334**

🛏 **SLEEPING P335**

# Index

Sights p000
Map Pages **p000**
Photo Pages **p000**

# Rome Maps

## Map Legend

### Sights
- Beach
- Buddhist
- Castle
- Christian
- Hindu
- Islamic
- Jewish
- Monument
- Museum/Gallery
- Ruin
- Winery/Vineyard
- Zoo
- Other Sight

### Eating
- Eating

### Drinking & Nightlife
- Drinking & Nightlife
- Cafe

### Entertainment
- Entertainment

### Shopping
- Shopping

### Sleeping
- Sleeping
- Camping

### Sports & Activities
- Diving/Snorkelling
- Canoeing/Kayaking
- Skiing
- Surfing
- Swimming/Pool
- Walking
- Windsurfing
- Other Sports & Activities

### Information
- Post Office
- Tourist Information

### Transport
- Airport
- Border Crossing
- Bus
- Cable Car/ Funicular
- Cycling
- Ferry
- Metro
- Monorail
- Parking
- S-Bahn
- Taxi
- Train/Railway
- Tram
- Tube Station
- U-Bahn
- Other Transport

### Routes
- Tollway
- Freeway
- Primary
- Secondary
- Tertiary
- Lane
- Unsealed Road
- Plaza/Mall
- Steps
- Tunnel
- Pedestrian Overpass
- Walking Tour
- Walking Tour Detour
- Path

### Boundaries
- International
- State/Province
- Disputed
- Regional/Suburb
- Marine Park
- Cliff
- Wall

### Geographic
- Hut/Shelter
- Lighthouse
- Lookout
- Mountain/Volcano
- Oasis
- Park
- Pass
- Picnic Area
- Waterfall

### Hydrography
- River/Creek
- Intermittent River
- Swamp/Mangrove
- Reef
- Canal
- Water
- Dry/Salt/ Intermittent Lake
- Glacier

### Areas
- Beach/Desert
- Cemetery (Christian)
- Cemetery (Other)
- Park/Forest
- Sportsground
- Sight (Building)
- Top Sight (Building)

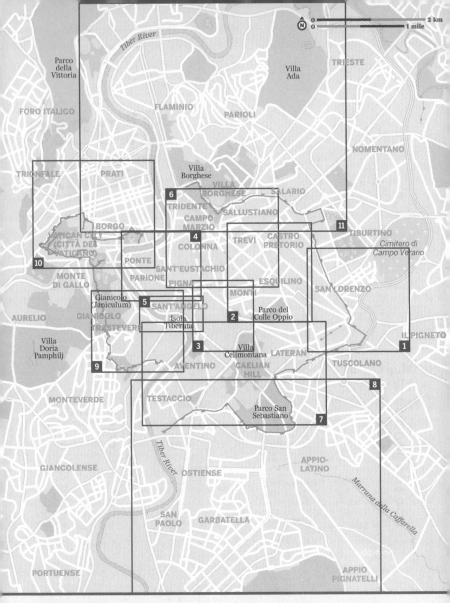

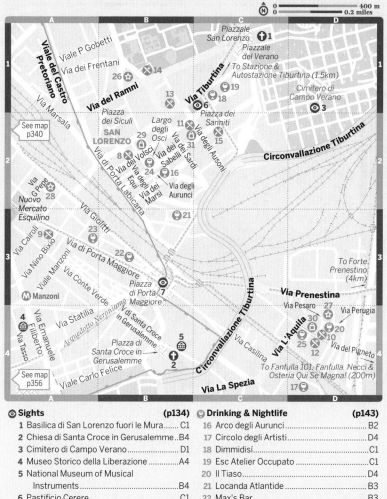

## Sights (p134)

| | |
|---|---|
| 1 | Basilica di San Lorenzo fuori le Mura.......C1 |
| 2 | Chiesa di Santa Croce in Gerusalemme..B4 |
| 3 | Cimitero di Campo Verano.......................D1 |
| 4 | Museo Storico della Liberazione.............A4 |
| 5 | National Museum of Musical Instruments...................................................B4 |
| 6 | Pastificio Cerere.......................................C1 |
| 7 | Porta Maggiore..........................................B3 |

## Eating (p140)

| | |
|---|---|
| 8 | Formula Uno..............................................B2 |
| 9 | Palazzo del Freddo do Giovanni Fassi.....A3 |
| | Pastificio San Lorenzo.......................(see 6) |
| 10 | Pigneto Quarantuno................................D4 |
| 11 | Pommidoro................................................B2 |
| 12 | Primo.........................................................D4 |
| 13 | Said...........................................................B1 |
| 14 | Sushiko......................................................B1 |
| 15 | Tram Tram.................................................C2 |

## Drinking & Nightlife (p143)

| | |
|---|---|
| 16 | Arco degli Aurunci...................................B2 |
| 17 | Circolo degli Artisti.................................D4 |
| 18 | Dimmidisí..................................................C1 |
| 19 | Esc Atelier Occupato..............................C1 |
| 20 | Il Tiaso......................................................D4 |
| 21 | Locanda Atlantide....................................B3 |
| 22 | Max's Bar..................................................B3 |
| 23 | Micca Club................................................A3 |
| 24 | Solea Club.................................................B2 |
| 25 | Vini e Olii..................................................D4 |

## Entertainment (p145)

| | |
|---|---|
| 26 | Instituzione Universitaria dei Concerti.....B1 |
| 27 | Nuovo Cinema Aquila...............................D4 |
| 28 | Teatro Ambra Jovinelli.............................A2 |

## Shopping (p146)

| | |
|---|---|
| 29 | Claudio Sanó............................................B2 |
| 30 | Iosselliani.................................................D4 |
| 31 | La Grande Officina...................................B2 |

# MONTI & ESQUILINO

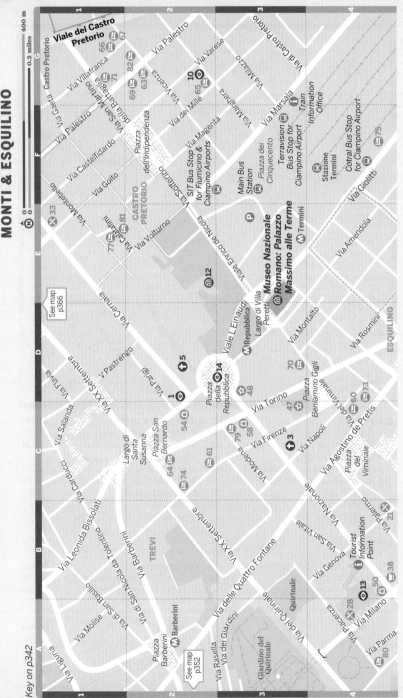

0
200 m
0
0.2 miles

See map
p366

See map
p352

Viale del Castro
Pretorio

Via Gaeta
Castro Pretorio
Via Villafranca
Via San Martino
della Battaglia
Via Palestro
Via Palestro
Via Castelfidardo
Via Golto
Via Montebello
Via Volturno
Via Cernaia
Via Palestro
Via Vicenza
Via dei Mille
Via Varese
Via Milazzo
Via Magenta
Via Marsala
Via Marghera
Via di Castro Pretorio

66
67
82
63
69
71
81
33
77
10
65

Piazza
dell'Indipendenza

CASTRO
PRETORIO

Via Soltterino
Via Cabralini

Viale Enrico de Nicola

SIT Bus Stop for
Fiumicino &
Ciampino Airports

Piazza dei
Cinquecento

Terravision
Bus Stop for
Ciampino Airport

Cotral Bus Stop
for Ciampino Airport

Stazione
Termini

Via Giolitti

Train
Information
Office

Main Bus
Station

75

Via Amendola

Museo Nazionale
Romano: Palazzo
Massimo alle Terme

Termini

Via Flavia
Via XX Settembre
V Pastrengo
Via Parigi
Via Salanda
Via Carducci
Via Leonida Bissolati
Via Cardini

Largo di Villa
Peretti

Repubblica
Viale L Einaudi

Largo di
Santa
Susanna

Piazza San
Bernardo

Piazza
della
Repubblica

Via Torino
Via Modena
Via Firenze
Via Napoli

Via Montalto

Via Rosmini

ESQUILINO

Via Nazionale

Via del Viminale
Via Agostino de Pretis
Via Beniamino Gigli

Piazza
Beniamino Gigli

Piazza
del
Viminale

1
5
14
54
61
64
74
79
58
48
3
47
70
60
73

TREVI

Via Leonida Bissolati
Via di San Basilio
Via Molise
V L Liguria
Via di San Nicola da Tolentino
Via Barberini

Piazza
Barberini

Barberini

Via Rasella
Via dei Giardini
Via delle Quattro Fontane
Via del Quirinale

Giardino del
Quirinale

Quirinale

Via San Vitale

Via Genova
Via Palermo
Via Milano
Via Parma

Tourist
Information
Point

21
38
50
13
28
80

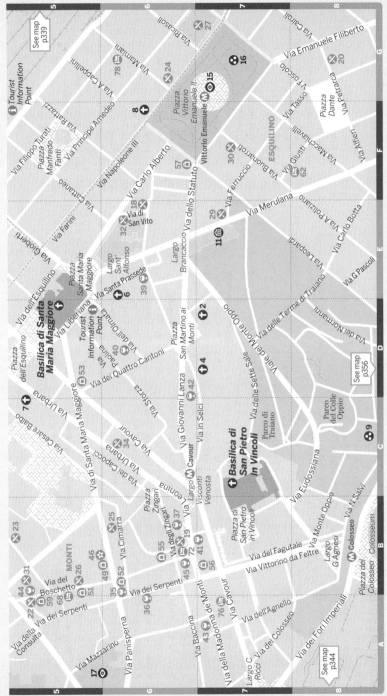

## MONTI & ESQUILINO *Map on p340*

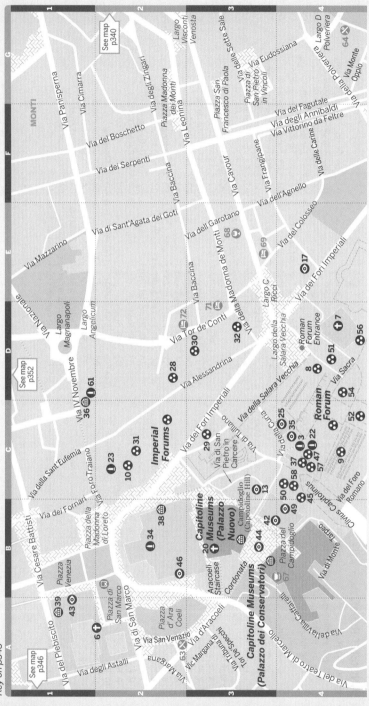

Key on p343

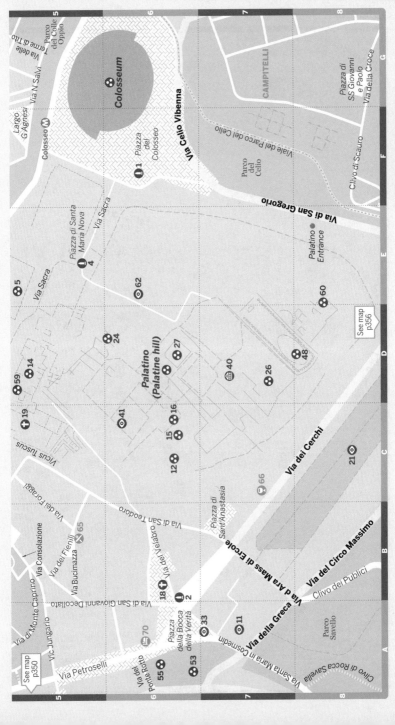

**Colosseum**

Via delle Terme di Tito

Parco del Colle Oppio

Via di N Salvi

Largo G Agnesi

Colosseo M

Parco del Celio

Piazza di SS Giovanni e Paolo

Via della Croce

CAMPITELLI

Clivo di Scauro

Viale del Parco del Celio

Via Celio Vibenna

Via di San Gregorio

Piazza del Colosseo 1

Palatino Entrance

Piazza di Santa Maria Nova 4

Via Sacra

Via Sacra

5

62

60

See map p356

24

27

Palatino (Palatine hill)

40

59 14

19

41

15 16

26

48

12

66

21

Vicus Tuscus

Via del Foraggi

Via di San Teodoro

Via di Sant'Anastasia

Piazza di Sant'Anastasia

Via dei Cerchi

Via del Circo Massimo

Via Consolazione

65

Via dei Fienili

Via Bucimazza

Via di San Giovanni Decollato

18

2

Via d'Ara Mass di Ercole

Clivo dei Publici

Clivo de' Publici

Via di Monte Caprino

Vic Jungario

70

Piazza della Bocca della Verità

33

11

Via della Greca

Parco Savello

See map p350

Via Petroselli

55

53

Via del Ponte Rotto

Via Santa Maria in Cosmedin

Clivo di Rocca Savella

Parco del Celio

Key on p348

CENTRO STORICO NORTH

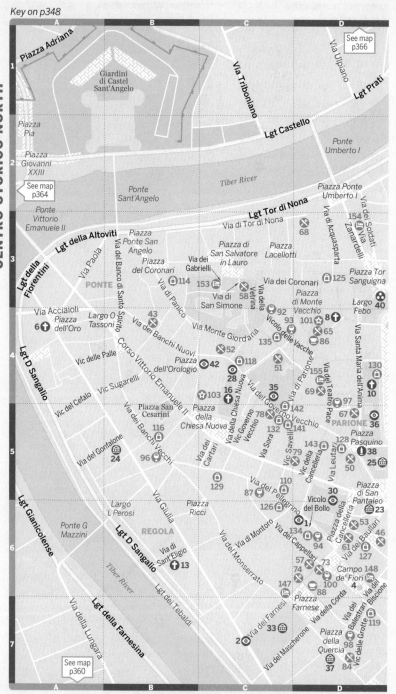

Piazza Adriana

Giardini
di Castel
Sant'Angelo

Via Triboniano

See map
p366

Via Ulpiano

Lgt Prati

Lgt Castello

Ponte
Umberto I

Piazza
Pia

Piazza
Giovanni
XXIII

Tiber River

Ponte
Sant'Angelo

Piazza Ponte
Umberto I

See map
p364

Ponte
Vittorio
Emanuele II

Lgt Tor di Nona

Via di Tor di Nona

Lgt della Altoviti

Piazza
Ponte San
Angelo

Via di Acquasparta

Via dei Soldati

Via
Zamardelli

Lgt della
Fiorentini

Via Paola

Via del Banco di Santo Spirito

Piazza
del Coronari

Piazza di
San Salvatore
in Lauro

Piazza
Lacellotti

154

Via Accialoli

PONTE

Via di
Gabrielli

Via dei Coronari

Piazza Tor
Sanguigna

6

Piazza
dell'Oro

Largo O
Tassoni

43

Via di Panico

114

153

58

Vetrina

Via della

125

Largo
Febo

40

Via dei Banchi Nuovi

Via di
San Simone

92

Via di Monte
Vecchio

101

8

65

Vic delle Palle

Corso Vittorio Emanuele II

52

Via Monte Giordana

135

93

86

Via Santa Maria dell'Anima

Vic Sugarelli

Piazza
dell'Orologio

42

118

51

155

130

10

Vic del Cefalo

Piazza San
Cesarini

103

16

28

35

69

97

67

Via dei Banchi Vecchi

116

78

Via del Governo
Vecchio

142

Via di Parione

Via del Teatro Pace

PARIONE

36

Piazza
della
Chiesa Nuova

Via della Chiesa Nuova

132

141

Piazza
Pasquino

128

38

Via del Gonfalone

24

96

Via dei
Cartari

79

143

50

25

Via Giulia

129

110

87

126

Vicolo
del Bollo

30

Piazza
di San
Pantaleo

23

Largo
L Perosi

Piazza
Ricci

1

134

Piazza della
Cancelleria

53

46

REGOLA

Via di
Sant'Eligio

13

Via di Montoro

Via del Cappellari

94

61

127

Ponte G
Mazzini

Via di Monserrato

57

73

Via dei Baullari

Lgt Gianicolense

Lgt D Sangallo

74

100

Campo 148
de' Fiori

4

119

Tiber River

147

88

Via della Corda

Lgt dei Tebaldi

Piazza
Farnese

Piazza
della
Quercia

Via della Lungara

Via del Mascherone

33

Via dei Farnesi

2

Lgt della Farnesina

See map
p360

98

37

84

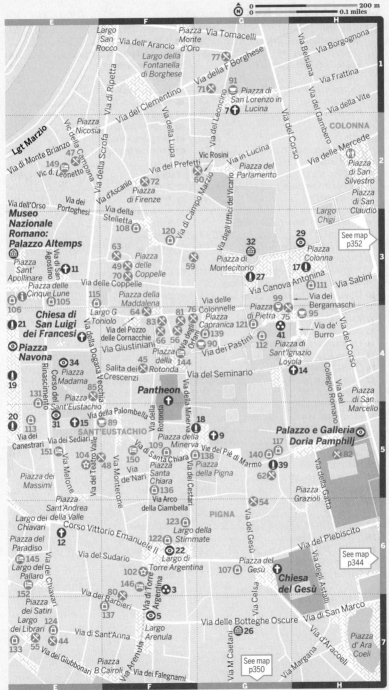

# CENTRO STORICO NORTH *Map on p346*

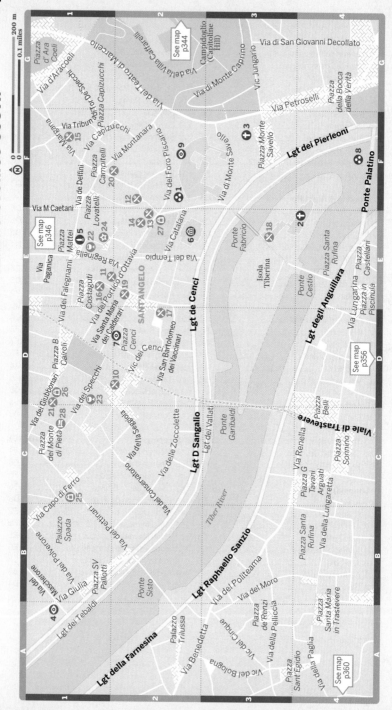

200 m
0.1 miles

Piazza d'Ara Coeli

Via di San Giovanni Decollato

See map p344

Via della Villa Caffarelli

Via del Teatro di Marcello

Campidoglio (Capitoline Hill)

Via di Monte Caprino

Vic Jungario

Via Petroselli

Piazza della Bocca della Verità

Via d'Aracoeli

Via delle Botteghe Oscure

Piazza Capizucchi

Via Tribuna

**15**

Via Capizucchi

Via Montanara

Piazza Monte Savello

**3**

Lgt dei Pierleoni

Via Margana

**20**

Via Campitelli

Via dei Foro Piscario

**9**

Via di Monte Save

**8**

Ponte Palatino

Via M Caetani

See map p346

Piazza Mattei

**22**

**5**

Piazza Lovatelli

Via Reginella

**24**

**12**

**14**

**13**

**27**

**1**

Via Catalana

**6**

Via del Tempio

**2**

**18**

Ponte Fabricio

Piazza Santa Rufina

Piazza Castellani

Via Paganica

Via dei Falegnami

Via dei Portico d'Ottavia

Piazza Costaguti

**11**

**16**

**19**

SANT'ANGELO

Isola Tiberina

Ponte Cestio

Piazza in Piscinula

Via Lungarina

Via dei Calderari

Via Santa Maria

**17**

Lgt de Cenci

Piazza Cenci

**7**

Vic dei Cenci

Via San Bartolomeo dei Vaccinari

See map p356

Piazza B Cairoli

Piazza del Monte di Pietà

**21**

**26**

Via dei Specchi

**23**

**10**

Via dei Giubbonari

**28**

Lgt D Sangalio

Ponte Garibaldi

Piazza Belli

Viale di Trastevere

Via Renella

Via Capo di Ferro

**25**

Via dei Pettinari

Via del Consorvatorio

Via delle Zoccolette

Lgt dei Vallati

Tiber River

Piazza G Tavani Arguati

Piazza Santa Rufina

Via della Lungaretta

Piazza Sonnino

Palazzo Spada

Via dei Polverone

Piazza SV Pallotti

Palazzo Pallotti

Via della Seggiola

Lgt Raphaello Sanzio

Via del Politeama

Via del Moro

Via del Maschterone

Via Giulia

Palazzo Trilussa

Ponte Sisto

Lgt dei Tebaldi

Via Benedetta

Vic del Cinque

Via della Pelliccia

Piazza de Renzi

Piazza Santa Maria in Trastevere

Piazza della Paglia

Lgt della Farnesina

Piazza Sant'Egidio

See map p360

**4**

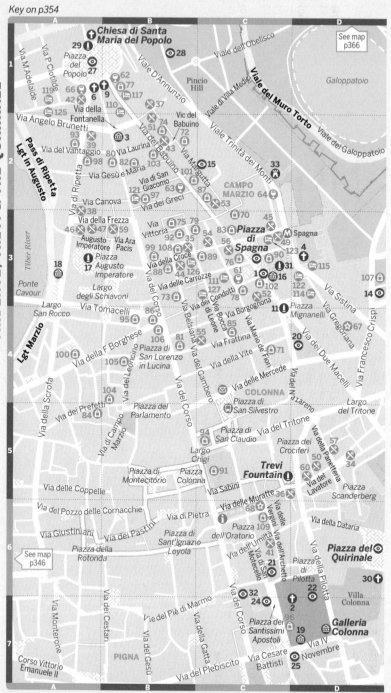

Key on p354

Chiesa di Santa Maria del Popolo

Piazza del Popolo

Pincio Hill

Galoppatoio

Viale dell'Obelisco

Viale di Villa Medici

Viale del Muro Torto

Viale del Galoppatoio

Via M Adelaide

Via P Clotilde

Via D'Annunzio

Via Angelo Brunetti

Pass di Ripetta
Lgt in Augusto

Via della Fontanella

Via del Vantaggio

Via di Ripetta

Via Laurina

Via del Babuino

Via Gesù e Maria

Via della Frezza

Via Canova

Via di San Giacomo

Via dei Greci

Via Margutta

Viale Trinità dei Monti

CAMPO MARZIO

Piazza di Spagna

Spagna

Tiber River

Augusto Imperatore

Via Ara Pacis

Piazza Augusto Imperatore

Via della Croce

Via Vittoria

Via delle Carrozze

Via dei Condotti

Via Borgognona

Via Bocca di Leone

Via Belsiana

Via del Corso

Via Mario de' Fiori

Via Sistina

Via Gregoriana

Via Francesco Crispi

Piazza Mignanelli

Ponte Cavour

Largo San Rocco

Via Tomacelli

Largo degli Schiavoni

Via della F Borghese

Via del Leoncino

Piazza di San Lorenzo in Lucina

Via Frattina

Via della Vite

Via delle Mercede

Via del Gambero

COLONNA

Via Nazareno

Via dei Due Macelli

Lgt Marzio

Via della Scrofa

Via dei Prefetti

Via di Campo Marzio

Piazza del Parlamento

Piazza di San Silvestro

Piazza di San Claudio

Via del Tritone

Piazza dei Crociferi

Largo del Tritone

Via della Panetteria

Piazza Scanderberg

Largo Chigi

Piazza di Montecitorio

Piazza Colonna

Via Sabini

Trevi Fountain

Via del Lavatore

Via delle Coppelle

Via del Pozzo delle Cornacchie

Via Giustiniani

Via di Pietra

Via dei Pastini

Via delle Muratte

Via delle Vergini

Via della Dataria

See map p346

Piazza della Rotonda

Piazza di Sant'Ignazio Loyola

Piazza dell'Oratorio

Via dell'Umiltà

Via del San Mocichello

Via dell'Archetto

Piazza di Pilotta

Piazza del Quirinale

Via Monterone

Via del Cestari

Vie del Piè di Marmo

Via della Gatta

Via del Corso

Piazza dei Santissimi Apostoli

Via della Pilotta

Villa Colonna

Galleria Colonna

PIGNA

Corso Vittorio Emanuele II

Via del Gesù

Via del Plebiscito

Via Cesare Battisti

Via IV Novembre

See map p366

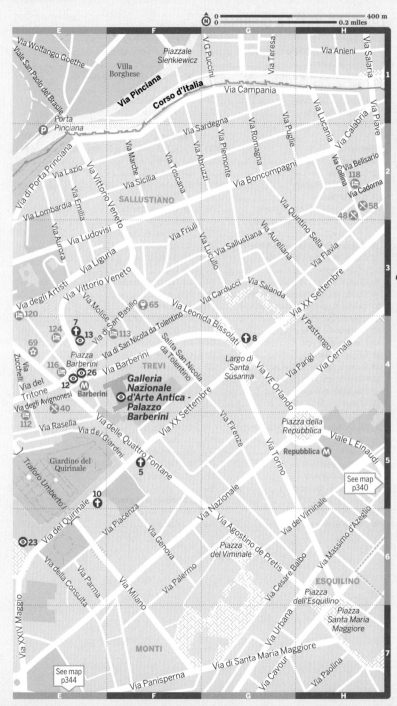

# TRIDENTE, TREVI & QUIRINALE *Map on p352*

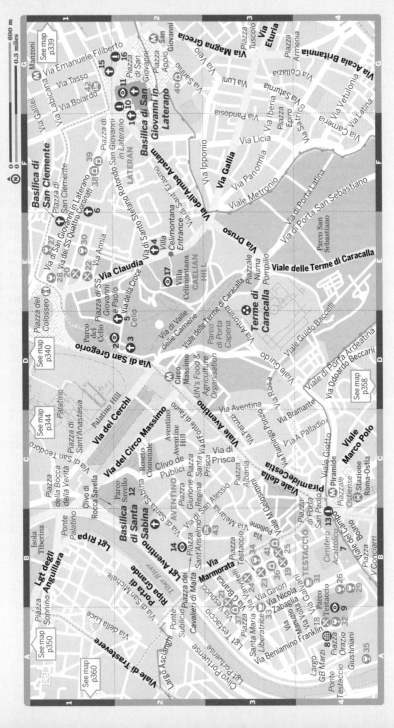

See map p339
See map p340
See map p344
See map p350
See map p360
See map p358

0 0
0.3 miles
600 m

# SAN GIOVANNI TO TESTACCIO

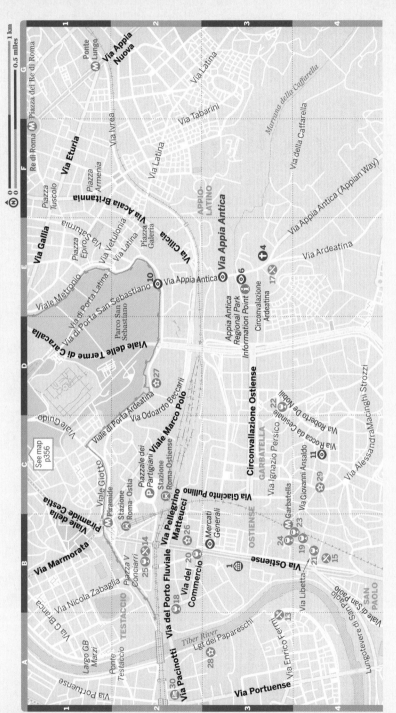

0 1 km
0 0.5 miles

See map p356

**SOUTHERN ROME & APPIA ANTICA**

Via Appia Nuova
Ponte Lungo
Piazza dei Re di Roma
Re di Roma

Via Eturia
Via Ivrea
Via Tabarini
Via Latina

Piazza Tuscolo
Piazza Armenia
Via Acaia Britannia

Via Gallia
Piazza Epiro
Via Vetulonia
Via Saturnia
Via Latina
Piazza Galeria
Via Cilicia

Via Latina

Via della Caffarella
Marrana della Caffarella

APPIO-LATINO

Via Appia Antica (Appian Way)

Viale Metronio
Via di Porta Latina
Via Appia Antica

Via Ardeatina

10
Via Appia Antica
6

Viale delle Terme di Caracalla
Via di Porta San Sebastiano

Parco San Sebastiano

Appia Antica Regional Park Information Point

4

17

Circonvalazione Ardeatina

Viale Guido

27

Viale di Porta Ardeatina
Via Odoardo Beccari
Viale Marco Polo

Circonvalazione Ostiense

GARBATELLA

Via Rocca da Cesinale
Via Roberto De Nobili

22

Via Ignazio Persico

Via Alessandra Macinghi Strozzi

Viale Giotto
Piazzale dei Partigiani
Stazione Roma-Ostiense

Via Giovanni Ansaldo

11

29

Piramide
Stazione Roma-Ostia
Via Giacinto Pullino

Via della Piramide Cestia
Via Pellegrino Matteucci

26
Mercati Generali

OSTIENSE

Garbatella
23

24
19
1
21
15

Via Ostiense

Via Marmorata
Piazza V Conciliari
25
14

18
Via del Commercio
20
Via di

1

Via Libetta

TESTACCIO
Via Nicola Zabaglia
Lago GB Marzi

Via G Branca
Ponte Testaccio
Via del Porto Fluviale

13

Tiber River
Lgt dei Papareschi

28

30
Via Pacinotti

Viale di San Paolo
SAN PAOLO

Via Enrico Fermi

Lungotevere di San Paolo

Via Portuense

**Via Portuense**

# SOUTHERN ROME & APPIA ANTICA

**TRASTEVERE & GIANICOLO**

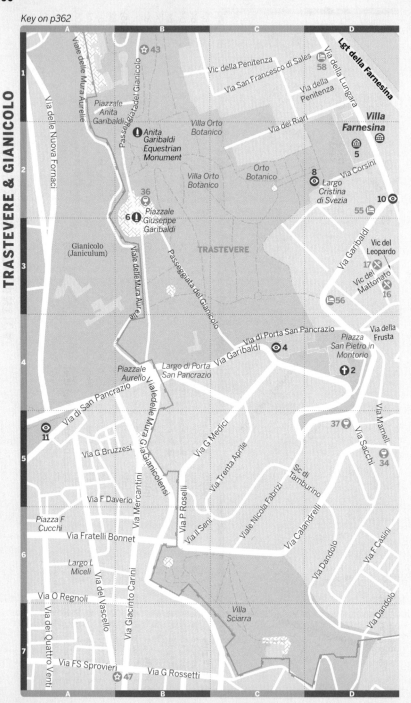

Viale delle Mura Aurelie

Via delle Nuova Fornaci

A 43

Passeggiata del Gianicolo

Vic della Penitenza

Via San Francesco di Sales

58

Via della Penitenza

Via della Lungara

Lgt della Farnesina

Piazzale Anita Garibaldi

Villa Orto Botanico

Via dei Riari

**Villa Farnesina**

5

Anita Garibaldi Equestrian Monument

Villa Orto Botanico

Orto Botanico

Via Corsini

8 Largo Cristina di Svezia

10

36

55

6 Piazzale Giuseppe Garibaldi

**TRASTEVERE**

Via Garibaldi

Vic del Leopardo

17

Vic del Mattonato

16

Gianicolo (Janiculum)

Viale delle Mura Aurelie

Passeggiata del Gianicolo

56

Via di Porta San Pancrazio

Piazza San Pietro in Montorio

Via della Frusta

Via Garibaldi

4

2

Piazzale Aurelio

Largo di Porta San Pancrazio

Via di San Pancrazio

Viale delle Mura Gianicolensi

37

Via Mameli

Via Sacchi

11

Via G Bruzzesi

Via G Medici

Via Trenta Aprile

Sc di Tamburino

34

Via F Daverio

Via Mercantini

Via P Roselli

Via il Seni

Viale Nicola Fabrizi

Via Calandrelli

Via Dandolo

Via F Casini

Piazza F Cucchi

Via Fratelli Bonnet

Largo L Miceli

Via del Vascello

Via O Regnoli

Via Giacinto Carini

Villa Sciarra

Via Dandolo

Via dei Quattro Venti

Via FS Sprovieri

47

Via G Rossetti

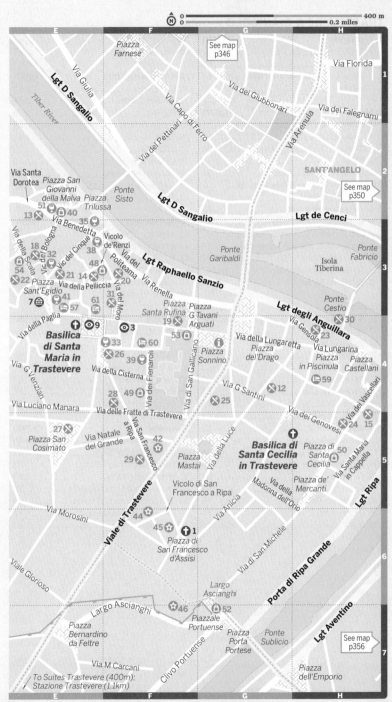

0    0    400 m
0    0.2 miles

E    F    G    H

Piazza Farnese

See map p346

Via Florida

Via Giulia

Lgt D Sangallo

Via Capo di Ferro

Via dei Giubbonari

Via dei Falegnami

Via del Pettinari

Via Arenula

SANT'ANGELO

Via Santa Dorotea

Piazza San Giovanni della Malva

Piazza Trilussa

Ponte Sisto

See map p350

51

13

40

Lgt D Sangalio

Lgt de Cenci

Via Benedetta

35

Via della Scala

Vicolo de' Renzi

Lgt Raphaello Sanzio

Ponte Garibaldi

Ponte Fabricio

18

Via del Bologna

32

Vic del Cinque

38

48

Via del Politeama

Via Renella

Isola Tiberina

Ponte Cestio

54

21

14

20

22

Piazza Sant'Egidio

Via della Pelliccia

31

Via del Moro

Piazza Santa Rufina

Piazza G Tavani Arguati

Lgt degli Anguillara

30

7

41

57

61

19

Via Gensola

23

Via della Paglia

9

3

53

Via della Lungaretta

Piazza del Drago

Via Lungarina

Piazza in Piscinula

Piazza Castellani

Basilica di Santa Maria in Trastevere

33

60

26

39

Via della Cisterna

Via dei Fienaroli

Piazza Sonnino

59

Via G Venzian

Via di San Gallicano

Via G Santini

12

Via Luciano Manara

28

49

25

Via delle Fratte di Trastevere

Via dei Genovesi

Via dei Vascellari

24

15

27

Via Natale del Grande

42

Piazza San Cosimato

29

Via San Francesco a Ripa

Piazza Mastai

Via della Luce

Basilica di Santa Cecilia in Trastevere

Piazza di Santa Cecilia

50

Via Santa Maria in Cappella

Via Morosini

Viale di Trastevere

44

Vicolo di San Francesco a Ripa

Piazza de' Mercanti

Lgt Ripa

45

1

Via Anicia

Via della Madonna dell'Orio

Piazza di San Francesco d'Assisi

Via di San Michele

Porta di Ripa Grande

Viale Glorioso

Largo Ascianghi

46

52

Piazza Bernardino da Feltre

Largo Ascianghi

Piazzale Portuense

Piazza Porta Portese

Ponte Sublicio

Lgt Aventino

See map p356

Via M Carcani

Clivo Portuense

Piazza dell'Emporio

To Suites Trastevere (400m); Stazione Trastevere (1.1km)

1

2

3

4

5

6

7

Tiber River

# TRASTEVERE & GIANICOLO *Map on p360*

## VATICAN CITY, BORGO & PRATI Map on p364

VATICAN CITY, BORGO & PRATI

Key on p363

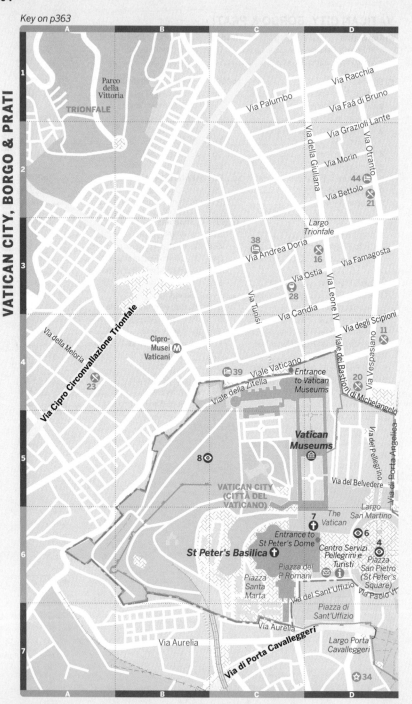

**A** **B** **C** **D**

1

Parco della Vittoria

TRIONFALE

Via Racchia

Via Palumbo

Via Faà di Bruno

Via Grazioli Lante

Via della Giuliana

Via Morin

Via Otranto

2

44

Via Bettolo

21

Largo Trionfale

38

Via Andrea Doria

16

Via Famagosta

Via Ostia

3

Via degli Scipioni

28

Via Leone IV

Via Candia

11

Via Tunisi

Via della Meloria

Via Cipro Circonvallazione Trionfale

Cipro-Musei Vaticani M

Viale dei Bastioni di Michelangelo

Via Vespasiano

4

23

39

Viale Vaticano

Entrance to Vatican Museums

20

Viale della Zitella

Via del Pellegrino

Via di Porta Angelica

**Vatican Museums**

5

8

**VATICAN CITY (CITTÀ DEL VATICANO)**

Via del Belvedere

Largo San Martino

7 The Vatican

6

4

6

Entrance to St Peter's Dome

**St Peter's Basilica**

Piazza dei P Romani

Centro Servizi Pellegrini e Turisti

Piazza San Pietro (St Peter's Square)

Via Paolo VI

Piazza Santa Marta

Via del Sant'Uffizio

Piazza di Sant'Uffizio

Via Aurelia

7

Via Aurelia

Largo Porta Cavalleggeri

Via di Porta Cavalleggeri

34

**A** **B** **C** **D**

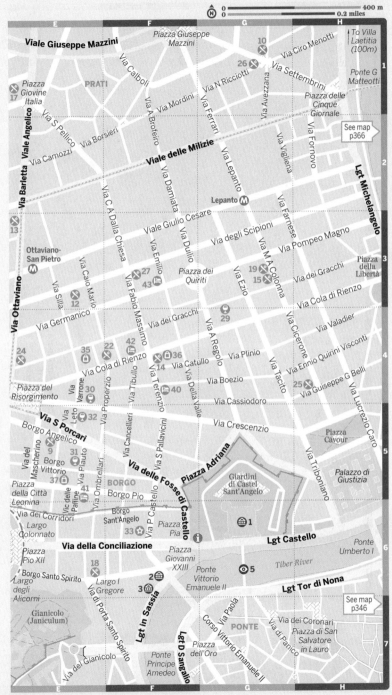

0    400 m
0    0.2 miles

**Viale Giuseppe Mazzini**

Piazza Giuseppe Mazzini

To Villa Laetitia (100m)

Via Ciro Menotti

Ponte G Matteotti

10

26 ✕

Via Settembrini

Via Calboli

PRATI

Piazza Giovine Italia
17 ✕

Via S Pellico

Via A Brofeiro

Via Mordini

Via N Ricciotti

Via Ferrari

Via Avezzana

Piazza delle Cinque Giornale

See map p366

Via Angelico

Via Borsieri

Via Camozzi

Viale delle Milizie

Via Damiata

Via Fornovo

Lgt Michelangelo

Via Barletta

Via C A Dalla Chiesa

Via Lepanto

Via Vigliena

Lepanto Ⓜ

Viale Giulio Cesare

Via Emilio

Via Duilio

Via degli Scipioni

Via Farnese

Via Pompeo Magno

Piazza della Libertà

13 ✕

Ottaviano-San Pietro Ⓜ

Via Caio Mario

Via Fabio Massimo

Piazza dei Quiriti

27 ✕
43 🏛

Via Ezio

19 ✕
15 ✕

Via M A Colonna

Via dei Gracchi

Via Cola di Rienzo

Via Ottaviano

Via Silla

12 ✕

Via Germanico

Via dei Gracchi

Via A Regolo

29 🍴

Via Cicerone

Via Valadier

Via Ennio Quirini Visconti

Via Giuseppe G Belli

24 ✕

35 ✕
22 ✕
42 ✕
14 🏛 36

Via Cola di Rienzo

Via Tibullo

Via Terenzio

Via Catullo

Via Plinio

Via Boezio

Via Tacito

25 ✕

Via Lucrezio Caro

Piazza del Risorgimento

30 ✕
32 ✕

Via Varrone

Via Leto

Via Propezio

Via Cancellieri

Via S Pallavicini

Via Della Valle

Via Cassiodoro

Via Crescenzio

Piazza Cavour

**Via S Porcari**

Borgo Angelico

9 ✕
31 ✕

Borgo Vittorio

37 🏛

**Via delle Fosse di Castello**

**Piazza Adriana**

Via Triboniano

Palazzo di Giustizia

Via del Mascherino

Via Plauto

Via Ombrellari

Giardini di Castel Sant'Angelo

Piazza della Città Leonina

41 ✕

Vic delle Palline

BORGO

Borgo Pio

Via dei Corridori

Largo Colonnato

Borgo Sant'Angelo

33 ✿

Via P Castello

Piazza Pia

🏛 1

Lgt Castello

Ponte Umberto I

Piazza Pio XII

**Via della Conciliazione**

Piazza Giovanni XXIII

ⓘ

📍 5

Tiber River

Lgt Tor di Nona

18 ✕

Largo I Gregore

2 🏛

Ponte Vittorio Emanuele II

See map p346

Borgo Santo Spirito

Largo degli Alicorni

Via di Porta Santo Spirito

3 🏛

Piazza dell'Oro

Via Paola

Corso Vittorio Emanuele II

PONTE

Via dei Coronari

Piazza di San Salvatore in Lauro

Via di Panico

Gianicolo (Janiculum)

Lgt in Sassia

Lgt D Sangallo

Ponte Principe Amedeo

Piazza dell'Oro

Via del Gianicolo

# VILLA BORGHESE & NORTHERN ROME

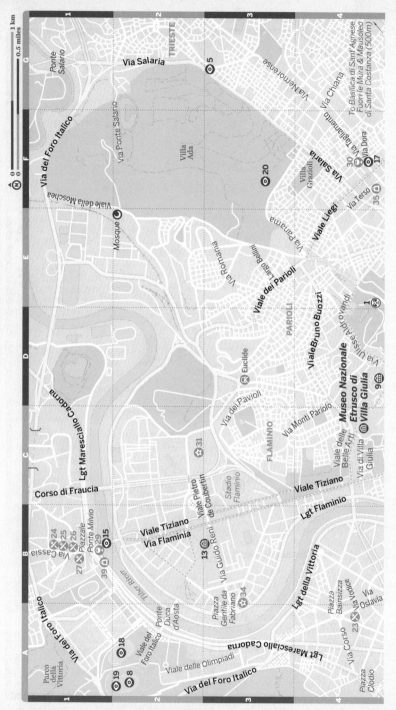

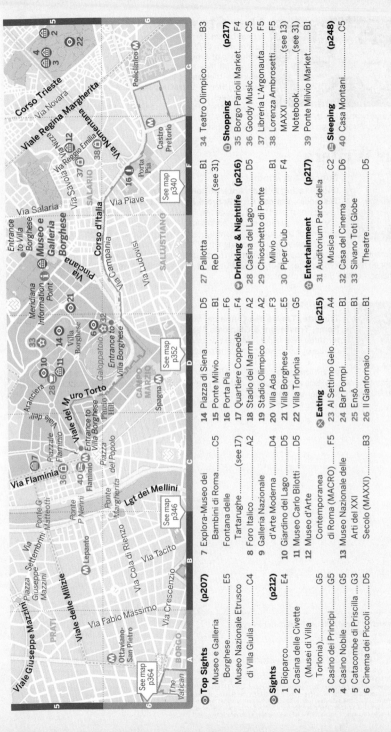

**VILLA BORGHESE & NORTHERN ROME**

## ⊙ Top Sights (p207)

| | | |
|---|---|---|
| Museo e Galleria Borghese | | E5 |
| Museo Nazionale Etrusco di Villa Giulia | | C4 |

## ⊙ Sights (p212)

| | | |
|---|---|---|
| 1 | Bioparco | E4 |
| 2 | Casina delle Civette (Musei di Villa Torlonia) | G5 |
| 3 | Casino dei Principi | G5 |
| 4 | Casino Nobile | G5 |
| 5 | Catacombe di Priscilla | G3 |
| 6 | Cinema dei Piccoli | D5 |
| 7 | Explora-Museo dei Bambini di Roma | C5 |
| | Fontana delle Tartarughe | (see 17) |
| 8 | Foro Italico | A2 |
| 9 | Galleria Nazionale d'Arte Moderna | D4 |
| 10 | Giardino del Lago | D5 |
| 11 | Museo Carlo Bilotti | D5 |
| 12 | Museo d'Arte Contemporanea di Roma (MACRO) | F5 |
| 13 | Museo Nazionale delle Arti del XXI Secolo (MAXXI) | B3 |
| 14 | Piazza di Siena | D5 |
| 15 | Ponte Milvio | B1 |
| 16 | Porta Pia | F6 |
| 17 | Quartiere Coppedè | F4 |
| 18 | Stadio dei Marmi | A2 |
| 19 | Stadio Olimpico | A2 |
| 20 | Villa Ada | F3 |
| 21 | Villa Borghese | E5 |
| 22 | Villa Torlonia | G5 |

## ⊗ Eating (p215)

| | | |
|---|---|---|
| 23 | Al Settimo Gelo | A4 |
| 24 | Bar Pompi | B1 |
| 25 | Ensō | B1 |
| 26 | Il Gianfornaio | B1 |
| 27 | Pallotta | B1 |
| | ReD | (see 31) |

## ⊙ Drinking & Nightlife (p216)

| | | |
|---|---|---|
| 28 | Casina del Lago | D5 |
| 29 | Chioschetto di Ponte Milvio | B1 |
| 30 | Piper Club | F4 |

## ⊙ Entertainment (p217)

| | | |
|---|---|---|
| 31 | Auditorium Parco della Musica | C2 |
| 32 | Casa del Cinema | D6 |
| 33 | Silvano Toti Globe Theatre | D5 |
| 34 | Teatro Olimpico | B3 |

## ⊙ Shopping (p217)

| | | |
|---|---|---|
| 35 | Borgo Parioli Market | F4 |
| 36 | Goody Music | C5 |
| 37 | Libreria L'Argonauta | F5 |
| 38 | Lorenza Ambrosetti | F5 |
| | MAXXI | (see 13) |
| | Notebook | (see 31) |
| 39 | Ponte Milvio Market | B1 |

## ⊙ Sleeping (p248)

| | | |
|---|---|---|
| 40 | Casa Montani | C5 |

# Our Story

A beat-up old car, a few dollars in the pocket and a sense of adventure. In 1972 that's all Tony and Maureen Wheeler needed for the trip of a lifetime – across Europe and Asia overland to Australia. It took several months, and at the end – broke but inspired – they sat at their kitchen table writing and stapling together their first travel guide, *Across Asia on the Cheap*. Within a week they'd sold 1500 copies. Lonely Planet was born.

Today, Lonely Planet has offices in Melbourne, London and Oakland, with more than 600 staff and writers. We share Tony's belief that 'a great guidebook should do three things: inform, educate and amuse'.

# Our Writers

### Duncan Garwood

**Coordinating Author, Ancient Rome, Centro Storico, San Giovanni to Testaccio, Vatican City, Borgo & Prati, Villa Borghese & Northern Rome**
Even after more than a decade living in Rome, Duncan is still fascinated by the city's incomparable beauty and hidden depths. He has worked on the past four editions of this guide and contributed to a raft of Lonely Planet Italy titles, as well as newspapers and magazines. Each job throws up special memories and this time it was visiting a chapel in the Vatican Museums that's usually closed to the public.

Duncan also wrote the Plan Your Trip and Understand sections, as well as the Transport chapter and part of the Sleeping chapter.

Read more about Duncan at:
lonelyplanet.com/members/duncangarwood

### Abigail Hole

**Tridente, Trevi & the Quirinale, Monti, Esquilino & San Lorenzo, Southern Rome, Trastevere & Gianicolo** Abigail moved to Rome in 2003 and lived there for three years. Her first son was born in Rome, she got married on the banks of nearby Lago Bracciano, and nowadays she divides her time between Rome, Puglia and London. She has worked on three editions of Lonely Planet's *Italy* and *Rome* guides, wrote the *Best of Rome* guide, and cowrote the first edition of *Puglia & Basilicata*. She also regularly writes on Italy for various publications, including *Lonely Planet Magazine*, *Wanderlust* and i-escape.com.

**Published by Lonely Planet Publications Pty Ltd**
ABN 36 005 607 983
7th edition – Feb 2012
ISBN 978 1 74179 856 2
© Lonely Planet 2012   Photographs © as indicated 2012
10 9 8 7 6 5 4 3 2 1
Printed in China